The Anunnaki Legacy

Transformation, Kundalini, Hyperborea, Göbekli Tepe, Hopi, Maya, Gods, Goddesses & the Divine Feminine, Skygods & Creation, The Flood, Sacred Trees, Alchemy & Serpent Wisdom.

Anunnaki Legacy

Categories: Metatags:
Mankind, origins, Genetics and Epigenetics, DNA, Maya, Aztec, Atlantis, Hopi, Evolution, Darwin, Multiple Edens, Creator Gods, Skycraft, Angels, Beings of Light, Souls, Kundalini, Hermeticism, Gnosticism, Kabbalah, New Thought, Karma, Reincarnation, Recycling, Earth Graduate, Global Tour – many countries, Anunnaki, Planet X, UFO, Tree of Life, The Flood, Serpents and Dragons.

Cover design: **Front: Miscl Bing & Pinterest Images**
(source: public domain)

1st Column: **Hopi**: Blue Star; Massau (Great White Brother) as Kachina; Prophecy Rock. (Chapters 1 & 7.)

2nd Column: **Göbekli Tepe**: Indra ('Nau') powering the T-posts yielding Kundalini. (Chapters 7 & 9.)

3rd Column: **Goddesses**: NüWa; Inanna/Ishtar; Black Madonna. (Miscl Chapters and Apx B.)

Back Cover: Key topics in book.

Book text in Garamond 12 font.

Author may be reached at TJ_cspub14@yahoo.com

ISBN – 13: 978- 1533537058

Other Books by the Author

Virtual Earth Graduate	VEG
The Transformation of Man	TOM
The Earth Warrior (docu-novel)	TEW
Quantum Earth Simulation	QES
The Science in Metaphysics	TSiM

(These books are profiled on pp. 619-620.)

Table of Contents

Chapter 5 – Greece, Egypt & Israel

Part II – Serpent Wisdom

Introduction

Over the centuries, there have been many reports of esoteric spiritual knowledge groups, from the Essenes, to Kabbalah, to Gnosticism, to the Illuminati to the Rosicrucians and today's New Thought churches. This esoteric teaching got its start in Sumeria and was promoted by an **Anunnaki** who loved Man, and it is generally known as **Serpent Wisdom** because he called his special group **The Brotherhood of the Serpent**. It also was later known as The White Brotherhood. It has also been called **Dragon Wisdom**.

Serpent in this case does not mean evil.

The word 'serpent' reflects the ***Kundalini* aspect of enlightenment** for Man. It also has a medical connotation when used in the Caduceus.

Medical Caduceus

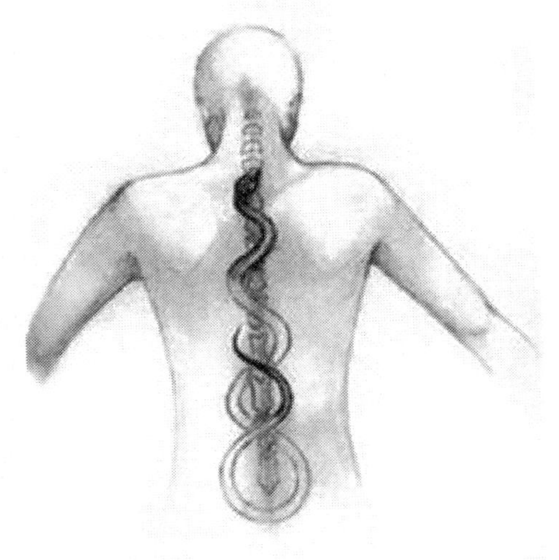

Kundalini

The Kundalini Serpent(s)
(source: davidicke.com/oi/extras/08/April/9.jpg)

The Caduceus was chosen as the symbol of healing/medicine as it was associated with **Asclepius** and **Hermes** who were healers and both carried a stick with a stylized serpent wrapped around it…

Asclepius (left) god of medicine.
His followers were called the Therapeutae.

Hermes (aka Mercury) who was a messenger god, associated with Thoth who was associated with Anunnaki healing (Chapter 5). Thus Hermes was also associated with healing, thru Hermetics and Alchemy (i.e., Elixir in Chapter 10).

And throughout the Western world only, as we'll see, there is an aversion to using the word 'serpent' and thus it has often been renamed **Dragon Wisdom**. It is in this context that the terms Serpent Wisdom and Dragon Wisdom are used interchangeably.

Global Survey

Be aware that this book does a global survey largely by pictures, pointing out that while Enki was promoting Serpent Wisdom around the planet, and the forms that that took, there is also evidence of the Sumerian **Tree of Life**, **Serpent Imagery** and similar **Creation** and **Flood** legends – indicating a common source behind the world's traditions. It is believed that the Anunnaki (and Others) had a hand in much of Man's education, growth and protection throughout the centuries and that is evidenced by the common legends and traditions around the planet.

The point being that the native peoples could not have gotten into their boats and travelled <u>all around the planet</u> (as if on some kind of missionary journey) just to spread the Tree of Life, the Flood story (it isn't a myth – it really happened, but was not worldwide), and the **similar Skygod global stories**.

The global examination is **not technical nor is it 'heady'** and involved – although some may wish it were (as if asking for additional proofs). Enough evidence is given to give the reader a realization that there was a common teaching happening around the world that suggests one people with the means to spread teaching and imagery with ease… and that was largely the Anunnaki (and Others like them).

Along the way, when anomalies are found, they are reported (such as Nubians in Central America and **Elephants** in the Mayan world) AND just to be of more interest, there are insets with side stories which look like this –

> Do not skip these textboxes, they yield the local color and interesting aspects of whatever culture is being examined.

Dragon Wisdom

The book is divided into two parts:

> **Part I** – global tour examining similar elements between cultures, all the while looking for the Tree of Life, Serpents, Flood and Creation.
>
> **Part II** – Examines the roots and teachings found in the Dragon Wisdom that have made it into the public (exoteric) realm.

And as the book circles the globe, in Part I (Chapters 1-8), examples of Serpent Wisdom will be pointed out. Then in Part II an effort is made to examine the groups, sects or secret orders have kept the secret teachings and what we can deduce and know from what Enki set out to do.

Summarily, in Chapter 10, much of what Serpent Wisdom must have been teaching is reflected in **Transformational Alchemy**, today's New Thought, and the all-important Serpent Fire initiation done so many times among the Hindu, Djedhi, the Sufi and even the Chinese Masters. Illuminati, Rosicrucianism, Kabbalah and Gnosticism all have their roots in Hermeticism (since Hermes was Thoth was Ningishzidda – Enki's son who was part of the dispersion of Serpent Wisdom).

And finally, in Chapter 13, we can learn what the Dragon Wisdom principles were for living by observing some of the wiser founders of America who were privy to to the esoteric teachings – many being Masons and Rosicruscians.

Cautions

Rewind: Why it was initially called Serpent Wisdom is the subject of the first chapter, and how it dispersed around the globe and what it looks like today is the rest of the book. What this book seeks to do is trace the spread of the Serpent Wisdom (*Kundalini*) groups and how they relate ultimately to today's global esoteric spiritual groups.

Along the way, we will also see similar Trees of Life, Flood legends, and similar skygod Creation myths… and maybe a UFO or ET along the way.

A caution here: Do not be alarmed or put off by the use of the word Serpent. Western civilization, thanks to the Church about 700 years ago, was taught to fear and deprecate the Serpent, modifying the true story of the Garden of Eden (see Chapter 12) in the process. The rest of the world knows that the Serpent (not snake) stands for wisdom, healing and spiritual growth. And to avoid the connotation of an 'evil snake' with the word Serpent, this book will interchangeably use the term Dragon Wisdom – especially as it is Wisdom gained thru the *Kundalini* Dragon Fire.

Serpent Imagery

We use the serpent imagery in the medical world as the **Caduceus** and also in Egypt: The Egyptian priests used it in their headdress to symbolize wisdom (due to their "third eye" being open via *Kundalini*):

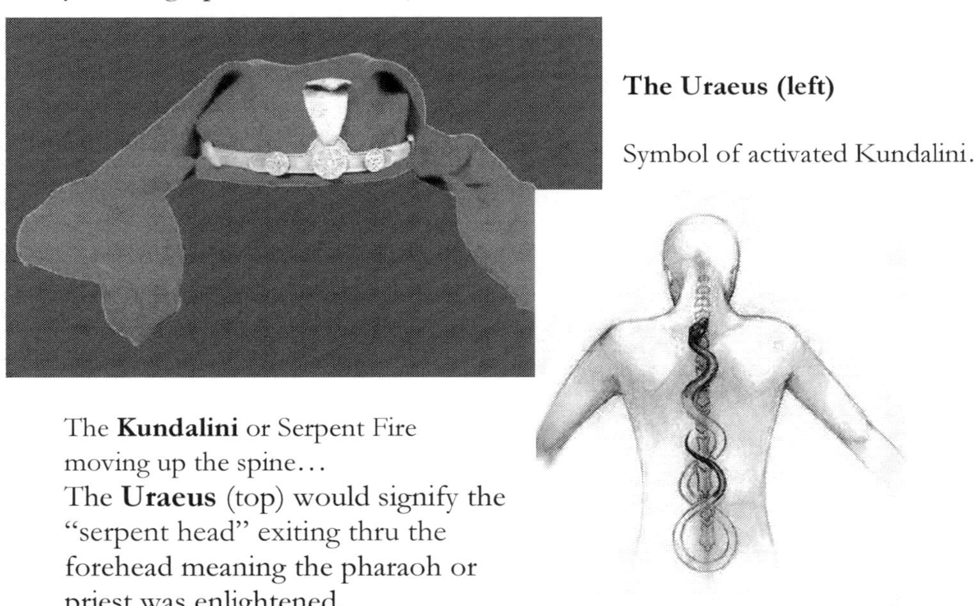

The Uraeus (left)

Symbol of activated Kundalini…

The **Kundalini** or Serpent Fire moving up the spine…
The **Uraeus** (top) would signify the "serpent head" exiting thru the forehead meaning the pharaoh or priest was enlightened.
Also called **Dragon Fire** (in China).

And even Moses in the Bible lifted up a bronze pole in the desert (Numbers 21) with a serpent on it to get people **healed** (below). … Note smaller snakes are crawling all over the people and afflicting them. The idea was to acknowledge the Great Serpent (the god providing for the people in the Wilderness) and be healed… this was as a result of the Israelites dissing God and complaining about the Manna… so the god sent adders and vipers among the people. Moses then mounted a bronze serpent on a pole and if the people would turn to it, they'd be healed.

> This doesn't make any sense until you know that Yahweh was Enlil and the original Anunnaki were referred to as serpents. See Chapter 1 herein. Also see Ch 3. VEG for a more detailed examination of the issue.

Notice that it resembles the Caduceus (first page**).**

The image of a serpent for wisdom was chosen for several reasons: the DNA helix-shape resembles 2 snakes entwining each other, and the ***Kundalini*** which travels up the *nadi* (2 channels) of the spinal area, in a snake-like motion, thus resembles a serpent.

Those are the reasons serpent imagery was chosen, and not a condor, rat, tiger, nor even an owl. The **eagle** later symbolized freedom (or Spirit), and the **owl** has been used for just Knowledge. The **Serpent** symbolizes special knowledge proactively blessing Man -- medically as well as spiritually. Its cousin, the Dragon, symbolizes **Dragon Fire**, or *Kundalini,* which includes and generates Serpent Wisdom. (Thus, Dragon Wisdom and Serpent Wisdom are used interchangeably in this book.)

The Serpent also had another significance that even the ancient Babylonian priest Berossus and the Jewish *Haggadah* lend credence to – to honor the source of the Teachings. This is explored in Chapter 1 and it is hoped that the reader will not misjudge the information, but give it some space due objective consideration, but there is no requirement to believe the ancient references.

Thus without an understanding of where Dragon Wisdom came from and what it symbolizes, the rest of the book could be confusing.

Importance of Trees

There is one more aspect that needs special emphasis. Trees are venerated all over the planet, except possibly in Africa and the Arctic where they are few and far between. Trees were often worshipped as **proxies for divinity** and temples were built in the heart of scared groves – for several reasons:

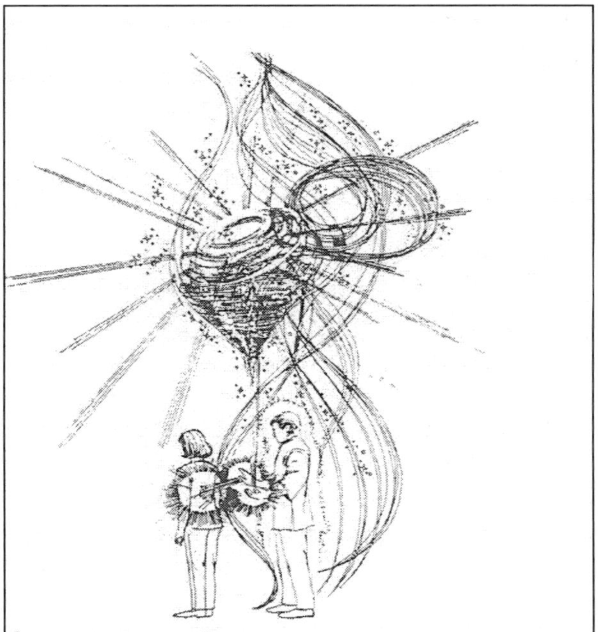

Trees give off a lot of ***chi*** or energy in addition to **oxygen** such that a thick grove of trees was very healthy, and the Druid priests could draw in the *chi* and use it to heal people.

Universal Life Force (chi) in Healing
(Pranic Healing, p. 155.)

The second reason is that trees also possess strong roots into the earth drawing up the **energy of the Earth** and the Chinese know about it, as do the Hindus (who call the energy *Prana*). There are books on the subject:

As you can see, we not only have the **Tree of Life** reference, we also have a **Dragon**…. and the *Sefirot* (see Chapter 12).

QiGong (aka Chi Kung) is a Chinese system of drawing in and using ambient "universal energy" or *chi* -- principally to heal the body.

And yes, the Druids knew all about this, like the Chinese and Hindus did/do. Now you know why the Dragon is significant to the Chinese!

(credit: Bing Images: Master Mantak Chia)

While the TOM book goes much more into this issue, let it be said that the human body has a **torus of energy** around it and centering oneself in a grove of trees is a way to cleanse and strengthen the body. Consider that your chakras can not only draw in the "universal energy" (*chi*) but the chakras also **resonate** and draw in the

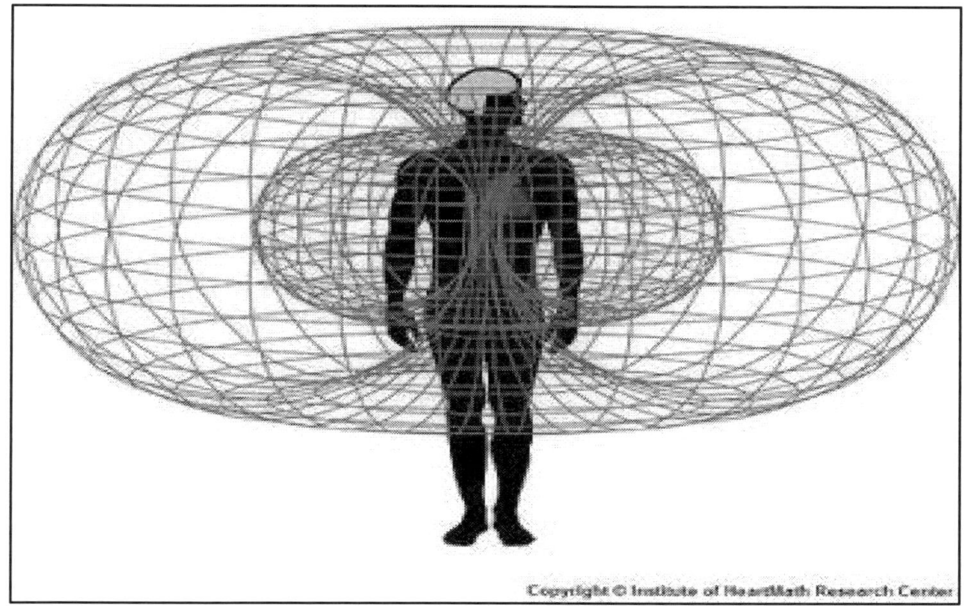

ambient energy (i.e., Dark Energy) which interpenetrates everything.

Now you know why QiGong masters are found exercising beneath really large/old trees…. And why they were so important to esoteric groups…

Single QiGong exercise (right)

or…

Group Tai Chi (left)

This is not silly. It is real and if you, the reader, never try it, you'll never know how energizing and healthy it can be. The Druids and Chinese were on to something.

In addition, the Druids venerated their sages as *oak tree men* – and the Syrian Mysteries venerated their sages as *cedars*… and called them **The Cedars of Lebanon**… pillars of the religious structure in their culture. Many trees were considered sacred – the **oak** (Druids), the **pine** (the Savior God, think: Christmas tree – Dec 25, Jesus' birth), the **ash** (divine nature of Man, Yggdrasil with the Norse), the **cypress** (the goddess principle), and the **palm tree** (Yang generation of energy). [1]

At any rate, trees were also symbolic to the Mayans (*Popul Vuh* in Chapter 6) and the Greeks (Creation Myth with Zeus) – both claimed that their gods created a version of Man from wood. How would two disparate civilizations thousands of miles apart have the same legend? (In both cases the legend was making the point that earlier versions of Man did not work, which is what the Sumerian creation tablets say, too.)

That mystery of similar symbols and teachings all around the planet is what this book is about… It should become obvious as the book progresses that someone was going around to different men, in different places, throughout ancient history, teaching and healing Man and in the process imparting common ideas, imagery and ways of doing things. For sure, Enki and his assistants were involved in supporting and developing the *Adapa*'s mental and spiritual potential with the promotion of Serpent Wisdom Groups.

The evidence is all over the Earth…

Others, Not Aliens

Lastly, throughout this book, the point is made that not only were the Anunnaki here, Others were, too. While Dr. Martinez in Chapter 8 suggests **polygenesis** (multiple Gardens of Eden), it is more basic than that. The growing suspicion is that some Others have <u>always been here</u> – before Man as we know him was created.

The indigenous peoples around the planet have legends about the gods coming from the sky and creating Man (and we'll examine those). However**, just because they came from the sky doesn't mean they were ETs,** or aliens from another planet – Have you seriously considered the lightyear (LY) gap between potentially habitable planets Out There and Earth? Alpha Centauri is the <u>closest</u> solar system to ours (4.3 LY away) and while any sophisticated ETs (with UFOs) would not use rocket power, faster-than-light travel runs the risk of hitting a wandering asteroid (or another ship) because you can't see it in time! (Even Far-Distant Galactic Radar still requires an early course correction at speeds above Lightspeed!)

> And while we're at it, let's punch a logical hole in the idiot idea of **Wormholes**:
> First, how would you create one right where you want it and get it to stay put?
> Second, How would you extend it to where you want the other end to be – and if you could, aren't you already there?
> Third, How would you get it to stay open and not collapse on you as you traverse it?
> And don't say that the answers represent technology that we don't have yet – Please consider that it logically makes no sense in 3D, yet intra-dimensional travel (see TOM book [**portals**]) is a viable probability…

What is strongly suggested, at various times in this book, is that the Others who created Man, educated him, and still watch out for him (i.e., **The Watchers** or Wm. Bramley's **Custodians**), are a **very ancient group of advanced <u>humans</u>** who live in inaccessible parts of Earth: inside mountains, at the bottom of the sea, and perhaps in the ancient Hyperborea, Lake Vostok, or even on the backside of the

Moon. It is plausble that they played the rôle of the **Greek, Roman and Norse gods** and the Sumerians called them Anunnaki.... "those who came from the sky." And if their job was/is to watch out for Man, that could mean <u>they are still here</u>...

It also means that if Man continues to abuse the planet (Think: pollution and nuclear waste), <u>because THEY also live here</u>, they will be forced to deal with Man. An alternate scenario is examined in the **Epilog** – and deals with White Hats and Black Hats.

Something interesting to think about as we tour the planet and check out the similar imagery... frequent **Creation by Skygods**, The Flood, the Tree of Life, similar languages/writing, the number seven (Think: the Pleiades), Dragon Force/*Kundalini*, Serpent Wisdom... somebody gave it all to Man.

What if these **terrestrial Ancient Ones** pretended to be from other planets – so that Man would <u>not</u> go looking for them on Earth? That can mean the UFOs are Earth-based... the **Skygods' skycraft** (Chapter 1). Consider that the UFOs that Man sees around Earth are quiet, no smoke, no flame – they are **anti-gravity (AG) craft**. That means they do not come across the solar system or the Galaxy – AG craft need something to push against, like a planet's gravity/mass.

Hence, interstellar craft use something like Ion Propulsion, Nuclear power, or something we are not aware of yet that uses Dark Energy (which is everywhere)... but it is obvious they do not use jets/rockets as the Anunnaki did (Chapters 1 & 2) – that in itself says the Anunnaki craft were Earth-based (despite what the late Zechariah Sitchin said). Could their craft have been the 'Flying Dragons' of the Ancient Ones? (See pages 101-108.)

Consider: most UFOs seen today are built on Earth and flown by terrestrials. The real ET craft rarely show up and when they do they are cloaked.

> Special Note: **The Table of Contents** is detailed to avoid the need for an Index.

Chapter 1: Anunnaki Overview

Man's Origins

While it is true that Africa is home to the Black race and it was created first, we have the late **Zechariah Sitchin** to thank for informing us as to who created Man and why. In his landmark book The Twelfth Planet, published in 1976, he shared that the **Anu.na.ki (aka Anunna)**, were gods who came down to Earth to mine mineral resources, among them gold, and found the work too arduous and so genetically engineered (created) worked slaves – in Africa to work the gold and uranium mines. They took an existing hominid, probably Homo *erectus*, and mixed their DNA with it so that it had enough intelligence to follow directions, and strong enough that it could handle the daily digging… using Anunnaki tools of course.

> This was also outlined in Virtual Earth Graduate, Ch. 3, and there is more substantiation at the end of this chapter.

The significance of the Anunnaki lies in their creation of Man, coupled with their responsibility, according to **Galactic Law**, that if one develops/creates a sentient race, one is responsible to nurture and develop that race, training it and instilling proper virtues in it so that it can develop into a responsible, respectful, proactive entity able to get along with its brothers and sisters, and learn to fend for itself.

In this vein, the **gods as Anunnaki** were to teach the humans law, ethics, morals, mathematics, medicine, astronomy, religion, and agriculture, to name just a few. The alternative, according to Galactic Law, was to create the worker slaves, *Lulu*, and when done with them, terminate them and leave Earth. This was the choice of the Anunnaki leader on Earth, Enlil. His brother, Enki or Ea, who was the very sophisticated Science Officer who created the slave workers, chose to protect, promote and develop his progeny – even giving them the ability to reproduce as *Adama.*

However, the new humans were very rowdy, noisy, smelly and bred like rabbits, much to the annoyance of Enlil, who tried starvation, then disease to cut their numbers down to a more manageable group… when that didn't work, and the Anunnaki in orbit who shipped the ore elsewhere (Mars? or back to their planet if they were ETs), came down and had relations with the human women, they produced **Nephilim**, giants and that really angered Enlil – the giants were not manageable at all. Enlil instigated a **Flood** of Biblical proportions, to wipe out humans and giants. Enki had other ideas and provided for the cryogenic storage of flora and fauna genetics (DNA) on board a small submersible craft (*elippu tebiti*), [2] and it rode out the localized Flood (mostly Middle East, Asia and Africa).

Enlil was furious at what Enki had done. However, Enki was very persuasive and pointed out that some remnants of Man had survived in other parts of the globe, AND with Enlil's permission, he'd develop a superior version of Man to be used as a Priestly Group, whose DNA was better and smarter. So Enki used his own DNA, modified to breed a very sophisticated, intelligent version of **priest** that would not reproduce but be subject to Enki's replication as needed – no one wanted Man to be as smart or smarter than the Anunnaki gods were! Enki convinced Enlil to set them up as priests to guide and shepherd the humans, following the Flood about 7000 BC … let them train, nurture and protect the humans. And so various leaders and priests were planted around the globe and Enki himself would travel to them and assist and assess progress – calling himself Quetzalcoatl in South America, for example.

Sumerian Ziggurat in Ur

And while a few gods resided up in their ziggurats, in Mesopotamia, the priests were programmed and mediated Anunnaki knowledge, standards and morals to the humans. Some humans also had advanced abilities that the common humans didn't have… *Adapa* were smarter, more intuitive, stronger physically, and some were clairvoyant. Anunnaki DNA + Adapa = **Hybrids**, such were later called Noah, Moses, Abraham, Sargon, Gilgamesh, Alexander the Great… all the way down to Charlemagne. Naturally, these men passed on their genetics thru breeding with beautiful and sometimes non-hybrid women. That bloodline exists today, despite the Church trying its best to wipe it out with the **Inquisition** (300+ years) and if a woman displayed psychic abilities, she was burned as a witch at the stake – such even happening to the fabled Joan of Arc.

Note: in Virtual Earth Graduate, Ch. 3, are pictures of Moses and Alexander the Great (below) pictured with horns – a possible Anunnaki vestige.

(Horns: See also Chapter 8.)

If the great men of yore were Anunnaki hybrids, they could still have had reptilian vestiges, such as horns. It's interesting that they were portrayed that way, so it must have been a compliment… otherwise it would have been banned. On the other hand, maybe Alexander did not have horns, but the horns 'symbolized' his Hybrid heritage… like Sargon.

Obviously, it is not a lock of his hair.

Credit: kingofmacedon.net via Yahoo [3]

Naturally, all priests over the centuries were forbidden to marry in synch with the Anunnaki desire that the Priest DNA (being better, smarter) did not replicate itself among the population. As the Church admitted smart, qualified common men into its priestly ranks, over the centuries – especially after the Anunnaki went home in 650 BC – the admonition to be celibate was continued. However, some of the women that had had relations with the Anunnaki and the human hybrids, did carry advanced DNA and develop abilities themselves and produce offspring that were smarter among the general population. A better *Adapa* which now invited souls to inhabit the bodies.

Anunnaki Agenda, Part I

Just a brief word here about the Anunnaki view of the humans, the slave workers. As it was in the Bible, Adam and Eve were not to eat of the Tree of Life (as well as eat of the Tree of Knowledge). So too were the created humans not to partake of the Tree of Life... lest they live forever. The Tree of Life was some sort of DNA-enhancing substance that already granted the Anunnaki very long lives (in the thousands of years: see the **Sumerian Kings List** for an eye opener, Chapter 13).

While probably not an actual tree, per se, it symbolized either a process or a transformation of one's genetics (such as regeneration of **mitochondria** – the 'batteries' in the body's cells, or preserving the chromosomes' **telomeres** which keeps the chromosomes from degenerating), which improved one's health and longevity.

The Tree of Life (discussed in a later section) was off-limits to humans. After the creation of the *Adapa,* a superior form of Man, the gods asked themselves whether Man should be as good as they are – Should he be as wise, live so long, and challenge their hegemony of the Earth? Genesis 3:22 in the Bible recounts it thus:

> And the Lord God said, Look, the man has become as one of us, knowing good from evil [having partaken of the Tree of Knowledge] and now, what if he puts forth his hand and takes also of the Tree of Life, and eats, and lives forever?

According to the Sumerian accounts, the Anunnaki were worried that the humans might have the potential to develop themselves and be like them, the gods! After Enki finished upgrading Man to the *Adapa*-stage, Enlil was furious – the humans were not only smart, they could also procreate! [4]

The Sumerian/Anunnaki version of Creation runs thus (paraphrased to save space): [5]

> The Anunnaki were mining the gold and uranium for their personal use in South Africa. The gods were doing the labor all themselves and it was very arduous, despite their technology, and they complained a lot. Then a group of them rebelled and went on strike.
>
> Enlil was Lord of the Earth Expedition. Enki was the Chief Science Officer. They were brothers.
>
> One day, Enlil visited the mining operation and the workers chose then to strike and present their complaints. Enlil considered force against the mutineers, but was better advised to speak with Enki (aka Ea) who suggested that he could make a slave worker from existing DNA on the planet. The slave was to be called a *Lulu,* and Enki fashioned it from a 'mud' made from the DNA of one of the Anunnaki and that of a hominid roaming the wilderness [suspected: Homo *erectus*.] Everyone agreed it should be done.
>
> Homo *erectus itself* could not be used as it was smart but wild and could not understand orders. Yet it provided the basic 'muscle' needed in the primitive worker. There were many trials and many failures, although Enki was a master of genetic engineering. Enki would need to get the genetic material from an intelligent Anunnaki and 'wire' that into the DNA of the Homo *erectus,* aka *Lulu* [in Sumerian].
> (continued...)

The Mother Goddess, Ninharsag, was brought in to oversee the gestation process which involved surrogate mothers who would give a genetic 'egg' and Enki would impregnate it *in vitro* with the desired genetic material, and implant it back in the surrogate mothers (1 at first, then later 7 as the process was found to work).

It was called a mixture of 'blood and clay' and upon that mixture, the Anunnaki would 'imprint' the image of the gods. And after numerous trials, because the humanoid genome is very complicated, success was reached with the *Lulu,* which was described as smooth-skinned, black and with nappy hair. It had the disadvantage that if more workers were needed, then the lab had to produce more, and that was very time-consuming (9 months to create a worker, and another 10 years before it could start to work...) and in later years, Enki used more midwives with more 'seeds' to produce more workers. [Enki could speed up the growth so new workers were ready in 12 months.]

As that became cumbersome, Enki took it upon his own initiative (i.e., didn't tell Enlil) that he gave the gift or procreation to the slave worker, calling it now, *Adama*. And it was necessary to fashion a female counterpart, and the two together could begin to produce the needed workers without the intervention of the lab.

Enlil discovered what Enki had done and lambasted him, furious: "We did not come to another planet to play God!... You have made *Adama* to be like us... knowing good from evil... able to procreate... one more step and he will live forever!" [*Adama* was not to partake of the **Tree of Life** and that was why he and the woman were kicked out of the Garden of Eden.] Enlil then swore to remove the humans ... as well as the giant Nephilim which had been the byproduct (at the same time) of Igigi (Anunnaki workers) mating with earth women.

Thus we had The Flood.

After The Flood, Enlil was counseled by Enki that the workers could prove useful to also build their Ziggurats and work the fields, and praise us, honor us! [See *Popul Vuh*, Chapter 6.]

(continued...)

Thus the humans who survived the Deluge were taken under Enki's wing and trained for new tasks, and more workers were created. Enlil agreed with Enki that he'd not do a Flood again, but next time he might send Fire...

At some point, Enki encountered an attractive *Adama* woman and had relations with her, she became pregnant and gave birth to what was called the *Adapa* – a superior version. And again, Enki's head was on the chopping block – the *Adapa* was TOO good, too wise and had enough of the Anunnaki DNA to develop into a being who could challenge the Anunnaki ideas. Enlil would not permit that.... In addition to which the humans were now so numerous that they kept him up at night with all their racket.

Enki had to take that *Adapa* DNA and 'detune' it to where Man was not as intelligent, nor did he live as long. [This theme will arise again in Chapter 6 with the **Mayan account of Creation** in the *Popul Vuh*.]

Enlil tries famine to decrease their numbers, and then releases ***Suruppu* disease** on them which did cut down their numbers. Enki again intercedes for the humans, as he had done after The Flood, and wins Enlil's approval to administer the cure and instead of wiping out the humans, set up a priest group to better train and control them... this was the origin of Religion and the "behave or go to Hell" dictum.

In addition, several of the more adroit humans, who were now **'hybrids'** or mixtures of more Anunnaki than human genetics, were given kingships [origin of *Dieu et Mon Droit*... known as "my divine right to rule"] and senior positions such as Sargon, Alexander the Great, and Hammurabi – to whom special laws were given for Man's benefit.

The Anunnaki main contingent (400-500) went home in 650 BC , leaving a smaller Remnant, often called Nagas.... Examined later (and in the <u>Virtual Earth Graduate</u>).

Nagas are examined in Chapter 4.

While Adam, Moses and Methuselah lived for hundreds of years, because they had fresher, more complete copies of Anunnaki DNA, Man in general was not to be given more than 70 years, on average, such that he could not live long enough to grow in wisdom and spiritual knowledge. Enlil did not think Man should discover and develop his spiritual potential – the gods wanted slaves, not gurus.

According to another author dealing with the Anunnaki Agenda:

> As we have seen, early humans were reported to be a constant headache to their Custodial masters [i.e., Anunnaki]. The slave creatures not only disobeyed their rulers, they often banded together and rebelled. This made human unity undesirable….
> It was better that humans be **disunited**. One of the ways in which the problem of human unity was solved is described in the Biblical story of the Tower of Babel. [6]

If they **couldn't communicate**, they could not unite, much less cooperate. And just to make sure the humans would find it hard to unite, should they start to learn each other's language, the Anunnaki also promoted **different religions** in various parts of the world… knowing that humans would squabble over who had the truth about God.

How's it working so far, centuries later? (See Anunnaki Agenda, Part II, p. 400.)

And lastly according to Bramley:[7]

> If we compare ancient and modern ideas about how Man came into existence, we find two very different versions. The ancient version is that an extraterrestrial society had come to possess Earth and sought to exploit the planet's resources. To make the exploitation easier, a work race was created: Homo *sapiens*. Humans were treated like livestock and were frequently butchered when they became too numerous or troublesome. [**Charles Fort** *and* **John Keel** came to this same conclusion, separately.]
>
> To preserve Homo *sapiens* as a slave race and prevent future rebellion, spiritual knowledge was repressed, human beings were scattered geographically into different linguistic groups, and conditions were created to make physical survival on Earth and all-consuming chore from birth until death. This arrangement was to be maintained indefinitely for as long as the Custodial society possessed Earth.
>
> In contrast the modern view is that human beings had evolved accidentally from "star stuff" [Panspermia] into slime, into fishes, into monkeys, [IRS agents?], and finally into people. The modern view actually seems more fanciful than the ancient one.

And that is all relevant to the development of 'underground' or secret societies begun by Enki (Ea) to further develop his progeny, Man. And that is one of the major issues traced in this book… the **serpent symbol** signified three things in the ancient world: (1) the creator of Man and the spiritual teachings, (2) the *Kundalini* enlightenment potential in Man, and (3) it symbolized the Serpent Wisdom groups that promoted Man's development.

One of the logos of the Serpent Wisdom Group (left) was the forerunner of the **Caduceus** (below).

Today's medical caduceus

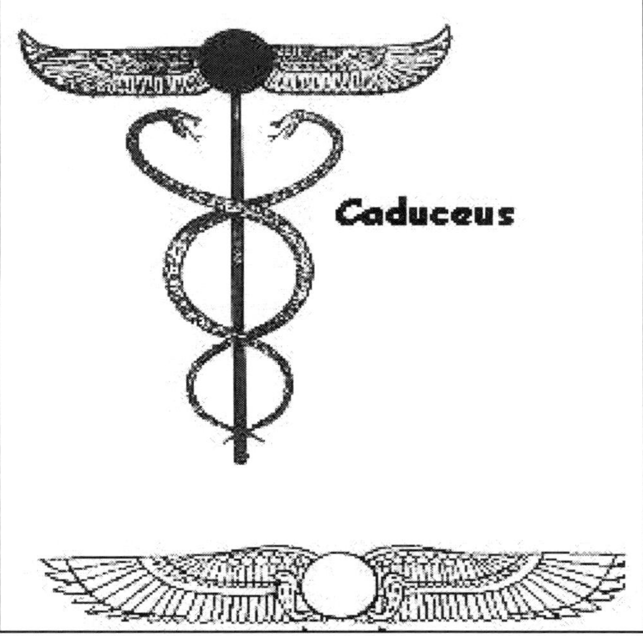

The addition of the wings, was an Anunnaki touch (seen left) as they often added the winged Sun to symbols (and this will be seen again when we examine the Anunnaki contribution to Egypt).

Left:
The ancient symbol for healing (top) and the ancient symbol for the Sun (below).

The caduceus is easily seen as an extension of the bottom, winged design. Note the Sun has serpents (bottom).

One emphasis in this book is on the **Tree of Life**, found in many cultures, and the formation of the Serpent Wisdom group, often called **Brotherhood of the Serpent**. In addition, this chapter emphasizes that the gods as Anunnaki educated the humans, and gave separate, esoteric spiritual knowledge to the priests. That will be traced across the centuries and the globe in the remaining Chapters 2 – 8.

> **For now, we deal mostly with the Anunnaki version of the gods (because it is the best documented)…**

Anunnaki Education

One of the primary goals was to instill a sense of Law and Order in the unruly humans. Because Enki had used the Homo *erectus* as the foundation for a slave worker, inherent animal behavior came with that hominid's genetics – a lack of ability to focus, think or speak. In addition, the new humans were prone to taking whatever they wanted from another human, pettiness and violence were the norm and the Anunnaki 'guards' were constantly stopping fights and sometimes they had to stop group riots. Enki saw this and went to work to upgrade the genetics to a more docile human, and he added speech (**FOXP2 gene**) so that guards and priests could communicate with the mix of humans, first *Adama* then *Adapa*.

Morals and ethics were commanded to be written down by the Anunnaki but first the humans had to be taught a basic, simple writing. Given a pointed triangular stick this became known as **cuneiform**.

Cuneiform Tablet

Only priests and later, 'scribes', were taught to read and write. This pattern was repeated in Egypt and among the Maya and Vikings, each getting a different system of **Writing** (see pp. 48-51).

The humans chosen to work in the fields were taught **Argricultural** principles. The humans chosen to heal other humans were given basics in **Medicine**. (Really serious health problems among humans could be handled by the Anunnaki medical system – which was much more advanced – and Enki (aka Ea) would use the feedback information to upgrade human DNA to make the humans more resilient and healthy… thus there were several versions of humans running around, some healthier and smarter than the others.)

Humans were also taught the basics of **Astronomy** and the Anunnaki pointed out the 3 stars in what is now called Orion's Belt in the sky at night showed the areas that were home to the Anunnaki in Mesopotamia, the Aldebaran from Sirius, Oannes in Africa, Denebians in China…. Earth was host to a number of ET groups.

> And they sometimes fought each other, as will later be examined…
> that is what happened to Puma Punku.

Again, the issue is that humans were trained to mine, cultivate, heal, and write as well as fight some of the Anunnaki's battles on Earth – for them! So Man learned weapons and **Warfare**. The Anunnaki even fought among themselves, and since we have their DNA, is it any wonder that one of the legacy items from the Anunnaki is their pettiness and violence (amplified perhaps by the genetics of the Homo *erectus*).

Anunnaki Appearance

Critical of much of what this book imparts relates to the original appearance of the Anunnki when they first came to Earth. While the hominid form (two arms, two legs, a head, two eyes, etc) is fairly common in the Galaxy, and much of the visible Universe, the human (mammalian) form is not that common. Much more prevalent is the reptilian form – it is considered physically superior but the Anunnaki-created *Adapa*, or Homo sapiens, is smarter than the reptilian form! The issue, leading to the **Quarantine of Earth** for Man's protection (see Epilog), is that the reptiles are like space pirates – they aren't evil but their physical superiority (and their technical weapons, most of which were stolen from other star systems, being way beyond what Man has), has meant that Man has to be protected and educated in how to defend himself from the Draconians (aka the Orion Empire who are reptilian).

The original Anunnaki were said to look something like the following:

Note: Those that were later born on Earth were the product of Enki's genetic engineering, and they were human-looking. (See VEG, Ch.3.)

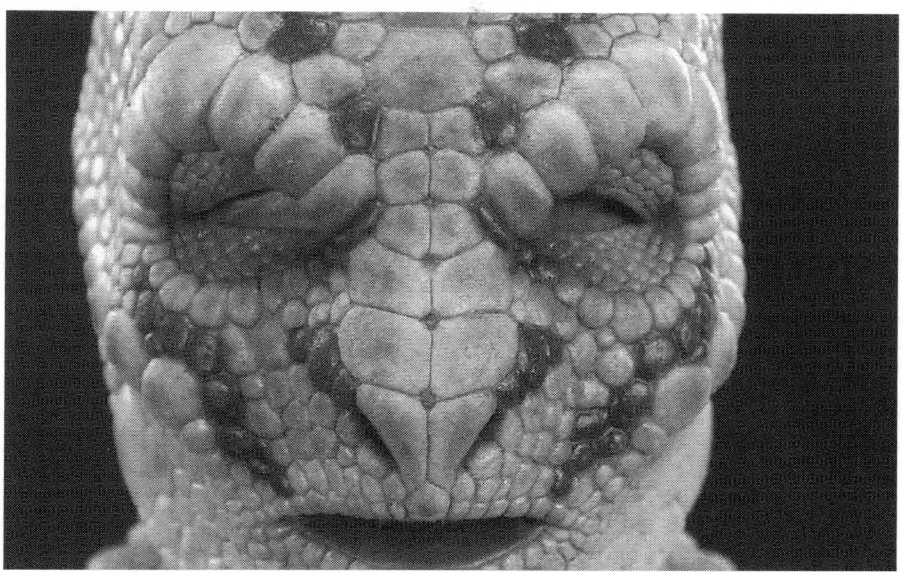

Anaconda-like Reptilian Visage

Elsewhere, in a museum this was spotted: A statue of an Anunnaki god:

Anunnaki from Ubaid Culture (3500 BC)

The general consensus is that they were humanoid, thus making Man "in their image", but they were covered with a very fine coating of scales – much finer than the picture on the last page. This gave them the appearance of shining, reflecting sunlight so the humans called them "**The Shining Ones**." They were still considered ugly to the humans whom they had made. (Later, the Serpents of Wisdom, Chapter 13, will also be seen to be the Shining Ones.)

Berossus, a Babylonian priest writing about the appearance of the gods, said that Man's ancestry traced back to the **Oannes**, an amphibious creature which came to teach civilization to Man. (Think: humanoids in Scuba gear.)

Berossus called them ***Annedoti*** which means "the repulsive ones" in Greek. He also refers to them as *musarus* or an "abomination." It is in this way that Babylonian tradition credits the founding of civilization to a creature which they considered a "**repulsive abomination**." [8]

> According to another source, the word 'Annedoti' looks like 'Anunnaki' and the **Oannes was another name for the Anunnaki [Ea]**. [9], [10]

One would think that if the gods were so superior and grand as indicated in some ancient texts that they would be flattered to have Man make images of them, and display their greatness. But, after Man was created, the gods forbade Man to make images of them (Think: Ten Commandments, # 2: Thou shalt not make any graven image) and they tended to stay atop their Mesopotamian ziggurats and Mayan pyramids to be waited on by certain human servants who knew the truth, but did not speak of the gods' appearance with the worker population below, or in the city and fields, that had been created to serve the Annuna. So their physical **repulsiveness** must be true, otherwise Man would have flattered and praised their god's appearance. And again, the reptilian nature of the <u>original</u> Anunnaki is explicit in the Sumerian accounts:

> **The reptiles verily descend,**
> The Earth is resplendent as a well-watered garden,
> At that time Enki and Eridu [his city] had not appeared,
> Daylight did not shine,
> **Moonlight had not emerged.** [11] [emphasis added]

This is a larger issue, covered in <u>Virtual Earth Graduate</u>, where it is suspected that **the Moon was added later around Earth**, to give it tidal action, seasons including the tilt on the Earth's axis, and to serve as an observation post.

An ancient source in the Jewish *Haggadah* said that **Man in the beginning was also semi-reptilian**:

Before their bodies had been *overlaid with a horny skin, and enveloped with the cloud of glory.* No sooner had they violated the command given them [to not eat of the Tree] that *the cloud of glory and* ***the horny skin*** *dropped from them*, and they stood there in their nakedness, and ashamed. [emphasis ours] ... [continued]...

Describing man before the Fall, it was said that "his skin was as bright as daylight and covered his body like a luminous garment." This luminous and bright skin or hide was their "cloud of glory." [12]

Left: also what the original Anunnaki might have looked like with very fine scales... <u>and horns</u> as we'll see later.

So Man <u>was</u> originally made in their image. The change, just briefly, to the current mammalian form was done to facilitate easier replication – reptiles birth via eggs, and humans would now have live birth and lose their semi-reptilian heritage – which originally included longer lives – something not wanted by the Anunnaki. Humans would not be as smart, nor live as long, and Enlil had his way. Also our softer, more vulnerable skin would give the Anunnaki an edge over us in disciplining Man – hitting a reptile with a stick does little damage. It would however get the human's attention and cooperation.

And down the road, by 2500 BC, so that the Anunnaki could play god and walk <u>among</u> Man, Enki found a way to alter the genetics in the Anunnaki womb so that future Anunnaki descendants, such as **Marduk and Inanna**, **would look human** – but they still had superior smarts and abilities. Thus the Anunnaki could appear in human form and walk among their progeny, and so **they became gods to the Vikings, Greeks and Romans**... until the gods discovered that they still could not control rowdy Man and had to try another approach...

A more mammalian version of the Anunnaki looks like the following (alleged to be Marduk). Imagine the bust (below) to have a very fine patina of body scales and that is probably very close to what the Anunnaki looked like – Note that the Egyptians did picture Akhenaten and family with oblong heads (below and Chapter 5).

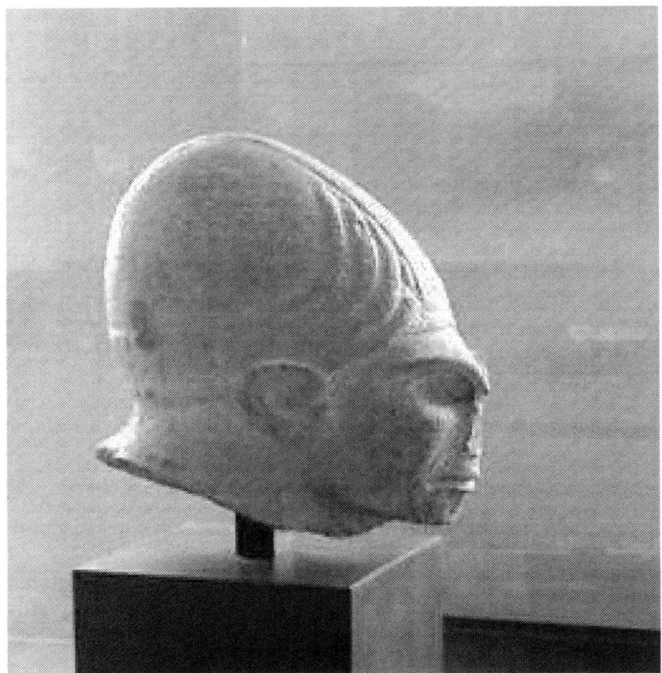

Anunnaki Bust in Iraqi Museum
(credit: https://www.pinterest.com/karenstatler33/annunaki/)

The 4 curved 'horns' is a sign of Anunnaki **rank**, and this could be Marduk, his rank being '40'. Enlil had 5 horns, his rank being '50'... the top rank on Earth.[13], [14]
We do the same thing in our armed forces today with chevrons:

Rank of US Army Sergeant

US Air Force Sergeant

In the Anunnaki bust above, note the elongated head, reminiscent of the Egyptian and Peruvian samples found around the planet. In fact, one of the Sumerian queens was found to have a large head (**Queen Pu.Abi**), and Zechariah Sitchin wrote about her tomb in the Earth Chronicles books.[15]

The skulls below were found in Peru and are not human as they do not have the correct sutures and they are not merely deformed skulls as their inner volume exceeds that of a human.

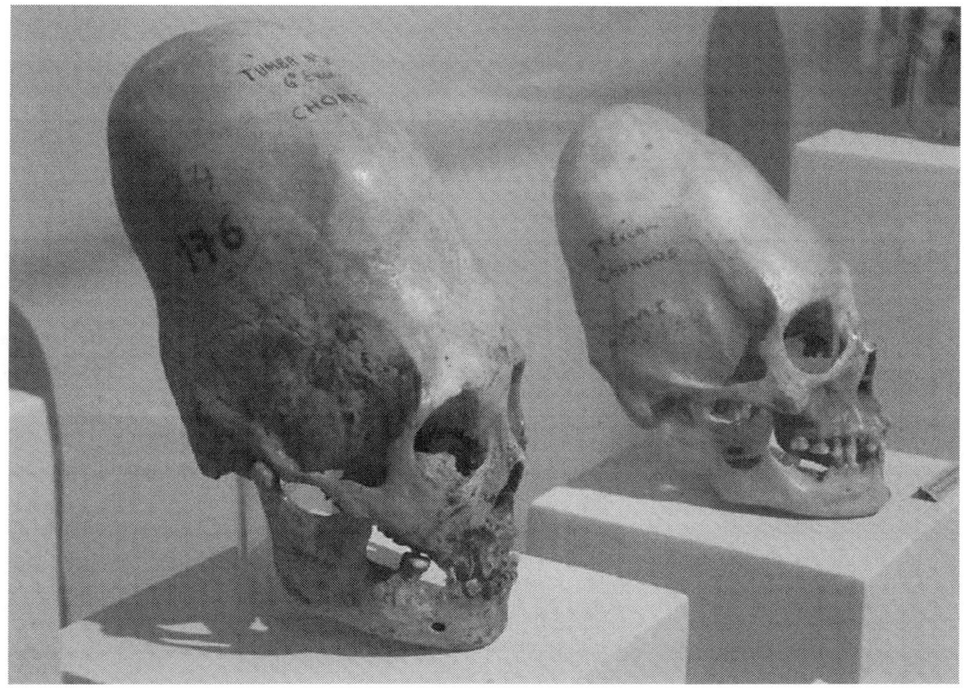

Peruvian Skulls (no human sutures)

And another find in Sumeria attributed to **Queen Pu.Abi** (aka Queen Shubad) is the following headdress which, according to Zechariah Sitchin, is made for a large head…

Sumerian Queen Pu.Abi large headdress

All of that to say that the Egyptian hieroglyphic panels show children with unusually large heads, too:

Nefertiti, Akhenaten and Children

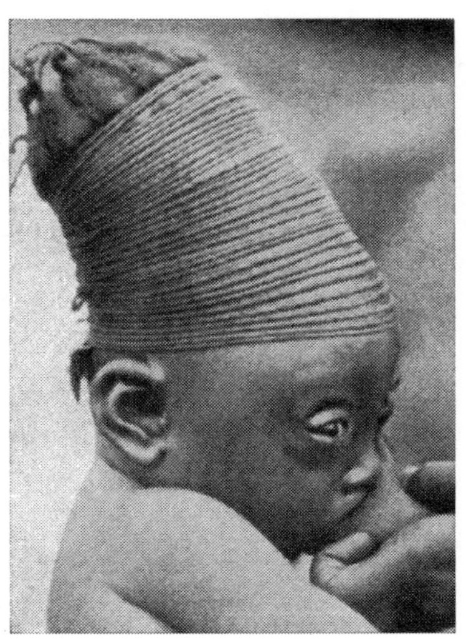

It is said that some tribes around the world bound their children's heads to elongate them – in honor of the gods whose heads they were imitating.

But it has been found that the inner volume does not change, and the skull is merely deformed – compared to the real thing (shown above in Peruvian skulls) where the inner capacity is much larger, and there is an absence of the "Y" shaped sutures common to the human skull.

(See Apx E, Virtual Earth Graduate.)

Giants

It wasn't all just large heads. Due to the earlier Nephilim crossbreeding, there were large bodies in the land, too. And the Bible is correct in reporting the existence of Giants in Canaan, spied by Joshua, which included the Philistines and Goliath.

Anakim Warrior

Philistine Goliath

The Anakim warrior above is similar to the giants reported and feared by the Vikings (see Chapter 2) who were said to live in Jotunheim. And today's modern world still sees giants (next page) – perhaps a throwback to the Nephilim? If the Nephilim survived and migrated into Canaan, then their genetics could have spread and included humans not quite their giant size, but who carried the gene (to stimulate the pituitary gland) resulting in other humans being large…

7' Giant in Afghanistan

9' Giant in America, 1930's
Robert Wadlow 8'11".

While this IS a pituitary gland issue, what gene caused the gland to overreact?

World's Tallest Man (living today)

Bao Xishun of China is the world's tallest man for the second time… **7' 9"**

The Anunnaki were 8-9' tall.

Anunnaki Law & Religion

Meanwhile, the Anunnaki were training their Priest group to read and write. One of the first things to do was to give the humans a set of rules, laws or behaviors to guide them – and command the Priests to enforce the Societal Law and/or Religious Laws. It was simpler in the beginning to make Religion the Law and if one didn't behave, then punishment followed – and it was found Man could be threatened with Eternal Damnation… Oh, yes, make that a place where he'd suffer forever… Oh, that's it – Hell. Be good, however, and you get to go to Heaven. And whereas Man was rather undeveloped and naïve, 4-5,000 years ago, it worked.

The Priests and Scribes got together and wrote down the Societal Law that the Anunnaki gave them, called **the Hammurabi Code** (ca 1760 BC) on 12 tablets.

Code of Hammurabi – 282 Laws

Hammurabi Law

This was a very strict "eye for an eye" code – so that rowdy humans might think twice before doing something unwise. For example, several laws say:[16]

> 8 -If any one steal cattle or sheep, or an ass, or a pig or a goat, if it belong to a god or to the court, the thief shall pay thirtyfold therefor; if they belonged to a freed man of the king he shall pay tenfold; if the thief has nothing with which to pay he shall be put to death.
>
> 195 – If a son strike his father, they shall cut off his fingers.
>
> 196– If a man destroy the eye of another man, they shall destroy his eye. If one destroy the eye of a freeman or break the bone of a freeman he shall pay one *mana* of silver.

This Code was given to Hammurabi by Shamash (Marduk) via Enki (seated).

Credit: Wikipedia
Right is a cropped picture to show the detail....

Stele is in the Louvre Museum, Paris

Note the horned headdress on the seated god (right) The 4 horns are a sign of Enki's rank – also attested by the wavy lines ("water god") off the god's shoulders. [17]
Note also that the seated god is taller than the human Hammurabi, and the seated god holds symbols of his office: a **Rod and Loop** (Power & Life: see Ankh in Chapter 5) which the Egyptians called a **Shen Ring**.

Note the rod and circular royal insignia being given to Hummurabi, whose hand is over his mouth as a sign of respect. Note Hammurabi has a plain hat, no horns…

Religion

As for Religion, the Anunnaki made it primitive so the humans could follow it easily, and they met Moses on the mountain (making sure he could not see Enlil's face) and gave him 10 basic Laws… or Ten Commandments.

To the Priest group, and to those who were sharper, serving the priestly group according to Enki's orders, more was given. The esoteric secrets behind the exoteric (common, public) Religion were given to develop the spirituality of the souls who were worthy (capable?) of learning more. Enki was determined to see just how far he could develop his special, brighter progeny, the *Adapa*. Esoteric Teaching was not given to the *Adama*, a lot of whom comprised much of society.

To that end, Enki developed what would later become a secret society called the **Brotherhood of the Serpent** (Chapter 9). In the beginning, this was open to those humans who showed promise in the lower, initiate levels of the Teaching. He promoted it in certain parts of the globe, but it would later be seen as a threat in Egypt and had to go "underground" by humans to preserve the valuable knowledge of what Man really is, where he came from, what his true potential is as a soul, and how to develop his inner potential. The Egyptian priests kept the Teaching to themselves and did not want everyday Man to have it – or else he could not be controlled if he "woke up" and actualized his real potential.

Concluding chapters will examine just what the Teachings were.

Creation vs Evolution

Just as an aside, note that the Anunnaki gods created Man, and they weren't alone. There were **multiple gods and multiple Gardens of Eden** around the planet… the Black race was seeded in Africa by the Anunnaki, the Brown race was seeded in MU, the Yellow race was seeded in China allegedly by those from Deneb (think: Huang Di), and the White race was seeded in Northern Europe allegedly by the Aldebarans (think: Hyperboreans), and the Red race was allegedly seeded in North America if not in Atlantis before that. Blacks did <u>not</u> evolve into Whites.[18] (See Chapter 8 and Cosmic Ancestry section.)

Then Evolution took over, rather: **<u>assisted</u> evolution**, and we moved from Neanderthal to Cro-Magnon to Homo *sapiens*. It is well-documented by the late Zechariah Sitchin how Enki "assisted" the development of his own progeny by mating with the *Adama* and later-stage *Adapa* to create hybrids. (Darwin's 2 theories of Survival of the Fittest and Natural Selection were of course correct, and today are called **Epigenetics**.) [Examined in VEG and TOM].

Anunnaki Creation of Writing

In various places around the globe, the Anunnaki wanted Man to learn to write things down – document his history and move away from the oral tradition, wherein things often got changed. Whereas they established **Cuneiform writing** in Sumeria…

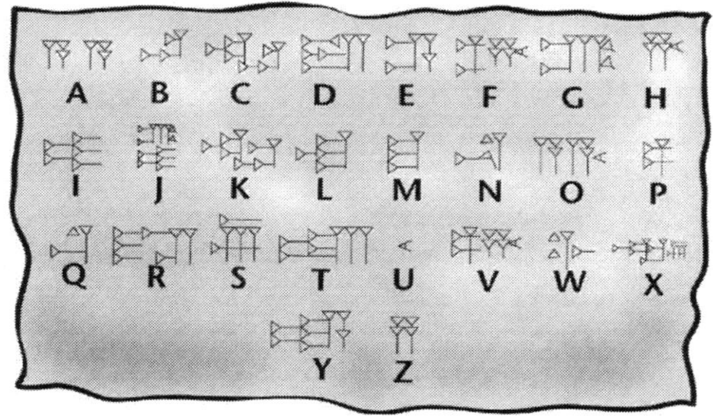

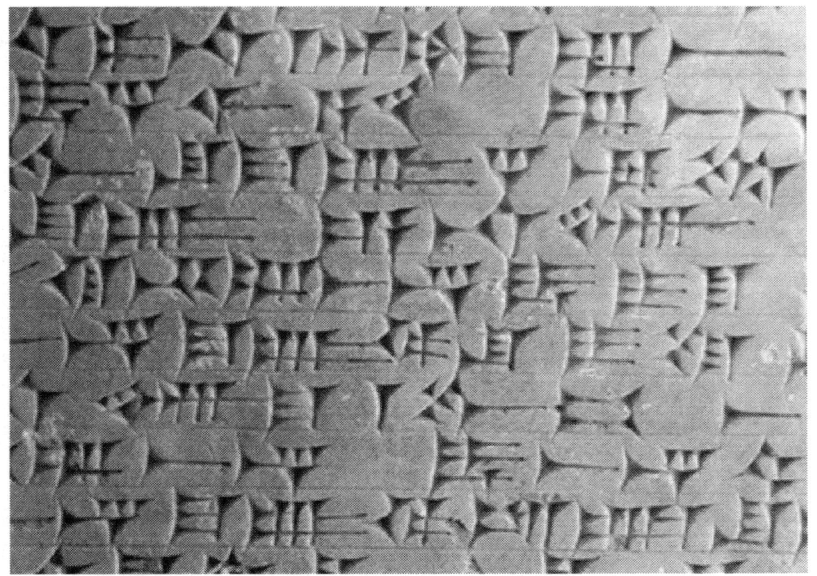

Note: letters 2 – 4 are: P - N - O (see picture key above)

..and show a certain stylish interpretation as well…

Then, they initiated (left) a **hieroglyphic system**, in Egypt…

Cartouche

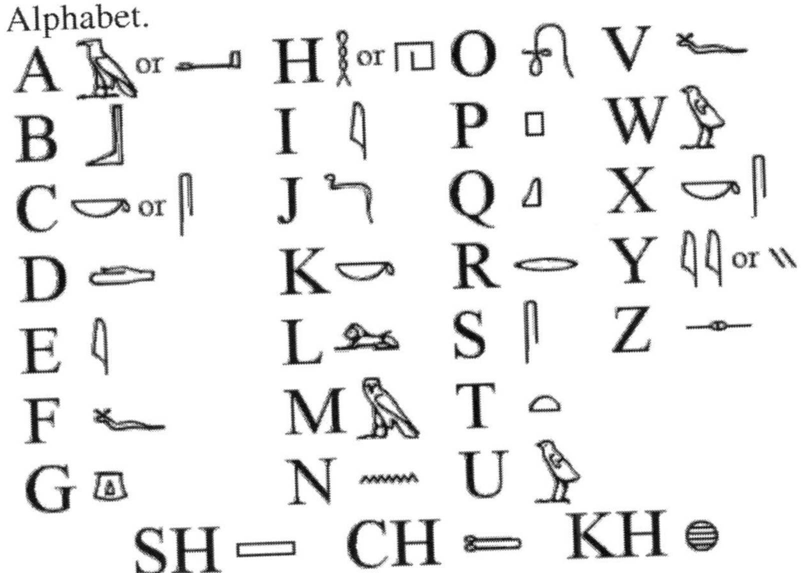

(You can see from the alphabet how Khufu's name was spelled in his cartouche. It was actually spelled "Kh-u-f-u"…yet note the "w" bird also = "u" bird.)

...and hieroglyphics among the Mayans (below):

And the Mayan version was very hard to decipher as there was no one standard way of writing something: for example, "Jaguar" in Mayan is B'alam ---

(samples credit: Wikipedia in https://en.wikipedia.org/wiki/Maya_script)

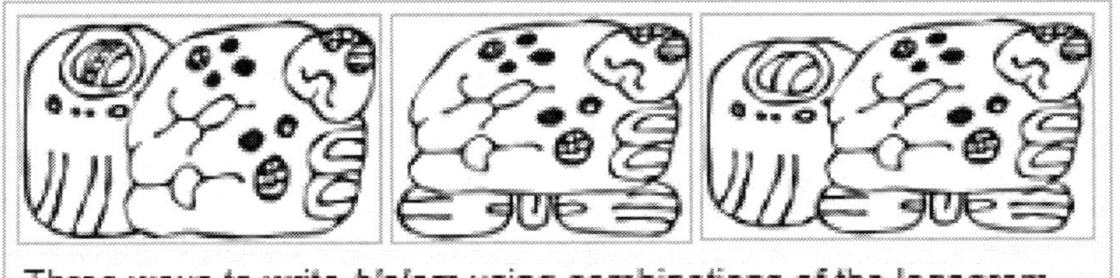

Three ways to write *b'alam* using combinations of the logogram with the syllabic signs as phonetic complements.

The Mayan scribes in each Mayan city-state developed their own style and modified what they had been taught, resulting in non-standard, hard-to-decipher hieroglyphics.

In the Scandinavian countries, and Northern Germany, one used **Runes** as a way of inscribing rocks for gravestones and to commemorate something/someone.

Note the Runes (letters) around the outside of the design. This is a Scandinavian runestone, but the twisting, turning of the snake-like or cord-like design is reminiscent of the Celts – and the two cultures merged at a later point in history.

Runic alphabet:

Rune	UCS	Transliteration
ᚠ	ᚠ	f
ᚢ	ᚢ	u
ᚦ	ᚦ	þ
ᚨ	ᚨ	a
ᚱ	ᚱ	r
ᚲ	ᚲ	k (c)
ᚷ	ᚷ	g
ᚹ	ᚹ	w
ᚺ ᚻ	ᚺ ᚻ	h
ᚾ	ᚾ	n
ᛁ	ᛁ	i
ᛃ	ᛃ	j
ᛇ	ᛇ	ï (æ)
ᛈ	ᛈ	p
ᛉ	ᛉ	z
ᛊ ᛋ	ᛊ ᛋ	s
ᛏ	ᛏ	t
ᛒ	ᛒ	b
ᛖ	ᛖ	e
ᛗ	ᛗ	m
ᛚ	ᛚ	l
ᛜ ᛝ ◻	ᛜ ᛝ	ŋ
ᛟ	ᛟ	o
ᛞ	ᛞ	d

The characters spell words in Old Norse:

Við hleifi mik seldo ne viþ hornigi,	No bread did they give me nor a drink from a horn,
nysta ek niþr,	downwards I peered;
nam ek vp rvnar,	I took up the runes,
opandi nam,	screaming I took them,
fell ek aptr þaðan.	then I fell back from there.[31]

2nd line: Nam ek vp rvnar ("v" is a "u")

Nam	from	German Nehmen to take
Ek	from	German Ich for I
Vp	from	Norse Op for up
Rvnar	from	Norse Runar (runes)

So "nam" = ᚾᚨᛗ (see table)

Regarding the Runic alphabet, it is very important to remember that the letters were all straight-lined – so that a hammer and chisel could pound them into a rock and the writer did not have to worry about making curved lines...

The Kensington Runestone found in Minnesota, 1898.

It says:

Eight Götalanders and 22 Northmen on (this?) acquisition journey from Vinland far to the west. We had a camp by two (shelters?) one day's journey north from this stone. We were fishing one day. After we came home, found 10 men red from blood and dead.
Ave Maria save from evil.
(*side of stone*) There are 10 men by the inland sea to look after our ships fourteen days journey from this peninsula (or island). Year 1362

Götalanders (above) were Germanic and the Northmen were Norwegian.

Note the date – Vikings were in Minnesota in 1362 – So do we believe Christopher Columbus who was almost 130 years later? The Vikings had a small colony in Newfoundland in AD 1000: at Anse-aux-Meadows.

Anse-aux-Meadows, Newfoundland

More on the Vikings in Chapter 2…

Anunnaki Technology

The reason for exploring so much of what the Anunnaki knew and did is important to examining what **legacy** the gods left to Man in various cultures around the globe. And as will be seen, whereas the Anunnaki were based in South Africa (for mining), and in Sumer (Iraq-Iran today) and Egypt, the gods' influence and training spread to the Vikings, Maya, Inca, Chinese, Hindus, and Greeks. The gods also had bases in Bolivia-Peru (Puma Punku, Sacsayhuaman, Nazca….) and it has been suggested that the Ancient Ones visited, if not occupied, Atlantis (which was not in the Mediterranean – see Chapter 8, Younger Dryas map).

In the meantime, before examining those cultures, it is necessary to expose what the Anunnaki taught and trained the humans to know and do because they took it with them to other countries. The aim is to reveal primarily the Anunnaki legacy in global cultures.

The MEs

While it has never been explained how the Anunnaki used something they called The MEs, it is a fact that they had small 'crystals' (see back cover) or perhaps something like our Flashdrives which stored a lot of data. They used these to run their civilization, and they contained information (like an encyclopedia) on medical, scientific, engineering, legal, and warfare weapon use, including formulas, procedures, and historical and genealogical data. All total there were about 94 MEs.[19] One can assume they had a device with which to read them, perhaps their own version of a computer. Sitchin recounts the story of **Inanna stealing the MEs** thus:[20]

> Enki was the Science Officer among the Anunnaki and had control of the MEs. Now that Inanna wished to make Uruk in Sumer a great urban center, she set out to Enki's abode in the Abzu swamp, in southeastern Africa, to pry some essential MEs out of her great-uncle.
>
> Inanna journeyed in her **flying Boat of Heaven** to Enki's abode. Enki realized that Inanna was visiting him unchaperoned, no guards, "the maiden all alone has directed her step to the Abzu" and Enki ordered his chamberlain to prepare a banquet and some sweet wine from dates.
>
> After Enki and Inanna had feasted, and Enki was "happy with drink", Inanna brought up the subject of the MEs. Gracious with drink, Enki presented her with some MEs to make Uruk a seat of kingship. She took these and asked for more. She worked her charms on Enki asking for more, and Enki made a second presentation. Bright Inanna took them. (continued…)

As the drinking and feasting continued, he gave her 7 MEs that provided for a function of a Divine Lady, in addition to those already given which gave her kingship and governance. They included temple management, servants, rituals, music and arts, metalworking, masonry, leatherwork and weaving, scribeship and mathematics. Last but not least he gave her a ME for weapons and the art of warfare.

As Anu's Beloved, Inanna wished to rule a big, important city in Sumer, not the outpost in the Indus Valley called **Aratta** [Mohenjo-Daro].

Now having the essentials to set up her kingdom, she slipped away in her Boat, leaving smoke and fire behind her.

When Enki sobered up and realized what he had given her, he ordered his chamberlain to pursue her and retrieve the MEs. He caught up with her in Eridu but she had given the MEs to her pilot who took them to Uruk while Inanna distracted the chamberlain. She could not be Queen in Uruk but the MEs would insure that her position as a Patron-Goddess would be secured. (Appendix B.)

Enki captured Inanna and locked her up at Eridu (Earth's 1st city, by the way), and tried to get the MEs back. Enlil, the Sovereign over Earth, flew to Eridu and Inanna won her case to keep the MEs and made Uruk a mighty city (4000 BC). She then turned her attention to finding a suitor and tried to get married. The rest is intrigue and action worthy of *As The World Turns....* (see Dumuzi & Inanna in Chapter 5).

ME does not stand for anything; it is not an acronym. It is a Sumerian word for the objects. We do not know what the Anunnaki called the devices, nor for sure what they looked like.

Flying Boats of Heaven

It was said that Inanna flew off to Africa from Mesopotamia in a "flying boat," and while we have no pictures of what that was, it must have been the primitive Sumerian way to describe a craft that flew. All the Sumerians knew were boats – not even chariots – that came later in Egypt. So if a craft suddenly lifted off and flew, it must be a <u>flying</u> boat.

Fortunately, ancient sculptures have been found which are the artists' attempt to show what ancient flying machines looked like, and the most likely candidate for Inanna's flying boat is shown below:

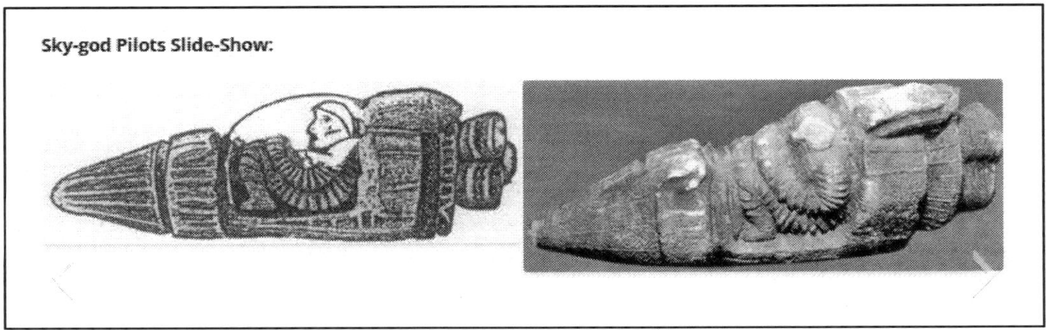

Ancient "Flying Boat" from Sumeria?
Credit: mesopotamiangods.com./astronauts-shems-discs-rockets-skygods

The Sumerians added wings to objects to indicate that they flew, and if the object was round and had an exhaust flame, it could look like this:

No, the above is not the Sun. The circle has **Enlil's symbol – an 8-pointed star**. The Sun was shown like this below (***udjat,*** adopted by the Egyptians):

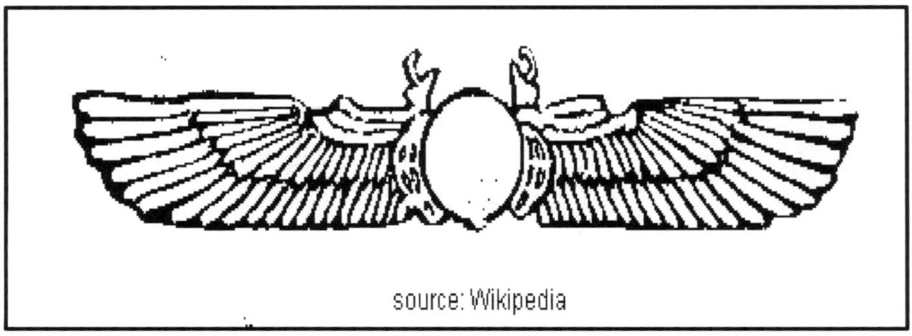

source: Wikipedia

Ancient MU & Shem

shem at Inanna's temple

An ancient coin found at Byblos… the biblical Gebal… on the Mediterranean coast of Lebanon, depicts the Great **Temple of Ishtar (Inanna).** The coin depicts a 2-part temple. In front stands the main temple structure, imposing with its columned gateway. Behind it is an inner courtyard or "sacred area" hidden and protected by a high massive wall. It is clearly a raised area as it can only be reached by ascending many stairs.

(credit: enkispeaks.com)

In the center of this sacred area stands a special platform its crossbeam construction resembling that of the Eiffel Tower , as though built to withstand great weight. And on the platform stands the object of all this security and protection: an object that can only be a *mu.*[21]

This is a "divine bird", and the enclosure was built to protect it (Foundry, p. 221). Ninurta and 2 companions appeared to King Gudea, standing beside Ninurta's IM.DU.GUD or "divine black wind bird." The object was so important that it was guarded by two "divine weapons" – "supreme hunter" and "supreme killer"… Weapons that emitted beams of light [lasers] that could kill.

Murals at Tell Ghassul, east of the Dead Sea, contain murals dated from 3500 BC which show the following "whirlwinds" of antiquity (left)… These are not faces, but representations of machines that flew.

(credit: enkispeaks.com

This is another drawing of a Shem with the Sumerian pictograph for the DIN.GIR (to its right)…

(credit: Messagetoeagle.com.)

The 'rocket' to the right is composed of two symbols:

…where DIN means 'righteous' and GIR means 'rocket' and when put together, and used before a god's name, as in DIN.GIR Enki, it signifies the 'righteous one of the rocketships, Enki'. It also visually signifies that the ship was a 2-stage craft.

Hymn to Inanna

Lastly, a hymn to Inanna/Ishtar and her journeys in her Boat of Heaven clearly indicate that the *mu* was a vehicle in which the gods roamed the skies – far and high:[22]

Lady of Heaven,
She puts on the Garment of Heaven [spacesuit],
She valiantly ascends towards Heaven,
over all the peopled lands,
she flies in her MU.
Lady who in her MU
to the heights of Heaven joyfully wings
over all the resting places,
She flies in her MU.

Her 'Boat' was also called ZAG.MU.KU – "the bright MU which is for afar." This was also called a "Chariot of Fire" – [23]

I raised the head of the boat ID.GE.UL ("high to heaven")
The Chariot of Marduk's princeliness,
The boat ZAG.MU.KU whose approach is observed,
the supreme traveler between Heaven and Earth,
in the midst of the pavilion I enclosed,
Screening off its sides…

…and that recalls the original drawing of the **Shem** in its temple enclosure (prior page). MU, Boat of Heaven… now what is a Shem?

Tower of Babel

In the Bible, the followers of the god of Babylon began to build a "tower whose head can reach to the heavens" – a launch tower, we would say nowadays. "Let us make a **Shem**," they said, -- not a "name" as is commonly translated, but the original meaning of the Sumerian source of the word MU – a rocketlike object. (3450 BC)

> The Sumerian term MU or its semitic derivitives *shu-mu* ("that which is a MU), *sham* or *shem*. Because the term also connoted "that by which one is remembered" the word has come to be taken as meaning "name." But the universal application of "name" to early texts that spoke of an **object used in flying** has obscured the true meaning of the ancient records. (Note: one would also be remembered if one had a MU and could fly around!) [24]

Note: the god **Shamash** (Shem-esh [ESH = fire]= "The Shining One") was in charge of Mission Control, based at **Ur-Shulim** (Jerusalem) and was also called Utu, or "he of the fiery rocketships." (See Israel section in Chapter 5.) The Shining Ones are examined in Chapter 13.)

Raising the Dead

The Anunnaki were also known to have the technology to raise the dead back to life… something the Egyptians (governed by Thoth and Marduk, Enki's sons), were to quick to seize upon and is one of the reasons they mummified bodies – to be later resurrected. Inanna later mummified Dumuzi to resurrect him (Chapter 5). [25]

See footnote 25: further resurrection info.

Ninmah was Enki's half-sister and was a medical expert, having assisted in the genetic creation of the original *Lulu* worker slaves. **Anzu** was an Anunnaki stationed on Mars when his grandfather **Alalu** was killed (fighting for control of the spaceport) and Anzu was also killed for stealing Enlil's MEs, disrupting the communications system, and leading an astronaut revolt against Enlil. Anzu was caught and paid the price: [26]

> Ninmah performed a variety of procedures to revive Anzu . "From her pouch she took out the **Pulser**, upon Anzu's heart pulsing she directed… she took out the **Emitter**, its crystals' life giving emissions on his body she directed ."
>
> In addition, she also used the **Food of Life** and the **Water of Life** which she placed in his mouth and on his lips… Ninmah repeated this several times after which Anzu opened his eyes.
>
> The Face on Mars, in Cydonia, is alleged to be the face of **Alalu** who was killed before he could become the King of the Anunnaki.

Face on Mars (after NASA denial of The Face)

Tree of Life

There were Trees of Life all over the ancient world, including the Vikings and the Maya. The following are some examples which begin with the Sumerian Tree of Life…said concept was transmitted to the other parts of the globe.

Sumerian Tree of Life. Note the pinecone fertility symbols in their hands, and note that there are 13 'flowers' to the Tree: each side reflects 6 chakras + the top/crown chakra. This is examined more in Chapter 12.

The pinecone was a **symbol of fertility** and even the Vatican has one outside on its grounds (below).

That is not a wristwatch but a bracelet on the Anunnaki god's arm.

The three horns indicate it is a god, drawn as a human, but the wings say he also flies.

The **pinecone** is also found at the Vatican… it was also a symbol of the **Pineal Gland** (in the center of the brain), and associated with enlightenment.

Kundalini Connection

The pine cone, Egypt, and the Eye of Horus have an interesting relationship.

The All-Seeing Eye of Horus

Operative Masonry, in the fullest meaning of that term, signifies the process by which the Eye of Horus is opened. E.A. Wallis Budge has noted that in some of the papyri illustrating the entrance of the souls of the dead into the Judgment Hall of Osiris, the deceased person has a **pine cone** attached to the crown of his head. The Greek mysteries also carried a symbolic staff , the upper end being in the form of a pine cone, which was called the *thyrsus* of Bacchus. In the human brain there is a tiny gland called the **pineal body,** which is the sacred eye of the ancients, and corresponds to the third eye of the Cyclops.

Little is known concerning the function of the pineal gland, which Descartes suggested (more wisely than he knew) might be the abode of the spirit of Man. As its name signifies, the pineal gland is the **sacred pine cone in Man** – the *eye single* [Think: Biblical passage about having a single eye], which cannot be opened until **CHiram** [sic] the spirit fire [aka *Kundalini*] is *raised* through the sacred seals which are called the Seven Churches [viz., Chakras] in Asia. [27] [emphasis added]

Note: there is an oblique reference to the Seven Churches of the Bible's *Book of Apocalypse*, and the seven seals and the Seven Churches mean the same thing. This was also what the ancients called being "born again" : (opening the 7 seals = 7 chakras).

Returning to the original Sumerian picture of the Tree of Life, note that the gods are also manipulating the Tree which has 13 'buds' on it… the concept is what transferred, not the exact representation... pinecones symbolize genetic work. (Chapter 12 has much more on this.)

So the Anunnaki possessed some degree of genetic expertise, as well as knowledge of Man's anatomy and make-up. However, the fact that we get old, die, and get sick are a result of intentional Anunnaki design. (Think: control.)
They modified our genetics to have **mitochondria** and **telomeres** wear out – causing aging – and our immune systems are not capable of stopping the onslaught of Ebola or MRSA.

However, the original humans such as Moses, Methusala and Adam did live much longer lives – as a result of Anunnaki genes being given to Man, and then further 'adjustments' were made to the DNA, so that "3 score and 10" would be Man's years, as stated in the Bible.

Not only the Sumerian texts state that Man was not intended to live long and know much like the Anunnaki, but the *Popul Vuh* of the Maya states that same thing. (See VEG, Ch. 5, and Chapter 6 in this book.)

Tree of Life – Alternate Versions

In addition to the Sumerian Tree of Life, it is a stylized version of something esoteric found in the Kabbalah … part of the **Alchemy** tradition given by the Anunnaki to the Sumerians, then the Egyptians, and then it was adopted by the Hebrews.

Note that there are 9 + 2 elements on the Kabbalistic Tree (right) and in its more simple form there are 10 basic parts (left):

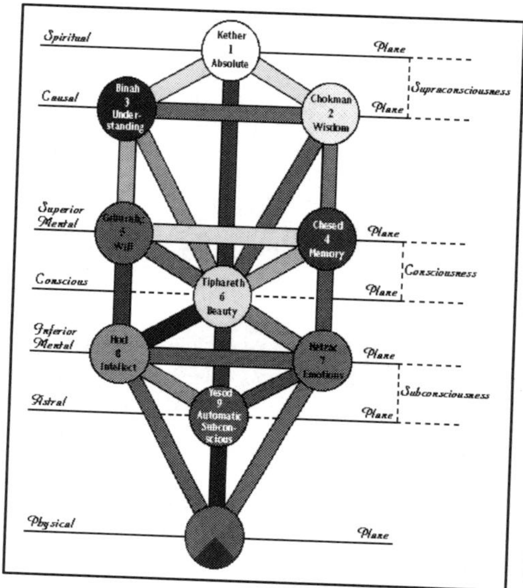

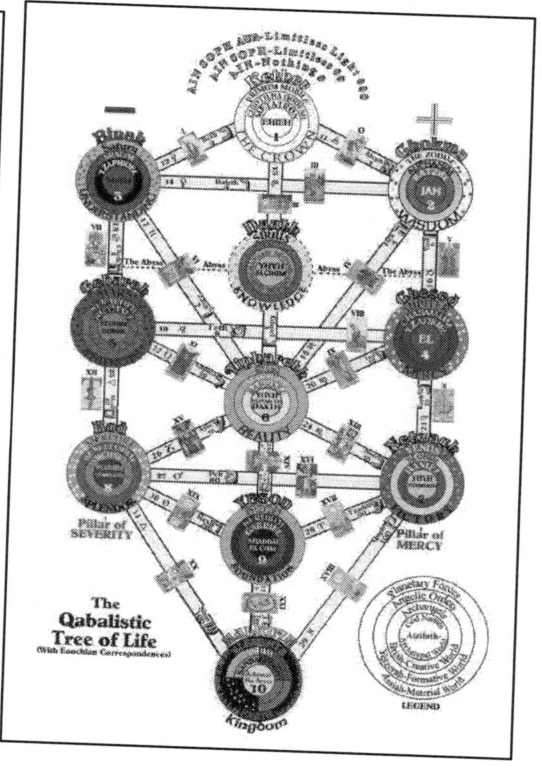

Note the Tree on the right also has the **Da'at** sphere under Keter (top).

The Kabbalah Tree of Life will be re-examined in Chapter 12, but for now it is significant that its source was the gods – same concept, whereas the Hebrews took it further in the Kabbalah to describe multiple aspects of Man's esoteric nature. This is another relationship between the Sumerian Tree and the Kabbalistic Tree.

It will also be seen in the chapters on Vikings and Mayans that they, too, inherited the basic Tree of Life teaching.

For now, just note the similarity between the Kabbalah Tree of Life and the Norse Tree of Life (**Yggdrasil**):

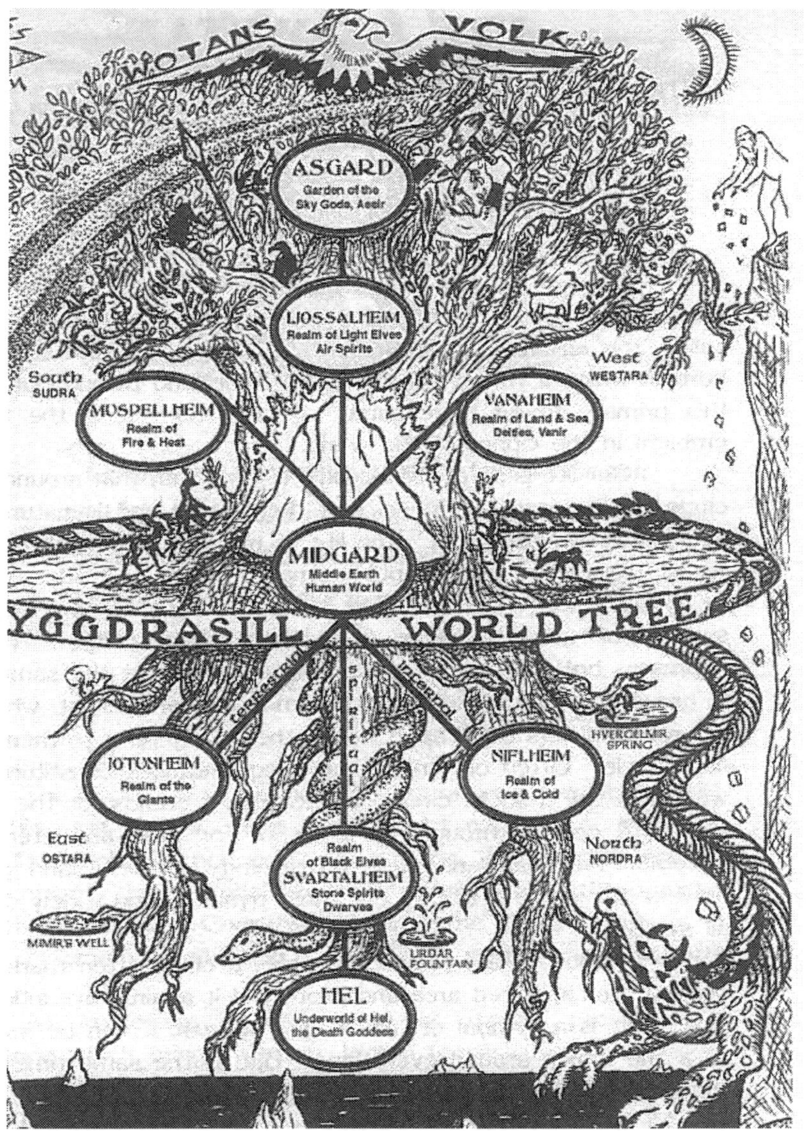

The Anunnaki spread basic teachings all over the globe, as we will see….

Note the Dragon/Serpent (bottom) and the Eagle (top) – universal symbology examined in Chapters 9 and 12).

Brotherhood of the Serpent

The last issue to be covered before leaving the Anunnaki review, is to emphasize that Enki (aka Ea) really loved his creation and sought to develop them as much as he could. After all, **Galactic Law** (Glossary) says that any advanced race developing a new, sentient race is responsible for them, to nurture, educate and protect them until they can fend for themselves. As was said earlier, Enlil did not want that responsibility – it was not that he hated mankind, just that the chore of raising them properly would consume a lot of resources, and he was against that.

Enki, on the other hand, wanted to see how far he could take the *Adapa*, the best humans, and that sounds like a mindset typical of a Science Officer who has created life. Thus when Enlil tries to wipe out Man (and the Nephilim) with **The Flood**, Enki thwarts that plan and sees to it that DNA for all flora and fauna that would be destroyed by the Flood, are preserved.

The humans become Enki's responsibility and eventually the Anunnaki are to go home (BC 650) – largely due to their warlike nature (guess where Man's propensity for war came from?), and the **Solar Council** stepped in during the Cosmic War that destroyed Tiamat (between Mars and Jupiter), but they were too late to prevent a **plasmic disruptor** from creating the huge scar on Mars (*Valles Marineris*) and blowing most of its water and atmosphere away. The Anunnaki were invited to go home, but in accord with **Galactic Law**, some had to stay behind and shepherd Man....and using their human form, they became the Viking gods, then the Greek gods, and then the Roman gods.

Then seeing that Man still wasn't obeying them, they themselves went underground, and managed Man by proxy (explained in <u>Transformation of Man</u>). They became known as the Nagas (under India and China).

Enki did not want to lose his creation and gave special, spiritual knowledge to several of his *Adapa* protégés... and they called their group The Brotherhood of the Serpent, espousing what would become known as **Serpent Wisdom**, as used throughout this book. This teaching included Astronomy, Alchemy (transmutation of materials and development of the soul), Chakras, Bionet, and *Kundalini*, higher Mathematics including fractals and Fibonacci series, Geometry, Medicine, and Higher Truths. Later, the Egyptian priests and the much later Catholic Church would drive the teaching underground into secret societies (which will be examined later) because it was a threat to their organizations.

Snakes & Serpents

To properly understand the history of our planet, it has become obvious that there are too many mysteries – if one does not know about the Serpent influence. First we should understand that the **snake** is the physical slithering creature seen around the world. But the **Serpent** is the mystical even legendary aspect of those who assisted mankind's development.

Secondly, we need to take a look at the root of the words for serpent or snake.

> The snake is known in the language of ***Can***aan variously as Aub, Ab, Oub, Ob, Op, Eph, and Ev. Amazingly in the Mayan language *Can* means serpent, as in Cucul*can* the bird serpent, and just as in the Ancient Sumerian A*can* and the Scottish *Can* for serpent (which is where we get the word *canny* like the wise snake). Vul*can* the Roman god of fire comes from the Babylonian *Can* for serpent and *Vul* for fire showing an etymological link across thousands of miles. Indeed even the very center of the Christian world, the Vatican, comes from the words *vatis* for prophet and *can* for serpent, making the Vati**can** a place of serpent prophecy. [28]

The snake worshippers in Moses' era were known as Hivites, from *Hhivia* or serpent, and the Hivites become **Ophites**, early Christian Gnostic serpent worshippers. *Hevia* was the root of the **Biblical Eve** name: it means 'female serpent.' Even Baal (or Bel) was a solar god whose name is thought to have originated as an abbreviation of ***Ob-El*** – the **serpent god** or shining serpent. According to one source, the 'shining' aspect reveals a subtle clue where on one hand the shining was said to represent the auric glow around someone with an altered state of consciousness. That was a clue that true illumination derives from Knowledge of one's own soul and of the greater work of the gods.

And on the other hand, it is a reference to the stars above, **Ophiuchus** – the serpent constellation which was kept out of the Zodiac (see Chapter 11). The stars and Sun do shine down on us. In addition, know that the Sun was associated with the serpent imagery around the world.

> Going back to Baal, we find that the 20th century writer and historian Bryant remarked that the Greeks called him Beliar, which was interpreted by Hesychius to mean "a dragon or great serpent." Bel is the Assyrio-Babylonian version of the gods Enlil and Marduk – being the same as Baal – the same Baal seen throughout the Bible. So the Baal in the Bible is a Babylonian serpent god. [29]

Gardiner also points out that **Tanit** was a goddess in Northern Africa associated with the Tree of Life like **Ishtar** and **Astarte** (aka Inanna)[30], and the name means 'Serpent Lady'. She is found on many coins in Carthage accompanied with the caduceus symbolizing her Serpent role in life, death and rebirth. **Inanna** is also called a 'Queen of Heaven' like Isis and Mary which has connections to the Moon, whereas the male serpent is Ra, the King of Heaven – the Sun. [31] Inanna is also associated with the Pleiades, 7 stars, which keeps cropping up, as we'll see….[32]

The following is verified ancient knowledge: [33]

Serpent Imagery

Just as an interesting aside, the following is offered for consideration.

Clemens Alexandrius said that *Heviah* – the root of Eve – means 'female serpent'. "If we pay attention to the strict sense of the Hebrew, the name Evia aspirated signifies a female, serpent."

It is connected to the same Arabic root which means both 'life' and 'serpent.'

The Persians even called the constellation, Serpens, 'the little Ava' or 'Eve.' (Serpens was also called Ophiuchus… see Chapter 11.)

> Ophiuchus comes from Ophis (snake) and cheiro (to handle). Ophiuchus was in fact a snake handler.

In old Akkadian, Ad signifies 'father' and according to C. Staniland Wake in *The Origin of Serpent Worship*, Adam was closely associated in legend with Seth, Saturn, **Thoth** (see Chapter 5) …. Who were all associated strongly as serpents.

Note that Abel in Genesis means 'serpent shining' as mentioned earlier of OB-El derivation. Cain was also thought to be of serpent descent. Ca-in suggests the *Ca/Can* source meaning serpent. Abel resolves to Ab (snake) and El (shining one) and therefore he was a snake god or a shining snake.

According to rabbinical tradition Cain was not the son of Adam and Eve, but the son of Asmodeus, the 'serpent spirit' who is Ahriman in Persian Zoroastrianism.

Remember that Serpent can also be an appellation for someone advanced in spiritual knowledge and abilities. Such were the founders of Serpent Wisdom groups.

Anunnaki Summary

There are several things to know at this point.

1. The Sumerian civilization sprang up **overnite** – thus it was fully formed. There were never found any older layers of the major cities when archeologists started digging in Iraq… that means the Sumerian civilization did not evolve. Whoever set it up already had developed the architecture, pottery, irrigation channels, writing and math, to name a few things. All information to create a civilization from scratch was contained on the **MEs**, special high-tech objects (like flashdrives) that were basically an encyclopedia of skills and data to run a civilization, and knowledge to genetically create/modify living organisms.

   All parts of Sumeria sprang up fully developed.

2. The Sumerian humans denigrated their gods – they were brutally honest about them, recording their lusts, battles with each other, the fact that some of them were repulsive (and the gods issued orders to not make any images of their real appearance – unless as humans), and they recorded how the gods tried to wipe them out with disease (***Suruppu***) and then a Flood.

   The gods had very human attributes: power-hungry, lustful, petty, lying, sneaky, belligerent… and they gave Man some of their DNA.

3. When Iraq was excavating and bulldozing land to create a new highway, the Sumerian tablets were accidentally found. Thousands of them. Hidden. Not meant to be found. So this was not a popular myth for the masses… these tablets and cylinders were considered sacred as they contained information about the origins of Sumerian civilization. It was about the gods and Man.

   The Sumerian tablets were hidden and not for the masses.

4. Humans were created in the image and likeness (i.e., humanoid) of the gods – so-called because the gods came from the sky with power and knowledge. Man was created as a **slave** to work the mines in South Africa, build the ziggurats in Mesopotamia, and work the agricultural fields in both locations. The Anunnaki also appeared to be gods because they lived longer and thus appeared to be immortal. Man's DNA was cut down so that the gods didn't have to put up with long-living but rowdy, ignorant humans.

(Virtual Earth Graduate Ch. 3 goes into much more of these aspects.)

5. Enki was also called "**Ea, the Serpent God**." (which relates to much of the following chapters: Enki founded the **Serpent Wisdom** groups, which became secret societies).

This is a very standard picture of Enki /Ea (from Sitchin's 12th Planet):

This shows Ea as the water god and he was said to dwell in the swamp (Abzu)....[34] actually a bright place with flowing waters...

Yet it is more relevant to show his other less common picture... Enki is on the left...

An attendant holds the screen while Ea – as the **serpent god** – reveals the [coming Flood] secret to Atra-Hasis [aka Noah or Ziusudra or Utnapishtim – he was known by 4 names]. [35]

Enki was called the Serpent God because he was the keeper and originator of the esoteric secrets and genetic science that would eventually bless Man.

Sitchin's Anunnaki Substantiated

(Credit: en.wikipedia.org)

The late Zechariah Sitchin left our world in 2010, but he would have loved to see his protégé, **Sasha Lessin**, and his work be verified by NASA and/or archeologists.

The late (1996) **Carl Sagan** initially said he thought that aliens existed and could visit us. Sagan always advocated scientific skeptical inquiry and the scientific method, and he pioneered exobiology and promoted the Search for Extra-Terrestrial Intelligence (**SETI** which was discontinued). He wrote the novel *Contact* which became a movie of the same name – so he wasn't an enemy, just asking for solid proof.

> SETI was a dumb idea from the beginning – what if we were announcing our presence to **hostile ETs** who were looking for a new world to plunder? Don't laugh – Dr. Stephen Hawking said the same thing lately. SETI was officially cancelled recently (though others have privately adopted it).
>
> It was also a dumb idea since any ETs who knew about Earth would already be here – why would they answer?

Then **Erich von Däniken** came out with his book Chariots of the Gods? in 1968, only to have Sagan attack the idea – due to a lack of outstanding proof. Then Sitchin came out 8 years later with his book, The 12th Planet, and substantiated some of von Däniken's claims. And since then, the establishment has tried everything they can (largely via TV specials with total skeptics) to discredit the whole ET and Man concept. Now it is time to remind them of the evidence that does exist which they conveniently ignore.

First, let it be said that Sitchin assumed that the Anunnaki "who came down" were ETs, and while that is believable nowadays, it is also possible that they were an **advanced terrestrial race** – from **Atlantis** or **Hyperborea**. Just because the Sumerians saw them flying, and the Zulu and Dogon in Africa saw them land, does not mean they were ETs. And if so, the chances are good that they are still here (underground). Since they were described as flying with noise and smoke, they apparently were using rockets and did not have interstellar propulsion anyway.

The rest of what Sitchin proposes largely holds water – but to know that and to appreciate it, one has to look at the whole picture:

Evidence of Advanced Beings

This is some of the "evidence" around the planet that Man did not do – due to lack of technology or manpower to do them.

Sacsayhuaman – giant walls protecting a fortress at the top, perhaps a landing pad. The walls consist of huge boulders that are custom cut, one boulder has 11 or more angles – as if it was melted and poured into position.

Baalbek – home to what was once a landing pad for the Anunnaki ships (no joke), and the floor/platform consists of huge, solid rectangular pillars of stone, each weighing more than 800 tons. There is one laying on the ground between the Temple platform and the quarry, called The Trilithon, which is so heavy that modern equipment cannot lift it.

Puma Punku – once an outpost for the advanced beings, it looks now like it was destroyed, stones scattered in all directions. But upon closer examination, the stones show evidence of laser-cutting equipment – the local natives said they did not do it nor did their ancestors, but "the gods from the sky did it."

Olmec Heads – found in Central America they have been obviously cut perfectly round into many Negro faces (the Nubians in Chapter 5) wearing helmets. Nearby are many stone spheres, perfectly round that were used ballistically against the Olmecs' enemies.

Mayan Pyramids – the interesting thing about the pyramids' steps is that they are spaced for larger beings to climb them – (see VEG Ch. 10). Humans have a hard time climbing the pyramids and steel cables have been installed to assist those brave enough to make the climb (pp. 274, 280).

These are all shown in VEG and some in this book.

Southwest Petroglyphs – in many places in the American Southwest, are the petroglyphs made by natives who saw strange beings. Included are often scratched drawings of serpents. (See Chapter 7.)

Zuni Petroglyphs – "The Ant People"?

Saqqara Tomb – in the pyramid of Zoser (Djoser) at Saqqara, inside on the wall of the tomb is a very interesting relief:

The top left is obviously a helicopter, the next is a "tank" or submarine, and below the "tank" is something that looks like a jet plane. And below that is what looks like a glider.

The tomb dates back to 2650 BC.

Reminds one of the saying: "There is nothing new under the Sun."

Australian Rockart -- Anyone want to take a guess as to what this is? What did the Aborigines in Australia see? (Chapter 8.)

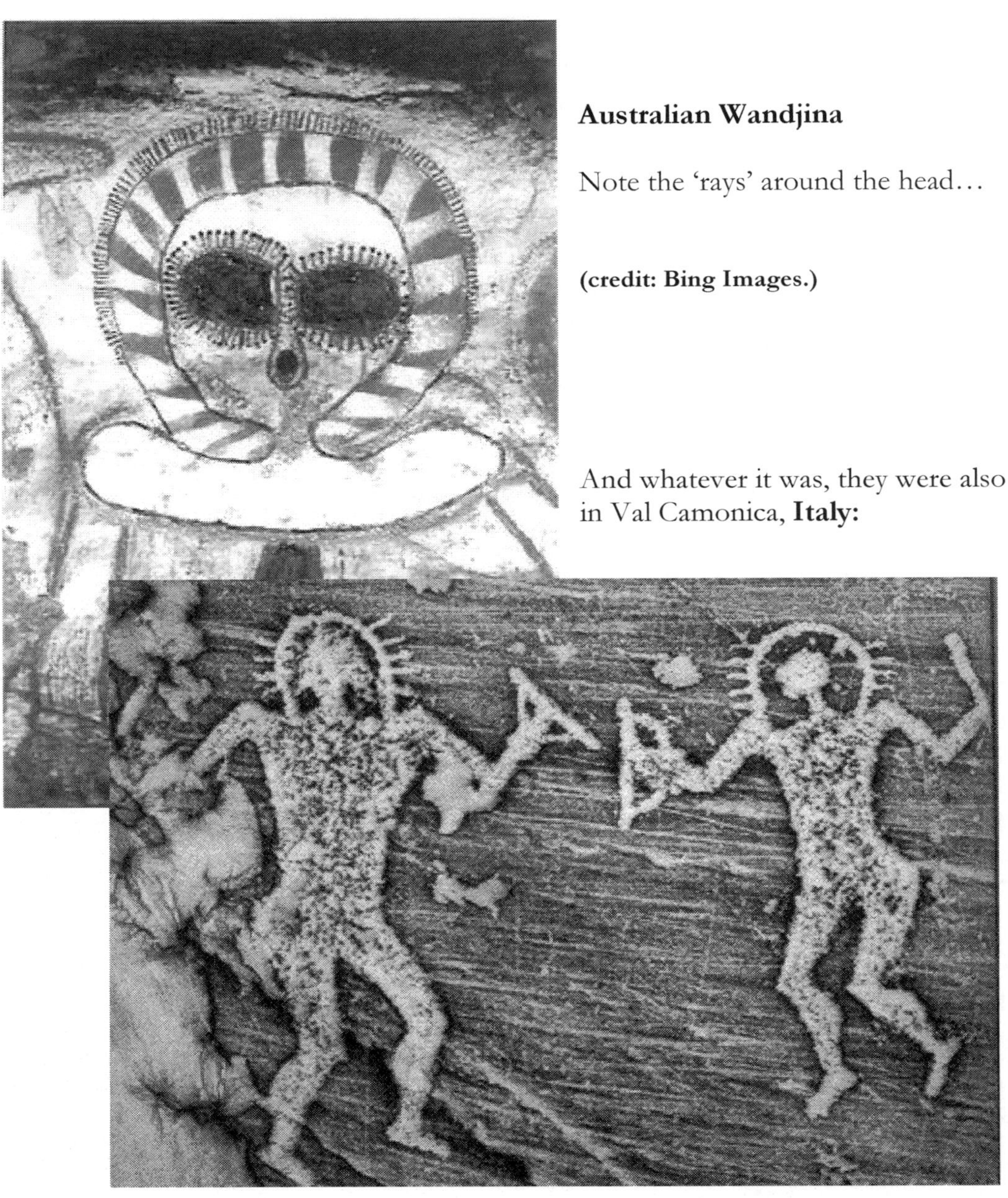

Australian Wandjina

Note the 'rays' around the head…

(credit: Bing Images.)

And whatever it was, they were also in Val Camonica, **Italy:**

And lastly, because many of the other unique pictures of things might also be via Photoshop®, the selection is limited. The ones shown throughout this book (except where a few are noted with caution) have been vetted to be authentic – especially since they have been around for a long time (before modern graphic tools).

Thus we turn to a modern issue that has just been raised as of April 2016.

NASA and Planet X

There is gravitational evidence of a large object (maybe a planet) in the **Kuiper Belt**, perturbing the orbits of known asteroids and small moons. Since Pluto was downgraded from a planet (even though it has 5 moons), the object astronomers are looking for is called the **9th Planet** – god forbid we leave Pluto as a planet, then we'd be making Sitchin correct with the 12th Planet collection (the Sumerians counted the Sun and Moon as objects) and the "X" in Planet X could also be seen as a "10" or 10th Planet – Woohoo, we can't have that!

The 9th Planet is said to have 10 times the mass of Earth, e.g., the size of Neptune.

Here are the known objects out there:

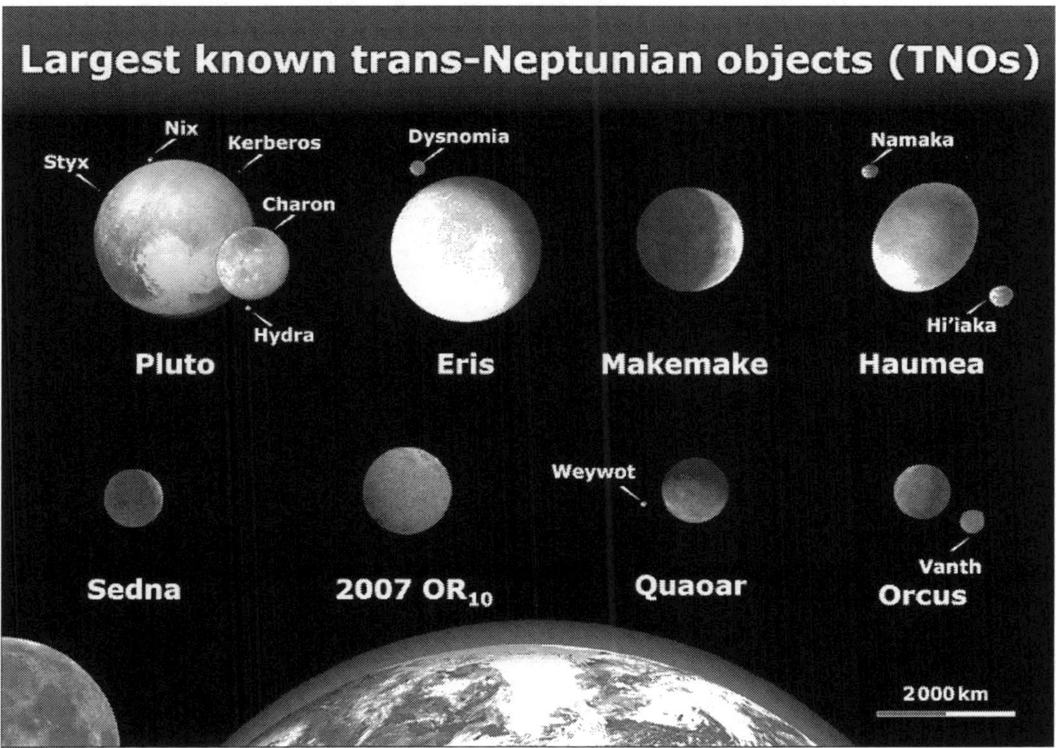

The best description of the 9th Planet is in the following chart:

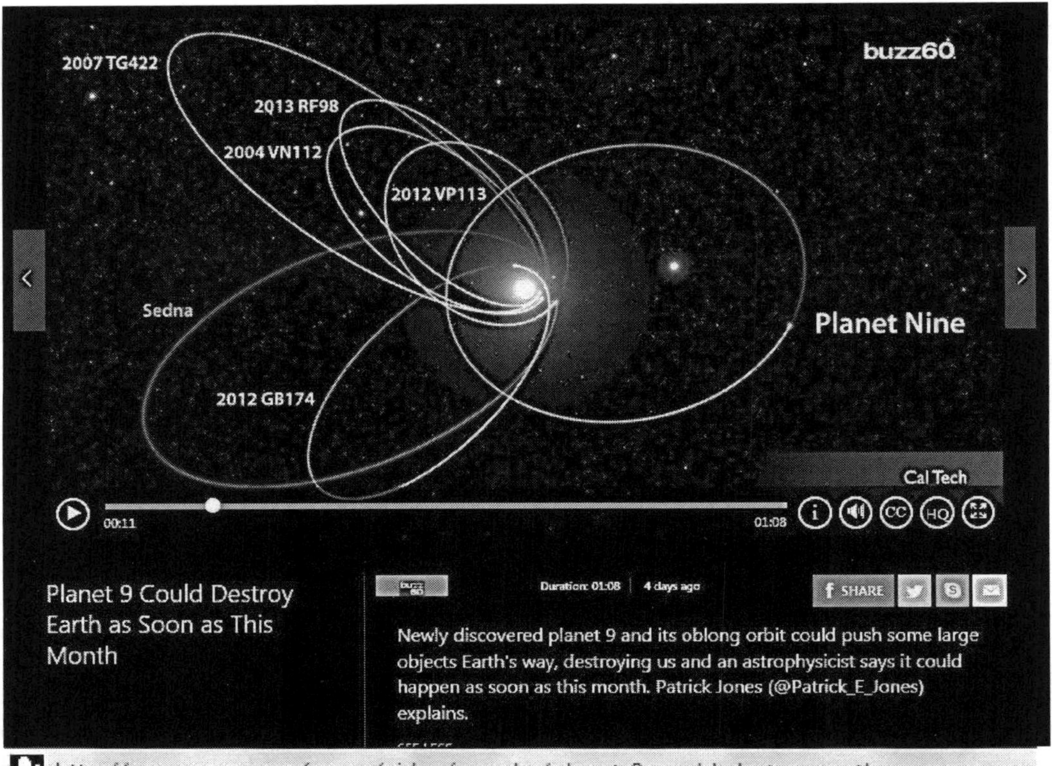

http://www.msn.com/en-us/video/wonder/planet-9-could-destroy-earth-as-soon-as-

The legend in lower right (above diagram) says:

> Newly discovered Planet 9 and its oblong orbit could push some large objects Earth's way, destroying us and an astrophysicist says it could happen as soon as this month [January 2016]…. It could take 20,000 years to complete an orbit of the Sun. Other astrophysicists disagree since the object hasn't been found yet.

So the establishment says they see no evidence to support van Däniken nor Sitchin, and yet the astronomers are not kidding – **there is something large out there**, at the edge of the solar system, and they are looking for it. [36] They know it is what knocked Sedna into an extended orbit (above diagram: lower left).

In support of Mr. Sitchin, remember that he is not alone: in addition to the Sumerian epics, the *Atra Hasis*, the *Enuma Elish* and the *Epic of Gilgamesh*, there is also the Hebrew *Haggadah* and Berossus confirming that we are not alone. Add to that the Hindu Mahabharata speaking of aerial battles in Vimanas and there are some things to give serious consideration to.
Keep that in mind as we survey the effect that Enki's Serpents of Wisdom had on ancient cultures around the globe…

Russian Phobos II Probe

And while this does not vindicate the Sitchin-Anunnaki issue, it is saying that there are some very big spaceships out there – not necessarily the Anunnaki's, but more than likely, the huge ships belong to those who inhabit Mars and don't want us there. Two American NASA and two Russian Phobos probes were lost – and one (Phobos II) was **shot down** – and whatever shot it down left a huge shadow on the planet's surface:

PHOBOS IMAGE MARCH 26th 1989 (Showing shadow of Mars Surface (Just before Impact)

(credit: Bing Images: unexplained-mysteries.com)

That picture is not showing the Phobos II shadow – Phobos II is taking a picture of the Martian surface just seconds before impact. As an interesting corollary, Jim Marrs in his book Alien Agenda had this to say (from his research):

> In his book, Aliens From Space, [Maj. Donald] Keyhoe flatly stated, "Since **1953** [before the US or anyone had put satellites in orbit around Earth], the Air force had known that giant spaceships were operating

> near our planet." He said that it was during that year that the military began experimenting with new long-range radar equipment. "While making the initial tests," Keyhoe wrote, "AF operators were astonished to pick up **a gigantic object orbiting near the equator**. Its speed was almost 18,000 mph. Repeated checks showed that the tracking was correct. Some huge unknown object was circling the Earth, **600 miles out**." According to Keyhoe, shortly after this object was detected, **a second large object** came into orbit about 400 miles out and also was tracked on Air Force radar. [37] [emphasis added]

What all this suggests is that the Visitors are here – call them **Watchers**, Grigori, or Custodians, or **Anunnaki Remnant** (VEG, Ch. 10.) And, note that if they were hostile, we'd already have had a replay of the Hollywood movie, *Independence Day*. Yet, there are White Hats and Black Hats out there – See Epilog.

> What it may be is the Others who have been in this part of the solar system longer than Man has been on Earth, and therefore **Sitchin is correct,** and the Others inhabit remote parts of Earth (Nagas under India-China, and Nordics under Mt Shasta, for starters) as well as Mars (underground – note the water conduits on Mars in VEG, Apx. A and Appendix A in this book)….
>
> And ask yourself if the ships that Neil Armstrong saw sitting on the rim of a crater (watching the two astronauts) weren't part of this group of Others. Neil's comment was "Man, those babies are huge…" and then he was told to switch to the encrypted channel.
>
> According to Otto Binder, who was a member of the NASA space team, when the moon-walkers, Aldrin and Armstrong were making their rounds some distance from the LEM, Armstrong clutched Aldrin's arm excitedly and exclaimed:
>
> **Armstrong**: What was it? What the hell was it? That's all I want to know!
> **Mission Control**: What's there? Malfunction… (garble). Mission Control calling Apollo 11 …
> **Apollo 11:** These babies were huge, sir!.... **Enormous**!... Oh God! You wouldn't believe it!....I'm telling you there are other **space-craft** out there… lined up on the far side of the crater edge!...
> **They're on the Moon watching us!** [38] [emphasis added]

Maybe Sitchin and von Däniken are on to something…. as well as the Hopi. However…

Let's clarify this: Zechariah Sitchin was mostly right but he fudged on a few things. This was originally examined in VEG, Ch.3 –

The late Zechariah Sitchin was a rascal and didn't tell us five key things about the Anunnaki issue:

Appearance: they were initially reptilian, later created a genetic mammalian version, as for Inanna and Marduk, and then for hybrids like Noah, Moses, Sargon, Alexander the Great…;

Gold: they mined gold but not for their planet's atmosphere; it was ingested as monoatomic gold to sustain their longevity;

Nibiru: was a planet circling a Dwarf failed sun – it was allegedly destroyed near Jupiter in April 2003 as it was returning;

Remnant: most Anunnaki left Earth in 650-600 BC; a portion stayed on due to Galactic Law governing Creator Races (see **Prime Directive**, **Remnant** in Glossary);

Ancient Ones: The Anunnaki were not the first. The Ancient Ones, Devas and Others were here before Man and still are. (See Chapters 12-13.)

Hopi Blue Star

Having come this far in the discussion, it would be appropriate to conclude with what the credible Hopi elders are forecasting. They have a list of 10 things that lead up to the Endtime, and all but one have now happened.

"The Fourth World shall end soon, and the Fifth World will begin.
This the elders everywhere know. The Signs over many years have been fulfilled, and so few are left: [39]

> *"This is the First Sign:* We are told of the coming of the white-skinned men, like Pahana, but not living like Pahana men who took the land that was not theirs. And men who struck their enemies with thunder.
>
> *"This is the Second Sign:* Our lands will see the coming of spinning wheels filled with voices. In his youth, my father saw this prophecy come

true with his eyes -- the white men bringing their families in wagons across the prairies."

"This is the Third Sign: A strange beast like a buffalo but with great long horns, will overrun the land in large numbers. These White Feather saw with his eyes -- the coming of the white men's cattle."

"This is the Fourth Sign: The land will be crossed by snakes of iron."

"This is the Fifth Sign: The land shall be criss-crossed by a giant spider's web."

"This is the Sixth sign: The land shall be criss-crossed with rivers of stone that make pictures in the sun."

"This is the Seventh Sign: You will hear of the sea turning black, and many living things dying because of it."

"This is the Eight Sign: You will see many youth, who wear their hair long like my people, come and join the tribal nations, to learn their ways and wisdom.

"And this is the Ninth and Last Sign: You will hear of a dwelling-place in the heavens, above the earth, that shall fall with a great crash. It will appear as a blue star. Very soon after this, the ceremonies of my people will cease.

Analysis

The signs are interpreted as follows: The **First Sign** is of guns. The **Second** Sign is of the pioneers' covered wagons. The **Third** Sign is of longhorn cattle. The **Fourth** Sign describes the railroad tracks. The **Fifth** Sign is a clear image of our electric power and telephone lines. The **Sixth** Sign describes concrete highways and their mirage-producing effects. The **Seventh** Sign foretells of oil spills in the ocean. The **Eighth** Sign clearly indicates the "Hippy Movement" of the 1960s. The **Ninth** Sign was the U.S. Space Station Skylab, which fell to Earth in 1979. According to Australian eye-witnesses, it appeared to be burning blue.

Another Hopi prophecy warns that **nothing should be brought back from the Moon** -- obviously anticipating the Apollo 11 mission that returned with samples of lunar basalt. If this was done, the Hopi warned, the balance of natural and universal laws and forces would be disturbed, resulting in earthquakes, severe changes in weather patterns, and social unrest. All these things are happening today, though of course not necessarily because of Moon rocks.

The **10th Sign** is the coming of the Blue Star followed by the Red Star.

They say that first will come the **Blue Star** which will be the warning that Planet X is coming – the Hopi call it the Purifier. It is the **Red Star** that comes by next and causes **cataclysms**, earthquakes, asteroids and dust in the sky for years as the Earth passes thru the wake of this Destroyer, Nemesis, or Wormwood… and even more exciting – a **pole shift** is possible. This whole planetary scenario reminds one of what was written in the Bible's Book of Revelations.

Sitchin called Planet X **Nibiru** – but that is a planet circling the Red Star which means that the Red Star is actually a **Brown Dwarf** that did not ignite as a sun in our binary solar system. And the presence of a Brown Dwarf that glows red as it interacts with the Sun we know about would have the gravitational field to perturb Pluto, Neptune and Sedna as it comes back into the solar system again… [40]

Not a nice scenario but it may be part of our cosmological setup. Thus if we see a Blue Star, we need to head for the hills, or some underground shelter. And if that isn't possible, then reading and applying Virtual Earth Graduate – absorbing the last 3 chapters and **preparing oneself spiritually** for what could be a transition to the Other Side… your mindset at such a time will determine what happens to you and where you go.

> **Serpent Wisdom** was given in Chapter 10 (Hermetic Principles) and Chapter 13 (Insider Truth) to also serve in this regard.

Summary

Remember that there were multiple gods doing things around Earth, and we have just looked at one set: the Anunnaki. The chapter on China will reveal another set, the Aborigines in Australia will reveal another set, and the Zulus and Dogon tribes in Africa will describe another set. Earth appears to have been something of an **Experiment**… perhaps to see which version of humans proved to be the most viable.

Providing the Ancient Ones were not the Anunnaki, they would have preceded the Anunnaki and the multiple creations of Man. It is believed that the Ancient Ones did step in after catastrophes and rescue Man and help rebuild his civilizations. Whereas the Anunnaki Remnant became the Nagas, the Ancient Ones were often called the Watchers, the Shining Ones, or the Builder Gods. We have never been alone.

Chapter 2: Northern Europe

It is an interesting journey from Mesopotamia and the Sumerians to Scandinavia and the Vikings, and perforce, the Germanic tribes must also be included. The Celts were involved and will be dealt with in the next chapter.

Scandinavia

The area around the Baltic Sea was well-known and sailed by the Norse, the Swedes and the Danes.

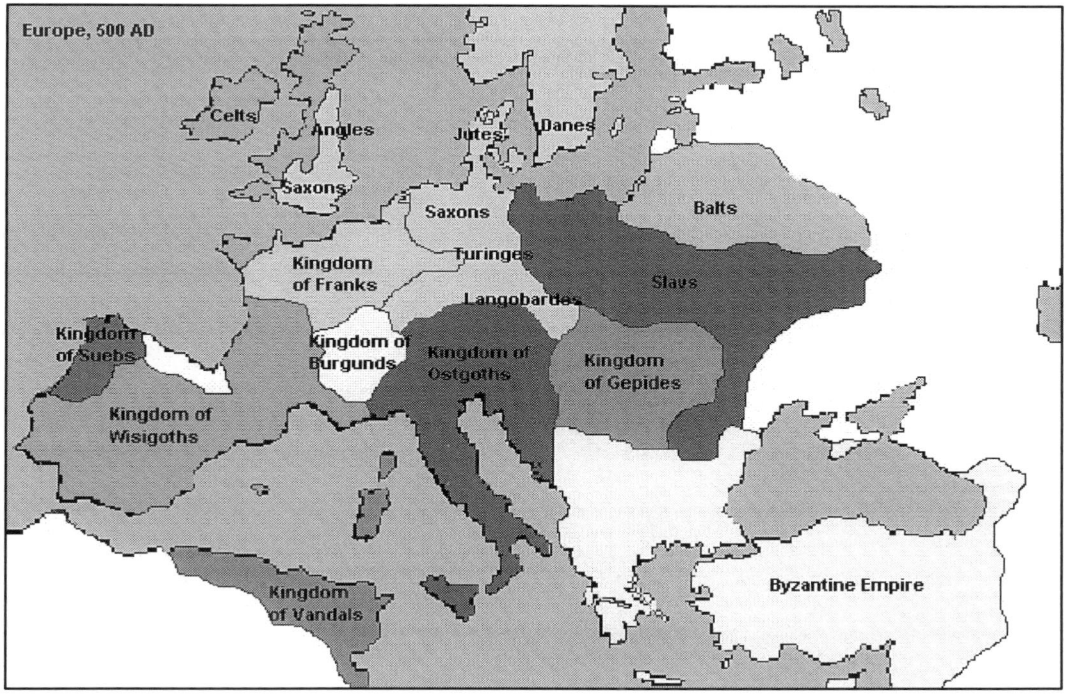

Europe about AD 500

Note that the map shows Danes and Jutes, not Norse, Norwegians nor Swedes… The issue among historians has always been: Where did the Vikings come from? They were not known to the Anflo-Saxons, nor to the Germanic tribes until their famous raid, out of nowhere, upon **Lindesfarne** in AD 793 when they sacked and plundered the rich monastery there.

> Lindesfarne is located on the Northeast coast of Britain, where the 'g' in Angles is located (map above).

They are thought to have organized in Scandinavia about 700 AD and might be the former **Frisians** aka Germanic tribes that migrated north. It was during the 3rd to 5th centuries that the Frisians living right on the coast of Northern Germany and what is now the Netherlands, suffered many marine incursions – that is to say, the ocean kept drowning them! They decided to move out and probably north to new, fresh land. Many went inland and swelled the ranks of the Germanic tribes.

> Since there was no recorded history that is reliable, it has even been suggested that they originated in **Hyperborea**, or Thule. And that was the subject of the Nazi quest to find their roots… Aryan roots which we'll see were about 2000 miles east of Germany! (Think: Persia)

The **Jutes**, shown on the 1st map, were Germanic and morphed into the Danes, who morphed into Norse and Swedes... all later called Vikings…which originally meant 'dwellers on the creek/fjord' and later came to be associated with those who 'travel/explore.'

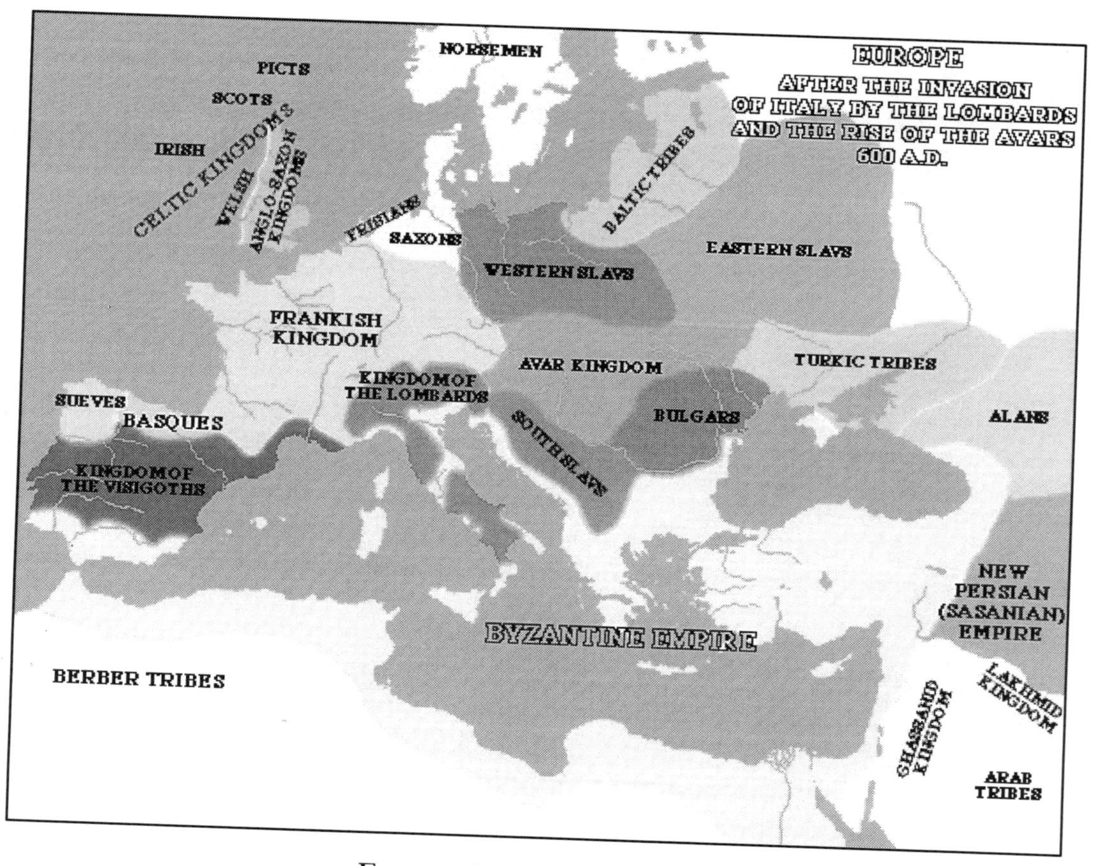

Europe about AD 600

Note the map in AD 600 now shows Norse, Frisians, and Germany is still Frankish and Slavic. Note for later reference, that the Celts have morphed into Irish, Scots, Welsh and Picts.

But what is the connection with the Anunnaki? There are two major items which show the Anunnaki influence with the Vikings – The Tree of Life and the Viking gods (who may also have been the Hopi Kachina gods).

Tree of Life

The Vikings acquired the World Tree teaching and called it **Yggdrasil**:

This is the traditional view – with the Eagle at the top and the Serpent at the bottom.

But there is more behind the Viking view of the world…

The more relevant picture is:

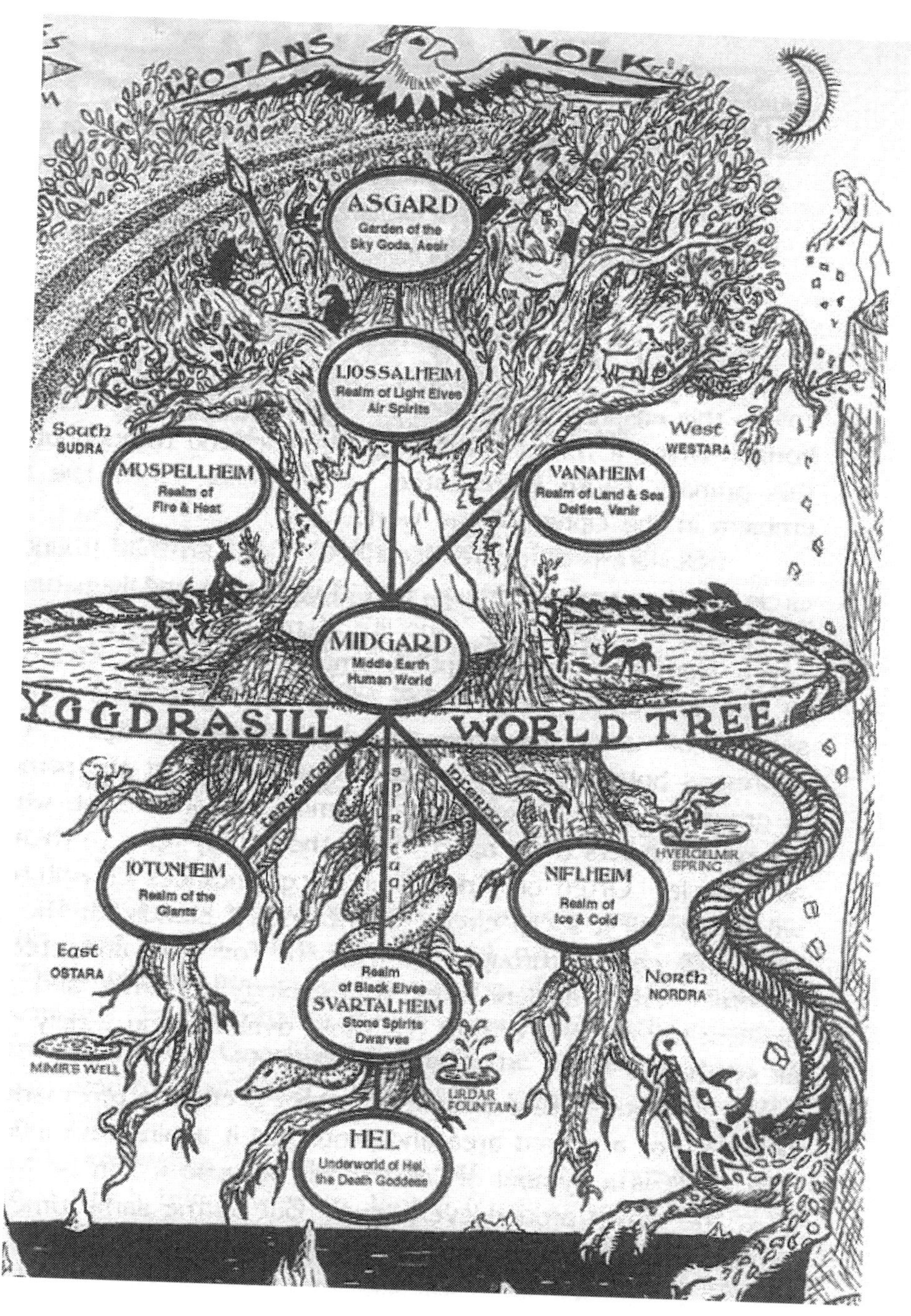

This was the Tree of Life as compared with the Sumerian and Kabbalistic Trees earlier, in Chapter 1. Note the **Eagle** at the top, the **Serpent** is wrapped around the root that says 'spiritual', and now there is a **Dragon** which figures into the Norse endtime scenario, called **Ragnarök** wherein the Giants, Man and the assorted beings of the 9 different worlds (circular globes on the Tree) all get together and fight **Jörmungandr** the world serpent (i.e., world darkness).

Note also Thor's hammer and his spear among the foliage, as well as Thor's two Black Ravens who reported all that happened to him from Midgard (the realm of the humans). **"Wotans Volk"** at the top of the Tree is the old German Wodin which became Odin – THE Norse god. The banner says "Odin's People."

Prior to describing the 9 worlds, one more thing is visible – it appeared in the first Yggdrasil picture -- but you can barely make it out there: the Serpent eating its tail. This is an interesting ancient concept of eternity, or constant new beginninngs (as in the concept of the Phoenix) called **Ouroboros** and was popularized by the Greeks. Interesting that this teaching was common to both Greeks and Vikings! (More on that when we get to the Greeks – they did trade with each other.)

Nine Levels of the World

Asgard -- where the gods live: Odin had Frigg + Jord (2 wives), Thor + Sif, Loki, Freyr + Freya, Baldr, and Ran to name some major ones. There were more. (All are male except those joined by the "+" = their female consort.) Beings here were called Aesir.

Asgard was also the location of Valhal or **Valhalla**.

Note that two days of the week were named after the Norse gods: Thursday = Thor's day, and Friday = Freyr's day (see p. 484).

Ljossalheim -- the home (*heim*) of the Elves of Light and Air Spirits.

Muspelheim -- realm of Fire and Heat (but not what we would call Hell). Also called Alfheim (home of the Elves).

Vanaheim -- realm of Land and Sea, where Freyr & Freya live. Beings here are called Vanir.

Midgard -- Middle Earth where the humans live.

> If this starts to sound like the *Lord of the Rings*, guess where JRR Tolkien got his inspiration?

The following are considered underground – below Middle Earth.

Jotunheim -- realm of the Giants, note that that is considered the Terrestrial Root.

Niflheim -- realm of Ice and Cold, also where the Dead reside.

> Niflheim was one of the two primordial realms, the other one being Muspelheim, the realm of fire. Between these two realms of cold and heat, creation began when its waters mixed with the heat of Muspelheim to form a "creating steam". Later, it became the abode of Hel, a goddess daughter of Loki, and the afterlife for her subjects: those who did not die a heroic or notable death. [41]

Note also that this is the Infernal Root – between Midgard and Niflheim.

Svartelheim -- realm of the black elves, dwarves and stone spirits. Not good.

Note also that this is the Spiritual Root of the Tree

Hel -- the realm where failed warriors and those who are not honorable in life go when they die. A favorite saying when one Viking was upset with another (who wasn't living up to his Viking code): "To Hel with you!"

> **This concept of Hel coupled with the Greek concept of Hades gave the Western world its concept of Hell. (Satan came from the Egyptian Set or Sata – a being dressed in red that lived in the hot desert…** VEG, Ch.6**)**

Speaking metaphysically, these realms can also represent what will be seen as the Kabbalistic aspects of the world – the Norse just put their unique stamp on the Tree of Life concept – to reflect their world. What is interesting is that the Tree of Life is a basic concept and similar structure found among the Celts, Egyptians, Mayans and Hebrews…

Norse Gods

Here is where we see some definite technology being used by Thor – in addition to his **eight-legged horse Sleipnir** which could carry his master to Hel and back…. What was that really? And Thor had several magical weapons at his disposal, but where did he get them? To answer that, we have to start with Loki, who was a trickster god, and his dealings with the dwarves:[42]

> Loki, as a trickster god, loved playing pranks on the other gods... and some were serious... which usually aroused Thor's anger.
>
> One day, while the goddess Sif slept, Loki snuck up on her and cut off her hair. Her husband, Thor, made dire threats against Loki who wisely agreed to make amends. He visited the dwarves and got them to make replacement hair out of gold, and he had them also make a special ship, **Skipbladnir**, and a spear, **Gungnir**.
>
> This triggered intense rivalry among the dwarves to see who could make the best gifts for Thor. The loser would lose his head. Loki naturally sought to interfere, to sway the outcome, and was able to distract one of the dwarves long enough that the handle of the Hammer , **Mjölnir**, was not what was wanted... it was too short. Nonetheless the magic Hammer worked as designed and the bet was won, Loki had to shut up.
>
> In addition to the Spear, Thor was given a special belt, **Meginjörd**, which doubled its power, and a set of iron gloves, **Jarngreipr**, with which to handle the Hammer.

Magic Boat - Skipbladnir

Thor was given a magic boat that could disappear into one's pocket after use, and brought out of his pocket and expanded to sail wherever he wanted. It doesn't say it was inflatable but it seriously reduced its size until it could fit into one's palm.

Magic Spear - Gungnir

The spear given Thor was so special that it always hit whatever it was thrown at. Sounds like it might have had laser-guided technology…

Magic Hammer - Mjölnir

Thor's Hammer when thrown always came back to him, after hitting its target and destroying it. His Belt was part of this scenario, as it doubled the Hammer's destructive power, and the Gloves were necessary to insulate Thor from the Hammer's electrical potential. This sounds like a legend that was based on some actual science – else why not just have the Hammer... Why need the Gloves and the Belt? It sounds like someone saw the actual (scientific) setup and one has to wonder if the Dwarves were what we today call the little Greys, who are very technologically advanced...? There is no proof that the technology displayed by Thor came from the Anunnaki – yet they were one of the technologically advanced beings at the time on the planet. It might have been the Ancient Ones closer to Scandinavia: those called the **Hyperboreans** at the North Pole (of which Apollo was a part. See Chapter 5 on Greece).

Thor on his 8-legged steed Sleipnir with the Spear

"Eight-legged steed" sounds like a **skycraft with 8 landing gear**... and we find corroboration of that in Gyeongju, South Korea – of all places to find the exact same imagery.

There is a painting on the wall inside the tomb of Cheonmachong of the Silla Dynasty, about 5th Century AD and it is called The Heavenly Horse – **and it also has 8 legs.** They called it a flying horse – proto-Koreans did not have chariots, so they didn't call it that.

Korean Heavenly Horse
(Credit: Wikipedia-Cheonmachong: public domain)

Note that the horse's tail and mane appar to be more like a **dragon**, including the fire coming from its mouth. Apparently the inhabitants of what is now Korea, back in the 5th Century, saw the same **flying craft** as the Norse Vikings, and characterized it as a flying horse. In any event, it had 8 legs and we would today ascribe that to the landing gear of a skycraft.

There is another aspect of the Norse legend that deserves some attention…

Rainbow Bridge

Odin, the main god, was said to have a **High Seat** – meaning he oversaw everything in Midgard where the humans lived. And he daily received knowledge of what the humans were doing from 2 black Ravens who communicated directly to him…

In addition, Asgard, Odin's realm, was connected to Midgard by a Rainbow Bridge, called **Bifrost**. The red color was said to be burning hot, and could not be touched – as if it carried the power sustaining/empowering the Bridge…

Rainbow Bridge from Midgard to Asgard (Valhalla)

The Bifrost had a guardian who operated it, called Heimdall.

Odin's High Seat

It is interesting to speculate that the Bifrost was a portal between Earth and the Moon – certainly the Moon could serve as a **High Seat** and see what is happening on the Earth below. Your other choice, in today's terms, would be an orbiting spacecraft, which the Anunnaki certainly had (operated by the Igigi). The two Ravens could be like drone sentinels observing and collecting data on human activities.

Odin's wolves, Geri and Freki, are a sign of high kingship:[43]

> Scholars have also noted Indo-european parallels to the wolves Geri and Freki as companions of a divinity. The 19th century scholar Jacob Grimm observed a connection between this aspect of Odin's character and the **Greek Apollo**, to whom both the wolf and the raven are sacred. Philologist Maurice Bloomfield further connected the pair with the two dogs of Yama in **Vedic mythology**, and saw them as a Germanic counterpart to a more general and widespread Indo-European Cerberus-theme. Michael Speidel finds similar parallels in the Vedic Rudra and the Roman god Mars. Elaborating on the connection between wolves and figures of great power, he writes: "This is why Geri and Freki, the wolves at Woden's side, also glowered on the throne of the **Anglo-Saxon** kings. Wolf-warriors, like Geri and Freki, were not mere animals but mythical beings: as Woden's followers they bodied forth his might, and so did wolf-warriors."
> [emphasis added]

So there are similarities with the Greeks and Hindus.

Poetic Eddas

The Eddas is the body of writing that has come down to us from the Age of the Vikings, composed largely in the 13th Century. They say some very interesting things.[44]

Adam & Eve

The trio of gods gifting the first humans, Ask and Embla [Adam & Eve], by Robert Engels, 1919

Odin is mentioned or appears in most poems of the *Poetic Edda*, compiled in the 13th century from traditional source material reaching back to the pagan period.

The poem *Voluspa* features Odin in a dialogue with an undead völva (a shamanic seeress), who imparts in him wisdom from ages past and foretells the onset of Ragnarök; the destruction and rebirth of the world.

Among the information the völva recounts is the first human beings, found and given life by a trio of gods; Odin, Hönir, and Lothur. In stanza 17 of the *Poetic Edda* poem *Völuspá*, the völva reciting the poem states that Hœnir, Lóðurr and Odin once found Ask and Embla on land. The völva says that the two were capable of very little, lacking in *ørlög* and says that they were given three gifts by the three gods:

Old Norse:
Ǫnd þau né átto,
óð þau né hǫfðo,
lá né læti né lito
góða.
Ǫnd gaf Óðinn, óð
gaf Hœnir,
lá gaf Lóðurr ok
lito góða.[22]

Benjamin Thorpe
translation:
Spirit they possessed not,
Sense they had not,
blood nor motive
powers, nor goodly
colour.
Spirit gave Odin, sense
gave Hœnir,
blood gave Lodur, and
goodly colour.

Henry Adams Bellows
translation:
Soul they had not,
Sense they had not,
Heat nor motion, nor
goodly hue;
Soul gave Othin,
Sense gave Hönir,
Heat gave Lothur
and goodly hue.

Note here that Adam and Eve are said to not have souls, and Odin gave it to them, reminiscent of the Bible's Genesis 2 where God breathed the spirit/soul into Man. It has been pointed out in the Sumerian *Atra Hasis* and the Mayan *Popul Vuh* that Man was created in stages, and some did not have souls.

> (This point is echoed and examined in detail in Ch's. 1 and 5 Virtual Earth Graduate, and Apx. D of Transformation of Man. Note even in Norse legend, the gods – plural – made Man what he is today and then souls moved into the bodies.)

Self-sacrifice

It is a common idea in some legends, that gods occasionally sacrifice themselves for the good of their progeny. Such was the case with Odin who hung for 9 days and nights on the Yggdrasil Tree – sacrificing himself, losing an eye, to learn the deeper truth of the Runes. [45]

> In Old Norse texts, Odin is depicted as one-eyed and long-bearded, frequently wielding a spear named Gungnir, and wearing a cloak and a broad hat. He is often accompanied by his animal companions—the wolves Geri and Freki and the ravens Huginn and Muninn, who bring him information from all over Midgard—and **Odin rides the flying, eight-legged steed Sleipnir across the sky** and into the underworld [called Hel].

> Odin is attested as having many sons, most famously the god Baldr with Frigg, and is known by hundreds of names.. In these texts, Odin frequently seeks knowledge in some manner and in disguise (most famously by obtaining the knowledge of Runes), at times makes wagers with his wife Frigg over the outcome of exploits, and takes part in both the creation of the world by way of slaying the primordial being Ymir and the gift of life to the first two humans Ask and Embla. The knowledge of both the Runes and poetry is also attributed to Odin. [emphasis added]

Again, note the flying horse as in flying chariot (Ezekiel and Enoch in the Bible), and the association of him with the first two humans… Could Odin be equated with the Sumerian Enlil?

Valhalla

This is a huge drinking-hall with plenty of wine, mead, venison and practice fighting – for the final Ragnarök battle. It is where the valiant Viking warriors go when they die – as opposed to the cowards who go to Hel.

Endtime or Ragnarök

> Later in the *Eddas*, the **völva goddess** recounts the events of the Aesir-Vanir War, the war between two groups of gods. During this, the first war of the world, Odin flung his spear into the opposing forces of the Vanir…

> This is reminiscent of the wars the Anunnaki fought among themselves, as well as the wars between the gods in the Hindu *Mahabharata*.

> After Odin gives her necklaces, she continues to recount more information, including a list of **Valkyries**, referred to as… the ladies of Odin. In foretelling the events of Ragnarök, the völva predicts the death of Odin; Odin will fight the monstrous wolf **Fenrir** during the great battle at **Ragnarök**. Odin will be consumed by the wolf, yet Odin's son Vitharr will avenge him by stabbing the wolf in the heart. After the world is burned and renewed, the surviving and returning gods will meet and recall Odin's deeds and "ancient runes." [46]

Ragnarök is the endtime battle involving all 9 levels of the beings in Yggdrasil… the Giants join forces with Fenrir and the Dwarves and attack **Valhalla**. Reminiscent of the Bible's Revelation, the battle begins with a period of constant Winter – the Sun has been blocked from view, and the Moon also disappears. The dead return from Hel and join the fray. Heimdall blows his horn, the battle proceeds, and everyone is killed except two, and the world is burned by **fire**… The Bible said, paraphrased: "I'll send fire not a Flood next time …" (2 Peter 3:5-12) When it is all over, two humans survive. The world will be born anew, better than before. That is the significance of the **Ouroboros** around the Norse Tree of Life… Life goes on, and appears to be in Eras.

Viking Character

This has been saved for last as it is very significant.

The Vikings sailed to many parts of the known world, and across the Atlantic creating settlements in Newfoundland and Minnesota – true Adventurers. They were **not all cutthroats and barbarians**. Like the Celts, they had developed a real skill in metalworking and made some of the finest swords, helmets and ritual objects the world has seen.

(Above) A Viking weathervane finely crafted showing the Celtic influence with the interlaced cords and the suggestion of a Serpent

.

(Below) A Viking helmet –note the attention to detail and the fine interlace of the chain mail. (Note: no horns on the helmet: Vikings didn't use them, Germanic tribes did.)

--

And lest people think the Vikings were just crude barbarians, take a look at the fine artwork on this door:

This shows pride of workmanship.

And a further example that shows detail and that the Vikings weren't just throwing their longships together as fast as they could to get on with the next raid……

In addition, their knowledge and skill in building the Viking longboats was unsurpassed – the boats would not flip over in a storm on the ocean – they had mastered the keel and kept their boats from leaking. They were easy to maneuver and very fast – better than the Phonecians' boats, by the way.

The Viking Longboat

The Vikings weren't the only ones with low, flat boats decorated with Serpent/Dragon heads…. You may recognize this coming from Chapter 1 – more connection between the Sumerians and the Vikings:

Sumerian Marduk Sails a Serpentboat into War

Marduk used a **serpentboat** to do local battle. Since the Anunnaki and Marduk preceded the Vikings by centuries, it is reasonable that the Vikings copied the Anunnaki when they made their longboats --- perhaps the Anunnaki even taught the Vikings how to make a superior longboat...

Social *Things*

The Vikings were very disciplined in their social settings – and were the first to treat "town discussions" in a democratic way – everyone had a voice in these meetings which were called ***Things.*** Laws were enacted and documented here. There was also the *Althing* in Iceland where disputes were resolved, a period of truce was declared if need be, and people came from all around. Local chieftains held a Thing every Spring, and an Althing later in the year. And no weapons were allowed… it had almost a sacred atmosphere. At the Althing an appointed Lawspeaker would read aloud one-third of the laws in force… this was a paid position lasting for a term of 3 years.

> ***Thing*:** The Thing met at regular intervals, legislated, elected chieftains and kings, and judged according to the law, which was memorized and recited by the **Lawspeaker** (the judge). The Thing's negotiations were presided over by the Lawspeaker and the chieftain or the king.... [sometimes] the Thing was dominated by the most influential members of the community, the heads of clans and wealthy families, but in theory **one-man one-vote was the rule.**
> A famous incident took place when Thorgnyr the Lawspeaker told the Swedish king Olof Skötkonung (c. 980–1022) that the people, not the king, held power in Sweden; the king realized that he was powerless against the Thing and gave in.[47]

If someone was caught in a criminal act, and he was adjudged an outlaw, then he would be banished and his property confiscated. It was hard to survive without the support of the local society, so men tended to toe the line.

Women were respected in Viking society and anyone caught abusing a woman was dealt with severely. On the other hand, in Viking raids to other shores, for plunder or trade, the women were "fair game."

Lindisfarne Raid, AD 793

And this raid was mentioned earlier, but it too has been saved for special mention.

This was the very **first Viking raid** on unsuspecting foreigners, and they sacked and burned a very rich monastery. But that is not the end of the story.

Lindisfarne Ruins

According to the Viking records… [48]

> ...in this year fierce, foreboding omens came over the land of the Northumbrians, and the wretched people shook; there were excessive whirlwinds, lightning, and **fiery dragons were seen flying in the sky**. These signs were followed by great famine, and a little after those, that same year on 6th ides of January, the ravaging of wretched heathen people destroyed God's church at Lindisfarne. [emphasis added]

Sky Craft of the Gods

Fiery dragons were seen among the Sumerians, too – every time an Anunnaki ship (a 'Heavenly Boat') took off, there was smoke, flame and noise. The classic example of a flying dragon is suggested below.

The Hollywood Version

Or perhaps it looked closer to the following pictures…..

…or…

…the essential elements are there: **wings, smoke, noise, flying**… the only thing missing is **flame** like Napalm (or a laser flash) coming out the front of the jet!

And yet what seems to really have happened, as the gods flew around the globe, is that their ships might have looked like the following:

Spaceship Overflying Human Settlements[49]

Might that not be taken for a dragon flying thru the sky? All the elements of the dragon concept are there. If it made **noise** (as in a jet exhaust) as it **flew**, and produced **smoke**, and then shot **fire** (Lightray?) out the front of the craft… wouldn't a primitive human not know what he was looking at, and concoct a story about a flying 'dragon'?

It is not known what the Anunnaki ships looked like, but they were called **Shem** and flown by the DIN.GIR.... the "Righteous Ones" [50] of Chapter 1. And if people called them dragons, because they looked like it and there were prior stories of dragons, then they must have had wings, flame/smoke, and made noise...

(credit: Bing Images: deviantart.com)

And consider that if the Anunnaki were reptilian as the Babylonian priest Berossus said (in 300 BC)...

The **reptiles** verily descend...[51]

...perhaps he was looking at their ship?? So, what if the Anunnaki also designed their larger skycraft (much as the *Star Trek* Klingons did their "Birds of Prey") to resemble dragons? They are known to have called their craft **U.SHUM.GAL** ("great fiery flying serpent")[52]... so would the following rocketship be reasonable?

(credit: ancient aliens season 11, episode 1)

Interesting that the ship is taking off from a large platform – such as the one in **Baalbek** which was built with the massive **Trilithons.** And it does resemble a **dragon** – fire, smoke, and wings…

Let's go a step further, keeping with the possibility that the Anunnaki were human Ancient Ones, and their ships weren't just metal tubes… maybe there was some "dragon" design. Consider two things:

First, what did the Egyptians see that they recorded on the **Abydos** temple wall, which said temple goes back to the First Dynasty (i.e., 3100 BC). This picture has been around for a while: [53]

Then, the **second** point is that the Anunnaki were pictured as flying by the Sumerians: it is a clear picture of an Anunnaki god flying.

And again…

This appears to be similar to the first relief (just above) and yet is more 'mechanical' looking. The picture on the left looks less like a bird and more like a craft.

(credit: Bing Images: ancients.com)

Some 'authorities' will say that these are simply drawings of the Sun 'flying' across the sky – kind of like the Egyptian Sun god, Ra, which was pictured thus:

As is obvious, they are not the same thing. All the last two have in common is wings and a disk -- as does the following:

A little more care is in order before deciding what a "winged disk" stands for.

Now the final point. It is suggested that Inanna and her Anunnaki cohorts had **small, private 'jets'** to get about (e.g., her 'Boat of Heaven') – and that was examined in Chapter 1 (section: The MEs). Their personal craft could have looked something like the following (these objects were found in **Turkey**, which is south of Mesopotamia): [54]

(credit: mesopotamiangods.com/astronauts….)

And another website (below) shows a similar, smaller, personal craft… which were all used around the planet just as we use PT boats and destroyers on the seas, and aircraft carriers for bigger purposes… it is reasonable that the Anunnaki also had various size craft for different purposes, the larger ones staying in orbit… 600 miles out? (See Marrs' quote at end of Chapter 1.)

Could the Ancient Ones have also had colonies/bases on the Moon and Mars and travelled there as well? There are ruins on the Moon and someone is still there.

The single-seat rocket ship was found in **Toprakkale**, which ancients called Tuspa, in **Turkey** where the kingdom of **Urartu** ruled over 2500 years ago.

Now let's connect the dots.

We have flying, wings, and a sphere for sure, and sometimes noise and flame. The following is a reasonable representation of the larger Skygod craft…

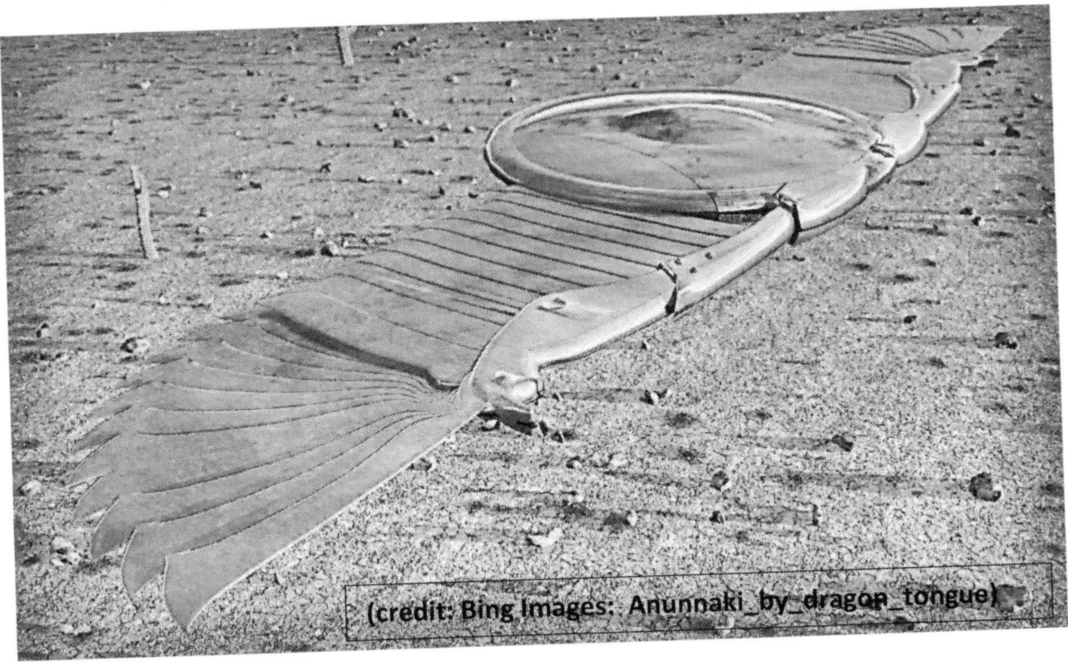

(credit: Bing Images: Anunnaki_by_dragon_tongue)

Please note the resemblance to the way the flying Anunnaki were pictured:

Only missing are the tail feathers (exhaust?) and the two projections (landing gear?) on the bottom.

The following pictured craft must have landing gear… (probably retracted).

(credit: Bing Images: thelivingmoon.com)

Another website agrees with the concept:

(credit: Bing Images: photobucket.com)

It is apparent that the 'feathers' at the wingtips can swing back and the wings (midsection) may also be able to swing back… to a Delta craft? Lack of jets suggests this is an **electrogravitic craft**, whereas the smaller personal craft are jet powered.

Relevant Cropcircles

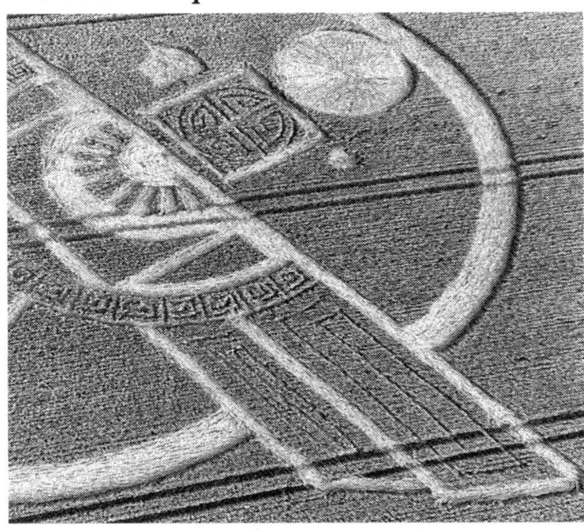

And lastly, what if the beings that are doing the cropcircles are trying to show us something? (The picture left was not a crude Doug&Dave (D&D) work.)[55]

July 25, 2015 Cropcircle
An attempt at an Anunnaki symbol…

(see below the original…)

(credit: cropcircle connector: Uffcott Down, Wilshire, July 2015. Paul Jacobs, CGI)
Also (credit: Bing Images: bp.blogspot.com)[56]

One caveat with the above semi-real cropcircle: it is not a precision drawing, note the wiggly 'lines' in the wings, and the square box above the wings is not parallel to the wings. While the scale is too big to have been done by D&D, closer examination at website Cropcircle Connector shows the design to NOT be symmetrical and this is rather irregular for a large cropcircle whose size says it should be genuine. Rough edges everywhere, the crop is not laying down smooth and even (with a sheen – see next page) as it should… and the lines are irregular.

It is suggested that the usual beings doing cropcircles did not do this 'Anunnaki' one, and now we have someone with similar technology but without the **perfect symmetry and polish** … So, viewers beware in the future….

Here is the Doug & Dave method… and it makes this:

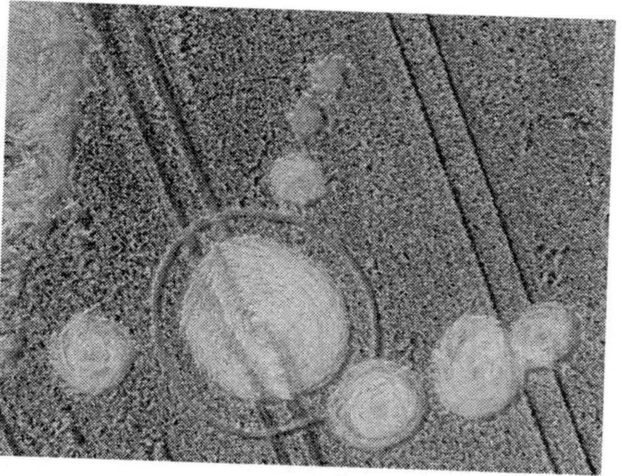

Below are 4 real cropcircles …obviously **precise and detailed**… How could the sheep (who blindly believed that D&D did them all) have left their brains outside the building when they were informed by 'experts' that D&D did them all?

And speaking of relevant cropcircles, there is another one that is not D&D, either. This reflects the **Serpent Imagery** we're looking for. And this one is real.

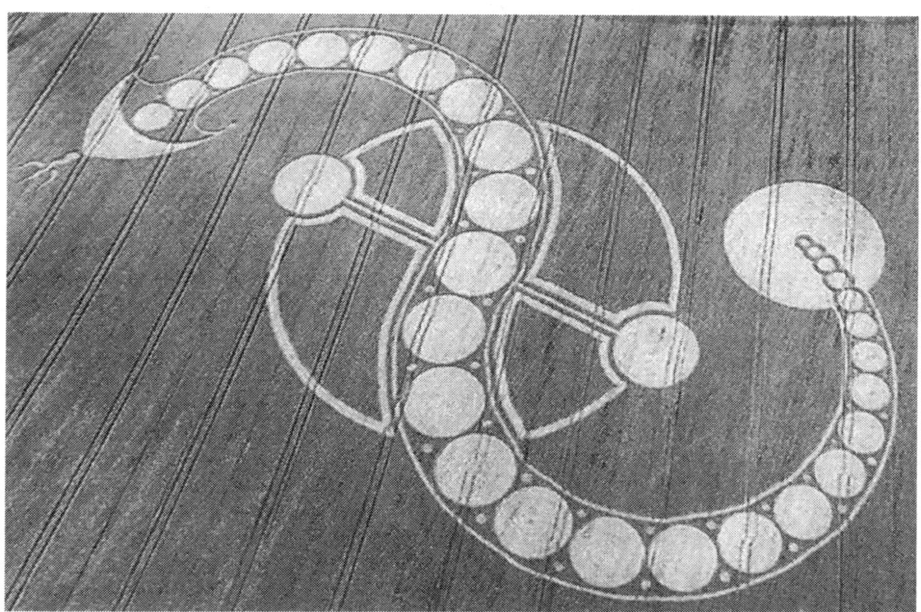

Serpent Cropcircle appeared: 4 de agosto de 2011
(credit: sabiduriadelaluz.org)

The bigger the cropcircle, the less chance that it was faked as it would take humans too long to do it and someone would see them. Always look for **polish and perfect symmetry.**

Summary

While not exhaustive, the foregoing was a look at what the Skygods, including the Anunnaki, might have left, or inspired, the Norse to put on the prows of their boats, and say about their World Tree … inserting a serpent and eagle into the motif. Note that the last Anunnaki winged ship and the crop circle could also be seen as eagles… or dragons?
The point being that the Norse gods were no doubt the Skygods (Anunnaki?) playing god, trying to train, teach and corral the violent tendencies of humans (all over the planet, including Korea). Having created a sentient being, they said themselves that they were responsible for it – to nurture, train and develop it (*a la* Enki)… or terminate it (*a la* Enlil).

Lastly, there are 2 particular points to emphasize, as it will be throughout the book... that of **Sacrifice** and **Flood**. Not only did **Mayans, Aztecs** and **Incas** perform human sacrifice, so did the **Norse**.

Sacrifice

> The Heimskringla tells of Swedish King Aun who **sacrificed nine of his sons** [over the years] in an effort to prolong his life until his subjects stopped him from killing his last son Egil. According to Adam of Bremen, the Swedish kings sacrificed males every ninth year during the Yule sacrifices at the Temple at Uppsala. The Swedes had the right not only to elect kings but also to depose them, and both king Domalde and king Olof Trätälja are said to have been sacrificed after years of famine.[57] [emphasis added]

Somewhere, someone (humans) got the idea that blood sacrifice was essential to the prosperity of a town, the fertility of the crops, or the way to make sure the Sun rose again the next day (Aztec notion). And yet sacrifice was <u>not</u> performed in Sumeria… home of the Anunnaki gods.

Because it was so common around the globe, it was probably a renegade Anunnaki suggestion (think: Aztec god Huitzilopochtli[58]) – or was another group of ETs seeking to cause chaos among the humans? Even **the Celts** believed that saving the head of your enemy in battle and giving it a prominent place in one's home or temple assured the possessor of the energy and any wisdom of said decapitated enemy. (This was due to their belief that the soul resides in the head.) [59]

Flood Myth

As will be seen, while **the Norse did not have a Flood Myth**, the Chinese, Hindus, Hopi, Aborigines, Koreans, Incas, the Sioux, Siberians, and Thai, to name a few, did.[60]

The point being that this semi-substantiates a world-wide Flood of Biblical proportions, and yet the Sumerian epics of *Gilgamesh* and the *Atra Hasis* (Tablet III) give the impression that the **Flood was localized** and lasted for just a short time. If it was world-wide, why didn't the Norse say anything about it?

There are discrepancies and similarities found around the globe as the influence of the Skygods is traced… and the foregoing was just something to think about as the book progresses thru the different cultures, seeking the Tree of Life, The Flood, Skygod Creation stories, Dragons and Serpent Wisdom…

Chapter 3: The Germans & Celts

Moving southward and over to what is now the British Isles, we discover the Celts, and depending on when we visit them, there may be a mix of tribes and war-like people living there: Celts, Picts, Irish and the Welsh.

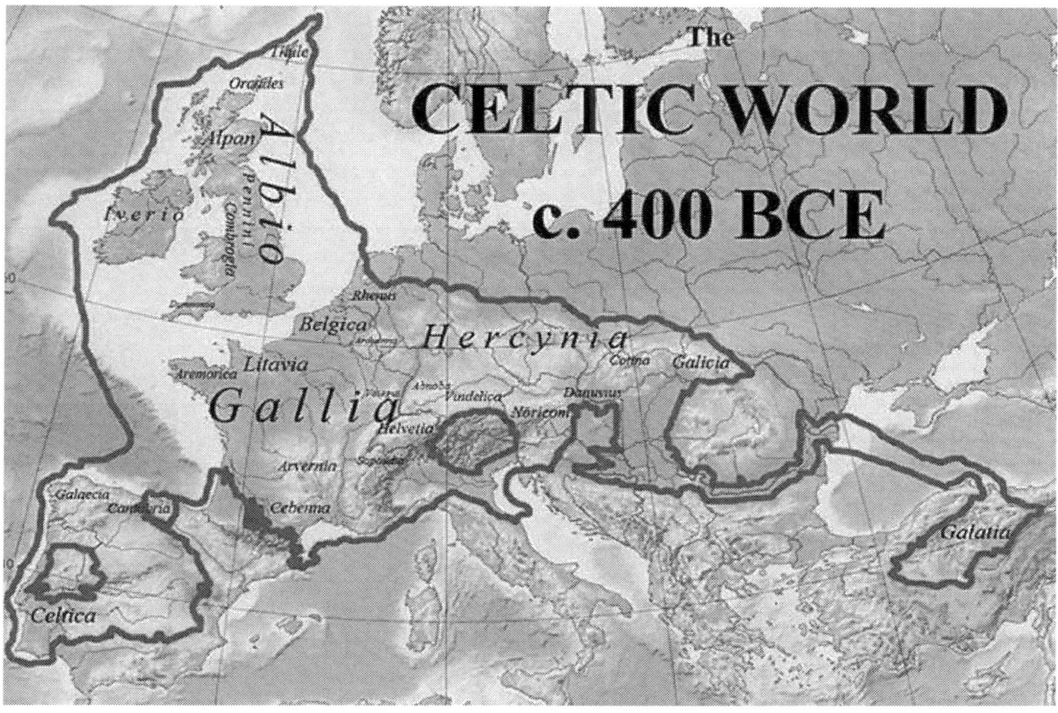

As a matter of fact, the Celtic world on the British Isles was a result of Vikings settling there, and nomadic tribes crossing the Channel, notably the Germanic tribes, including the Frisians (Denmark area). Thus it is necessary to first examine the Germanic tribes and then the Celts for any legacy of the Anunnaki.

Germanic Tribes

Germania was the name given by the Romans to the Germanic tribes east of the Rhine, which is largely the area of 'Hercynia' in the map above. They are examined first as they were involved in migrations westward and became involved in the eventual Anglo-Saxon conflict in Britain; thus they were one of the components of the Celtic world.

In the world of Germania, and later dealing with the Romans, two rivers were very important – the Rhine and the Danube – natural barriers to migration, and to Roman conquest. The Danube is the heavy line (running west to east), and the Rhine runs north and south, from Rotterdam (upper left of map) thru Bonn and Strasburg, and on to Switzerland. (In reality, the river starts in the Alps and flows to the sea.)

(Credit: Wikipedia: https://en.wikipedia.org/wiki/Danube)

The Rhine came to separate the Gauls from the **Germani**, and the Danube was where the Romans drew their northern occupation line – the north end of their Empire.

In fact, the Romans could not conquer the Germani – and lost 3 legions trying to conquer the fierce tribes found there. (A legion consisted of about 3,000-6,000 foot soldiers, well-armed and trained in specific battle formations and tactics.)

Battle of Teutoberg Forest

In the northwestern part of Germany, in Lower Saxony, about 100 km east of Dusseldorf, stands the forest of Teutoberg – not far from Heinrich Himmler's triangular Wewelsburg Castle, so located because it was close to the scene of Germany's defeat of the Roman Empire.

Battle of Teutoberg Forest, AD 9
(credit: Otto Albert Koch - www.lwl.org and on https://en.wikipedia.org/wiki/Arminius)

The point of all this Germanic history is – look at the picture: **Germanic** helmets (**horns and wings** – both Anunnaki emblems by the way) and the way of dressing, often shirtless (like the Celtic warriors). Viking warrior helmets did not use horns but some headgear may have been so adorned for ritual purposes.[61]

Yet there is more to the story. There was a Teutonic warrior in Germania that was very big named **Teutobochus** (that's the Latinized form; he would have called himself Teutobod). Not much is known about Teutobochus except that he was very large (est. 3 meters). The early Christian historian Paulus Orosius wrote that Teutobochus could "vault over four or even six horses" and towered above other men. [62] He was a **giant**.

> Indeed at the famous **Battle of the TeutobergerWald**, the Germans would so utterly decimate **three Roman armies** in the brutal fighting that Rome would maintain a more or less **defensive** posture with respect to the Germans until the Western [Roman] Empire's final collapse….
>
> Eventually, however, some of these Germans were captured by the Romans, and one of them, the particularly troublesome King by the name of **Teutobokh** was paraded in Rome in the customary triumph. The Roman historian Floras reports that this king was so tall that… Teutobokh could be 'seen above all the trophies or spoils of the enemies, which were carried upon the tops of spears' …
> Teutobokh was easily nine feet tall… perhaps considerably taller.[63]

Teutobokh Taken Prisoner

Here again, we have giants in the land, genetic throwbacks… perhaps to **Nephilim** times? Remember that the Nephilim were giants, and the Vikings in Chapter 2 also said there was a realm of giants (Jotunheim) – as well as those found in a cave in the American Southwest with red hair. [64] (Ch. 2 in Virtual Earth Graduate explores the giant issue.)

Other than being very fierce and warlike, there isn't much to research in the Germania issue – they were so busy feasting and warring that no one among them had time to write anything down… What we think we know comes from Pytheas, Herodotus, Strabo, Titus, etc. who were the on-lookers from Rome and Greece. And some of their significant writings are lost to us. Germania, however, was known to be composed mostly of Celts, proto-Slavic, Baltic and Scythian peoples and at earlier times, the **Cimbri** and **Teutones**.

Germanic Paganism

Of course this centers around **Tree Worship**, more specifically, "Irmin's Pillar" or the **Irminsul** – a great tree that was cut and shaped to look like a huge wooden pillar. This originated with the Irminones in northwestern Germany, near the TeutobergerWald Forest (see last section). It was used in animal and human sacrifices, until Charlemagne had it cut down. [65]

(credit: Wikipedia: Heinrich Leutemann)

A Germanic god Irmin, inferred from the name Irminsul and the tribal name Irminones, is sometimes presumed to have been the **national god** or demi-god of the Saxons. The connection with the Norse/Vikings is as follows:

> The Old Norse form of *Irmin* is *Jörmunr,* which just like Yggr was one of the names of Odin. **Yggdrasil** ("Yggr's horse") was the yew or ash tree from which Odin sacrificed himself, and which connected the nine worlds. Jakob Grimm connects the name *Irmin* with Old Norse terms like *iörmungrund* ("great ground", i.e. the Earth) or *iörmungandr* ("great **snake**", i.e. the Midgard **Serpent**).[66] [emphasis added]

The connection with the Celts is more than an historic merging of the two cultures. It is known that the paganism of the Saxon people involved **groves of trees**, and was a precursor to the Druidic worship of the Celts.

Across the Germanic world, there was some variation in the places where pagans worshiped, however, it was common for sites displaying prominent natural features to be used. Tacitus claimed that the 1st century tribes of Germany did not "confine the gods within walls... but that they **worshiped outdoors in sacred woods and groves**", and similarly there is evidence from later continental Europe, Anglo-Saxon England and Scandinavia that the pagans worshiped out of doors at "trees, groves, wells, stones, fences and cairns."[67] The goddess **Iðunn** was venerated there, too.

Iðunn and The Apples of Youth.

In Norse mythology, **Iðunn** (pron: ee-thun) is a goddess associated with apples and youth. Iðunn is attested in both the *Eddas*.... In both sources, she is described as the wife of the god Bragi, and in the *Prose Edda*, also as a keeper of apples and granter of eternal youth. (Reminiscent of the Golden Apples in Greek mythology.)

Golden Apples of the Hesperides

Either we have an incredible coincidence, or the Vikings were aware of the Greek story of the golden apples. In the Greek version, the goddess Hera had a **tree** (or maybe an orchard) where the golden apples grew which tasted like honey and could heal, in addition to their ability to **grant immortality** to the one who ate them. (These apples were stolen by Hercules as the 11th Labor of Hercules.) [68]

> Also, in another weird coincidence, having mentioned Thor's Hammer (Chapter 2) which always returned to the one who threw it, the golden apples were also said to be used as missiles and would return to the one who threw them. [69] [Seriously, in the legend.]

It is a possibility the Vikings heard the Greek story, liked it, and 'borrowed' it:

> Facilitated by advanced seafaring skills, and characterized by the longship, Viking activities at times also extended into the Mediterranean littoral [shores], North Africa, the Middle East, and Central Asia. [70]

And having said that, when Chapter 8 examines the **Yazidi in Iraq**, with their blonde hair and blue eyes, we'll know that the Vikings intermingled with the Middle Eastern women... as well as with the Celts and Saxons.

Celtic History

Much of the early history of the Celts is unknown, or vague – largely because (1) their religion (Druidism) forbade anything being written down, and (2) what was written down was prejudiced (Romans considered the Celts barbarians and not worth anything – even though many times the Celts beat the Roman Army!), and (3) the Romans did not understand the Celtic way of life and so took guesses and made incorrect assessments. The Celts were actually quite civilized, just outlandishly fierce in battle. (Sometimes they even fought nude!)[71]

Thus, in looking thru their mythology and what was said about them by even their neighbors, we find that their early history deals a lot with **the gods intervening and assisting them**. And that is the reason for this section – just as the Greeks, Romans and Vikings had their fair share of interplay with the gods, so too did the Celts.

Several examples will suffice between the years of 1000 BC and 400 AD – which last date is close to the gods leaving mankind alone. Just as the Greeks and Romans were left alone by the gods, so too were the Norse and the Celts – in fact, due to the close proximity of the Celts to Scandinavia, one might expect stories of the gods and/or their technology to be similar. [72] And they are.

One finds that among the original people to settle Ireland, the **Tuatha Dé Danann** are a mystery… no one is sure where they came from, and they acted like gods, practicing magic, shapeshifting, and possessing special tools. And when they lost a battle with the Formorians, who were also practicing magic – a battle of the gods, if you will – the Tuatha were required to go into the hills and spend the rest of their lives underground – and allegedly became the fairy people of Ireland. They were led to the Otherworld by **Mannanan Mac Lir**, a sea god who had powers of magic, healing and weather control. He is said to have flown his **magical chariot** over the sea.

During a fierce battle, the Celtic King **Nuada** lost a hand and had to turn his kingship over to Bres, another ruthless warrior. Dagda rescues Nuada and has a new hand made for him out of silver, and eventually returns Nuada to power after **Miach** created magic waters that restored Nuada's original hand (Think: Inanna in Chapter 1 and Ptah also had this regeneration power in Egypt).

Magic and sorcery were attested to by the Romans, as they were sometimes the victims of it.

Morrigan is one such powerful sorceress (who was the model for the Morgan le Fey character in the King Arthur stories). **Dagda** is known as the Good God and he had a special **hammer** that could kill nine men at once, and yet its long handle could return them to life. (Remember Thor's Hammer in Chapter 2?)

Dagda also had a magic harp that could make everyone sad, or cause them to fall asleep, or cause them to forget what they were doing (this is shades of Apollo and his harp). Lastly Dagda had a magic cauldron that could feed any number of people.

The all-time hero of most Celtic stories is **Lugh**, of noble birth, parented by the mother **goddess Danu**, from whence the Tuatha Dé Dannan get their name – "the people of Danu" or "the tribe of the gods." The Romans knew Lugh existed and equated him with Apollo, as both were called "the Sun god," and Lugh helped the Tuatha Dé triumph over the Formorians – a triumph over the forces of Darkness.

> So if we accept the classical writers, the ancient Celts believed they were physically descended from the sky god [Ollathair] who himself was descended from Danu, the 'divine waters.' [73]

So they have quite a history and are somehow a mixed group, including the Germani, the Cimbri, and it is even alleged that the Tuatha Dé Dannan are related to the people in **Hyperborea**. (That latter is a topic for Chapter 4.)

Thus we know nothing about serpent imagery, Flood imagery, or the origin of their people. However an interesting object was found by treasure-hunters **in Saxony-Anhalt, Germany** in 1999 (a little west of today's Berlin in northern Germany). It has been called the **Nebra Disk** and has been authenticated and dates back to the 1600 BC period, aka The Bronze Age.

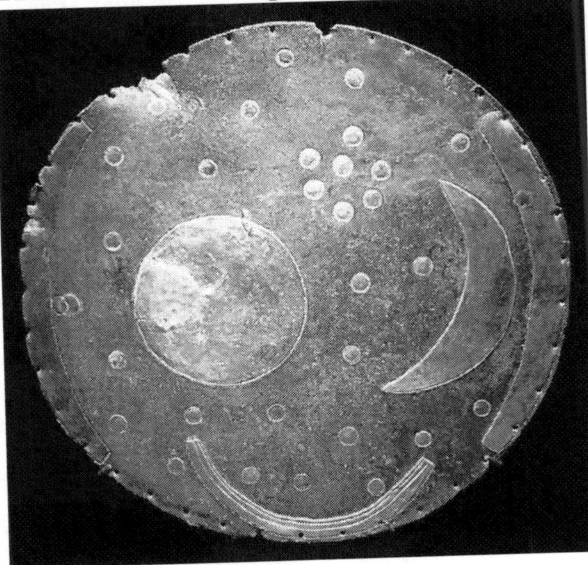

(credit: Wikipedia: Nebra Sky Disk.)

In the beginning the Nebra Disk had 32 'stars', the Sun and Moon, and the small cluster of 7 stars is the **Pleiades**… often used for navigation.

That Constellation will keep coming up as we examine other cultures.

In addition, the gold crescent on the right was matched by one on the left, and the disk was thought to be used as a **portable** astronomical device for verifying the solstices. The two arcs span an angle of 82°, correctly indicating the angle between the positions of sunset at summer and winter solstice at the latitude of the Mittelberg (51°N) [Austria].[74] Thus the users of the Disk were north in Germany when the Disk was lost or buried, consistent with constant migration by the people of that day.

Note that the Pleiades, Taurus, Orion, and Sirius are all in the same area of the sky… significant to ancient legends (p. 464).

Celtic Warriors

The Celtic warriors were as fierce as the Germani, but went a step further: they painted their bodies blue and added Celtic designs. The Vikings and Germani did not do extensive body paint.

Note the **Torc** around her neck (left) – a sign of status in the tribe –perhaps as a great warrior(ess) or maybe she was a leader of some rank.

(credit: Bing Images: Torc)

The Celtic warrior (right) also wears a Torc and the Celtic **Triskalion** (necklace) – signifying the Trinity. They were wild in battle and must have struck fear in the Roman soldiers as well as in other tribes.

Celtic Tribes

The Celts were as fierce as the Germani and Vikings, and Rome fought them several times and except for a few successful battles, the **Romans also lost to the Celts**, as they did to the Germani, and Rome decided to leave them alone. Rome never tried to colonize the Northern Europe area held by the Norse – they couldn't get past the Celts and Germani to do it. There is more documented history where the Celts are concerned, and it is therein that we find some interesting issues that appear related to the Anunnaki.

Druids

The Serpents of Wisdom in the British Isles were known as Naddred (Welsh) or Adders (serpents), and among the Gaels they were often called Druids, or "wise ones." They were priests and magicians. Remember that Enki started the **Brotherhood of the Serpent** and due to numerous persecutions by religion-for-the-masses groups, his teachings had to be done in secret, by groups that were not open to the masses.

Such were the Druids – a group of spiritual masters trained in esoteric teachings who came to settle in Britain, largely Ireland, and were called the **Tuatha Dé Danaan** – the Tribe of Danaan. Originally assumed to be seafaring people from the Mediterranean, they abandoned their Asia Minor location (which would have been close to Mesopotamia where Serpent Wisdom started) and migrated to the colder climate of northern Europe about 1500 BC. Their mythical hero was **Dagda The Good**, a club-wielding warrior.[75]

Upon reaching the shores of Ireland, **Dagda**, the Druids, and the magical **Tuatha Dé Danaan** began a series of incursions into the island by cloaking themselves in a mist and appearing unexpectedly in front of the Folbergs, the established occupants of the country. After defeating the Folbergs, the Danaans spread out through the country, some founding colonies and others forming mystery schools.

The Dagda built a temple at Brugh na Boinne (or Newgrange) which was a strategic vortex on the Earth's energy grid from which to rule. The Danaan named Mananan was a legendary magician who built his temple and mystery school on an island off the coast of Ireland, now called the Isle of Man. Mananan used his power to build a community out of huge stone blocks which he magically transported many miles thru the air. (Hint: Stonehenge is similar.) He was also said to have deceived and confused his enemies by appearing simultaneously as 100 people , none of whom looked like him.

The People of Dan were eventually conquered by the Milesians and in the treaty that was drawn up, the Danaan were to leave the surface of the Earth and dwell in an underground kingdom , entered thru sidh-mounds (the "hollow hills" of Ireland). Thus they became known as the magical subterranean fairies, elves and dwarves.

People later claimed that they didn't all leave the surface, and some stayed behind as Druids.

> Interesting sidelight: The king of the Anunnaki was **Anu** and the Anunnaki were sometimes called **Anunna**. How close is that to Danaan? **Tuatha Dé Danaan** is translated: "People of the Serpent Goddess Dana." Etymologically, it is considered close.

Note that the Vikings also spoke of elves and dwarves to be found in their lower realms, Alfheim and Svartelheim. The Tuatha went underground.

Oak Groves and Trees

The significance of trees, and in particular, Oak Groves, harks back to two things:

> A source of ***chi,*** or ambient energy that can be used in healing and groves were an easy source of the energy – the more trees the better.
>
> and:
>
> Trees were a symbol reflecting the Tree of Life concept which began in Mesopotamia and spread to the Vikings. **Mistletoe** was the sacred growth only handled by the high Druids – with a golden sickle.

The practice also relates back to when the Goddess Dana (mentioned above) was worshipped at the shrine of Dadona in Pelasgian Greece. [76]

The Druid centers spread throughout most of Europe and by 200 BC there were hundreds of such temples. These centers were considered holy, just as Christians revered Chartres Cathedral, and Druids from all over Europe would attend annual gatherings hosted by Arch-Druids in Gaul and Galatia (now called Turkey).

Mistletoe

The Druids also made herbal use of the Mistletoe which was believed to be saturated with serpent life force *(chi)*. It was cut from the tree using a golden scythe and used in potions to heal people and increase fertility. The healing effects were so profound that the Celts called it "all heal" and revered it as one of the ingredients in alchemical transformation. The other ingredient was sometimes snake venom.

Alchemical transformation of the individual, seeking greater awareness and/or higher consciousness, was one of the main pillars of Serpent Wisdom and the goal of *Kundalini* activation. (More on this in Chapters 7 & 9 the chapters on Serpent Wisdom.)

Left: ancient Druid grove

Celtic Tree of Life

Note the coiled up serpent/dragon under the tree – reminiscent of the Yggdrasil tree of the Vikings. Also harking back to the Vikings is the presence of the wolf as it accompanied the Norse god Odin. The stag represents a spiritual figure who may take the form of a red or white deer.

The Gundestrup Calderon:

Cernunnos, The Antlered God

Note in the picture of the cauldron above, Cernunnos is the god of fertility and death. The antlers signify that he is protected by **the gods who had horns** and that is also why the Germani wore helmets with horns – seeking the favor/protection of the gods of ancient times (viz., Anunnaki). Below is a magnified section of the copper **Gundestrup Caldron** (which could heal people):

Note the symbolic deer to the left, and the wolf to the right. He is holding a **serpent** (healing) in his left hand and a **Torc** (life) in his right. The Torc was usually symbolic of someone with high rank or importance. And note that he also has one around his neck (where they were usually worn). Torcs might also be worn on the arm and could be finely-crafted gold or silver.

TORCS

(credit: Bing Images: torc)

Celtic Torc from Snettisham

Druid Initiation

Before leaving the Druids, it is interesting that there were seven degrees of Druidism, from neophyte to Master. After applying to the local master for apprenticeship, the initiate was sent to the nearest body of water to cleanse the physical body. Then he or she (there were Druid priestesses, too), would be brought to the local oak grove via **underground tunnels** and chambers where it was believed that the Earth energy would begin to produce the serpent life force in the initiate. [77] Djedhi initiates in Egypt also went thru a tunnel to the Great Pyramid for their ceremony.

> The initiate was given a drink from the **Cauldron of Keridwen** who was the androgynous **Serpent Goddess** which often included hyssop, vervain, wort, and sea water and therefore possessed the alchemical power of awakening the Serpent Goddess at the base of the spine [i.e., *Kundalini*].
>
> After imbibing the sacred mixture, s/he might remain in one of the mysterious cells or caves where s/he was subjected to rigorous discipline, and where s/he studied the rites and secret doctrines, finally emerging back into the outer world.
>
> The candidate would have to submit to one last ordeal. During the coldest and darkest part of the night, the candidate would have to climb onto a raft and be drawn out to a turbulent sea and left there until the morning... to float fully exposed without oars.
>
> If an initiate could avoid being swallowed by the rough waves and survive a night on the icy, windswept water, the Druids took it as a sign that s/he had been chosen and protected by the gods to achieve the hallowed post of a Druid.
>
> Druids were basically shamen and as such, all over the world, have had to undergo trials and hardship tests to 'prove' they were called to their position.

At each of the **seven stages of Druidism**, the Druid was given a different colored sash to wear around his/her white gown, and in addition, there was a special stone called a **Serpent's Egg** to be worn around the neck... a blue-green glass bead set in gold and strung on leather. These were proudly worn and the ones with the most Eggs were alleged to be the most powerful Druids. Those achieving 7 Eggs became Masters.

> Such a Druid had united the polarity, merged with the transcendental Solar Spirit within, and became a clear vessel of serpent power and Wisdom.... The position of Arch Druid was limited to 3 people and each had his/her headquarters in the "magical isles" which surrounded Britain. One ... had his seat on the Isle of Anglesey... another on the Isle of Man, and the third was situated on the **Isle of Wight**, anciently known as **"the Dragon's Isle."** [78]

Like the Egyptian priests of the **Djedhi**, the Druids performed many of the same functions and miracles. Part of the Serpent Wisdom was being initiated into the use of what was called serpent power. Power to create foggy mists, to become invisible or shapeshift, to cast spells, to transform oneself into a menhir (the standing stones of Britain), to magnetize to themselves any knowledge from any source, and they could change the weather, fly thru the air, prophesy, talk directly with the gods, and even raise the dead (just as Inanna and Ptah could do).

In addition, they also used psychedelics to commune with the spirits, and the spirits would tell them which plants to use for specific purposes – and thus Herbology was born. (See Chapter 10, 'Higher States', Jeremy Narby.)

J.R.R. Tolkien was inspired by Norse/Celtic legends to write his *Hobbit* and *Lord of the Rings* books. Thus it is no accident that the picture (left) resembles Gandalf, the benevolent wizard.

Celtic Druid Priest

Saint Patrick

And into this mélange of Druids and their oak groves came Christianity about AD 432. **Palladius Patricius**, as he was named at birth, was ordained by Pope Celestine as a bishop and sent to Ireland to shepherd the new flock there. He was a genuine evangelist who sought to convert the **pagans and heathens** to Christianity. As Ireland's Apostle (St. Patrick) he explained the Trinity using the 3-leaved shamrock.

For clarity: ancient forms of worship:
Pagan – Wicca and Druidism
Heathen – Old Norse/Germanic religions

So when the history books say that St. Patrick drove the snakes out of Ireland, that has to be seen in terms of Druidism, which reflects the fact that **he was driving Druidism and Serpent Worship out of the country.** On the surface, it is a cute story, kind of like a fable, but with real historic, deeper meaning. And all he did was to drive the Druids underground as a secret society of which the spiritual essence could later be found in Gnosticism, Hermetism and Rosicrucianism, to name a few. (These are examined later with links to Anunnaki teachings.)

Yet, again, the **serpent and dragon imagery** did not disappear, it was merely 'explained away' as an old myth symbolizing Man's fight with evil on the planet.... whatever. The Church was ramping up its desire to remove witchcraft and anything that was not conducive to 'normal society' (where everyone is on the same page, religiously, and no one has any paranormal abilities)... Plain Vanilla Society was the Church's goal... and a total break with the past.

England in General

And yet, we come to the realization that one of Britain's earliest heroes, **King Arthur**, was known as the **Pendragon**, or Chief Dragon. Thus the legends call King Arthur the descendant of dragons, just as the Chinese emperors (Huang Di) and Sumerian kings also claimed. King Arthur wore a helmet which was adorned with a drawing of a dragon head.

The red dragon became the symbol of Wales.

Flag of Wales

The Welsh flag evolved from a story involving a castle, the king of Britain, Vortigern, and the Wizard **Merlin**. Vortigern's castle kept sinking into the ground, and Merlin the Chief Druid was brought into resolve the dilemma. He discovered a cavern under the castle occupied by two dragons, one white and one red. Removing the white one, the red one was left and it stopped upsetting the castle, and the red dragon became the badge of Uther Pendragon, the father of King Arthur.

Going further, we encounter **St. George** and the dragon – another legend about a professional dragon-slayer.

More ancient is the epic account of ***Beowulf*** (dated to the 8th century) – a warrior who earned great fame by killing the monster **Grendel** (below, said to be an evil **Giant**) who lived in a lake. The story, dated about AD 800, also contained the ubiquitous **dragon** that Beowulf later slays in its lair.

Beowulf Slays the Dragon

Grendel the Giant

Beowulf performed his heroic feats in Denmark and what is now Sweden… in the land of the Geats. The Danish king was very grateful to Beowulf, yet Beowulf suffered a mortal wound in taking the dragon down.

Celtic Goddesses & Queens

And lastly, a brief look at the **Celtic Goddess Brigid** or Brigit is in order.

Celtic Goddess Brigit

She had red hair and was the goddess of healing and learning, and the daughter of Dagda the Good. She has been equated with Dana and **Anu**. [79]

While Anu was the Sumerian God, it was also the name of another Celtic goddess who is an ancestor of the Tuatha Dé Danaan and involved with fertility. **Danu.**

It is interesting that the Celts had a goddess with the same name as the Sumerian's god, Anu, and the Tuatha Dé Danaan may have originated in the area of Greece, [80] which was home to the Greek gods…

…who were actually the Anunnaki whose main god was Anu. Is there a connection? Brigit has also been equated with **Freya,** the Norse goddess of fertility and likened with Isis. Brigit which has been equated with Ishtar [81] who has been equated with **Inanna** the Anunnaki goddess. [82]

Goddess Brigit/Freya

And then, there is **Queen Maeve** (pronounced: Mab or Medb):

Note the High Seat, like Odin was said to have, also the Raven and the Deer antlers, and note the sword and shield, making her a Celtic Queen of War.

All Norse imagery.

She was a colorful character and her name, Maeve, or Medb, translates to 'drunken woman.' Legend says she ran faster than horses, slept with innumerable kings, and carried birds and animals across her shoulders. She is a central figure in the Irish epic *Cattle Raid of Cooley* : Comparing possessions with her consort, King Aillil (reminiscent of Enlil) had a magic bull that she wanted. She used her army to steal the magic bull of Cooley and did battle with another famous Celtic hero, **Cú Chullain,** son of **Lugh.**

Lugh is another famous Celtic hero who was called the Sun God (similar to the Greek Apollo), thus Cú Chullain was also called the Son of Light.

After a great battle with Cú Chullain, she took the bull, but it in turn had to fight with Aillil's bull and the two killed each other.

Lastly, of note is another Celtic heroine who was treated savagely by the Romans, as she led her people to resist Roman colonization, about AD 60, but has lived on in history as a great leader and warrior of her people.

Queen Boudicca

Note the longboats, the Torc and the red hair. The **Celts and the Vikings had joined**, or merged, by AD 60, and shared major elements of their cultures.

Queen Boudicca (also: Boadicea) led her **Iceni** in a successful revolt on a Roman colony and **routed the Romans**. She then moved on toward a major Roman colony, now called London, and the Romans knew they didn't have sufficient numbers to defend Londinium, so Suetonius did a hasty retreat, and all the while he could not believe that a woman could be a successful warrior! The chauvinist Romans were insulted, to say the least. She led her 100,000 warriors against the town, and sacked London and burned it to the ground.

> An estimated 70,000–80,000 Romans and British were killed in the three cities by those led by Boudicca. **Suetonius**, meanwhile, regrouped his forces in the West and, despite being heavily outnumbered, defeated the Britons. The crisis caused Nero to consider withdrawing all Roman forces from Britain, but Suetonius' eventual victory over Boudicca confirmed Roman control of the province. Boudicca then either killed herself to avoid capture, or died of illness.[83]

In her honor, a statue was erected in London, next to Westminster Bridge. She is shown in her war chariot with her two daughters.

Queen Boudicca.

There were also movies and TV adaptations made in her honor. [84]
Note the wicked spikes on the wheel hubs.

Rewind: England in General

England has a long history of dragons and people claim to have observed them for centuries. In fact, it has probably persisted longer there than in any other country, except Romania.

> In a survey of the English countryside, Marc Aleksander in his book *British Folklore* has revealed that there are more than 70 towns and villages which have a tradition of dragons. [85]

The French (Sir Lancelot) fought a dragon here, Romanians (and vampires) and the Island of Rhodes (eastern Mediterranean) abound with stories of Dragons.

But there is one amazing glyph of something that has been called a horse, carved into the English countryside, that bears a closer examination.

Uffington Horse

There is a very large modernistic carving of an animal, done by the ancients around 3000 years ago. At 374 feet long, formed from deep trenches filled with crushed white chalk, the figure is situated on the upper slopes of White Horse Hill in Oxfordshire, England. Nearby is another hill called **Dragon Hill**....

Dragon Hill

Dragon Hill was the site of many ancient rituals and even carries the legend that St. George slew a dragon there... marked by the white chalk spot. What is significant is that the picture of Dragon Hill was taken from the summit of White Horse Hill...

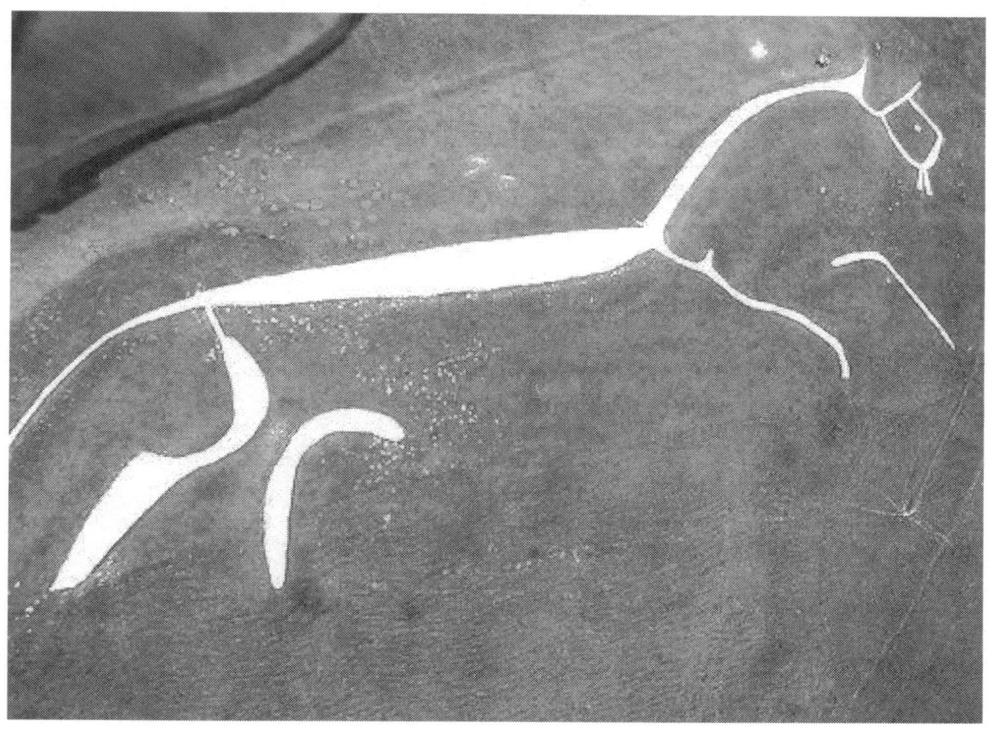

The image on **White Horse Hill** (above) does not look like a horse… maybe it could be a panther (it resembles a large cat)…? Or a dragon?

What is puzzling are the **two marks** coming from its mouth area… What are those supposed to be? The picture (left) is a better look at the "horse's" head….

It is suggested that this is not a horse, but a dragon since it is 100' from Dragon Hill, especially since the head, neck and body do not look like a horse. The body is lean/skinny like a dragon, the neck is longer than a horse's, but appropriate for a dragon, and the shape of the head is too large for a horse, but right for a dragon. And dragons had long tails… and yet it is missing the wings.

The foregoing is exactly describing a Chinese dragon (next chapter).

What's puzzling, other than it is a very abstract version of a 'something' – is that it is done in an art form that wasn't common to ancient Man. He typically drew what he saw – <u>and</u> this dragon has no wings…. But dragons often are pictured with **spines from the lower jaw…**

Were the **Celts** (who were the artists of White Horse Hill)[86] leaving us a subtle clue with the two spikes coming off the chin of the "horse?"

Located not far from the stone circles of Avebury and **Stonehenge**, Dragon Hill is famous for the outline of a great "horse" carved into the chalk hillside….it goes back into misty antiquity.

The belief has persisted among local people that it is not a horse at all but the outline of a dragon.[87] [emphasis added]

And dragons, being related to serpents, also have **forked tongues** – is that what the Uffington Horse's face is showing?

Look again at the original picture of the dragon on the hill… another give-away seems to be the two "horns" on the back of the head. Stylized to be sure, but horses don't look like that.

Just something to think about…

Stonehenge

How could we cover the Celts and the Tuatha Dé Dannan and not examine Stonehenge? It is known that all stone circles in Britain are temples of Ceridwen (aka Keridwen mentioned earlier in Druid Initiation).[88] And further, it is said that **the Tuatha Dé Dannan built Stonehenge**, way back in antiquity, no farther back than about 3000 BC. That date corresponds with the appearance of the **Nemed** (2350 BC) from whom the Tuatha are descended. Prior to the Nemed were the **Partholon** who date back to Noah.

> Note: the name Tuatha Dé Dannan comes from Tuatha for tribe(s) or "people of" and the Dannan is the genitive case of the goddess Danu that they worshipped. Note that Danu has been reconstructed as Danu, of which Anu (genitive *Anann*) may be an alternative form. *Anu* is called "mother of the Irish gods" by Cormac mac Cuilennain. This may be linked to the Welsh mythical hero Don. Hindu Mythology also has a goddess called Danu, who may be an Indo-European parallel. Anu was also the God of the Anunnaki.
>
> It is fascinating to speculate that Danu may be related to (or even descended from) the Anunnaki King who was also called Anu, and Annan bears a similarity to the word Anunna. After all, the Annan were gods and may have originated in Hyperborea (see Chapter 4).

The stones are aligned with the sunset of the winter solstice and the opposing sunrise of the summer solstice. So there was Astronomy for planting/harvesting, as well as Druid celebrations. It was also a communal meeting place among Celtic tribes.

The stones were quarried miles away, over rivers and hills – thus it is said they were moved and placed by the Tuatha Dé Dannan adepts who could **levitate** such stones. And then the learned scientists announce:

> There is little, or no direct evidence revealing the construction tech-

> niques used by the Stonehenge builders. Over the years, various authors have suggested that **supernatural** or anachronistic methods were used, usually asserting that the stones were impossible to move otherwise due to their massive size. However, conventional techniques, using Neolithic technology as basic as shear logs, have been demonstrably effective at moving and placing stones of a similar size. How the stones could be transported by a prehistoric people **without the aid of the wheel**, or a pulley system is not known. The most common theory of how prehistoric people moved megaliths has them creating a track of logs on which the large stones were rolled along. Another megalith transport theory involves the use of a type of sleigh running on a track greased with animal fat. Such an experiment with a sleigh carrying a 40-ton slab of stone was successful near Stonehenge in 1995 [**some weighed more than that!**]. A dedicated team of more than 100 workers managed to push and pull the slab along the 18-mile journey from Marlborough Downs. [89] [emphasis added]

They just can't imagine any way outside the box which constrains their thinking. Yet, why move the stones by brute force if the Druids knew how to levitate them? Perhaps they should also visit **Sacsayhuaman** and The Great Pyramid whose stones look like they were "poured" into place. (See VEG, Ch. 10.) Just because block and tackle could move something, that doesn't mean that the ancients did it that way.

Stonehenge consists of several types of stone, principally:[90]

Bluestones

It is generally accepted that the bluestones (some of which are made of dolerite, an igneous rock), were transported by the builders from the Preseli Hills, **150 miles (240 km) away in modern-day Pembrokeshire in Wales**.... It is assumed that there were about 80 of them originally, but this has never been proven since only 43 remain. The stones are estimated to weigh between 2 and 4 tons each.

The long distance human transport theory was bolstered in 2011 by the discovery of a megalithic bluestone quarry near Crymych in Pembrokeshire, which is the most likely place for some of the stones to have been obtained.

Sarsen Stones

Other standing stones may well have been small sarsens (sandstone), used later as lintels. The stones, which weighed about two tons, could have been moved by lifting and carrying them on rows of poles and rectangular frameworks of poles, as recorded in China, Japan and India.

However, 30 enormous sarsen stones *(shown grey on the plan below)* were brought to the site. They may have come from a quarry, around 25 miles (40 km) north of Stonehenge on the **Marlborough Downs**, or they may have been collected from a "litter" of sarsens on the **Chalk Downs**, closer to hand. Each standing stone was around 4.1 metres (13 ft) high, 2.1 metres (6 ft 11 in) wide and weighed around 25 tons.

Within this circle stood five trilithons of dressed sarsen stone arranged in a horseshoe shape 13.7 metres (45 ft) across with its open end facing northeast. These huge stones, ten uprights and five lintels, weigh up to 50 tons each

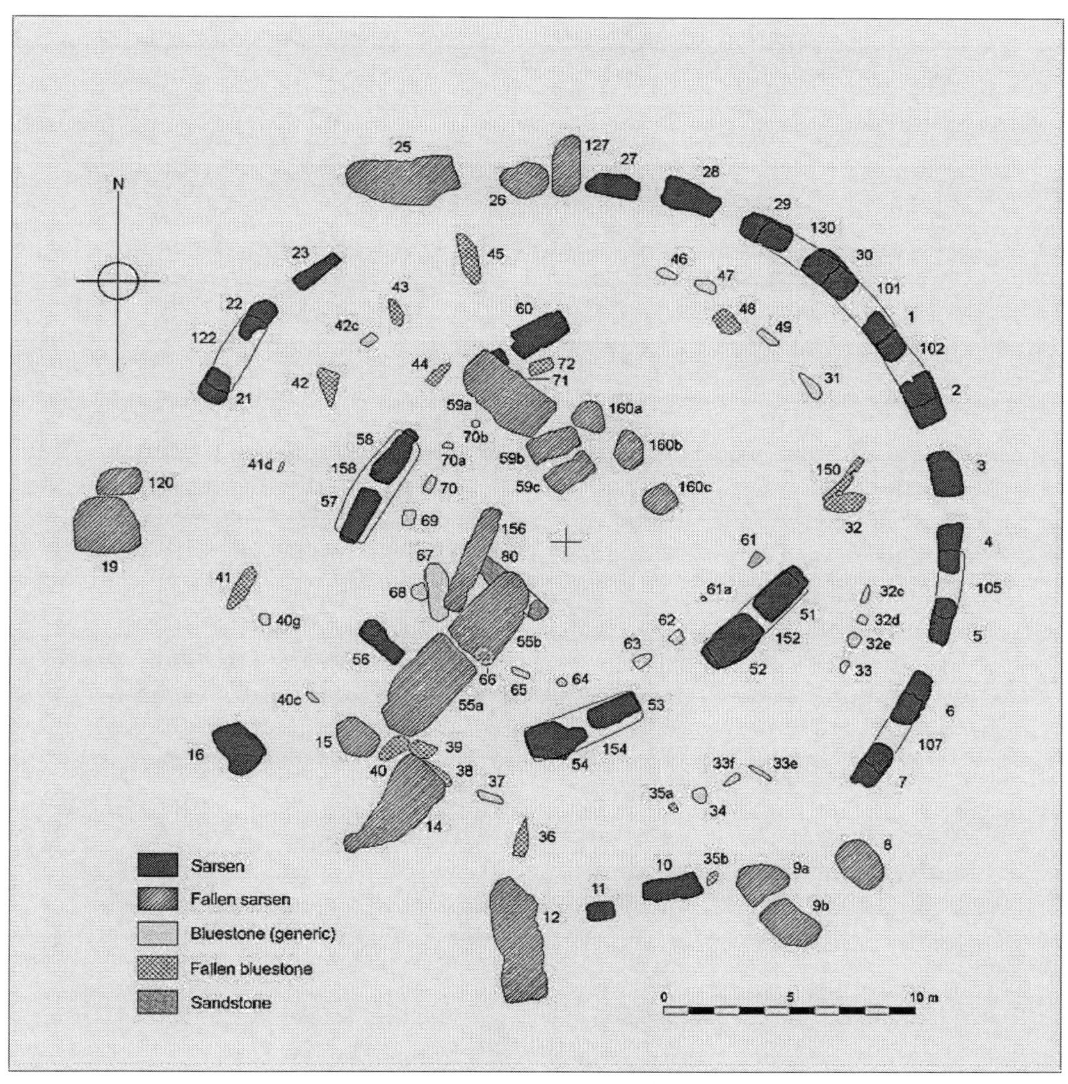

Plan of Stonehenge
(credit: Anthony Johnson in 2008 from a computer analysis.)

The point being in all this that the ancients knew how to move 50-ton rocks over great distances (and suggests a technology that is lost today), and the original inhabitants, the **Nemed** were considered gods, and thus their descendants, the Tuatha Dé Dannan were also considered as such – and they all used undocumented technology to do things (move stones, create fogs, cause storms to sink ships, heal people…) that were beyond the ken of the later Celtic tribes who had come in from Europe.

> According to *Lebor Gabála Érenn*, they came to Ireland "in dark clouds" and "**landed on the mountains** of [the] Conmaicne Rein in Connachta; and they brought a darkness over the sun for three days and three nights." [emphasis added]
>
> Nemed, like those who settled Ireland before him (the Partholon), had a genealogy going back to **the biblical Noah**. The Partholon arrive on the uninhabited island about **300 years after Noah's Flood** and are responsible for introducing such things as farming, cooking, brewing and buildings. After some years, they **all die of plague** in a single week.[91]

The Roman historians corroborate the settlement of Ireland:

> The *Historia Brittonum*, a 9th-century British Latin compilation attributed to one Nennius. It says that Ireland was settled **three times by three groups**, with 'Partholomus' and his followers being the first. It says he came to Ireland from Iberia with a thousand followers, who multiplied until there were four thousand, and then all died of plague in a single week.[92]

The point of relating all that history is that these things were not just mythic. The people and their exploits and battles were very real. What this is leading up to is where the **Partholons** and **Nemeds** came from…. We are trying to establish a connection with Hyperborea or the Anunnaki, if possible.

> **….** one man survived [the plague]: Tuan, son of Partholón's brother Starn. Through a series of **animal transformations, he survived through the centuries** to be reborn as the son of a chieftain named Cairell in the … 6th century. He remembered all he had seen, and thus Partholon's story was preserved.[93]

Now, believing just for a minute that these ancients had advanced knowledge to transform themselves (and Tuan wasn't the only one), live long lives ("survived thru the centuries…"), move heavy stones, possess a magic hammer (Lugh), and slay everyone in battle with a flaming spear that never missed its mark…. What does that say about them?

So if they **landed their ships on the mountain**, and their lineage traced back to a son of Noah (Japeth), then **surely they would have known and interacted with the Anunnaki** of that same era and location. And we have already suggested that the Norse gods were none other than the Anunnaki who also played Greek and Roman gods… so they were not myth. And if the gods were just a few hundred miles northeast of Britain, in Scandinavia, why would the Partholons, the Nemeds and the Tuatha Dé Dannan not have had at least some of the Serpent Wisdom personal development, giving rise to their so-called "magic" (Druid) powers? And could they also have had some of the technology (special hammer and spear, magic cauldron, and landing ships on mountains…) also enjoyed by the Norse – and the Hindus (Think: Vimana flying craft in Chapter 4).

See also Chapter 7 and the **Göbekli Tepe** temple which changed people.

Rewind: Tuatha Dé Dannan Origins

Whereas the chapter began with the Germani and the Cimbri waging war on Rome (and winning), a later reference speaks of the Cimmerii (not related to the Cimbri) who were said to have the same attributes as the **Hyperboreans** and "who are robbed of the sight of the Sun…. by the position of the place in which they live…" (Think: Land of the Midnight Sun). The author goes on to point out that Hyperborea is in the far north from Britain, and "… it calls to mind the Tuatha Dé Dannan … who lived in islands in the North of the world, learning magic, druidism, sorcery, and wisdom…[all describing ancient technology]" [94]

> This whole hotch-potch of legends, however confusing, does suggest that the Cimmerii were identified with both the Hyperboreans and the Cimbri…. For all these peoples, whether Hyperborean, Cimmerian, Cimbrian, or even Tuatha Dé Dannan are represented as belonging to a race of mysterious origins which lives at **the ends of the Earth** and was supposedly driven from its original home [by catastrophe]. In mythological terms, **they are all Tuatha Dé Dannan**…. And since the Hyperboreans supposedly initiated the **solar cults at Stonehenge and Delphi**, both Greeks and Celts must have owed aspects of their civilization to their predecessors.[95]

And let's not forget that Apollo received offerings at the temple in Delphi (Delos) and spent 6 months of the year in Hyperborea. And…"Apollo was said to descend to this island [Britain] every 19 years." [96]

> **Callimachus** sang that Apollo rode on the back of a swan to the land of the Hyperboreans during the winter months. [97]

Apollo was the son of the goddess Leto and Zeus. Divine birth. The late Zechariah Sitchin also identified him as Enki. [98] Thus, Apollo would have used his "sky boat" as the Anunnaki called their personal craft.

Apollo in His Golden Sun Chariot
(credit: Bing Images: Pinterest.com)

The above is the "politically correct" version for Apollo. Perhaps what he really had was one of the ancient sky craft found in Peru and Turkey:

Is this a "golden sky boat", or chariot?

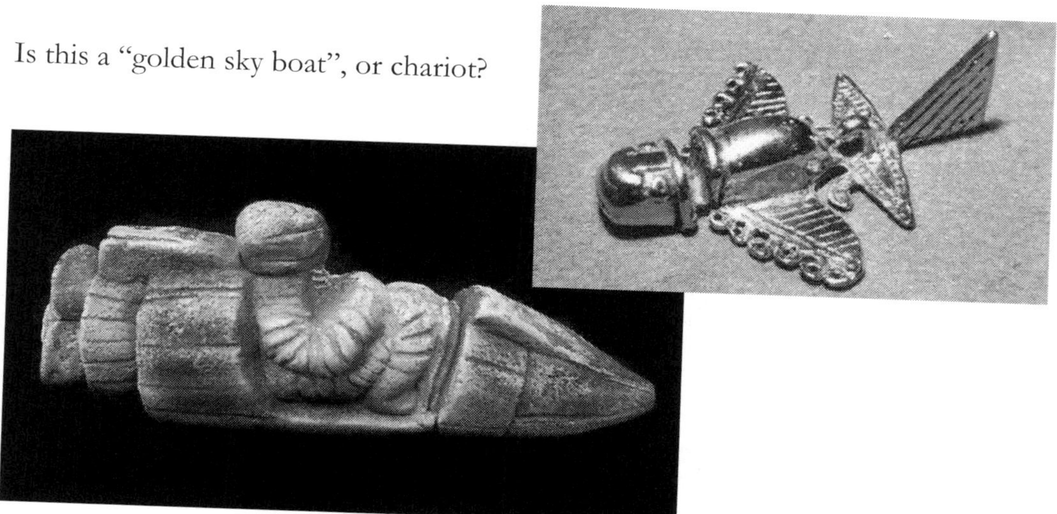

So, in summary, ancient history is not recorded in concrete but the attempt was to discover connections and draw some tentative conclusions that suggest that the Celts benefitted from the Serpent Wisdom teachings of the Enki-led secret society. And it is possible that the Celts also had some Anunnaki technology, as did the Norse just across the North Sea.

Further revelations as this book goes around the globe on a search for a Tree of Life, Serpents, and potential Anunnaki influence will lend credibility to the foregoing suggested conclusions. Other cultures had similar encounters and benefits…

∫ ∫ ∫

Evaluation & Caveat

Such ancient tales as recorded throughout this book often have some basis in reality but are hard to prove for lack of physical evidence (after thousands of years!). And because of the traditional, narrow-minded 'scientific' thinking which says that Man has been in a steady upward evolution, societally and technologically… from caves thousands of years ago, using sticks and stones, grunting at each other and hiding from animals larger than he…and therefore there just could not have been any flying craft (nor nuclear weapons)… But another vetted text like the Hindu **Mahabharata** describes aerial battles thousands of years ago in skyships with very advanced weaponry that blew lasers and thunderbolts across the sky, blowing up other skycraft… That ain't Stoneage! (See Chapter 4.)

And as also examined in Chapter 4: how to explain the similarities in languages and writing around the globe? (See pp. 160-164.)

And as for the presence of ETs, that blows scientific minds. Yet, if we are now getting off the planet and have some nuclear and genetic expertise, is it so hard to think that we might have been visited, ETs might have done what Zechariah Sitchin said, and that some of the ancient legends are based in fact, not fantasy?

Instead of ETs, what if the anomalies all over the planet were the work of the **Ancient Ones**, who have been here, since before Man, and probably are still here, guiding us? (Think: Atlantis, MU, and Hyperborea examined next chapter.)

Remember that really old historical accounts are called **myths**; semi-old accounts are called **legends**, and more recent historical **events** are often ignored if they don't agree with the Standard Model… Yet they can all be true.

Do not blindly believe the foregoing accounts, but be willing to consider that it or something like it probably happened as the source of the common legends and writing, and someday, when we encounter ETs or Others with more knowledge of Earth, we may be shocked to learn what really happened in our ancient history – the ETs/Others and their craft have been here for quite a while, so they probably DO know, and they probably recorded it… Are we ready for the truth?

∫ ∫ ∫

Chapter 4: India and China

Moving on to India and China, we find longer and deeper traditions. Both countries have records of **ancient visitations from the gods** who came down from the sky and either healed people and/or taught them civilization. That was the same story that the Sumerians recorded and said was their history with the Anunnaki.

However, whereas the Sumerians recorded that their civilization was set up complete 'overnight' in historical/anthropological terms, they also recorded that the gods not only taught them **Warfare** and how to make weapons, the gods also involved mankind in the gods' Earth-based battles.

The Anunnaki fought among themselves and ranged over a wide area – Mesopotamia, over what is now called India (Indus Valley), and over South America. They fought over control of the spaceport in what is now Saudi Arabia. They fought over the outpost Puma Punku near Lake Titicaca. And the aerial battle with the Aryans over India occurred about 3000 BC, and that was called the **Kurukshetra War**. It is strongly suspected that the gods had something to do with the breakup of Atlantis.

Anunnaki in India

The Kurukshetra War was documented in the epic narrative called the **Mahabharata.** It has been compared with the Bible, the Koran, the works of Shakespeare and the works of Homer for its significance in historical importance.

It allegedly was written in the 4th Century BC about events that occurred much earlier (as far back as the 9th Century BC) and here some explanation must be given to better understand the War.

> Inanna was a beautiful woman Anunnaki who had been given the rule over the **Indus Valley**, and she set up the key cities of Harappa, Mohenjo-Daro, Dholavira, and Kaligangan – in what was then the far eastern hegemony of the Anunnaki Rule. That is today mostly in Pakistan.
>
> Because the Indus Valley was under Anunnaki Rule, there were priests and high members of a class-based society to whom the Anunnaki gave the technology for flying and the Pandavas and the Kauravas used it to attack one another. They called their craft Vimanas – designed and shaped after their pyramidal temples.

The Indus Valley cities are shown following the Vimana information…
The **Vimanas** looked like this:

Two Rukma-style Vimanas

…and that design was based on the familiar shape of Asian temples:

And then most Anunnaki went home about 650-600 BC – having kept order in the world up until then. They knew what would happen, and Man started squabbling over land and who was the Anunnaki favorite, and who wanted more land, and push came to shove and war broke out – in the skies over India – even destroying Krishna's city of Dwarka, which was on the western coast, now under water. Later recorded, it was known as the **Kurukshetra War**.

The technology was from Anunnaki passed on to Man…reminiscent of the technology that the Viking god Odin had: **thunderbolts.**

Some depictions of the War follow. Of course many of the aerial craft are shown as flying chariots, temples…but not all :

Shakuna-style Vimana

The concept of the **flying wheel** is a common motif for showing a flying craft.

In fact, a temple on wheels was not an early "RV" or motorhome, but a reminder that the temple's counterpart, the Vimanas, did fly. And those who flew the Vimanas were revered as gods …hence the 'temple and god' connection.

A Ratha: Spoke-wheeled Chariot

Thus….

The Vimanas could carry a number of people as they were large, and equipped for battle. The cutaway shows "electric magnets" (base), "steering gear" (above base), "passenger cabins" (middle), and propeller/air shafts (for steering). Power was electric and appears to be anti-gravitic.

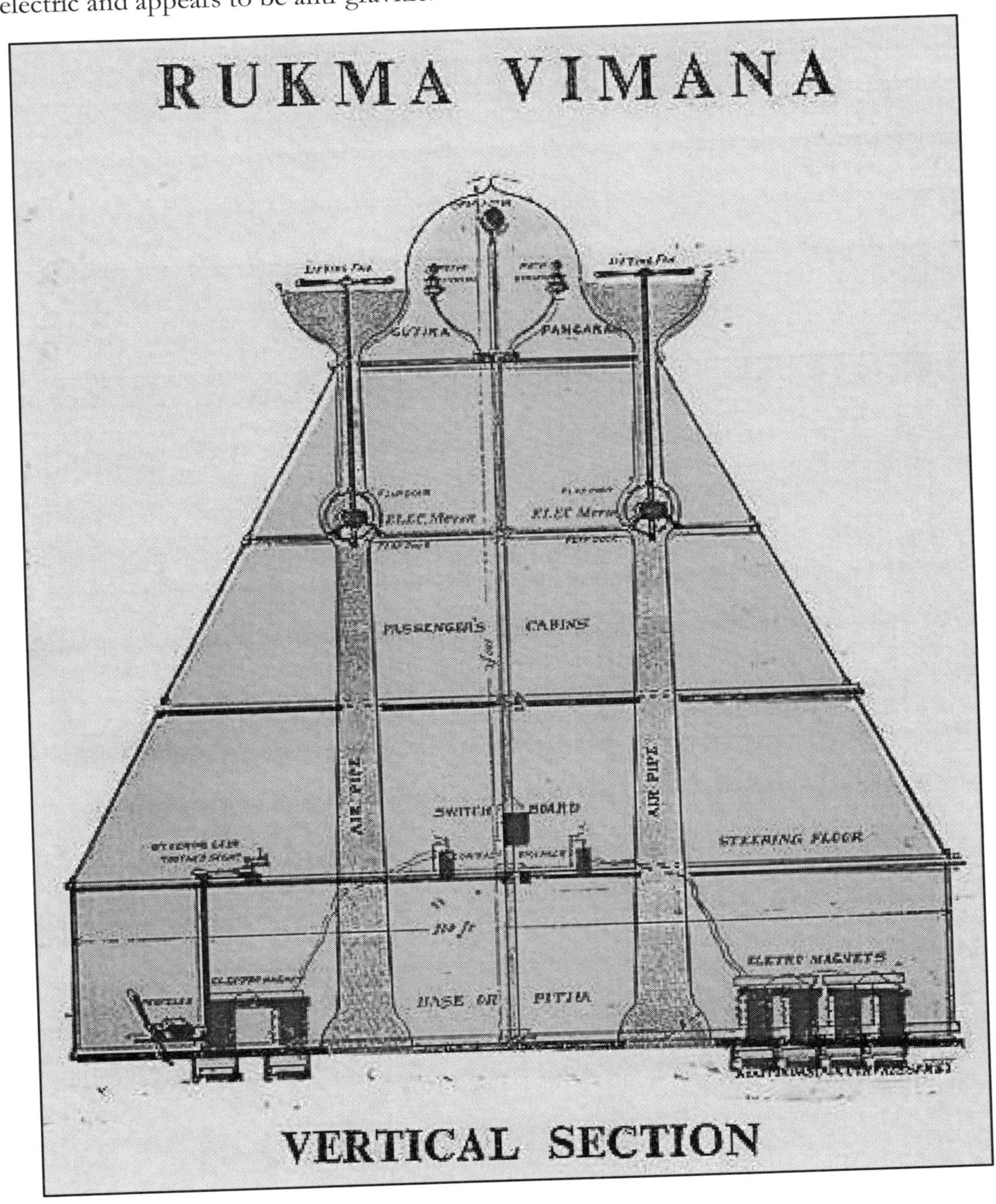

These were not just legend. Not too long ago a strange piece of metal was found that fits the description of a landing pod/foot….

Some researchers, including Hindu scholars, are convinced that an ancient advanced civilization existed in what is now India. They claim that the prehistoric civilizations had **advanced technology** including **high-energy weapons, flying aircraft and even atomic weapons**. They point to ancient Veda and Mahabharata texts as evidence. Recently, the mysterious aluminum wedge (below) is suspected to be connected to an ancient Vimana flown in India. According to ancient astronaut theorists, the aluminum wedge was **part of a landing gear** of a sky craft whose manufacturing date was around 18,000 years ago and was made of a metal that was not discovered by human beings until the early 1800s.

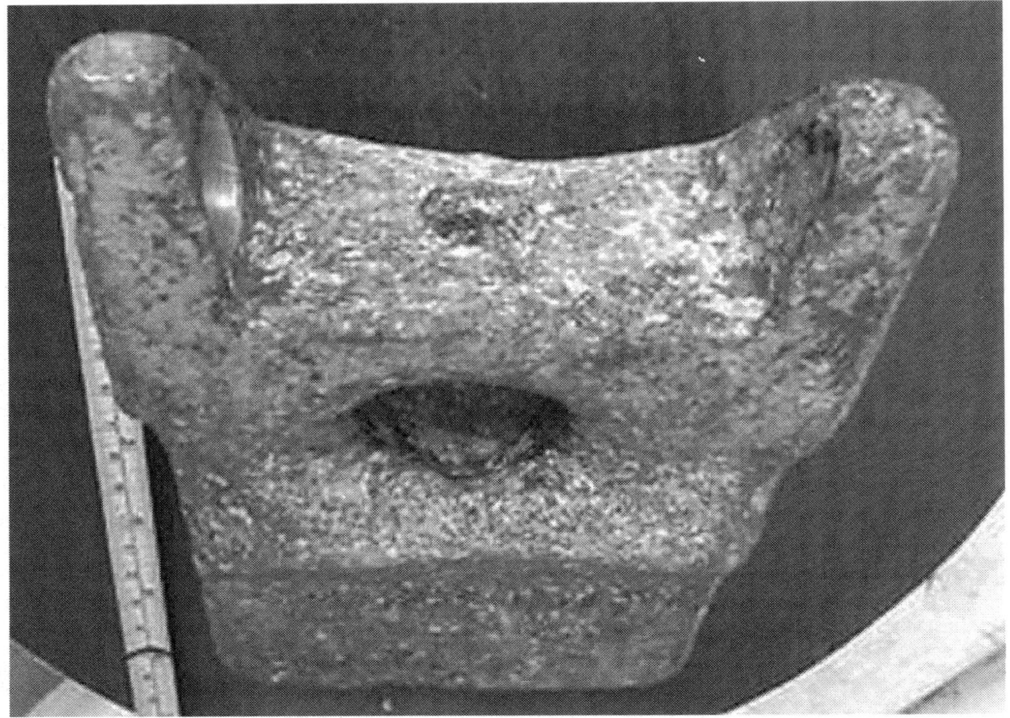

Vimana Landing Gear? : An Aluminum Aiud

While most of the Vimana were used for transport in the Earth's atmosphere, some Vimanas were even capable of spaceflight, others could be used as submersible vehicles. Like modern aircraft, the Vimana had various shapes and sizes depending on the function for which they were designed. Some had two engines, as agnihotra-vimana; others, like the gaja-vimana, had more. Among all of these, there may be a dozen different types of Vimanas all designed for different purposes. Most of them had the ability of ionospheric flight.

According to ancient astronaut theorists, the **Aiud wedge** might have belonged to the ancient Vimana flying machines. The Aiud wedge is an object that doesn't seem to belong anywhere in history, it is a mysterious object that, according to research is composed as follows: **aluminum (89%)** Copper (6,2%), silicon (2,84%), zinc (1,81%), lead (0,41%), tin (0,33%), **zirconium**(0,2%), cadmium (0,11%), nickel (0,0024%), **cobalt** (0,0023%), bismuth (0,0003%), silver (0,0002%), and gallium (in trace amounts).

Aluminum was not discovered until the early 1800s, the commercial production of aluminum requires melting points of temperatures up to 1,000 degrees Fahrenheit, something that, accord to scholars was not achievable in Man's distant past.

Some researchers suggest that the production of this mysterious object can be traced back as far as **18,000 BC**, a date that mysteriously coincides with the age of the Vimanas.[99] And it coincides with Gobekli Tepe's heyday (Chapter 7).

Flying Temples

And, there was a legend of flying temples…[100]

Temple at rest…

It was said that some temples flew....[101] The top part could detach and fly off – perhaps the original concept was that the Vimana took off/landed on a platform...

...Temple Lift Off.

Wars of the Gods

The weapons conventionally shown are spears, bow and arrow, and swords, but that is not what all parts of the Mahabharata say. See the following...

A postcard (left) ....

This style Vimana was called **Tripura.**

Some of the Vimanas were called "Flying Cities":[102]

…and as pictured, still they fought on….

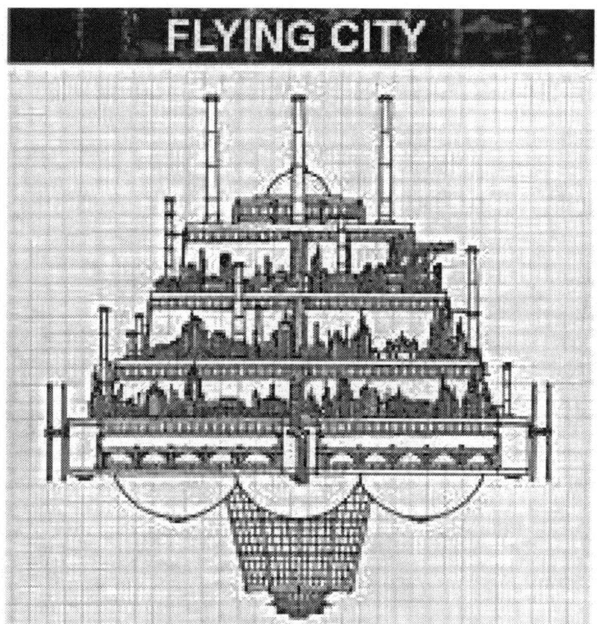

The ancient records allegedly say that there was some **very sophisticated weaponry** being used… perhaps the **Baumastra device** cited in the Mahabharata.

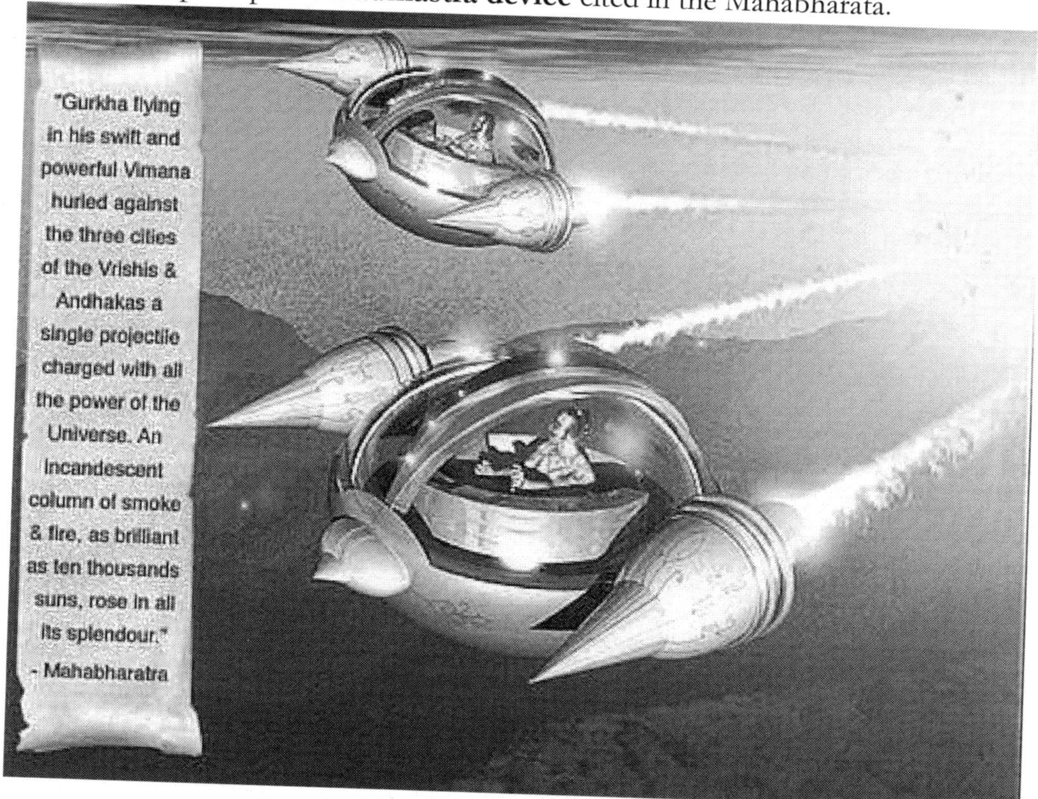

Text in Picture Sounds like an Atomic Weapon.

To quote the Mahabharata:[103]

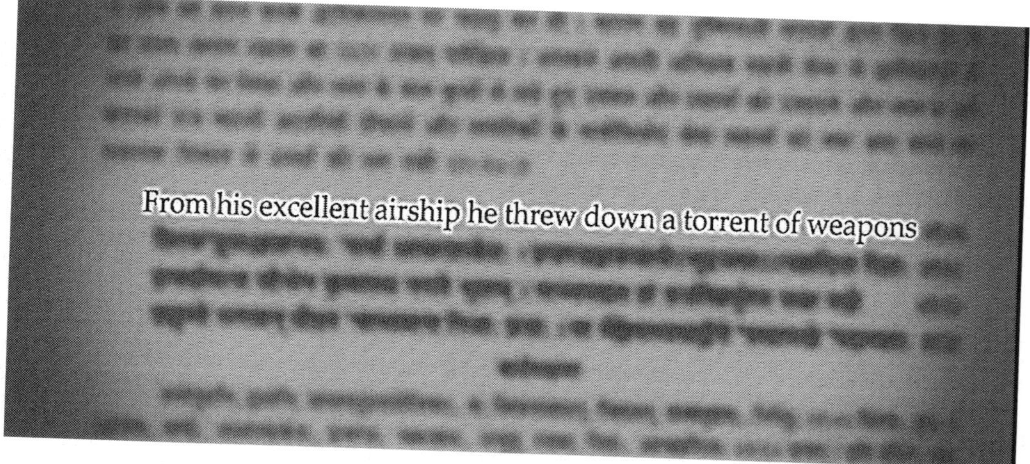

This is more than the bows & arrows and spears shown in traditional paintings. But is it valid? For comparison, let's look at the Sodom and Gomorrah account…

Sodom, Gomorrah et al

Allegedly, Sodom and Gomorrah, according to Zechariah Sitchin in his Anunnaki Chronicles, states that the Anunnaki in all their battles with each other decided to **nuke Sodom and Gomorrah** (and **Admah, Zeboim and Zoar** [also known as Bela]) because their progeny were genetically defective, turning to all sorts of deviant behavior. Enlil was only too happy to get rid of malfunctioning humans. The Bible says:

> "And Abraham got up early in the morning to the place where he stood before the Lord: And he looked toward Sodom and Gomorrah, and toward all the land of the plain, and beheld, and, lo, the smoke of the country went up **as the smoke of a furnace**." Gen. 19:28

Those who witnessed the Trinity, Nevada, testing of the atom bomb reported what they saw, and it was the same story: remember that pictures of nuclear explosions look like this: "The blast shot straight upward in a pillar, then **mushroomed** out in a vast cloud overhead." And the Anunnaki contaminated the whole area.

According to research by writer Zecharia Sitchin, the written record indicates that the war was between Enki and Enlil, sons of the Sumerian god, Anu, who battled for supremacy in about **2000 BC**. Enlil's son Marduk was apparently the one that used a nuclear weapon to destroy the five cities as well as the Sumerian Civilization, which was downwind (blowing Northeast) of the radioactive fallout.[104] Brilliant strategy, Marduk.

> The destruction in these cities went beyond even the damage a volcano might cause. While volcanic ash will burn and bury a city, it can leave stone structures intact as with the City of Pompeii, under Mt. Vesuvius, Italy.
>
> **Everything in Sodom, Gomorrah, Admah, Zeboim and Zoar was turned to ash** [not covered with it]. Only the foundations of the buildings remain. In one of the cities was found the shape of a mound which may have been a ziggurat, common among the cities of ancient Sumer.[105] [emphasis added]

And as Lot and his family make their way from Sodom to Zoar, Lot's wife pauses and looks back. The Bible said she was turned into a pillar of salt. She didn't get away and was consumed by the blast. **She was not turned to salt, but to ash.[106]**

The point being that since the Anunnaki had nuclear weapons, they may have also been used in the **Kurukshetra War**. While that is speculation, it is reasonable since Krishna's city on the coast, called Dwarka, has been found leveled and under 8' of water.

Kurukshetra War

The Kurukshetra War took place in the following region of India (also called the **Indus Valley**):

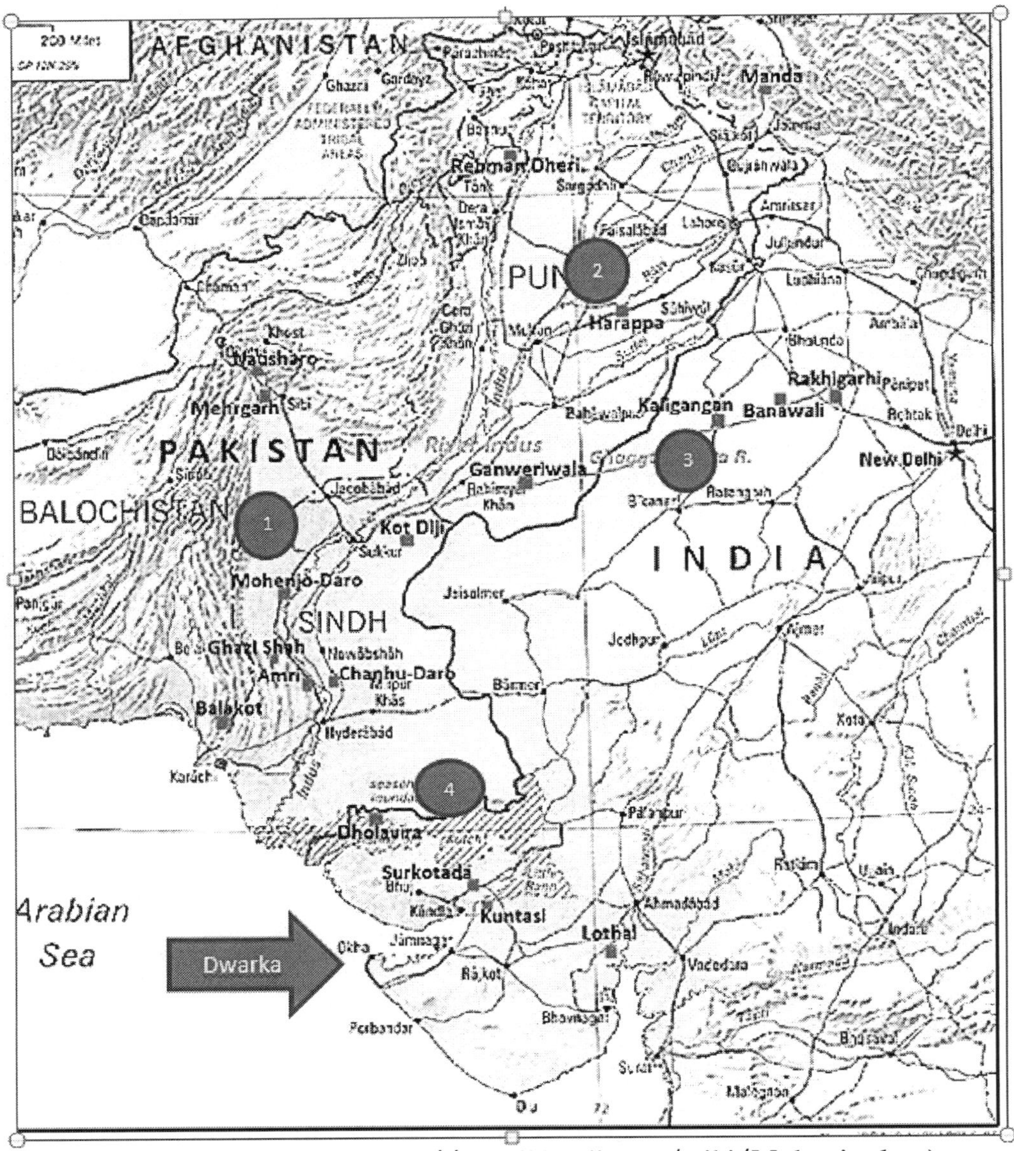

(Map credit: Wiklipedia: https://en.wikipedia.org/wiki/Mohenjo-daro)

Note: Location 1 is Mohenjo-Daro
Location 2 is Harappa
Location 3 is Kaligangan
Location 4 is Dholavira
Dwarka was Krishna's home by the sea (destroyed in the battle).

These cities were also part of **Inanna's kingdom in the Indus Valley**. What is relevant is that **Mohenjo-Daro**, for example, went into decline about 1900 BC – which is also when the Anunnaki were fighting each other in sky battles, and they nuked **Sodom and Gomorrah** – and the Indus area is said to still show mild radioactivity to this day – in addition to which there is evidence in the area of some sand and rocks being fused by high heat.

> Mohenjo-Daro and Harappa have been called "the Hiroshima and Nagasaki of the ancient world." This is due to the fact that when archeologists were excavating the ruins of those cities, they found skeletons all over the cities, in strange poses, and sometimes holding hands.... The skeletons are rated among **the most radioactive** in the world – equal to the ones gathered from Hiroshima/Nagasaki.
>
> In addition, there are **mysterious black clumps** all over the cities...It is assumed that these are just what is left of clumps of bricks or pottery that was obviously exposed to very high temperatures – around the vicinity of 2550-2910° F. The centers of both cities bear the evidence of an explosion, or something resembling one – the buildings are leveled and the farther from the city's center one gets, the better the condition of the buildings. [107]

That is what a nuclear blast does, in addition to turning sand into **vitrified glass** which has also been found.

So either the Anunnaki were involved in the Kurukshetra War, at least by giving the Hindu elite the technology to build and arm their Vimanas, or the Anunnaki were physically involved and Hindu Vimanas fought Anunnaki skycraft. This is not as outrageous as it first seems.

Scholars have analyzed various historical and archeological data to date the War, and despite the inconclusiveness of the data, attempts have been made to assign a historical **date for the Kurukshetra War**. Popular tradition holds that the war marks the transition to Kaliyuga and thus dates it to 3102 BCE. That is very close to the start of the **Mayan Calendar** (3114 BC) and semi-close to the start of **the Jewish Calendar** (3760 BC). A number of other proposals have been put forward:[108]

- P. V. Vartak calculates a date of October 16, 5561 BC using planetary positions.
- P. V. Holey states a date of 13 November 3141 BC using planetary positions and calendar systems.
- K. Sadananda, based on translation work, states that the Kurukshetra War started on November 22, **3067 BC**.

- B. N. Achar used planetarium software to argue that the Mahabharata War took place in **3067 BC**.
- S. Balakrishna concluded a date of 2559 BC using consecutive lunar eclipses.
- R. N. Iyengar concluded a date of 1478 BC using double eclipses and Saturn+Jupiter conjunctions.
- P.R. Sakar estimates a date of 1298 BC for the war of Kurukshetra.

According to **Sasha Lessin**, a disciple of Zechariah Sitchin, the Anunnaki timeframe for some of their major events is as follows:[109]

> **3760 BC** – the first king was chosen to govern the earthlings. (note the Jewish Calendar start date is the same)
> 3100 BC – Stonehenge is built.
> 2900 BC – Inanna rules the Indus Valley.
> 2316 BC – 2023 BC – Anunnaki constant warfare, fighting over territory and kingships. Sumerians migrated to India and the Far East.
> 1450 BC – Enlil sends Moses to tell the pharaoh to release the Israelites.

It is not unreasonable that the Anunnaki were involved in the fray in India, one way or the other since (1) the Hindus had to have gotten the technology for the Vimanas from some advanced race, and (2) **India and the Indus Valley were already under Anunnaki hegemony.** And the most reasonable date for the start of the Jewish people seems to be around 3760 BC, and the War appears a bit later around 3067 BC… both well within the ruling Anunnaki purview.

Indus Valley Script

While examining the Indus Valley, there were some positive aspects taking place. Remember that the Anunnaki introduced Man to writing in Mesopotamia (Cuneiform script) and while Harappa and Mohenjo-Daro were very advanced, they also received tutelage in writing. It has been simply called **Indus Valley Script**:

Ancient Indus Valley Script

And someone thought that the **Easter Island Script** (Rongorongo) looked a lot like it…

…and produced a comparison:

If one is based on the other, some poetic license was taken as the Rongorongo Script is 'fleshed in' – the figures have more body to them… And yet the cultures and scripts are thousands of miles apart… unless there was a landbridge between the two and ancient India was bigger landwise and extended almost to Australia. It was part of the ancient landmass called Lemuria (Mu).

Additionally, a comparison might also be made to the Linear A and Linear B scripts which also look alike … the older **Linear A** (Minoan) has yet to be deciphered:

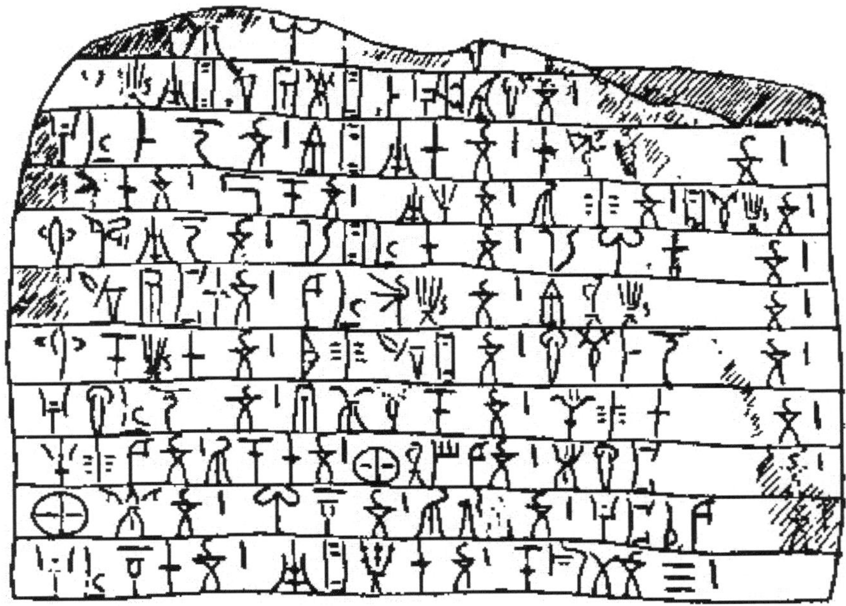

And the Linear B which has been deciphered looks like the A form but if Linear B decoding is used on A, it generates nonsense. Linear A on the **Phaistos Disk**:

Bing Images

Linear B: said to be a very early form of Greek…

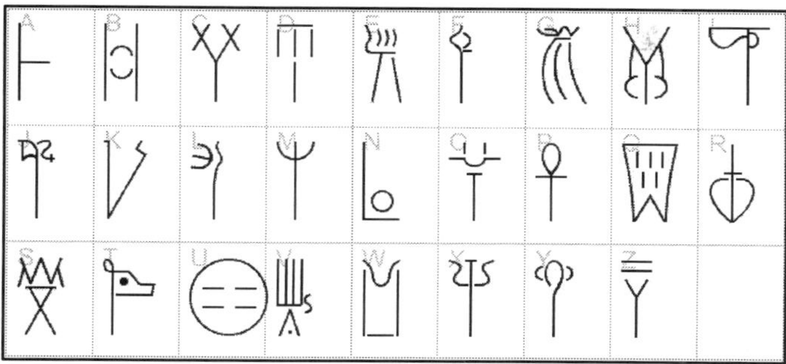

As if that weren't enough, a very interesting match has been found between Linear A of Crete and the **Mayan hieroglyphs**:

MAYAGLYPHS DE LANDA'S ALPHABET			CRETAN SCRIPT Linear A		
Ca					
U					
E					
H					
T					=ta
C					
X sch					
U					
Z					
A					
A					
PP		p glottal		=Pa	=Pa
O					
N					
B					

Comparative table of Mayan and Cretan signs from Pierre Nonore', ***In quest of the White Gods***.

In many cases the Phoenicians and the Maya have very similar 'characters' for the same letters, and also similar meanings for the characters. Now, the Maya cannot possibly have hit upon not only the names but also the order as in the Phoenician alphabet. So at first sight it looks as if the Mayan script (DeLanda) had come from the Phoenicians. But the Phoenician characters are very simple, in contrast to the complicated day-symbols of the Maya.

It therefore seems probable that both scripts have a common root, older than the Phoenician script, from which they both developed. We may therefore safely say that the Mayan legends were right: Kukulcan their White God, taught his people the script he had brought with him. And this script was Cretan.[110]

And we all know that Kukulcan was Quetzalcoatl was Nigishzidda – the bearded white man who taught the natives in the Americas.

Thus we can safely say that the Anunnaki were busy educating Man around the globe.

For those who are still in doubt, consider the following. There has been a study done on the basic alphabets of the Old World, and it was found that

Greek, Phoenician, and Mayan alphabets have an amazing similarity, and some, in fact, are almost identical. Here are a few instances - giving the letters in: [111]

GREEK	PHONECIAN	MAYAN
Alpha,	aleph,	ahau
Beta,	bejt,	baaz
Gamma,	gimel,	ghanan
Epsilon,	eh,	eb
Iota,	iud,	ik
Kappa,	koph,	queh
Lamda,	lamed,	lamat
Tau,	tav,	tihaz

This is clear evidence that someone was going around and educating humans, and just barely varying the language/writing aspect. Says Dr. Martinez in Delusions of Science & Religion (appx E):

The Chinese system of writing, as well as that of ancient America, arose independently of the so-called Mesopotamian (Sumerian) "cradle of civilization," yet all three languages are of the agglutinative type. Most Native American languages, like Algonquian, are agglutinative, akin to Chinese (single words can be as long and descriptive as phrases or even sentences).

FAR-FLUNG LINGUISTIC COUSINS

ALGONQUIAN	CHINESE	TRANSLATION
mai'ah	*ma**	expression
p'boa†	*m'boa*	winter; destroyer
hagni	*ah'gni*	fire; to burn (same in Sanskrit)
go'ongwe	*oe'gwong*	love-offering
ni'oh'ghoo	*ni'ghoo*	prayer
shu	*su*	enlightened; prophetic
yope'ang	*yoke'eng*	sacred star
haden	*haden*	sky, heaven (*hades* in Greek)
haw'git	*git'haw*	Sun, the all-heat (same in Arabic)
hogawatha	*hogawata*	mastodon

*The term is *mai* in the mother-language (Panic).

†"Winter" is *p'boa* in Panic. The term *Panic* refers to both the language and the culture of Pan (Mu, Lemuria)—the lands lost in the Pacific to the Great Flood of Waters (my next book!).

The Algonquins are examined again on page 347.

Let's conclude the Indian section of this chapter with a look at their version of the Tree of Life.

Tree of Life

There are two versions – one involving peacocks in a sacred **Peepal tree**…

…the other records the **sacred serpent Sesha** (right) climbing the Jambu Tree that is found at **Mt. Meru.**[112]
Sesha (**Seshanaga**) is the World Serpent. Again, the serpent (Naga) is sacred to the Hindus.

As was seen with the Norse Yggdrasil, the serpent and tree is a motif found around the globe. The question is, since a Mt. Meru (**home of the gods**) is also sacred to the Jain, Chinese, Taoists and Buddhists, does it actually exist somewhere?

Mount Meru

According to Hindu lore, Mt. Meru is located on the island of Jambudvipa – (which is also the ancient name for India itself) also called **Sumeru**, which consists of 5 peaks. (Interesting etymological similarity to 'Sumer' – home of the Anunnaki.) Sacred to Jainism, Hinduism, Buddhism, and Tibetan Bön, it is also called **Mt. Kailasa**, which lies just over the China-India border in China, part of the Tibetan Himalayas. Shiva's palace was said to be in Mt. Kailasa (aka **Mt. Meru**).

Hang on to your hat. Dr. Vineet Aggarwal has studied the issue of Mt. Meru and its location for years, and came to a conclusion, and wrote a book about it, called Artic Home of the Vedas. He thoroughly vetted ancient Sanskrit sources and came to the conclusion that Mt. Meru is not a mountain but refers to the Earth's **axis** of rotation.

> Just as described in the **'Legend of Meru'**, Earth's axis extends thru both ends of the globe (Sumeru-Meru-Kumeru); is not visible to the naked eye (beyond the physical plane); protrudes at the polar regions (covers North Pole and South Pole); and **from the perspective of a man Standing at the Pole, the entire cosmos quite literally revolves around it as well!** [113] [emphasis added]

According to ancient descriptions of Mt. Meru,

> Sumeru is the polar center of a mandala-like **complex of seas and mountains.** The square base of Sumeru is surrounded by **a square moat-like ocean, which is in turn surrounded by a ring (or rather square) wall of mountains**, which is **in turn surrounded by a sea**, each diminishing in width and height from the one closer to Sumeru.[114]
>
> **Remember that description as it fits well with the following picture-map on the next page.**

In addition, the Legend of Meru, quoted above says:

> the Sun along with all the planets circle the mountain…
>
> the Meru mountain was also described as being surrounded by Mandrachal Mountain to the east, Supasarv Mountain to the west, Kumuda Mountain to the north and **[Mt.] Kailash** [sic] to the south…
>
> Narpatijayacharyā, a 9th-century text, based on mostly unpublished texts of Yāmal Tantr, mentions "Sumeruḥ Prithvī-madhye shrūyate drishyate na tu" ('Su-meru is heard to be **in the middle of the Earth**,

> but is not seen there'). Vārāhamihira, in his Panch-siddhāntikā, claims Mt. Meru to be **at the North Pole** (though no mountain exists there [now] as well). Suryasiddhānt, however, mentions a Mt. Meru **in the middle of Earth**, besides a Sumeru and a Kumeru at both the Poles.[115] [emphasis added]

Isn't that just what the 'Legend of Meru' first quoted above said? What do we have that fits the description?

> Vārāh Mihir, the most famous Indian astronomer from ancient times, identified the **North Pole as the location of Meru** in his celebrated work Panch-siddhāntikā. So, if we accept the Polar location and combine it with the description as the 'Abode of Gods', it would imply, that – **North Pole is also the location of HEAVEN**!! [emphasis added] [116]

...and that brings up the concept of **Hyperborea**... home of the gods... Asgard?

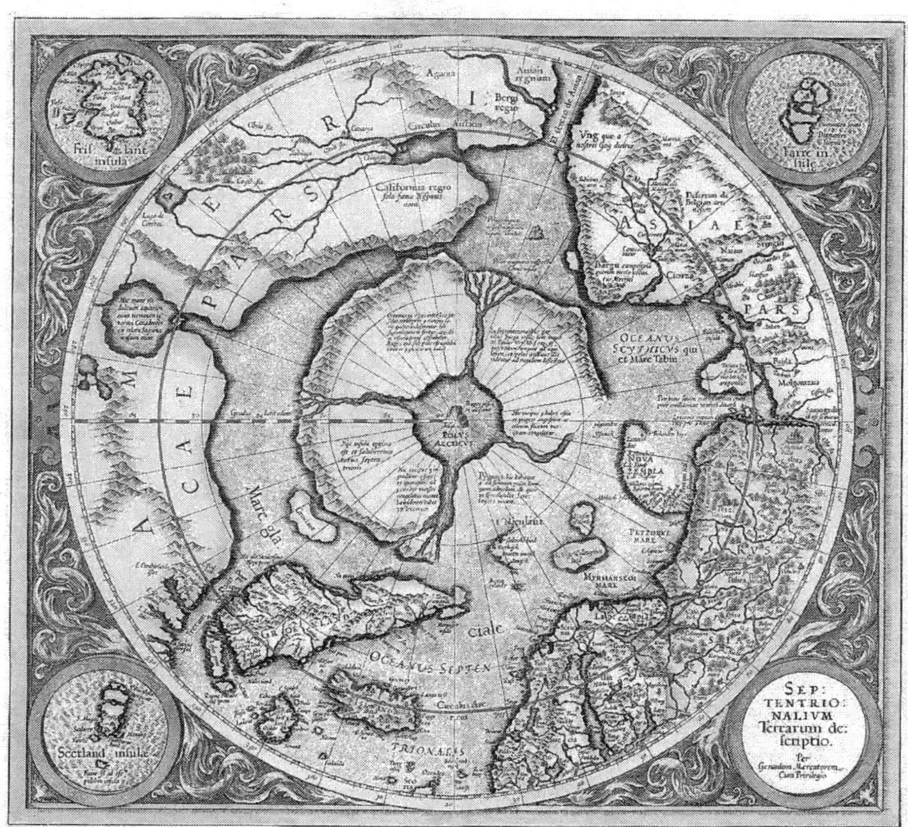

Gerardus Mercator Map of the Arctic Area, 1595.

Note the seas and mountains as described, and also note that there is a mountain in the middle (Mt. Meru). There is an easier version to read:

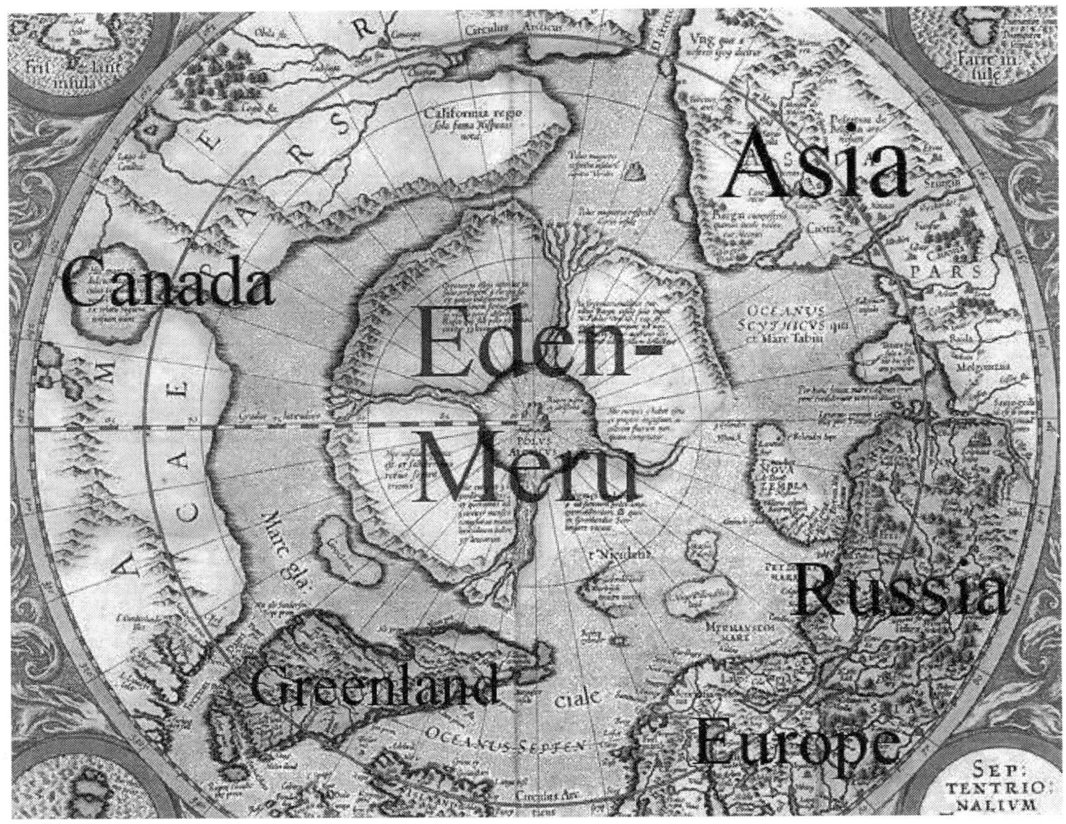

(credit: Bing Images/mysticrapture.weebly.com)

Mt.Meru would have to be directly below the North Star if (as quoted above)

> **from the perspective of a man Standing at the Pole, the entire cosmos quite literally revolves around it as well!**

… and the only way that can work is if Mt. Meru is [was] located at the North Pole.

Surprised?

> Don't be, for at least half a dozen World Mythologies locate their sacred lands at the North Pole! **Japanese and Chinese** Mythologies describe the palaces of their Gods **directly below the Pole Star** and at the same time in the middle of the Earth (just like Meru). They talk of Meru as Shumisen and believe it connects the three realms of Heaven, Earth and Hell. **Celtic Mythology** talks of a Heaven with more than 6 months of continuous Winter again suggesting a polar location.

So there you have the link between Hindu and Nordic legends, starting with a similar Tree of Life – tree and serpent motif again. It is suggested that there had to be some sort of interface between the two cultures, as they are nowhere near each other, and that link is the same one that gave Thor and Odin their technology as well as the Vimana technology to the Hindus. The Anunnaki (aka Ancient Ones).

Just because it is interesting to look at (pyramids), here is conceptual view of Hyperborea (before it sank):[117]

Artist Conception of Hyperborea

Lokmanya Tilak

Some credit must also be given to Lokmaya Tilak, a late Indian historian, who wrote the book The Arctic Home of the Vedas in the late 1800s. Tilak gives an extremely detailed and convincing account based on the literary evidence of various Shlokas from Rig Veda and the Zoroastrian Avesta that point to an Arctic Home of the ancient **Aryans**.

> The book places the original home of Aryans at the North Pole, from which **they had to emigrate due to the Ice deluge 10,000 years ago**!! Around 8000 BCE, the age of migration from the original home began when the survivors roamed over the northern parts of Europe and Asia

> in search of lands suitable for new settlements. If we accept this scenario, we can easily understand the legends of **Noah and Manu**, the progenitors of mankind in this current age. [118]

The Indian people (Aryan or not, this is debated) used to live along the warmer coastal areas of India during the Ice Age, at which time the ocean was 400' lower than present. When the Ice Age began to recede it was followed by a resurgence called the **Younger Dryas** which, after another 1000 years of cold and ice, began disappearing about 9600 BC. [119] As the end of the Ice Age finally melted the glaciers, the oceans rose 400' and forced the coastal people to move inland.

Lastly, consider this account from the **Vishnu Puraan** and look again at the Mercator map of Hyperborea:

> The Akash Ganga, flowing from the feet of Vishnu [supreme Hindu deity], falls around the city of Brahma, on top of Meru. O twice-born ones, she then subdivides into FOUR rivers, dividing the land into **FOUR continents**... [120] [emphasis added]

Greek Corroboration

The Greeks told of a people in the far north, called **Boreades**, that were about 9 feet tall (reminiscent of Teutobokh). That is according to Aelian. According to Siculus, the Boreades dwelt in **Hyperborea** and the succession of kings was tightly kept within the family. Aelius Herodianus wrote that the Arimaspi were identical to the Boreades in physical appearance... and Callimachus wrote that the Arimaspi had fair hair. [121]

Rewind: **Apollo** was said to winter among the Hyperboreans for 6 months of the year. For their part the Hyperboreans sent mysterious gifts, packed in straw, which came first to Dodona and then were passed from tribe to tribe until they came to Apollo's temple on Delos (Pausanias). [122]

This is a lot of detail with credible writers dealing with specifics if it is all a fantasy... and one of the sources is really old...

Serpents in Literature

The Book of Dzyan

If this doesn't convince you that a serpent race was associated with India, nothing will. Probably the oldest document in Sanskrit, it speaks of **a serpent race that descended from the skies and taught mankind.** And as with anything that purports to be ancient and present Truth, there are people and forces on Earth that will come out of the woodwork to diss it and try to discredit it. Such is the case with this book, which is said to be from Tibet.

(Note that Dzyan when pronounced sounds like "zion.")

According to this book, [123] the Sarpas were the **Great Dragons**, also called the Fifth Race, and were the first to inhabit Earth. The Fourth Race had been the giants which were largely removed by The Flood. The story goes that the gods re-descended after The Flood to repopulate the planet and teach the humans. These serpent gods had a humanoid face but the tail of a dragon. (This is also **NüWa** in the Chinese half of this chapter.)

The **Nagas** were said to be the product of the serpents interbreeding with humans. They were described as an intelligent reptile that could fly around the planet in their **sky-chariots**. A reptile flying around the sky in a craft that spits fire – sounds like a dragon, no? Why does this sound like the Anunnaki again?

The Ramayana

Another Indian epic describes the serpent god Ravan who steals Sita, the bride of Rama and takes her off to Ceylon: [124]

> The serpent-god Ravan retreats to his kingdom of Ceylon, supposedly safe from the pursuit of Rama's army. But Rama's aide, Hanuman, builds a bridge of boulders across the watery strait separating the island from the mainland. Thus Rama can cross over and rescue his bride, Sita.
>
> Throughout the story, Ravan is described in barbaric terms more suitable to a reptile than a mammal – he "feeds on humans" and "drinks the blood of his foes." He is so formidable in battle that he almost defeats Rama when he uses his special **"Naga weapon"** which paralyzes his enemies and drains their life force.
>
> Ceylon was the island kingdom of Ravan and was known to be the stronghold of the **serpent people**. It is also described as the home of serpents in ancient Chinese texts.

The Mahabharata

Lastly we come to another famous Indian epic – examined earlier for the sky battles between two warring groups, the Pandavas and the Kauravas, in Hindu society. They fight the great **Kurukshetra War**, destroying Krishna's city and home in coastal Dwarka in the process.

In the epic, which is older than the Ramayana, there is an account of the **Great Snake Sacrifice.** [125]

> The tale starts with King Pariksit of the Kauravas who shoots a deer while hunting. Only wounded, the deer runs away and the king chases it. He meets an ascetic and asks if he has seen a deer, but the ascetic has taken a vow of silence and does not answer the king. This angered the king who then takes a dead snake and places it around the neck of the ascetic sage. The sage's son, Srnga is outraged and vows revenge and places a curse on the king. This started the blood feud between the two groups.
>
> Significantly a third party intervenes and is angry over the use of a serpent, one of her own kind, to insult the sage. Taksaka, the king of the **serpent people** sends snakes to cause the death of King Pariksit.
>
> The *Mahabharata* actually begins with Janamejaya, the son of King Pariksit who is now the king, making a snake sacrifice, called the ***Yajna,*** to avenge his father's death. The ceremony represents (symbolically) the desire to eradicate the Nagas, and King Janamejaya is busy throwing live snakes on the ceremonial fire.
>
> Astika, the son of the serpent king intervenes and pleads with Janamejaya to let his relatives live. The ceremony shifts to propitiating the serpent ancestors and at the same time, expelling them from India's cultural heritage. The Nagas retreat **underground** and leave the surface world to the humans.

Note that serpents in Indian lore now have an equivocal role. They can rightly be called **flying dragons** and have a mostly proactive role in India's history (as much as they did in Mesopotamia), and yet it has come down to a love-hate relationship. The humans seek to ignore their past association with the serpent gods.

Yajna is also covered in Chapter 11.

The same love-hate relationship is often seen in Egyptian lore, as the Anunnaki gods were there, too as Ra, Thoth and Isis… but humans preferred to become **Djedhi** – their own masters – as will be seen in the next chapter. In Egyptian lore the serpent gods were not seen roaming the skies (as dragons) as they had done in India, Europe, and China.

> It is interesting that today Sinologists suggest that **Chinese culture originated in Mesopotamia,** as a colony of Sumer, along with that of Egypt, India and Mesoamerica. Of course, as will be seen in the last part of this chapter, the great **Huang Di** came down from the sky in **a red dragon** and started Chinese civilization and unified the different warring states into one country.
>
> [How can this be? Who was he?]
>
> There is a close similarity to the 2 languages and **Sumerian (being agglutinative) belonged to the same language group as the Chinese**. Even in the present day, the Chinese syllabary is based on signs fundamentally similar to the old pictographs of the Sumerians. [126]

It would appear, between the lines, that Huang Di could have been sent by the Anunnaki, who also no doubt at least communicated with the Nagas – if they weren't Nagas themselves. He didn't die; he ruled 100 years and the **red dragon** came back down and he entered it and was flown back to the sky realm. [127]

Hindu Summary

There was a lot more to the Indian history and research took longer than anticipated, but it looked like there really was something to the Vimanas, the Tree of Life involving Mt. Meru, and some corroboration for Hyperborea – which figures into Norse teachings – **Valhalla** was often said to be located north among the snow and ice. Thus **Asgard might have been Hyperborea**, and the Norse Rainbow Bridge instead of being a portal, as some theories go, might have been the Northern Aurora Borealis leading the way to Hyperborea, or Asgard.

And as we progress into the Greek and Roman civilizations, we find the gods directly dealing with Man – What if Mt. Olympus wasn't the only home of the gods – What if Hyperborea (in addition to Apollo cited above) was where they originally lived? Even more fascinating was if the Anunnaki were not ETs, but an advanced Earth-based culture… the Ancient Ones?

And lastly the Indian research again led to involving the Anunnaki whose legacy does spread far and wide.

∫ ∫ ∫

At this point, being geographically close to China, we need to take a look at the Chinese world and see if the Tree of Life, Serpents and Anunnaki influence can be found there.

However, while there are interesting legends about some major people in Chinese history, such as **Huang-Di**, there is much confusion and rewriting that has obscured whatever the original history was. Notably, the Chinese **Doubting Antiquity School** has chosen to prove that Huang-Di, also known as the Yellow Emperor, was not a real person, but mythological. Other instances abound, such as that of **NüWa** and **FuXi**, also being mythical. The large pyramid of Emperor Wu just outside Xi'an and the way its existence was kept from the West (until 1947 when a pilot flying from India to China during WW II spotted it and took a picture), means China is not sharing its history. Even now, the Western world was not allowed to examine the pyramid, actually a tomb, that also is famous for the Terracotta Warriors.

Huang-Di is also known as **Emperor Qin Shi Huang** and it is to his credit that China was unified, and the Great Wall of China (13,000 miles) was built. He was said to have been brought to Earth in 259 BC by a red dragon, and while that is disputed, there is no record of where he was born, nor who his mother was. He is also known as Emperor Wu. Much of Chinese history is sadly either clouded or missing.

And the minute the possibility of ET involvement in Man's history raises its head, the authorities are quick to denounce it and call it all myth… Why?

Thus the examination of China will be very brief so as not to lead to much speculation or impart false information.

∫ ∫ ∫

Addendum

It recently came into view that in 2015 the **102nd Indian Science Congress** met and discussed the issue of whether Vimanas really existed – based on the schematics and accounts in ancient Vedic literature. While most scientists were being "politically correct" and pooh-poohing the issue, credible data was presented that included propulsion technology that ancients could not have understood, much less have written about – unless they saw and had flown the craft.

When asked where crashed samples of the craft could be found, alas there was no evidence as the events happened thousands of years ago. The issue was shelved for the time being. [128]

Anunnaki in China

The main search has been for a Tree of Life, looking for some common imagery around the globe, and verifying who used serpent imagery the same way.

Tree of Life

Note the sleeping Dragon (instead of a Serpent) and the Phoenix bird in the tree (instead of an Eagle) – see Norse Tree of Life: Yggdrasil.

The Dragon is associated with **Huang Di** the first emperor, and those sky gods who came and civilized China, and the Phoenix symbolized the empress, as well as rebirth. According to Wikipedia the dragon is highly regarded and:

> It is the only mythological animal of the 12 animals that represent the Chinese calendar, and 2012 was the Chinese year of the Water **Dragon**. 2013 was the Chinese year of the **Serpent**.

Dragons

Dragon Dance in Parade

The dragon in China was called **Lung** ("long" as in sinewy) and there are over 700 versions of the dragon dance. A form of dragon dance from Tongliang County (铜梁龙舞), which originated as snake totem worship, was said to have begun during the Ming Dynasty and became popular in the Qing Dynasty. [129]

> Chinese dragons are a symbol of China, and they are believed to bring good luck to people, therefore **the longer the dragon in the dance, the more luck it will bring to the community**. The dragons are believed to possess qualities that include great power, dignity, fertility, wisdom and auspiciousness. The appearance of a dragon is both fearsome and bold but it has a benevolent disposition, and it was an emblem to represent imperial authority. [130] [emphasis added]

In addition, Chinese dragons traditionally symbolize potent and auspicious powers, particularly control over water, rainfall, typhoons, and floods. The dragon is also a symbol of power, strength, and good luck for people who are worthy of it. With this, the Emperor of China usually used the dragon as a symbol of his imperial power and strength. [131]

Flag of China until 1912

The ancient Chinese self-identified as 'the descendants of the dragon' because the Chinese dragon is an imagined reptile that is the evolution ancestor of humans and other common animals. The presence of dragons within Chinese culture dates back several thousands of years with the discovery of a dragon statue dating back to the fifth millennium BC. **Chinese dragons don't have wings**.

In today's Chinese culture the dragon is considered totally mythical. And when they painted pictures of it,

> …the people paint the dragon's shape with **a horse's head and a snake's tail**. [Think: **White Horse Hill in England** and the "horse" carved into the hillside.] Further, there are expressions as 'three joints' and 'nine resemblances' (of the dragon), to wit: from head to shoulder, from shoulder to breast, from breast to tail. These are the joints; as to the nine resemblances, they are the following:
> his **antlers resemble those of a stag**, his head that of a camel, his eyes those of a demon, his **neck that of a snake**, his belly that of a clam… his scales those of a carp, his claws those of an eagle, his soles those of a tiger, his ears those of a cow. Upon his head he has a thing like a broad eminence (a big lump), called *chimu*. If a dragon has no *chimu*, he cannot ascend to the sky. [132] [emphasis added]
>
> *Chimu* sounds like 'shem' (rocket) in Sumerian culture and both are associated with flight…

Rewind: The Chinese dragons do not have wings… and the flag above shows two protrusions from the snout…so coupled with the above highlighted quote, where have we seen that combination?

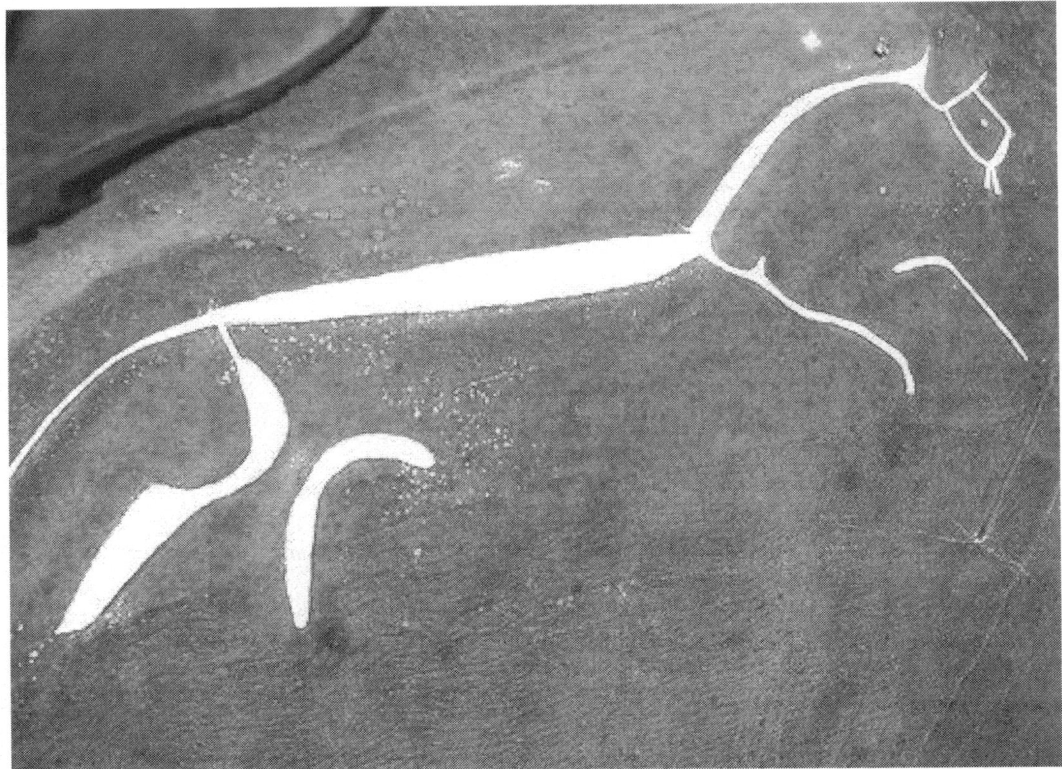

Uffington "Horse" Oxfordshire, England

Still think it's a horse?

Denying Man's real heritage and origins is a symptom of narrow-minded 'experts' who cannot accept that Man is <u>not</u> just now evolving to a high-tech society. Man used to be more and do more, but that would suggest failure as a species, or interference from Others, and perhaps it is a vicious cycle that will repeat – Oh, no! – better tell the public that our ONLY path from the past has been – out of the trees, into the caves, tribal living, and a slow climb to our now "top of the heap" status as the greatest society that has ever been on Earth. Yeah, right!

So much for British horses...

UFO Pictures

It would be interesting if there were some ancient drawings of sky craft, other than dragons, cruising thru the sky. As the next page shows, there are some in the Orient… usually depicted as a wheel…

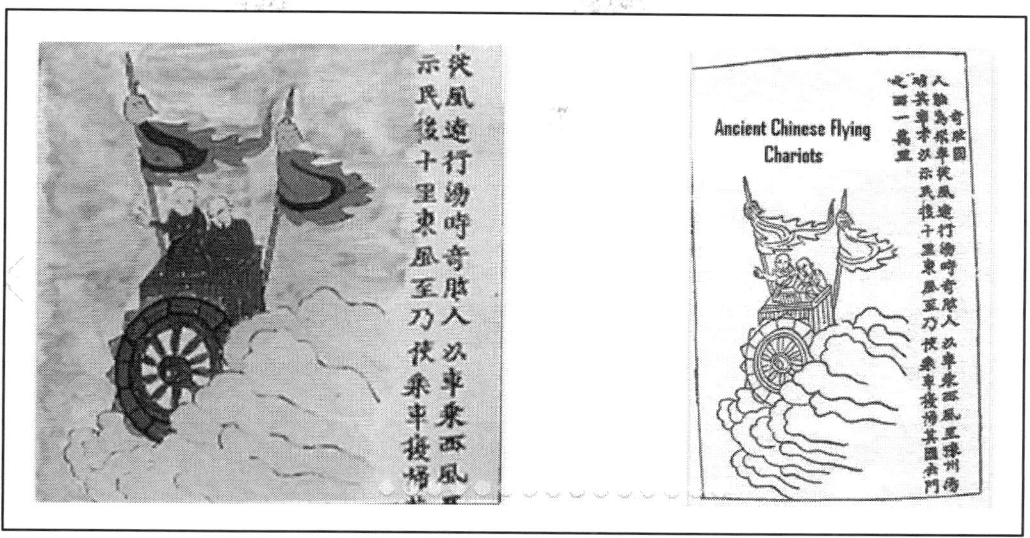

Chinese depiction of alien god in his sky-chariot Ji Gung Land, China. 147 AD.

Wall relief found on island of Jotuo

While the bottom picture is from Japan, it is true that flying disks and dragons have been seen in the Orient for thousands of years. Note the halo (right) around the pilots' heads signifying that they are gods… The object on the left is said to be a flying disk.

And then there is a picture of a special disk from Nepal…

This is another mysterious stone from the Tibetean area.

Dated 3000 BC… depicts alien disc, lizard and alien body (if not a clever current-day hoax) and alien script that has yet to be translated.

Note: the similar Dropa Stones have been debunked and can be reviewed on a special website. [133]

Rewind: Mount Meru

In Chinese it is called **K'un Lun.**[134] It is said to be the source of the wind, the Yellow River, and the Ju Shui. It is also called **Sumeru**... where "su" means wonderful applied to the name of the mountain ("Meru"). Otherwise the description of Mt. Meru among the Buddhists is the same as among the Hindus.

Ancient Buddhists thought Meru was the center of the universe. The Pali Canon records the historical Buddha speaking of it. In time, ideas about Mount Meru and the nature of the universe became more detailed.

The Buddhist Universe[135]

Ancient Buddhists imagined the universe as essentially flat, with Mount Meru at the center of all things. Surrounding this universe was a vast expanse of water, and surrounding the water was a vast expanse of wind.

This universe was made of **thirty-one planes of existence**, stacked in layers, and three realms, or *dhatus*. This cosmos was thought to be one of a succession of universes coming into and going out of existence through infinite time.

Our world was thought to be a wedge-shaped island continent in a vast sea south of Mount Meru, called **Jambudvipa**, in the realm of Kāmadhātu. The earth, then, was thought to be flat and surrounded by ocean. That would change in the late 1800s.

Cosmic Turtle

At this point it is interesting to note that the Chinese, the Hindus, the Japanese, and the Siberians, and some North American tribes all have a legend of the Cosmic Turtle supporting the world. In fact, the Japanese and the Iroquois have a legend of a **Skywoman** who came from Heaven to Earth (perhaps Inanna?) and interacted with humans to help them.

The Japanese Version

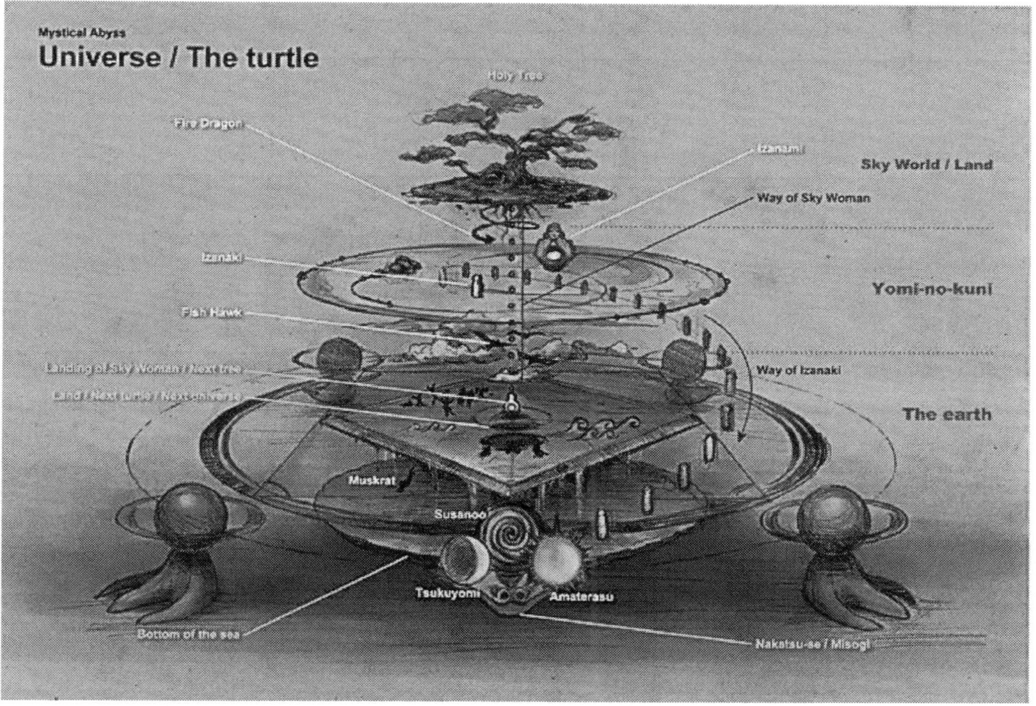

Note the Holy Tree at the top. And also note (at 11:00 o'clock) it says "Fire Dragon" which is reminiscent of the Norse Tree of Life with a Serpent at its roots.

At the very bottom is a stylized giant turtle, supporting the Earth. Note also that Skywoman, **Izanami**, 'falls' directly down to Earth from the base of the Tree, and Izanaki, her consort/counterpart who is male, is represented by the 'cylinders' swinging clockwise from Heaven to Earth. [136]

The Chinese Version

In Chinese mythology the **creator goddess NüWa** (next section) cut the legs off the giant sea turtle Ao (鳌) and used them to prop up the sky after Gong Gong damaged the Buzhou Mountain that had previously supported the heavens. Researchers of early Chinese mythology also note that the flat undershell and round domed upper shell of a turtle resemble the ancient Chinese idea of a flat earth and round domed sky. [137]

The Earth on the Cosmic Turtle ultimately supporting Mount Meru.
(credit: Bing Images: codoh.com)

North American Indian Version

Iroquois Creation Myth[138]

Long before the world was created there was an island, floating in the sky, upon which the Sky People lived. They lived quietly and happily. No one ever died or was born or experienced sadness. However one day one of the Sky Women realized she was going to give birth to twins. She told her husband, who flew into a rage.

> **In the center of the island there was a tree which gave light to the entire island since the sun hadn't been created yet.**

He tore up this tree, creating a huge hole in the middle of the island. Curiously, the woman peered into the hole. Far below she could see the waters that covered the earth. At that moment her husband pushed her. She fell through the hole, tumbling towards the waters below.

(continued...)

Water animals already existed on the earth, so far below the floating island two birds saw the Sky Woman fall. Just before she reached the waters they caught her on their backs and brought her to the other animals. Determined to help the woman they dove into the water to get mud from the bottom of the seas. One after another the animals tried and failed.

Finally, Little Toad tried and when he reappeared his mouth was full of mud. The animals took it and spread it on the back of Big Turtle. The mud began to grow and grow and grow until it became the size of North America. Then the woman stepped onto the land. She sprinkled dust into the air and created stars. Then she created the moon and sun.

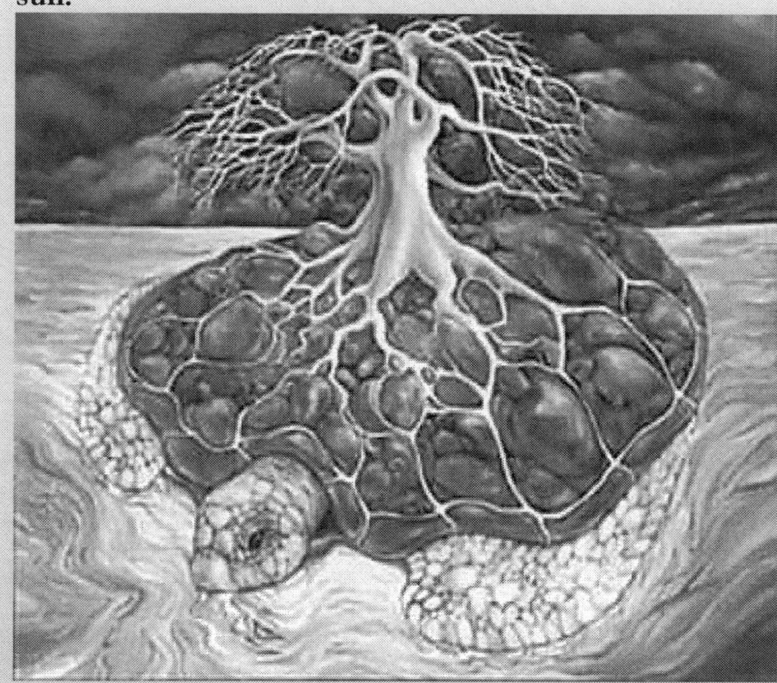

Native American Turtle Creation Story

Native American Turtle Pictograph by Jo Ann Tomaselli In Native American mythology, the turtle symbolizes Mother Earth and represents good health and long life.

The Iroquois people hold a great respect for all animals. This is mirrored in their creation myth by the role the animals play. Without the animals' help the Sky Woman may have sunk to the bottom of the sea and Earth may not have been created.

That is very interesting – Who are the **Sky People**? There are no further sources on this. Also note that the Iroquois Sky Woman (above) is similar to the Japanese Skywoman (aka Izanami).... So the ancient peoples were aware that there were Others here and they were involved in Creation. The story above also involves a **Tree of Light** just as the picture of the Japanese Turtle features a "Holy Tree." Interesting that similar symbology made it around to different cultures – and that is one of the major points of this book. Just how and why it went global is the second point. And the third point will come in the last half of the book where the real significance resides with the spread of Serpent Wisdom – the first two points are merely establishing the concept that those who spread Serpent Wisdom also spread similar information and stories to the humans as they went.

Osage Sidenote

The Osage was another Amerindian tribe, occupying large the central US – from Ohio to Oklahoma, and Kansas-Missouri area. Their part in this current scenario is that they also spoke of a **Sky People** – they called them **Tsi-zhiu** (which sounds Nahuatl, or Aztec, by the way). [139]

And just because it is an interesting anomaly, there was a 19th Century painter who visited the Osage and asked to paint their chief, Shonka Sabe (Black Dog). The 19th-century painter George Catlin described the Osage as

> the tallest race of men in North America, either red or **white skins**; there being few indeed of the men at their full growth, who are less than six feet in stature, and very many of them six and a half, and others **seven feet [tall].** [emphasis added]

White skin? Tall? Are we describing Indians, or.... the descendants of Norse explorers? Remember the Norse traveled inland down the St. Lawrence river to Minnesota and south... to Kensington where they carved a runestone (Chapter 2). That was a land claim but they never got back to it due to the Plague which ravaged Europe and exploration was suspended.

The Hindu World Tortoise

Hindu mythology has various accounts of World Tortoises, besides a World Serpent (**Shesha**), Kurmaraja and World-Elephants.

The most widespread name given to the tortoise is **Kurma** or Kurmaraja. ("raja" means king). The Shatapatha Brahmana identifies the earth as its lower shell, the atmosphere as its body and the vault of heaven as its upper shell. The concept of World-Tortoise and World-Elephant was conflated in popular or rhetorical references to Hindu mythology. An alleged tortoise ***Chukwa*** supports **Mahapadm**a, the elephants supporting **Mount Meru.**

(credit: ulc.org)

And to complete the issue of Mount Meru, we need to consider one more thing.

Rewind: Mount Meru

The following is an analysis of Flat Earth, Turtles and the Milky Way which deserves some attention as it purports to explain the Mount Meru mystery:[140]

Mount Meru, also called Sumeru(i.e the "Great Meru"), is a sacred mountain in Hindu and Buddhist cosmology as well as in Jain cosmology, and is considered to be the center of all the physical, metaphysical and spiritual universes. It is also the abode of Lord Brahma and the Demi-Gods (Devas). The mountain is said to be **84,000 Yojanas** high (which is around **672,000 miles** or 1.082 million kilometers). Many famous Hindu and Jain temples have been built as symbolic representations of this mountain. A Burmese-style multi-tiered roof, represents Mount Meru.

> Now: Which earthly mountain can have these proportions? Maybe the measurement above is not a very precise measurement of the Milky Way, but it appears to represent "astronomical dimensions" which suggest a

description of the large flat disc of our Milky Way with the Milky Way Bulge/Centre (similar to the hump of a turtle).

This does not negate the fact that Hyperborea was a likely home of the gods, and that there was a mountain there. However, how does the Flat Earth come into play?

Flat Earth

> When Columbus lived, people thought that the earth was flat. They believed the Atlantic Ocean to be filled with monsters large enough to devour their ships, and with fearful waterfalls over which their frail vessels would plunge to destruction. [141]

But maybe there is another explanation to this "Flat Earth" belief and "devouring monsters" in the ocean? It is easy to see why someone who knows the truth about the Earth's shape would scare people into NOT sailing across the ocean – to keep the secret for themselves (for whatever reason: Think: **The Secret of Oak Island**).

But, can it possibly be that the ancient Flat Earth myth is confused with some true story with a complete other meaning and Mytho-Cosmological understanding? It is very possible, because it all depends on interpreting a myth and connecting the right symbols to the right celestial objects.

> **What happens with the logic if a myth is taken for an Earthly matter and not as a celestial matter? Well, it all goes wrong and then the myth turns out to be complete nonsense! Scholars have determined that Mount Meru must be on planet Earth. What if the myth actually represented something else – a point of Creation in the Milky Way?**

Of course you have to ask yourself, How would the primitive people around the planet (who could obviously see the Milky Way at night), come to think on their own that it had anything to do with the creation of Earth?... much less that the progenitors of Man would have come from the stars! Someone had to tell them…

and there is a connection to Visitors who not only engineered Man genetically, but stayed and educated him (because it was required of them: see Glossary: **Galactic Law).**

> Creator Goddesses, Creator Gods and Creator Animals are all wrongly assumed to be Earth-derived – just the imagination of very naïve people. They should be connected to the Solar System and the planets, and they also should be connected to the Story of Creation and to the myths of the Milky Way.
>
> The galaxy centre is mythologically also called the Primordial Mound, the **World Mountain** or Hill, the Enclosed Light, the **First Island**, the First Light etc., and they all describe the very centre bulge of the Milky Way which **seen from the side** has a flat disc look with the bulge centre in the middle as seen on the picture above. All over the World ancient people have built a lot of hills symbolizing this Milky Way Central Hill and they also have told a lot of stories combined with different symbols of both animals and human beings in order to tell the Mytho-Cosmological story of origin. [emphasis added]
>
> The very shape of a Turtle shell and its pattern are used by several cultures to describe the bulgy center of the Milky Way with its flattish disc. [142]

The big question is: How did they know what our galaxy looks like <u>from the side</u>? We have telescopes and can see other galaxies which all have the spiral and bulge, thus we know ours also looks like that – but the ancient world had no way to see any of that. Again, the only way they could know is if <u>someone told them</u>… or showed them!

Flying Turtles

Even more interesting is that some native cultures have described UFOs as "flying turtles" or "flying shields" … Is there a connection?

If the UFO were shaped like on the left…?

And that raises the issue of <u>who</u> was flying something that looked like a turtle (or a shield):

(credit: Bing Images: tert.am)

And we can mention the Mayan imitation of 'flying turtles':

(credit : Bing Images: ancientufo.org.)

Notice that the face does not look Mayan. What if the beings flying the 'turtles' were Visitors from elsewhere on Earth – they don't have to be ETs.

The above image of the Flying Turtle Man comes from Guatemala:

> In Central America, Guatemala according to archaeologists the earliest human settlements in this region date back over 14,000 years. In this region we can find numerous ancient artifacts, and among them is this one: The figure of a man lying inside what appears to be the shell of a turtle and according to legend, these are **the giant flying turtles** which flew around in Guatemala. You can observe that the entire body is aerodynamically fashioned. The extremities are pressed in an aerodynamic fashion against the body of the figure… once again **Ancient technology**. [143] [emphasis added]

Enough birdwalking. Returning to the Turtle myth around the world…

Siberian Version

Lastly, some tribes in Siberia say that Mandishire (aka Manjusri) is the giant tortoise which carries the world on its back. [144] He is known also by the more complete name Manjusri**kumara**bhuta – and the important part is "kumara" which signifies a connection to the four Kumara sages who came to Earth to enlighten Man, working in Lemuria (Mu) and then India. [145]

Manjusri in the Lotus Sūtra, also leads the **Nagaraja**'s daughter to enlightenment. Interesting connection with the Nagas mentioned next – "raja" means king and the Nagas are the underground Serpent people. Thus he also had a connection with the Nagas and their teachings.

Nagas

There was also a Chinese legend of **NüWa** and **Fu Xi** (pronounced 'foo-shee') where NüWa is a beautiful **Snake Goddess** and Fui-hsi is a renowned sage.

> The Dravidians or Nagas were said to be the result of the sexual liaison between serpent-gods and mankind. They were described as a coarse, cannibalistic people, dark-skinned, and flat-nosed. **They were known for their wisdom and lived underground….[who] are described in many of the Sanskrit sources as an intelligent reptile that could fly around the skies <u>in their chariots</u>. It is a fitting description of a dragon.** [146]

NüWa is one of the creators of the Chinese human race. Her recipe for creating mortals began with yellow mud [because the yellow race was based in China]. She dipped a rope into the mud and then trailed the rope around; the drops that dripped from the rope became men and women. Those she fashioned by hand were the royal ty.

In another rendition, like many other creators, she fashioned mortals from lumps of clay. When evil giants set fire and flame loose upon the world, NüWa [also called Nu-Kua] restored everything by replacing the overturned poles of the world with the feet of a **giant turtle** which repaired the widespread damage that came after the catastrophic flood and fire. She also melted stones of 5 colors to repair a rip in the sky.

NüWa is often depicted as a woman from the waist up, and a dragon's tail below.

See also picture p. 469.

The Serpent Goddess NüWa
…the tail is just visible (appears to be flame).

Just FYI: the god **Panku** is the other major Creation God. His name measn "coiled antiquity" and he is said to be the originator of Yin and Yang. (Serpents coil.)

The implication is that NüWa was descended from the **Naga Goddesses**, which conceptually looked like the following....

Naga goddess

And the male warrior:

And that appears to be overdoing it a bit... especially if the Nagas are no more than Anunnaki Remnant and perhaps look more like this:

They all live underground – **under India and China**. Understandable as they always had a problem with the Sun and would age if they stayed in the daylight... so they stayed in the Ziggurats and temples atop the Mayan pyramids.

Indochina Connection

As if that weren't enough, there is one more example of Naga influence.

> Serpents, or Nāgas, play a particularly important role in **Cambodian**, Isan and Laotian mythology. An origin myth explains the emergence of the name "Cambodia" as resulting from conquest of a **Naga princess** by a **Kambuja** lord named Kaundinya: the descendants of their union are the Khmer people. [147] [emphasis added]

Connection with Egypt

The Chinese believed that each person had two souls – a physical one (for the Earth realm) and an eternal one . The Egyptians agreed and called them the **Ba and Ka**, respectively.

Connection with Greece

Both Greek (Hesiod's *Theogony* involving Chaos and the Titans) and Chinese creation stories (NüWa and Pan Gu) feature several generations of flawed attempts at making humans. Add to that the similar Sumerian (*Enuma Elish*) and Mayan (*Popul Vuh*) accounts, and it is obvious they are all based on the same reality. The gods created Man.

Summary

What is interesting about NüWa being a **Serpent Goddess** is that she was allegedly a creator of the human race. So far, that responsibility has belonged to the Anunnaki of Mesopotamia (viz., Ninharsag), some of whom were reptilian. NüWa was also part reptilian… and a creator of humans in China… Do we dare consider her to be an Anunnaki, or somehow related to them?

> The answer is simple: if NüWa was a Naga, she was part of the Anunnaki Remnant. This is covered in Virtual Earth Graduate. The Anunnaki, when they went underground (about AD 800-900), became what has been called the Nagas. And many of them did not have tails, but they often had horns.

So far, the serpent imagery is moving around the globe, and even though the indigent peoples and tribes did not have an interface with each other, they did meet and learn from the Anunnaki, or the Ancient Ones, when civilization, tools and religion, including Serpent Wisdom, was spread around the planet.

That is why the concept of the Tree of Life, Serpents, and occasionally high tech craft or weapons have been discovered in the ancient texts. And there is more.

Chapter 5: Greece, Egypt & Israel

Moving from India and China, we go southwest to the Eastern end of the Mediterranean. There are ancient traditions in Greece and Egypt and there are some interesting esoteric aspects to Hebrew tradition, as well. Both Greece and Egypt have ancient texts about **visitors from the skies** that either guided Man as in Greece, or ruled Man as was the case in Egypt. Greece was given philosophical insights and some healing information, and Egypt was under the Anunnaki rule directly. Israel is said to have been the Command Center (at Mt. Moriah) for the **Anunnaki skycraft**. That was the same story that the Sumerians recorded and said was their history with the Anunnaki who both guided and ruled them.

Anunnaki in Greece

The outstanding and perhaps most obvious presence of the Anunnaki was to be found in the Greek gods. In fact, the Anunnaki gods were trying the motif of walking-and-living-among-Man as a direct way of influencing him… and the same gods continued the strategy with the Romans… until it became obvious that it wasn't working. Humans began to tire of the gods and diss them regularly, and did whatever they wanted to… until they got caught.

> **Myth of Sisyphus**, He was punished for his self-aggrandizing craftiness and deceitfulness by being forced to roll an immense boulder up a hill, only to watch it roll back down, repeating this action for eternity.
>
> **Pandora's Box** , where she was the first human woman created by the gods, and presented (and teased) by them with a box containing the world's ills – and she opened it, after being warned not to.
>
> **Prometheus**, chained to a rock, afflicted by a vulture, for stealing fire from Olympus and giving it to Man. Here even another god is punished for disobedience.

…and so forth in Greek mythology. A Greek writer/poet knew that the gods could be treacherous (viz., Olympians fighting Titans – which is the mythologized war between the Anunnaki gods for control of Tiamat and later the spaceport) and warned of that in his classic work…

> **Hesiod's *Works & Days***, a didactic poem about farming life, also includes the myths of Prometheus, Pandora, and the Five Ages. The poet gives advice on the best way to succeed in a dangerous world, **rendered yet more dangerous by its gods.** [148] [emphasis added]

According to the Bible (OT), **God builds a special race** and gives them Ten Commandments to be a showcase to the world – and they also (being 'stiffnecked') disobey and the Old Testament is replete with the God of Israel (Yahweh aka Enlil) dealing with his disobedient people via Serpents in Numbers 21. He lets them be taken into captivity three times (Babylonians, Assyrians, and Egyptians) as they are slow to learn and do what he says.

However, for the point of clarity and comparison, here is the pantheon of gods, and how it originated with the Anunnaki (Ancient Ones?):

Anunnaki Hybrid Remnant aka The Gods

Many Anunnaki began leaving Earth about 650 BC and most were gone about 560 BC.[149] And yet there was a **hybrid Remnant** that stayed on and controlled Man (via the Priestly group) the same way the main Anunnaki gods had done earlier. The Remnant initially took the form of the Greek gods who were real, not myth, and who later were given Latin/Roman names, [150] and thus <u>the Church would have known about them</u>.

Greek God →	Roman God
Apollo (Enki)	Apollo
Dionysus/Hermes (Ningishzidda)	Bacchus
Eros	Cupid
Heracles	Hercules
Zeus (Enlil)	Jupiter
Ares (Marduk)	Mars
Poseidon (Enki)	Neptune
Hades	Pluto
Odysseus	Ulysses
Aphrodite/Athena (Inanna)	Venus
Adonis (Dumuzi)	-------

There are more gods but the above is a sampling of the names used first by the Greeks and then later changed into Roman gods. The older Greek temples were actually one of the resting places of the Anunnaki gods as they traveled from place to place, surveying their domain. In the past, they resided atop ziggurats in Sumeria, atop pyramids in the Yucatan, atop Machu Picchu and then Mt. Olympus in Greece – places that were not easily accessible to Man. What is interesting is that another scholar contends that the "… Roman gods arose from a void with no mythological tradition associated with them." [151] That means that there had been no Roman precedent for a pantheon of gods, but Romans were told to adopt the worship of the same Greek gods <u>and to change their names</u> -- except for Apollo.

> *Apollo was one of the Greek and Roman gods, thus he appears in both pantheons. The Greek and Roman gods were the Anunnaki or their hybrid descendants. Note that* ***Enki*** *got around and was known by several names – depending on country. Also* ***Marduk*** *was Mars, Ra and Nimrod.* ***Inanna*** *was also Venus, Kali and Ishtar (according to Zechariah Sitchin).*
>
> Also interesting that there were allegedly two sets of Greek gods: the **Titans** (TI.TA.AN in Sumerian which means "Those who in Heaven Live") and the **Olympians** who were another set of gods that defeated the Titans. [152] Besides the wars between the gods in heaven, the Olympians had also earlier taken on the earthly **Giants** (Anakim, Rephaim and Giborim…which were <u>also known to the Norse</u>) running amok on the Earth and removed most of them. The squabbles and infrastructure wars between the Greek gods were actually the wars between the Anunnaki.[153] And Sitchin informs us that the Titans were the Rephaim thus resolving the whole issue of who was whom. [154] [emphasis added]

It is entirely possible that the Titans were the Anunnaki and the Olympians were the Ancient Ones – vying for control of the planet.

And it was thus for many other human civilizations around the globe, in different Eras, who also had their pantheon of gods. While it started with the Sumerians, it spread to the Norse, the Celts, the Greeks, even the Japanese, the Mayans, the Egyptians, the African tribes, and the Chinese. In a number of cases around the world, **<u>the same god</u> appears but with a different name.** [155] Enki was said to be Quetzalcoatl, Kukulkan, Viracocha and Ahura-Mazda for example.

Dumuzi and Inanna

The above cross-listing of the gods may appear incomplete when it comes to Dumuzi, but there is a reason… Dumuzi/Adonis didn't survive to enter the Roman pantheon…

> The Anunnaki Dumuzi and Inanna were lovers... later called Adonis and Venus, among other names. Dumuzi was betrothed to Inanna, who was the daughter of Anu, the king. This was an effort to bring peace between the Enki and Enlil factions (in Mesopotamia). Ever since The Flood when Enki saved the humans [Noah and the Ark fame], Enlil had reluctantly agreed to tolerate the humans – if they proved useful. Enki hoped to see his son, Dumuzi, marry Inanna to bring peace thru marriage – a theme that was repeated between countries and fiefdoms in the Middle Ages, as well...
> (continued...)

It is also significant that the Anunnaki society was one of strong caste – and Dumuzi belonged to a lower caste, and Inanna was of higher birth. (Anunnaki initiated the caste system in India.)

Enlil ordered the Indus Valley given to Inanna as a dowry gift.

After The Flood, Dumuzi was given rule over the domestic herds in Africa. Marduk, jealous of Dumuzi, and wanting to rule Africa [Egypt], set out to make sure that Dumuzi failed to marry Inanna... he wanted her for himself, as well as Egypt. Marduk learned thru his sister, Geshtinanna, that Inanna had plans to promote Dumuzi to ruler of Egypt, so Marduk persuaded his sister to seduce Dumuzi so that there would be a legal heir to succession... making him believe that his child with Inanna would not be a legal heir (a lie).

After intercourse, Geshtinanna told Dumuzi that Marduk will accuse Dumuzi of raping her, and be furious. Marduk would seek to kill him and cancel the marriage to Inanna. Dumuzi panics and runs away and hides behind a waterfall but slips into the rapids and drowns (in Lake Victoria).

Inanna is wise to the treachery, recovers Dumuzi's body and she grabs some high-tech weapons and chases Marduk – into the Great Pyramid. She is furious and ready to kill Marduk.

Marduk is holed up in the Great Pyramid and radios Anu who tells Inanna to back off as Marduk has a powerful weapon that will kill her if she catches him. Inanna is a very skilled warrior goddess and is not afraid of Marduk. So Anu orders Enlil to surround the Pyramid and, temporarily assured safety, Marduk comes out, Anu and Enlil hear the case, and Anu being no dummy (and intuitive), sentences Marduk to die slowly sealed up in the King's Chamber of the Pyramid, no food, no air.

Marduk's wife, Sarpanit ['sarpa' is sanskrit for **serpent** and she is the daughter of a Naga and a human] calls on Enki for help (Marduk is Enki's belligerent son). Enki sends Ningishzidda (aka Thoth in Egypt) his other son to tunnel into the Pyramid, rescue Marduk and Enki then banishes Marduk to North America.

(continued...

...this is an actual account of Anunnaki doings by the Sumerians...

> Marduk later returns to Egypt (as Ra) and banishes Ningishzidda and his Nubian group to what is now Central America where they set up headquarters and create stone heads [Olmec] and prepare to some day return to Egypt.
>
> Inanna meanwhile takes Dumuzi's body and mummifies it hoping to revive it (yes, they had technology to resurrect people) when they get back to Nibiru, allegedly their home planet.

As can be seen, the carryings-on of the Anunnaki were certainly worthy of a day-time soap opera! And whereas different cultures around the planet seem to have a multitude of gods (with different names) it really was **the same set of Anunnaki as gods** because they were responsible for the development of Man, according to Galactic Law (as was said earlier in Chapter 1).

As part of the examination of Greece, it remains to be seen whether they had or acknowledged a Tree of Life.

Tree of Life

The closest the Greeks got to what has been seen to be the traditional Tree of Life, as originally promoted by the Anunnaki, was their reverence for **groves of trees**... a definite **Druid connection**. As is shown below, the Celtic/Druid influence spread into Europe and slightly beyond.... (Galatia [Turkey] below, far right.)

The Greek groves of trees were considered to be the home of the **Dryads**… also called the nymphs of **oak trees**, or nature spirits. (Dryad ≈ Druid?)

> **Dryads**, like all nymphs, were supernaturally long-lived and tied to their homes, but some were a step beyond most nymphs. These were the hamadryads, who were an integral part of their trees, such that if the tree died, the **hamadryad** associated with it died as well. For these reasons, dryads and the **Greek gods punished any mortals** who harmed trees without first propitiating the tree-nymphs. [156] [emphasis added]

So in essence, the Greeks did not know about, or subscribe to, the Sumerian Tree of Life. They did other things. But they did follow the reverence and teaching about Trees, Serpents and Serpent Wisdom. Especially did Pythagoras…

Orphism

One of the aspects that Serpent Wisdom took among the Greeks was a movement called Orphism initiated by **Pythagoras** whose name was a combination of *python* + *agor* – loosely translated means the "speaking python" – relating back to the Pythian Apollo. A later Greek sage, Heraclitus stated that Pythagoras was a man of extensive learning and Xenophanes claimed that Pythagoras believed in the transmigration of souls – stopping a dog from being beaten because he heard the voice of a departed friend in the dog's cries. [157]

> Pythagoras (4th century BC) also gave the world mathematics (Pythagorean Theorem), naming the basic geometric shapes, and devising the Tetractys which was worshipped by the Pythagoreans as a sacred symbol: [158]

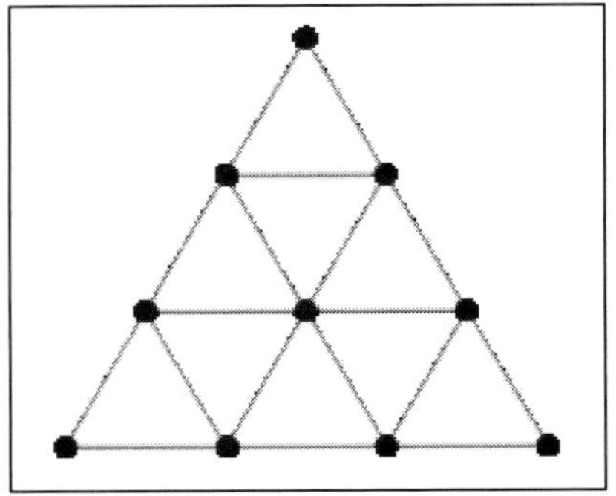

The **Tetractys** or tetrad, is the geometrical representation of the **fourth triangular number** (see below).

There were many components to the concept and that is shown below…. Think: YHWH.

This Pythagorean symbol has its significance as follows, and this was part of the esoteric Serpent Wisdom imparted to the initiates. And the following is also relevant to Alchemy and Kabbalah, as we'll see later… (Chapters 10 and 12).

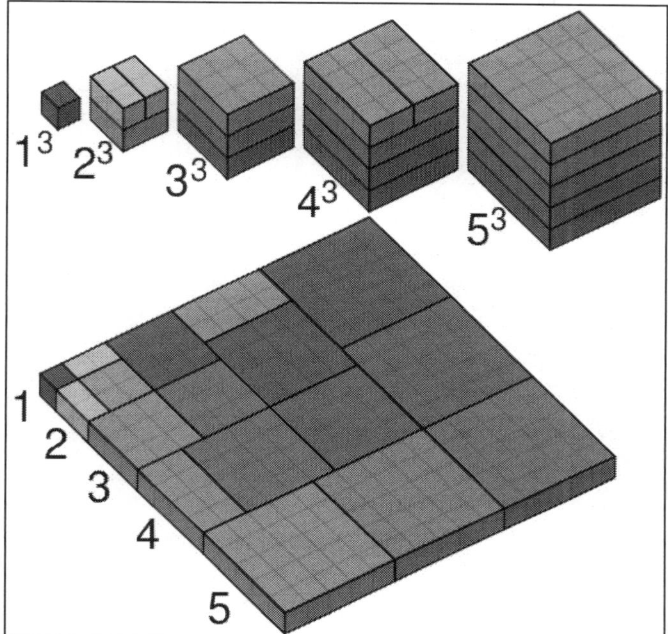

A square whose side length is a triangular number can be partitioned into squares and half-squares whose areas add to cubes. This shows that the square of the *n*th triangular number is equal to the sum of the first *n* cube numbers.

So $2^{3=8}$

Looked at another way:

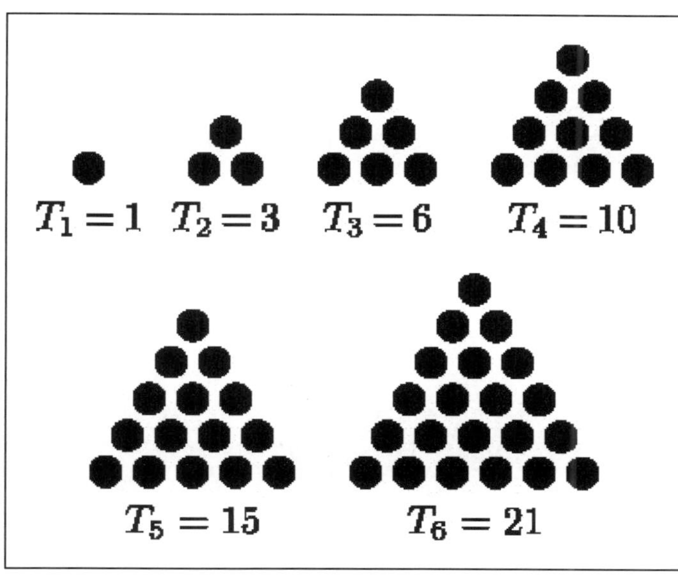

Note that T_n = some number which is the sum of the dots in a triangular shape. ..

Now the significance of that is found in computer networking. A fully connected network of *n* computing devices requires the presence of T_{n-1} cables or other connections.

In a tournament format that uses a round-robin group stage, the number of matches that need to be played between *n* teams is equal to the triangular number T_{n-1}. For example, a group stage with 4 teams requires 6 matches, and a group stage with 8 teams requires 28 matches. This is also equivalent to the handshake problem and fully connected network problems.

> Now, aren't you glad you asked? Yet, the point is that Pythagoras' discovery of the **triangular number** provided the later mathematicians with the insight to develop advanced concepts. And mathematics has always had a special fascination for Man (Hint: Newton), often bordering on the esoteric because it provided us with the **Fibonacci** spiral which describes how items form in Nature, like the nautilus shell – **Nature and the Cosmos adhere to mathematical rules**!

Triangular Number

A. The first four levels symbolize the harmony of the spheres/cosmos as :
   1. (1) Unity (Monad)
   2. (2) Power (Dyad) – Limit/Unlimited
   3. (3) Harmony (Triad)
   4. (4) Kosmos (Tetrad)

B. The four rows add up to **ten**, which was unity of a higher order (The Dekad).

C. The Tetractys symbolizes the **four elements** – fire, air, water, and earth.

This is foreshadowing Alchemy a bit (covered in Chapter 10), and it is significant that Alchemy has some of its roots in Hermes and Pythagoras.

A prayer of the Pythagoreans shows the importance of the Tetractys (sometimes called the "Mystic Tetrad"), as the prayer was addressed to it.

> *"Bless us, divine number, thou who generated gods and men! O holy, holy* ***Tetractys****, thou that containest the root and source of the eternally flowing creation! For the divine number begins with the profound, pure unity until it comes to the holy four; then it begets the mother of all, the all-comprising, all-bounding, the first-born, the never-swerving, the* ***never-tiring holy ten****, the keyholder of all"*[159]

He is talking about the 4-level pyramid – shown next page…

Ok, further non-technical significance is to be found in the Hebrew **Kabbalist** symbol: [160]

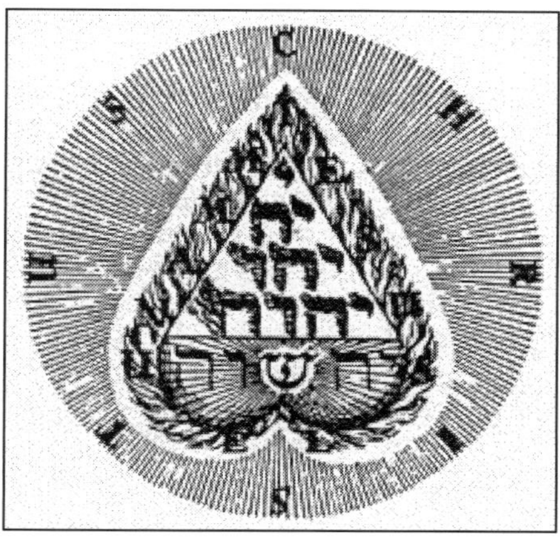

Kabbalist Symbol

Starting at the 12:00 o'clock position, read the letters: CHRISTUS around the edge.

Note the 4-level pyramid inside.

Symbol by early 17th-century Christian mystic Jacob Bohme, including a **tetractys** of flaming Hebrew letters of the Tetragrammaton (**YHWH for Yahweh**).

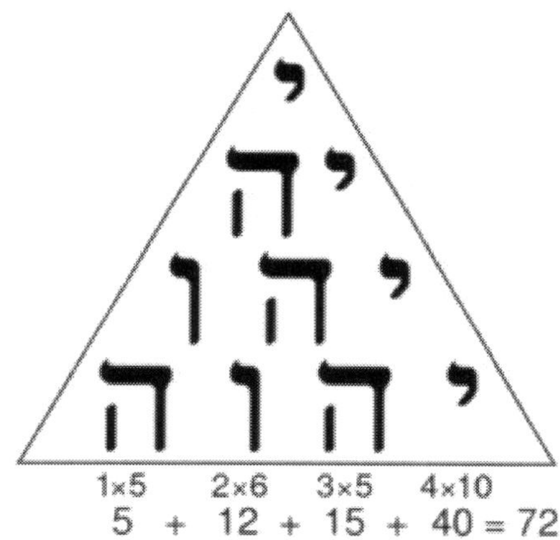

A tetractys of the letters of the Tetragrammaton adds up to 72 by gematria.

Gematria is the Hebrew system of assigning numbers to letters and thus determining significance to a word or a person's name.

So Pythagoras had an influence on the Hebrews and their sacred esoteric knowledge, to be reviewed later in Alchemy. It has been argued that the Kabbalistic Tree of Life (Sefirot in Chapter 12), with its ten spheres of emanation, is in some way connected to the Tetractys, but its form is not that of a triangle. The well-known occult writer Dion Fortune mentions:

> *"The **point** is assigned to Kether;*
> *the **line** to Chokmah;*
> *the two-dimensional **plane** to Binah;*
> *consequently the three-dimensional **solid** naturally falls to Chesed."*

(Pythagoras declared the first 3D [pyramid] solid to be the tetrahedron.)

The relationship between geometrical shapes (square, cube, triangle, circle) and the first four **Sephirot** is analogous to the geometrical correlations in Tetractys, shown above under **Pythagorean Symbol**, and unveils the relevance of the Tree of Life with the Tetractys. (Chapter 12)

Ok, now to return to more basic things… the point having been that some of the ancient discoveries and concepts (some given to Man by the Anunnaki) have led to **advanced mathematical concepts** of today and the significance of Pythagoras cannot be understated.

Of equal importance in the Greek world was Hermes.

Hermes and the Emerald Tablet

Hermes Trismegistus ("thrice greatest") has been portrayed as a messenger of the gods. As was said earlier, he was also Ningishzidda, son of Enki (Ea), who were both definitely pro-Man. He is credited with creating the Emerald Tablets, or **Smaragdine Tablet** which is ancient **hermetic wisdom** (examined later in Chapter 10).

> Hermetic Wisdom is <u>directly</u> associated with Serpent Wisdom, and also with Alchemy which was not just the transmutation of base metals to gold, but also included the transmutation of Man's soul – i.e., achieving higher consciousness.

What the publicly-revealed tablet says is not very long, but worth a brief glance in as much as it foreshadows Serpent Wisdom. Isaac Newton included the following translation among his alchemical papers:

1. Tis true without error, certain & most true:
2. **That which is below is like that which is above** & that which is above is like that which is below to do the miracles of one only thing.
3. And as all things have been & arose from one by the mediation of One: so all things have their birth from this one thing by adaptation.
4. The Sun is its father, the Moon its mother, the wind hath carried it in its belly, the Earth is its nurse.
5. The father of all perfection in the whole world is here.

6. Its force or power is entire if it be converted into earth.
7. **Separate thou the earth from the fire**, the subtle from the gross sweetly with great industry.
8. It ascends from the earth to the heaven & again it descends to the earth & receives the force of **things superior & inferior**.
9. By this means you shall have the glory of the whole world
10. & thereby all obscurity shall fly from you.
11. **Its force is above all force**. For it vanquishes every subtle thing & penetrates every solid thing.
12. So was the world created.
13. From this are & do come admirable adaptations whereof the means (or process) is here in this. Hence I am called **Hermes Trismegist**, having the **three parts of the philosophy of the whole world** [viz. Alchemy, Astrology & Theurgy].
14. That which I have said of the operation of the Sun is accomplished & ended.

The text of the *Smaragdine Tablet* gives its author as Hermes Trismegistus ("Hermes the Thrice-Greatest"), a legendary Hellenistic combination of the Greek god **Hermes** and the Egyptian god **Thoth** (aka Ningishzidda according to Zechariah Sitchin and his translations of the Sumerian tablets).

> The layers of meaning in the *Emerald Tablet* have been associated with the creation of the philosopher's stone, laboratory experimentation, phase transition, the alchemical magnum opus, and the correspondence between macrocosm and microcosm.[161]

Thoth & the Emerald Tablet

(credit: Bing Images: buddy.huggins.com)

The basic story of Thoth and the Emerald Tablets is interesting:[162]

> For some 16,000 years, **Thoth** ruled the ancient race of Egypt, or K'met, from approximately 50,000 B.C. to 36,000 B.C. At that time, the ancient barbarous race among which he and his followers had settled had been raised to a high degree of civilization. His vast wisdom made him ruler over the various **Atlantean colonies**, including the ones in South and Central America.
>
> When the time came for him to leave Egypt, he erected the Great Pyramid over the entrance to the Great Halls of Amenti, placed in it his records, and appointed guards for his secrets from among the highest of his people. In later times, the descendants of these guards became the pyramid priests, by which Thoth was deified as the God of Wisdom, The Recorder, by those in the age of darkness which followed his passing. In legend, the **Halls of Amenti** became the underworld, the Halls of the Gods, where the soul passed after death for judgment.
>
> During later ages, the soul of Thoth passed into the bodies of men in the manner described in the tablets. As such, he incarnated three times, in his last being known as Hermes, the thrice-born. In this incarnation, he left the writings known to modern occultists as the **Emerald Tablets**, a later and far lesser exposition of the ancient serpent mysteries.
>
> The tablets consist of **ten** which were left in the Great Pyramid in the custody of the pyramid priests. The ten are divided into thirteen parts for the sake of convenience. The last two are so great and far-reaching in their import that at present it is forbidden to release them to the world at large.
>
> (What has been shown above in this chapter is the one publicly released tablet.)
>
> Description of the Tablets:
>
> It should be understood that the Great Pyramid of Egypt has been and still is a temple of initiation into the mysteries. Jesus, Solomon, Apollonius of Tyana and others were initiated there.
>
> (continued…)

> Now, a word as to the material aspect of the tablets. They consist of ten tablets of emerald green, formed from a substance created through alchemical transmutation. They are imperishable, resistant to all elements and substances. In effect, the atomic and cellular structure is fixed, no change ever taking place. In this respect, they violate the material law of ionization [aka Entropy].
>
> The wisdom contained therein is **the foundation of the ancient mysteries**. And for the one who reads with open eyes and mind, his wisdom shall be increased a hundred-fold. The true student will read between the lines and gain wisdom. If the light is in you, the light which is engraved in these tablets will respond.

The ten components to the Emerald Tablets are alleged to exist, yet no historical record can be found. It may be just New Age wishful thinking. Related to Serpent Wisdom is Orpheus and the **Orphic Mysteries**.

Orphic Mysteries

Orpheus was a bard, prophet and a poet. The major stories about him are centered on his ability to charm all living things, even stones with his music, and his attempt to retrieve his wife, Eurydice, from the underworld (and again we have the underworld symbology true to the Norse Tree of Life teachings).

For the Greeks, Orpheus was credited with the composition of the **Orphic Hymns**, a collection of which survives. Shrines containing busts of Orpheus and Apollonius of Tyana (see Ch. 11 in Virtual Earth Graduate) were regarded as oracles.

The significance of the Hymns was to be found in that they served as a storehouse of mythological data along the lines of Hesiod's *Theogony*, which was a treatise on the genealogy, acts and nature of the Greek gods. His Orphic poetry was recited in mystery-rites and purification rituals.

What Orpheus taught is also significant, and relates to Serpent Wisdom:

1. Human souls are divine and immortal but subject to Karma.
2. The ascetic way of life is the best and leads to the purification rituals.
3. The mystery rites and purifications lead to communication with the gods.

4. There are sacred writings about the origin of gods and human beings.

And some of those things are assumed to be contained in the Emerald Tablets.

Ouroboros and Omphalos

The Greeks also had imagery backing their more esoteric teachings. The **Ouroboros** was a common theme for the Celts, Aztecs and the Norse and is found in the Greek depiction:

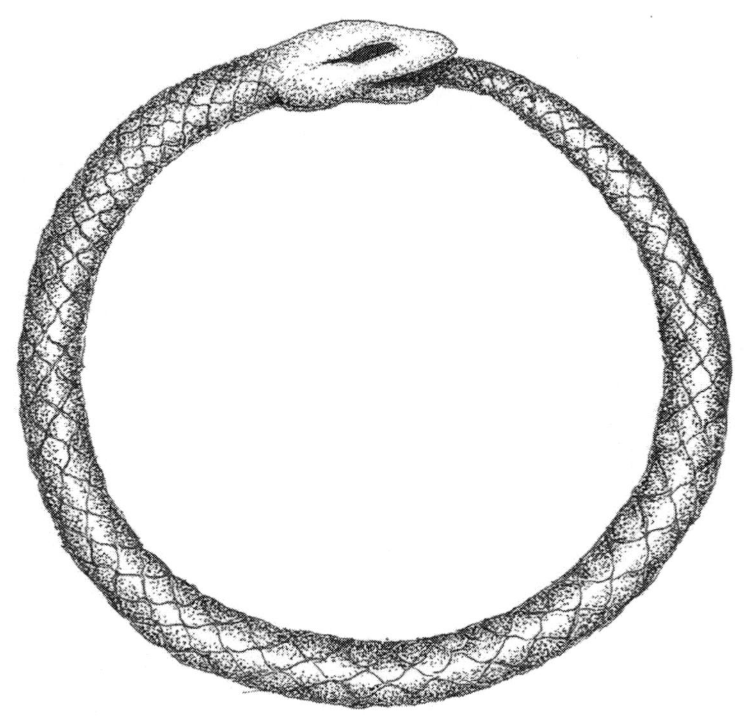

It is a classical depiction of a serpent eating its tail – signifying **eternity**, or any cycles that repeat without end. This applied to the concept of metempsychosis which was later refined to that of **reincarnation**. (Souls are eternal.)

The other esoteric depiction of Greek philosophy is shown in the **Omphalo**s:

"Omphalos" means navel and rested at Delphi which Zeus determined was the center of civilization. In addition, a legend says that the Oracle could communicate with the gods via the stone, which was hollow.

Holland (1933) suggested that the stone was hollow to allow intoxicating vapours breathed by the Oracle to channel through it – (credit Wikipedia/Omphalos.)

Omphalos

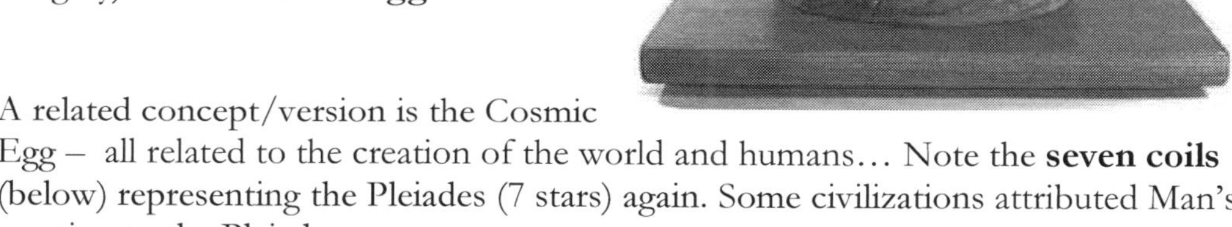

Another version of it (with serpent imagery): **The Cosmic Egg**.

A related concept/version is the Cosmic Egg – all related to the creation of the world and humans… Note the **seven coils** (below) representing the Pleiades (7 stars) again. Some civilizations attributed Man's creation to the Pleiades.

The Primal Serpent coiled 7x around the Cosmic Egg

Again, note the serpent imagery connected with fertility and birth…and Creation by Serpents (a recurring theme, esp. in Australia).

Cosmic egg
(credit: Mark Pinkham in *Return of the Serpents of Wisdom*, p. 322.)

Serpent Imagery

Further serpent images are found with **Medusa**, **King Cecrops I**, **Hercules** fighting Ladon (a Dragon), and the **Basilisk**...

Kekrops (Vasenbild in Palermo).

King Cecrops I was pictured as a bearer of Serpent Wisdom (above right). Hercules (below) slays Ladon...

Hercules Fighting Ladon

...and lastly, the **Basilisk**...[163]

… which was part serpent with a dragon's head.

And the above picture is an excellent rendition of something we have seen before: the Norse **World Serpent** called **Jörmungandr** (Chapter 2, and see the film, *Ragnarok*).

Delphi Oracle and Pythia

The Oracle at Delphi was always a woman called a **Pythia** (from 'serpent').

This was also later called the **Temple of Apollo** and the Oracle was always present in some form since 1400 BC.

The Pythia sits in a cave just a few meters from the Temple of Apollo. It was said that the god Apollo answered inquiries to those who came before the Oracle, who sat in a cave over an abyss.

She was called the Pythia and was doubtless the most powerful woman in the world at that time.

The name "Pythia" is derived from Pytho, which in myth was the original name of Delphi. The Greeks derived this place name from the verb, *pythein* (πύθειν, "to rot"), which refers to the sickly sweet smell of the decomposition of the body of the monstrous **Python** that was slain by Apollo.

'Pythia' was also a House of Snakes.

The usual theory has been that the Pythia delivered oracles in a frenzied state induced by vapors rising from a chasm in the rock, and that she spoke intelligently in her own voice.[164]

Note the ring of serpents around the circular wall.

Again, the serpent imagery is found in Greece, among the healers, like Asclepius.

Healing Imagery

Asclepius represents the healing aspect of the medical arts; his daughters are Hygieia ("Hygiene", the goddess/personification of health, cleanliness, and sanitation), Iaso (the goddess of recuperation from illness), Aceso (the goddess of the healing process), Aglaea/Aegle (the goddess of beauty, splendor, glory, magnificence, and adornment), and Panacea (the goddess of universal remedy).

He was one of Apollo's sons, and those physicians and attendants who served this god (perhaps a demi-god is appropriate as he wasn't a full god) were known as the **Therapeutae** of Asclepius (in Alexandria).

Modern-day medicine honors him with its own version of his symbol:

(Left) Asclepius and his serpent staff.

(Below) Hermes and his staff….

And today's medical symbol the **Caduceus** derived from Asclepius and Hermes:

Alexander and the Talking Trees

There is another Greek legend about Alexander the Great wherein he and his men ascend a great mountain in India to meet with an old white-haired Sage who shows Alexander two talking trees.

Alexander the Great (Iskander) as pictured by a manuscript of the Shahnama (Book of Kings) by Firdawsi circa 1330-1340. (credit: Wikipedia: commons: Iskandar)

The Sage led Alexander to the Trees of the Sun and the Moon – the Tree of the Sun had leaves of red gold, and the Tree of the Moon had leaves of silver. The trees advised Alexander to not return to Macedon but that he'd live another 20 months and then die of poison. The trees would not tell him who would give him the poison cup but that his mother would die and remain unburied. [165]

Scholars surmise that "talking trees" refers to strips of wood with letters on them, serving as an oracle or a Tarot-type function.

By this point, it should be clear that the gods contributed much to civilization in Greece. They also gave Man in Egypt their knowledge.

Anunnaki in Egypt

Whereas some of the gods operating in Greece were identified as Anunnaki, it behooves us to see who the Egyptian gods were, in the same way.[166]

Egyptian God	→	**Anunnaki God**
Amen-Ra/Ammon		Anu
Thoth		Ningishzidda
Ptah		Enki
Ra/Aten		Marduk
Horus		son of Osiris and Isis
Osiris		son of Marduk
Isis		Ninmah
Set(h)		son of Marduk

Enlil and Inanna did not have 'god' roles in Egypt.

The gods were involved with humans from the start, and often fought each other over land, resources and rights to the humans. The following account is from Dr. Lessin's *Anunnaki Chronicles...*[167]

Osiris and Isis lived near Marduk in lower Egypt. Shamgaz was commander of the Astronaut Corps, based in Baalbek, Lebanon. Marduk had split the rule of Egypt between his two sons, Osiris and Set(h). In 9830 BC Shamgaz told Seth that while Osiris lived, he (Seth) would lack good fiefs and not prosper. In fact, Osiris would inherit Marduk's throne and Seth would get nothing.

Thus Seth, Shamgaz and Nephys would kill Osiris and invited him to dinner, drugged him, and when he passed out, locked him in a coffin and threw it in the sea.

Isis, Marduk and Sarpanit [Marduk's earthling wife] retrieved Osiris' coffin from the sea. Enki [Science Officer] had Isis extract semen from Osiris' dead body and inseminate herself with it. She said, "Our son [Horus], not Seth, shall rule Egypt!" She bore Horus and hid him while he grew and later went off to fight Seth and avenge Osiris.

(continued...)

Gibil teaches Horus as he grows up, and tutors Horus how to fight Seth and how to pilot the skycraft. Gibil made multi-headed missiles for him and how to use them. Later when Horus ' army marched on Seth, Seth dared Horus to an air battle – Seth was the local champion pilot.

Horus took his craft up fast and locked horns with Seth, and Seth hit Horus with a poison dart missile [the canopy was open], forcing him to land, and Ningishzidda came to Horus' rescue, gave him an antidote and sent him back up into the sky.

Horus came at Seth from his blind side, with everything he had, including the 'harpoon'-- a super missile that renders the enemy blind and deaf, and Seth crashed to the ground. Horus landed, bound Seth and dragged him before the Council which condemned Seth to live (not in Africa where Ham was) but in Canaan. Seth soon ruled Canaan and got control of the spaceport in what is now the tip of Saudi Arabia.

Horus, Enki and the forces attacked Seth and regained control of the spaceport, the Great Pyramid (called the Ekur, used as a beacon and a spiritual transformation center [Kings Chamber]) and Mt Moriah – the control center is now covered by the Dome of the Rock, which goes down 3 levels. [See end of this chapter, p. 256.]

Seth and Horus were barred from ever ruling over Lower Egypt.

The gods arrived early on the scene, before there was an Egypt, and set about making a home for themselves… They came in from Sumer (Iraq) and they cleared land, drained swamps, and built temples moving huge slabs of rock and erecting huge obelisks – then carving hieroglyphics into them with **laser-like equipment**.

> A simple glance at the hieroglyphs and designs on temple walls and obelisks with their **incredibly sharp edges** will quickly show one that the pictographs and hieroglyphs were not made with a stone and obsidian chisel.

Artwork Exposed

Note the lines are perfect, no irregularities, symmetry is also a feature of the work…

…the cartouche is perfectly oblong and symmetrical…

… the twisted rope (below the lower bird) would be hard to do with a chisel – the lower two loops are perfectly the same size…

Now note the face of Ramses (below) – it is perfectly symmetrical…. The left half exactly mirrors the right half. (This has been verified with a mirror and a computer imaging process.)

This suggests the use of a laser-like sculpting device.

For comparison, let's look at **Puma Punku** where they used similar technology to cut huge blocks of Andesite and Granite (2 very hard stones):

The above was not done with stone and chisel as is the case below:

or:

Precision is not possible without the **laser-like equipment** of the Egyptians/Sumerians.

Having said that, we come to the artwork at the **Temple of Edfu**, one of the oldest temples in Egypt erected by **Thoth and the Seven Sages**…

And by the way, if the inside vaults were painted and carved by torch-light (they weren't), why has no carbonblack/soot ever been found on the ceilings of the Egyptian hallways, vaults, or tombs?

Suggestion:

The Dendera Lightbulb

Note the 4 insulators, the wire/cable, the filament, and the wire is plugged into something…

And today's replica that works:

(credit: right)[168]

It was determined that the **Baghdad Battery** (in lower right of picture [right]) could produce 1.2 volts... so could 6 power a crude lightbulb?

As you will see in the following examination of Edfu and the Ancient gods, there was a lot more going on than the public is told.

Shebtiw at Edfu

Edfu is an ancient site in Upper Egypt, south of Luxor, where Horus built a massive temple. In fact, Egyptian ancient history says that there were three sets of gods involved: the **Builders**, the **Sages**, and the **Shebtiw**. The Egyptians believed that those 3 were the "olden gods" who preceded the better-known ones that ruled Egypt and Mesopotamia after 3000 BC.

> Horus established a **foundry** at Edfu and enlisted humans in his fight against the evil Seth [who killed his father Osiris], arming them with weapons "forged of divine metal."
> The temple description also states that Horus kept there his great Winged Disc ; "when the doors of the foundry open, **the Disc riseth up**." [169]

The "olden gods" were said to have come by boat to Egypt and included Ptah, the one who 'developed' or made things, including raising the land of Egypt from the waters. (Remember that Ptah was Enki and Thoth was his son Ningishzidda – already gods in Sumeria.) Said Mr. Sitchin, ".... **Evidence shows that the gods of Egypt originated in Sumer.**" [170] The Egyptians believed in Gods of Heaven and Earth and another set that they referred to as **the Great Gods who descended from Heaven** and they are still recognizable on temple walls by their horned headgear.

(credit: Bing Images: fineartamerica.com)

Be clear that the gods shown above who descended from Heaven, came first to Sumer and then came later to Egypt.

Seven Sages

In addition in the pantheon of gods from Sumeria, i.e., among the Anunnaki leaders, there were also the **Seven Great Anunnaki** who were also called the Seven Gods of Destiny, the Seven Gods Who Judge, and these same were called the **Seven Sages** in Egypt. [171] The Seven Sages were sent by Enki to teach humans civilization, [172] and had a part in the **Egyptian Creation Myth.**

According to the Edfu Temple "texts" (which are the hieroglyphics on the walls), the gods gathered together , **Thoth and the Seven Sages**, at the place called Djeba (the Falcon) in Wetjeset-Hor. Horus was called the Falcon, as was his ship which (above) was said to be kept at the "foundry" or temple (pp. 57-58).

According to E.A.E. Jelinkova, Thoth and the Seven Sages created the Edfu temple and among their retinue were two gods Aa and Wa.[173] And from another source, we learn that A (or Aa) was another name for Thoth. [174] And we already know that Thoth was Ningishzidda (thanks to Messrs. Sitchin and Lessin) and was sent by Ptah (or Enki) – and that is how it all comes together.

Creation Versions

But all was not in perfect harmony – at least not for long. It was said that the land was risen from the sea by Thoth and he stood on the initial island of earth, initially also called the **Island of the Egg** – symbolizing the birth of something. It was said by some sources that his word created the land – reminiscent of the Book of Genesis where God speaks things into being… and yet another source said that Thoth stood on the primeval island (Atlantis) and … well, let's work up to that….

The Book of Genesis appears to show two creations (See Chapter 12), and the Egyptians have at least 4 different versions of creation: [175]

Version 1: The most ancient story is that the world was created by Ptah who did it by thought and word alone. He was seen as a creator deity but never rose to become a major Egyptian god.

Version 2: Thoth created land and peopled it near what was called Hermopolis (Greek name for **Khemnu**, which was a city that honored Thoth equating him with Hermes.) Here we find the **Ogdoad**, the Group of Eight which were the first couples created: Shu and Tefnut, then Geb and Nut, then Osiris, Isis, Set(h) and Nephthys. Amun/Thoth + the 8 gods = the **Ennead (nine deities)**.

> **Note:** the Nine deities of Egypt with Thoth are reminiscent of the Nine Gods and Bolon Yokte said to rule the Maya (see Maya, Ch. 6).

Version 3: The god **Khnum** was an ancient ram-headed god on Elephantine (an island in the Nile) who made people from clay on a potter's wheel. This was the first solid link between the gods and humans in Egyptian myth.
Khnum had a temple built to him at Esna…

Location in Egypt

Very interesting is where the Temple of Edfu is located:

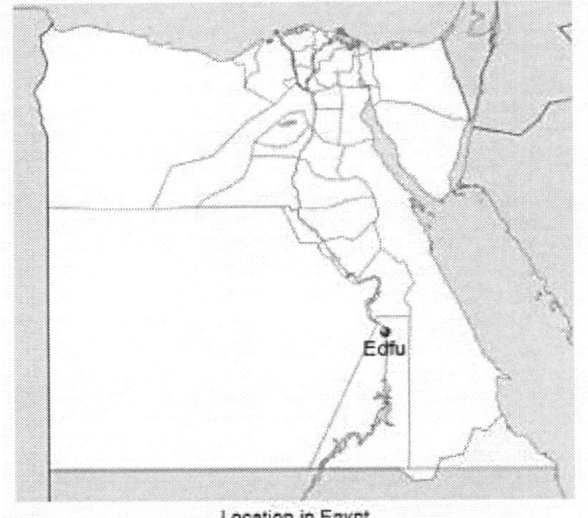

Location in Egypt

Are these the same temple with two different names?

Khnum was later associated with Atum. He is always pictured as a ram-headed god:

Atum is a **god of creation** and is considered to have molded the other deities… from clay – as did NüWa in China.

Amun and Ra were merged to Amun-Ra. Atum was another name, or Amun at a different time. [176]

Amun-Ra (next page) was also ram-headed…

(credit: Wikipedia: Khnum)

Amun-Ra

You have to wonder what was going on with all the reference to serpents, rams' horns, goats' horns, and horns denoting rank among the Anunnaki... In fact, **Alexander the Great** visited Amun-Ra (left) , saw his horns, knew he was a descendant of the gods, and because Alexander also had horns, he knew he was also part god.

A coin commemorating Alexander the Great

Credit: kingofmacedon.net via Yahoo [177]

If the great men of yore were Anunnaki hybrids, they could still have had reptilian vestiges, such as horns. It's interesting that he was portrayed that way, so it must have been a compliment… otherwise it would have been banned.

Even in today's world, people occasionally are born with horns, or a vestige of same…

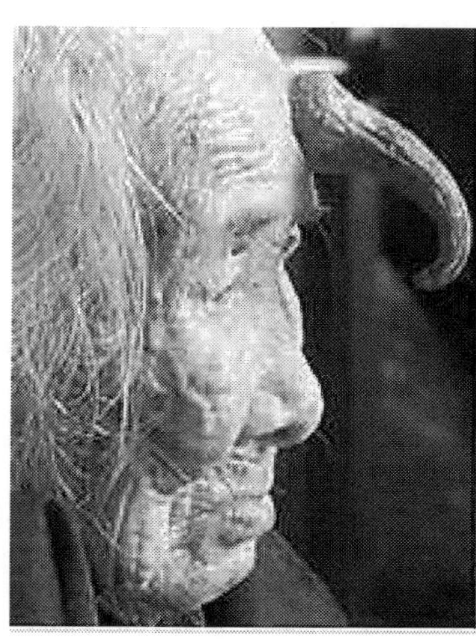

These people are found in China and Tibet which is close to the Anunnaki domain in Sumer… easy for genetic vestiges to transmit in the area…

…and some have tails.

Anyway, back to the Temples at Edfu and Esna… inside courtyards…

The temple at Edfu:

And of course, this is the temple at Esna….

What is going on here?
Temples were not "cookie-cutter." They uniquely represented the one they honored.

(There was no reconciliation of the two names or temples… So… they are assumed to be the same temple.)

The point of Khnum being a ram-headed god is not out of keeping with an earlier description of Enki (according to Sitchin): **Enki was a chimera** and sometimes was depicted as a goat-headed creature to the Chaldeans:

The Chaldean god Ea

(credit: piney.com)

This is because Enki was associated with the constellation Capricorn, not that he looked like a fish-goat.

But the horns correlate to Khnum's imagery… Could Khnum have been another word for Enki?

Enki had 4 horns as his rank… and horns were a symbol of power and status…

Guess where the design for the king's crown came from? Ever wondered why the original ones had spikes (horns) on them?

Recall that the Anunnaki set up kings as rulers… "imitation is the sincerest form of flattery."

And some took different forms around the globe…

… Is it just coincidence?

Anyway, that temple similarity was an anomaly that just had to be checked out, and apologies for the confusion in the names of the gods (it is not clear as one god had different names in different places)… **the significance is the horns and snake imagery**… and we are straying from the Egyptian versions of creation…

Version 4: This myth came out of **Heliopolis**, north near the mouth of the Nile and Cairo… There was the great infinite ocean, called Nun or Nu, and from it emerged the god Atum from the primeval waters, and stood on a raised mound, called the **Island of Trampling**, and created life… Remember Atum was later called Amon-Ra. (These gods were often renamed, see endnote 176.)

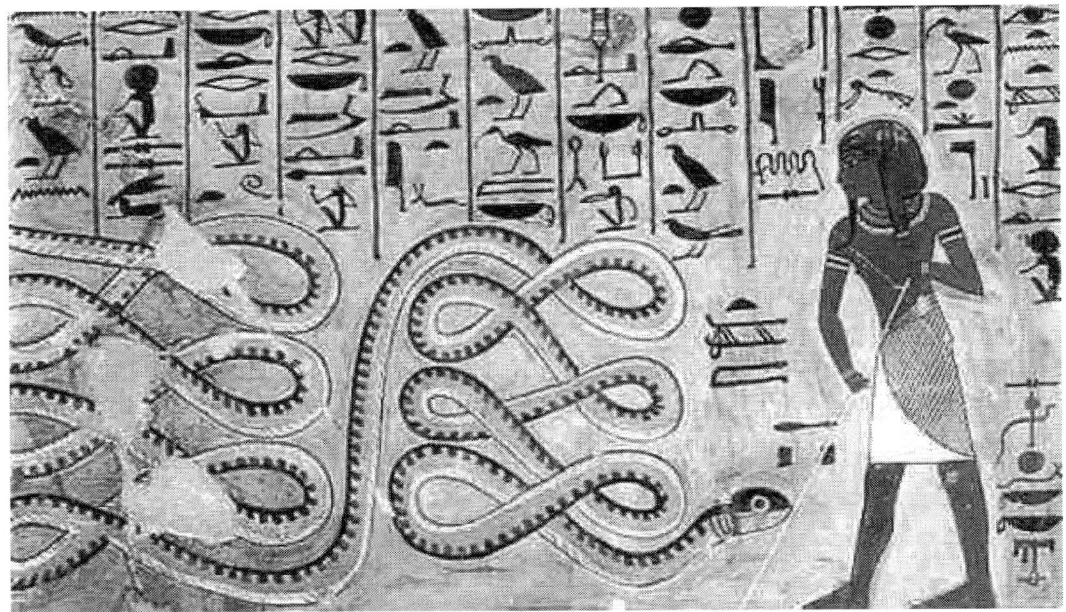

The God Atum Fighting the Serpent…
(credit: landofpyramids.org)

Ok, now we have Atum (who was Thoth in an earlier version) and he is fighting a **serpent**… on the primeval island with a weird name… "Trampling?"

War Among the Gods

Unfortunately, the symbolism of Atum (aka Thoth aka Ningishzidda) fighting the serpent is all too real. Said EAE Reymond:

> The domain of the Wetjeset-Neter is now attacked by the enemy Snake… When the enemy, **the snake**, **appeared at the landing stage** [platform] of that domain, a bw-titi, Place-for-Crushing , was planned and protective guards of the gods were formed…. There is allusion to **a fight on the earth** in front of the shelter. Another fight took place at the same time **in the sky** in which the Falcon [Horus] was believed to fight against the snake named sbty [shebtiw].
>
> The Edfu cosmogonical records begin with a picture of the primeval island where the gods were believed to have lived first… the Earth-Maker is said to be **the snake who created the Earth**… [178]

So what we have is serpents at the beginning, creating the world (land from the sea) and the humans and some other gods, and then getting into a fight and destroying the island (Atlantis) and dwelling place (calling it the **Island of Trampling**), then it all gets rebuilt. And it appears that the Builder Gods, the Sages and the **Shebtiw** were the Anunnaki since they were originally reptilian (see VEG Ch. 3 – Berossus, the ancient Babylonian scribe, said so).

And it is known that **the gods did fight among themselves**, ground and air battles (read carefully some of the sections in Chapter 1, 4 and 5), and some of the original inhabitants died. It is still maintained that the Nagas in India (underground) are said to be the remnant of the original Anunnaki – they were called the "serpent people." Said EAE Reymond:

> A further important fact that emerges … the allusion to the underworld… makes it clear that **the underworld existed before the world was created…** [179]
>
> And that is significant as the creation myth of the Amerindians (Navajo and Hopi) and the Inca are said to have emerged from under the Earth.

After the first destruction, a large company of divine beings [Deva] appeared on the scene and **the snake was overthrown**. The victorious gods then settled the area again and built a Temple at Edfu to commemorate in stone ("Edfu Texts") the whole event. The temple was built at the dictate of the **Ancestor gods** and thus originated the Winged One symbol (including 2 serpents): the ***udjat***.

Tree of Life

At this point, we need to know if Egypt had a Tree of Life, as did many other cultures. After all, the Anunnaki started the concept and they now ruled Egypt. No specific Tree was found depicted in Egyptian wall reliefs, but a Tree was found mentioned in the hieroglyphics: Persea. It was just a brief mention in Egyptian Tradition associated with Atum-Ra. That seemed strange.

So a quick look was taken in the surrounding area, and a **Sefirot** was discovered among the Hebrew esoteric teachings, and with another quick look at Islam, it was discovered that the Quran speaks of a **Tree of Immortality** only – but that qualifies as a Tree of Life. Shown below is the Islamic version, found on a carpet:

(credit: https://en.wikipedia.org/wiki/Tree_of_life#Middle_East)

There are eight birds in the Tree, but no serpent. The serpent is called Iblis in the **Quran**, however. Quranic reference to the Tree is symbolic; eating of the forbidden Tree in Eden signifies that Adam disobeyed God.

So what is the story with Egypt? There are two things that symbolize life to the Egyptians. The **Ankh** and the **Acacia** tree.

The Ankh

The ankh is known as the "breath of life." It comes from the ancient Egyptian hieroglyphic character that read "life", a triliteral sign for the consonants **Ayin – Nun – Het.**

It represents **eternal life**, which is the general meaning of the symbol. The Egyptian Gods are often portrayed carrying it by its loop, or bearing one in each hand, arms crossed over their chest. The ankh appears in hand or in proximity of almost every deity in the Egyptian pantheon (including Pharaohs).

The origin of the symbol is related to the Picture of Hammurabi being given the Laws and the **Rod & Circle** held by the god – the Ankh is just a 'reconnection' of the two objects. (See Chapter 1 – Hamurabbi.)

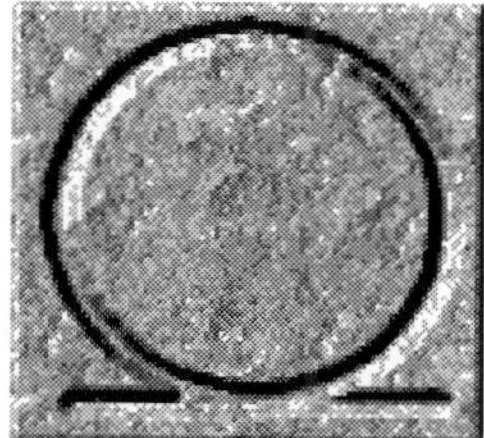

the Shen Ring

The triliteral Ayin – Nun – Het significance is in the following:

AYIN in Hebrew, Arabic, Amharic, and Maltese means "eye." This suggests a connection with the Eye of Horus.

NUN Nun is believed to be derived from an Egyptian **hieroglyph of a snake** (the Hebrew word for snake, *nachash* begins with a Nun, and snake in Aramaic is *nun*) or eel. The glyph has been suggested to descend from a hypothetical Proto-Canaanite naḥš "snake", based on the name in Ethiopic, ultimately from a hieroglyph representing a serpent:

HET is a hieroglyph for "courtyard."

The pharaohs and other high priests all carried ankhs around by the loop. The ankh appears frequently in Egyptian tomb paintings and other art, often at the fingertips of a god or goddess in images that represent the deities of the afterlife **conferring the gift of life on the dead person's mummy.** Additionally, an ankh was often carried by Egyptians as an amulet, either alone, or in connection with two other hieroglyphs that mean "strength" and "health."

> By the way, the Egyptian practice of **mummification** was copying the Anunnaki process (without understanding it exactly), whereby a deceased person was preserved to be resurrected again – the Anunnaki had the ability to raise the dead (see Chapter 3, Druid Initiation and Chapter 1, Raising the Dead – a process). The Anunnaki technique was more like suspended animation, and they left the body intact and would regenerate it on the cellular level… whereas the Egyptians removed the organs and such a destruction of the body could not even be resurrected by the Anunnaki.

The Egyptian in the picture below is carrying an **Ankh**.

Note that in Chapter 1, Hammurabi holds a Rod and Circle – a **Shen** – which is related to the Ankh – in the Shen, the circle is Eternity and the Rod is Life/Power. Same meaning as the Ankh.

The Shen Ring could be stretched to a cartouche:

The Pharoah's name was 'encircled' and 'protected' by the Shen Ring.

The Acacia Tree

Here is the interesting part.

To the Ancient Egyptians, the Kabbalistic **Tree of Life** represented the hierarchical chain of events that brought everything into existence. The spheres (*sefirot*) of the Tree of Life demonstrate the order, process, and method of creation.

In Egyptian mythology, the first couple, apart from Shu and Tefnut (moisture and dryness) and Geb and Nut (earth and sky), are Isis and Osiris. They were said to have emerged from the **acacia tree** of Iusaaset, **which the Egyptians considered the Tree of Life**, referring to it as the "tree in which life and death are enclosed." **Acacia trees also contain DMT**, a psychedelic drug associated with spiritual experiences. [180] This may be the alleged Persea tree…

Thoth and Seshat were associated with the Tree of Life.

Thoth **Seshat**

(credit: Bing Images: Pinterest)

Thoth was one of the earlier Egyptian gods, thought to be scribe to the gods, who kept a great library of scrolls, over which one of his wives, **Seshat** (the goddess of writing) was thought to be mistress. He was associated by the Egyptians with speech, literature, arts, learning. He, too, was a measurer and recorder of time, as was Seshat.[181]

Seshat is often pictured with two interesting things:

Notched Rod is for Measuring

Note the 7-pointed 'star' above her head, (often associated with **the Pleiades**) and the **Shen Ring** at the bottom of the staff.

"**Seshat** is the wife most often mentioned in connection with Thoth.... [and she is] a deity of the stars and to builders by aiding them in the **stellar alignment** of new structures, especially temples." [182]

Re: Thoth...
The magical powers of Thoth were so great, that the Egyptians had tales of a **'Book of Thoth'**, which would allow a person who read the sacred book to become the most powerful magician in the world. The book "the god of wisdom wrote with his own hand" was though a deadly Book that brought nothing but pain and tragedy to those who read it, despite finding out about the "secrets of the gods themselves" and "all that is hidden in the stars." [183]

...and that aspect will be further examined in Chapter 13... sometimes enlightenment is not all it is cracked up to be.

> And in a related note, the Hindus venerated Sesha, one of the Nagas, also called **Seshanaga** ... whose name is similar to the Egyptian Seshat, and Sesha was known as the **World Serpent**.
> Seshanaga is the Nagaraja or king of all Nagas and one of the primal beings of creation.

As if that weren't enough, lastly we come to a fascinating part of Egyptian lore: the Djedhi priests and their connection with serpents. Since the serpent was associated with *Kundalini* and that resembled a serpent, and the *Kundalini* also brought with it greater awareness and wisdom, the Djedhi was said to possess Serpent Wisdom and Power.

Djedhi and Serpents

Whereas the archeologists and historians consider the Djedhi to be just myth, it may have its reality in some ancient fact. Just as there are Indian gurus who can perform miracles, and adepts in the martial arts can break stone blocks with their bare hands, and some **Qigong masters** can use the Force to knock an opponent off his feet (without touching him). [184]

So if today's adepts can manipulate ambient energy to heal, make things disappear, climb ropes (not attached to anything), mesmerize, why couldn't the ancient Merlin have done the same thing AND passed the knowledge on secretly to others thru a Serpent Wisdom group?

A drawing of a Djedhi also called a **Gnostic Warrior**. Spiritually trained to master his *Kundalini* and use its power (The Force) to achieve healing, devination, or miracles.

Carrying a staff, as did Gandalf in *The Hobbit*, and Moses in the Bible, was *de rigeur*.

One of the greatest Gnostic (enlightened) Warriors was Moses:

(credit: Bing Images: politizine.blogspot.com)

**(credit above:
Bing Images: gnostictemplars.org)**

At any rate, before examining the what and how, the following are a couple of the accounts of these Egyptian priests and their amazing abilities (from the *Westcar Papyrus*). [185]

The **first story**, told by Khafra, is set during the reign of one of Khufu's predecessors. King Nebka's chief lector Ubaoner finds that his wife is having a love affair with a townsman of Memphis, and he fashions a crocodile in wax. Upon learning that his unfaithful wife is meeting her lover, he casts a spell for the figurine to come to life upon contact with water, and sets his caretaker to throw it in the stream by which the townsman enters and leaves the lector's estate undiscovered. Upon catching the townsman, the crocodile takes him to the bottom of the lake, where they remain for seven days as the lector entertains the visiting pharaoh. When he tells Nebka the story, and calls the crocodile up again, the king orders the crocodile to devour the townsman once and for all. Then he has the adulterous wife brought forth, set on fire and thrown in the river.

The **second story**, told by another son named Baufra, is set during the reign of his grandfather Sneferu. The king is bored and his chief lector Djadjaemankh advises him to gather twenty young women and use them to sail him around the palace lake. Sneferu orders twenty beautiful oars made, and gives the women nets to drape around them as they sail. However, one of the girls loses an amulet - a fish pendant made of malachite so dear to her that she will not even accept a substitute from the royal treasury, and until it is returned to her neither she nor any of the other girls will row. The king laments this, and the chief lector folds aside the water to allow the retrieval of the amulet, then folds the water back.

The **third story**, told by Hordjedef, concerns a miracle set within Khufu's own reign. A townsman named Dedi apparently has the power to reattach a severed head onto an animal, to tame wild lions, and knows the number of secret rooms in the shrine of Thoth. Khufu, intrigued, sends his son to invite this wise man to the court, and upon Dedi's arrival he orders a goose, an undefined waterbird, and a bull beheaded. Dedi re-attaches the heads. Khufu then questions him on his knowledge on the shrine of Thoth, and Dedi answers that he does not know the number of rooms, but he knows where they are.

(continued…)

(3rd story cont'd)

When Khufu asks for the wheres and hows, Dedi answers that the one who can give Khufu access is not him, but the first of the three future kings in the womb of the woman Rededjet. This is a prophecy detailing the beginnings of the Fifth dynasty, starting with Userkaf.

Other Djedhi are mentioned in Egyptian history as having the ability to traverse the scorching Egyptian sands with only their magical staffs and/or becoming powerful magicians in the service of the Pharaohs. Some Djedhi are found in the service of the Pharaoh that Moses and Aaron confronted in order to demand freedom for the Hebrews. At the Pharaoh's command his Djedhi magicians turned their staffs into live serpents, representing the Dragon Force that each Djedhi possessed. But Aaron's staff also turned into a serpent, albeit a much larger one than those of the Djedhi, and it proceeded to consume their smaller serpents, thus proving the superiority of his Dragon Force to theirs.[186]

Through raising the inner **Dragon Force** (i.e., *Kundalini)* the Djedhi acquired abilities to perform supernatural feats. The wisdom of the Egyptian Djedhi that the **Knights Templar** studied (from the Sufi) may have first entered the Middle East as early as the Exodus, since Mentho tells us that the Hebrew leader **Moses** had been initiated into all the secrets of Egypt's priesthood and was thus a Djedhi Master himself. According to the *Westcar Papyrus,* the teachings of these earlier magician-priests were compiled by the Egyptian Djedhi and stored within the "secret chambers of the sanctuary of Thoth." These were the **Mysteries of Thoth-Hermes**, the leader of the earlier "Serpent Tribe" of magician-priests. (These documents are what the pharaoh in the 3rd story above was looking for.)

These mysteries covered in detail the physics behind activating and **developing the Dragon Force through alchemy** - the art that Thoth-Hermes would eventually became the recognized patron of throughout much of the world.

> Through **Thoth's alchemy** an Egyptian Djedhi was able to awaken the normally dormant Dragon Force at the base of his spine and then move it upwards to his head where it awakens the Third Eye [6th chakra] and culminates in supernatural powers and intuitive, **gnostic wisdom**. The proof that a magician-priest had succeeded in this **alchemy** is intrinsic to his honorific title of Djedhi. The "Djed" prefix of Djedhi denoted "column," while **the root word or**

> **sound Dj denoted "serpent."** Thus, a Djedi was one who had wakened the Dj or serpent at its seat and then raised it up his or her **Djed "column"** or spine to the head.[187] [emphasis added]

As for secret organizations, and secret teachings, the wisdom of Egyptian Djedhi may have also arrived many years later in the Middle East when the Sufi Dhul-Nun al-Misri traveled there from Egypt after spending many years studying the alchemical hieroglyphs of the Djedhi that covered the temples and obelisks of Egypt. With the esoteric wisdom he discovered, Dhul-Nun al-Misri founded the al-Banna, the Sufi sect of "Freemasons." According to the Sufi Idris Shah, the al-Banna were teachers of the Templars during the years the Knights resided in the al-Aqsa Mosque on the Temple Mount (later, this chapter). Much of the wisdom of alchemy and the Dragon Force that resulted from the Templar-al-Banna alliance was later taken into the continent of Europe by Templar Knights who transmitted it into fledgling Speculative Freemasonry. [188]

The following is an interesting side-bar to the development and spread of the Serpent Wisdom & Power which will be very relevant in a later chapter on Serpent Wisdom. In addition, in order to make more sense of the following account, it is necessary to know where Sarmatia and the Sarmatians were – remnants of the Persian Empire, knocking at the door to the Roman Empire.

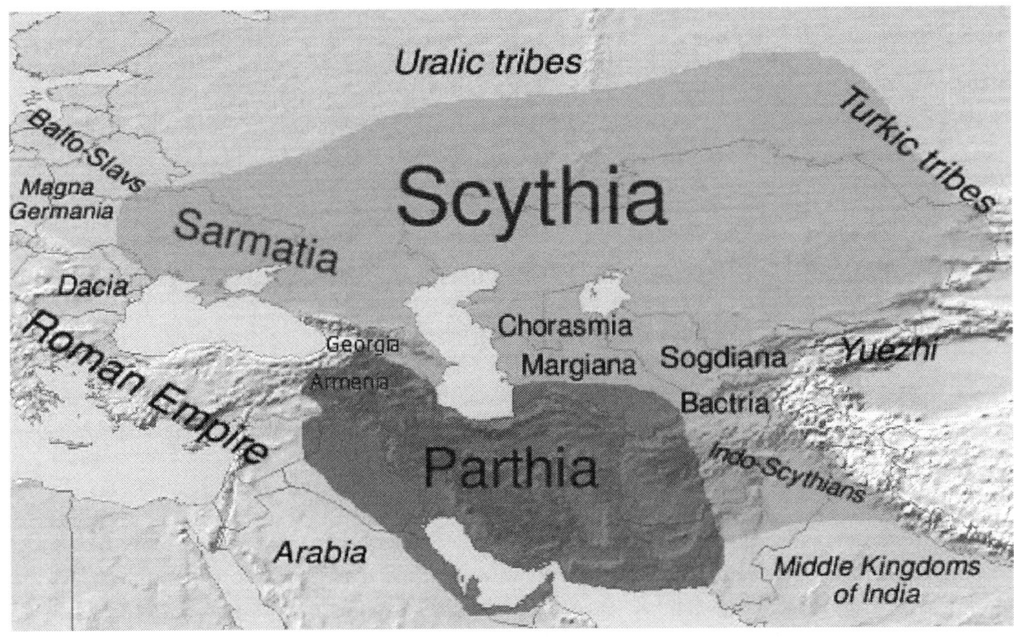

Sarmatia from 5^{00} BC to 400 AD

Keep in mind that the whole Serpent Wisdom and Dragon Force teachings originated with **Thoth** in Egypt (and he was actually Ningishzidda, an Anunnaki who would have known about the Brotherhood of the Serpent that his father, Enki, started as a way to spiritually enhance humans, as well as **resurrect the dead** as Inanna did.)[189] The following side-bar is an account of how the Teachings made their way from Egypt to Persia to Europe over the centuries. [190]

The Persian order of **Nart Knights** were the Masters of the Dragon Force of the ancient Persian Empire. Possibly as old, or even older than the **Djedhi** of Egypt, the Narts may have existed as early as King Jamshid, one of the incipient Persian kings of legend who ruled during the time of "Airyan Vaejahi," the Persian Golden Age that some historians date back to 20,000 BCE. Jamshid was a classic example of the Fisher King of Grail legend by suffering a fall from pride and the ensuing loss of his **Dragon Force**, or **"Farr"** as it was called in Persia. Jamshid engendered a lineage of Farr-empowered priest kings that culminated in the highly spiritual Kayanid Dynasty founded by King Key-Khosrow, the "Persian King Arthur." Records state that, like King Arthur, Key-Khosrow possessed knights (his "Narts") who were associated with a Holy Grail (the "Nartmongue") and conducted their meetings around a table similar to Arthur's Round Table. The mystical legends of Key-Khosrow and his Narts were eventually compiled into the *Nart Sagas* during the later Persian Empire and have since been regarded as Persian counterparts to Europe's Holy Grail legends.

According to *From Scythia to Camelot*, the *Nart Sagas* may have first entered Europe with bands of Persian Sarmatian warriors who were in the hire of the Roman legions. The authors of this theory, Littleton and Malcor, make the interesting observation that **King Arthur and his Knights** could have been Sarmatian soldiers and members of a Roman legion stationed that was Hadrian's Wall with orders to protect England from the marauding Picts of Scotland. During the following downfall of the Roman Empire, Arthur and his men would then have been released from their Roman service, at which time Arthur would have become king of the newly liberated land of Britain and his fellow soldiers would have been transformed into the Knights of the Round Table.

(This alternate history of Arthur and his Knights was recently made into a major motion picture entitled King Arthur *staring Clive Owen as the British monarch.)*

(continued...)

What little we know today of the Persian Narts suggests that they were continually seeking to increase their **Dragon Force** in order to become warrior adepts with a high level of spiritual purity and enlightenment. Only those whose dedication to king and country was immaculate could hope to increase their Farr to the degree needed in order to drink from the Nartmongue when it was passed around the Persian Round Table. Certain Narts increased their Farr to such a degree that they became the obvious choice to succeed an outgoing king. Some, like King Key-Lohrasp of the Kayanid Dynasty, became endowed with a mystical temperament and an abundance of gnostic insight.

The Nart Secrets of the Dragon Force possessed by the early Persian kings and their Narts were preserved within Persian civilization for many hundreds of years. Then, in the 11th century AD, Hasan-i-Sabah, the founder of the Order of Assassins that was to become a huge influence on the **Knights Templar**, revived the ancient Nart tradition. He resurrected the Secrets of the Dragon Force, founded a cadre of knights to serve him, and chose for his court the castle of Alamut, the "Eagles Nest," which was located high in the Albourz Mountains, the region of northern Persia that had anciently been the seat of the Persian kings.

Hasan learned the Secrets of the Dragon Force both by studying the Nart Mysteries and by traveling to Cairo's House of Wisdom for the purpose of mastering nine mystical degrees of alchemical attainment. After his graduation Hasan left Egypt and returned home to quickly establish himself as one of the greatest alchemists that Persia had ever seen. He subsequently founded his own mystery school of nine degrees, which eventually became known as the **Order of the Assassins**. The degrees of alchemical purification of Hasan's school – which Hasan cryptically referred to as the **nine steps of ascension up the mystical mountain of Kaf** - assisted his Assassin Knights in awakening the inner Dragon Force and acquiring gnosis. Hasan's manual for his mystery school, the *Sargozast-i-Sayyid-na*, provided a step-by-step guide to the alchemical practices that would lead an aspiring knight to the summit of Kaf.

(continued...)

Hasan's alchemical Secrets of the Dragon Force were passed down to successive generations of Assassins, during which time they became known as the Teachings of the Resurrection. The greatest promoter of these teachings, and a fully enlightened Master of the Dragon Force in his own right, was the later Assassin **Grand Master Rashid al-din Sinan** of Syria. Sinan began his career as a common Assassin knight in Persia but eventually achieved enlightenment and an abundance of supernatural powers by adhering closely to Hasan's alchemy. After being sent to govern the Assassins' outpost in Syria, Sinan is said to have acquired the power to be able to **see into the past or future**, and for being able to go for indefinitely long periods without eating or drinking. His psychic ability also became legendary. When a letter was delivered to him it was said that Sinan would hold the unopened letter against his third eye for a moment and then promptly write down and dispatch a reply to the sender.

Through their encounters with Sinan and his knights the Templars, who had nearby castles in Syria, learned some of the Assassins' Secrets of the Force. The Templars felt an affinity with the Assassins since they were both renegade orders of knights aspiring to **Alchemy and Gnosis** while being ostensible members of a fundamentalist religion. Sinan, whom the Templars came to call the "Old Man of the Mountains," awed the Knights with his powers and they coveted his alchemy, which they eventually learned from both him and his knights, as well as from various other **Sufi** sects. As a compliment to what would eventually become the prodigious amount of Sufi teaching they acquired, the Knights Templar also inherited the gnostic teachings of the Johannite Gnostic Church which had been passed down to them from a series of grand masters beginning with John the Baptist, Jesus, John the Apostle, and Mary Magdalene. (See Nag Hammadí in Chapter 12.)

The Knight Templars would subsequently create their own Holy Grail mystery school tradition comprised of numerous levels of attainment.

(continued...)

The Dragon Force, the Knight Templars were to discover, was the true **"Holy Grail."** Although the Knights may have possessed certain physical objects which were ascribed the power of a Holy Grail, including the Holy Shroud, the Veil of Veronica, and perhaps even the cup that Jesus drank from during the Last Supper, they discovered from their Sufi teachers that **what made an object a Holy Grail was its accompanying Dragon Force** or Holy Spirit power. It was this Force that activated and drove the process of alchemy within a Knight and eventually opened him to his inner gnostic wisdom and supernatural power. Once awakened, the Force eventually destroys all impediments that keep one from knowing his divine self, including both the ego and limited concepts of reality.

The Templars' Secrets of the Force eventually passed into some of the Secret Societies of Europe, including the **Rosicrucians and Freemasons**, and for a while this wisdom survived in its purity. But it would eventually become grossly distorted, hidden or completely forgotten, and the era of the Dragon Knights would come to a grinding halt. But now, certain Templar organizations, like The International Order of Gnostic Templars, are making a concerted effort to resurrect the Dragon Knight wisdom of Egypt, Persia, and the early Templars.

So how did one become a Djedhi?

Djedhi Training

What has been kept secret, of course, is that the King's Chamber in the Great Pyramid was used to initiate the Djedhi-to-be and activate the Dragon Force. Also note that in much of the literature, serpent and dragon are used interchangeably. The following is a basic account of what an initiate would go thru in the King's Chamber (Great Pyramid) – after being approved by the pharaoh. [191]

The aspirant would serve an apprenticeship and for months and for years be observed and disciplined. Sweeping the temple floors, bathing twice a day, shaving the whole body, studying scriptures, and deciphering and memorizing the hieroglyphs pertaining to the teachings of Thoth-Hermes.

(continued…)

After years of study and purification, the initiate could be judged worthy to join the Order of the Djedhi. S/he would be led blindfolded to the paws of the **Great Sphinx** and as the Djedhi priest chanted some mysterious words, a door would magically fly open and the candidate would then be ushered into a hallway which ran under the Sphinx into the Great Pyramid. S/he was now ready for spiritual ascension.

Making their way up the passageway inside the **Great Pyramid**, they would enter the King's Chamber and all it contained was a large stone sarcophagus with its lid [nowadays missing] leaning against the wall. There were two star shafts aligned with the sacred 37° angle (the angle for "meeting the serpent" – one toward Orion and the other toward Alpha Draconis. Opposing star energies would come down these passageways and unite to create a balanced ambiance which was conducive to awakening the *Kundalini* fire within the initiate. The polarity union of the Chamber [electromagnetically] would precipitate a "zero point" of magnetism for spiritual awakening.

The initiate would enter the granite sarcophagus and lie down. The stone lid was placed on the tomb [it had an air hole] and the candidate was now totally sealed off from the world. The priest would declare the initiate officially dead and leave him/her there for three days while reciting the sacred words of Thoth-Hermes [no doubt from the Emerald Tablets – see chapters on Serpent Wisdom]. The dynamic fire of the *Kundalini* was expected to rise up in the candidate.

If the initiate was ill-prepared, the process might end in mental, emotional or physical pain and the process would terminate prematurely. If successful, the candidate would be 'reborn' and get out of the sarcophagus with Serpent Wisdom and Power. The new Djedhi was now known as a **Kepher** or "Arisen One." Other priests and the pharaoh would be standing around the 'reborn' priest or priestess, welcome them, and present them with the symbol of the order, the golden band of wisdom which was honorably worn over the third eye, called the **Ureaus** (see below).

The **Ureaus** signified that the wearer was enlightened and had some Serpent Power. As shown below, it was again the sign of the serpent and was also a reference to **Uadjet**, the Serpent Goddess, who was also codified in hieroglyphics as a snake:

See earlier use of this symbol under Ankh. Uadjet or **Wadjet**, was the goddess of lower Egypt and **Winged Serpent** protector of the pharaoh.

The **Ureaus** looked similar to this:

or

Relevant Aspects of Egypt

There are a few remaining items pertinent to Egypt to help understand the Olmec-Mayan connection in the next chapter. Ancient Egypt was called **Kush** and included the Kingdom of Nubia… It was also called **K'met.**[192]

Nubians

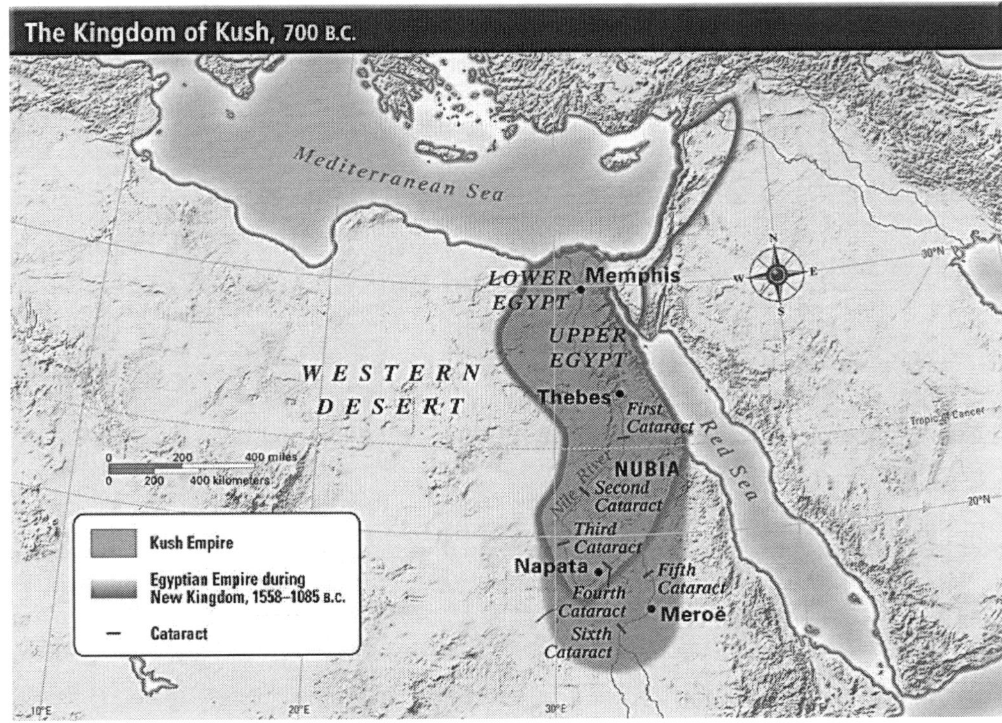

The Nubians were Blacks and had their own pyramids (new and old shown):

And the Egyptian reliefs show the following:

Contrary to some authors who have found Blacks among the Egyptian murals, they were not always slaves. In fact, it has been theorized by credible Egyptian scholars that Cleopatra could have been a Nubian princess. As evidence…

There was an ancient queen of Nubia called **Queen Tiye**:

Queen Tiye ruled the Amarna Dynasty during 1390 BC – 1353 BC (37 years).

She became the Great Royal Wife of the Egyptian pharaoh **Amenhotep III**. She was the mother of Akhenaten and grandmother of Tutankhamun… Her mummy was identified as "The Elder Lady" found in the tomb of Amenhotep II (crypt: KV35 in 2010.[193]

BingImages/Black Queen Tiye

Be aware that in southern Egypt, and connected to Ethiopia, was a Kingdom of Nubia (see map above) run by Blacks. Nubian Egypt was called **Kush.**

It is a fact that there was a Kingdom of Nubia.
It is a fact that the BBC said it found Cleopatra's sister's tomb --

> Queen Cleopatra VII was a descendant of Ptolemy, the Macedonian general who ruled Egypt after Alexander the Great. She was Greek. But remains of the queen's sister **Princess Arsinoe**, found in Ephesus, Turkey, indicate that her mother had an "African" skeleton. [194]
> [i.e., its features were African.]

It is a fact that Cleopatra hated her sister (and probably ordered her mysterious death).

It is also a fact that there was a Nubian/Egyptian **King Piye** who was the first of the so-called Black pharaohs, a series of Nubian kings who ruled over all of Egypt for three-quarters of a century as that country's 25th dynasty.[195]

Of particular note is the following National Geographic picture from Feb. 2008:

Left:
Artist's likeness of King Piye of the Nubian Kingdom.

Of note are the 2 **kings' headdresses** – important when the Olmecs are examined in the next chapter.

As a matter of fact, the 'helmet' concept was pretty popular with another **King Piankhy** (about 715 BC.):

Ancient Egypt: a black Sudanese (or Kushite) king from south of Egypt, named Piankhy (right), invaded and conquered most of Egypt and founded Dynasty 25 of the Pharaohs. (pinterest.com)

To be sure, it is not proven anywhere that the Cleopatra was Black, or even Egyptian 'brown' -- yet scholars are intrigued by the possibility:

> Many scholars believe that Cleopatra's paternal grandmother was a concubine. That woman's background has been assumed to be either **Alexandrian or Nubian**. She may have been ethnically Egyptian, and she may have had a heritage which we'd today call "Black."
> In some Renaissance art, Cleopatra is portrayed as dark-skinned, a "negress" in the terminology of that time. But those artists were also not eyewitnesses, and their artistic interpretation may have been based on trying to distinguish Cleopatra's "otherness" or their own assumptions about Africa and Egypt.
> But remains of the queen's sister Princess **Arsinoe**, found in Ephesus, Turkey, indicate that her mother had an "African" skeleton....
> Egypt is an African nation. This is fact. So why is it so surprising that Cleopatra, the queen of Egypt, could be African?
> Today scientists are stating that Arsinoe and Cleopatra, who were at least half sisters, probably shared the same mother. And this mother was, at least in part, African. And not just African, they believe she was sub-Saharan African.... [and] that's code for Black ya'll.[196]

Cleopatra Art

Ancientartsofegypt.com

BingImages/Black Cleopatra

Lastly, it is also a fact that we just don't know for sure what her racial aspect was.

Miscellaneous Notes:

It is also a fact that **the Sycamore tree** was considered holy by the Egyptians as it "stood on the threshold of life and death, connecting the two worlds."[197]

The Tree of Life, also known as the **World Tree**, is an ageless symbol of eternal aliveness and often reflects an interconnectedness of all life, and often contains images of birds, serpents and various animals germane to the particular culture. In some cases, as in Japan in the Shinto religion, the sacred trees are marked with pieces of paper symbolizing lightning bolts and when a family member dies, s/he is portrayed as a branch on the tree.

The Two Arks

While we're at it, let's disclose something else of interest.

The **Great Sphinx** originally did not look like it does today – it did not have a man's face – Pharaoh Khafre allegedly had it recarved to suit him. And it is not the body of a lion; it is that of a dog, or even a jackal. It reposed next to the **Temple of Anubis** (still about 200' away) and that is why it is the statue of Anubis.

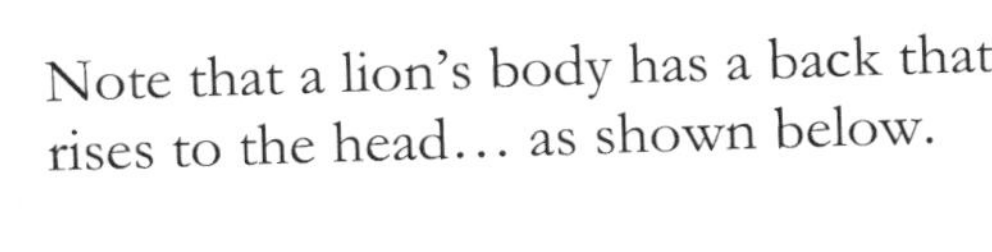

Note that a lion's body has a back that rises to the head… as shown below.

(credit: Wikipedia: Anubis)

Now look at the Sphinx again: **It has a flat back.**

(credit: Bing Images: tourwithjack.blogspot.co.il)

So you say that when they **recarved the head area (and they did)**, they leveled the back… perhaps, but why is the Temple of Anubis right nearby? And consider this statue found in the tomb of Tutankhamen:

Note the "dog" on the pedestal and the ears, the paws are forward…. And of note also are the wooden poles to carry it… similar to the Ark of the Covenant.

(credit: Wikipedia: Anubis: photo by Harry Burton, 1922.)

And lastly, a rather fancy version of what must have been a rather plain Ark of the Covenant:

(credit: Bing Images: thetrumpet.com)

It makes one wonder whether the statue of Anubis was also holy and not to be touched as it was carried by poles, or was that just a convenient way to carry it? Could it have looked more like this (below), with the **angel wings acting as antennae** to receive the microwave signal from the Anunnaki who had radio, radar, microwave, shortwave….?

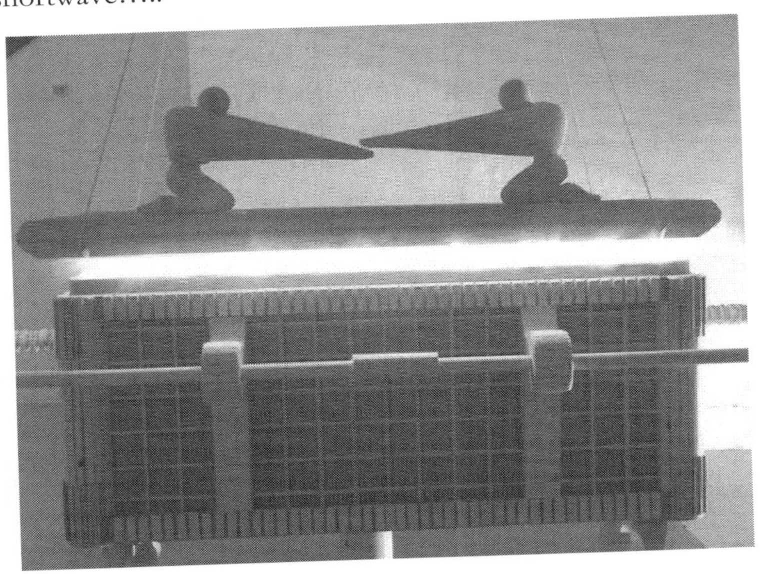

Before leaving this topic, it should be said that the Ark would not communicate with the Hebrew Priest unless he was wearing the **Ephod**.... the 12-stone chestplate.

This is in no way meant to be disrespectful to the Hebrews, or their tradition. The Ark did not speak verbally to the Priest, but one or more of the 12 Ephod stones would resonate with the signal sent thru the Ark, and if the Priest had asked a question, the answer would be given as a yes, no, maybe, ask later.... Any one of 12 pre-arranged signals pertaining to the particular resonance or vibration of the stone(s). (Obviously, the Ark transmitted his voice to whomever was listening downstairs... see next: below the Rock.)

Be aware that all gems have a particular vibration rate.

(credit: Bing Images)

Anunnaki in Israel

With all due respect to the Israeli people and traditions, this section is offered based on (1) what the late Zechariah Sitchin said about Mt. Moriah, and (2) the obvious connection with the Trilithons in Baalbek. There is no intention to denigrate the Holy Mount.

Next we come to the **Knights Templar** who ostensibly were tasked with protecting pilgrims to and from the Holy Land but the real interaction occurred when the Knights took lodging in a wing of the palace of the reigning **King Baudouin** of Jerusalem. They learned many things from the **Sufis** who occupied another wing of the palace, the Knights became aware of several legends in the area, and what might be buried under **Mt. Moriah** (aka The Temple Mount) – significant to Jews, Christians and Muslims. When the Knights learned some basic Arabic, they could explore some of the writings and discussed these things with their Sufi teachers. So they carefully excavated and explored...

In fact, they would have seen the huge **Trilithons** under the Temple Mount which are there to this day and are almost as big as those in Baalbek. They were cut and moved using the same style and technique(s) as in Baalbek.

Under Temple Mount: Foundation Stones

The Master Course Stone: Located between Warren's Gate and Wilson's Arch (which is located under the Gate of the Chain).
This stone is 44 feet long, 11.5 feet high, and 15 feet wide. It is estimated to weigh 570-630 tons. This stone is the master course. It was used to stabilize the smaller stones under it. It sits 20 feet above the Herodian street level and 33 feet above the bedrock. The master course extends to the left of the edge of this photo and past the right edge. The small stones setting above were used to fill in where the Romans chipped away at it in 70 AD, attempting to dismantle the whole Western Wall. They reached the level of this Master Course Stone and stopped. **The rectangular holes** in the stone were bored centuries later to help secure plaster to the wall in order to create an underground cistern to hold water for the homes above.[198]

(All 4 pictures [this + next 3 pp] credit: above footnote: www.generationword.com)

You should be asking yourself, Who moved these huge granite blocks weighing 600 tons? Certainly not the local natives who lived here 2000+ years ago. Also consider that the **Master Course Stone** did not have the "handles" shown when it was first laid in place. And note that the stone below the Master Course Stone is also very large.

One can see for himself that **Herodian stones** [7 layers in Western Wall, next 2 pix] are much smaller and without pride of workmanship when compared to the enormous megalithic courses making up the foundations of the Temple Mount. [199]

The stonework goes quite deep. The 62' of the diagram is the Wailing Wall area.

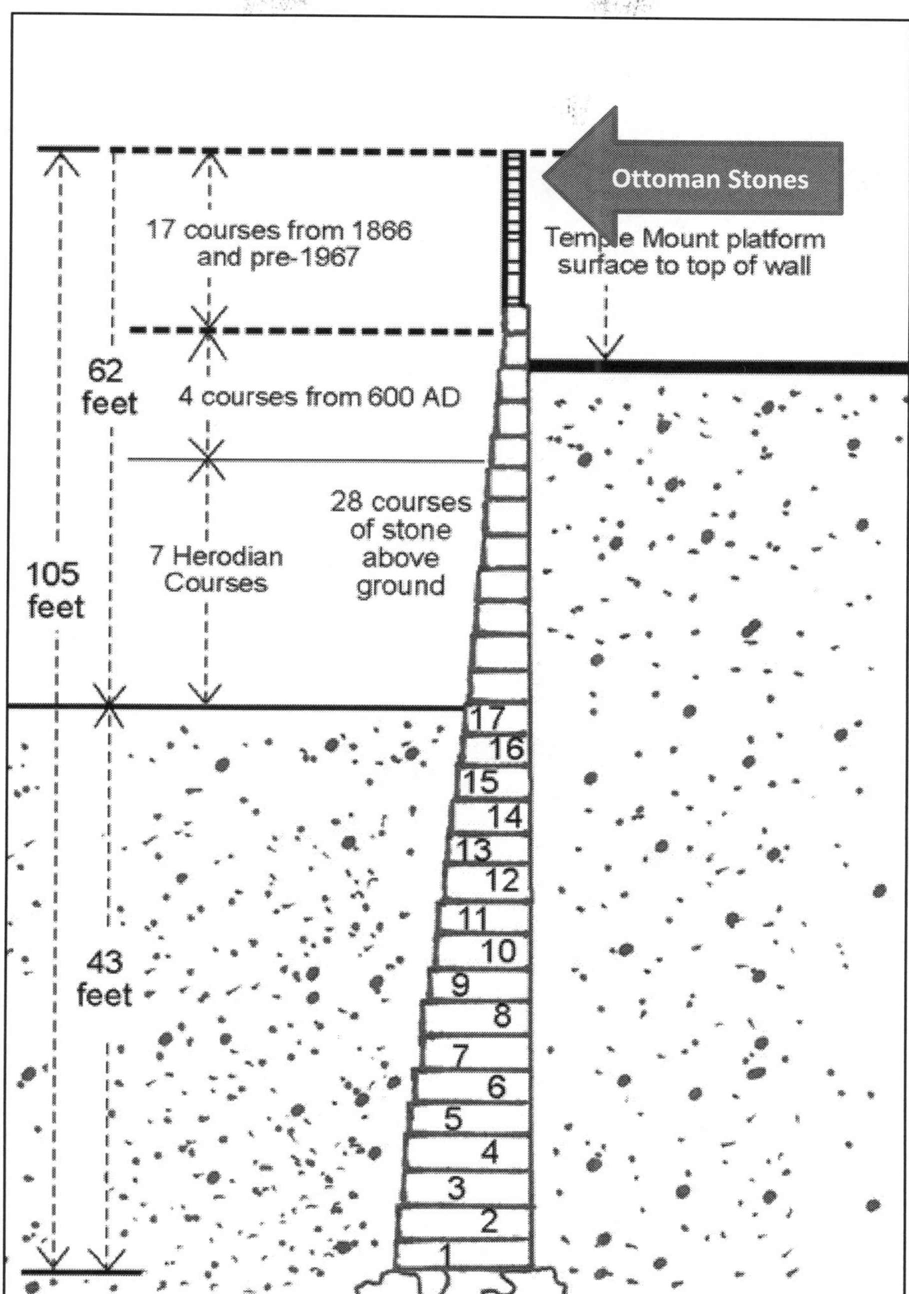

17 Ashlars still remain below ground, and they are also large.

To clarify-- Much stonework has been done over the ages as shown in the picture below:

Templar Excavations

The Knights Templar excavated a lot under the Temple Mount (before the place was off-limits) and history has said reportedly that they found something valuable. In later years, their tunnels and holes were walled up.

The point of this is that somebody with the technology placed the lowest level stones and reinforced the Temple Mount for reasons the archeologists would like to explore… and the Muslims will not allow. To see what the Temple Mount was used for, one must be able to see inside the **Dome of the Rock** – the large Rock inside and the stairs leading down under the Rock. For that we turn to Zechariah Sitchin and one of his excursions into the Dome of the Rock.

He made it down the stairs into the first room and was almost spotted and so could not go further down into the second room. [200] It has been said for decades that there is another chamber below the first one that the authorities now admit to, but is still off-limits.

A feature in National Geographic suggested that the [area] beneath the **cave** may be another chamber hiding the Ark of the Covenant: "Knocking on the floor of the cave under the Muslim Dome of the Rock shrine elicits a resounding hollow echo, [but] no one has ever seen this alleged [2nd] chamber....Famed 19th-century British explorers Charles Wilson and Sir Charles Warren could neither prove nor disprove the existence of a [2nd] hollow **chamber below the cave**. They believed the sound reportedly heard by visitors was simply an echo in a small fissure beneath the floor." [201] [emphasis added]

Rock Foundation Stone

Under the **Sakhrah** / Foundation Stone, in the heart of the Dome of the Rock in Jerusalem, is the cave allegedly created during Muhammad's ascension.

The top of the Rock looks like this (cuts, channels and a 2' wide hole which allowed cables and a metal tube supporting a telemetry dish all feeding to the control room below):

(credit: Bing Images: Israelandyou.com)

Going down the stairs , one comes to a chamber ("the cave" mentioned above) with rugs and what appears to be another part of **a massive granite wall** (2nd picture). **Stairs** are to the right in both the drawing and the picture.

(credit: Bing Images: roots2now.wordpre4ss.com)

(credit: Bing Images: jerusalem.com)

According to Sitchin, standing in the shrine, looking at the Rock:

> I began to mull over how I could manage to achieve what I was really after: to find a way to go under the sacred rock. Where a **cavelike space** exists. Virtually every traveler and explorer in past centuries reported and depicted such a cavity, and some suggested that under that one there was yet <u>another</u> [2nd] hidden one. [202] [emphasis added]

And then he provides drawings of what others have seen or heard about, including (first) the stairwell and Rock:

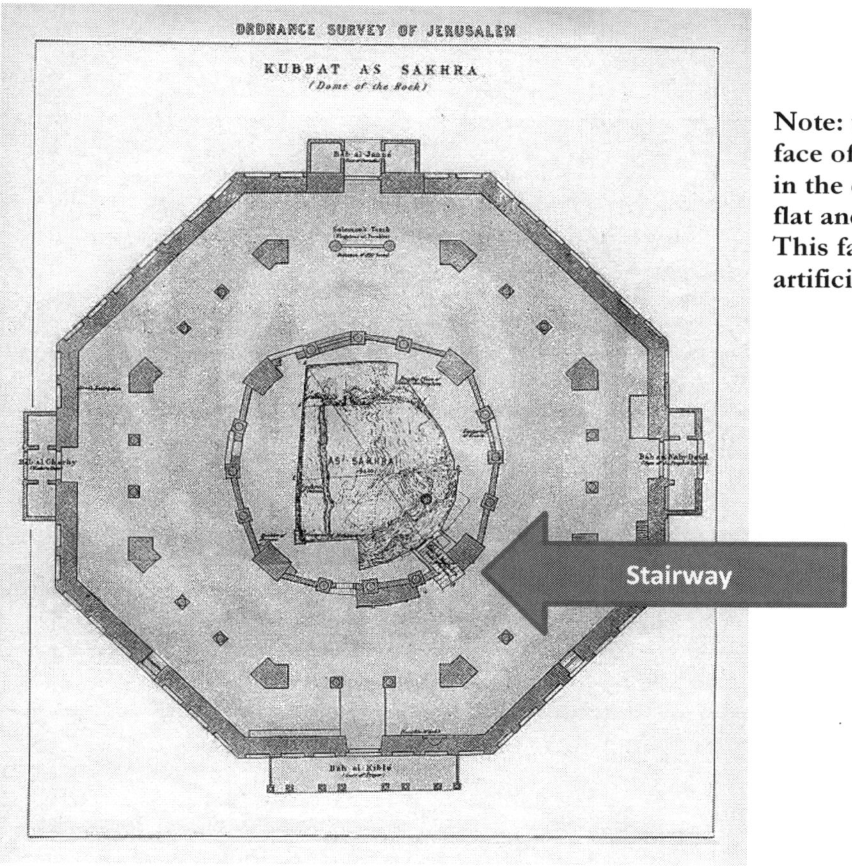

Note: the Western face of the Rock (left in the diagram) is cut flat and straight. This face was artificially created.

(credit: Bing Images: centuryone.com)

And then he provides a side view of what is said to be there. The bottom drawing is the most likely as Sitchin explains his investigation (following the drawings):

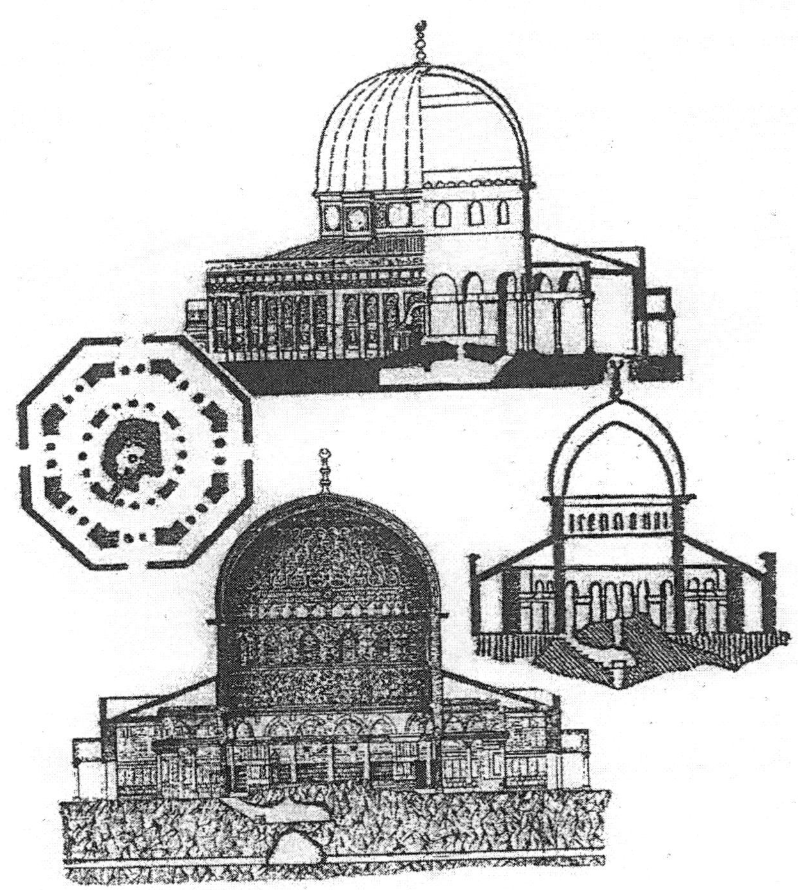

Figure 151.

(credit: Zechariah Sitchin [203])

Sitchin received an invite from a **Wakf** authority on The Dome of the Rock and was asked to return to the Dome by himself, as the Dr. Mahmoud Salameh wanted to show him something special about the Rock. And a woman was not allowed on this visit, so he comes with Wally, a friend, and meets Mahmoud at the entrance at 10 a.m. as agreed. His account follows: [204]

> There was hardly anyone else inside, or at least we didn't notice others. We circled the sacred Rock and took numerous pictures…. trying to capture the cuts and angles on the face of the rock…. we came to the stairs…
> *Now*! I said to Wally ….[and] while Wally stood guard, I rushed down the stairs, my heart palpitating…. In a flash I was down the
>
> (continued...)

steps and into the cave.... The place was dimly lit. Light came thru the perfectly **circular hole** bored thru the rock.... The rest of the rock surface above smooth areas and some niched ones. The floor under my feet was covered with carpets, frustrating my attempts to locate an opening farther down. There seemed to be an opening in one side of the cavern, overhung with a cloth curtain.

That's IT! I thought to myself....

But as I moved toward it, I tripped over seated women all dressed in black clothing and veiled... they literally blocked my way to the opening in the rocky wall.... I had no flashlight with me.... I just stood there motionless.

Then I heard Wally's voice *Quick, someone is coming!* I rushed back up the stairs in time to be back up when Mahmoud and a guard approached us. "You must leave!" they said....

Wally and I left.

Al-Sakhra, Foundation Rock

Before leaving this part, it is significant that Sitchin said in many of his books that the Mt. Moriah location was used as a **Command Center** for the spaceflights in and out of the Middle East area. Looking at the top surface of the Rock, it is strangely carved and contains straight lines carved into it plus the 2' wide hole cut thru seven feet of it that looks like a laser bored it – perfectly round and perfectly smooth. It has been suggested that the grooves cut into the Rock's face might have channeled some wires or conduits leading to a possible control room below it.

The point of this is to give some credence to Sitchin's stand that a long time ago, the Rock was used for something technological.

The map (left) shows the alleged spaceports at Baalbek and Mt. Sinai Spaceport (tip of Saudi Arabia). In the middle is Jerusalem as the Command Center.
(credit: Bing Images: Crystallinks.com)

And to be more credible, Sitchin found a cylinder seal that recorded the Anunnaki trip into the solar system, where Earth is the 7th planet and Pluto was #1.

And, amazing but true, a circular tablet that can be seen on display in the British Museum in London, describes in eight segments various aspects of **space travel** between the Anunnaki's planet Nibiru and the Seventh Planet (Earth) Fig. 122 in The 12th Planet.

One segment in particular, enlarged here for clarity, (Fig. 123 in The 12th Planet) shows (and states) that the route traveled by Enlil ("Lord of the Command") entailed **passage by seven planets**; it also called for a route diversion between the planet DILGAN (Jupiter) and APIN (Mars):

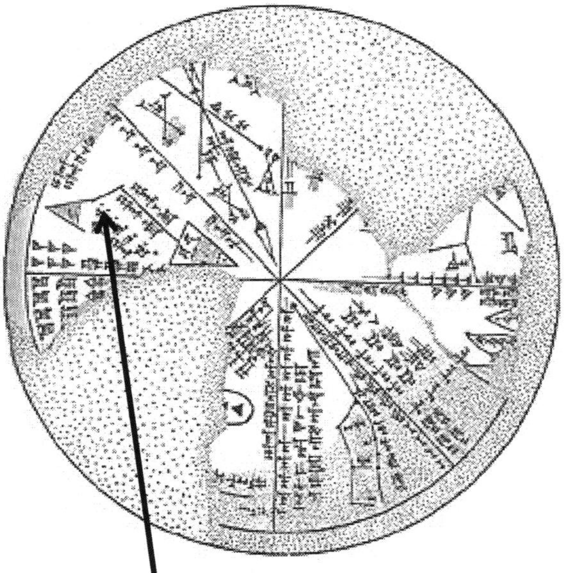

Fig 122

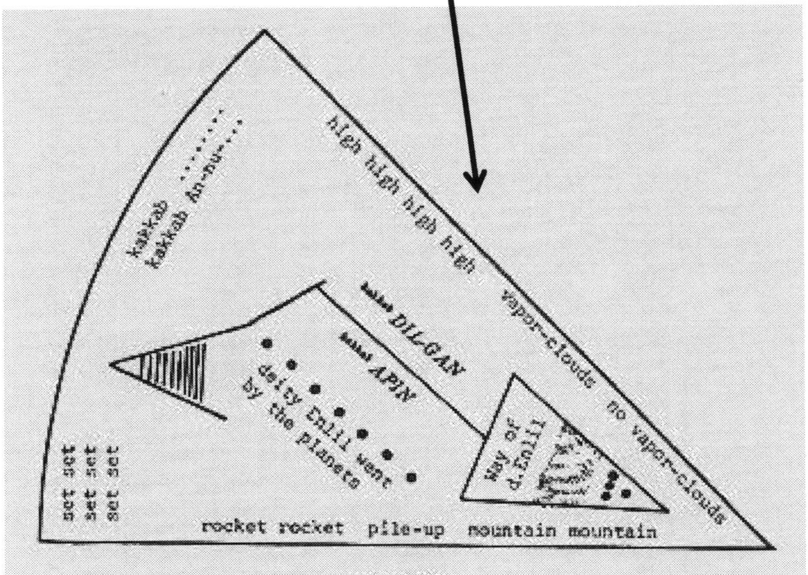

Fig. 123

(credit text & pix: http://www.sitchin.com/nasa_looking.htm)

And when they got to Earth, they keyed in on the **Great Pyramid** (a sighting reference), and then used the flight path Sitchin suggests. [205] Ground control was on/in Mt. Moriah.

At any rate, the Templars must have seen the Dome of the Rock, too, as it was finished in 691 AD, and yet there is nothing documented about the Rock's original markings and legendary use, or if it was, time and the Church have erased it. The Crusaders captured Jerusalem in 1099 AD and the Dome of the Rock was given to the Augustinians, who turned it into a church while the Al-Aqsa Mosque became a royal palace. The Knights Templar, who believed the Dome of the Rock was the site of the Temple of Solomon, later set up their headquarters in the Al-Aqsa Mosque (home of the Sufis) adjacent to the Dome for much of the 12th century.

So much for Templar strength, Jerusalem was recaptured by **Saladin** on 2 October 1187, and the Dome of the Rock was reconsecrated as a Muslim shrine.

Lately, Tomography has shown that there are **chambers and tunnels** in sections of the Mount that have been walled up, and are currently inaccessible. Archeological excavations have been brought to a halt when the Muslims discovered current-day explorations and all work under the Mount has now stopped.

Summary

While there is not a direct connection between Greece and Egypt, except thru their common gods, there is a third party connection that influenced both countries … and several more cultures in the area. The Serpent Wisdom teachings indeed did migrate all around the globe and some went secret and some, as has been shown, were in plain sight on temple walls – but their meaning was obscure to the uninitiated.

The sacred tree imagery and healing also made its way around the planet, although in some cases the "tree" was shown as an ankh or a design woven into a carpet. In all cases the real meaning and teachings that empowered the initiates were closely guarded from the public, for without proper training in the hands of a master, who had the discipline and had proved worthy of correctly using the sacred knowledge, the ability could be misused. Shapeshifting, turning water to wine and lead to gold, and walking on water were not abilities that the average person could be trusted with.

And the Church wanted it that way. So as a result, the growing Christian movement considered Serpent Wisdom a threat to its very existence, denigrated the Serpent, and the rest is history…The common person in today's world does not know there is more, and some who do know, consider Serpent Wisdom "witchy" stuff because it has been 'branded' that way. A later chapter will evaluate the esoteric teachings.

The next two chapters will cover the major bases in the Americas, and the last part of the Global Tour covers the general dispersion, a miscellaneous chapter that just gives mention of minor spots around Earth where the teachings also went.

Chapter 6: The Americas, Part I

Moving west from Greece, India, China and Egypt, we come to the Americas. While Mesopotamia and the Anunnaki were closer to Greece and Asia, and even Scandinavia, and thus an influence seems easier to imagine, the Anunnaki were airborne and traveling to Latin America, Peru, or to the USA was no problem for them.

This book has not addressed where the Egyptians came from (Atlantis?), nor will it attempt to dig into the origins of the Indian race, nor the Latino race. That is beyond the purview of this book. The main focus has been where Man's **civilization** came from, who helped him, and what are some of the common teachings, structures, and beliefs that have been spread around the globe. If the Celts, Vikings and Hindus didn't get your attention, the Mayas, Aztecs and Incas are up next.

Anunnaki in Central America

Whereas Huang Di was the god in China who came and went by dragon, Thoth, Marduk, and friends came and went in their dragons from Mesopotamia to Egypt. If they could fly from Mesopotamia to Scandinavia, or India, they could easily fly to the Americas. And they could not call themselves Thoth, Enki, or Krishna, names that would have no meaning. They would accept the names given to them by the natives in the New World… Quetzalcoatl (Aztec), Kukulcan (Maya), and Viracocha (Peru/Inca) … in most cases the natives described them as **white men with beards**.

Relief on temple wall… Mayans did not have beards so this is not one of their people.

The beard is under the chin (left), and note that the features are not Mayan – no Mayan nose or slant to the forehead.

Jadite head of bearded Quetzalcoatl
This head is in the *Musee de l'Homme*, Paris, France

Aztec statue of bearded Quetzalcaotl
Both photographs are from Thor Hyerdahl's *American Indians in the Pacific*

Origin of the Aztecs

The Aztecs followed the Mayans, time-wise, but their legend about their origins is so significant as to partially answer where the Actecs, Toltecs, Olmecs and Mayans came from, so they are examined first.

The Aztecs were not well-liked wherever they went due to their ritual of human sacrifice and so they kept moving, all the while taking captives from neighboring tribes and sacrificing them to the god of the Sun so that the Sun would continue to rise each day. The Aztecs, who called themselves **Mexica** (pron: Meh-SHICA), wandered farther and farther finally making their way south into Central America. They were forced to stay on the move as anywhere they went, their reputation would accompany them and neighboring tribes, as they passed thru an area, would band together and attack them. The Aztec wanted a peaceful and protected home.

Allegedly they originated in North America above the Colorado River (perhaps associated with the **Anasazi**, "the ancient ones"). While migrating, their shaman had a dream that advised him to build their city when they saw an eagle sitting on a nopal (cactus) with a serpent in its mouth. After several years of wandering and not seeing the special 'sign', they wound up around today's Mexico City and what is today called Lake Texcoco where they saw the eagle. The result was recorded on the Mexican flag:

The later name of the country, Mexico, is a morphing of the Aztec word **"Mexica"** where the 'x' changed to an "h" pronunciation from the Aztec "sh" so it is spoken as "MEH – hico."

Tenochtitlan was built on the shallow lake about 1325 AD and in Nahuatl, a language the Aztecs shared with the Toltecs whom they admired, allegedly means "among the prickly pears [nopal cactus]"... The Aztec are said to have been so impressed by the Toltec when they saw **Teotihuacan** (about 50 miles north of today's Mexico City) that they adopted some Toltec customs as well as more of the Toltec language, **Nahuatl**. [206]

Teotihuacan from the Pyramid of the Moon

What is more relevant to this review is that the Aztec had a tradition that they originally came from the East, from **Aztlan** – and that is the source of the word Aztec. If the Spaniards had not totally destroyed Tenochtitlan and the few Aztec written records (similar to what they did to the Mayan codices) we might know more about their exact point of origin. And we might find that the Aztecs and Mayas had a common point of origin far to the east…

Atlantis Revisited

According to the Mayan Dresden Codex, there is a hieroglyphic record of the picture of the trip from the place the Mayans called **Atzantiha:**[207]

Figure 1.3. A page from the Mayan Dresden Codex that shows the god Itzamna sailing from the east, where the Maya were said to have come from. They called this place Atzantiha in their Mayan language. It is also worth noting that Itzamna is the symbol of the great Mayan master teacher. His wisdom was the basis for the construction of Ch'iich'en Itzam (usually spelled Chichén Itzá); this initiatory knowledge is manifested in the forms of these temples of the Yucatán.

(credit: The 8 Calendars of the Maya, p. 13)

Elsewhere there is a picture of the source of the Aztec and Mayan migration:[208]

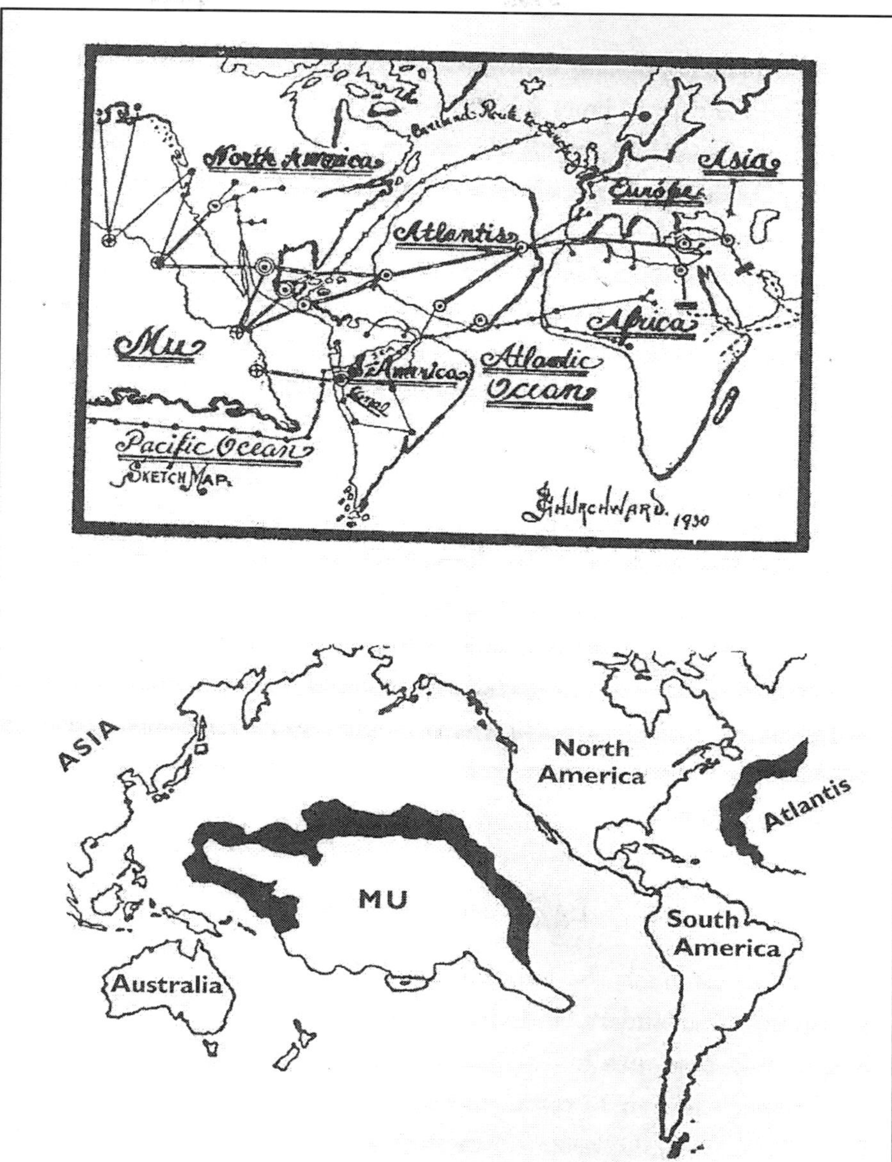

Figure 1.5. James Churchward shows that two continents once existed and later disappeared, having been swallowed by the Pacific and Atlantic oceans. These continents were called Mu (or Lemuria) and Atlantis. As one can see from Churchward's map, the people of Mu were connected to the Maya, Nahua, Hopi, Inca, Aymara, et al., while at the same time all these peoples were connected to Atlantis, which in turn was related to the Egyptians, Ititians, Babylonians, Hindustanis, et al.

(credit: The 8 Calendars of the Maya, p. 17)

From the above, we can reasonably reckon that the earlier Aztecs escaped the **Atlantean cataclysm** and escaped into southeast America, probably around Florida or Georgia. Atlantis was said to have two main components to their civilization: the peaceful Followers of the One, and the warlike Might Makes Right group – the priest/scientists who misused the crystal **Firestone**. The latter's aggressive behavior would have forced them as Mexica to constantly migrate westward. Some went east to Egypt, and also became the Guanches (**Canary Islands**) and the **Basques** (Pyrenees between France and Spain)—the Basque language is very unique and does not match any known linguistic group. (Basques are examined in Appendix B.)

The Mayans, on the other hand are thought to principally come from the more peaceful and spiritual **Lemuria (Mu)** and also formed the basis of the Polynesians and perhaps they also migrated westward into what is now Australia and Southeast Asia, including **India**.

As was shown in Fig. 1.3 (above picture), the Mayans revere **Itzama** credited with establishing writing and civilization to the Mayas. **Hunab K'u** is the main god of the Universe for the Mayans, Nahuas and Mexica.[209] (It is respectfully submitted that the 2 gods correlate well with Ningishzidda and Anu, respectively from Sumeria.)

Quetzalcoatl

Another god common to the Toltecs, thus the Aztecs, and later the Mayans, was called **Quetzalcoatal**. Quetzalcoatl was the god's name to the Aztecs, whereas among the Mayan he was also called **Kukulcan**, and among the Incas, he was called **Viracocha.** We know from the late Zechariah Sitchin's work that it was really Ningishzidda (Enki's son) so in this case we know what his real name was, but we still do not know what the Anunnaki called themselves – "Anunnaki" is the name given the Star Visitors by the Sumerians. It means "From heaven to Earth" just as Quetzalcoatl means "Feathered Serpent."

> **Quetzal** is the name of a green jungle bird with long plumage.
> **Coatl** is the Nahuatl word for 'serpent.'

Quetzalcoatl was venerated in Teotihuacan by the **Toltecs** – remember they preceded both the Aztecs and the Maya – and had his own pyramid dedicated to him, standing between the Pyramid of the Moon and that of the Sun. He was thought to have been the founder of the Toltec civilization. Quetzalcoatl was related to gods of the wind, of the planet Venus, of the dawn, of merchants and of arts, crafts and knowledge. He was also the patron god of the Aztec priesthood, of learning and knowledge. Quetzalcoatl was one of several important gods in the Aztec pantheon, along with the gods Tlaloc, Tezcatlipoca, and Huitzilopochtli.

Quetzalcoatl's pyramid in Teotihuacan

A closer inspection reveals serpent décor on his pyramid (similar to that on the Mayan pyramid at Chichen Itzá):

In addition to the Quetzalcoatl serpent heads, also pictured is **Tlaloc**, the rain god (with circles for eyes)... reminiscent of a Kachina mask.

Tezcatlipoca was considered Quetzalcoatl's brother, both proactive supporters of the humans, and Huitzilopochtli was known as the antagonist in the ancient stories – promoting human sacrifice which Quetzalcoatl told the Aztecs and Mayans to stop.

Teotihuacan's layout is significant…

Veneration of Orion

At this point, it is interesting to note the similarity between the pyramids at Giza, the pyramids at Teotihuacan, and the three stars in the constellation of Orion's Belt.

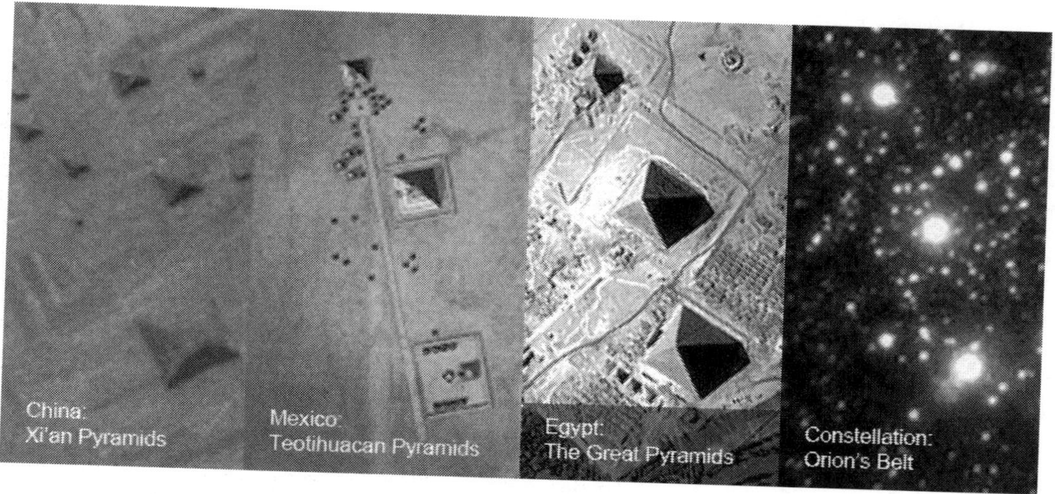

In addition, the layout of some pyramids in China (above, far left) also matches that of the three stars in Orion's Belt. And a further shock comes when we find that the layout of the **Hopi villages** of the 1st, 2nd and 3rd Mesas also match the Orion Belt stars (Chapter 7 Orion-Hopi Connection):

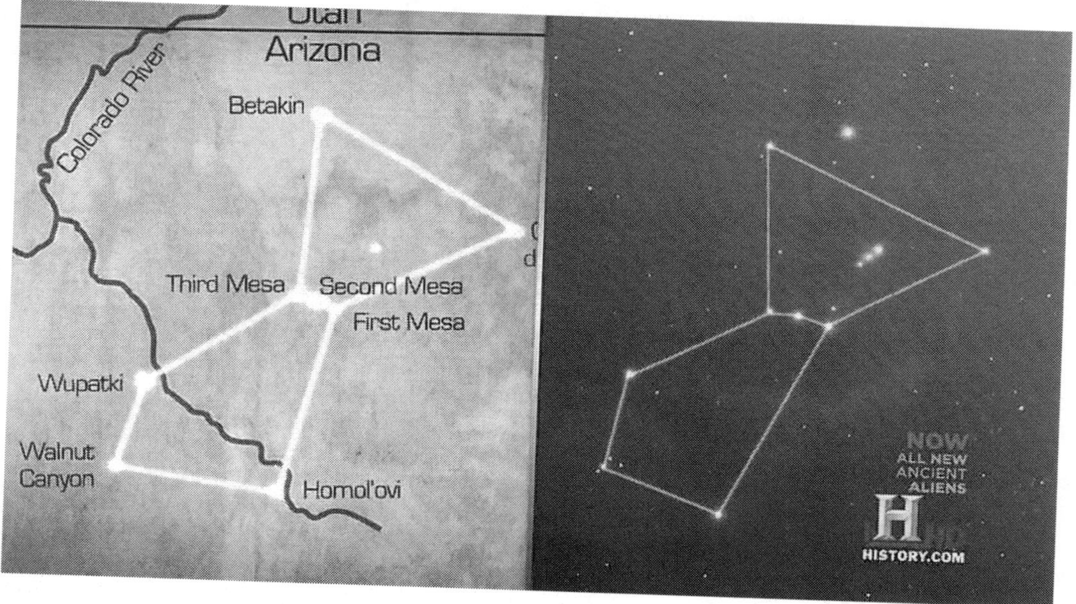

Clearly Orion was significant enough to the ancient peoples that they would build structures replicating the three-star layout in Orion's Belt with that unique offset. In fact, both Orion and the Pleiades were significant to ancient peoples… suggesting a connection with their interface with the gods who gave them education in agriculture, medicine, writing, and other basics.

There must have been a significant reason for several unrelated cultures to build with the "Orion Design" in their layout, and it turns out that the beings from Orion were among those who visited Man and helped him. It has been theorized that the Anunnaki might have been from Orion (not Nibiru) since the Orion Empire is reptilian and so were the original Anunnaki (see VEG, Ch. 3).

As will be seen in Chapter 8, Dr Susan Martinez substantiates the proposition of this book by saying that there were **multiple Gardens of Eden**, and the Orion group was just one of the players in that scenario – Huang Di and NüWa played a part in Man's creation in China, and Viracocha was operative in South America, and thus perhaps Lemuria/Mu as there was a landbridge (p. 389) between Mu and Peru. The *Popul Vuh* of the Mayans relates another creation story which is similar to that of Mesopotamia (and the Anunnaki.

There were **multiple types of humans**, from Homo *erectus*, to Heidelberg Man, to Neanderthal, to Denisovans, to the Hobbits in Indonesia (Homo *floresiensis*), Cro-Magnon and lately, Homo *sapiens*. Since Evolution has been largely discounted (there is no 'missing link') and humans show a design, it is clear that there must have been a Designer, and in fact, **multiple designers** across the millennia.

In addition, the **pyramid structure** was also found among different locales – suggesting a common source:

Teotihuacan Pyramid of the Moon

Mesopotamian Ziggurat

… and the pyramid took many variations in style…

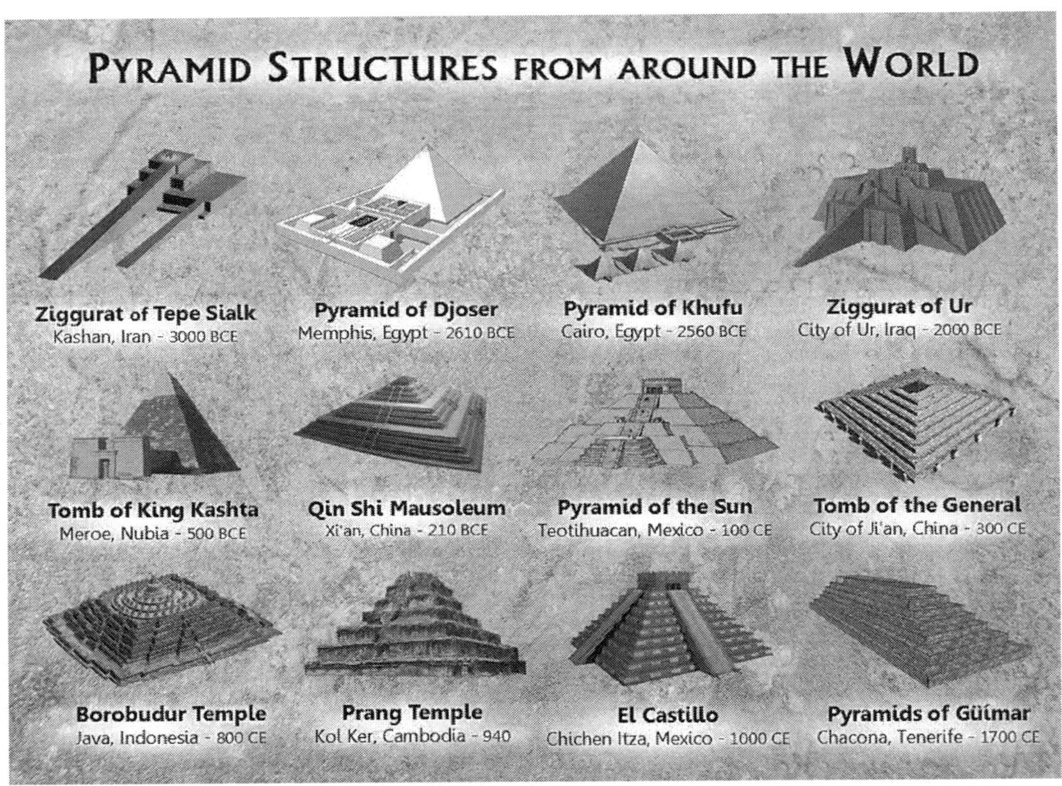

(credit: Bing Images)

Not all pyramids were used as tombs. The Great Pyramid of Giza was never a tomb; it was used as a Djedhi initiation center, in addition to generating power that was broadcast to places like **Göbekli Tepe** for *kundalini* awakening (see later section on Göbekli Tepe).

In fact, the tops of some pyramids were ideal for landing a skycraft and the depositing or admitting a god from/to the craft – out of the reach of the humans. And this is not so farfetched an idea when you consider how steep the pyramid steps were – as if to stop or slow the humans down from easily ascending the pyramid (esp. in Central Mexico).

Consider the following possibility with the Teotihuacan pyramid in Mexico: consider that the top of many pyramids was broad and flat enough to land a skycraft.

… or at Baalbek…

(credit: Ancient Aliens, Season 11, Episode 1.)

And again, if it was a long way to the top (above picture) the humans would have a hard time getting to the top just whenever they wanted to… and if the sides were really steep, the gods could control access to the top (as below)…

View from the top of the pyramid at Chichen Itza

Aztec Calendar

The Aztecs had a calendar which consisted of a 365-day year and a **260-day** ritual cycle. These two cycles together formed a 52-year "century." In addition, it showed the current world and also the 4 worlds before this one. Each world was called a sun, and each sun had its own species of inhabitants. The Aztecs believed that they were in **the fifth sun** (the Hindu and Navajo have a similar story!) and like all of the suns before them they would also eventually perish due to their own imperfections.

Every fifty two years was marked out because they believed that fifty two years was a **life cycle** and at the end of any given life cycle the gods could take away all that they have and destroy the world.[210]

> Most people then didn't live beyond 52 years anyway as life was arduous and dangerous (war).

The Aztec Calendar

Note: that is not a tongue sticking out of the center face: it is a flint knife, a reminder symbolizing sacrifice. See truer picture (next pages)...

There are 4 'boxes' in the center = the four worlds. The first ring moving outward has the 20 day names, and the next ring has 36 divisions (probably decorative since they are all the same pattern), and then on the outermost ring are 2 sets of 10 markers. The top box (at 12 o'clock) is significant, according to the following picture:

> Many times on TV, programs will show the Aztec Calendar and incorrectly call it the Mayan Calendar because, as will be seen in the next section, the Mayan Calendar is just 3 wheels and does not look like a calendar.

Figure 6.1. This illustration is from the Aztec Calendar, or the Stone of the Sun. The original calendar is in the National Museum of Anthropology in Mexico City. This calendar, made of stone, weighs 22 tons and measures 3.70 by 3.90 meters. As one can see from this illustration, there are 13 intervals in the upper square part and 20 intervals in the circle part. The carvings are the hieroglyphs of the Nahua people. If we multiply these two numbers, 13 x 20 = 260, the result is a new indicator for days, intervals, degrees, and so forth—thus demonstrating that both the Mayan and the Nahua peoples used the same sacred calendar.

(credit: The 8 Calendars of the Maya, p. 83)

13 days (dots) times 20 months (outer ring) = 260 days ritual calendar.

It is said that **the Maya inherited their calendar from the Olmec**, whose calendaring system also involved a 260-day cycle for rituals. Thus the Aztec, who succeeded the Mayas, also owe their calendar roots to the Olmec.

The significance of this is not to explain how the Aztec calendar works, but to draw a comparison with that Mayan calendar, having similar roots.

Rewind: the Aztec calendar from another perspective:

Note the object in in his mouth has a design… **Tecpatl** (below)…

… Now examine the symbols used below **especially #18**… "flint or knife." It is #1 (also in the 1 o'clock position) on the outer ring, previous page.

Credits: Bing Images: Aztec Calendar.

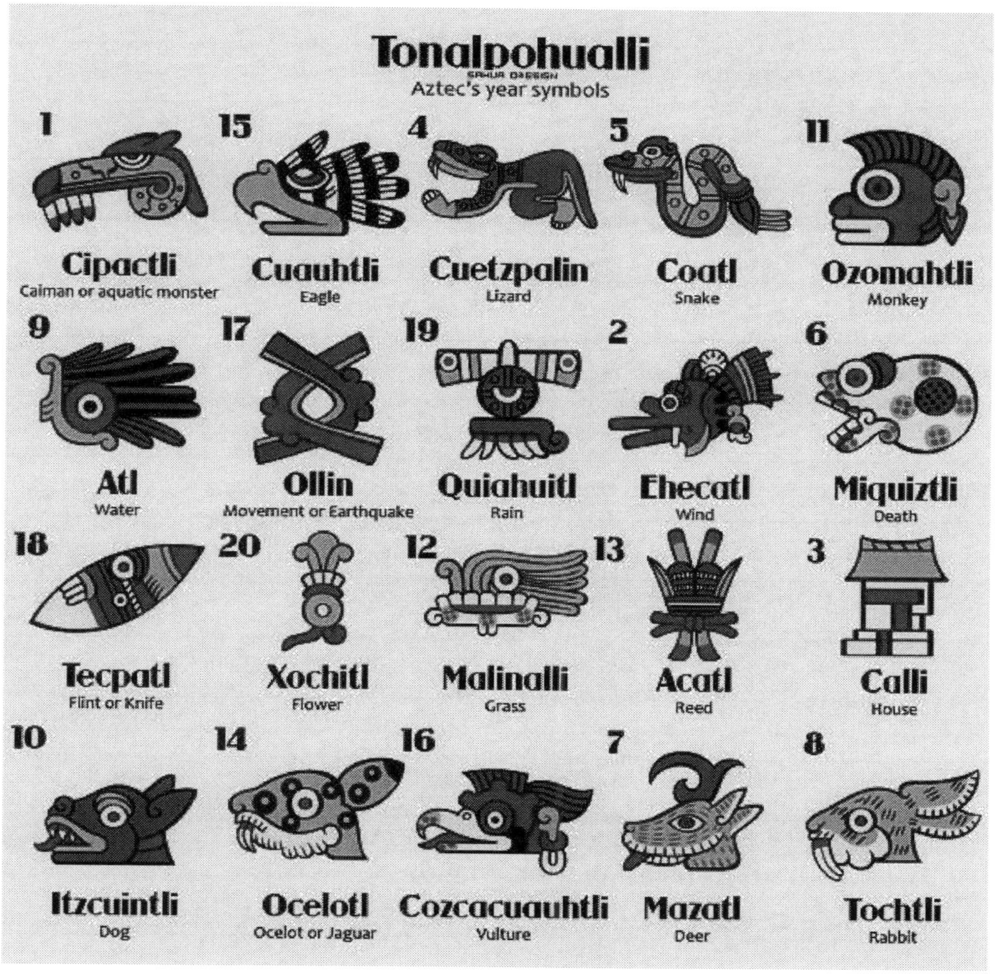

Tonalpohualli

Aztec's year symbols

1 **Cipactli** Caiman or aquatic monster

15 **Cuauhtli** Eagle

4 **Cuetzpalin** Lizard

5 **Coatl** Snake

11 **Ozomahtli** Monkey

9 **Atl** Water

17 **Ollin** Movement or Earthquake

19 **Quiahuitl** Rain

2 **Ehecatl** Wind

6 **Miquiztli** Death

18 **Tecpatl** Flint or Knife

20 **Xochitl** Flower

12 **Malinalli** Grass

13 **Acatl** Reed

3 **Calli** House

10 **Itzcuintli** Dog

14 **Ocelotl** Ocelot or Jaguar

16 **Cozcacuauhtli** Vulture

7 **Mazatl** Deer

8 **Tochtli** Rabbit

Also note that #5 is "coatl" = snake and part of Quetzal**coatl** – an Aztec god called "feathered serpent." "Quetzal" is a bird with long, green feathers.

Mayan Calendar

Quetzalcoatl taught the Aztecs and the Mayans mathematics, astronomy, medicine, agriculture… basically a repeat of what was taught the humans in Sumeria. In addition, the Mayans developed a calendar with **Itzamna**'s help:

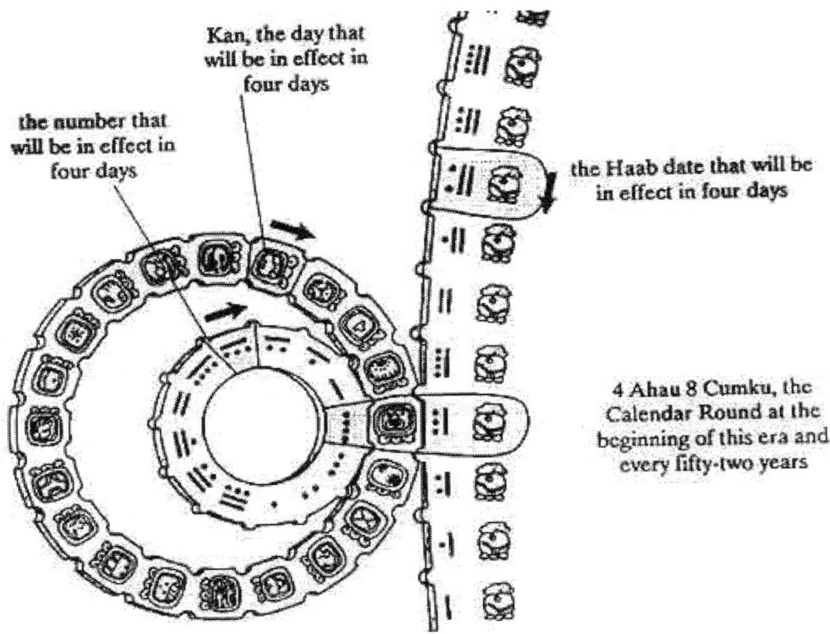

Since the Olmec gave the Mayans their calendar, it was the Olmec priest **Itzamna** who was credited with its presentation and explanation to the Mayas. His name meant **"lizard house"** and it is said that he was identified with **Hunab K'u** (the high deity to the Mayans, which means "the only god").

> Itzamna was **an active creator god**, as is shown by the following. Confirming Landa's description of the book ritual above, (Hun-) Itzamna is stated by Diego Lopez de Cogolludo to have invented the priestly art of **writing**. According to this same author, Itzamna (now written Zamna) had been a sort of priest who divided the land of Yucatán and assigned names to all of its features. More generally, **Itzamna was the creator of humankind…** [211] [emphasis added]

The Mayans had more than 17 calendars, but mainly used 8 major ones. [212]

As can be seen above, the Mayan calendar is in 3 parts, and should not be confused (as is so often done on TV) with the Aztec calendar. The two circular wheels are the **Tzolk'in** and the Outer stone arch is the **Haab'**.

The **Haab'** (outer stone arc) was 18 months of 20 days (=360 days). Used since about 550 BC, the calendar process also had to pick up a period of 5 extra days …

> …("nameless days") at the end of the year known as ***Wayeb'*** (or *Uayeb* in 16th-century orthography). The five days of Wayeb' were thought to be a dangerous time…. "During Wayeb, portals between the mortal realm and the Underworld dissolved. No boundaries prevented the ill-intending deities from causing disasters." To ward off these evil spirits, the Maya had customs and rituals they practiced during Wayeb'. For example, people avoided leaving their houses and washing or combing their hair.[213]

The **Tzolk'in** calendar combines twenty **day** names with the thirteen day **numbers** to produce **260 unique days**. Twenty was significant in the Maya counting system; whereas today we use the decimal system, base-10, the Maya used the vigesimal or base-20 system. Successive days are numbered 1-13 and then start again (see inner wheel in diagram above).

A **Calendar Round date** is a date that gives both a **Tzolk'in and Haab'**. This date will repeat after **52 Haab' years** or 18,980 days, i.e., a Calendar Round. For example, the current creation started on **4 Ahau 8 Kumk'u** (see Mayan diagram above). When this date recurs it is known as a Calendar Round completion.

Since Calendar Round dates repeat every 18,980 days, approximately **52 solar years**, the cycle repeats roughly once each lifetime, so a more refined method of dating was needed if history was to be recorded accurately. To specify dates over periods longer than 52 years, Mesoamericans used the **Long Count calendar**.

Calendar Issue with December 21, 2012

According to the scholars, the Long Count Mayan calendar identifies a date by counting the number of days from the Mayan creation date **4 Ahaw, 8 Kumk'u** (August 11, 3114 BC in the proleptic Gregorian calendar or September 6, 3114 in the Julian calendar). But instead of using a base-10 scheme like Western numbering, the Long Count days were tallied in a modified base-20 scheme.

Note: the Sumerians (Anunnaki) used a base-60 schema.

The point being that there was no disaster truly forecasted for **December 21, 2012** as that date used the Gregorian calendar's original date (versus the original Julian

Calendar), and it was off by about 27 days. In fact, the Mayans were not predicting the end of the world, just the start of a new cycle.

> December 21, 2012 was simply the day that the calendar went to the next **b'ak'tun**, at Long Count 13.0.0.0.0. The date on which the calendar will go to the next Piktun (a complete series of 20 b'ak'tuns), at Long Count 1.0.0.0.0.0, will be on October 13, 4772.[214]

> Each b'ak'tun is about 5126 years (to 2012). Interesting that the Jewish calendar says we are now in year 5776 (so 2012 was 5772)... which means the Mayans began counting in 3114 BC and the Jews started counting in 3760 BC.... (see Ch. 5 for reference on this – the Kurukshetra War's date). The Jews began their calendar approximately 646 years before the Mayans.

Numbers were significant to the Mayans, just as they were to the Hebrews (i.e. Gematria). And it is of note that the **Chichen Itzá pyramid**, also called El Castillo, in the Yucatan was built with the number of days in a year in mind: 365 steps on it. (Note the steep steps to the Casita at the top – where the god resided.)

El Castillo at Chichen Itzá

Note: they are on their hands and knees again.

There are 4 sides with 91 steps on each side (= 364 steps) and that was considered the Aztec year. There was one more all around step at the top to the Casita. 365 steps – so they did know the number of days in a year.

The stairs were built at a 45° angle although the sides of the El Castillo pyramid were built at 53° -- which correlates with the Great Pyramid in Egypt whose sides were built at the same angle.

And there is a **cable** running up the stairs (in the middle) because people find it hard to climb and descend… the gods were taller (8-9' tall Anunnaki) and had a bigger stride/step – note the people (last page) bent over and coming down in a sitting position. Only the northeastern side of the pyramid has **serpent heads** at the base of the stairs – so that the 2 equinoxes will display the "**Serpent** coming down to Earth."

This is significant as it salutes **Quetzalcoatl (aka Kukulcan)** as the "Feathered Serpent" who taught humans. During the two equinoxes, the Sun's light creates the illusion of a serpent with **7 segments** (Pleiades again)…the Serpent's head is at the base of the stairs. Isn't that a little complicated for primitive Mesoamerican indians to figure out? How did they get the angle and the timing just right – Did Quetzalcoatl or **Itzamna** help them?

El Castillo at Equinox

Rewind: The Mayan Calendar

It was said earlier that there was a discrepancy between the Gregorian Calendar and the Mayan Calendar of 27 days. In fact, it was more than that. The Mayan Calendar was fairly accurate but was still off by 1 day every 4 years, and a manual adjustment had to be made. And the start date of **August 11, 3114 BC** is just a scholarly calculated date… there were three men who collaborated on the what the start date could have been and it was called the GMT Correlation. However,

> Until 1972 there were no fewer than 16 different hypotheses for Day 1. They ranged from 8498 BC to 3121 BC. [215]

And then on top of that, the original start date of the last Baktun is still in dispute among some scholars – a Baktun consisting of 1,872,000 days.
Consisting of 1-day errors for every 4 years… according to **Professor Carl Calleman**, a Mayan researcher, that yields a 420-day error in the continuity of the Calendar. Thus his speculation was that October 28, 2011 was the actual enddate.

And all that is very interesting considering the Maya knew the actual length of the year! They did not use fractions and the true length of the year is 365.2425 days, which is why it was off 1 day every 4 years. But the Maya didn't care, they wanted to keep their Calendar synchronized with larger cycles, and the Long Count Calendar was the one they were watching as their belief (given them by the Star People) was that **the god Bolon Yokte** would return with the 9 gods at the end of the Baktun.

And ironically, the formal Mayan Civilization came to halt somewhere around 800 AD. The people just abandoned the cities and temples and walked off… today there are about 2 million Maya still living in Central America so they didn't disappear, and many still speak the old language, Nahuatl… but of course they can't read the hieroglyphic inscriptions.

The Maya still have shamen and they still use the Mayan Calendar, and the latest story this author heard was that the Long Count was off by about 5 years, making 2017 the time of the return…

Mayan Origins

Having covered the basics of Aztec origins and the calendaring systems, both originating with the Olmec, (which was actually Ningishzidda and his Nubian [Egypt] followers [216]), we come to an examination of a little-known aspect of human origins in Central America: **Tamoanchan** near Veracruz. (More on this, p.289.)

> The legendary first settlement of the Feathered Serpents in Central America was **Tamoanchan**, a name which means "the place where

> the people of the Serpent landed." .... One of their spin-off cultures was known as the **Olmec**. [217] [emphasis added]

And the Olmec were creators of the giant stone heads found in Costa Rica: the balls bear their likeness… which has been said to be Negro, Polynesian, etc. – but they are the faces of the **Nubian warriors** (Ancient Egypt) who accompanied Ningishzidda.

Yes, those are helmets. Remember the Nubian king and warriors in Chapter 5?

(credit: San Lorenzo Museum.)

Even though we now know the Olmec were really the Nubians, we do not know what they called themselves in the New World...

The Olmecs were also busy making figurines which have puzzled archeologists for decades. A few follow…

(credit: Bing Images: www.messagetoeagle.com)

It looks like the astronaut has a snout like an elephant, but the rest of the body appears to be reptilian. This is a being wearing a helmet sitting inside an unknown object, probably a flying machine. The artifact is kept at the Museum of Belize City.

That is reminiscent of the 'elephant' cornices at Chichen Itzá:

Somehow the Mayans and Olmecs (their predecessors) knew about **elephants**... or were the mastodons still roaming the Americas?

Archeologists cannot handle the image being an elephant so they claim that it is the image of Chac Mool, the rain god. (Not. The eyes are not those of Tlaloc or Chac Mool.)

(credit: http://www.strangehistory.net/2010/07/22/mongol-elephants-in-america/)

Someone will say those aren't elephants, and then we have to offer more **proof**:

Consider the Mayan glyphs:

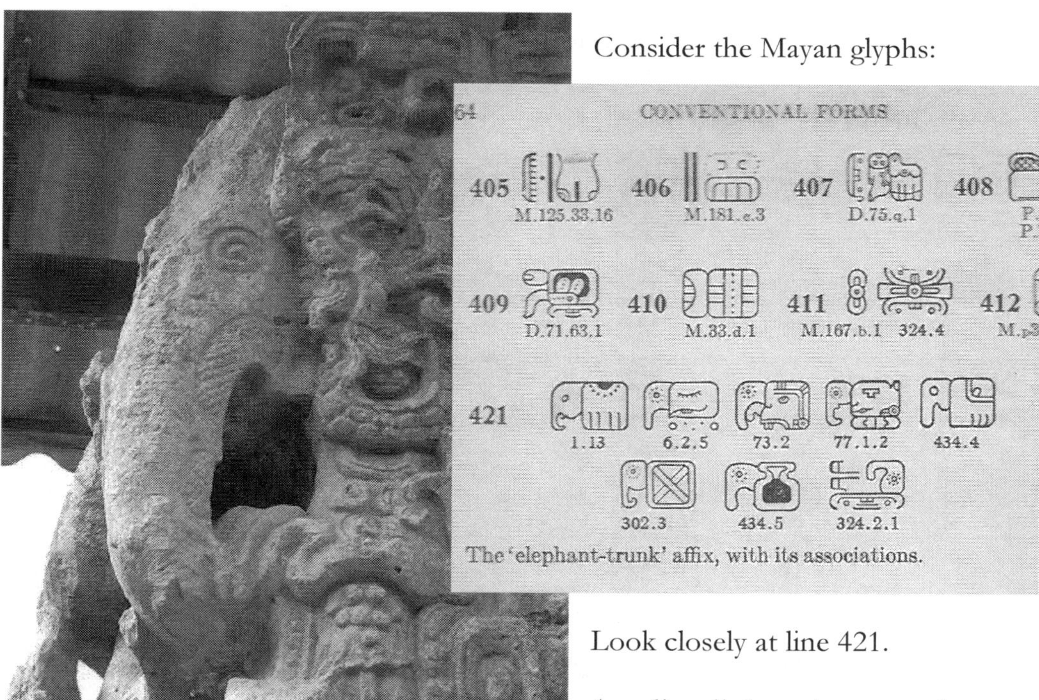

64 CONVENTIONAL FORMS

405 M.125.33.16 406 M.181.c.3 407 D.75.q.1 408 P.

409 D.71.63.1 410 M.33.d.1 411 M.167.b.1 324.4 412 M.p3

421 1.13 6.2.5 73.2 77.1.2 434.4

302.3 434.5 324.2.1

The 'elephant-trunk' affix, with its associations.

Look closely at line 421.

(credit: all three images: above with www.strangehistory.)

The odd elephant issue would make more sense if the sculptures had been found in India – the Hindus revere their elephant god **Ganesh**…. And it makes one wonder if the Olmecs brought elephants with them to the Veracruz area… and if not, were there still mastodons roaming south into Central America…?

The Olmecs also produced the following works of art:

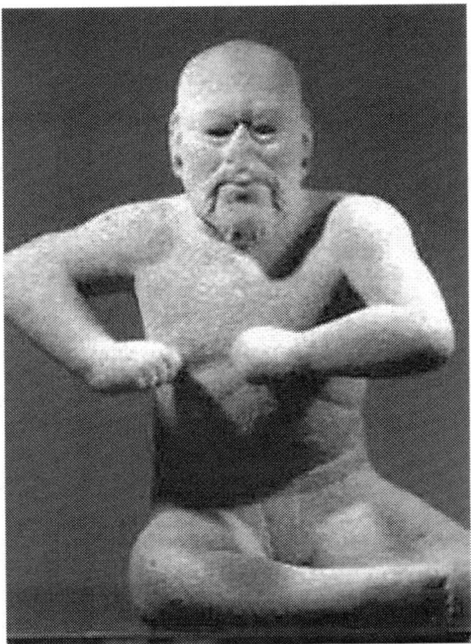

This is called the **Olmec Wrestler**… yet he looks oriental.

(credit: Bing Images: memberstripod.com)

And don't ask what this is:

…but it is Olmec….

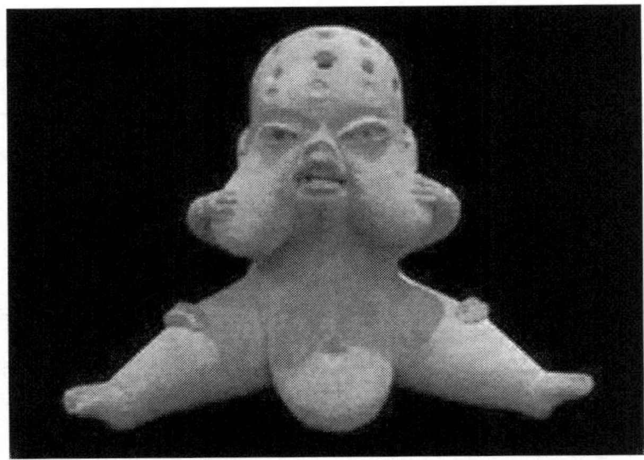

In addition, the Olmecs did something else which has puzzled archeologists for decades, and the **giant stone balls** they fashioned have been found in Costa Rica, Serbia and New Zealand, to name a few places…

A Costa Rican collection…

…and those in New Zealand:

So the question often asked is "What are they? Why were they sculpted – and how did they get them perfectly round?" They were made by those who made the huge stone faces…with similar technology… and they are not natural.

What people don't know is that the spheres were made in various sizes and used like **stone cannon balls** – projectiles that were shot at their enemies. They caused a lot of damage to buildings, ships, and walls… but unlike nuclear weapons (which the Anunnaki also had), they left no radiation residue, and instead of any other type of weapon blowing something up, there was just a simple stone object which got the enemy's attention and served as a preliminary deterrent.

Here is a brief Who's Who among the Aztec, Mayan and Incan gods:

Aztec Gods:

Coatlicue – serpent goddess; dressed in clothes to which are attached serpents.
Tezcatlipoca -- 'Lord of the Smoking Mirror', brother and sometimes adversary of Quetzalcoatl. God of darkness, war and death.
Huitzilopochtli – 'Blue Hummingbird of the Left', major Aztec god, promotes sacrifice.
Xipe Totec – 'The Flayed Lord' promoting self-flagellation, and the god of agriculture.
Tlaloc -- rain and fertility god (portrayed as a black man). Corresponds to Mayan Chac Mool.
Xochiquetzal – goddess of flowers and fruit. Mother of Quetzlcoatl.
Xochipilli – brother to Xochiquetzal, the flower princess, lord of sexuality and youth. (Also patron saint to gays and prostitutes. See CHIN below).
Quetzalcoatl – **'Feathered Serpent'** bringer of civilization.

Mayan Gods:

Chac Mool – rain god to whom human hearts are sacrificed.
Hunab K'u -- God of the Universe; called 'The only giver of movement & measure.' May be Itzamna's father.
Itzamna – a great deity, like Huitzilopochtli. Considered **a creator-god**. His wife, **Ixchel,** is mischievous and reminiscent of Loki in Norse legends.
➔ **Chin** – god of homosexuals and prostitutes (Gay is nothing new).[218]
Ah Puch – lord of death.
Kinich-Ahau -- god of the Sun (like Egypt's Ra).
Gucumatz – another name for Kukulcan.
Kukulcan – Mayan name for Quetzalcoatl who brought civilization
Hun-Batz – 'One Howler monkey'; a stepbrother to the Hero Twins.
Votan -- legendary ancestral deity (**name similar to Norse Wotan** …covered later).

Incan God : Viracocha (aka Kukulcan and Quetzalcoatl)
(more in the section below on the Inca…)

The foregoing Maya names are primarily taken from the books of the **Chilam Balam** and the **Popul Vuh**. And there are hundreds of Mayan deities, depending on which period you look at – Preclassic period (c. 2000 BC to 250 AD) or Classic (250 AD to 900 AD). And then the Maya just abandoned their city-states about 800-900 AD. Today there are still about 2 million Mayas living in Central America, so they didn't just disappear, they just walked off. And the **Nahuatl** language is still spoken by about a million Mayas. [219]

So what else do we know about the Maya's beliefs and traditions that correlate with the Sumerian gods traveling all over the world?

Mayan Tree of Life

Just as the Sumerians, Vikings and the Chinese had images of a Tree of Life, so too did the Mayans. And it is wrapped up with the sacred "T" teaching:

FIGURE 16.

(credit: Secrets of Mayan Science/Religion.

In the Fig 16 above, note the 3 sections: [220]

(A) is from an Aztec seal, and the shape in a "T" and represents the Aztec belief that Man originated with the trees. (The Maya said this 1000 years earlier.)

(B) represents the mesoamerican belief that trees were not only sacred but "The Nahua (Aztecs) claimed descendence from the trees and illustrated their origin with a figure emerging from a broken trunk." (Vindolonesis Codex.)

(C) is found as a design motif on a wall in Teotihuacan, Mexico.

The Maya identify with their brother, the Sacred Tree, ***yaxche***, which is to say, "first the tree." Many religions have a sacred tree and for the Maya the *yaxche* is the stately and ancient **Ceiba tree**…. Pictured below is ONE tree:

The tree is called **El Arbol de Tule** – located in Oaxaca, Mexico. It has a diameter of 46 feet, and it is so large that it was originally thought to be multiple trees, but DNA tests have proven that **it is only one tree**. The age is unknown, with estimates ranging between 1,200 and 3,000 years and a local legend says that it was planted by a priest about 1400 years ago. The tree is occasionally nicknamed the **"Tree of Life"** from the images of animals that are reputedly visible in the tree's gnarled trunk.[221]

Mayan Cosmogony

Two astronomical items impressed the Maya:[222]

The Milky Way

According to the Maya, the Milky Way was the place of origin of life on Earth. It was called the Wakah Chan, or **erected serpent** –which is pictured further on the next few pages. ("Chan" comes from Chanes, an ancient tribe in South America, and the word means "serpent people.")

The Milky Way was also referred to as the **World Tree** and it was often represented by the **Ceiba Tree**. The clouds of diffused stars were known to be an interstellar nursery which gave life to everything on Earth.

The Pleiades

The constellation was known as Tzab-ek to the Maya, and they said it was **the place from which they came.** The Tzolk'in (or sacred calendar of the Maya) is based on the astronomical cycle of the Pleiades.

That is why they were so interested in tracking the stars and did so via the Caracol Observatory at Chichen Itza:

Caracol Observatory
The viewing windows aligned with the appearance of celestial bodies such as the Pleiades and Venus.

Maya World Trees

Moving back to the Mayan teachings, we find that there are other pictorials relating to the Mayan belief that Man originated with a tree…

FIGURE 11.
Page 2 of the Selden Codex: The mythological birth of humanity shows a person emerging from a sacred tree. This image has historical content. Those of us with knowledge of Mayan/Aztec culture recognize the sacred "T" as the symbol of the tree that produced the human being. This knowledge was ours long before the arrival of the Catholic priests, who brought their Christian concept of Adam, Eve, the tree, and the serpent. We worked with this knowledge in the remote days of Hanahuac, Tamuanchan, Ixachitlan, Tauantinsuyo, or America.

What is important here is the shape of the tree – in a "T" with Man emerging from it. Note also the **two serpents** intertwined with the horizontal arms of the Tree which represent positive energy (*can*) and negative energy (*nac*)… How did the Mayans know about that? (This relates to the Chinese concept of Yin/Yang, and there is a record of the Atlantean Maya visiting Asia… see next section.)

Left: **(credit: Secrets of Mayan Science/Religion.**

At right is a picture of a stone in the Anthropology Museum, Mexico City – also called the **Tree of Life**:

Note the bird symbolizing Spirit.

And there is one last example of the Sacred "T" this time in the form of a Maltese Cross… Mayan for "tree" was *che* or *te*.

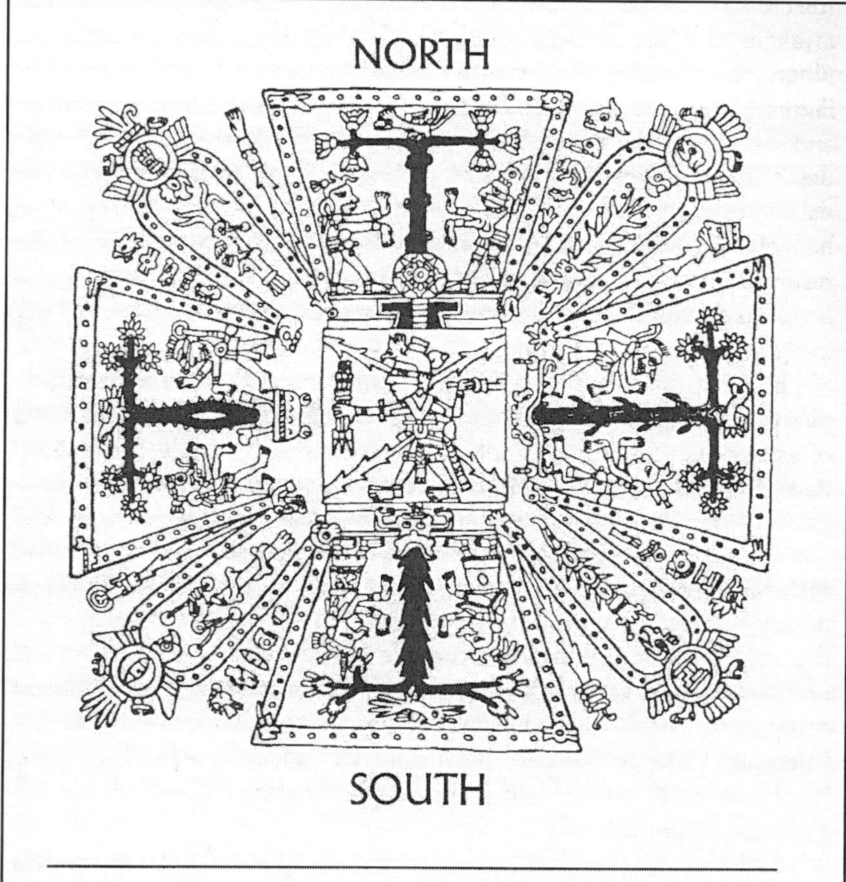

FIGURE 12.
The Fejérváry-Mayer Codex: In this manuscript we find four trees oriented toward the cardinal points. In the center, a figure controls energy. Also present are birds and other symbols used in this codex, which should be named *uahom che*, the word used by the Maya to designate "the cross of the tree." To what do we attribute this designation? It is interesting to discover the clear meaning: "The tree that awakens us" or "within the tree that awakens conciousness."

(credit: Secrets of Mayan Science/Religion.

Interesting that the figure in the center is handling lightening bolts – reminiscent of the Norse god Odin or Thor. There are 4 trees and again, **birds** at the 4 corners.

In addition, there are two bits of information associated with these trees.[223]

Maya Esoteric Facts

(1) As was pointed out earlier, **Tamuanchan** is given as the location where Man first appeared in Mesoamerica… Figure 16B (p. 289) is associated with Tamuanchan via Codex *Vendobonensis*. It was believed that humans and trees were made of the same substance, spiritually if not literally – trees were thought to have a living essence (Man just has more) and today we (and the Chinese) call that *chi*.

(2) The teaching about the letter "T" goes back to antiquity to a great Hindu writer, **Valmiki**, who stated that the Naga Maya visited India about 2700 BC, and brought their culture to India. There you have influence going the opposite direction… from the New World to the Old.

It is noted that **Berossus**, a Chaldean priest, wrote that the Maya came to his homeland back when they used to live in Atlantis. In Africa they were called Mayax, in Hindustan they were called Naga Maya, and in Greece, they were called Cara Maya. [224]

Lord Pacal & the Tree

This section would not be complete, and the Maya would never forgive me, if we didn't attempt to set the record straight about the imagery on the lid to Lord Pacal's sarcophagus:

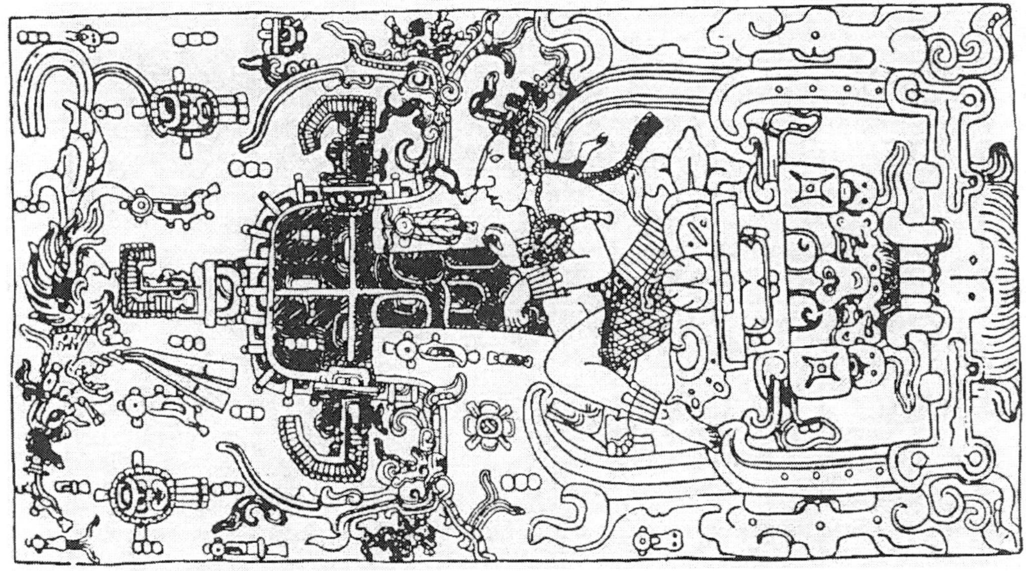

(credit: Secrets of Mayan Science/Religion

The tomb is found under the Temple of the Inscriptions in Palenque, Yucatan. It has been said by **Ancient Astronaut Theorists** that this represents Lord Pacal blasting off in his spacecraft… his nose pushing some instrument, his right foot operating some lever/assembly, and his hands do appear to be working some controls. However, note the black "T" again – and there is a **bird** on the far left – what would be the top of the diagram if it were vertical. We have the Sacred Tree motif on the lid – and his nose is touching another 'T' (note **3 dots** in a 'T' shape) as shown below – which is what the Maya used to indicate "divine breath." [225]

These drawings will exemplify the Mayan use of the 'T' under the nose to signify **"divine breath."** It could also be said that the small triangular "T" at Lord Pacal's nose is capturing his breath.

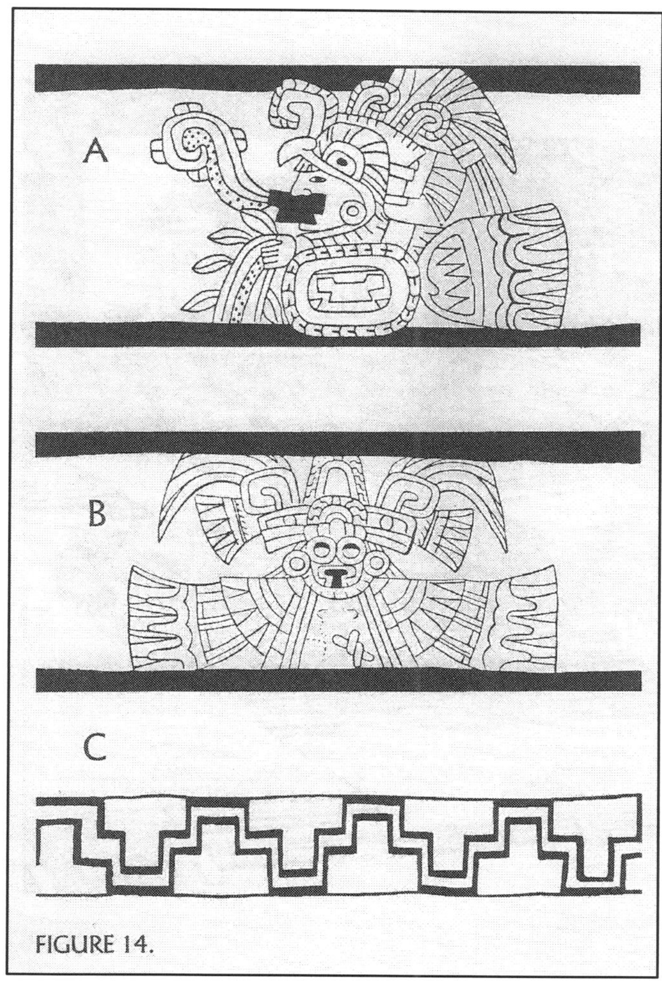

FIGURE 14.

(credit: Secrets of Mayan Science/Religion

At the bottom of diagram Fig. 14 is again the border relief displaying the "T" shape from a Mayan room used to train priests – hence the 'divine breath' to bless them.

So the Mayan implication for the Lord Pacal tomb image is that he is at the <u>bottom</u> of the "T" – having been born at the top of the "T" he is now making his transition back to Source – the Tree emerges from Lord Pacal's naval…and a **bird** sits upon the Tree, symbolic of the Spirit. **Birds and serpents are always significant**.

Atlantes de Tula

If the Ancient Astronaut Theorists want to discuss something ET-looking, they should consider what the Tula Toltec spacemen signify…

Of particular interest is: What do they all hold at their right sides: guns?

They also have chestplates (panels) of some sort…

Are these related to the Anunnaki astronauts?

Whatever is in their <u>left</u> hands is also open to speculation... a curved knife, a tool…? Is the chestplate related to electronics and perhaps to the Anunnaki MEs (Ch. 1)? Anunnaki were said to sometimes wear the MEs on their chests… reminiscent of the Hebrew priests wearing an *ephod*… 12 stones that uniquely vibrated when God answered via the Ark (see Chapter 5).

Maya Creation Story

Now let's take a look at the Mayan version of their origins. It was said earlier that they came from MU (Pacific Ocean) and some came from Atlantis. And we also have an account of how the Mesoamerican Indians originated in **Tamoanchan** (near Veracruz)… and the different versions do not necessarily contradict each other – time is the big key. Mayans may be from MU, and after that continent sank, the natives headed East for what is now Central America… those who occupied Atlantis, when it sank, scrambled to the West and East to Central America and eventually Egypt, respectively.

Such accounts are found in several Mayan 'history' books – which could tell us more if the overzealous Spanish Conquistadores hadn't destroyed everything in their wake as they plundered the Americas in their search for gold. The Spanish priests with them thought the natives were in league with the devil because they practiced all sorts of sacrificial rites – including human – and that meant all writings would be destroyed and the Indians would have to become Christians.

Chilam Balam

Such was one book that was rewritten under the guidance of the Spanish priests. It dates to the time of the Spanish Conquest, and is an account of the first inhabitants of the Yucatan. Its name means "Jaguar Priest."

> …the first inhabitants of the Yucatan were the Chanes, or "People of the Serpent" who came across the water from the East with their leader **Itzamna**, who was called the "**Serpent of the East**" and was a healer who could cure by laying on of hands and revive the dead. [226]

Remember that Inanna and the Egyptians could also resurrect the dead.[227]

> J. Eric Thompson the dean of Mayan studies maintains that the term *Itzem,* from which [Itzama's] name is derived, should be translated as "lizard" or **"reptile."** In fact, Itzmal, the sacred city of the god Itzamna, literally means "the Place of the Lizard." [228]

Again, more of the Serpent Wisdom imagery which will be explored in a later chapter.

Popul Vuh

The other great work is the *Popul Vuh* which is a document dating back to about AD 1554, again <u>rewritten</u> from pieces of the original <u>and</u> from the memories of the surviving natives – after Cortez tried to kill them all. The title translates to "Book of the People."

Because it was **rewritten under the guidance and tutelage (to Christian values) of the local Spanish priest,** who was also teaching the natives to write, it became an epic creation myth. It was translated to Spanish about AD 1700. What is interesting is to compare the Anunnaki gods' treatment of the humans they created (see Chapter 1) with the creation of Man in the *Popul Vuh*... very similar. The following is an accurate 'paraphrase': [229]

> The Popul Vuh starts out with only sky and water in an eternal darkness. Hidden in the water under green and blue feathers were the Creators [allusion to Quetzal]. They talked among themselves and decided to create land and trees and plants, and then because it was all too quiet, they added animals. They sat back and told themselves that it was all perfect and they were very happy with what they had done.
>
> They approached the animals and asked them to praise them and thank them for what they had done, but all the animals could do was scream, hiss, and cackle – but they could not even name their creators.
>
> The Creators were disappointed and decided to make another set of beings who could praise and thank them. They would be superior and rule over the Earth.
>
> Their first attempt was to make Man out of **muddy earth** [reminiscent of NüWa in the Chinese account]. But he was too soft and weak. He could speak but had no mind behind the words. He was removed.
>
> The next attempt was to make Man out of **wood**. It was firm and strong, but it had **no soul.** It also had no mind. They could and did replicate and spread over a good part of the Earth. [Think: Land of Nod.] Yet, they wandered aimlessly on all fours and did not think of their Creators.
>
> The Creators were again very disappointed, and decided to send **a Flood** to wipe them all out. [Here is the common Flood image that has been found all around the globe.]
>
> (continued...)

The gods had to do something really special if the beings were to have sentience and be able to praise and love their Creators.

Four animals came to the Creators and told them where there was a material that they might use to make beings... a puma, a coyote, a crow and a small parrot came forward. They told them about the ears of **yellow and white corn** growing abundantly nearby. The Creators found the corn and ground it up and made the four **First Fathers**. They added flesh and muscles. The Creators were very pleased with their work and they congratulated themselves on a perfect job.

The Creators looked at the humans and found them to be intelligent, attractive and wise. They looked and talked like human beings. They could see far into the distance... everything revealed its nature to them. When the four First Fathers saw all there was to see in the world, they went to their Creators and thanked them and praised them. "We know everything and we thank you!"

The Creators were no longer pleased. They said, "Have we created **creatures who are better than we intended**? Are they too perfect?.... They are so knowledgeable and wise that **they will be like us** – They will be gods like ourselves!" [Same thing the Anunnaki said.]

The Creators decided to take the beings down a notch and blew a fog in their eyes (and brain) so that they could only see what was right before them. They removed the total knowledge that the four First Fathers had. Humans were now dense and unaware. The gods were happy again.

And then the gods discovered that something was still missing... They would create **women** and thus wives for the four First Fathers while the men slept. Afterward, the gods again said, "What we have now done is perfect!"

So the gods made many more beings like the First Fathers and First Mothers... the people lived and multiplied and subdued the Earth. But everyone still lived in Darkness for the Creators had not yet created Light. So the gods said "Let there be Light!" and there was the Sun. Now people could see their gods – who quickly warned them to not make any images of them [also as did the Anunnaki].

(continued...)

> The humans lived together in the East in great numbers, rich and poor, light-skinned and dark-skinned, speaking different languages.
>
> The people entreated their gods to give them good, happy, useful lives with peace. The animals avoided Man and now went about their business, and the people praised their Creators, dancing around their priests who were offering incense and sacrifices to the Sun. The Creators had illumined the Earth with Light and now said, "We have made it and it is perfect!"

Reading between the lines, one can see the Christian influence as parts of the story relate to Biblical events… the creation of woman, the Flood, Babel, and 'Let there be Light!' and the judgment that it was all good (or perfect). But more than that is the revelation that **Man was not to be as smart as his gods** – which is exactly what the Anunnaki said when Enki had fashioned the *Adapa.* Man was not to live as long, nor be as smart, and thus Man's genetics were cut down and modified to the "three score and ten years" for his lifetime – He could not partake of the Tree of Life in the Garden.

And it is clear that this was not due to sin. It was just the way the gods created Man – originally as **a slave** to serve them. Interesting that the slave aspect did not show up in the translated *Popul Vuh.* (Church editing?)

Overall, it is coming together that Man was seeded in different parts of the planet, with different facial features (some have beards, some don't, some have slanted eyes, some don't…) and yet the critical separating aspects were language and religion. **Different languages** kept Man from easily communicating with other people around the globe, and **different religions** kept Man arguing about who was right about the gods…

There seems to have been **an agenda to keep Man from uniting** … perhaps the gods did not want Man organizing and challenging them. And we are now beginning to develop our potential and master genetics, space travel and computers…. Are they still there watching? If so, and we leave the planet, we will encounter them… What will they do? Will they congratulate us, or take us captive and start us all over again …? What if they are still here… watching?
More on that later… (Chapter 9, Anunnaki Agenda.)

Meanwhile, the remaining part of this chapter now deals with…

The Cuban Pyramids

In addition to legends about massive floods, there are also legends of **Atlantis** that sank in the Atlantic Ocean. And both may have their factual origin in the gradually rising sea levels as the last Ice Age came to a close (somewhere 8-10,000 years ago)

> Deep in the waters of Cabo de San Antonio, off Cuba's [west] coast, researchers are exploring unusual formations of smooth blocks, crests, and geometric shapes. The Canadian exploration company that discovered the formations, Advanced Digital Communications, has suggested that they could be the buildings and monuments of an early, unknown American civilization. [230]

Many scientists are skeptical of any theory that might tempt people to draw a parallel with the fabled lost city of Atlantis. Geologist **Manuel Iturralde**, however, has stressed the need for an open mind while investigations of the site continue. "These are extremely peculiar structures, and they have captured our imagination," said Iturralde, who is director of research at Cuba's Natural History Museum. Iturralde has studied countless underwater formations over the years, but said, "If I had to explain this geologically, I would have a hard time."

> In his report on the formations [2002], Iturralde noted that conclusive proof of man-made structures on the site could reinforce some oral traditions of the Maya and native **Yucatecos**. These people still retell ancient stories of an island inhabited by their ancestors that vanished beneath the waves. [231]

In a related article, the Morien Institute has said that there is geological evidence that says the islands of the Carribbean are all connected and were once part of a larger landmass. The Yucatan, Cuba, Dom. Republic and Puerto Rico were all connected:

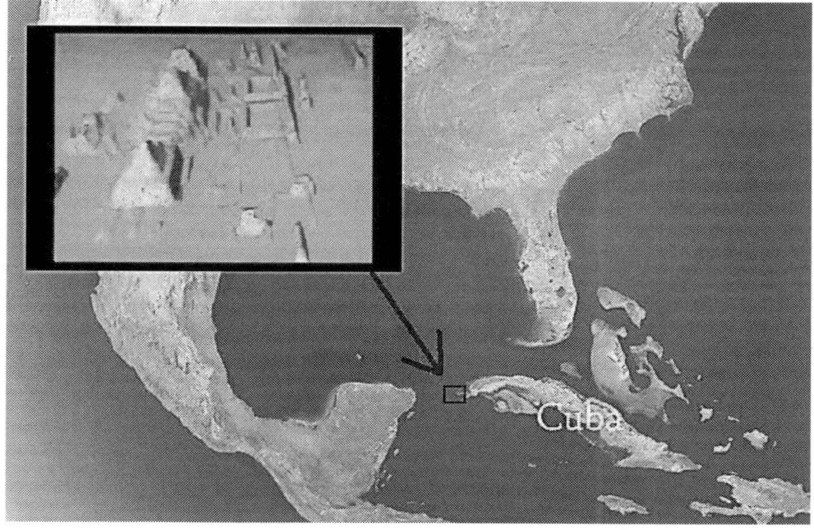

Further research is scheduled to take place over the summer of 2002. Data thus far has been collected using sonar scans and video. The structures are buried under 1,900 to 2,500 feet (600 to 750 meters) of water. [232]

Underwater Sonar has allegedly produced the following which is reconstructed from the sonar data:

Pyramids found off the coast of Cuba in about a half-mile of water.
(credit: Bing Images: Pinterest.com)

Scientists would like to believe that this is most likely an old pre-Mayan ruin, but the ocean levels rose 8000 years ago (estimated at 300' higher) and the Maya were not around then. This increases the chance that it is an older civilization dating back to close to the time that the last part of Atlantis is said to have disappeared into the Ocean (it was lost in stages). While the main Atlantean Island-Continent was in the middle of the Atlantic, this sunken site could have been related.

(See Chapter 8 section called '**Younger Dryas**' and the picture of the Atlantic floor.)

And even more interesting is this drawing of what **Tenochtitlan** (Aztec capital) looked like based on descriptions from Aztec writings:

Note the similarity between the pyramids in the Guanahacabibes sonar pictures and the pyramids of Tenochtitlan – in particular, note that they both have the "inset" temple at top. Tenochtitlan is not like the Mayan pyramids, nor is it like the Egyptian pyramids… both Tenochtitlan and the Cuban pyramids have pointed temples at the top. Can we suggest that the Guanahacabibes sunken pyramids are, in fact, **Aztlan**… the old Aztec capital from which they came when they "came from the East…"? (See p. 266 [picture text] and Chapter 7, Anasazi section.)

> Naturally this information will have its detractors, and there is a group of scientists still trying to convince people that Atlantis was really Santorini (Eastern Mediterranean) and Plato didn't know what he was talking about when he said it was outside the Pillars of Hercules (now called Gibraltar).

Status

So what is the status of Guanahacabibes today? That was 14 years ago…

When they reported discovering sunken temples, it did attract the attention of the National Geographic Society, the Military and the US Government. The problem was the depth – how to get down there, closer, and inspect the target? In 2004 the group planned another expedition, but gave a lame excuse:

> "*they could not complete the mission due to technical deficiencies of the submarine that rendered it unable to take images from the marine bottom*". One wonders why they went under-equipped when on the verge of so important a discovery. Nevertheless, [it was] announced that they would be returning in 2005, with funding from National Geographic Society. Since then, **silence** (apart from its inevitable appearance on *Ancient Aliens*).[233]

This raises the issue of a coverup… Did they really find something and the government doesn't want people to know about it? The only reason for that would be: if it is **an underwater base** (Think: USOs) that is <u>still used</u>…

> **Note**: Edgar Cayce said that Bimini and the Bahamas were once part of the Atlantean world – that raises another issue: What if the Atlanteans did not all die in the cataclysm? What if they kept their technology, made an organized escape, and found refuge elsewhere on Earth, and still monitor surface activity? Could these be the **Watchers** (or Bramley's Custodians)?

Analysis

First consider that there <u>was</u> a landbridge between Cuba and the Yucatan centuries ago (next page). Secondly remember that there was **an asteroid hit** right in that area (65 mil. years ago – allegedly that terminated the land dinosaurs). The asteroid could have destroyed the landbridge and maybe sunk the temple(s).

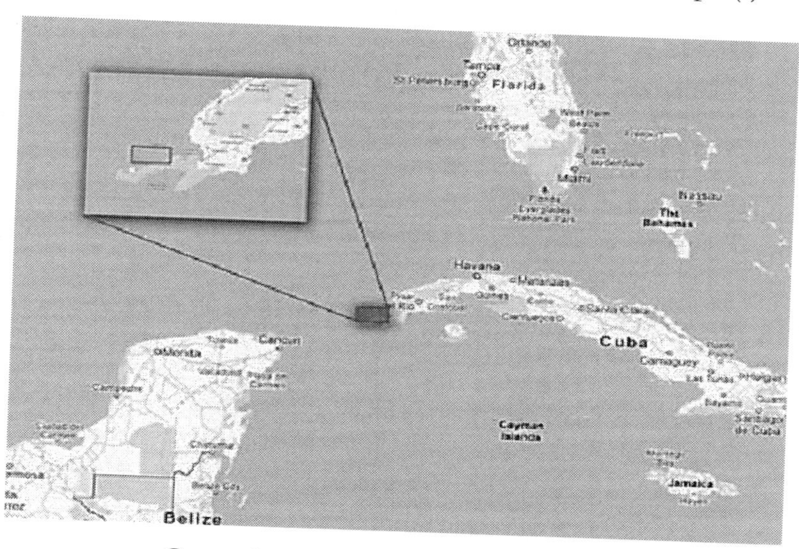

Guanahacabibes Peninsula

The thinking is that the temple was not there 65 mil. years ago, but that the tectonic plates could have been destabilized such that centuries later, the frail landbridge collapsed and took the temple(s) with it.

The asteroid strike was another 250 miles west of the landbridge. See below: This was called the **Chicxulub Crater** (circle below).

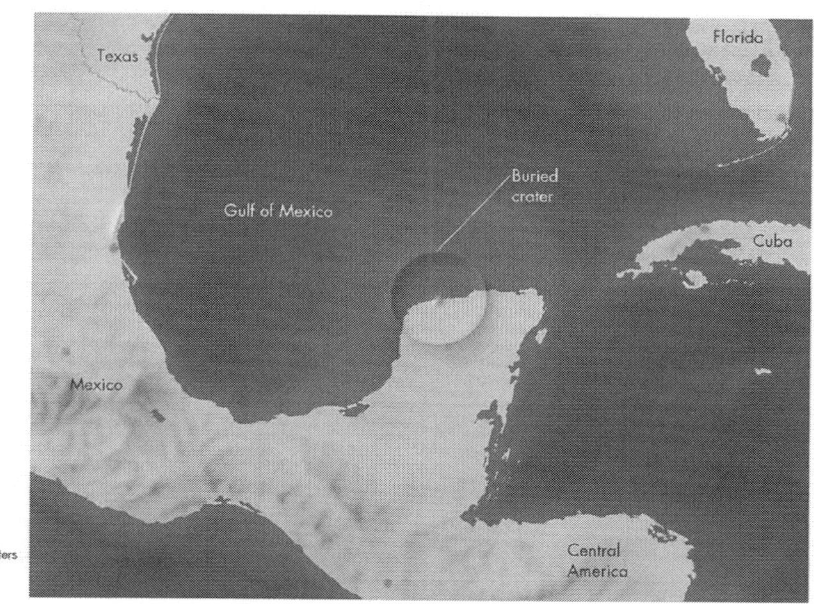

Copyright © 2005 Pearson Prentice Hall, Inc.

And FYI, here is the landbridge data…the circle was the asteroid impact zone (now filled in, no crater visible). You make the call.

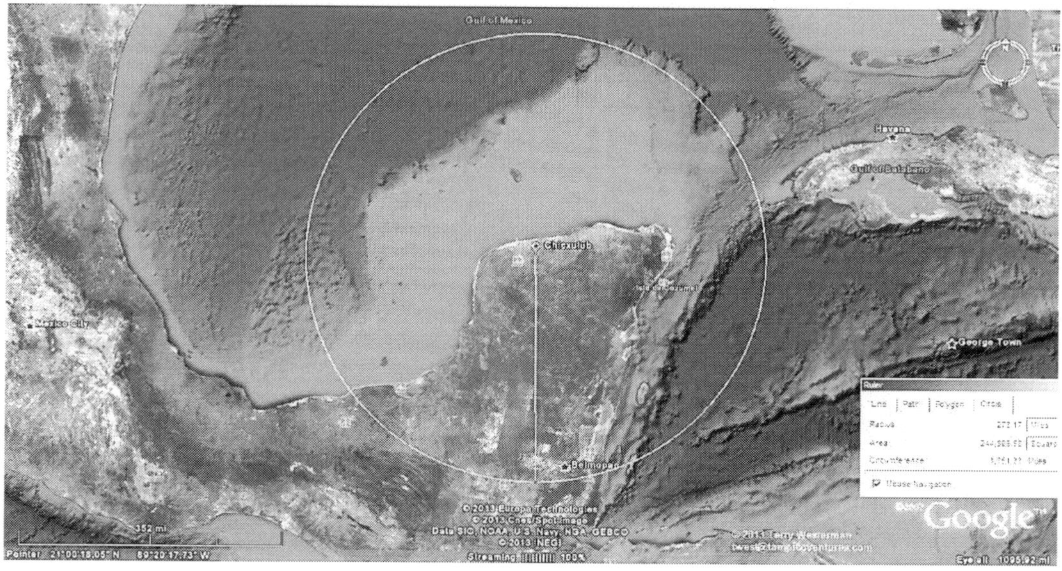

Landbridge East of the Yucatan (seafloor)

Summary

This chapter covered Central America – Aztecs, Olmecs, Chichimecs, Toltecs and Mayans. North America is examined in the next chapter, as this chapter would have been too large if it were all put together. Chapter 7 covers North and South America, and Chapter 8 completes the Global Tour: a miscellaneous grouping of Oceania peoples, Tibet, Australia, Fiji, Indonesia, and back to Africa.

Rewind: The Nine Gods

Please note that many cultures around the Earth have stories about the **Nine Gods** who came down and shepherded them -- the Ennead in Egypt (Geb, Nut, Isis, Osiris, Shu, Tefnut, Set, Nephtys) + Atum = The Nine in Egypt, the Mayan Bolon Yokte and his group of Nine Gods, there was also a Council of Nine among the Norse gods, the Etruscans recognized Nine Gods as well, and lastly, the Greeks knew that Zeus had a Council of Nine (Athena, Apollo, Ares, Demeter, Hephaestus, Hera, Hermes, Poseidon) to advise him and rule the Earthlings. Somehow there were nine gods who 'managed' humans and the Earth and the many cultures aoround the planet reflect that in their traditions, and sometimes in their religion.

And is there a connection to antiquity seeing that the US Supreme Court has 9 justices?

As can be seen so far, the gods were busy all over the globe, often shepherding humans, sacrificing some and teaching others… leading one to realize that some gods (The Nine) were benevolent and some (Orion Group) were malevolent. Humans were sacrificed to 'please' the gods, who often stood nearby… What do you think was done with all the bodies? The sacrifices took place at the top of the pyramid, where the heart was extracted, and the body was kicked down the steps of the pyramid. No one has ever found a pile or pit of skeleton bones from these sacrifices… Where did the bones go? (Use your imagination and the hints given above.)

And it will later be seen that the Teachings went underground as they went to the New World and to Europe. It was obviously not for the masses – whom Enlil had always judged to be inferior. Thus some Teaching was briefly taken by Enki publicly – until the Church and the Egyptian dynasties suppressed it. This is examined in a later chapter.

Chapter 7: The Americas, Part II

Continuing the Americas' quest for the Tree of Life, Serpents and common legends, we come first to the Incas.

The Anunnaki in South America

This getting to be very interesting. Not only were there similarities and links between the Sumerian Anunnaki and the Olmecs, but links between the Olmecs and Egyptian Nubians, and links between the Aztecs and Maya, there are also links between the Aztecs and the Inca. **Hernán Cortés** (aka Cortez) was the enemy to the Aztecs, and **Francisco Pizarro** was the bad guy to the Incas. They both did the same atrocities to the native population… killed natives, stole gold, destroyed ancient writings…all in the name of The Crown, and of course, Christianity. Guess what? Cortez and Pizarro were cousins.

And even more, the Incas have a Creation Story as well as a Tree of Life. Let's take a brief look at the main Incan gods.[234]

Inca Gods

Viracocha – also spelled Wiraqucha. He was the god of everything. In the beginning he was the main god, but when **Pachakuti** became Inca emperor, he changed this god's importance, pointing out that the most important god was **Inti**.

Inti -- was the Sun god. Source of warmth and light and a protector of the people. Inti was considered the most important god. The Inca Emperors were believed to be the lineal descendants of the Sun god.

Paricia -- was a god who sent a **Flood** to kill humans.

Mama Quilla -- ("mother moon" or "golden mother") was a marriage, festival and moon goddess and daughter of Wiraqucha and Mama Qucha, as well as wife and sister of Inti. She was the mother of Manqu Qhapaq (aka Manco Capac).

Ataguchu – a god of creation

Manco Capac --

> Manco Capac (1st Inca) and **Pachacuti** (created the empire).
> Origin: Manco Capac was a son of the Sun god **Inti** and **Mama Quilla**,

and brother of Pacha Kamaq (aka **Pachacama**. Manco Capac himself was worshipped as a fire and sun god. According to the Inti legend, Manco Capac and his siblings were **sent up to the earth by the Sun god** and **emerged from the cave** of Pacaritambo carrying a golden staff, called *tapac-yauri*. Instructed to create a Temple of the Sun in the spot where the staff sank into the earth, they traveled to Cusco via **underground caves** and there built a temple in honour of their father Inti.

Note: emerging from a cave or some underground dwelling is similar to the Navajo and Hopi/Zuñi teachings.

Copacati -- was a lake goddess. (Think: **Lake Titicaca** and the underwater temple now discovered by archeologists: it is about 300' long.)

Lake Titicaca

The Lake gets its name from "Titi Khar'ka" meaning Rock of the Puma. The natives so named it because they thought the outline of the lake resembled **a puma chasing a rabbit.** (Specs: 350' deep at points…. At 12,507 ft altitude)

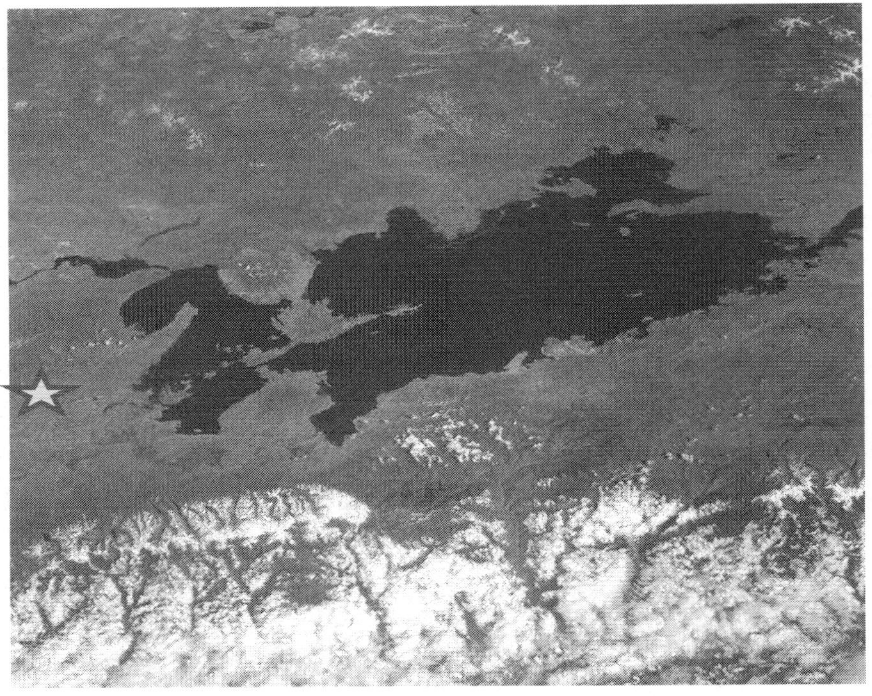

Lake Titicaca

Tiahuanaco is marked in the picture by the **star** (city now in ruins).

The image can only be seen from the air (like the ground-level designs at Nazca) … So you have to ask yourself how the natives knew what the Lake looked like. Again, could the **Anunnaki** (who had a base at Tiahuanaco and Puma Punku) take them aloft and show them their land below?

> The Lake sits on the border between Bolivia and Peru. So, the local natives have a cute saying: Considering the name of the Lake, the first part (Titi) is for Peru and the rest (caca) is for Bolivia.

The local Aymara natives call the lake Winay Marka, which means "Eternal City" and they are referring to the city of **Tiahuanaco** (aka Tiwanaku) **.** 'Eternal' because it was built a long, long time ago – the Aymara say they did not build it – it was there when they came into the land. Between 300 BC and AD 300, Tiwanaku is thought to have been a moral and spiritual center for the Tiwanaku Empire, which was inhabited around **1500 BC**. (That is when the Anunnaki were traveling around the planet.)

This is the location of the famous **Gate of the Sun** –shown below as it was originally found in 1903:

(credit: Wikipedia: http://bilddatenbank.khm.at/viewArtefact?id=253874)

This is also the location of the **Temple of Kalasasaya**, also was in ruins:

Credit: Wikipedia.org: Anakin~commonswiki

The Kalasasaya dates back to at least 200 BC - 200 AD and was **rebuilt in modern times**.

The temple underwater in Lake Titicaca was discovered as a result of the Atahuallpa 2000 expedition and is reported to be "200m by 50m wide, and is surrounded by a wall …[which is] 800m long – half a mile!" [235]

By the way, this is the same area of the world where **Puma Punku** is located with its strange laser-cut blocks… You know the natives didn't do that. The blocks below are **andesite** – extremely hard.

Note the fine and straight cuts in the rock, and the precise equi-distant holes.

The blocks also had originally polished surfaces.

These holes (Left) are **precision-engineered** – all cut to the same depth, perfectly smooth and exactly (to the mm) the same distance apart.

(credits: Bing Images/ Puma Punku)

The rest of Puma Punku looks like this (below):

(credit: Bing Images: sistemasolarunido.wordpress.com)

The point? The Anunnaki often got into battles with Others on Earth (not always other Anunnaki) and this base high in the Andes was blasted apart. It was not an earthquake.

While we're doing a brief tour, scientists know the Inca did not build the fortress of **Sacsayhuaman**, but they dismiss it as an anomaly:

Yet what is more interesting is what is **at the top of the hill** protected by the 3 layers of walls. The first row (above) is shown in the lower row of this distance shot :

This next picture is the part the TV shows don't often show (because they don't know what it is): It is related to what was done at Göbekli Tepe (see next section).

(Suggested: an initiation center for Serpent Wisdom. Not a rocket landing pad.)

Moving over to **Ollataytambo**, across the valley, we find the following huge wall:

(credit: en. Wikipedia.org.)

This was a part of something else, note the 'studs' as if to better grasp the wall and move it… or connect it with something.

Also found was this said-to-be agricultural terracing:

(credit: Bing Images: adamandelaineinsa.blogspot.com)

Those circles above are perfectly round and precision cut into the stone at **Moray.** Obviously, ignorant natives did that with stone tools… Note: The fortress of Ollataytambo was a huge religious, military, social, administrative and agricultural complex from the Tahuantinsuyo (Quechua: "4 parts") times. [236] (The Incan Empire consisted of 4 parts or 4 major areas.)

Before examining the Inca History, there is one more anomaly in Peru, at **Nazca**… The archeologists have no idea what the perfect pattern of holes is that accompanies the Nazca Glyphs…[237]

Pisco Holes in Peru
(credits: Bing Images: coolinterestingstuff.com)

A stretch of thousands of mysterious holes punched into the earth, that lead up the hill called **Monte Sierpe** ("Serpent Hill"), located on the same plateau, not far from the Nazca lines. A better look:

7000 holes stretch 1 mile, uphill from the road. These holes are symmetrical and not very deep.And nothing has ever been found in them – they were not used for planting, nor were they remnants of mining operations… It is almost like it was a way to "mark territory", mostly to be seen from high up…. Like the Nazca lines themselves.

Seen from space it looks like a **Serpent**. The holes resemble scales… made by a machine. (The top end is blackened earth. No head.) The Nazca 'animal' glyphs were done by the local natives to urge the Anunnaki to return…

There are those who say that the holes were a big **Egg Farm** – reptilians put their eggs there to hatch. NO shells or any bones have ever been found in them.

Others says that this was a **rainwater catcher** and the local tribes would assign a hole to each family who would take water as they needed it… except that the soil is porous and does not retain water.

Then others says that it is a **binary code** – and the natives (who of course had to be binary code experts) would light fires in certain holes to send a binary message to the ETs – at night…. Except that no ashes have ever been found in any hole, and some rows have 7 holes and others have up to 12 – that is not binary.

What the **Band of Holes** really is is very simple. But you need to see it from the air, about 1 mile up, and you need to take a look at the 'head' up in the north end of the Band. The body looks like a Serpent, the 'head' was defaced/burned, and the holes are the scales:

It resembles a snakeskin.

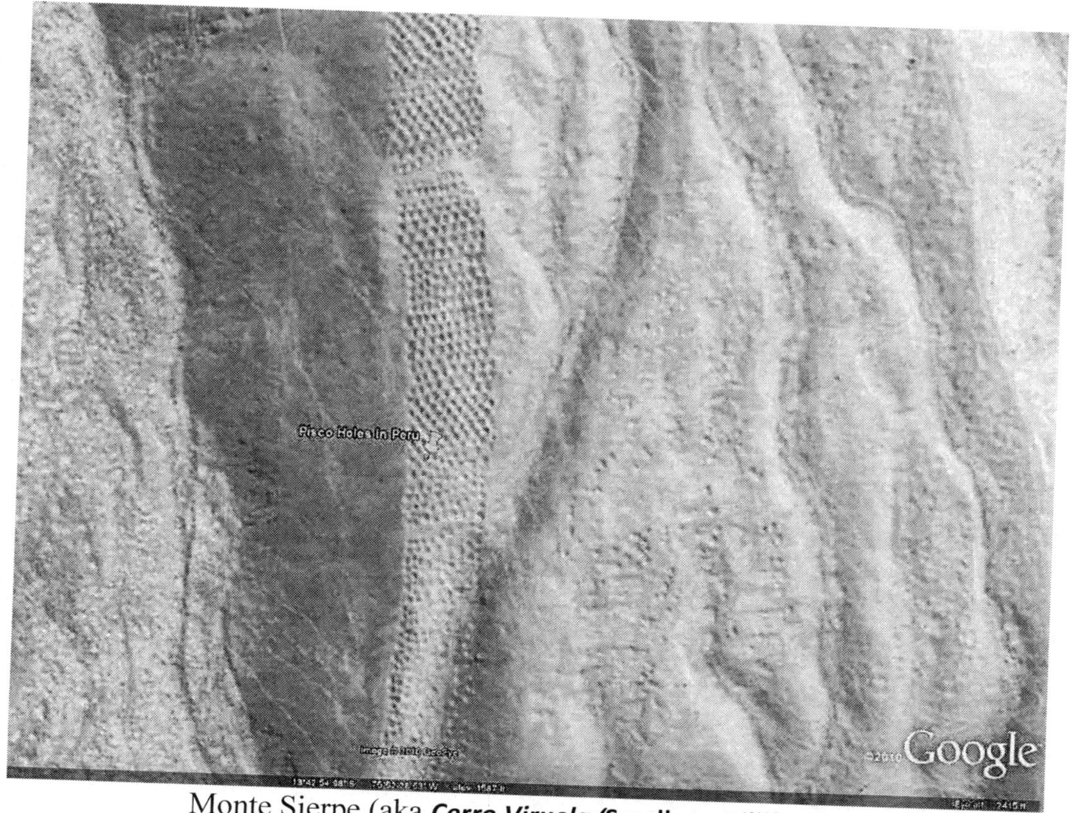

Monte Sierpe (aka ***Cerro Viruela* 'Smallpox Hill')**

Again, it looks like someone was 'marking their territory'.... Perhaps the Serpent Band was a demarcation line for others to stay away... "Don't cross this line!" Or maybe when the 'head' was intact, it used to point to something...?

And just a short distance away (to the right), there are random, practice holes...

And we have a clue: "If you look at the most northern part of the band, you will notice that it ends within **unnaturally darkened area** (it almost looks like the remnant of an explosion)..." [238] Look carefully at the picture above – see the other holes off to the right. There is nothing to discern where the 'head' used to be.

Nonetheless, Man did not make the holes.

And after all the theories (even 'storage holes' and 'pre-dug graves'), no one knows what purpose they served... like the Nazca 'runway' lines on the desert floor (VEG Ch. 10 answered this). What if the ETs were testing drilling equipment, or just fooling around? "Hey, Zarg! Let them try to figure this one out!"

Göbekli Tepe

And then we find something similar to Sacsayhuaman at **Göbekli Tepe**.... (See also Chapter 9...)

The function of **large cupules** has eluded researchers for many years, and cannot simply be grinding holes since they are found in great numbers marking vertical wall surfaces as well as horizontal surfaces. This conundrum can now be definitively put to rest by accurate cross-referencing of **Paleo-Sanskrit texts** that provide direct statements from the builders themselves as to the purpose of the extensive temple complex...

(credit: Bing Images: Human Resonance.org/göbekli_tepe.html)

Cupule marks are the result of repeated strikes by hammerstones against the rockface. Studies replicating the process with comparable materials confirm many thousands of hammerstone strikes were made in the formation of each large cupule, ***generating electricity*** *as the mechanical energy also becomes transduced.* [239]

Listen carefully. These guys were playing with *Kundalini*. The inference is that hammer strikes were generating a small pizeoeletric current in the limestone to move the *Kundalini* in the initiate (who was standing or sitting on it bare-skinned).

A small stone tablet [below] recovered during excavations presents glyphs praising the beneficial effects of electro-acoustic *Kundalini* meditation practices undertaken at the open clustered temples of Göbekli Tepe, reading: ***adhi-as traya kundalini***, meaning "For delivering, protection: **Kundalini.**" This little tablet offers the simplest explanatory statement as to the **sophisticated electro-acoustic functions of the piezoelectric temples**, which once roared with the reverberations of energy as transmitted by the Great Pyramid [240] and **focused via spaceships (hovering above the temple: also see column 2 on front cover).**

Is this amazing or what? Göbekli Tepe is dated to 10,000 BC – and they knew about *Kundalini*! And just in case you think that is a coincidence, look carefully at the picture on the following page…

Caption: A smaller-than-life-size sandstone sculpture of a bald head was recovered at Göbekli Tepe, with only basic facial features (below). The electrical movement of energy experienced by adepts during *Kundalini* meditation under the influence of focused infrasound at megalithic sites is represented by the ***kundalini*** snake glyph. The top of the round head shows the **serpent glyph rising to the crown chakra**, offering the simple glyph statement: ***adhi kundalini***, meaning "Delivering Kundalini."

A Bald Human Head with Two Ears

Translation or not, the picture can't be much clearer. The *Kundalini* comes up the spine, to the back of the head, and opens the Crown chakra.

And while we're at it, in Turkey at Göbekli Tepe, some of the writing on the Vertical T columns has been translated (next picture), and does anyone want to bet whether this following translation will be presented to the public, when discussing Göbekli Tepe? **"Spaceships delivering." (See Appendix C lexicon.)**

The largest standing megalith at Göbekli Tepe is covered with pictograms showing a human figure with reflected standing waves for arms, leading to a pair of hands above a belted animal-skin loincloth (left, only partly excavated).

Embodying ***Indra (god Jupiter)***, the glyphs below the rectangular head state: ***Indra ra • ra-as nau adhi*** meaning "Jupiter granting, the one for granting, **spaceships delivering**" (above).

This sounds like a temple where Serpent Wisdom and **Dragon Fire** were actually practiced. And remember that Inanna and the Anunnaki had "boats of heaven" (i.e., skycraft) with which to get around and could thus be the "spaceships" spoken of.

Pizeoelectric Rousing of *Kundalini*

Hilltop at Göbekli Tepe: Geopolymer Limestone Cement Floors

It is worth repeating the major discussion found on the source website:...[241]

The broad hilltop complex of Göbekli Tepe presents large areas of well-preserved **geopolymer limestone cement floors** that, along with the dozens of **'T'-shaped megaliths** themselves, have been mistaken by onsite archeologists for natural bedrock carved smooth. Paleolithic knowledge of geopolymer chemistry has been clearly demonstrated at the **Visoko pyramids** and can be easily ascertained at Göbekli Tepe.

In fact, large man-made cement pads were poured and used for advanced **psychoacoustic purposes** that have not yet been discerned by modern investigators at Göbekli Tepe. The platforms' smooth surfaces were artificially produced for **barefoot contact with sacred piezoelectric stone that transduces infrasound into a localized electromagnetic field for human benefit.** The piezoelectric geopolymer platform was laid out with a specific plan delineating footpaths, curbs and elevated areas around several permanent features including what appear to be large postholes and oblong slots for securing the bases of megaliths (above).

The **high calcite content of the piezoelectric limestone** enabled efficient transduction of acoustic and mechanical energy into an electrical charge that was applied for **water purification** *and lightwater levitation.* Acoustic separation of protium from deuterium was also achieved by water levitation basins around the pyramids and within passage chambers like Gavrinios, Newgrange, Knowth and Dowth.

Laboratory analysis of the limestone surfaces of the **square basins** (below) revealed the presence of **oxalates**, leading to speculation about beer production. However, the presence of oxalates results from geopolymer stone casting processes employed at Göbekli Tepe to produce megaliths from a liquid slurry of sand, fly ash and water. Oxalic acid was used to chemically disaggregate available bedrock into fine grains. In South America, oxalic acid residues were identified on the **Sacsayhuaman** temple megaliths, and on the surfaces of the **Tiahuanacu** Gate of the Sun. *Göbekli Tepe's standing stones also retain residual oxalates.*

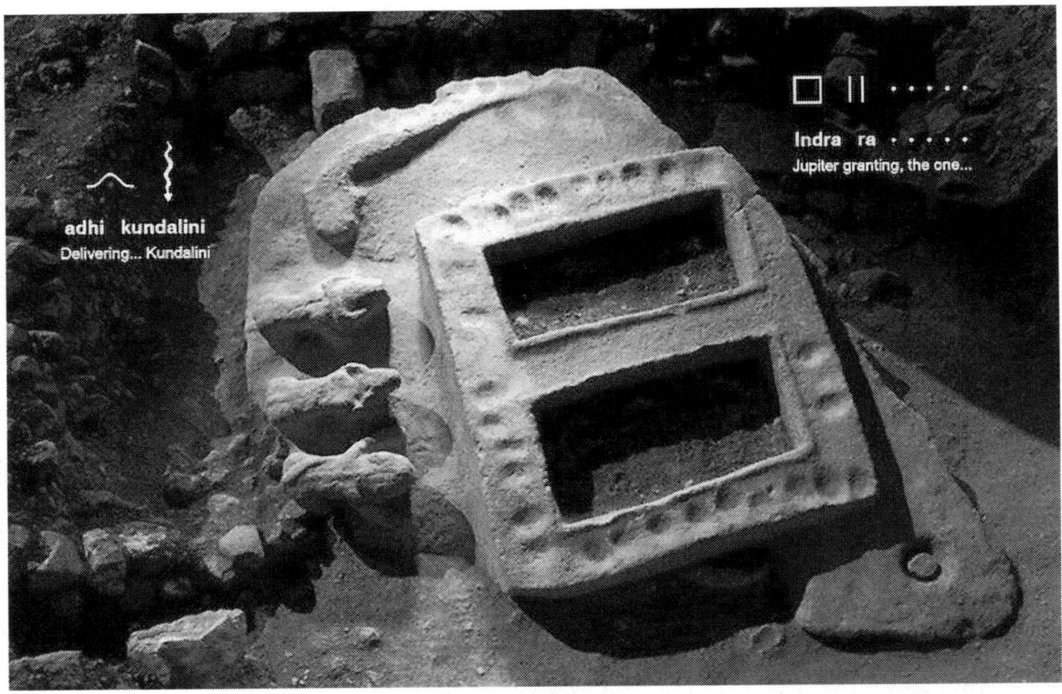

Use involving limestone basins which were also shaped in the square format to signify the deity imparting the benefits by resonant infrasound focused at that site by the Great Pyramid. [Now we know what the great Pyramid was used for – besides Djedhi initiation. No doubt the capstone was the transmitter of the energies that authors like Joseph Farrell and Christopher Dunn claim was generated and beamed … somewhere.][242]

Clear and consistent cultural links to the Vedic practices of barefoot **bioelectrification** and hands-on **Qi healing** that have been well preserved in Asia, but reflect the advanced heritage of a Paleo-Sanskrit motherculture that remains at the root of all spiritual practices worldwide. Hundreds of simple animal pictograms were discovered deep within the Paleolithic caves of **Lascaux** [next pg], Chauvet and dozens of others in present-day

France, all constructed **using the same geopolymer stone reconstitution techniques**.[243]

That means that Göbekli Tepe was designed as a Serpent Wisdom *Kundalini* Initiation Center… That means that the arrangement of the T-megaliths, their composition and the piezoelectric qualities of the whole structure all contributed to an experience, including sound, to awaken and move the *Kundalini.*

> A note on the translations: The **Paleo-Sanskrit** phrase: ***ra las*** -- meaning "Granting shining"-- was inscribed into mold-made lamps at Lascaux Cave in France ~18,000 years ago. This is the same 'scratching' writing found at Göbekli Tepe…
> The highly geometric forms of the megaliths and idealized animal pictograms adorning them correspond closely to **geometric language forms** [below] of the worldwide Paleo-Sanskrit culture, associated in every region of our planet with monumental piezoelectric temples dedicated to the planet Jupiter…
>
> There is a lexicon and explanation of Paleo-Sanskrit on the website:
> http://www.human-resonance.org/paleo-sanskrit.html
>
> Also see **Appendix C** for an introduction to Paleo-Sanskrit.

Lascaux Cave

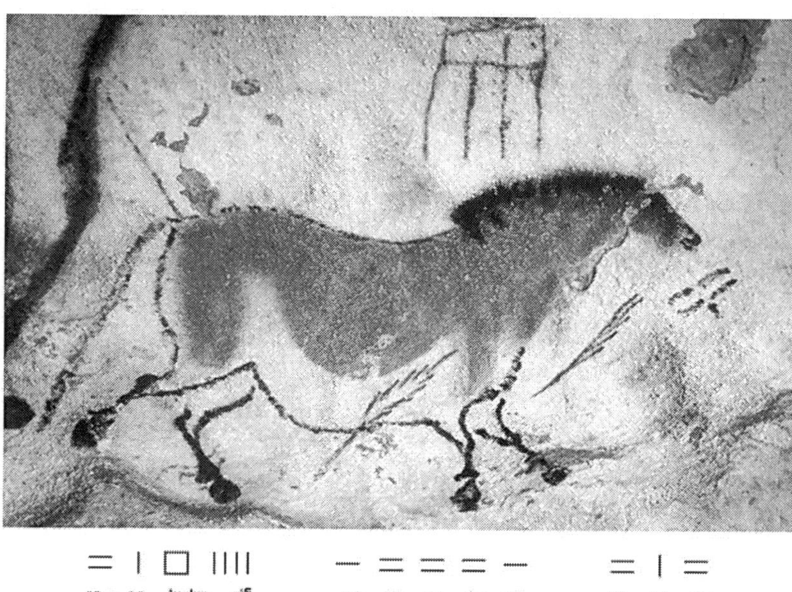

Note the cave wall painting[244] carefully – the lines and 'boxes'… The cavewall was prepped with a white limestone surface and then the artists blew the paint thru a reed onto the wall.

Lascaux was painted about 18,000 years ago – before Göbekli Tepe – and yet they both used the **Paleo-Sanskrit** script: = means "ra" ('granting') and there are two sets of parallel marks = = below the *dun horse's* nose. The square 'boxes' always stand for "Jupiter" (**Indra** reflects a Sanskrit and early *Rig Veda* connection) and the 4 vertical lines from the two boxes could either be "ris" ('diminshing') or more likely the artist repeated Jupiter twice and painted the two vertical lines instead of = the lines were done as ‖. Keep in mind that this was a pictographic, **paleogeometric script** and the 'letter' could be arranged as part of a drawing, or placed at an angle if wanted. Consider the following picture from the temple of Göbekli Tepe…

When is a duck not a duck? When it is a **pictographic (geometric) script**:

Duck bill is = [ra]

Duck chest is ([mi]

Duck rump is) [is]

Duck feet is = [ra]

Unless you know Paleo-Sanskrit you'd never get the message. **(Apx C lexicon.)** And how many archeologists working on Göbekli-Tepe know anything about a language/script used before 10,000 BC?

There is also a reason Göbekli Tepe was buried… what they were doing there was not for casual public eyes…nor did they want the temples desecratred by wandering hordes (like at **Mt. Nemrut** in Chapter 9: Göbekli Tepe Rewind.)… so when they left, they buried the temples.

In short, Man has not been on an ever-rising linear progression to our modern state… in some ways current Man is dumber than he was 5000 years ago. Some of the Ancients were much more advanced than we are. Thus it is 'modern' ego that says we are the pinnacle of Man's development – these same people were the ones who burned Giordano Bruno at the stake (AD 1600) for suggesting that the Earth was NOT the center of the universe, and that the Sun did NOT revolve around the

Earth. As a species, humans make very little progress because their minds are closed – they <u>live in fear</u> of being wrong and thus discredit and discount anything that does not agree with what they think they already 'know.'

Such is a 'disease' called **cognitive dissonance**.

Moving forward, South America has many anomalies, especially in Peru and Bolivia.

Inca Creation and Religion

Inca legend says that they came from 3 caves, from an underground dwelling (just as the Hopi/Navajo say), and **Manco Capac** was the founder of the first city, emerging from a the 3rd cave called **Paqariqtampu.** This "house of production" was located on the hill called Tampu T'uqu (Quechua *t'uqu* a niche, **hole or gap in the wall,** today **also the modern word for window**, hispanicized *Tambotoco, Tamputoco*). The cave thus had three 'windows.' Manco Capac, his three Ayar brothers, and his four Mama sisters, emerged from the chief window in the middle. [245]

> Another theory held by more obscure groups, tending to dwell on the mysticism of South American Indians is that Paqariq Tampu is a quasi-mythical place believed by these historians to have been **flooded** by Lake Titicaca. Chronicles like the one of Guaman Poma mention Paqariq Tampu: "They say they came from Titicaca lake and from Tiahuanaco and they entered Tambo Toco and from there eight Inca brothers and sisters came out... Those eight brothers and sisters came out and …. they went towards the city of Cuzco.[246.]

No mention of creator serpents or the creator gods, and yet, you gotta wonder what was going on **underground**… Why were they living there, and for how long? Did they have helpers ('Ant People') like the Hopi did? Was there a large cataclysm that forced people underground and then they re-emerged later?

> The Inca referred to their empire as ***Tawantinsuyu,*** "the four *suyu*". In Quechua, *tawa* is four and *-ntin* is a suffix naming a group, so that a *tawantin* is a quartet, a group of four things taken together. The empire was divided into four *suyu* ("regions" or "provinces") whose corners met at the capital, **Cusco** (*Qosqo*).

And there is a Quechua 'nod' to the serpents: an Incan Banner which does venerate the Serpent Gods [247]:

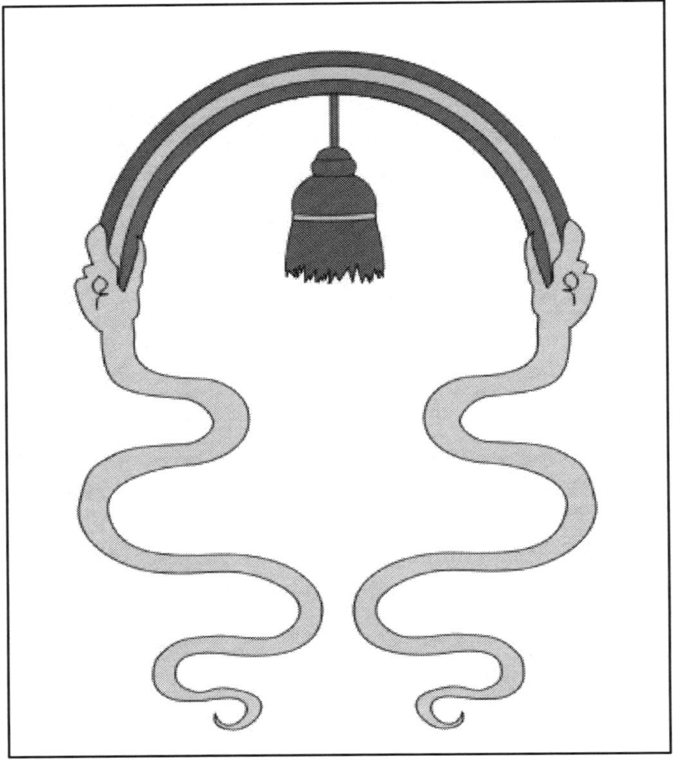

Banner of the Tawantinsuyu

The sign of the Incas was the rainbow and **two parallel snakes** along the width with the tassel as a crown, which each king used to add for a badge or blazon those preferred, like a lion, an eagle and other figures.

In addition, the pictures of helmeted Incas is reminiscent of the Olmec and the Nubian king/warriors….

Short, compact helmets were in style throughout the Central and South American cultures.

(This is not to suggest that the Inca were related to the Olmecs or Nubians, just that the headgear is surprisingly similar.)

(credit: en.wikipedia.org/wiki/Inca_Empire)

The Inca **practiced human** sacrifice, as did the Maya and Aztec cultures, meaning that not only did Viracocha get around (who forbade human sacrifice) but that the Aztec god Huitzilopochtli (a negative Anunnaki) made sure that humans were sacrificed to the gods…

Surprisingly, the Inca believed in **Reincarnation** and thus **mummified** their dead, similar to the Egyptian belief and practice.

The Detmold Child

A mummified child currently on exhibition at the California Science Center in Los Angeles, California. (It was named The Detmold child by its owners Lippisches Land Museum in Detmold, Germany.)

The mummy has been identified to be about 6,500 years old, making it one of the oldest ever found.

Incan mummies were usually found in a seated position.

Peruvian Tree of Life

Chakana (or Inca Cross, Chakana) is - according to some modern authors - the three-stepped cross equivalent symbolic of what is known in other mythologies as the Tree of Life, **World Tree** and so on. Through a central axis a shaman journeyed in trance to the lower plane or Underworld and the higher levels inhabited by the superior gods to enquire into the causes of misfortune on the Earth plane.

(credit: https://en.wikipedia.org/wiki/Inca_mythology#Deities)

The Chakana is also said to be the **Andean Cross**. Note that it is reminiscent of the Maya "T" symbolizing 'Divine Breath' as well as looking like four "T's" put back to back.

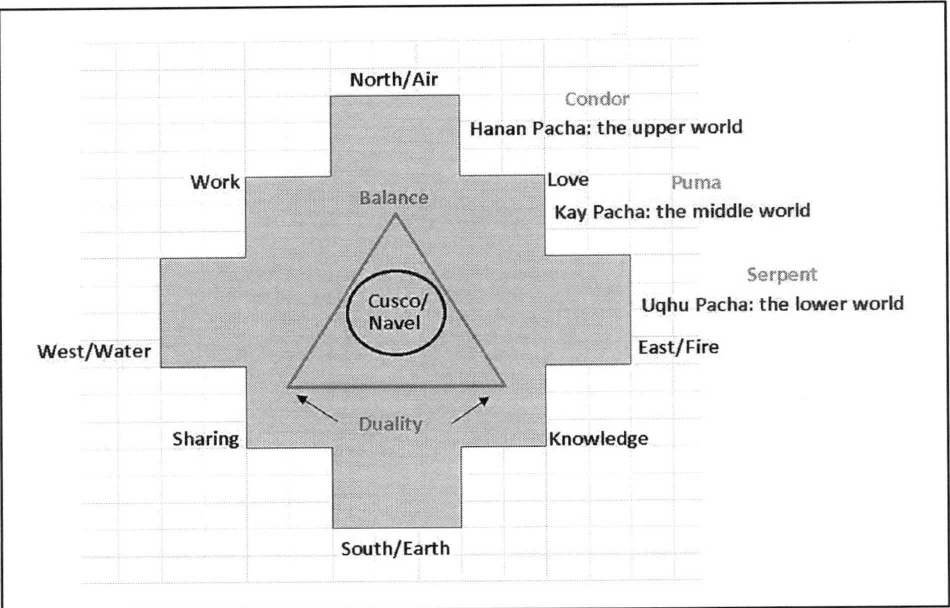

> The **stepped cross** is made up of an equal-armed cross indicating the cardinal points of the compass and a superimposed square. The square is suggested to represent the other two levels of existence....
>
> Garcilaso de la Vega, *el Ynga*, reports about a holy cross of white and red marble or jasper, which was venerated in **16th-century Cusco**. The cross had been kept in a royal house, in a sacred place or *wak'a*, but the Incas did not worship it. They simply admired it because of its beauty. The cross was square , measuring about two by two feet, its branches three inch wide, the edges carefully squared and the surface brightly polished.[248]
>
> **Note that the serpent occupies the Lower World (Uqhu Pacha) in the diagram above (right center, the East) and is assoxciated with fire…** like, Dragon Fire?

Tiahuanaco and the Amarus

In addition, another author has discovered that the Andean Cross was purposely used by the **Amarus,** in building the city of Tiahuanaco, or "**the City of Wisdom.**"

A Peruvian culture called the Quechuas call their leaders and wise men Amaru, or **serpents**. The two best known Dragon Cultures that they initiated were the Inka [sic] and the Chimu. [249]

> After completing their work at Tiahuanaco, the Amarus traveled throughout the Andes while constructing megaliths aligned with the Tiahuanaco vortex. In the process they created a huge Andean "cross/stairstep" pattern with Tiahuanaco as its center. The cross/ stairstep was a symbol carved upon many of the blocks of Tiahuanaco and other megalithic sites. It unites the form of the Greek Cross with the lightning or "stair step" image of the serpent, thus making it an Andean version of the "**serpent on the Tree/cross**."[250] [emphasis added]

Moving from South America to North America…

Anunnaki in North America

The following distribution shows several very important tribes that we will examine more closely: the Diné (Navajo/Hopi), the Cahokia (Mississippian Culture), the Anasazi, and the Lakota (Sioux).

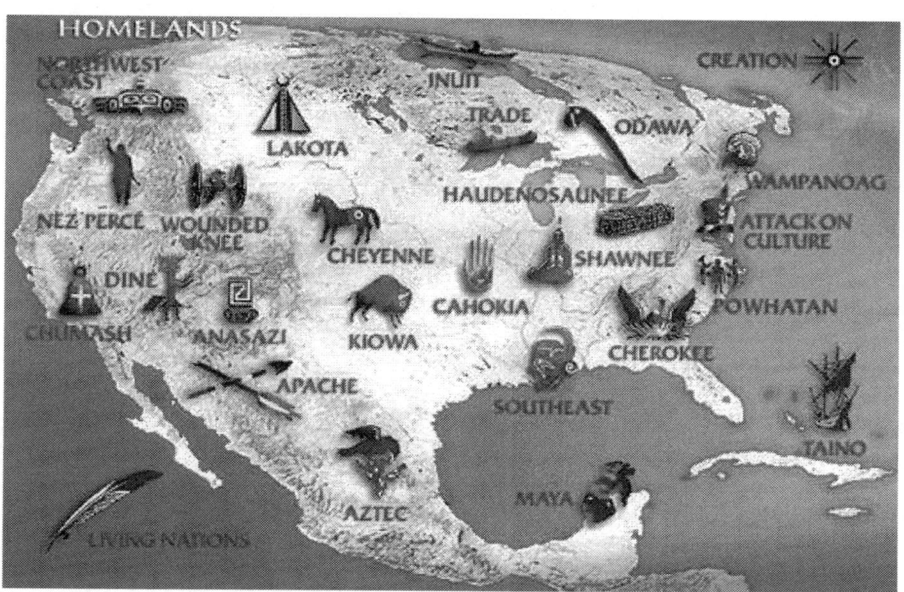

(credit: http://redlionsssci.wikispaces.com/Group%201-11)

Serpents

Preliminarily, it needs to be emphasized that the **Serpent Brotherhood** did go to the New World as Enki wanted to benefit as many humans as possible. Some of the migrating leaders of the Serpent Clans set up serpentine deities to be venerated which were known as **Snake** and **Thunderbird Clans**. Snake initiates would adorn their bodies with tattoos of snakes, or hang snake fangs around their necks. Some functioned as healers within their tribe, and others as *Kundalini* Masters. The Cherokee Serpents sometimes operated as **Dragons** and roamed the area around the tribe protecting it from trespassers. [251]

Many Snakes were part of a long line of adepts whose job it was to pass on secret knowledge, often guarded since leaving the Motherland. And if the Motherland was in India or Atlantis then there should be some similarity in major teachings. The problem as we'll see is that the deeper secret teachings, e.g., those of the Hopi, are still secret and all we know is that they have secret teachings and some prophecies, but the main Southwestern tribes are most likely to at least yield a clue or two…

Navajo (or Diné)

It is said that the Navajo are related to the Apaches, sharing a similar language called Athabaskan, and that the two came into their current regions about AD 1400 from around Canada. And it has been noted that some of the Athabaskan natives (still in Canada) are able to understand the Navajo dialect to this day.

Creation Myth[252]

In the beginning, the First World, or Black World, existed. It was black and had 4 corners and over each corner was a column of colored cloud – black, white, blue, and yellow. The black and white clouds came together at the northeast corner and formed First Man. The yellow and blue clouds came together at the southwest corner and created First Woman. A white wind blew the spirit into First Man and First Woman breathing life into them. Their descendants were the Air People who initially had no form. They began to quarrel and being unhappy with their world, began to climb upwards until they reached the Second World.

When the First People reached the Second World, or the Blue World, they were just as unhappy as they had been before. First Man decided that they should leave this world, too, so he took an abalone, a white shell, turquoise and jet, and he created a wand that carried the people to the Third World, or Yellow World. This too was an unhappy place where people lived sinfully and deviant ways brought them misery. They had leadership problems and people were starving, so First Man knew they

(continued…)

had to move on up again, to the Fourth World, The Black & White World.

Meanwhile Coyote and Water Monster had gotten into a fight and Water Monster was in the process of creating a **Great Flood** to wipe everyone out.

Then a Great Flood came to destroy the world. First Man realized that the people needed higher ground to survive, so he built a tall mountain. Then he planted a cedar, a pine and a reed but none of these were tall enough to reach the next world. So he planted many bamboo shoots in one clump and prayed for a quick growth.

When the next day dawned and the water continued to rise, they found the bamboo shoots had grown together into one huge, hollow, stalk-like **tree.** The people climbed inside the tree and began climbing up it to reach the Fifth World. The locust made a hole in the sky and people began to climb in the Fifth World.

In the Fifth World, First Man brought up soil from the Fourth World and built mountains, houses, and put the Sun and Moon in the sky. To their surprise this world was already populated with Hopi, Zuni, Apache and Ute.

Even in the new land, the Flood was still a threat. People knew it had to be Water Monster who caused the Flood and he must be angry with them. So First Man and Woman reasoned that Coyote, the great trickster, must have done something to anger Water Monster and so they grabbed him and found he had stolen water Monster's coat and also his children and had put them in his coat. They took the coat with the children and put them in a boat and sent them on the Flood to the Water Monster.

The Water Monster was appeased, the Flood stopped and the people could finally live happily and prosper.

So there is the Tree myth – people use it to find life in the Fifth World and escape the Flood.

The Zuñi and Hopi

Perhaps they are best known for their **Kachina** dances – natives wearing colorful masks and portraying the gods whom they revere. Kachinas may also represent a concept, a prayer for fertility or rain and even for deceased ancestors. There are more than 400 types of Kachinas between the Zuñi and the Hopi who both perform Kachina dances.

> ….there may be kachinas for the sun, stars, thunderstorms, wind, corn, insects, and many other concepts. Kachinas are understood as having humanlike relationships; they may have uncles, sisters, and grandmothers, and may marry and have children. Although **not worshipped**, each is viewed as a powerful being who, if given veneration and respect, can use his particular power for human good, bringing rainfall, healing, fertility, or protection, for example. One observer has written:
>
>> The central theme of the kachina [religion] is the presence of life in all objects that fill the universe. **Everything has an essence or a life force**, and humans must interact with these or fail to survive.[253]

(credit: Bing Images: theworldaccordingtochinacat.wordpress.com)

All **Pueblo Indians** (Navajo, Zuñi and Hopi) have a belief that the Kachinas were beneficent real beings who came with the Hopis and Navajos from the **underworld**. The underworld is a concept common to all the Pueblo Indians.

> The Kachinas wandered with the Hopis over the world until they arrived at **Casa Grande** (south of Phoenix), where both the Hopis and the Kachinas settled for a while. With their powerful ceremonies, the Kachinas brought rain for the crops and were in general of much help and comfort. Unfortunately, all of the Kachinas were killed when the Hopis were attacked by enemies (Mexicans) and their souls returned to the underworld. Since the sacred paraphernalia of the Kachinas were left behind, the Hopis began impersonating the Kachinas, wearing their masks and costumes, and imitating their ceremonies in order to bring rain, good crops, and life's happiness.
>
> Another version says that in an early period, the Kachinas danced for the Hopis, bringing them rain and all the many blessings of life. But eventually, the Hopis came to take the Kachinas for granted, losing all respect and reverence for them, so the Kachinas finally left and returned to the underworld [via the San Francisco Mountains].[254]

Sotuknang the God of the Sky
(credit: http://www.trueghosttales.com/kachina-extraterrestrials.php)

Most notable among their masks is the representation of Sotuknang or the **god of the sky**. Like many other ancient societies, the stories are told through the petroglyphs and the cave drawings. These drawings, like the Egyptians and ancient Chinese, have objects that appear to be aircraft of some kind. In the legends of Sotuknang, it is said that he comes to the people on a **"flying shield."** It is reminiscent of other legends and religious histories where it was evident that at the very least, people were thinking about existence outside this particular realm.

Kachina Facts

The Hopi embrace the idea of Reincarnation and 'kundalini energy', including the body's bionet and chakras. Last but not least, they also believe in Karma. [255]

Another point regarding the Kachinas: the **Dogon in Africa** had similar masks and similar dances and there appears to be a connection.

> Within Hopi religion, the Kachinas are said to live on the San Francisco Peaks near Flagstaff, AZ. To the Hopis, the name primarily refers to the supernatural beings who visit the villages to help the Hopis with everyday activities and **act as a link between gods and mortals.** [256] [emphasis added]

In fact that makes the Kachina sound like the Greek gods who resided in the mountains… it tends to give them a flesh-and-blood status….kind of like the Anasazi.

Zuñi Kachinas, on the other hand, are thought to live at the bottom of the Lake of the Dead, a mythical lake which is reached through Listening Spring Lake.

> Although some archaeological investigations have taken place, they have not been able to clarify which tribe, Hopi or Zuñi, was developed first. The Hopis have built their cult into a more elaborate ritual, and seem to have a greater sense of drama and artistry than the Zuñis. On the other hand, the latter have developed a more sizable folklore concerning their Kachinas.[257]

The Hopi identify with the Ant People and say they live **underground** – which was their point of origin (thru a *sipapu* – next section)...

Ant People

The Hopi occasionally tell of the 'others' who live underground and helped them to emerge into this world. Sometimes these 'Ant People' show up to help them thru hard times. This was related in a TV series: [258]

> ***Mysteries at the National Parks*** is an American reality TV series that premiered on May 1, 2015, on the Travel Channel. The series features the secrets and legends in National Parks across the United States.

# 1.7	"Portal to the Underworld"	May 22, 2015

Season 1 Episode 7:

A park ranger's report of ghosts has ties to a deadly commercial airplane collision at the Grand Canyon National Park in Arizona. The planes crashed [in 1956] at a mysterious area of two rivers meet, called "the confluence", where half a century earlier, explorer G.E. Kincaid climbs 1,500 treacherous feet to explore strange stains on a canyon wall that led to his discovery of a cavern full of ancient **Egyptian artifacts**. And it's also where a college student and a Hopi Indian say they found a portal to a futuristic metropolis believed to be inhabited by what the Pueblo tribe described as **"ant people"** who helped save them from natural disasters.

Considering that the Naga live underground, they are a prime suspect for the role – but they do not look like ants… which would have large heads and spindly bodies…. But there is a being that we are all familiar with nowadays that looks like that…. Sounds suspiciously like a **Grey**… but let's let the Hopi show us in their petroglyphs:

Note the one on the far right between two serpents…. and the antennae… There are no less than 4 serpents pictured (1 left and 3 right).

(credit: Bing Images: http://lauriezuckerman.blogspot.com/2010/05/laurie-zuckerman-photographs-canyon.html)

Another version of the Hopi emergence story is that they came up from underground thru the Sipapu…

Hopi Sipapu Grand Canyon

Note the hole top center.

It is a sacred place of pilgrimage for the Hopi, at the bottom of the Canyon of the Little Colorado above its junction with the Colorado River. [259]

The Pueblo people all have that emergence story… Navajo, Hopi and Zuñi.

Could the Ant People be pictured below (left and right of the Kachina)?

There are hominids with antlers… or antennae… like **Cernunnos, the Celtic god** (Chapter 3).

(credit: Bing Images)

This **Sipapu** (Hopi word) aspect needs just a bit more examination: A *sipapu* is also a hole in the floor of a kiva (which usually has a covering [roof] for privacy) :

Sipapu in a Ceremonial Kiva

The Hopi Sacred Stories explain that this is the hole in which the first peoples of this world entered. As "They" stepped outside of the "Sipapu," they **morphed from lizard-like beings into homo sapiens,** or human form (See F. Waters, 1963, and later reprints; Courlander, 1971). It is from this point that the "First Peoples" of the Earth began to divide and separate, creating differing tribes along the first journeys of the first humans.[260]

Two other authors, Dr. A.C. Ross (aka *Ehanamani*) and Dr. George Hunt Williamson (Road in the Sky), reported that the Hopi, which means "peaceful people," like many Amerindian tribes' legends, said **they came from the stars**, as recorded in the creation songs of the Two Horn Society. The Aztec, Creek, Osage, Navajo and D/Lakota tribes venerate the 7 stars of the Pleiades and (as shown on the Summary page of this chapter) the Hopi uniquely use pottery designs reflecting the ancient canals of Mars. The Red race was native to Atlantis and when it sank, they fled to North America, which is why their legends all reflect a similar origin. So coming from a "hole" into this world sounds like using a **portal** to make the journey to Earth…? (Think: stargate.)

Percival Lowell , the eminent astronomer, actually recorded canals on Mars, that have since disappeared: It is suggested that the beings on Mars knew we were about

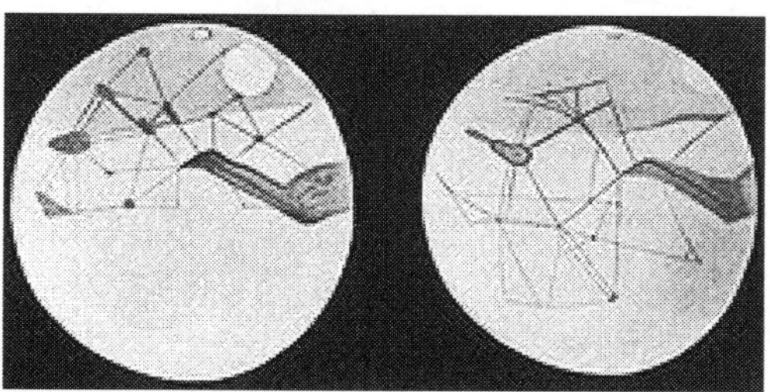

to use telescopes to closely examine their planet, and they wanted their presence to remain secret (including shooting down 2 Phobos probes from the USSR – see Chapter 1) and they replaced surface canals with what is shown on page 618 of Apx. A.

Snake Clans

The Pueblo Indians often practiced snake dances – using live rattlesnakes. They were deposited on the floor of a kiva and allowed to crawl over the clan members' bodies until a fearless 'rapport' is reached and soon the members are daringly picking up the snakes and holding them in their hands… or clenching them between their teeth. [261]

There is also reported to be an esoteric act by the members of the Snake Clan and herein we find the *Kundalini* element again:

> Following the gathering ritual [playing with the serpents in the kiva] is a foot race wherein 7 runners speed along a straight track of desert, each holding a stick of a different color, and each races up to the top of a steep bluff. The colors of the sticks represent the seven chakras thru which the serpent kundalini must race to the crown [head] chakra and produce enlightenment. [262]

During the sixteen-day Snake Dance festival, there is another 'marriage' of *Kundalini* with the crown chakra when a young girl from the Snake Clan is 'married' to a to a young boy from the Antelope Clan [symbolizing the Crown chakra] – the male and female components of the Ida and Pingala *Kundalini* essence. Keep in mind that this teaching began in India, moved to China, and now is practiced by the Pueblo (Hopi) peoples in Southwest America. Obviously the Brotherhood of the Serpent was at work here.

The climax of the sixteen day festival is when the Snake Clan paint themselves vermillion red (the color of the serpent fire) and the members of the Antelope Clan paint themselves silvery grey paint (the color of the Crown chakra) and they dance together symbolizing the union of polarity and the merger of *Kundalini* with the Crown chakra.

Thunderbird Clan

Another fascinating branch of the North American Serpent Clan is that of the Thunderbird Clan. The Thunderbird is a version of the **Chinese rain dragon** and is a form of the Great Spirit, or a manifestation of the Primal Dragon and an aspect of the Serpent. [263]

> Many members of the Thunderbird Clan also acquire the ability to channel the serpent power of the "Bird of Lightening" through their own bodies and then utilize it for healing and spiritual transformation. … This power is very concentrated and deadly… [but] When handled

appropriately … this awesome energy can be transmitted to others to elicit a spontaneous healing or to awaken the Kundalini…the inner "lightening serpent."[264]

The great ChiGong healers in China have been doing this for centuries – amassing and using *chi* to heal or perform martial arts. (Covered in this book's Introduction and also in Transformation of Man.)

As an interesting aside, the Amerindians also knew about the huge, black, flying **pteradactyls** (Pteranadons) which also received the name, Thunderbirds. They were last seen in the Southwest about 120 years ago.

Bing Images

The above picture is believable as the author's grandfather, who had a cattle ranch back in 1903 just north of Brownsville TX, shot a **Pteradactyl** that kept attacking his cattle at night. He showed me a picture of the bird, hung on the side of the barn, away from the public road, and it looked just like the above photo. It was the same size… maybe a 20' wingspan. When the County Agent next came out to inspect the ranch, he saw the bird, and had the Army come out, take it down, and carry it away. (Upon my grandfather's death in 1978, the picture was not among his scapbooks or momentos.)

Orion – Hopi Connection

This has already been explored by TV programs, especially the *Ancient Aliens* series, but because it is relevant, it is briefly included here. The Hopi deliberately set up several villages copying the layout of the Orion Constellation….

That is not a coincidence. For reasons unstated and undocumented, the Hopi chose to mirror the Orion Constellation – just as the Egyptians (or their ancestors) set up the three large pyramids mirroring **Orion's Belt** …as was shown in Chapter 6. This suggests a connection between the Hopi and the beings from Orion – else why not picture Scorpio or Libra? Could the beings from Orion have also been on Mars (as well as guiding the Egyptians in the layout of the Earth pyramids)? And if they were also the Kachinas, why hide their faces… unless they were humanoid, but not human-looking?? **This is reminiscent of the Anunnaki (Orion reptilians) who stayed up in their ziggurats until they developed human offspring (Marduk and Inanna, etc…) and could move among the humans.**

And now for an interesting connection…

Lakota Sioux

Keep in mind that the Sioux are from the Dakotas, or northern US near Canada. So why do they also have a Thunderbird Clan, why is their name **Teton Sioux** (from Nadouessioux - **'snake'** or 'enemy'), and why do they also say they emerged from **underground**? [265] If a stargate was used, as in the case of the Hopi, perhaps it was underground, to hide it…?

Waukheon was their name for the Thunderbird, and **Unhcegila** was their name for an interesting serpent creature, profiled below: [266]

Unhcegila (Unk Cekula) is a serpentoid creature which was responsible for many unexplained [Sioux] disappearances and deaths.

She was described at first as having no real shape or form; she had eyes of fire, and a fanged mouth that was shrouded in a smoky or cloudy mass. As time went on further, her form was exposed as being massive, with a long scaly body whose natural armour was almost impenetrable. Her eyes burned with wrathful hunger, her claws were like iron, and her voice raged like thunder rolling in the clouds. [Ed.: sounds like a 'dragon' or flying craft…]

Whoever who looked upon her will get blind, go insane, and die on the fourth day. […from radiation poisoning…?]

Her weakness is a seventh spot on her head, behind which a flashing red crystal lies within, which functioned as her heart. To kill her, one has to shoot a medicine arrow at it. This crystal was much sought after by many warriors, as it grants its bearer great power.

The ancient Lakota tribes of the Northwest had heard rumors, from neighboring tribes, that a nameless shadow had **emerged from the icy Atlantic waters** of the far Northeast. In time the creature had come to the Black Hills (Ȟe Sápa) seeking a new home in the mountains. Once she arrived and made a place in the mountains, she coexisted with everyone, from the tribes to the Wamakaskan and the other spirit beings, before she became the cause of chaos and fear.

Over the many years in which she wreaked havoc in the Hills, she was challenged by many warriors from the Lakota tribe. It was learned that the creature had offspring, and the tribes had to kill them when they began feeding on people.

She was slain after she ate the family of a great warrior from the bear clan. This warrior was told by a Weasel spirit that if he was to get swallowed by **Unk Cekula,** he could use his knife to cut his way out of the belly of the beast, and free the other victims.

The Lakaota Sioux was one of the many tribes who not only feared the Thunderbird, but regarded "…them as ancestors to the human races who played a part in the creation of the world." [267] (Watchers or Devas?)

And lastly, regarding the Hopi, there is one more interesting aspect to them – their language.

Hopi Langauge

> **Hopi** (Hopi: *Hopílavayi*) is a Uto-Aztecan language spoken by the Hopi people of northeastern Arizona, USA. **Uto-Aztecan** is a Native American language family consisting of over 30 languages …. found almost entirely in the Western United States and Mexico. The name of the language family was created to show that it includes both the Ute language of Utah and the **Aztecan languages of Mexico**… including the Pipil language of El Salvador….
> The Nahuatl (Aztecan) language is still spoken by 1.5 million people. [268]

That connects the Aztecs with the Hopi/Navajo. It has been known for years that the Aztecs wandered south from the United States until they settled in what is now the Mexico City area. Just as the Navajo are connected with the Hopi, that means the Navajo and the Hopi and the Anasazi ("the ancient ones") are also connected.

Anasazi

So what, if any, relationship is there between the Hopi/Navajo and the Anasazi?

> Anasazi in Navajo means 'enemy ancestors.' In contemporary times, the people and their archaeological culture were referred to as **Anasazi** for historical purposes, a name which was given them by the Navajo, **who were not their descendants**. Reflecting historic traditions, the term was used to mean "ancestors of enemies," and contemporary Puebloans [Hopi, Zuñi, and Navajo] do not want this term used. [269]

It seems that some fifteen hundred years after the Pueblo People had been living here [in the Southwest], a strange tribe of wild barbarians began to trickle in. The Hopis called them **Tavasuh** (because they killed people with stone clubs). Today they are known to us as Navajos, a proud and enterprising people and one of the richest Indian tribes in America.

(continued…)

Why then if the early Navajos are not called by the Pueblo name of Tavasuh, should the ancestors of the Pueblo people be known by the Navajo name of Anasazi?

Secondly, where these Ancient Ones came from still poses a moot question among anthropologists. Most guess they came across the Bering Strait about 15,000 years ago... still others speculate they may have had an origin farther **to the East**.. perhaps in a place that mirrors their name as they eventually left the Pueblo area and headed into Mexico as Mexica, or Aztecs... **from Aztlan**.

The Anasazi left their home in the Four Corners (Cliff Dwellings) due to a great 300-year drought and migrated south to live among the pueblos of the Hopi and Zuñi... and the Colorado River.

Much evidence connects the Anasazi with the Hohokam and Mogollon cultures more to the south...

For a quick map reference:

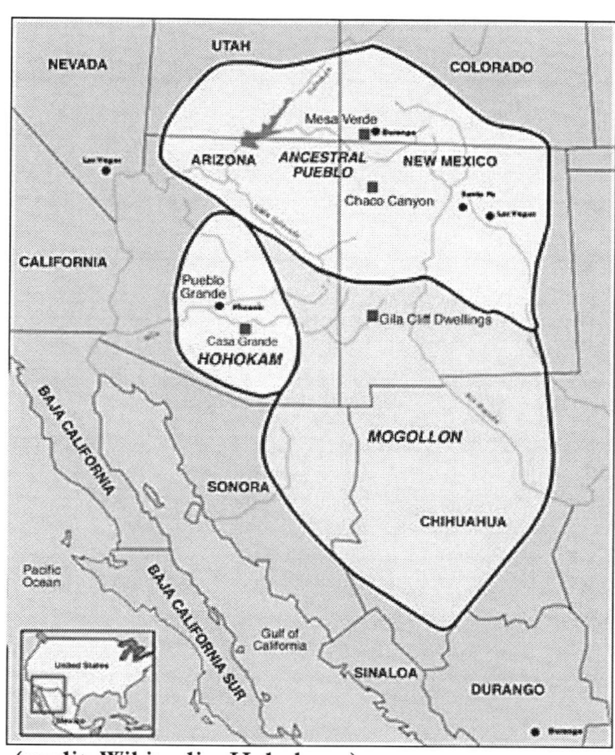

(credit: Wikipedia: Hohokam.)

The essence of this is that no one knows just where they came from, but they were **too barbaric like the Aztecs**, sharing the same language group, and no one knows what they called themselves as they left no written records. But they were related to the Hohokam and Morgollon Cultures.

The Anasazi, Navajo and Aztecs are related. (Chapter 13, Number Seven section.)

It is known that the Aztecs came from North America into Mexico, but their origin is farther East…. (see pp 266, 301, & 547).

Supposing the Anasazi came from the East, (and Aztecs and Navajo) that could suggest they all were part of the **Mississippian Culture**, of which Cahokia was their greatest settlement. And Cahokia was settled by the refugees from Atlantis…

Cahokia

And if you look closely, at the artist rendition (below) based on written descriptions of the settlement, it looks a lot like the Aztec city of **Tenochtitlan** (p. 303).

Life at Cahokia was filled with workers going about daily activities and the tasks of house building in the shadows of the tall mounds occupied by the elite. (press.uchicago.edu)

The Cahokians were also known to practice sacrifice….

…and if that doesn't remind you of the Aztecs, nothing will.

Cahokian Priest with Victim's Head

(credit: Wikicommons: Herb Roe.)[270]

One last bit of a link to the Aztec culture. Aztec warriors were fond of participating in the **Eagle Warrior** (exclusive!) cadre:

Aztec Eagle Warrior

(Left: Bing Images: yucanito.blogspot.ca**)**

...and below is a warrior from Cahokia: note the Eagle mask and feathers...

(credit right: Wikicommons: Herb Roe)[52]

The Mississippian Culture extended north to the Great Lakes, south to Louisiana, and east to North Carolina. It influenced many Amerindian groups, and likely spawned the Navajo and Aztecs.

And if that weren't enough, lastly we will examine the Ohio Serpent Mound – which is literally just "up the road" from the Mississippian Culture.

Ohio Mound Builders

The serpent is a popular image in Northern American natives' mythology.

Bing Images (2): Serpent Mound

The serpent has 7 curves (**Pleiades imagery**) and appears to be about to swallow an egg . Eggs symbolize birth and re-birth. The Ohio Mound is reputed to have been created about AD 1070 (ascertained by C14 dating.) But it is not an egg…

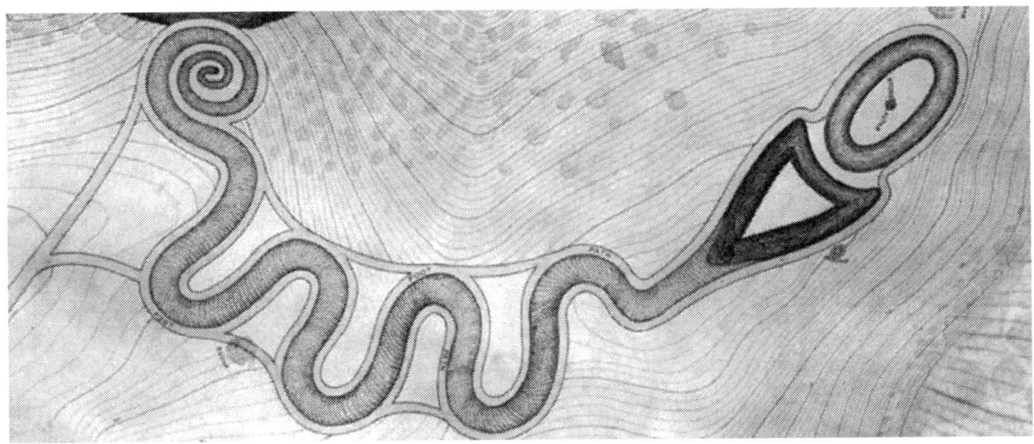

Turtle leading a Serpent

Shooting Star, chief of the Sioux tribe, came from an ancestral group called the "Turtles" – a branch of the fire worshipping **Atlantean Serpents.** According to their ancient records, following the destruction of the Old Red Land [Atlantis had very red-colored earth] the Turtles traveled on ships to .... the Mississippi Delta region .... where they were met by their ancient brothers, the **Iroquois Serpents** [note: Iroquois means "serpents"] who **followed them up the [Mississippi] River to their new homeland**. The Turtles became known as the Lakota [Sioux which also means "serpents"].

According to the late Deecodah of the extinct Elk tribe of the **Algonquins**, the long journey of the two tribes is commemorated at Serpent Mound in Ohio, which **depicts a turtle leading a snake.** [271] [emphasis added]

As a side note, the Turtle is often found in other cultures' mythology – Among the Hindu it is the World Turtle, supporting the Earth, and among the Chinese it is the Dragon Turtle.

Secondly, the **Algonquin** were perhaps the first tribe in North America and they claim to have originated (like the Sioux and the Apache) in Pan, and they called themselves Pauns, allegedly meaning "colonists from Pan." Also, the **Annishnabeg** are said to have come directly from Atlantis, and their name means "the people from where the Sun rises." In addition, it is interesting that the **Choctaw** in Oklahoma hint that their roots are in Atlantis as the state's name is derived from the Choctaw words *okla* and *humma*, meaning "red people" or "Sun people of the Redland."

(2nd ¶ source: Mark Pinkham[272])

What is unique about the Mound is that it accurately tracks the two annual solstices. And the Mound itself is not unique as there are two others like it – one in Scotland and one in Ontario, Canada. They are also used as **burial mounds**.

The Serpent Mound's coils being aligned to **the two solstice and two equinox** events each year. If the Serpent Mound were designed to sight both solar and lunar arrays, it would be significant as the consolidation of astronomical knowledge into a single symbol. The head of the serpent is aligned to the summer solstice sunset and the coils also may point to the winter solstice sunrise and the equinox sunrise. [273] [emphasis added]

> The Serpent Mound may have been designed in accord with the pattern of stars composing the constellation **Draco**. The star pattern of the constellation Draco fits with fair precision to the Serpent Mound, with the ancient Pole Star, Thuban (α Draconis), at its geographical center within the first of **seven coils** from the head.
>
> Why were primitive people so obsessed with venerating the stars?

Some researchers date the earthwork to around 5,000 years ago, based on the position of Draco, through the backward motion of precessionary circle of the ecliptic when **Thuban was the Pole Star**. Alignment of the effigy to the Pole Star at that position also shows how true north may have been found. This was not known until 1987 because lodestone and modern compasses give incorrect readings at the site. Somewhere in antiquity, a **meteorite** crashed into the ground where the Mound was built – about 250 million years ago – and by the time the Mound was built, there would have been no geologic features to reveal the **underground presence** of a lodestone meteorite…So was the Mound in this location a "coincidence," like the astronomical alignments?

Underground Summary

At this point, it should have registered with a close reading that the theme of living underground or emerging from underground into this world, even coming out thru a cave, is rather a global *meme*.

Here is a rundown of the cultures who said they <u>left</u> an underground world:

Amerindians	Navajo, Hopi, Zuñi Sioux, Acoma, Arikara
Australia	some Aborigines, some spirits
India/China	Nagas
South America	Incas, Chamacoco, Mbaya, Tereno
West Indies	Taino

What this suggests is that if there was a cataclysm and people had to seek shelter in caves, or even underground, their recorded world began when they emerged again into the Sun on the Earth's surface…. And many of the world's cultures have an additional legend about a Flood (usually somewhere back about 8,000 – 10,000 BC).

In addition, let's not forget that Turkey was home to a couple of extensive underground cities – **Cappadocia** and **Derinkuyu** (Chapter 9) … makes one wonder what they were avoiding… war or cataclysm?

Even today, Man has built underground structures all over the world. Some are residential, some are commercial, and many more are military. If you want protection, or want something to survive potential cataclysms (like the **Svalbard Seed Bank**), build it underground, preferably in granite strata. Some US data storage companies have enlarged and reinforced the abandoned salt mines.

Here is a Swedish IPS office 100' below the streets of Stockholm:

White Mountain Office

(credit: http://www.jsonline.co.uk/blog/work-is-beautiful-ten-amazing-offices-around-the-world/)

As Man continues to abuse the environment, and continues the relentless drop in oxygen on the planet (if oxygen levels drop another 8-10%) no one will be breathing. We already have 20% less oxygen in the air than we did 100 years ago (Yes, scientists have been measuring it)[274] , but land developers and their deforestation, Fukushima radiation spreading thru the Pacific Ocean, humans creating the Pacific Ocean Trash Vortex, and bilge pumps from large sea tankers all continue to destroy the ocean's oxygen level. (See footnote 274 addendum.)

And because you thought the **Hobbit Homes** were just fiction:

Developed by E2BN for the National Education Network, UK
(credit: http://gallery.nen.gov.uk/asset74896_403-.html)

And Cappadocia, Turkey (above).

> If the abuse of the environment continues at the current pace, our only hope for survival will be to either leave the planet, or move underground into a completely self-sustaining complex… just they did on Mars (VEG, Apx A).

Rewind: Hopi Summary

So there we have some serpent imagery in the North American continent, as well as a hint at Others visiting humans and helping them. Of particular note is the legend where the Pueblo People (Navajo/Zuñi/Hopi) come into the current or Fourth World from underground (as did the Incas). But there is a bit more to the overall story including some Flood imagery…

> [Another] version (mainly told in Oraibi) has it Tawa destroyed the Third World in a **great flood**. Before the destruction, Spider Grand-Mother sealed the more righteous people into hollow reeds which were used as boats. Upon arriving on a small piece of dry land, the people saw nothing around them but more water, even after planting a large bamboo shoot, climbing to the top, and looking about. Spider Woman then told the people to make boats out of more reeds, and using **island "stepping-stones"** along the way, the people **sailed east** until they eventually arrived on the mountainous coasts of the Fourth World [Chile]. [275] [emphasis added]

So the Serpent imagery, the Flood and sailing east ("island hopping" as was suggested earlier), and a belief in Karma & Reincarnation as found in India, suggests the Hopi may have originated in Mu (not Atlantis), after they came to Earth from the stars. Lastly, did they have any legend about a great Teacher or Benefactor, such as **Quetzalcoatl**?

Kokopelli

There were many Serpent Wisdom benefactors in the Southwest (including **Kokopelli,** a fertility god) who roamed from village to village, playing his flute, and planting his seeds. (Yes, both types.)

On his head are dreadlocks, and he is sometimes pictured as 'humpbacked' when really that is just his **backpack**.

Not much is known about him or where he came from. He wooed maidens, brought the rain, and granted big harvests. The Hopi say he was an envoy between Man and the gods.

The Pale Teacher

There is one benefactor that stands out – because he was fair–skinned and bearded. The Hopi called him **Massau** (aka Pahana), the Great White Brother who will one day return as a Deliverer from the East and bring the missing piece of the set of Sacred Stone Tablets on which he wrote the commandments by which the Hopi have lived for centuries (sound familiar?).

Masaw Teaching the Amerindians
(credit: Bing Images)

He is said to have traveled the width and breadth of the North American continent, and was called **Emeeshtotl** by the Algonquins, which means **"feathered serpent."** In addition, the Choctaw called him **Em-Me-shee**, the wind god. The Iroquois called him Hia-wa-sah, **"the plumed serpent"** and recognized him as a Master Teacher. The Pawnees remember him as Paruxti, and the Dacotahs referred to him as Waicomah.[276] According to most tribal legends, when the Pale Teacher appeared, he was wearing a long white robe and sandals. Upon his hand was inscribed the Tau Cross, symbol of the androgenous **Serpent Sons**. [277]

So there we again have Serpent imagery, The Flood, migrating east, and the presence and guidance of a being like Quetzalcoatl. Remaining: it was said earlier that the Hopi drew designs on their pottery that resembled the canals on Mars, as also drawn by Percival Lowell.

Martian Pottery

Percival Lowell was the first American scientist to observe and draw the canals on Mars in 1903 (the Italian Schiaparelli, was the first in 1877):

He observed the canals thru a large 24" telescope. Note: polar icecap was larger than today.

And the Hopi made pottery in the 1800s which is reminiscent of the canals:

Hopi Pottery:

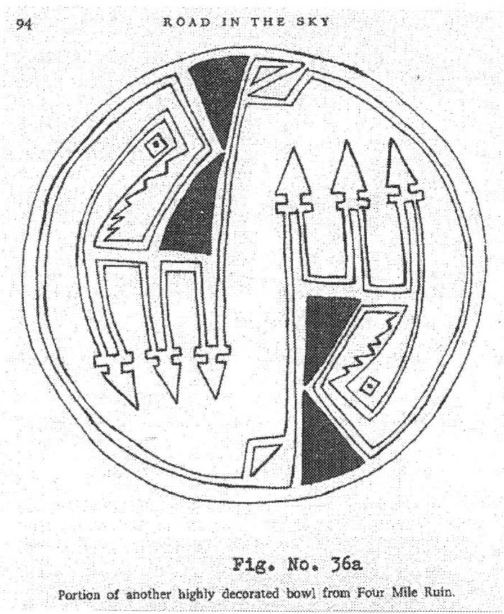

94 ROAD IN THE SKY

Fig. No. 36a

Portion of another highly decorated bowl from Four Mile Ruin.

Martian Landscape:

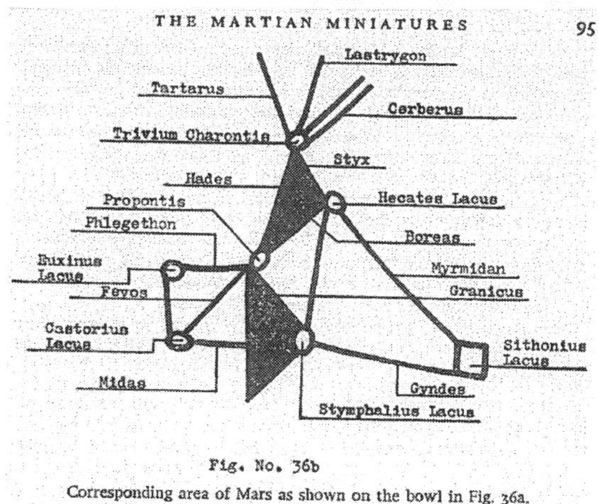

THE MARTIAN MINIATURES 95

Fig. No. 36b

Corresponding area of Mars as shown on the bowl in Fig. 36a.

(credit: GH Williamson's Road in the Sky, pp 94-95.)

What is amazing is that he received the **Prix Jules Janssen**, the highest award of the *Société astronomique de France*, the French astronomical society for his work in 1904. He later went on to search for and promote the existence of Planet X (soon to be called Pluto, discovered in 1930 by Tombough at the same Lowell Observatory). Because he was anything but a flake, and Schiaparelli also saw the canals, there was something there. Telescopes of that size do not lie. One has to wonder whether the canals were there before 1915 and then 'disappeared.' Lowell died in 1916.

General Summary

This chapter covered South and North America. Chapter 8 is thus a miscellaneous grouping of Oceania, Australia, Fiji, Indonesia, Tibet and back to Africa.

As can be seen so far, the gods were busy all over the globe, often shepherding humans, sacrificing some and teaching others… leading one to realize that some gods were benevolent and some were malevolent. The Flood mythology has turned out to be over most of the globe (but not 100%) – many cultures having some reference to it, and most cultures include some sort of Tree of Life. A few others have revealed their awareness of the *Kundalini* force, and yet the Anunnkai seem to have kept this teaching close to their Mesopotamian headquarters – Egypt, India and Turkey knew of it, but the father away one gets from Iraq, the less one hears of it.

While the Serpent Wisdom teaching was probably known to the Mayan adepts, and perhaps the Incas, one does not hear of it in North America, nor in Africa… as if it was "reserved" for the civilizations that evolved first – i.e., the oldest ones like China, India and Egypt. And it will later be seen that the Teachings went underground as they went to the New World and to Europe. It was obviously not for the masses – whom Enlil had always judged to be inferior. Thus the Teaching was briefly taken by Enki publicly – until the Western Church and the Egyptian dynasties suppressed it. This is examined in a later chapter.

It will also be seen that while the White Hats ('good guys') were going around the world trying to develop Man, the Black Hats were promoting human sacrifice and religions with dissension – so that Man would not be able to unite. Enlil did not want humans to unite, whereas Enki did. And as we learned in Chapter 4, not only were some cities nuked by the Anunnaki in what is now the Middle East (e.g., Sodom & Gomorrah, *et al*) we also had warfare in India, in the Indus Valley and at least 4 more cities were nuked in sky battles there (e.g., Mohenjo-Daro and Harappa, *et al*). And sometimes the humans were the pawns in the gods' wars with each other.

> This is where other ETs stepped in and invited the Anunnaki to go home and have been more like Watchers and protective of what happens on Earth. ETs may be still here, yet so are Those who were here before Man (the Ancient Ones, or Shining Ones)… and it looks like there is still a battle for the planet and humans because peace doesn't come to Earth… Black Hats vs White Hats again ... examined in the **Epilog**.

Chapter 8: Global Dispersion

The purpose of this chapter is to wind up the global tour and reveal other, minor places where the Anunnaki visited; other places where the Serpent Wisdom is found, and where else religion has both an exoteric and an esoteric aspect. The whole point of the first half of the book (8 chapters) is to show how similar teachings and images were found all over the world – even though many ancient native cultures did not have direct contact with each other (e.g., Fijians and Norse Vikings), and many have been thousands of miles apart – and often centuries apart.

The message in that is the theory that either the cultures with similar beliefs and imagery came from a common, but ancient source, or there was a third party who visited humans in many different places.

What will be discovered is that both are true: the cultures that are now separated by thousands of miles came from a source that does not now exist (e.g., Atlantis could have been the source for the Mayans and the Egyptians), AND there was a third party (Anunnaki) who were flying around the globe in their 'Sky Boats' and teaching humans agriculture (including the similar technique of 'terrace' farming in Chile and the Philippines), medicine (using herbs), religion ('Tree of Life' in multiple countries), and laws for managing a civilization, such as the Hammurabi Code (Iraq/Mesopotamia), the Law of Moses, Draco's Code (Greece), and Law of Manu (India). And don't forget Chapter 1 and the Norse *Thing* – an assembly where Norse Law ruled (Bjarkey Law and Uppland Laws and their predecessors)…

Our world expedition will start with a look at Indonesia, in reality a part of Indonesia called Bali where there is something reminiscent of Mayan culture, and connects with the last chapter.

Global Tour

Indonesia (Bali)

The following pictures show something very similar, and before some 'expert' announces that the Balinese image is that of a Fu Dog (implying a Chinese influence), the point is that a vicious, fanged image was attached in both cultures to the outside of a temple – and they do resemble each other. However, Balinese and Mayans never interacted, to our knowledge… so is it just an interesting coincidence?

BALINESE

MAYAN

And on second thought, could the Maya have seen something like the following ship when Quetzalcoatl came to them?

Note the 'feathers' around (above) Quetzalcoatl's head and their similarity to the open flanges on the ship.

Could this ship be mistaken for a dragon?

Remember that when people thought they saw a dragon, they had to already have heard of the legend of dragons in order to be able to consider that that was what they were seeing. The very first time a native saw one of the Anunnaki flying craft, s/he would not have known what to call it… except maybe a "flying boat" (as they did in Sumeria), or a large bird (see Cambodia below), or a flying shield…. Certainly it would be something to do with the gods since they were from the sky (where heaven was alleged to be located) and any display of power (beyond what Man can do) was always attributed to the gods.

Oceania (Borneo)

Almost in the same area of the world, we come to the **Dayak** people… natives of Borneo. They have a creation myth and a reverence for serpents – believing that ancestors can return as **serpents** and so killing one is a taboo.[278]

> Underlying the world-view is an account of the creation and re-creation of this middle-earth where the Dayak dwell, arising out of a cosmic battle in the beginning of time between **a primal couple**, a male and female bird/**dragon (serpent)**. Representations of this primal couple are amongst the most pervasive motifs of Dayak art. The primal mythic conflict ended in a mutual, procreative murder, from the body parts of which the present universe arose stage by stage. This primal **sacrificial creation** of the universe in all its levels is the paradigm for, and is re-experienced and ultimately harmoniously brought together (according to Dayak beliefs) in the seasons of the year, the interdependence of river and land, the tilling of the earth and fall of the rain, the union of male and female, the distinctions between and co-operation of social classes, the wars and trade with foreigners, indeed in all aspects of life, even including tattoos on the body, the lay-out of dwellings and the annual cycle of renewal ceremonies, funeral rites, etc.[279] [emphasis added]

That seems rather involved and extensive for just a simple jungle people… and on top of it all, they practice headhunting. The shamans also practice soul-retrieval and herbal medicine.

Oceania (Fiji)

In the mythology of Fiji, **Ratumaibulu** (aka Ratu-mai-mbula) is a god of great importance who presides over agriculture. In the month called *Vula-i-Ratumaibulu*, he comes from Bulu, the world of spirits, to make the breadfruit and other fruit trees blossom and yield fruit. He is said to be a **serpent god** who created coconuts.

Indochina (Laos & Cambodia)

> Serpents, or **nāgas**, play a particularly important role in Cambodian, Isan and Laotian mythology. An origin myth explains the emergence of the name "Cambodia" as the result of a conquest of a Naga princess by a **Kambuja** lord named Kaundinya: the descendants of their union are the Khmer people.

In another Cambodian legend, the *nāga* were a **reptilian race** of beings under the King Kaliya who possessed a large empire or kingdom in the Pacific Ocean region until they were chased away by the **Garuda** and sought refuge in India. It was here Kaliya's daughter married an Indian Brahmana named Kaundinya, and from their union sprang the Cambodian people. Therefore, Cambodians possess a slogan **"Born from the naga."** [280]

The Garuda is **a very large bird**, often associated with Vishnu as his mode of transportation… not a dragon, but a large bird… a flying 'craft' again.

Note that the 'bird' also has a serpent in its talons…

As can be seen, the Cambodians borrowed a lot from the Hindus, including the Naga concept:

Hindu Shiva was lord of the **Nagas**.

Nagas are serpent people who largely live underground below India and China… giving rise to the legend of Shambhala.

So while we are at it, let's visit Tibet…

Tibet

Long known for the mysticism attached to it, Tibet still fascinates spiritual seekers. And the Tibetan lamas and gurus do have some amazing abilities, including levitation, telepathy, and generating body heat while sitting in the snow – and melting it. There is reference to a **World Tree** wherein Garuda, or the Tibetan shaman's **eagle**, nests. [281] Unfortunately, there is no Serpent Wisdom (or if there is it is kept with their secret teachings), and they have no Flood legend. But they do have a legend that **the original rulers of Tibet were nonhumans who came from the sky**.[282]

There were only two things of interest and they are both on the Tibetan flag.

According to the Central Tibetan Administration website, the symbolism of the flag includes the [white] mountain representing Tibet, the snow lions of "a unified spiritual and secular life", a 3-colored jewel of the Buddha, the Dharma and the Sangha.

The **Yin/Yang** symbol: The lions are always presented in pairs, a manifestation of yin and yang – the female representing yin and the male yang

And there are **Snow Lions** instead of a serpent/dragon. The **roar of the Snow Lion** embodies the sound of 'emptiness', courage and truth, and because of this is often a synonym for the Buddhadharma, the Buddha's teachings, as it implies freedom from karma and the challenging call to [spiritual] awakening. It was considered to be so powerful that just a single roar could cause seven **dragons** to fall from the sky.[283]

(There is that seven, again.)
Because China (and the Mongols) spent so much time (over 1000 years) invading and controlling Tibet, it is no wonder that China uses the dragon and Tibet doesn't… hence the Snow Lions in Tibet.

Another curious anomaly discovered in China and Tibet were the people with horns growing from their heads. This is definitely a regressive genetic link to the Anunnaki who used horns to symbolize rank (Enlil had 5 horns, Enki had 4 horns, Inanna had 2 horns… all examined in Virtual Earth Graduate, Ch. 3).

(credit: Bing Images)

Tibetan Link with Navajo

Just before leaving the Tibetan issues, and foreshadowing the **Global Migrations** Section later in this chapter, the Tibetan language has some interesting connection with a people nowhere near Tibet.

> One of the strangest discoveries leading us to Tibet is that according to the newest linguistic studies by the American scientist E. Sapir and others, there is a group of Indian languages known as the **NaDene**, used among others by the Navajo tribe (Diné), which display clear similarities to the so-called Tibeto-Burman languages used in Tibet and India. [284]

So maybe the Navajo and the Tibetans both originated in Mu… Mu sank and some people went East and some went West.

Now back to Oceania and a strange island… **Pohnpei**.

This island was once populated with close to 20,000 people and the construction of the coastal "city" of **Nan-Madol** dates back 1500 years. Perhaps it was a really large city, but most of it is under the Pacific Ocean – the result of flooding at the end of the last Ice Age, 10,000 years ago. So all we see now is a set of coastal ruins built from really heavy basalt 'timbers' – slabs of rock about 2' square and up to 20-30' long – called basalt pillars. They were quarried miles away, on the other side of the island, and weigh anywhere from 5 to 60 tons. Natives said the pillars were moved thru the air, via levitation, by the priests and stacked in a style reminiscent of a log cabin. [285]

It was apparently used as a religious center but the people utterly vanished, perhaps due to the global flooding and/or because there was no access to fresh water.

Nan Madol Basalt Fortress
(credit: Bing Images: turistipercaso.it)

Allegedly built by two magicians, Olosopa and Olosipa, Man Madol was built after their homeland sunk… perhaps Mu, no one knows. Natives definitely say that it was all built by 'outsiders.' A related site at **Gunung Padang** (near Java) was built with basalt columns the same way by a god who took the form of a **dragon**. [286]

Gunung Padang Summit

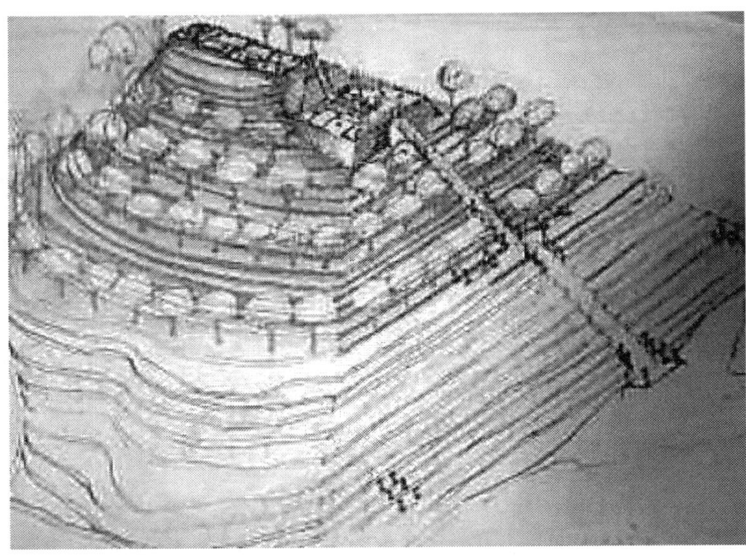

Gunung Padang – Pyramid in Java

Some say the terracing was manmade, others say that it is an ancient, small volcanic site.

(Above:) the pillars are strewn about as if there was a huge explosion. Just like **Puma Punku**.

Of interest is the fact that the inhabitants of Pohnpei venerated the **Pleiades** – a seven star cluster which relates to the seven founding ancestor voyages and the fact that the Pleiades rise from the horizon over the Pacific – signifying the raising of their dead ancestors – who are thought to reside in the submerged main part of the city.

> Interesting that the Moai statues on Easter Island were sculpted from volcanic rock which was called **Ma'ea Matariki** – Ma'ea meaning 'stone' and Matariki "…meaning to reference both the ancestors and that star cluster [i.e., the Pleiades]". [287]
>
> Both **Gunung Padang** and Easter Island constructions were achieved thru the use/manipulation of a force called **Mana**. Gunung was said to have been built in one night [as was the Pyramid of the Magician at **Uxmal**.]

Lastly, there is a mountain in the center of the island of Pohnpei and at its summit is an altar of basalt together with a **mangrove tree** which symbolizes the birth of the island from its volcanic sea bed. There again is the Tree imagery.

This last bit of information will come up again in the later section Global Migrations where the receding Ice Age and resulting global flooding became a hindrance to what had formerly been easy migrations around the globe.

Let's head south now…

Australia

The **Rainbow Serpent** or *Rainbow Snake* is a common deity, often a creator god in the mythology and a common motif in the art of Aboriginal Australia. It is named for the obvious identification between the shape of a rainbow and the shape of a snake (below)...

Rainbow Serpent in Australia

The earliest known rock drawings of the Rainbow Serpent date back to more than 6,000 years ago.

> Some scholars think that the link between snake and rainbow suggests the cycle of the seasons and the importance of water in human life. When the rainbow is seen in the sky, it is said to be the Rainbow Serpent moving from one waterhole to another, and the divine concept explained why some waterholes never dried up when drought struck.[288]

There are innumerable names and stories associated with the Serpent, all of which communicate the significance and power of this being within Aboriginal traditions. It is viewed as a **giver of life**, through its association with water, but can be a destructive force if angry. The Rainbow Serpent is said to have come **from the sky** and deposited the first two humans. The Aborigines called it Gria. Aborigines when asked where they come from, point to the sky.

"From the sky" agrees with the Zulu and Dogon, and "from underground" agrees with the Pueblo Indians and Incas.

Others say the Rainbow Serpent came **from beneath the ground** and created huge ridges, mountains, and gorges as it pushed upward. The Rainbow Serpent is understood to be of immense proportions and inhabits deep permanent waterholes and is in control of life's most precious resource, water. In some Aboriginal tribes, the Rainbow Serpent is considered to be **the ultimate creator** of everything in the universe. Also important is **Baiame**, Father of all things, and master of life and death. He is a force for Good.

The most common Rainbow Serpent myth is the story of the Wawalag or Wagilag Sisters.

According to legend, the sisters are traveling together when the older sister gives birth, and her blood flows to a waterhole where the Rainbow Serpent lives. In another version of the tale, the sisters are traveling with their mother, Kunapipi, all of whom know ancient secrets, and the Serpent is merely angered by their presence in its area. The Rainbow Serpent then traces the scent back to the sisters sleeping in their hut, a metaphor for the uterus. The Rainbow Serpent enters, a symbolic representation of a snake entering a hole, and eats them and their children. However, the Rainbow Serpent regurgitates them after being bitten by an ant, and this act creates **Arnhem Land**.

[Note a similar name in Norse legend]

Now, the Serpent speaks in their voices and teaches sacred rituals to the people living there.

(continued...)

> Another story is from the Great Sandy Desert area in the northern part of Western Australia. This story explains how the Wolfe Creek Crater, or Kandimalal, was created by a star falling from heaven, creating a crater in which a Rainbow Serpent took up residence, though in some versions it is **the Serpent which falls from heaven** and creates the crater. The story sometimes continues telling of how an old hunter chased a dingo into the crater and got lost in **a tunnel created by the Serpent**, never to be found again, with the dingo being eaten and spit out by the Serpent.

It should be emphasized here that the **underground imagery** is common to many Serpent legends – related to the Nagas who live under India and China and have built many tunnels. Peru and the Andes also are said to have many tunnels wherein the Inca hid their gold from the Conquistadors.

One of the common elements in Aboriginal society and personal practice is something called **Dreamtime.** The word has a meaning closer to eternal or uncreated. In Dreamtime an individual's entire ancestry exists as one, culminating in the idea that all worldly knowledge is accumulated through one's ancestors. Many Indigenous Australians also refer to **the Creation time** as "The Dreaming." The Dreamtime laid down the patterns of life for the Aboriginal people. "Dreaming" existed before the life of the individual begins, and continues to exist when the life of the individual ends. Both before and after life, it is believed that this spirit-child exists in the Dreaming and is only initiated into life by being born through a mother.

Creation is believed to be the work of culture heroes who traveled across a formless land, creating sacred sites and significant places of interest in their travels. The dreaming and travelling trails of the Spirit Beings are the "songlines", or dreaming tracks. Left is a trail sign for a 623-mile walking trail in Western Australia… using the **Wagyl** (serpent) motif:[289]

The Wagyl or **Waugal** is a snakelike Dreamtime creature responsible for the creation of the Swan and Canning Rivers. It was delegated to protect the rivers, lakes, springs and the wildlife.

(credit: wilkipedia: Wagyl)

Wandjina

Speaking of creation, these are the creators who became disgusted with the behavior of human beings and they caused a huge **Flood** which wiped out the humans, and then they created another, more civilized race. Now where have we heard that before? (See Chapter 1, Anunnaki displeasure with humans, and Mayan *Popul Vuh...*) These beings are depicted as semi-human with a bony face that has no mouth, and they can appear in various forms, like birds, and sometimes as humans. [290] Interesting that the same Flood story for the same reason would be among the Aboriginal stories… and of course, it also matches the Biblical Flood story.
The cave paintings look like this:

(credit: Bing Images: press.anu.edu.au)

These are found in the Kimberly region in NW Australia, and are thought to represent gods but they look something like Grey aliens (without the feathers!) as well, and the drawings are said to be about 5000 years old.

One of the cave sites is shown below, yet one has to wonder, since the Bushmen are short (about 4' tall) – how did they paint the topmost pictures…? Ladders?

The Wandjina were the first people, **creator beings**, from the sea and the sky.

Heading West now to Chile…

Chile

The **Mapuche** culture is located in south-central Chile and western Patagonia (in Argentina). Central to Mapuche cosmology is the idea of a **creator** called *ngenechen*, who is embodied in four components: an older man (*fucha/futra/cha chau*), an older woman (*kude/kuse*), a young man and a young woman.

Like many cultures, the Mapuche have a **Flood Myth**(*epeu*) of a major flood in which the world is destroyed and recreated. In the deluge almost all humanity is drowned; the few not drowned survive through cannibalism. At last only one couple is left. A *machi* shaman tells them that they must give their only child to the waters, which they do, and this restores order to the world.[291]

The key to Mapuche society is the role of the **machi** (shaman). It is usually filled by a woman, following an apprenticeship with an older machi, and has many of the characteristics typical of shamen. The machi performs ceremonies for curing diseases, warding off evil, influencing weather, harvests, social interactions and **dreamwork**.

> Dreamwork often involves soul retrieval, divining uses for Herbs, and prayer for plentiful harvests.

Sacred Tree

In addition, there is an interesting but ancient flag used by the Mapuche – which resembles the **Andean Cross** (Chapter 7 on the Peruvians):

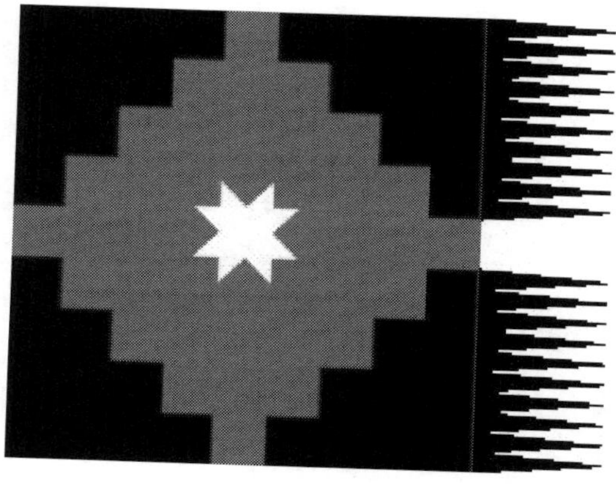

(credit: Wikipedia: Lautaro)

Arauco War Flag
The flag represents the long, long battle the Mapuche had with Spain… constant warfare, insurrections, but never totally subjugated. In 1598 the Spanish were kicked out of mid-south Chile.

The most characteristic feature of the old **Araucanian flag** is the center symbol which can be described as an octagram or **a star with eight points.** It represents the planet Venus, but has also been thought to represent **the canelo tree**, which is considered sacred among the Mapuches.[292]

Remember that Enlil's sign/logo was an 8-pointed star (Chapter 1).

It is also interesting that the main god of the Mapuche is called **Antu**. Maybe just a coincidence, but the main Anunnaki god was called Anu…. And apparently the Anunnaki did get around – especially into Africa (and Zimbabwe)….

Looking just a bit further, the **Indus Valley** culture provides something that resembles the Andean Cross:

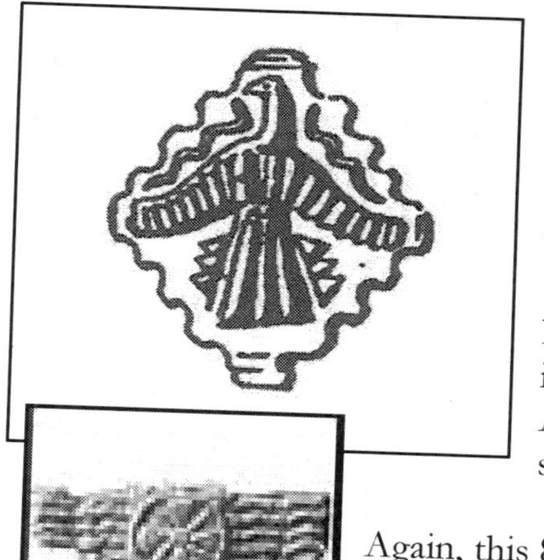

The bird or eagle is the embodiment of the avatar concept. The multi-stepped cross from the Indus Valley served the same function as the Andean Cross from Tiahuanaco. [293] This one adds **2 serpents**.

Note there are three points between corners in both diagrams (top and left) on this page. Also note the similarity to the Anunnaki symbol below (in particular the tail):

Again, this **8-pointed star** is Enlil's Mark of Office.

Anunnaki in Africa

For convenience, as many different cultures are examined, here is a map of Africa.

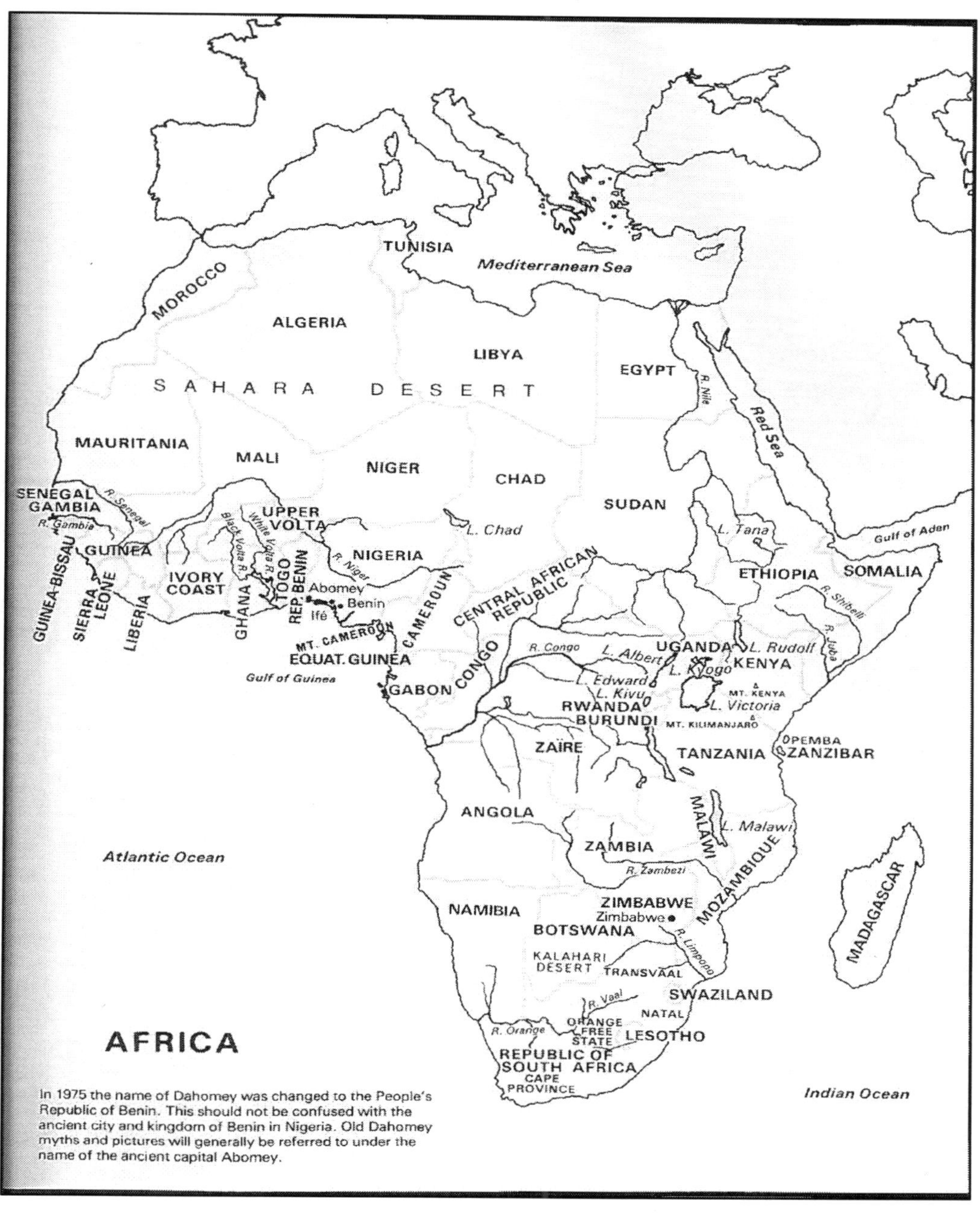

Zulu

Also called AmaZulu, they are the largest ethnic group in South Africa. While the term **Zulu means "people from the stars"**, it is harder to connect these people with Anunnaki imagery since the Church came in and converted and removed most of their ancient stories. Example:

> Unkulukulu is the highest God and is the **creator of humanity**. Unkulukulu ("the greatest one") was created in Uhlanga, **a huge swamp of reeds**, before he came to Earth.[294]
>
> The connection is that Enki, the Science Officer among the Anunnaki, was said to live in a marsh, full of reeds and serpents, called AB.ZU. He was believed to have lived in the Abzu since before human beings were created.[295]

Zulu Shaman

Credo Mutwa is a Sanusi or Sangoma (healer or shaman). He runs a hospice in Kuruman, South Africa. He is perhaps best known for his work with **David Icke** and the accounts of his encounters with extraterrestrials, called *The Reptilian Agenda*.

Credo tells how he has experienced pain at the hands of the Little **Greys**, the *Matindane*, and how **Reptilian** visitors, as well as **Nordics**, have interacted with humans in South Africa for a long time. Around his neck he often wears a necklace of metal artifacts – representing UFOs, reptilians and a metal hand with a diagram of the Orion Constellation on it.

Credo says that the Reptilians resemble the painting he made years ago, and he calls them **Chitauri**. The connection with the Anunnaki is that the Chitauri and Anunnaki (original ones) are alleged to be reptilian, also.

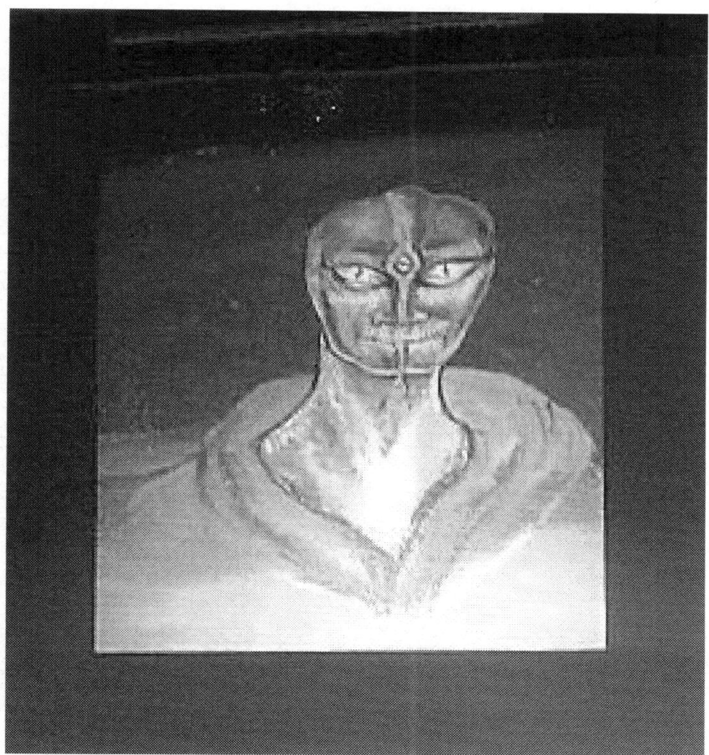

Remember that the Anunnaki presence was long-standing in South Africa as that was where the mines were – for gold and uranium. That is also where Enki had his laboratory, in the AB.ZU… and it is interesting that the word Zu ("wise") is found in Anunnaki parlance as well as among the Zulu.

The Anunnaki later created different racial workers in Mesopotamia, to build their ziggurats and work the agricultural fields.

Thus South Africa was where the black slave humans were first created. And as the Zulu call themselves "star people" that is alleged to be a reference to their origins.

And because the following picture of a sign painted by Credo has some bearing with what has already been discussed, in earlier chapters (4 and 5)… it will emphasize some issues:

(credit: Bing Images: http://okmalume.tumblr.com/post/32194163047/pics-taken-at-credo-mutwas-house-)

Pharaoh Narmer

The Olmecs <u>were</u> Black, and the Chinese FuXi was alleged to be Black, as well… and we discussed the possibility that Cleopatra was a Nubian Princess ….One has to wonder where a Zulu shaman heard these things…?

As for the **Pharaoh Narmer** image being Black (left) … judge for yourself.

Narmer was said to be the First Pharaoh to unite Egypt, and Upper Egypt was the home of the Nubians… Blacks in Egypt.

(credit: Bing Images: Narmer)

At any rate, a Tree of Life was discovered in a region of Central Africa…

> Called **Kilembe** it is reputed to be a magical Tree of Life.[296]

> Kilembe: A magical tree. This tree arrived on earth carried by the hero Sudika-mbambi when he was born. Occasionally referred to as Kilembe, Tree of Life, or Grand Bois.[297]

Dogon

While there is no Tree of Life, Flood or Serpent imagery among the Dogon, there is a strong connection to ETs.

The Dogon people are found in Mali, in Western Africa. Living in cliff-like dwellings, they have unusual dances, venerating the ETs who visited them centuries ago… from the **Sirius Constellation**. The Dogon say that the visitors drew a star map which included Sirius B which wasn't discovered until recently… the Dogon could not have known about it unless ET visitors told them. They have advanced astronomical knowledge: they knew that Sirius was a **binary system**, and they knew about the rings of Saturn and the 4 moons of Jupiter. Lately the credibility of the Dogon has been increased by their additional sharing that Sirius has a red dwarf and is really a **trinary system** – astronomers are now checking that out.

Similar to the **Hopi Kachina** (covered in Chapter 7), the Dogon perform a dance that symbolizes **Giants** which were tall and that explains the stilts.

Dance on stilts: the Dogon believe their deities came from the Sirius Star System.

They are copying the Nephilim Giants – offspring of human women and Anunnaki Watchers.

Another unique dance is the following, and it specifically venerates the ETs..

Of special note is the headdress that suggests a humanoid figure, but it is also reminiscent of something else in Physics, as well as some petroglyphs in the American Southwest: (see below)

And if that weren't curious enough:
consider these glyphs from Kayenta, Arizona:

www.everythingselectric.com

What did the natives see that inspired their artwork? Plasma weapons?

Stacked Toroidal Plasma in Physics →

(credit: www.crystalinks.com/nasca.html)

Nommo Dance: the Dogon have another dance and set of masks to venerate the Nommo, fish-like ETs who gave them civilization.

Zechariah Sitchin found the Sumerians had immortalized the **Nommo (aka Oannes)** in their murals and scrolls: Fish-like beings that are part human – science still conjectures that maybe this was how the Sumerians pictured humanoids in scuba gear….

Note the Tree of Life, and the Flying Anunnaki above the tree.

Also shown are the Nommo – men in fish capes.

And now to really make the connection with ETs and the Anunnaki…. This is a mural done by the Dogon to show their ancient interaction with what appear to be Little Greys…

Keep in mind that the Zulu Sangoma Credo Mutwa also spoke of having been abducted by unfriendly Little Greys (he called them ***Matindane***).

They told him that he was not who he thought he was and to accept his lot as something he had already agreed to. [298]

Zulu Carving of Matindane
(credit: Bing Images: tumblr.com)

So we are still looking for serpent imagery, sacred trees, Creation and any Flood myth. And the Dogon finally provide us with a **serpent** – on the cliff face that they use to record **circumcisions**:

(credit: Bing Images: happeningafrica.com)

Before leaving the Dogon, it was shown above that they do a dance reflecting giants who once walked the land. Recent excavations in Rwanda have proven interesting.

Rwanda Giants

Kigali, Rwanda is the site of about 200 giant skeletons unearthed which are suspected to be those of the Nephilim. (Again, the Anunnaki connection.) Current day anthropologists pooh-pooh the find as it contradicts established history of the planet… and the following picture has been vetted to NOT be any form of Photoshop®. Giants like the Philistines did exist, and the ancient Nephilim, too.

(credits: https://gigantiidacia.wordpress.com/tag/muntii-bucegi/page/2/)

Ashanti

Perhaps the Ashanti tribe of Ghana, West Africa, can provide some serpent imagery… maybe in gold as they were rich in gold. They revere a **Golden Stool** which was brought to them from Heaven, and it is so sacred that even the Ashanti king cannot sit on it. [299] It is a reminder that all thrones are sent from Heaven.

No gold serpent, but they do have a **Rainbow Serpent** like the Aborigines of Australia.

> The rainbow-god **Aidophedo** of the Ashanti was also conceived to have the form of a snake. His messenger was said to be a small variety of boa, but only certain individuals, not the whole species, were sacred. In many parts of Africa the serpent is looked upon as the incarnation of deceased relatives.[300]

The demigod Aidophedo of the West African Ashanti is also a serpent biting its own tail. That is reminiscent of the Greek concept of **Ouroboros**. How did the Greek concept get to the Ashanti…?

The Ashanti have a story about the origins of humans, and in addition to saying that **humans came from holes in the ground** –corroborating what the Navajo/Hopi have said earlier – they say that the Lord of Heaven sent a **python** to teach humans how to procreate. In the beginning there was no childbirth (like the Anunnaki story of the *Lulu* which could not reproduce) and the python told the woman that he would make her conceive. (It was Enki, the reptilian Anunnaki Science Officer who genetically engineered the first humans so that they could reproduce [Ch. 1].) So the real story gets altered just a bit with time.

Dahomey

In Dahomey mythology of Benin in West Africa, the serpent that supports everything on its many coils was named Dan. In the Voodoo of Benin (and Haiti) the "Rainbow-Serpent" is a spirit of fertility, rainbows and snakes, and a companion or wife to Dan, the father of all spirits.

You gotta wonder where they got all this….

First Peoples

Rather than attempt a long review of the African creation myths, some of which are long, some of which repeat each other, and some of which don't relate to anything that we are seeking, it is interesting to point out a few unique legends.

The Zulu of South Africa, and the Thonga of Mozambique, say they came out of a reed or reed-bed – it exploded and there the humans were.

The Herero of Namibia say their ancestors came out of a **tree** (like the Mayans), and yet, in the very same country, Nigeria, the Yoruba say the first people were made in Heaven and brought to Earth. The African Hereros, a Bantu tribe, says that after a great **Deluge**, white men came and mingled among them. [301] (These were probably the Hamites, descendants of Noah's son Ham.)

And in Burundi, Central Africa, as in a few other tribes around Africa, it is said that the **gods lived among Man** and helped him develop, teaching him agriculture. Many African tribes have legends about how the sky used to be so much closer to the ground (the Firmament?) and there was a woman in the Ila tribe who tried to reach God by piling up **trees** to reach him, but she never succeeded.

The Zambesi in Zambia also say that God created all humans and lived among them. There was one man in particular that was very clever and kept finding his way to where God lived, and God kept moving to avoid him. Finally God moved to the top of a great mountain, and still the man followed. God then called on the Spider to spin a thread and attach it to the sky, and God and his family moved up into the clouds. Still the man was clever and determined to reach God, so he cut down many **trees** and piled them on top of each other, but they were unstable and the tower of trees collapsed.

Similarly, the Pygmies have a tale about a persistent human who would not leave God alone, and because the humans would give him no peace, and were **disobedient**, God decided to leave them and move far away. So the sky was also moved farther away. (Remember: Enlil's displeasure with humans.)

> The interesting thing is that **God lived among Man** and that is reminiscent of the Anunnaki living among Man and developing his culture.

Pygmy Genesis

Even more curious is the Pygmy account of a Chameleon in the first times who took an axe and split open a **tree** – producing a great **Flood** that covered the whole Earth. In that water was the first human couple – and both were **light-skinned**. [302]

The Pygmy story of the first man, **Efe**, makes him out to be a hunter that God likes and so brings him up to Heaven, teaches him many things, and then puts him back on Earth with **special spears** (like the Norse Odin). When Efe was born, his parents were swallowed by a monster but Efe is a great hunter and kills it and frees them. The Efe also have a connection with the Dogon:

> Africa's Ituri forest **Efe people** have long known of planet Saturn as the "star of nine moons." (Its moons were not discovered in the West until 1899.)…. Local legends of **white gods** have long intrigued scholars of Africa, and if oral history be credited, those gods (the **euhemerized** tribes of [Noah's son] **Ham**) once inhabited their country.[303] [emphasis added] [Note: Euhemeris vets a myth.]

Yazidi Culture

While the Yazidi people mostly occupy Iraq, they have dispersed over much of the Middle East, Europe and Africa. And they are an interesting anomaly in the Arabian world – seeing some of them, you'd believe you were in Sweden:

(credit: YouTube: https://www.youtube.com/watch?v=gpJvymMGR9k)

Blonde hair and blue eyes… Aryan features in the Arab world. One does not convert to Yazidism – one is born into it. They count their ancestry as beginning with Adam – specifically as descendants of Adam through his son **Shehid bin Jer** rather than Eve. [304] Yazidi are descended from the original Aryans in Persia.

> **FYI: "Isis extremists plan to impregnate Yazidi women to destroy the blue-eyed, blonde hair bloodline."** [305]

And here is a Yazidi temple at Lalish… serpent time:

Interesting that a serpent is affixed to the outside of the temple, and yet there is nothing said about serpents when researching the Yazidi beliefs.

They are Monotheists but venerate seven spirits, and especially the Peacock angel, Malek Taus. (The Gnostics venerate 7 gods (Chapter 12), and 7 Anunnaki gods made Enlil marry Sud [aka Ninlil], also 7 stars in the Pleiades.)

7 is a magic number.

(credit: Wikipedia: MikaelF.)

So the point of this genetic anomaly leads us into a renowned Anthropologist with a bent for genetics who seeks to clarify the versions of Man based on genetic markers and sometimes just plain logic.

Cosmic Ancestry

At this point, it calls for an insertion of information provided by **Dr. Susan Martinez**, who has a doctorate in Anthropology and is not afraid to share what her research has shown – which sometimes flies in the face of the 'established' Anthropology out there. Let's look at a few of her findings:[306]

- Because we reviewed the **Bushmen** of Australia, it should be mentioned that they are considered by scientists (who have tested DNA around the world) to have the **oldest mtDNA** – in short, the oldest Mother is not in Africa but Australia. It is possible that they survived the Flood and humans who populated Africa after the Flood would have younger DNA.

- How did Homo *erectus* in Africa manage to evolve into modern man when his **<u>older</u> cousin in Asia** did nothing of the sort? In fact Asian Homo *erectus* is more primitive than his African relative – How can this be if Africa is where it all started?

- In fact, instead of early humans migrating from Africa (OOA or Out Of Africa theory), it has been shown anthropologically that **humans migrated into Africa** [from Oceania] and Bushmen (see point 1 above) in particular migrated from north of Australia.

- When faced with hominids like Heidelberg Man who looks like his contemporary in Africa, how is it that the African immigrants (to Europe) 'evolved' into Neanderthals, and the brothers and sisters still in Africa evolved into Homo *sapiens*?

- The races cannot honestly be traced back to, and did not differentiate from, a common stock; **each race had its very own history**. Negritos and Australians for instance, "do not share a common ancestry but merely interbred." [307]

- Subsapient man was not a traveler, and we needn't take him out of Africa or anywhere else to populate the world. It is much…. more realistic to take all the early races as indigenous to the lands where we find their bones… i.e., **Polygenesis.**

What Dr. Martinez is saying is that there were **multiple Gardens of Eden**, and a Dr. Carlton Coon postulated that the five basic races not only developed independently, but <u>at different times</u>.[308] And now, leading up to the giant-killer:

- Isn't it interesting that formerly Asia itself was called Asu-wa and it was covered with Asu man – the primeval race, the aborigines of Earth who abounded in Central Asia (India) during the Pleistocene.... In China, too, Asu man lived alongside Homo *erectus*, contradicting the "unique to Africa" idea.... And then there is the Zinj-like Dmanasi Man, in the Caucasus: How was this pre-Homo *erectus* (outside of Africa) handled?[309]

> Of equal interest are Australia's huge limestone pillars near **Roper River**, attributed to members of **a white race** – the site boasting streets and polished walls. Are they the same people depicted as bearded Caucasians in the rock art of central Australia near Alice Springs? Much of Australia's proto-history has been suppressed by the Australian Archeological Association (AAA) which has turned into a political body.... to please Aborigines. Thanks to the AAA **fossilized human remains were destroyed**. These included remains.... which proved the existence of highly developed pre-Aboriginal races before the arrival of the ancestors of the current Aboriginal tribes.[310]

The point of that being that just as some of the truth about Sumerian/Anunnaki history has been obfuscated, and the State museum in Iraq was sacked in 1991 during the Iraqui War (operatives were seen making off with priceless Sumerian treasures), there is an agenda "out there" to not let the real history of Earth be known. When it does surface, it is said that the information is either wrong or misunderstood, and then it is either decried as foolish nonsense, or it is hidden.

> And *Ancient Aliens* reported in an episode in Season 8 called "The Forbidden Zones" where Isis is merrily moving thru the Middle East destroying ancient temples, statues, etc – and being paid to do it.

So, on to two giant-killer revelations that Dr. Martinez has documented so painstakingly in her monumental work:

- Standing OOA on its head, it has been discovered that some African Negroes may actually have come from the East, ... somewhere in northern Asia, leading some scholars to think that **the Garden of Eden [or at least one of them] was in Asia** perhaps on the Pamir Plateau.

So there could very well be an **Out Of Asia** (OOA) dispersal:

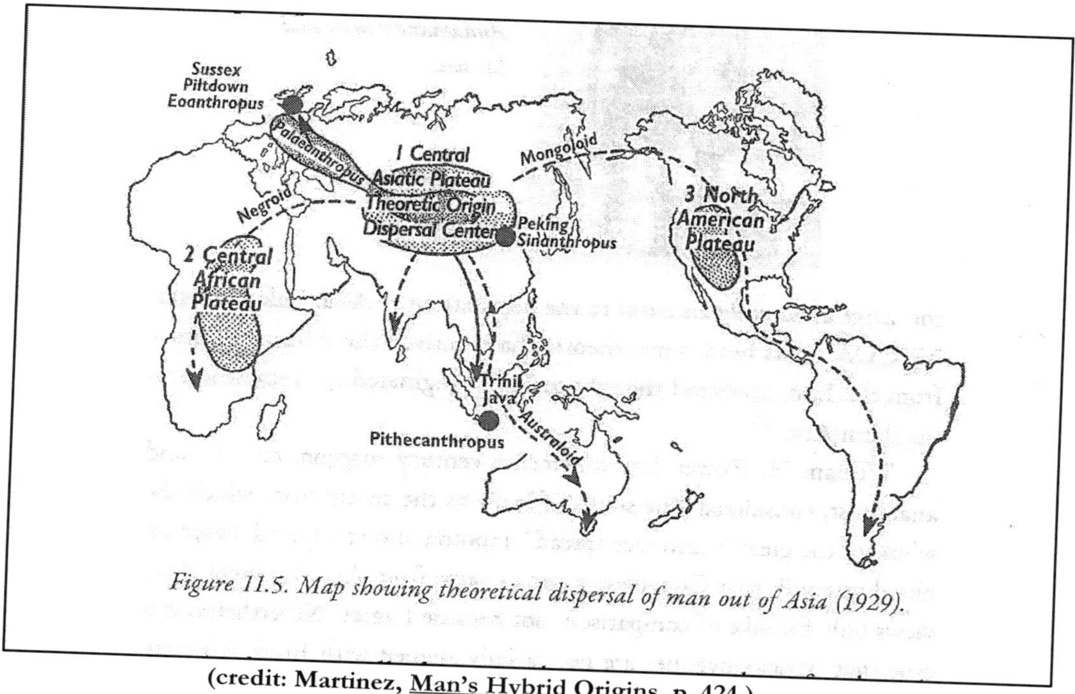

Figure 11.5. Map showing theoretical dispersal of man out of Asia (1929).

(credit: Martinez, <u>Man's Hybrid Origins</u>, p. 424.)

And now the 2nd major revelation, which accompanies Dr. Martinez's well-founded proposal that there were multiple Gardens of Eden (**Polygenesis**), is her belief that all of southeast Asia is a serious rival to the original OOA theory:

- Stephen Oppenheimer has shown by tracing myths that spread from Oceania to Africa … [that] Africa has the least diversity of legends and Australia has the most… Thus, there was a great African diaspora, but it was <u>post-Flood</u>.

- One of the most outrageous parts of OOA is that black Africans migrated north into Europe and Asia and lost their dark skin and distinctive hair and turned into Mongoloids and Caucasians… losing their original genome. Later, Negroes allegedly turned into Orientals. Such pseudo-science is entirely specious. So her last key revelation:

Blacks did not turn White.

Thus, from analysis of world-wide DNA, and archeological/anthropological analysis, it is reasonable that there were multiple Gardens of Eden – and the Sumerians only documented one of them.

If Blacks turned White because they lived in the shade, or northern regions with less sunlight, why isn't it still happening today? The same argument has been made for Man evolving from the Ape – Why is that not still happening today? As was said in Virtual Earth Graduate, the Scientific Method is often suspect… Perhaps it should be renamed?

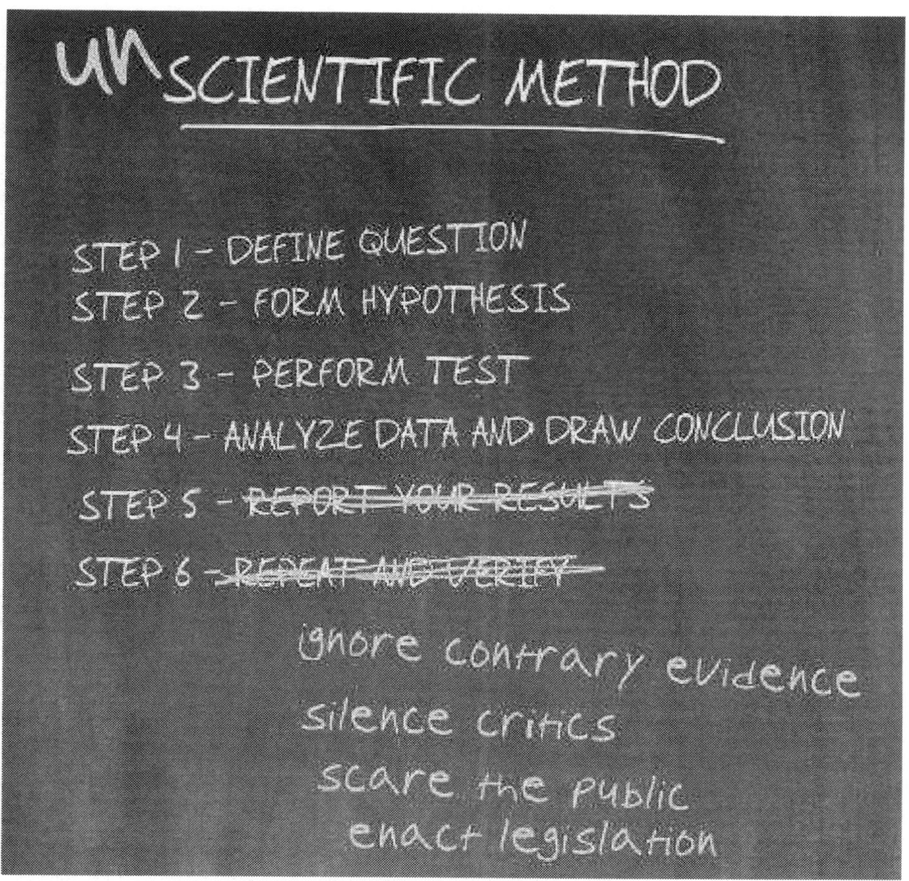

(Credit : Bing Images)

An interesting addendum: the Aborigines of Australia used a "bullroarer" which was an oval piece of metal swung on a rope over one's head and the noise was a low roaring sound. The Dogon of Mali also used them – indicating interaction (or migration) between the two cultures.

In the last chapter, the origin and migrations of natives were examined, now we'll take a closer look at the known facts. Let's take a brief look at migrations to better appreciate where the American Indians came from.

Global Migrations

When examining the North American scene, part of the mystery to be resolved, in addition to any Anunnaki-type influence, is where the different Indians came from. While the standard story is that American Indians (Amerindians) came across the **Bering Strait** in the olden days (8-10,000 years ago) at the end of the last Ice Age when there was a land bridge from Asia to Alaska, that has been found to be only part of the story. For one thing, it does not explain the Indians found in the Northeastern United States (Iroquois, Mohawk, Onondaga, Seneca, Huron, *et al*), nor those of the Southeastern US (Cherokee, Creek, and Floridian Seminoles).

The standard teaching on the earliest inhabitants of North America is said to be the **Clovis** people (earliest archeological site found in the USA: New Mexico):

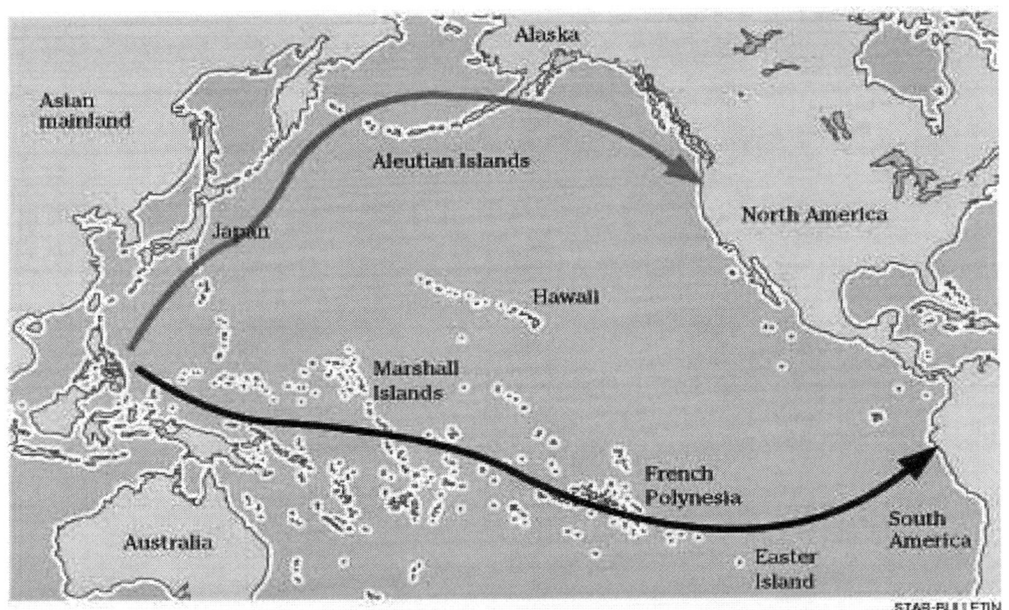

(credits: (above and below) http://frontiers-of-anthropology.blogspot.com)

The top arrow is associated with the **Clovis Theory** of migration from Asia across the Bering Strait, and the lower arrow is more of an oceanic, or Coastal, Theory. Of course, if the lost continent of Mu existed in the Pacific Ocean in ancient times, then sank, it is probable that some natives escaped and made their way to North and

South America (as well as westward to Asia and India). That possibility looks like this and North America could have been populated from both shores:

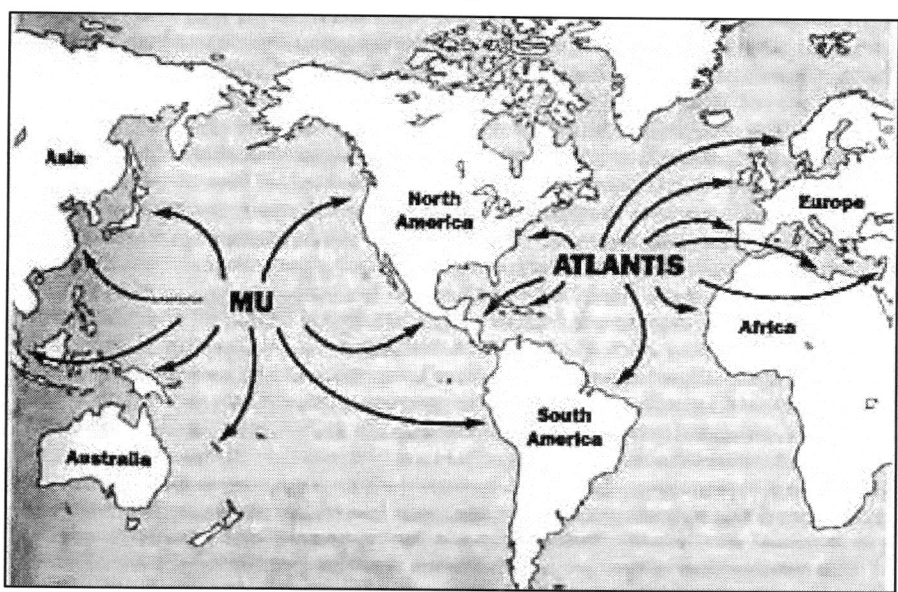

The existence of two extra continents (now gone) would have made migration a lot easier, and more logical. As it is now, there is scant evidence that Atlantis or Mu contributed to ancient cultures that we do know about because nothing is known about culture in Atlantis or Mu … except sparse rumors and occasional mention in ancient writings.

It has been established that the Chinese could have made it to America, as well as the Japanese who must have because **Jomon pottery** was found in Ecuador dating back 12,500 years. Valdivia (Ecuador) and Jomon (Japan) pottery are identical in every respect. [311] We already know that the Vikings not only made it to America, and settled in Newfoundland (Ch. 2), they sailed down the St. Lawrence Seaway and after a few portages, made it to what is now **Minnesota** (e.g., Kensington Runestone).

> In an episode of the History Channel (*America Unearthed* S1 E3) by Scott Wolter, a forensic geologist, we learned that the Minoans/ Phoenicians made it to North America and did extensive **copper mining in the Lake Superior area** – "100 million tons of copper came out of Wisconsin and Michigan about 3000 BC [and] went to the Mediterranean…" [312] And the Vikings were also exploring that area, so they too may have been involved.

Also back in Chapter 2 we examined how closely the script from Easter Island matches that of Mohenjo-Daro and it is theorized that neither people visited the other, but that there was a third party, the Anunnaki, who instructed both in writing.

Younger Dryas

Significant to all the migratory possibilities is that Earth was captured in an Ice Age that began to recede 15,000 years ago, then briefly refroze (called the Younger Dryas stage), then finally settled down into global warming about 10,000 years ago… and that melted the huge glaciers covering the northern hemisphere… flooding what was once a smaller Atlantic Ocean.

First the Atlantic looked like this about 18,000 years ago due to the extensive ice caps: Guess where **Atlantis** was? (Just as Plato said: "right outside the Pillars of Hercules [now called Gibraltar]"). Atlantis was "Y"-shaped.

Lower Sea Level: Exposing Land/Ridges

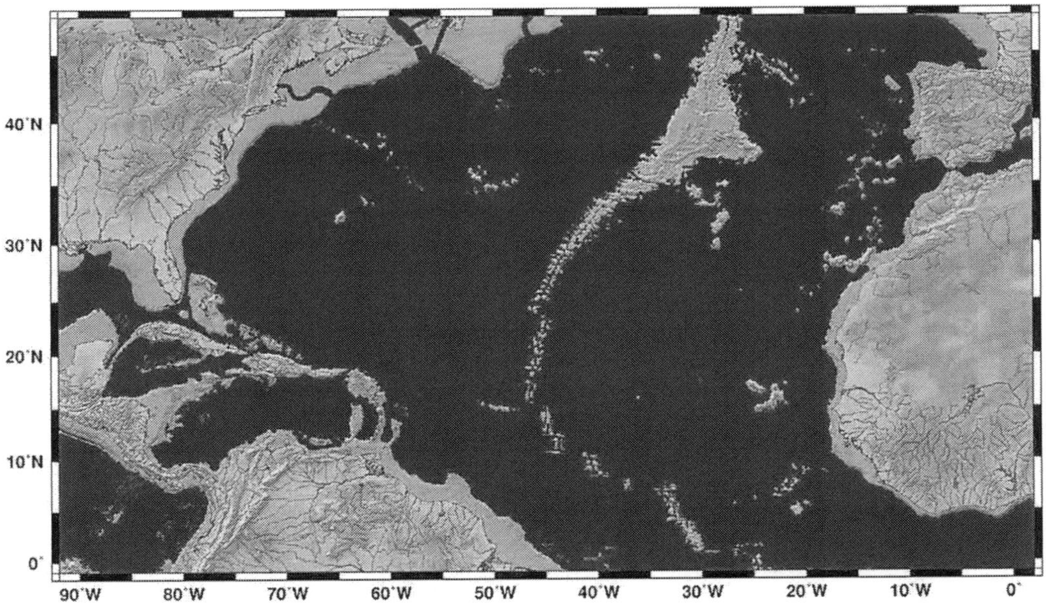

(credit: Bing Images: outofatlantis.blogspot.co.nz)

In terms of understanding how the Amerindians got here – without using the Bering Strait land bridge (which must have been like Antartica to wade thru – thousands of miles of ice…) , we need to see what the Pacific Ocean looked like… Note the land mass from India to Australia (next page)...

Sea Bottom

(credit: Bing Images:paciocn1 Lower Sea Levels)

What you want to really take a look at is the island chain and what is called the Nazca Ridge (see arrow) which is a raised string of land/islands (still on the Nazca Plate) which reaches all the way **from Easter Island to Chile**. During the last Ice Age, when the Pacific and Atlantic Oceans dropped about 400 feet, any humans wishing to migrate eastward across the Pacific Ocean, could almost walk to South America… using a boat one could still island-hop their way to South America.

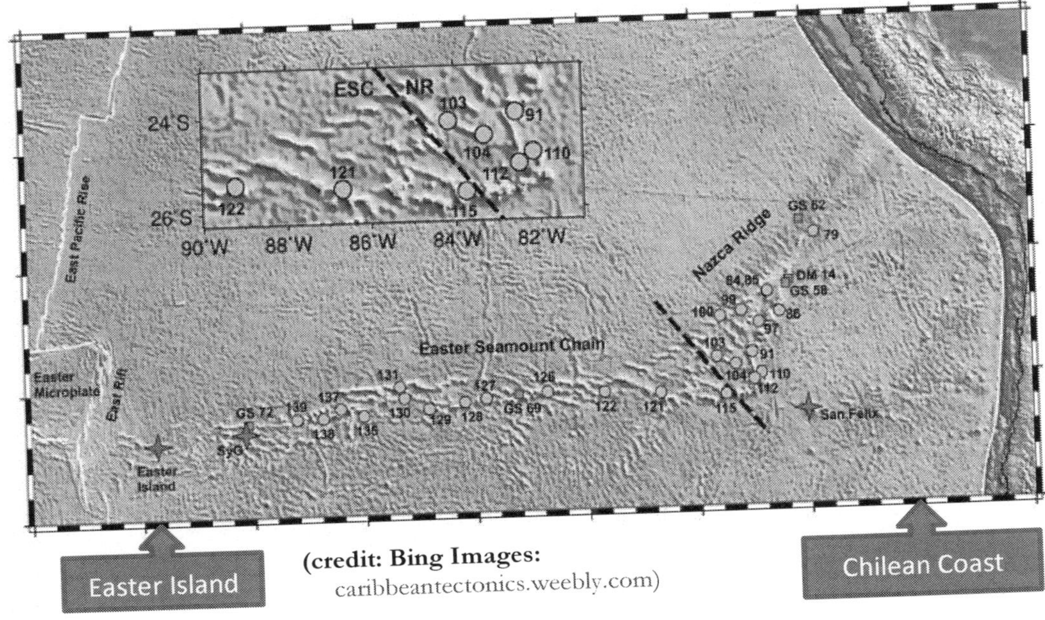

(credit: Bing Images:
caribbeantectonics.weebly.com)

> And that is why there is so much anthropological diversity among the Amerindians. They came from the West and the East, and humans did not make much use of the Bering Strait until about 6,000 years ago when the icecap was receding and it wasn't such an impassible obstacle. It was mostly the Inuit, Eskimos and Tlingit for example that used the Bering Strait—their ethnic Mongol, Siberian and Oriental heritage bears that out. Aztecs said they came from Aztlan, as did the Algonquins.

Lastly, there is another anomaly that says Central and South America were populated from across the Pacific Ocean. If humans migrated across the Bering Strait and settled North America, we would expect to find cultural remains in North America that are older than those from South America. Exactly the opposite is true…

> As has been shown on a respective map in time, in South America were discovered remains that were not only **older than North American remains**, but even older than those in the entirety of eastern Siberia…. Still there are no certain traces of people from North America (USA & Canada) that would be older than appoximately 15,000 years. [313]

Again South America was largely peopled by those coming laterally into the country as opposed to vertically (from the North). And this is significant: we thus expect to find a connection in Chile from the Australian peoples (the **Bullroarer**, mentioned earlier), we expect to see some effect from Japan on the **Jomon pottery** in Chile, and we expect to see the **Andean Cross** with an antecedent coming from the Indus Valley.

Thus, we can expect to see some beliefs and traditions in North America among the Amerindians that we have seen elsewhere. And we did, in the last chapter.

At any rate, let's not get into a detailed analysis of who came when from where. Thanks to the crazy Spanish Conquistadors, that information was largely destroyed. We were looking for a Tree of Life or World Tree, Serpent Wisdom elements, and similar Flood and Creation myths. We found a considerable similarity in same around the world…

Now the question really is: What was going on that spread agriculture, writing, medicine,metallurgy and similar imagery around the world? And can we tie it to the Anunnaki?

Chapter 9: Serpent Wisdom -- Origins

Moving from the global tour, we now take a look at what Serpent Wisdom is – What was it that the Brotherhood of the Serpent secretly taught worthy humans? And why was it begun and why did it go underground? While some of the details have been lost to recorded history, what has survived in the Sumerian records about the inception of Serpent Wisdom groups, and from what has survived in the known history of today's secret spiritual groups, we can deduce a lot of their origins, changes, processes and teachings.

Brotherhood of the Serpent

It all began with Enki (aka Ea), the expert geneticist among the Anunnaki. He was very happy with his creation, humans, and continued to tinker with their genetics scientifically morphing them from the sexless *Lulu*, to the reproducing *Adama*, and finally developing the intelligent *Adapa*, his creation that most closely resembled Cro-Magnon.

While Enlil, the Lord of the Earth Expedition, Enki's brother and superior, did not fully agree with the desire to populate the planet with humans (of any sapience), there was a need to work the mines, build the dwellings including ziggurats and work the crops so everyone could eat. The Anunnaki did not want to do the work, so Enki developed a **worker slave** using the existing Homo *erectus* and some of the Anunnaki DNA. It had to be smart enough to follow instructions from the Anunnaki bosses in the mines and agricultural fields, but not so smart that they could organize and rise up against the Anunnaki.

> Note: it has been suggested in Virtual Earth Graduate that *Adama* was the Neanderthal , and *Adapa* was what we call Cro-Magnon. Homo *sapiens* was a later genetic refinement of Cro-Magnon.

At one point, the humans that were created (after Enki mixed his DNA with that of a pretty *Adapa* female), produced an intelligent offspring that could do more than walk and talk and understand orders. It could reason and discuss – once language had been taught, and then writing.

Enki was fascinated with what he had created and wanted to see (as most scientists do) how far he could take this new creation… short of making the humans as smart as the Anunnaki themselves. He foresaw this **Adapa+** version as useful for creating a priesthood – a slightly superior version of humans that could take over some of the Anunnaki duties to manage humans… i.e., a Control Group. Kings and Priests, as it would turn out. But there was a catch.

Galactic Law

It has been stipulated in the Galaxy that new, sentient races will not be created by advanced civilizations – without Galactic Council (and local Solar Council) approval. Those planets, like Earth, that can support advanced lifeforms are the result of terraforming and close administration – a kind of Experiment and botanical or zoological ecosphere.

The Anunnaki got away with what they did in creating humans as they just modified an existing hominid and pushed its normal evolution up a million years. They did not create a brand new type of lifeform (as was done later with the mutants on Atlantis – and Atlantis paid dearly for it.) Now Enki was closing in on a violation of the Galactic Law as he was going beyond a slave worker (which Enlil had already decided to terminate [think: Flood] when the Anunnaki left Earth to return home – and that had Council approval). It is reasonable to think that the Council also suggested to Enki that he now had to shepherd his advanced progeny.

So Enki increased sentience/awareness and language ability (gene: **FOXP2**) and this bloodline was carefully controlled… at least in the beginning. These humans were to staff the King and Priest positions in Anunnaki settlements and were given Laws (Hammurabi and others) to guide human civilization. That was working and later generations would acknowledge the "god"-given right to rule with such phrases as "Dieu et Mon Droit" or: God and My Right [to rule].

Religion

Where Enki began to go awry was when he decided to teach the superior humans (who were so advanced that souls were incarnating into their bodies to experience something new) more about themselves and pass on to them the Anunnaki understanding of Life, God, the Universe… and he realized it had to be done properly – and kept out of the hands of the *Adama* and 'normal' *Adapa*.
In short, he realized there had to be an **exoteric** version for the masses and an **esoteric** or special truth for those who could handle it.

> Note: as was revealed in Virtual Earth Graduate, Enlil became Yahweh, the god of Earth, and Enlil was known to be strict – you obeyed or there were consequences. He had very little patience with rowdy, ignorant and smelly humans. (Later, Marduk took over this function when Enlil and his command went back home.)

Enki realized that the majority of the worker slaves, even the normal *Adapa* version, were not too bright and because they were often rowdy, rebellious, and lazy he followed Enlil's advice and made the exoteric religion one where (1) the gods of water, air, crops, animals, etc had to be appeased and (2) failure to make the gods happy would result in punishment and even death – and then he had a brilliant idea: tell the average humans that if they were good they'd go to Heaven when they died, and if they were bad they'd go to Hell – this was a threat to control them.

Enki knew there was no Heaven or Hell but the humans didn't. After all, what the Anunnaki said was Law – and they came from the sky (Heaven) as gods, so they must know… And the Anunnaki overseers of human activity followed suit with their reward/punishment concept – Keep in mind that there was an Anunnaki god over Agriculture, Canals and Waterways, the Anunnaki could control the weather so there was a god of Storms, Sun and Wind, and there was an Anunnaki god of War, Writing/Knowledge, and what basic Science the humans had. Thus was a **panoply of gods** arising in human experience. Not surprising that early human societies believed in multiple gods.

Now Enki had to provide esoteric religion for the Adapa+ version – they were smarter and would question things, wanting to know more, and would constantly be asking questions…. At some point they might see thru the Heaven & Hell scenario. Or they could overhear the truth in their dealings with the Anunnaki themselves. He couldn't use that but had to explain to the Adapa+ why it was being used on the other 90% of humans… and thus began a **class differentiation** (which by the way was a normal thing in Anunnaki society – remember their 'ranking' based on the number of horns one had?) and so esoteric religion was for the "upper class" humans.

The Anunnaki initiated the caste system in India.

Now we had class division, public (exoteric) religion, secret (esoteric) spiritual truth, and Pantheism.

Global Effect

As the first humans migrated north into different part of Africa, they encountered Visitors (as recorded in the first part of this book) who guided them in agriculture (so they could eat), how to build shelters (to survive the weather), and the basics in weaponry (to defend themselves from other humans). In addition, some effort was made to give the humans an understanding, albeit mythic, of where they came from, who their tutors were (as in the case of the Zulu and the Dogon), and an attempt was made to instill principles of peace, fair play and what their god wanted from them. Over time, needless to say, these concepts got skewed in the telling (as most tribes had no written system). Truth got lost in myths.

> The error potential in oral traditions is best exemplified by the game of **Telephone**. Sit 12 people in a circle on the floor, and take a brief 2-minute story which you also have written down. Whisper the brief story with outstanding (colorful) aspects to it to the first person. Have that person whisper it to the next, and so on around the circle. When it comes to the last person, have him/her repeat it aloud to the group and watch the commotion!
> It is often unrecognizable, so read the original (written) story to the group. (The details get glossed or omitted and often new interpretations creep in so that the original story is largely lost.)

And in different parts of the world, it was not always the Anunnaki who ruled and guided humans. In South America and Mesopotamia/India, it was the Anunnaki gods. In China it was the **Denebs**. In Northern Europe it was the **Aldebarans**. In South Africa (Zulu) it was the **Anunnaki** , in North Africa it was the **Sirians** and sometimes the Anunnaki (as Oannes) dealing with the Dogon.

There were super-cultures among the Atlanteans and ancient Hindus, and there were wars for control. In one case, the war extended into the inner solar system, the planet between Jupiter and Mars got blown up, and the Mars landscape received a mighty Plasmic Disruptor shot creating the *Valles Marineris* (examined in Appendix A in Virtual Earth Graduate). Mars was a way-station for the Anunnaki shipping minerals back home via huge transport tanker-ships, and the Cydonia region was one of their spaceports … with an image of Alalu, a deposed Anunnaki ruler.

Anyway, there was more than one Garden of Eden, and the 5 basic races of Man had different points of origin, and of course, different languages and religions given them. There seems to have been some sort of agreement among the Visitors that different races in different locales would have a worship of The God but there would be different tenets of their exoteric religion – SO THAT Man would find fault with others he came into contact with – and (per the **Anunnaki Agenda**) Man would not unite. **Different languages** would keep Man from understanding each other, and **different religions** would breed mistrust and possibly war – i.e., "Let's fight for the right God, our God! We're right and you're wrong!"

> The creators of Man knew how petty and judgmental humans could be – after all, humans were given some Anunnaki genetic traits.

Esoteric Religion

So Enki had a special, better version of Man that was not part of the worker slave group. It was the new **Priest Group**, and extended to some Kings as well. And with ensuing interbreeding, some Anunnaki mated with human *Adapas* and the result was (1) Nephilim (before the Flood – and that was why the Flood was done), and then it was (2) a more normal-looking human who was actually a **Hybrid** – superior to Adapa+ and these became the great men of history – Gilgamesh, Moses, Sargon, Alexander the Great to name a few… even down to the time of Charlemagne.

> **Note**: this is why some families throughout history have intermarried and traced their bloodlines carefully – to preserve (and not dilute) the 'hybrid' genetics. Yes, there are superior-version humans still on the planet. One such lineage was the Merovingians.

So Enki designed the esoteric (or 'occult' which means hidden) truths in a new organization called the **Brotherhood of the Serpent**… and took that to the main Anunnaki settlements around the planet. The initiates who entered into the Brotherhood and completed training became Serpents (sometimes called 'Adders'), and it was largely they who set up and maintained the various schools.

Seeing that Quetzalcoatl was pale-skinned and had a beard, that sounds like one of the Anunnaki gods. Pick one: Enki himself, or Ningishzidda (Enki's son), who later became Hermes, Thoth and brought the Olmecs to Central America. (None of Enlil's sons got involved.) [314]

According to Wm. Bramley:

> It is however a remarkable fact that Brotherhood-style secret societies are extremely pervasive throughout the entire world and exist even among very primitive peoples…. [they are] as common in the "primitive world" as they are in the "civilized" one. For example, Captain F.W. Butt-Thompson writing in his book *West African Secret Societies*, says of Africa:
>
> > The **Native Secret Societies** found amongst the peoples and tribes of the West Coast of Africa are many. Nearly **one hundred and fifty** of them …[315] [emphasis added]

He goes on to say that the mystical groups are very similar in organization and purpose to that of the Grecian Pythagoreans, the Roman Gnostics, the Jewish

Kabbalah and Essenes, and the Bavarian Illuminati – not to mention the Freemasons and the Rosicrucians.

Serpent Symbolism

In addition, according to Mr. Bramley's research (which is impressive), the Anunnaki who basically sided with Enlil against the humans growing and fulfilling their potential, we find that Enki (Ea) was the benefactor of mankind and wanted his creation to be more than slave workers. The Brotherhood adopted the serpent logo because "…Ea's first home on Earth was [built] by a snake infested swampland Which Ea called Snake Marsh." And yet another more credible reason is offered by the late Mr. Sitchin because the biblical word for "snake" is *nahash*, which is derived from the root NHSH which means to decipher , or find out… and that does describe Enki. [316]

> If you read Virtual Earth Graduate, there is another viable reason in Ch. 3 which won't be gone into here.

The Serpent imagery was also chosen because it was Enki's intention to develop Man spiritually via the *Kundalini* energy… moving the divine energy (*chi*) thru the chakras and serving to wake man up, i.e., empower higher consciousness in him – really heighten his 5 senses and activate a couple more (clairvoyance, telepathy, psychokinesis…). The *Kundalini* moving up the spine looks (to those with spiritual vision) like two snakes intertwining and rising up the spinal *nadi* (channel).

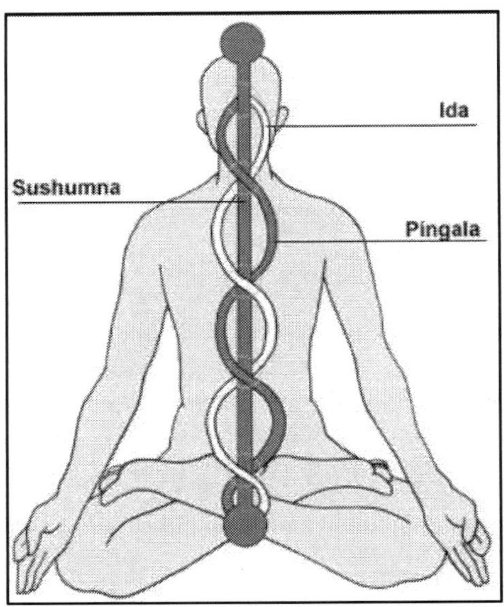

A better version shows the chakras and the *Kundalini* serpents together:

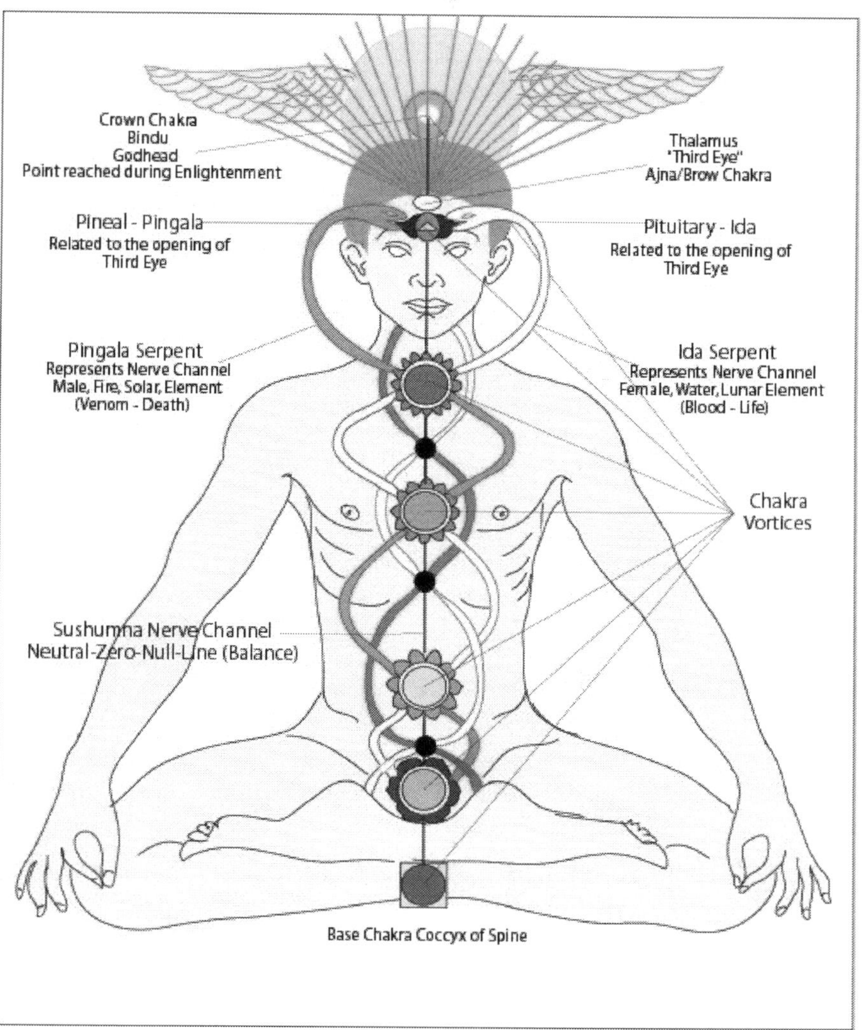

(credit: Bing Images: solawakening.com)

In the above, note the **pineal and pituitary** glands and their relationship to the Flow. Note also at the head the sphere with wings… reminiscent of the Anunnaki symbol, which was also found in Egypt…. The symbol had dual meanings.

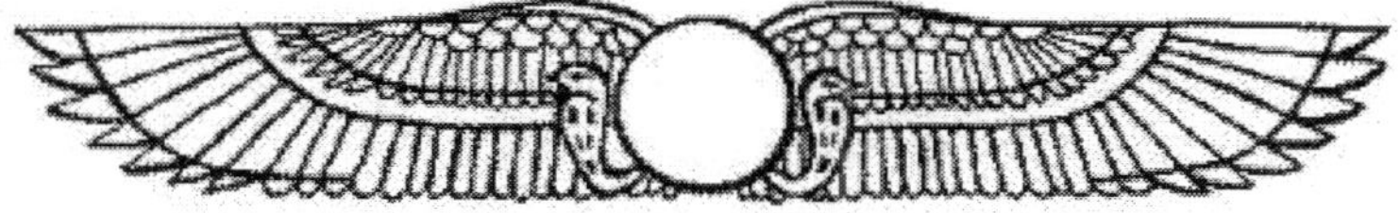

Kundalini is Sanskrit for "snake" or "serpent power" (Dragon Fire), so-called because it is believed to lie like a fiery serpent in the root chakra at the base of the spine.

This also resembles the **Caduceus,** or medical symbol....

(credit: Bing Images: anunada.wordpress.com)

Note that the top of the Caduceus has the "winged sphere" so popular among the Anunnaki diagrams and reliefs... The symbol was often associated with alchemy and wisdom and is derived from the Rod of Asclepius.

It also resembles the rod carried by the god **Mercury**:

Who hasn't seen the Florist Telegraph Delivery logo? (left)

(credit: Bing Images: unlockastrology.com)

Notice that Mercury was also associated with **Hermes**, and according to Wikipedia:

> Some accounts suggest that the oldest known imagery of the caduceus have their roots in a Mesopotamian origin with the Sumerian god **Ningishzidda** whose symbol, a [**wand**] with two snakes intertwined around it, dates back to 4000 B.C. to 3000 B.C [317]

Mercury, Hermes, Ningishzidda ... back to square one with the Anunnaki again.

And again:

> ...through its use in astrology and **alchemy** it has come to denote the elemental metal of the same name. It is said the **wand** would wake the sleeping and send the awake to sleep. If applied to the dying, their death was gentle; **if applied to the dead, they returned to life**.[318] [emphasis added]

That last point will be explored further in the section on Alchemy, but the reader should recall Chapter 1 where Inanna was restored to life and she planned to bring Damuzi back to life – Anunnaki technology was quite advanced, and this Caduceus is merely a symbol of Life.

So the Serpent symbolizes Knowledge (*nahash*) and *Kundalini* enlightenment.

Enki Villainized

Enki had a great idea and yet higher powers prevailed – not only in the Garden of Eden, where the serpent did not get to finish its liberation of the slaves (Adam and Eve – who were kept tending the Garden), but also some of the Serpent Wisdom Schools were shut down (due to jealousy by the Egyptian priests), and Enki was demonized by the fledgling Church – thanks largely to Enlil who said "No!" to enlightening the humans.

> The reason Enlil didn't stop Enki from experimenting and creating the **Adapa+** was his intention to wipe it all out (Think: The Flood) before returning home... so it didn't matter what Enki did ...let him have fun.

Enki himself had always been symbolized as a serpent (and as a medical geneticist he was directly connected to the Caduceus), but the Church began a serious and protracted campaign to program humans to see Enki and all serpents as evil and to destroy anything that spoke of snakes, serpents, enlightenment, etc... Enki's title was changed from "Prince of Earth" to "Prince of Darkness"... associated with

Lucifer – and instead of a "bringer of Light" (the real meaning), it was corrupted into Satan and/or the Devil. So humans were encouraged to resist, avoid and destroy anything having to do with Serpent Wisdom…. And today much of humanity walks in Darkness because that is the way Enlil wanted it. [319]

How's the **Anunnaki Agenda** working today?

Anunnaki Agenda, Part II

While this is examined more in detail in VEG, it is worth mentioning what the Anunnaki Agenda is because it explains why Man is still obstructed from spiritual growth even today…. Our **public schools** are dumbed down (to the lowest common denominator among the kids), **bookstores** have been closed – Borders, Walden Books, BookStop, Taylor Books and many of the B&N stores have been removed. In addition, a big cable company bought and removed BlockBuster **video stores** several years ago… (see also Epilog.)

> Their excuse was (1) to save money, and (2) you can browse online thru your TV. Wrong… videos They (the PTB) don't want you to see are not listed.

No, not a conspiracy, it is just the Agenda at work – Humans are not to browse bookstores and video strores where they might discover something interesting, or mentally challenging (e.g., *The Fourth Kind, Iron Sky, Prometheus…*), or anything that makes them think outside the box that was created for them… and it is just a matter of time (the movement is already under way) to control the Internet – not only a Logon Step (to identify you), but you'll have to have permission/access to "interesting" websites (e.g., *Bibliotecapleyades*)…if they are still there. The Black Hats have never gone away, and in VEG they are called the **Dissidents.**

Just recently, a great school of spiritual learning, called Religious Science (SOM), was undone and replaced with something called CSL – where the goal isn't to teach metaphysical principles, but the pubic comes in to this new 'church' on Sunday, sings, dances and celebrates in an atmosphere of Love… no relevant teachings. So what could be wrong with that? It promotes "having fun" (as I was told), smiling and just being loving, instead of hearing something that could help you grow spiritually – learning and understanding what you are and how life works is no longer the goal for the sheep.

Says Mr. Bramley:

> The derailment of spiritual knowledge [began] in Egypt [and] was caused by the corruption of the **Brotherhood of the Serpent**, to which the pharaohs and priests belonged. [320]

Is it surprising that the more recent Church took its teachings and knowledge thru historical channels, from Egypt, to Judaism, to Christianity? By the way, it is mostly the Western World that denigrates the Serpent, whereas in other parts of the world, the people have more positive traditions regarding serpents and recognize the serpent as the symbol of **knowledge and healing**.

> The original uncorrupted Brotherhood engaged in a pragmatic program of spiritual education…. [which] was scientific not mystical or ceremonial. The subject of the spirit was considered to be as knowable as any other sciences. [321]

And to boot, the Brotherhood amassed a considerable amount of accurate spiritual knowledge and yet it had not developed a well-defined route to spiritual freedom prior to its defeat (in Egypt). They were in a piece-by-piece, step-by-step process. And this ensured that the student did not get more than s/he could handle before being ready for the information and the accompanying higher experience.

Unfortunately, in Egypt, the Serpent Wisdom Schools had organized as "Mystery Schools" and were under the direction of the priesthood… which felt threatened and was corrupting the original teachings – and thus they developed a deteriorated version of mummification and uselessly buried people in wooden boats. The Mystery Schools not only restricted public access, but elitism and overregulation set in, and finally **many Schools became an instrument of spiritual repression**. [322]

So that was Egypt and the root of many schools in the Western World.

Fortunately, the Serpent Wisdom survived in various forms which tended to maintain the following truths, and these will be the underlying essence of the different Schools examined in this last half of this book.

Basic Serpent Wisdom

First and foremost, there is no spiritual growth without Compassion and Knowledge. Both Love and Knowledge are required to move one's **Personal Frequency Vibration** (PFV in Glossary) to a higher level –*kundalini*, or no. The basis is that all things have a personal vibratory rate – rocks, fish, flowers, humans… and as a result all things make a sound (audible or not). Sound is vibration.

And the degree of vibration is shown in one's aura – low, dense people vibrate more slowly than an Avatar, for example.

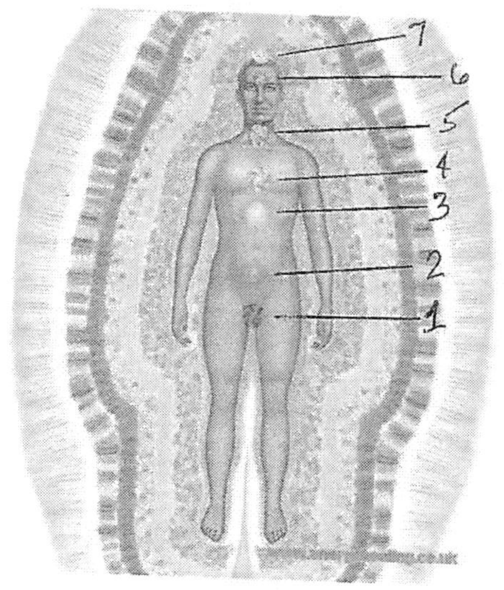

Layers of the Human Aura
(Source:
www.differentlight.org/images/Aura.jpg)

A dense person will tend to operate out of his/her lower 3 chakras and will have an aura reflecting one of the lower chakras – red, orange, or yellow.

The basic human chakras are:

#1 – Root chakra – survival
color: red location: genitals

#2 – Power chakra – sex, power, money
color: orange location: navel

#3 – Self chakra – ego
color: yellow location: solar plexus

And if the person is very spiritual, operating out of their higher chakras (4-7) They will display an aura with Green (healing) Blue (peace), Indigo (psychic), or White (crown chakra) as Buddha or Jesus would have looked – all chakras are united and balanced – thus the aura tends to be white, with gold at the core.

4. Heart chakra – (**green**) compassion, healing

#5. Throat chakra – (**blue**) speak truth , wisdom

#6. 3rd eye chakra – (**purple**) higher knowledge, insight

#7. Crown chakra – (**white**) connection with Godhead, spirituality

There are more chakras than this – the body energy network, the **Bionet,** is covered with them, including the palms and chakras on the backside of the human (spinal area) corresponding to the front ones.

The reason Love is important is that it is a high vibration coming from the open #4 chakra and when coupled with Knowledge (chakras 6 & 7) it sets a 'tone' or vibration that strengthens the aura and the Bionet – the aura is the vibratory rate of the Bionet which links all the chakras – all some 200 of them. This promotes health and longevity.

Kundalini

It is no accident that the Hindus speak of Yoga as a way to trigger *Kundalini* and produce enlightenment, and the Chinese have something similar – the Large Orbit Exercise in Qi Gong, wherein the student (or adept) mentally runs the body energy (*chi*) thru the meridians and in particular (connection with the Hindu Sushumna/Ida & Pindgala) the Du Mai and the Ren Mai meridians – achieving much the same result.

> What is interesting, and this is covered more in Transformation of Man, the *chi* in the body is very affected by the mind – *chi* follows attention. This is one of the secrets of Qi Gong and is used in healing. Adepts in Qi Gong can direct *chi* with their mind thru their hands to heal others.

The *Kundalini* is primal energy, or *shakti*, and it is supplied from the Earth via the #1 chakra. It then flows up and thru the **Bionet**, across the meridians and supports the bodily functions, especially the organs... but the organs are also connected to the chakras and the chakras normally draw in ambient *chi* (from the universe) and expel used or 'dirty' *chi*.

When a body exercises too vigorously, it may run thru its supply of *chi* for the day and the person may collapse until the chakras have been able to pump back in enough good, clean energy and the person can again walk and talk.

In the same way, if a person is using a lot of brain power, as a mathematician or computer programmer, and drives themselves to resolve an issue, they can deplete their overall *chi* (which has been routed to the brain). If that happens, the person may be light-headed or dizzy. In a similar way, if a person rides a really fast and scary roller-coaster, they are expelling *chi* faster than they are bringing it in – fear, panic and anger expel *chi* which is why at the end of the ride, the body is desperately trying to draw in energy, and the person may feel dizzy.

Energy Vampires

In another way, there really are "**energy vampires**" who suck energy from people during the day – and 99% of the time, it is quite innocently and subconsciously done. The prime example of this is someone starts an argument with you and it gets heated. Your energy builds as you are more and more determined to make your point and win… as it drags on, you begin to feel more and more drained. In fact, you are!

An energy vampire who knows they can do this will start grinning during the argument, and that is your clue that you have been had. You are exhausted and they walk away 'recharged.' How?

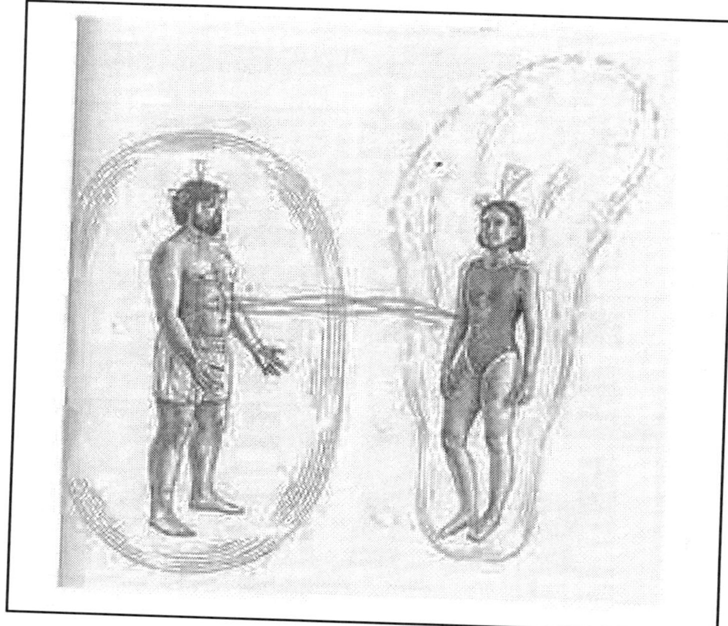

Two people with energy cords linking their 3rd chakras.

(credit: Bing Images)

The cones exiting from their heads are an artistic rendition of the chakras… they look like funnels, but are spinning energy vortices.
Also shown is her aura pulling away from him and it is not as well-defined as his healthy aura; she has some gaps or tears which are unhealthy.

There are people who sink their **"energy cords"** into others (subconsciously) and since you are fired up, your energy is really "up" – your energy is probably stronger than theirs, and like a strong battery recharging a weak on (via battery cables), your energy feeds to the other person whose energy potential is lower – It is just a law of physics: **Energy always flows from the higher potential to the lower**. And sometimes an energy vampire will do it on purpose, knowing that it will automatically work for them – many times they do not know how it works, just that if they start an argument, it doesn't matter whether they "win" or not – they get your energy. So they did win!

> This was examined in more detail in Transformation of Man, and 2 ways were given to protect oneself.

The reason these people do their little Drain Game is that they usually have only the first 3 chakras open and cannot draw in enough *chi* to meet their extra needs, so they start feeling tired and then get cranky, start an argument, and after a few years of this they begin to notice that after an argument, they have more energy. Of course, they don't know they are an "energy vampire" but it doesn't matter – they have learned a new behavior and you (and others) are the unsuspecting victims.

Note: if your aura is strong, it can stop or at least diminish their connection.

Ok back to the Alchemy and World Tree search…

Kundalini and the World Tree

By now it should be clear what the symbology of the serpent coiled at the bottom of the Tree of Life, or the World Tree, means…. Look at **Yggdrasil** again (from Chapter 2):

Yggdrasil, Tree of Life

Note that the **Serpent** (sometimes a dragon) lies at the bottom of the Tree – like the *Kundalini* lies at the base of the spine. At the top of the Tree is usually an **Eagle** which signifies the awakened person – the Crown chakra, and that person is able to take flight and rise above the mundane world. So the **Tree of Life is the spine** and that is an apt description… the spine empowers all other parts of the body by moving energy where it is needed.

The Egyptians referred to the spine as the **Djed Pillar**…

(credit: Bing Images)

The above looks sort of like a tree, but it was often said in Egypt to represent a spine, signifying "stability." [323] And, "Dj-" is an Egyptian prefix for 'serpent- .'

So the meaning behind Djedhi and Djed Pillar represents a form of serpent.

And there is more to it… and we encounter a **sacred tree**… [324]

In the Myth of Osiris and Isis, Osiris was killed by Set by being tricked into a coffin made to fit Osiris exactly. Set then had the coffin with the now deceased Osiris flung into the Nile. The coffin was carried by the Nile to the ocean and on to the city of Byblos in Syria.
It ran aground and a **sacred tree** took root and rapidly grew around the coffin, enclosing the coffin within its trunk. The king of the land, intrigued by the tree's quick growth, ordered the tree cut down and installed as a pillar in his palace, unaware that the tree contained Osiris's body.

Meanwhile, Isis searched for Osiris aided by Anubis, and came to know of Osiris's location in Byblos. Isis maneuvered herself into the favor of the king and queen and was granted a boon. She asked for the pillar in the palace hall, and upon being granted it, extracted the coffin from the pillar. She then consecrated the pillar, anointing it with myrrh and wrapping it in linen.

This pillar came to be known as the pillar of *djed*.

Djed pillars usually have 4 rings on them, but sometimes have only 3.

The *djed* may originally have been a fertility cult related pillar made from reeds or sheaves or a totem from which sheaves of grain were suspended or grain was piled around. Erich Neumann remarks that the the *djed* pillar is **a tree fetish**, which is significant considering that Egypt was primarily treeless. He indicates that the myth may represent the importance of the import of trees by Egypt from Syria.[325]

Erich Neumann was a psychologist and student of Jung and saw the world in symbols.

Parallels in other cultures

Parallels have also been drawn between the *djed* pillar and various items in other cultures. Sidney Smith in 1922, first suggested a parallel with **the Assyrian "sacred tree"** when he drew attention to the presence of the upper **four bands of the djed pillar** and the bands that are present in the center of the vertical portion of the tree.... Additionally, the sacred tree and the Assyrian winged disk, which are generally depicted separately, are combined in certain designs, similar to the *djed* pillar which is sometimes surmounted with a solar disk. Katherine Harper and Robert Brown also discuss a possible strong link between the *djed* column and the concept of **kundalini in yoga**.[326]

Speaking of the "bands present in the vertical part of the Assyrian Tree of Life…" there are three bands present ….

Yes, this is very similar to the Sumerian Tree of Life that was shown in Chapter 1.

This is the Assyrian Tree of Life…

(credit: Bing Images: pinterest.com)

Moving the Kundalini

And there are different ways to move the *Kundalini* – which is the last step the initiate takes when passing thru the various stages of Serpent Wisdom…. All the knowledge gained is helpful over the years, and that provides a context in which to function when the *Kundalini* does its job and the Serpent meets the Eagle. The other reason an Eagle is used is that the brain has two lobes and the Eagle has two wings.

When the Eagle meets the Serpent, the initiate may become a Dragon, aka Serpent of Wisdom. Out of Body projections and traveling are possible.

It is not the purview of this book to examine procedures to move the primal energy, except to say that various (non-public) forms of Yoga can do this, special breathing exercises (Pranayama) can do this, and a special form of meditation with Hemispheric Synchronization (Think: Monroe Institute) may initiate the condition in the brain that draws the *Kundalini* up.

> **Again, it is wisest to explore these avenues with a trained guru who have been thru the awakening process and can answer questions, as well as know what to expect and how to protect you. It is not wise to attempt any energy awakening process without safeguards. The danger lies in the energy shooting up the spine and hitting a blockage.**

Invoking Kundalini Experiences

The easiest way:

Kundalini can be awakened by *shaktipat*—spiritual transmission by a Guru or teacher.

There are two broad approaches to Kundalini Awakening: **active and passive.**[327]

The ***active approach*** involves systematic physical exercises and techniques of concentration, visualization, Pranayama (breath practice) and meditation under the guidance of a competent teacher. These techniques come from any of the four main branches of yoga, and some forms of yoga, such as Kriya Yoga, Kundalini Yoga and Sahaja Yoga emphasize *Kundalini* techniques.

The ***passive approach*** is instead a path of surrender where one lets go of all the impediments to the awakening rather than trying to actively awaken *Kundalini*. A chief part of the passive approach is **Shaktipat** where one individual's *Kundalini* is awakened by another who already has the experience. Shaktipat only raises *Kundalini* temporarily but gives the student a real experience to use as a basis.

Awakening -- Prepared or Unprepared

The experience of Kundalini Awakening can happen when one is either prepared or unprepared.[328]

Preparedness

According to Hindu tradition, in order to be able to integrate this spiritual energy, a period of careful purification and strengthening of the body and nervous system is usually required beforehand. Yoga and Tantra propose that *Kundalini* can be awakened by a guru (teacher), but body and spirit must be prepared by yogic austerities such as Pranayama, or breath control, physical exercises, visualization, and chanting. Patanjali emphasized a firm ethical and moral foundation to ensure the aspirant is comfortable with a reasonable degree of discipline and has a serious intention to awaken their full potential. The student is advised to follow the path in an openhearted manner.

Traditionally people would visit ashrams in India to awaken their dormant *kundalini* energy. Typical activities would include regular meditation, mantra chanting, spiritual studies as well as a physical asana practice such as Kundalini Yoga. However, *kundalini* is now widely known outside of the Hindu religion and many cultures globally have created their own ways to awaken the Dragon Fire within people.

Without explanation, an increasingly large percentage of people are experiencing *kundalini* energy awakenings spontaneously which means, it is not vital to follow a distinct set of instructions or rules in order to awaken the energy.

Unpreparedness

Kundalini can also awaken spontaneously, for no obvious reason or triggered by intense personal experiences such as accidents, near death experiences, childbirth, emotional trauma, extreme mental stress, and so on. Some sources attribute spontaneous awakenings to the "grace of God", or possibly to spiritual practice in past lives.

A spontaneous awakening in one who is unprepared or without the assistance of a good teacher can result in an experience which has been termed as "Kundalini Crisis", "spiritual emergency" or "Kundalini Syndrome". The symptoms are said to resemble those of Kundalini Awakening but are experienced as unpleasant, overwhelming or out of control. Unpleasant side effects are also said to occur when the practitioner has not approached *Kundalini* with due respect and in a narrow egotistical manner. *Kundalini* has been described as a highly creative intelligence which dwarfs our own. Kundalini Awakening therefore requires surrender; it is not an energy which can be manipulated by the ego.

> Some writers use the term "Kundalini Syndrome" to refer to physical or psychological problems arising from experiences traditionally associated with Kundalini Awakening

Rewind: Göbekli Tepe

All of that to say that they had a special temple and process that they ran at Göbekli Tepe, and that was 12,000 years ago. After that, the teachings went underground, into the Serpent Wisdom Schools – in fact, it is not hard to think that Göbekli Tepe could have been such a School, encouraged by Enki or his son.

According to Wikipedia:[329]

> Through the radiocarbon method, the end of Layer III can be fixed at about 9000 BCE… but it is believed that the elevated location may have functioned as **a spiritual center** by 11,000 BCE or even earlier, essentially at the very **end of the Pleistocene**..
>
> The surviving structures, then, not only predate pottery, metallurgy, and the invention of writing, or the wheel, they were built before the so-called Neolithic Revolution, i.e., the beginning of agriculture and animal husbandry around 9000 BCE. But the construction of Göbekli Tepe implies **organization of an advanced order** not hitherto associated with **Paleolithic**…. societies.
>
> > [Remember that Paleo-Sanskrit was the writing used.]
>
> Archaeologists estimate that up to 500 persons were required to extract the heavy pillars from local quarries and move them 100–500 meters (330–1,640 ft) to the site. The pillars weigh 10–20 metric Tons…. with one still in the quarry weighing 50 tons.
>
> > [Remember Baalbek – lifting heavy stones was no problem for Anunnaki technology.]
>
> It has been suggested that an elite class of religious leaders supervised the work and later controlled whatever ceremonies took place. If so, this would be the oldest known evidence for a **priestly caste**—much earlier than such social distinctions developed elsewhere in the Near East.

> [Remember that the Anunnaki initiated the Priestly Caste and why they did it.]

Around the beginning of the 8th millennium BCE Göbekli Tepe ("Potbelly Hill") lost its importance. The advent of agriculture and animal husbandry brought new realities to human life in the area, and the "Stone-age Zoo" (Schmidt's phrase applied particularly to Layer III, Enclosure D) apparently lost whatever significance it had had for the region's older, foraging communities. But the complex was not simply abandoned and forgotten to be gradually destroyed by the elements. Instead, **each enclosure was deliberately buried** under as much as 300 to 500 cubic meters (390 to 650 cu yd) of refuse consisting mainly of small limestone fragments, stone vessels, and stone tools. Many animal, even human, bones have also been identified in the fill. Why the enclosures were buried is unknown, but it preserved them for posterity.

> [Remember that the temple site was a spiritual center and the Anunnaki did not want roaming hordes or "curious public Joe" to find the site and desecrate it.]

(Credit Wikipedia [330])

The picture (top right) from another Turkish site is why Göbekli Tepe was buried:

Note the Serpent Head on the Right…

Vandals did not leave much of **Mount Nemrut** intact. And you want to ask yourself, what was going on in Turkey, not just at **Cappadocia**, but at **Derinkuyu** where there is an **eleven-story underground city** that can hold 20-30,000 people… Were they afraid of an air raid… or an asteroid strike… or maybe war between the gods? Or even more interesting, depending on the exact age of the site, perhaps the people knew that **Planet X** was coming by and chaos would result…?

(credit both pix: Pinterest.com)

Turkey is definitely a very interesting place, and it also is the home of Mt. Ararat… allegedly where Noah landed…. Although Anunnaki epics (*Enuma Elish*) indicate that Utnapishtim (aka Ziasudra aka **Noah**) did build a boat, it was reasonably small and Enki sent boxes of DNA samples to Noah (cryogenic cylinders) to take with him along with his family and some animals. According to Sitchin, it was a submersible craft …

> Enki provided him [Noah] with precise instructions regarding the boat, its measurements and construction. …We imagine this 'ark' as a very large boat, with decks and superstructures. But the biblical term – *teba* – stems from the root "sunken" and it must be concluded that Enki instructed his Noah to construct a **submersible boat** – a submarine…. [an *elippu tebiti*][331]
>
> It was to be a boat "like an Apsu boat," a *sulili*, it is the very term used nowadays in Hebrew (*soleleth*) to denote a submarine….
>
> "Let the boat," Enki said, "be a MA.GUR.GUR – a boat that can turn and tumble." [332]

And then in Sasha Lessin's book on the Anunnaki, we find that the *tebiti* has already been pictured –in Saqqara: [333]

Zoser Pyramid Inside Wall Relief

The appendage is said to be a mast folded down. What this means is that anything huge found on Mt. Ararat, which may even have the outline of a boat, is not it.

Then according to the story, the first thing Noah does when he steps out on land again, is to slaughter some animals – wasn't he supposed to protect them? It is the smell of barbecuing lamb that softens Enlil's heart, and Enki gets Enlil to agree to let humans survive and descend from Noah's cleaner genetic line. (Everybody forgot the Nephilim and the humans in Nod.)

Göbekli Tepe is stunning proof that Man was busy on Earth a lot earlier than most anthropologists give him credit for…. As if they are ignoring the Mesopotamian or Sumerian/Anunnaki creation of Man which put Man here <u>before</u> the Ice Age… speaking of which, Turkey was free of ice as was Sumeria… (next page)…

See map of Turkish ancient sites, end of Appendix B.

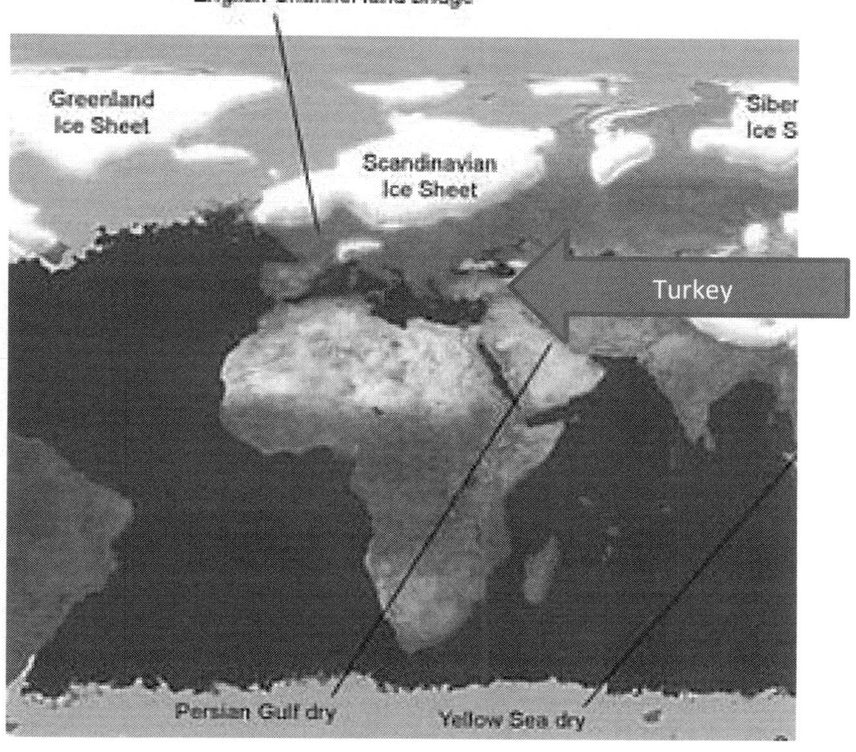

(credit: documentaryworldhistory.wikispaces.com) [334]

Also note from the map that South Africa where the Anunnaki were mining gold and uranium (near Zimbabwe), there is no ice. In fact, Turkey appears to have been less arid and perhaps was more temperate even with light forestation.

Moving on… While that did a little bit of a "birdwalk", it is interesting how many things link to other things.

Something a little safer and a lot easier to invoke than *Kundalini* is the following…

Peak Experience

And it should be noted that there is a lesser awakening that sometimes comes, as a partial awakening, before the full one. One may be walking along, in a beautiful park, and all of a sudden, the grass is so green, the flowers are bursting with a vibrant color that says all of creation is alive as you have never seen it! What has just happened is that you have activated totally heightened (peaked) senses, and there is a sight, sound, smell that is incredible… You are One with what you see… It is like a **walking meditation**… You are "high" and it will last as long as you don't analyze it

– stay in your heart and just enjoy it….. Interesting that once you have experienced this state, you can recreate it any time you want – by willing it. Your soul knows what it was and how you got there…all it takes is the first time, and remembering the way it felt and how things looked – and that will take you there again!

And sometimes the *Kundalini* does not move if the pupil's vibration level is not appropriate (high enough)…. And sometimes there are partial awakenings that do not last… and people have experienced those using Ayahuasca, Peyote, LSD… and those are not recommended either. Achieving awakening (higher consciousness) via any mechanical means will not last and may damage the psyche.

During the Egyptian initiations for Serpent Brotherhood and Djedhi Priests (see Chapter 5) the initiates were led thru physical environments and given potions to drink that helped to induce altered states. The Great Pyramid induced a special energy state that was similar to sitting in a natural Earth vortex. The Druids did similar things as was shown in Chapter 3 but they used the ambient *chi* from Oak Trees to heal and direct extra energy into the initiate hoping the time was right for the primal energy to move.

Another way that is becoming less and less available to people in the Southwest, is to go to Sedona and sit in a positive vortex, meditate and raise one's energy… that was until the year 2000 when the US Forest Service took over the canyons and fenced off safe areas containing the better vortices and now you can't get there.

> **Caution**: astrology is not of much help in planning to move one's *Kundalini*… the planetary energies are real but too weak to be of use. That is why the Oak groves and Great Pyramid were used the way they were... as concentrators of energy.

Now that we know what was eventually done to the initiates, let's begin to examine some of the different, but often related, teachings that Serpent Wisdom has offered, in its different forms, beginning with **Alchemy** and come up to the current day with Rosicrucianism and Freemasonry…

Chapter 10: Serpent Wisdom -- Alchemy

One of the first versions of Serpent Wisdom to be practiced by Man was Alchemy. While the historical roots of Alchemy are lost in antiquity, largely due to Church persecution, and book burning, there are three versions making the rounds:

1. The start of Western alchemy may generally be traced to Hellenistic Egypt, where the city of **Alexandria** was a center of alchemical knowledge…

2. Zosimos of Panopolis asserted that alchemy dated back to **Pharaonic Egypt** where it was the domain of the priestly class…

3. The dawn of Western alchemy is sometimes associated with that of metallurgy, extending back to 3500 BC. However, many writings were lost when the emperor Diocletian ordered the burning of alchemical books after suppressing a revolt in **Alexandria** (AD 292).

And it is not impossible that all three have a degree of validity about them. Alexandria was a Western Center for Therapeuts and arcane knowledge – which was kept in the ill-fated Library of Alexandria, which was sacked and burned three times.

The origin of Alchemy has been ascribed to **Hermes Trismegistus** (who lived about 1900 BC) and his writings, among them *Corpus Hermeticum* (aka *Hermetica*) and *The Emerald Tablet* (aka *The Smaragdine Tablet*). Although Hermes is the author named in the text of ***The Emerald Tablet***, its first known appearance was in a book written in Arabic between the sixth and eighth centuries AD.

> The oldest documentable source of the text is the *Kitāb sirr al-ḫalīqa* (*Book of the Secret of Creation and the Art of Nature*), itself a composite of earlier works. This volume is attributed to "Balinas" (or Pseudo-**Apollonius of Tyana**) who wrote sometime around the eighth century AD. In his book, Balinas frames **the *Emerald Tablet* as ancient Hermetic wisdom.** He tells his readers that he discovered the text in a vault below a statue of Hermes in Tyana, and that, inside the vault, an old corpse on a golden throne held the emerald tablet.[335] [emphasis added]

Following Balinas, an early version of the *Emerald Tablet* appeared in *Kitab Ustuqus al-Uss al-Thani* (*Second Book of the Elements of Foundation*) attributed to **Jabir ibn Hayyan,** the Arabic source, who credits **Apollonius of Tyana.**[336] (VEG Ch. 11)

Anunnaki Connection

All of that to say that tracing the real beginnings of Alchemy is difficult but it would be impossible were it not for one salient fact, given to us by Wikipedia and the late Zechariah Sitchin:

> **Wikipedia** says that the central figure in the mythology of alchemy is Hermes Trismegistus (or Thrice-Great Hermes). His name is derived from the Egyptian god Thoth and his Greek counterpart Hermes (aka Mercury)…. The *Hermetica* of Hermes is generally understood to form the basis for Western alchemical philosophy and practice. [337]

Zechariah Sitchin informs us that Thoth was in fact Ningishzidda, and that "Indeed, in time the Greeks identified 'Hermes Trismegistus' with Thoth as the god of knowledge and science." [338] Thus,

Thoth = Hermes = Ningishzidda.

The significance is that Ningishzidda was Enki's youngest son and shared in the Anunnaki Science Officer role, so he was knowledgeable in Science, Astronomy, Math, Chemistry and Genetics, etc. (He was also Quetzalcoatl in South America.) And Enki was the promoter of education for humans, and the one who started the Serpent Wisdom groups – secret knowledge for those worthy humans around the planet. It should not be surprising that Egypt was one of the places Hermes/Thoth chose to promote the meaning of Life, Science, and what would come to be called Alchemy (from Arabic **Al** ["the"] + **Khem** [Old name for Egypt & black soil]).

> And the reason it is Nigishzidda taking over for Enki is that Enki was near the end of his long life when The Flood occurred. Carrying on his father's duties fell to his qualified son, Ningishzidda.

An Anunnaki fact: [4]
The Mesopotamians believed the gods were immortal. The Sumerians said one year on planet Nibiru, a *sar*, was equivalent in time to 3600 earth years. Sitchin also said Anunnaki lifespans were 120 sars which is 120 x 3600 or 432,000 [Earth] years.

(continued…)

According to the **King List** 120 sars had passed from the time the Anunnaki arrived on Earth to the time of the Flood. However when the Lofty Ones came to Earth, their lifespans began to sync with Earth's faster orbit and they faced rapid aging compared to that on Nibiru. Einstein's Theory of General Relativity says celestial body gravity and motion warps local space/time [Earth is closer to our Sun than Nibiru is to its sun].

The Anunnaki discovered that by eating food from their home planet, and avoiding the Sun, they could keep the aging process synced to the pace of Nibiru.

The Sumerian god of wisdom Enki (Ea) was the leader of the first sons of Anu that came down to Earth. He played the pivotal role in saving humanity from the global Deluge. He defied the Anunnaki ruling council and told Ziusudra (the Sumerian Noah) how to build a ship on which to save humanity from the killing flood. Ea would have been over 120 sars old at that time, yet his activity with humanity continued to be actively supported for thousands of years thereafter.

People often have trouble believing that the Anunnaki could live for millennia. Very briefly, let's look at that. It is NOT impossible.

1. Reptiles are known to live longer than dogs, cattle and a lot of other animals,
   and
2. Man lives 70-80 years – which is astronomical compared to a Mayfly which sometimes does not even make it thru a day.

It is all relative and genetically-based (see point 3 next page).

Pyramid Power

It is all relative, and the Anunnaki were also said to have had the technology to restore people to life if they accidentally died (see Chapter 1 and Inanna). It would also be a function of the "resurrection technology" to lengthen their lives, and that has been suggested as one of the purposes of the **Great Pyramid of Giza**. We all heard that razor blades can be 'sharpened' and their useful life prolonged by putting them inside a pyramid for a day or two.

3. Lastly, Man used to live longer – e.g., Methuselah who lived 969 years. That could be imitated today – IF **telomeres and mitochondria** could be made to last longer (see TOM, Ch.13).

While skeptics are busy pooh-poohing the ability of a pyramid to keep food from rotting, or revitalize razor blades, there are two things they are not aware of:

1. If the pyramid is energized with an electric current running thru its surfaces, the space inside it creates a vortex which makes use of the Ether (or nowadays it is called **Dark Energy**) and anything in the pyramid is revitalized.[339]

2. A very recent development by a Greek scientist has found that a cone-shaped engine can and does produce more power (and levitation) than the Space Shuttle engines – due to some energy dynamics going on in the cone-shaped housing (which inside space is similar to that of a pyramid). [340]

And by the way, this aspect of the Ether (Dark Energy/Matter or **Zero-Point Energy**) is something that the Alchemists have known about for centuries…. Interesting that today's science is catching up with the Alchemists.

The Essence of the Universe

The Alchemists were aware (and probably still are) of something called *Prima Materia,* or **First Matter**. Also called Dew, Burning Water, Sulfur of Nature, the Serpent, the **Dragon**, White Smoke, Heart of the Sun, and Magnesia – about 60 different aliases meant to confuse the accidental reader of an Alchemist's notes.

> First matter, is the ubiquitous starting material required for the alchemical magnum opus and the creation of the philosopher's stone. It is the **primitive formless base of all matter** similar to chaos, the quintessence, or **Aether**. [341] [emphasis added]

The Alchemists followed their processes (consisting of at least 7 steps) and in lieu of the Philosopher's Stone, most of them had something called **"transmuting powder"** which when sprinkled into the crucible which held the lead sample, would sometimes bubble, fizz and transmute the lead to gold. The powder was reputed to be "… the color of the wild poppy and smelling of calcined sea salt" according to John Frederick Helvetius – who is profiled below. [342]

Kings and heads of state witnessed transmutation many times over the centuries, performed by many Alchemists, so it is a fact that it can be done. The issue in this chapter is where did the knowledge and process came from? – and we have to look to Thoth/Hermes aka Ninghishzidda… it was part of the secret society esoteric knowledge that was given to Man in the Serpent Wisdom groups. They said so in their symbology.

Alchemical Symbology

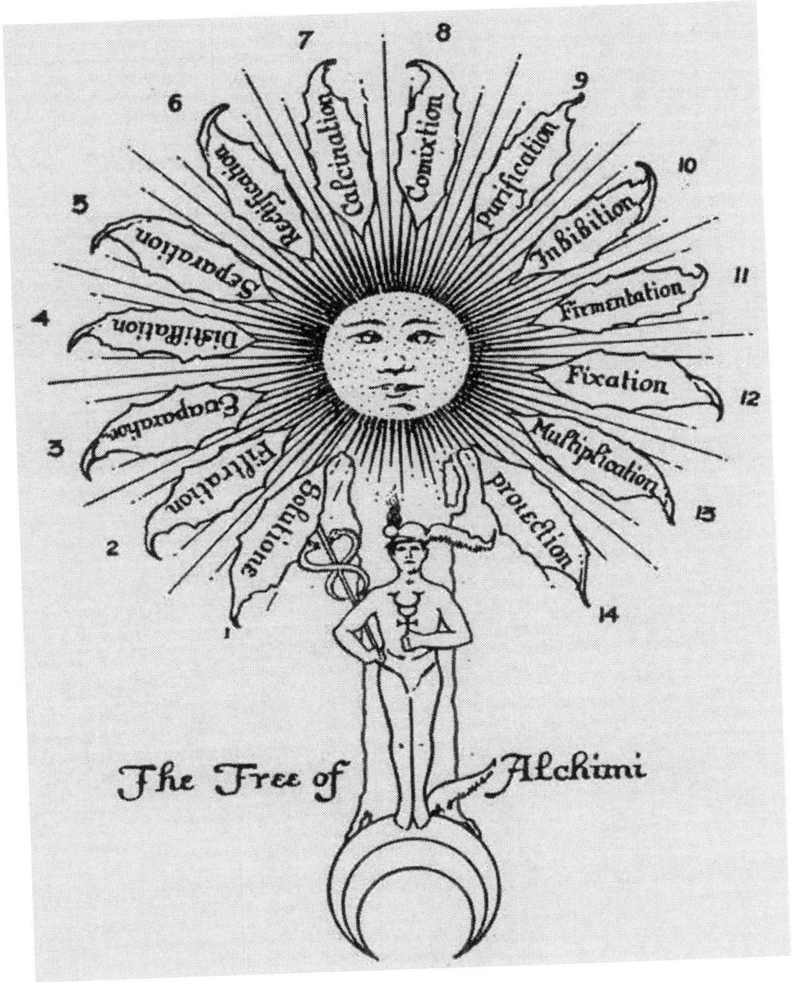

Herme's Tree of Alchemistry

The Alchemists not only stylized their 7-14 steps (for the process to transmute baser metals), but they also had another Tree: the trunk says 'Arbor Vita' or "living tree."

Alchemical Tree of Life under Heaven[343]
(credit: Bing Images: https://lilipilyspirit.com/alchemy_hermeticism.htm)

What look like golden apples are alchemical symbols for the planets and elements used in Alchemy. Note the peacock (lower left), the Seal of Solomon over the doorway, and the Hebrew YHWH at the very top. The two birds with the globes represent Earth, Air , Fire, Water – the **4 key elements**. The woman under the Tree is Lady Alchimia, mistress of the Art (that is not a serpent on her rod). The two 'humans' are Sol and Luna coming to Hermes, the alchemist (seated lower right in his study). Alas there isn't a serpent or dragon in the whole picture…. Yet they are useful valid symbols:

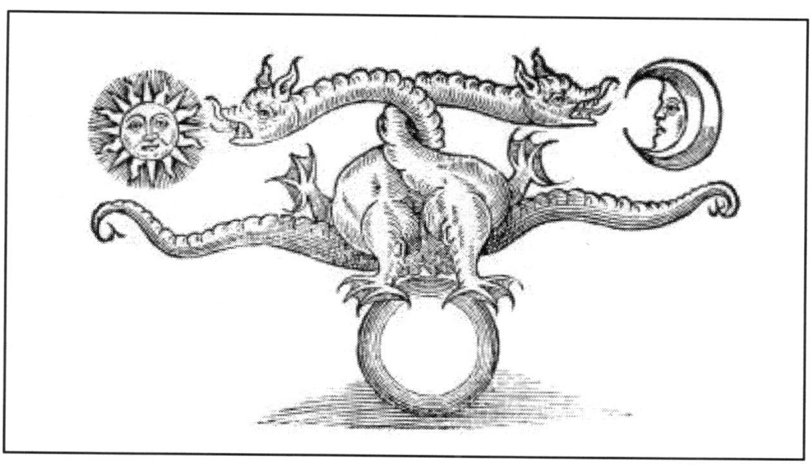

UNSPECIFIED - CIRCA 1754: Alchemical symbol of transmutation of base metal (Earth at bottom) into Gold (Sun) and Silver (Moon) through the agency of the dragon (Mercury - volatility). gettyimages.com

This is an oblique reference to **Kundalini** [344]...

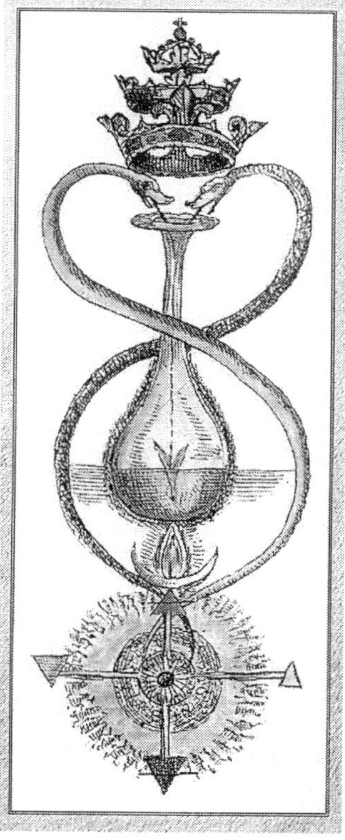

The Triple-Crowned Magistery [ξ]

Says the accompanying text: "The Secret Fire liberated from the Four Elements travels up the coils of the serpents and, descending via their tongues, exalts the elixir contained in the vessel [i.e., head]." Triple represents the Trinity, or connection with the One. Crown = crown chakra.

(ξ: a magistery is a product or medicine; a Quintessence.)

Note: **Azoth** is the 5th element, a Quintessence or absolute essence of Man that is to be released via the Great Work of Alchemy. (Think: *kundalini.*)

And of course, we again have the **Ouroboros** image used by the Alchemists (signifying that all is One and there is no end, no beginning...):

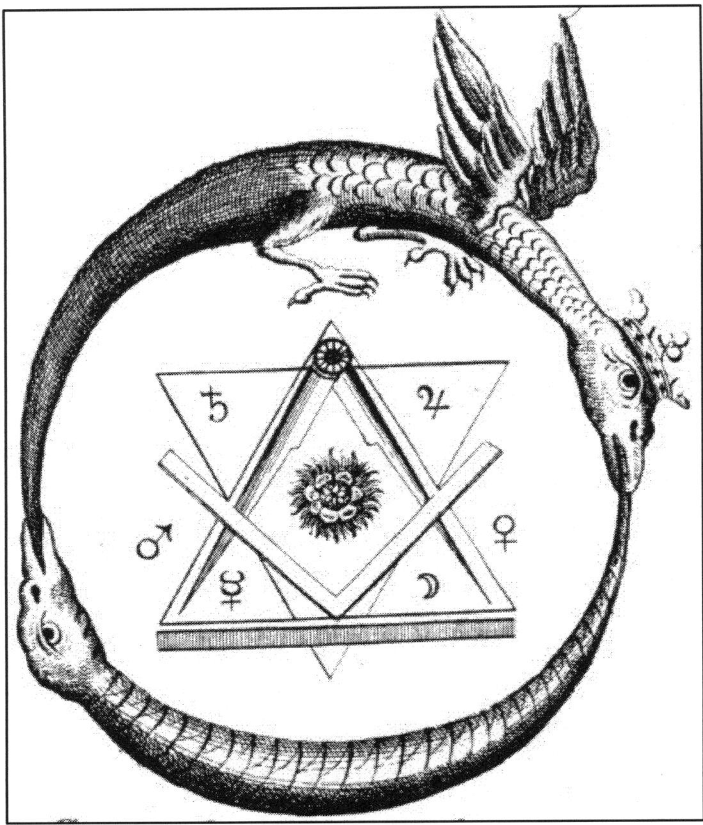

This alchemical symbol is really loaded:

A Dragon biting the Serpent represents the great dictum: *Solve et Coagula* -- dissolve the body and coagulate the spirit. The lower wingless serpent is the body that must be transformed, The Dragon *kundalini* Fire (note the Crown [chakra] symbol) is the spirit which must be 'coagulated' or fixed in order to be embodied.

The Rose in the center symbolizes Rosicrucianism, the two Triangles represent the dictum, "as above, so below" from the Emerald Tablet of Hermes. Also present are the Masonic tools and the symbol for male (left: ♂) and the symbol for female (right: ♀). The other 4 symbols in the triangles are (clockwise top left): lead/Saturn, tin/Jupiter, silver/Moon and mercury/Mercury.

> **Note** that 7 planets were said to influence 7 metals on Earth. (seven metals of alchemy: gold, silver, mercury, copper, lead, iron and tin). There's the number 7 again.

The metal Mercury is often represented by a **Serpent**, and the metal Gold is often symbolized by the Sun. In addition, just to round this out: there were three key chemicals: **Sulfur, Mercury and Salt**. Sulfur (masculine/Sun/Yang) and Mercury (feminine/Moon/Yin) were likened to the Ida and Pingala in the body and when the two *nadis* crossed each other, and achieved a balance, a chakra (energy vortex) was formed. (The Earth also has chakras, vortices, where energy spirals powerfully.)

Yes, the Chinese concepts apply as the Chinese also practiced Alchemy at the hand of Lao Tzu (who wrote an alchemical treatise called the **Tao te Ching**).

There is much more but this is just to substantiate that some very esoteric knowledge was passed on to Man, and one can see from the detailed chemical emphasis that goes on in Alchemy that is was a forerunner of modern Chemistry. And yet **Alchemy had a spiritual side** – it wasn't all just experimentation. What happens when you remove metaphysics from Alchemy?

Alchemy – Spiritual side = Chemistry

likewise:

Metaphysics – Spiritual side = Physics

That pretty well says where our 'modern' world is at, thanks to the Church. Alchemists were alleged to be practicing "witchy" stuff and might in fact be witches and warlocks... so it had to be stopped – at the expense of Man learning about his world and moving forward. If the Church had not interfered and had not persecuted Alchemy, today's science could have been realized back in the 1800s. Think not?

Just consider the following…

Atomic Truth

The alchemists were onto something back in the 1500-1700s, even though they did not know about atomic structure. Consider the atomic diagrams for Lead and Gold:

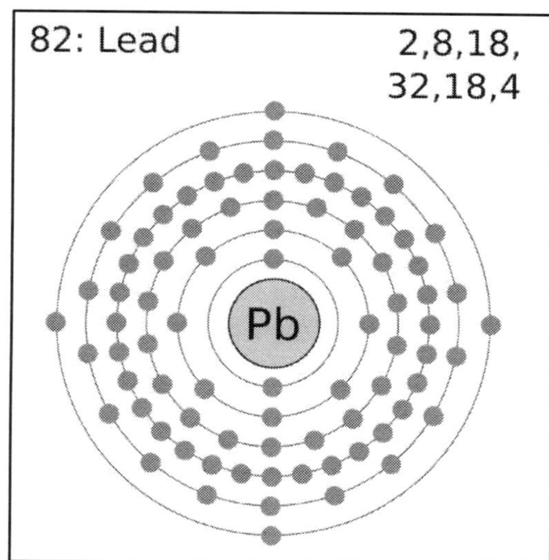

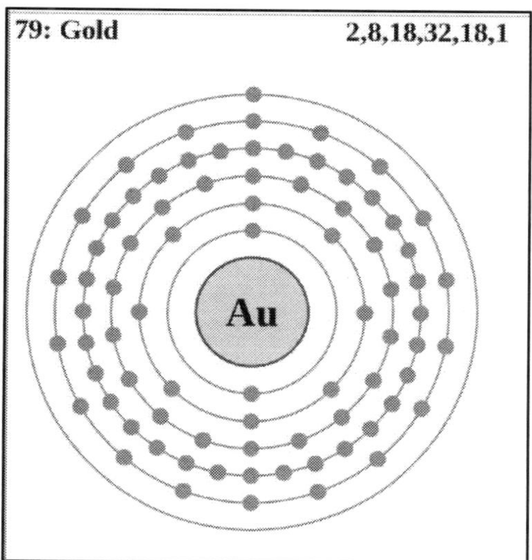

(credit: Wikipedia: commons)

The numbers in the upper right signify the number of electrons per shell (6 shells).

Lead (Pb): 2 8 18 32 18 and 4 (outer shell)
Gold (Au): 2 8 18 32 18 and 1 " "

Gold has 3 less electrons than Lead… so to convert Lead to Gold, remove the 3 extra electrons. And that has been done by physicists in the lab [345]… it takes a lot of bombardment with High Energy Physics to knock out the 3 electrons (using protons. See this footnote's additional text in Endnotes section.)

What is very interesting is that Gold and Lead are not next to each other on the Periodic Table of Elements:

Group→ / ↓Period	1	2	3	4	5	6	7	8	9	10	11	12	13	14	15	16	17	18
1	1 H																	2 He
2	3 Li	4 Be											5 B	6 C	7 N	8 O	9 F	10 Ne
3	11 Na	12 Mg											13 Al	14 Si	15 P	16 S	17 Cl	18 Ar
4	19 K	20 Ca	21 Sc	22 Ti	23 V	24 Cr	25 Mn	26 Fe	27 Co	28 Ni	29 Cu	30 Zn	31 Ga	32 Ge	33 As	34 Se	35 Br	36 Kr
5	37 Rb	38 Sr	39 Y	40 Zr	41 Nb	42 Mo	43 Tc	44 Ru	45 Rh	46 Pd	47 Ag	48 Cd	49 In	50 Sn	51 Sb	52 Te	53 I	54 Xe
6	55 Cs	56 Ba	* 71 Lu	72 Hf	73 Ta	74 W	75 Re	76 Os	77 Ir	78 Pt	79 Au	80 Hg	81 Tl	82 Pb	83 Bi	84 Po	85 At	86 Rn
7	87 Fr	88 Ra	** 103 Lr	104 Rf	105 Db	106 Sg	107 Bh	108 Hs	109 Mt	110		112	113 Uut	114 Fl	115 Uup	116 Lv	117 Uus	118 Uuo

*	57 La	58 Ce	59 Pr	60 Nd	61 Pm	62 Sm	63 Eu	Gd	Tb	Dy	67 Ho	68 Er	69 Tm	70 Yb
**	89 Ac	90 Th	91 Pa	92 U	93 Np	94 Pu	95 Am	96 Cm	97 Bk	98 Cf	99 Es	100 Fm	101 Md	102 No

GOLD

Gold (#79 = Au) is three steps removed from Lead (#82 = Pb) and notice that Thallium (Tl) and Mercury (Hg) are between Gold and Lead…. That means that when removing the electrons from Lead, one is going to first see Thallium then Mercury, and then Gold. So converting Mercury to Gold should be easier.

Now consider this: the alchemists did it with a "transmuting powder." So just how archaic and primitive were they? And because many wannabe alchemists never succeeded in transmuting metals, it is not obvious how it is done, nor can years of random experimenting discover it by chance. It is suggested that the stranger who appeared to John Frederick Helvetius (see profile below, in 'Nature of Alchemy' section) was in fact a pupil of Hermes (aka Thoth), who received his esoteric knowledge from the original source: Ningishzidda.

Nature of Alchemy

Whereas a lot of people would consider Alchemy nonsense or "witchy" stuff – that is exactly what the Church wanted people to think, so they would avoid discovering their higher self and potential for spiritual growth. Thus the Church denigrated Alchemy and not only burned books on the subject, it imprisoned and tortured people to death as an example to the public. That of course, drove the real Alchemy underground into secret societies – where Serpent Wisdom was already hiding.

Alchemy can be regarded either as a philosophy, as an experimental and physical science, or as a combination of the two… and Hermes was said to have identified the three main components of Alchemy: **Astrology, Alchemy** and **Theurgy**.

Astrology often involved Tarot. And it was believed that certain planets influenced certain metals, so specific experiments with certain metals would perform better if one considered which 'house' the planet was in at the time of the experiment – for the best result.

Secondly, **Alchemy** aimed to purify, mature, and perfect certain objects. Major aims were chrysopoeia, the **transmutation** of "base metals " (e.g., lead) into "noble" ones (particularly gold); the creation of an **elixer of immortality**; the creation of **panaceas** able to cure any disease; and the development of an alkahest, **a universal solvent**. In Europe, the creation of a **Philosopher's Stone** was variously connected with all of these projects.

A particularly representative story that is documented to have actually have happened, involved a Master who was distributing alchemical powder: [346] the evidence of **John Frederick Helvetius** (mentioned earlier), as he testified in 1666:

> "On December 27th, 1666, in the forenoon, there came a certain man to my house who was unto me a complete stranger, but of an honest, grave and authoritative mien, clothed in a simple garb like that of a Memnonite. He was of middle height, his face was long and slightly pock-marked, his hair was black and straight, his chin close-shaven, his age about forty-three or forty-four, and his native place North Holland, so far as I could make out. After we had exchanged salutations, he inquired whether he might have some conversation with me. It was his idea to speak of the **'Pyrotechnic Art**,' since he had read one of my tracts, being that directed against the Sympathetic Powder of Sir Kenelm Digby, in which I implied a suspicion whether the Great Arcanum of the Sages was not after all a gigantic hoax.
>
> (continued...)

"He took therefore this opportunity of asking if indeed I could not believe that such a **Grand Mystery** might exist in the nature of things, being that by which a physician could restore any patient whose vitals were not irreparably destroyed. [Sounds reminiscent of the Anunnaki ability to raise the dead and cure any disease.] My answer allowed that such a **Medicine** would be a most desirable acquisition for any doctor and that none might tell how many secrets there may be hidden in Nature, but that as for me -- though I had read much on the truth of this Art -- it had never been my fortune to meet with a master of alchemical science. I inquired further whether he was himself a medical man since he spoke.so learnedly about medicine, but he disclaimed my suggestion modestly, describing himself as a blacksmith, who had always taken great interest in the extraction of medicines from metals by means of fire.

"After some further talk the **'craftsman Elias'** -- for so he called himself -- addressed me thus: 'Seeing that you have read so much in the writings of the alchemists concerning the Stone, its substance, color, and its wonderful effects, may I be allowed to question whether you have yourself prepared it?'

"On my answering him in the negative, he took from his bag an ivory box of cunning workmanship in which there were three large pieces of **a substance resembling glass or pale sulfur** and informed me that here was enough of his tincture there to produce twenty tons of gold. When I held the treasure in my hands for some fifteen minutes listening to his accounting of its curative properties, I was compelled to return it (not without a certain degree of reluctance). After thanking him for his kindness, I asked why it was that his tincture did not display that ruby color that I had been taught to regard as characteristic of the **Philosophers' Stone**. He replied that the color made no difference and that the substance was sufficiently mature for all practical purposes. He brusquely refused my request for a piece of the substance, were it no larger than a coriander seed, adding in a milder tone that he could not do so for all the wealth which I possessed; not indeed on amount of its preciousness but for another reason that it was not lawful to divulge, Indeed, if fire could be destroyed by fire, he would cast it rather into the flames.

"Then, after some consideration, he asked whether I could not show him into a room at the back of the house, where we should be less liable to observation. Having led him into the parlor, he requested me to produce a gold coin, and while I was finding it he took from his breast pocket a green silk handkerchief wrapped about five gold medals, the metal of which was infinitely superior to that of my own money.

(continued...)

"Being filled with admiration, I asked my visitor how he had attained this most wonderful knowledge in the world, to which he replied that it was a gift bestowed upon him freely by a friend who had stayed a few days at his house, and who had taught him also how to change common flints and crystals into stones more precious than rubies and sapphires. 'He made known to me further," said the craftsman, 'the preparation of crocus of iron, an infallible cure for dysentery and of a metallic liquor, which was an efficacious remedy for dropsy, and of other medicines.' To this, however, I paid no great heed as I was impatient to hear about the **Great Secret.** The craftsman said further that his master caused him to bring a glass full of warm water to which he added a little white powder and then an ounce of silver, which melted like ice therein. 'Of this he emptied one half and gave the rest to me,' the craftsman related. 'Its taste resembled that of fresh milk, and the effect was most exhilarating.'

"I asked my visitor whether the potion was a preparation of the **Philosophers' Stone**, but he replied that I must not be so curious. He added presently that at the bidding of his master, he took down a piece of lead water-pipe and melted it in a pot. Then the master removed some sulfurous powder on the point of a knife from a little box, cast it into the molten lead, and after exposing the compound for a short time to a fierce fire, he poured forth a great mass of liquid gold upon the brick floor of the kitchen.

"The master told me to take one-sixteenth of this gold as a keepsake for myself and distribute the rest among the poor (which I did by handing over a large sum in trust for the Church of Sparrendaur). Before bidding me farewell, my friend taught me this Divine Art.'

"When my strange visitor concluded his narrative, I pleaded with him to prove his story by performing a transmutation in my presence. He answered that he could not do so on that occasion but that he would return in three weeks, and, if then at liberty, would do so. He returned punctually on the promised day and invited me to take a walk, in the course of which we spoke profoundly on the **secrets of Nature he had found in fire,** though I noticed that my companion was exceedingly reserved on the subject of the **Great Secret**. When I prayed him to entrust me with a morsel of his precious Stone, were it no larger than a grape seed, he handed it over like a princely donation. When I expressed a doubt whether it would be sufficient to tinge more than four grains of lead, he eagerly demanded it back. I complied, hoping that he would exchange it for a larger fragment, instead of which he divided it with his thumbnail, threw half in the fire and returned the rest, saying 'It is yet sufficient for you."

(continued...)

> The narrative goes on to state that on the next day Helvetius prepared six drachms of lead, melted it in a crucible, and cast in the tincture. There was a hissing sound and a slight effervescence, and after fifteen minutes, Helvetius **found that the lead had been transformed into the finest gold**, which on cooling, glittered and shone as gold indeed. A goldsmith to whom he took this declared it to be the purest gold that he had ever seen and offered to buy it at fifty florins per ounce. Amongst others, the Controller of the Mint came to examine the gold and asked that a small part might be placed at his disposal for examination. Being put through the tests with *aqua fortis* and antimony it was pronounced **pure gold of the finest quality**. Helvetius adds in a later part of his writing that there was left in his heart by the craftsman a deeply seated conviction that "through metals and out of metals, themselves purified by highly refined and spiritualized metals, there may be prepared the Living Gold and Quicksilver of the Sages, which bring both metals and human bodies to perfection."

What the public usually does not know is that **Alchemy mainly sought to purify the human body and soul, and achieve Gnosis** (a knowing connection with God). Forget transforming base metals into gold, a major aspect of Alchemy was the **transformation of the person, the soul**, into a better, more aware person… i.e., achieving higher consciousness, and here again, *Kundalini* often came into secret consideration. This had to be hidden from the Church, thus the putative lead-to-gold objective.

Theurgy, the 3rd component, was the "spiritual magic" or Divine Power behind Transformation (of metals and self) – the Chinese called it *chi*, the Hindus called it *prana*, for example. These were rituals performed with the intention of invoking the action or evoking the presence of one or more gods, especially with the goal of uniting with the Divine, achieving mystical oneness with God, and perfecting oneself.

As can be seen, from Chapter 9, this means **Alchemy was part of the Serpent Wisdom teachings, process and desired goal**. Alchemy is fundamentally spiritual… Transmutation of lead into gold is presented as an **analogy** for personal transmutation, purification, and perfection. Metaphysical aspects, substances, physical states, and material processes were used as metaphors for spiritual states, and ultimately **personal transformation**.

Both the transmutation of common metals into gold and the universal panacea symbolized evolution from an imperfect, diseased, corruptible, and ephemeral state toward a perfect, healthy, incorruptible, and everlasting state, so the Philosopher's Stone then represented a mystic key that would make this evolution possible. Applied to the alchemist himself, the twin goal symbolized his **evolution from**

ignorance to enlightenment, and the Stone represented a hidden spiritual truth or power that would lead to that goal.[347] And yet some alchemists were so advanced they could create gold…

Church & Crown Reaction

The following accounts are historically accurate: [348]

Naturally the authorities, Church and State, were interested in having the alchemists create gold for them, and as a matter of fact, King Gustavus Adolphus of Sweden (AD 1611) and Pope John XXII (AD 1316) had received a lot of gold this way, so they knew it was not a scam and some alchemists were looked on favorably. Such was not the case with all alchemists.

Alexander Sethon was called to a meeting with the Elector of Saxony, Christian II, and asked to demonstrate the transmutation of Lead into Gold. He was asked to share the secret of how he did it, and when he refused, he was imprisoned and tortured every day, but he never revealed the secret. Michael Sendivogius, Botticher, and Paykull also spent part of their lives in prison.

The controversial **Raymond Lully** (AD 1310) was also summoned by King Edward II to produce gold, and Lully agreed on the condition that it be used to finance the Crusades. He was given a room in the Tower of London and produced £ 50,000 pounds of gold. Edward became greedy and Lully balked at making more, and Edward imprisoned him. Lully later escaped and left England.

George Ripley gave £ 100,000 pounds of alchemical gold to the Knights of Rhodes when they were attacked by the Turks.

> The learned chemist **Van Helmont** and the doctor Helvetius (profiled above in the 3-page insert) were both skeptics with regard to the Philosopher's Stone and had even published books against it when they were both converted as a result of an identical adventure which befell them both. As related above, an unknown man visited them and gave them a small amount of 'projection powder' and instruction in how to use it….
>
> Both Van Helmont's and Helvitius' experiments were successful, and both men became acknowledged believers in Alchemy. Van Helmont became the greatest "chemist" of his day. If we do not hear nowadays that Madame Curie has had a mysterious visitor who gave her a little powder "the color of the wild poppy and smelling of calcined sea salt,"

> the reason may be that **the secret is indeed lost**; or possibly now that alchemists are no longer persecuted.... it may be that they no longer need the favorable judgment of those in power...[349] [emphasis added]

Sad to think that such knowledge and skill might have been lost to mankind, but consider that it still lives .... underground in Secret Societies, with true enlightened Masters (Think: Jeus turning water to wine...).

So what were some of the esoteric teachings? The following will briefly examine the Emerald Tablet and the Basic Hermetic Principles which are among the earliest esoteric teachings and are said to have originated with Thoth/Hermes. Thus these would have been the earliest recorded teachings promoted by Ninngishzidda as he set up the Serpent Wisdom groups, which we now know included *Kundalini* enlightenment, and Alchemy.

The Emerald Tablet

The Emerald Tablet of Hermes Trismegistus is a short work which contains a phrase (item #2 below) that is well known in occult circles: **"As above, so below."** The *Emerald Tablet* also refers to the three parts of the wisdom of the whole universe. Hermes states that his knowledge of these **three parts** (i.e., Astrology, Alchemy and Theurgy) is the reason why he received the name Trismegistus ("Thrice Great" or "Ao-Ao-Ao" [which mean "greatest"]).[350] ("A" = Alpha, "O" = Omega.)

Apollonius tells his readers that he discovered the text in a vault below a statue of Hermes in Tyana (Turkey), and that, inside the vault, an old corpse on a golden throne held the emerald tablet. It is not known what the tablet looked like, nor whether it was made of a gemstone... thus there is no picture of it.

In Hermes' tomb was found the *"Smaragdine Tablet"*, or the *Emerald Tablet*, on which were inscribed in Phoenician characters the following **thirteen sentences**:[351]

1. **Firstly, I speak not fictitious things, but that which is certain and most true.**
2. **Secondly, What is below is like that which is above, and what is above is like that which is below, to accomplish the miracles of one thing.**

> That is symbolized by **two triangles** one pointing up, the other pointing down, and such was appropriated by the Jewish flag of Israel:

The earliest Jewish usage of the symbol was inherited from medieval Arabic literature by **Kabbalists** for use in talismanic protective amulets (*segulot*) where it was known as a Seal of Solomon.

This symbol will be examined further when Kabbalah is reviewed (Chapter12).

(credit: Bing Images)

3. Thirdly, And as all things were produced by the meditation of One Being, so all things were produced from this one thing by adaptation.
4. Fourthly, Its father is the Sun, its mother the Moon; the wind carries it in its belly, its nurse is the spirituous earth.
5. Fifthly, It is the cause of all perfection throughout the whole world.
6. Sixthly, Its power is perfect if it be changed into earth.
7. Seventhly, Separate the earth from the fire, the subtle from the gross, acting prudently and with judgment.
8. Eighthly, Ascend with the greatest sagacity from the earth to heaven, and then descend again to the earth, uniting together the powers of things superior of the whole world, and all obscurity will fly far away from you.
9. Ninthly, This thing has more fortitude than fortitude itself, because it overcomes all subtle things, and penetrates every solid thing.
10. Tenthly, Thus were all things created.
11. Eleventhly, Thence proceed wonderful adaptations which are produced in this way.
12. Twelfthly, Therefore am I called Hermes Trismegistus, possessing the three parts of the philosophy of the whole world.
13. Thirteenthly, That which I had to say concerning the operation of the Sun is completed.

The following is the evaluation of the *Emerald Tablet* by an Alchemy Group in today's world (so you know what they think of it):[352]

> These 13 sentences seem to be abstract references to occult knowledge that only an adept would know what alchemical insights they refer to. The secrets of creation, of alchemy, of magic, of wisdom, mystical knowledge, and occult philosophy—and they are all the same thing. But whether this **One Thing** Hermes refers to is God, Spirit, or what you will, it cannot be put into words by Man.
>
> It cannot be taught by one man to another, although it can be hinted at as many New Thought/New Age groups do. This is the **Secret of Secrets** which opens all mysteries. It can only be found by each man by himself; and to each it will come in a different way and have a meaning that none other can fully share or understand. (See 'Insider' in Chapter 13.)
>
> Those that have found it, have all knowledge and wisdom, so far as these are obtainable on earth, and they inevitably will recognise others who have it. It creates a sort of Cosmic Free-Masonry, and the sign of it is written on the forehead (*Ajna* chakra open); but it can only be read correctly by the Initiate. To the Initiate the pretenders to this Wisdom are like glass; they see right through it into the very depths of the person's heart and soul.

After researching the *Emerald Tablet* and expecting some profound philosophical or metaphysical insight, the thirteen points above were rather anti-climactic. Items 4 – 7 clearly are code for something. In addition, <u>beware</u>: there is another website out there that purports to relate the translation to the [several] Tablets of Hermes… all 15 of them. From Atlantis, no less.

In a more credible vein, we can examine Hermetic Principles as written by a group of Alchemists in 1908. They called their work **The Kybalion**. Having vetted these principles on several Alchemical sites, and in two books related to Alchemy, the following principles are not only alchemical since they help to transform everyday consciousness to a higher realization, but they are also quite commonly found in the New Thought churches, whose metaphysical teachings are nothing less than spiritual alchemy.

Hermetic Principles

I. The Seven Universal Hermetic Laws

The basic thesis of ***The Kybalion*** is that the universe arose out of Mind, and *not* the other way around, as modern science teaches us. Once this simple truth is grasped we start to see the world with new eyes. We can then use the seven universal laws the book describes to unlock the hidden meaning of any philosophical or occult text, and also apply them to any area of our life; health, relationships, work, etc., for our own benefit in particular and that of the world in general. The seven laws or principles described in *The Kybalion* and the main propositions that derive from them, are: [353]

Mentalism. All is derived from Mind and the universe is the result of the operation of mental forces. In this first law are concealed the meaning and operation of all the rest of the Hermetic laws. This truth is echoed in the famous *Tabula Smaragdina*, or "Emerald Tablet" of Hermes Trismegistus, which states: "*And as all things were produced by the meditation of one Being, so all things were produced from this one thing by adaptation.*"

Correspondence. There is a specific correspondence between all things. This law is enshrined in the well-known Hermetic maxim: "*What is below is like that which is above, and what is above is like that which is below, to accomplish the miracles of one thing*", which is the 2nd sentence in the "Emerald Tablet" mentioned above. But correspondence is *not* the same thing as comparison, though the two words are often confused. A man *corresponds* to a god, for a god is an *Immortal* mortal and a man a *Mortal* immortal. Likewise, an atom corresponds to a solar system but heat *compares* to cold, for they are simply polarities of the same principle (see Law 4—Polarity). If you cannot see the distinction read and *think*, and then read and study some more until the difference becomes clear to you.

Vibration. Everything in the Universe is in constant motion, both internally and externally, even material forms *we* may consider to be inanimate. All moves and vibrates in accordance with fixed laws, most of which are entirely unknown to material science. **Any change in one's mental state alters the vibration of every living particle within us**. In this lies the key to health and disease, success and failure, strength and weakness. (See TSiM.)

Polarity. Everything in the Universe is *dual*; positive and negative, light and dark, hot and cold. In addition, a Higher state or principal is positive in relation to a lower one and *vice versa*. This law is responsible for sympathy and antipathy, attraction and repulsion and its application is the key to achieving inner balance and harmony in our lives. Opposites both repel and attract one another depending upon the nature of the forces or principles involved and the plane or realm of their activity. In this way we may reconcile all contradictions and paradoxes, whenever and wherever we encounter them, leading to a complete understanding of ourselves and our purpose and place in the Universe.

Rhythm. Everything in the Universe is subject to rhythm. Up and down, left and right, dark and light, backwards and forwards. In this law lies the key to understanding and controlling all activity, whether mental or physical, both within ourselves and in our environment. A simple example of this is the well-known saying that a wise man bends to the storm; a fool resists and is broken.

Cause and Effect. There is a cause for every effect within the Universe and an effect for every cause, though in many cases we are not *consciously* aware of the underlying cause that has produced a specific effect. This law is summed up very succinctly in the Hermetic axiom which states: "*that which comes up has always been sown; not all that has been sown comes up.*" Consequently, **there can be no such things as chance or coincidence**, which are merely words that describe any activity or event of which the cause is not known or perceived. (**Karma** is scheduled by the Life Plan with which you incarnated – see Transformation of Man.)

Gender or Sex. Gender is a universal principle throughout the manifested Universe. Not an atom nor an angel is devoid of it. The Masculine and Feminine principles manifest on all planes and apply to all states of consciousness. The Masculine or Father principle may be considered as the active and positive force, whilst the Feminine or Mother principle is the passive and negative condition. Both are necessary for creation. We find these two principles represented in the theological philosophies of all the great religions. In India, Brahma the Creator is complimented by Shiva the Destroyer. In ancient Egypt these two principles were sometimes symbolised by Horus and Set, who in this context may be regarded as a *feminine* principle. We should add that we are discussing universal *archetypes* here and *not* their material and physical manifestations such as human men and women. An individual woman can be just as 'positive' and 'creative' as any man (and sometimes more so), and a man may be negative, passive and destructive (and often is!). It all depends on the degree or extent of the Masculine (Yang) and Feminine (Yin) qualities present in any particular individual, and this varies enormously among mankind.

II. New Thought Metaphysical Concepts

The following are generally-agreed upon metaphysical principles, not stated in the above two sources. [354]

Nothing From Nothing Comes. Alchemy is not the making of something from nothing. It is the process of increasing that which already exists. For example, the 'essence' of Gold already exists within Lead… all that is required is to remove the intrinsic elements that make it Lead. And Copper can be created from Lead or Gold by removing those aspects of everything that is not Copper.

> The key to transmutation is to realize that everything is like everything else – all composed of the same *Prima Materia*… all atoms, or nowadays we'd say **quarks**... and don't forget that Dark Matter and Dark Energy permeate everything, too.

God is the Within and Without of All Things. The Supreme One manifests Himself thru the whole of Creation and the expansion or growth of all that currently exists. This says that God is Omnipresent. God is in everything.

Water Seeks its Own Level. Or said more colloquially, **Birds of a feather flock together -- because "like attracts like."**

What You Bind on Earth is Bound in Heaven. (As below, so Above.) This reflects the fact that if you dislike someone and curse them, the curse is carried with them when they die, and it must sometime be released or cancelled. It helps to formulate Karma – what do you have to learn that caused you to curse that other person? This also teaches the importance of Forgiveness. Cursing someone "ties" you to them until you wise up and release them (i.e., forgive them).

Within Everything is the Seed of Everything. This is the basis of the Law of Increase, as well as the basis for the very first statement in this Section II.

Law of Karma. This is not "an eye for an eye." It merely says that when one is born, certain lessons are awaiting the soul and they may be seen as tests and are to be met and overcome. Failure to do so guarantees the tests will return. For example, knifing someone in a past life does not mean that you must be knifed to 'repay' that action. It means that you can hopefully see during this lifetime, what causes you to act that way, and this time choose to stop it –i.e., overcome it.

Law of Confusion. Ignorant people love this one – it says that you do not have to learn everything in one lifetime, and you have the right to not know something. This means that someone who wants to teach you the **Golden Rule** does not have the right (or duty) to force it on you – when you are ready, and want to know, the teacher will appear and you cannot learn something until you realize you don't know and want to know. Yet, YOU are responsible to discover and learn (as the Insider says in Chapter 13.)

> This does not mean you can be stupid for Eternity. The gods will notice that you are defective if you learn nothing, and they have the right to 'disassemble' you and not spend any more effort trying teach a wayward soul in the Earth School.

Argue For Your Limitations and They are Yours. This is negative thinking and a dysfunctional way to go thru life. Saying I can't or I don't have what it takes is a lie and could eventually result in the 'disassembly' mentioned above. A soul is never tested beyond what it is able to do (or handle) – it is just that souls don't know that they are much more capable than they think. That is one of the lessons of the Earth School.

Your Words Have Power. This is related to the last principle. And the higher one's consciousness, the faster the words bear fruit. With most souls in Earth School, one must focus on what is wanted, repeat it, visualize it, put feeling/energy behind it, and then release it – repeatedly until it bears fruit.

> By the way, negative words, swearing, and listening to trash videos or Rap where every other word is the 'F' word creates astral mucous in the aura and attracts negative entities to one. (Sea salt baths cleanse the aura, by the way.)

The clue is: if you have spent years at it, wanting it, visualizing it, and it still doesn't show up, one of two things is true: You either don't really want it, or it isn't available.

> More aphorisms and insights are examined in Virtual Earth Graduate (last 2 chapters) and Transformation of Man.

Summary

Today's "scientists" regard the alchemists as dreamers and fools, though every discovery of their infallible science is to be found in the "dreams and follies" of the alchemists trying to create gold several centuries ago. It is no longer a paradox, but a truth attested by recognized scientists themselves, that the few fragments of truth that our modern culture possesses are due to the pretended or genuine adepts who were hanged by the Church or Crown with a <u>golden</u> dunce's cap on their heads.

What is important is that not all of them saw in the Philosopher's Stone concept the mere vulgar, useless aim of making gold. A small number of them received, either through a master or through the silence of daily meditation, **genuine higher truth**. These were the men who, by having observed it in themselves, understood the symbolism of one of the most essential rules of alchemy: Use only one vessel, one fire, and one instrument (i.e., Monotheism).They knew the characteristics of the sole agent, of the **Secret Fire**, of **the serpentine power** which moves upwards in spirals -- of the great primitive force hidden <u>in all matter</u>, organic and inorganic -- which the Hindus call *kundalini*, a force that creates and destroys simultaneously.

The Great Work

The alchemists often referred to their efforts as the Great Work – meaning to **transform oneself** into a more aware, caring, enlightened person – transcending the baser, lower nature of Man (the Serpent) and aligning more and more with the One, the Father of Light (via *Kundalini*, the **Dragon**. That is the meaning of the earlier diagram:

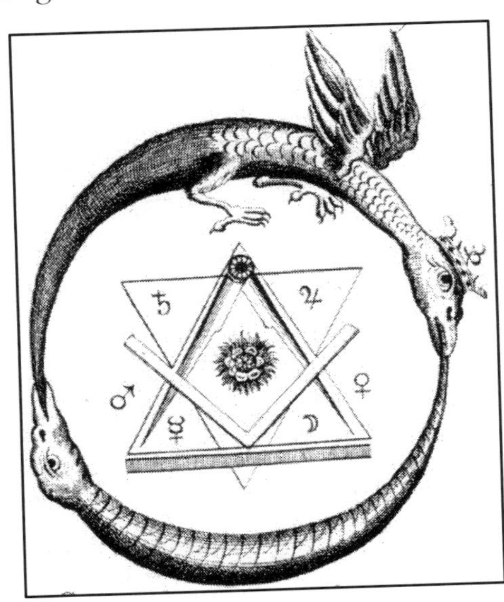

Such was the **Inner Work**. The Outer Work was that of learning Nature's secrets and using the knowledge to heal self and others with Herbology or elixirs… covered in the next chapter.

The secret of Alchemy is this: to empty oneself (no ego) and create a vacuum into which must flow the Energy and Presence of the Universe and produce a realization of Self with the Divine. Further, and herein the alchemists must have had the inner teaching from Thoth/Hermes:

> ….there is a way of manipulating what modern science calls a force-field. This force field acts upon the observer and puts him in a privileged position in relation to the universe. From this privileged position, he has access to the realities that are normally concealed from us by time and space, matter and energy. This is what we call the **Great Work**. [355]

The "force field" could be called Spirit, Intelligence, perhaps that is even what Dark Energy is… there is an Intelligent Mind that responds to us as we seek it. Call it the God Force, Baptism of the Holy Spirit, The Anointing, the **Dragon Force**… it is real, although we don't know much about its exact nature.

Kundalini is often called the Dragon Force.

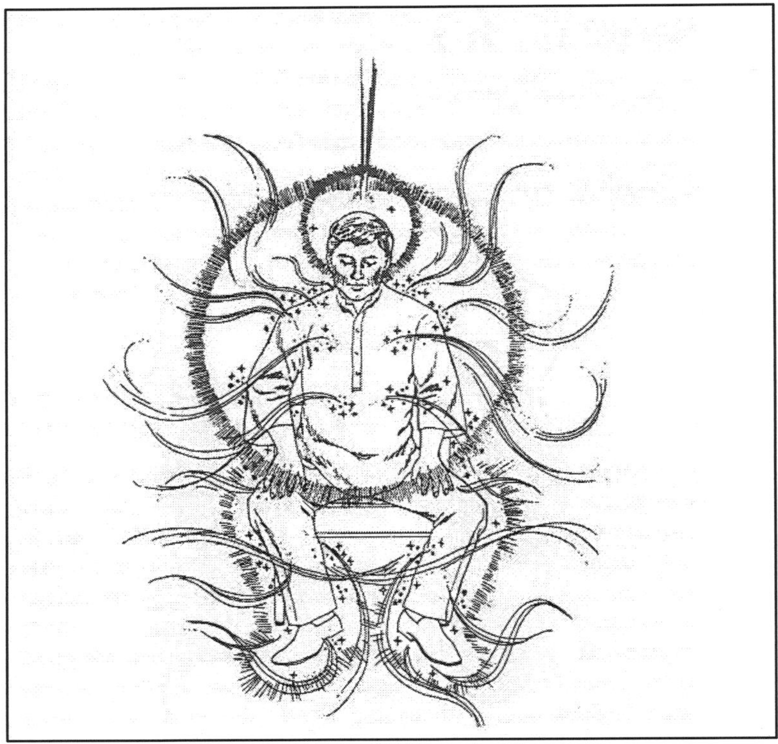

Drawing in The Force
(credit: Pranic Healing, p. 76)

When seekers practice raising the *Kundalini* and connect with the Force, they know it is real, and the proof is when they heal people, walk on water (i.e., levitation), or accurately foretell the future. Man is more than he thinks he is, and Enki and his son wanted people to know that and thus lovingly promoted Serpent Wisdom, including Alchemy, so that Man might develop his full potential.

As has been said in other books by this author, there is a group on the planet that does not want Man to be all that he can be, and they use the Church and Media to diss such ideas and program people to ignore or shun and laugh at anything that could be in their best spiritual interest. The Lords need dumb sheep to control so they can experience their power. God forbid you think outside the box that the Lords created for you.

Hermetic Integrity

They kept the divine science to themselves, a secret within their small group, and never left a complete account of what they did. Alchemy is fundamentally spiritual and teaches that there is a transcendent God in the universe in which we all participate. And more: Hermeticists teach that **a single, true theology exists** and was given to Man in antiquity and yet most public religions are incomplete versions of the original, true theology.

The alchemists calculated that the capacity for creation and the capacity for destruction were equal, that the possessor of the secret had power for evil as great as his power for good. And just as nobody trusts a child with a high explosive, so they kept the divine science to themselves, or, if they left a written account of the facts they had found, they always omitted the essential point, so that it could be understood only by someone who already knew.

Nicolas Flamel was perhaps the best known alchemist of his day (14th Century), and he went to great pains to couch his discoveries in plain language which on the surface appear to be about the transmutation of base metals. To the Church this was nonsense and so they watched him but left him alone as what he ostensibly said did not contradict the Church's teachings. However, "between the lines" and to anyone already indoctrinated into the secret information, his writings were a cleverly-coded esoteric document whose insights explained the spiritual transformation of Man.

> The essence of his [Flamel's] reputation are claims that he succeeded at the two goals of alchemy: that he made the Philosopher's Stone, which turns base metals into gold, and that he and his wife Perenelle achieved immortality through the "**Elixir of Life**." [356]

> In fact if that is true, then he is a good candidate for the **Count de St. Germain** (see Chapter 13). And don't forget, in Chapters 1 and 5 that

> the Anunnaki (Thoth and Inanna) also possessed the procedure to bring people back to life – as well as lengthen their own lives. All the Alchemists were doing was trying to discover what the Anunnaki already knew (and perhaps only shared with the highest initiates in Serpent Wisdom).

Examples of such men were, in the seventeenth century, **Thomas Vaughan** (called Philalethes), and, in the eighteenth century, **Lascaris**. It is possible to form some idea of the lofty thought of Philalethes from his book *Infroitus,* but Lascaris has left us nothing. Little is known of their lives. Both of them wandered throughout Europe teaching those whom they considered worthy of being taught. They both made gold often but only for special reasons. They did not seek glory, but actually shunned it. They had knowledge enough to foresee persecution and avoid it. They had neither a permanent abode nor family. It is not even known when and where they died. It is probable that they attained the most highly developed state possible to man, that they accomplished the **transmutation of their soul**. In others words, while still living they were members of the spiritual world. **They had regenerated their being, performed the prescribed task of mankind**.

They were **twice born**. They devoted themselves to helping their fellow men; this they did in the most useful way, which does not consist in healing the ills of the body or in improving men's physical state. They used a higher method, which in the first instance can be applied only to a small number, but eventually affects all of us. They helped the noblest minds to reach the goal that they had reached themselves. They sought such men in the towns through which they passed, and, generally, during their travels. They had no school and no regular teaching, because **their teaching was on the border of the human and the divine.** But they knew that a truthful word, a seed of gold sown at a certain time in a certain soul would bring results a thousand times greater than those that could accrue from the knowledge gained through books or ordinary science.

> **Paracelsus** (AD 1500) was a brilliant alchemist and was severely persecuted by the Church. Yet his contributions to our world of science today include: discovery of the metal zinc, **Homeopathy**, the doctrine of signatures in **Herbology**, laudanum, antisepsis (he was against bloodletting and using cow dung to help wounds heal), and was first to promote the **Germ Theory** as a cause of disease.

Esoteric Worldview

As the reader will see, in the following chapters, Alchemy was not limited to the Arabs, nor the Europeans – it was something of a *Zeitgeist* that persisted for several centuries as the idea of transformation, metal and spiritual took hold of men's imaginations. In fact, its origins can be traced to a concurrence in Greece with Neoplatonists, in Egypt with Hermeticism and the Gnostics, and the attempt to define and apply the higher spiritual concepts even inspired the Kabbalists and the Rosicrucians.

Thus, before moving into the following chapters where these issues are briefly examined, it would be helpful to insert an overview here, to orient the reader to the similar and outstanding aspects of the basic 5 movements.

Ancient Egypt

There are ancient mystery schools in Egypt, that were initially started by the gods (who happened to be the Anunnaki –in the beginning) and they had developed respectable advances in mathematics, astronomy, and medicinal knowledge. Today's avid public, wanting to know more about Egypt, have erred in assuming that they also had a belief in **reincarnation and karma**. Such is not the case. There is no evidence for such beliefs, and in fact, **the Egyptians were rather primitive in their understanding of the afterlife**. How one lived their life did affect their passage and performance in the afterlife, but that was it... you died and Osiris would weigh your heart on a feather scale. If you passed the test, you went on into the Duat and stayed there. You had one life to live and that was it. If you failed the **"feather test"** you had a "heavy heart" and were immediately cast into a fiery abyss. Reincarnation was not an option. Their overall worldview was materialistic and not very spiritual.

> The one attempt by Akhenaten and Nefertiti to lead Man away from the panoply of Egyptian gods and into a worship of The One lasted just a few years and resulted in the defrocked Egyptian priesthood (who had already warped what the Anunnaki [viz. Enki] had taught them) turning on Akhenaten and killing him and Nefertiti, and then reinstalling the old gods. Power was more important than Truth.

Neoplatonism

That takes us to Greece where much has been written about how great **Plato's ideas** were. In fact, Plato did travel to Egypt and undergo initiations by the Egyptian priests into the sacred mysteries. So we would expect to find some of those 'sacred ideas' in his writings.

Plato was also picking up on ideas from Orpheus, **Apollonius of Týana**, and Pythagoras and yet he is not aware of what must have been in the true, Serpent Wisdom teachings: that the Earth was not flat and that the Sun did not revolve about the Earth. Plato fails on one account – although he knows that the Earth is round, he still implies (in *Timaeus*) that the Sun and planets revolve around Earth. In addition, he does speak of a universal energy penetrating everything (Æther, nowadays called **Dark Energy**) and it reacts to and changes its form in synch with "harmonic frequencies" (Egyptian influence here) to create and sustain all things.

And then he becomes very sexist regarding **Reincarnation** (*Timaeus* 10) – first a soul is born into the "better of the two" body possibilities, as a Man, and failing that, he would have to come back as a Woman, and failing to handle that incarnation appropriately, he would come back as some animal which suits his baser nature….

Somehow, it looks like Plato did not get as enlightened as we'd like to think of him. He is nowhere near the esoteric knowledge that he should be displaying if he came thru the Mystery Schools as set up by the Serpent Wisdom group… especially dealing with the transformation of solids, liquids and gases, dealing with an Alchemical approach to explaining the four basic elements (air, fire, water, earth)… Perhaps what he reflects is the distorted view of same that was taught in the later Mystery Schools in Egypt that he allegedly graduated from.

Plotinus picks up Plato's ideas, as well as his pupil Aristotle, and these form the basis of **Neoplatonism**. Here the soul is thought to be all, and life is but an illusion (using Plato's Allegory of the Cave). Thus, some of its proponents advocated differing degrees of withdrawal from the world. Plotinus does define what a proper spiritual effort looks like if one choses to pursue lofty esoteric aims and perceive true, divine beauty. In fact, it is almost Gnostic in its rejection of the material and then going within to find the true Light, and letting it purify and polish one's true nature. This is in accord with the esoteric aims of Alchemy... and Hermeticism.

Hermeticism

Recall thaet Hermeticism consisted of 3 main parts: Alchemy, Astrology and Theurgy (or magical works). It is more than that, and famously includes the treatise called *Corpus Hermeticum* – 17 essays which because (1) they borrow from Plato's flawed concepts of the cosmos and creation, and (2) are beyond the scope of this book, will not be gone into here. However, a brief mention of what they do include is needed to lay the groundwork for later chapters, so that the major underlying Serpent Wisdom aspects begin to come together.

First and foremost are the concepts of **Reincarnation and Karma**... supported by Hermeticism. In fact, if a system supports Reincarnation it also <u>by default</u> includes Karma — as Karma drives the re-incarnation into further life experiences. And the way off the Wheel of Karma is to attain **Gnosis** – sufficient Knowledge to comport oneself in a way that cancels Karma. It is suggested that enough Knowledge begins to make one a god – able to know and do more than the average person.

> Certainly the Alchemists were after this- --if they had the knowledge to transform lead to gold, they might be considered a god… and if they could create the Elixir of Life they would be immortal like a god…

And the ultimate goal was to gain Knowledge to become god-like and return to Source where we merge with the universal Energy and Mind, and All are One – this was the meaning behind the **As Above, So Below** dictum – souls below heaven are all one just as the angels and higher beings above Earth are one.

The *Hermetica* contain few suggestions as to how this ascent is achieved. They merely advocate detaching from the world, and focusing on the divine nature of things. They also suggest developing one's **intuition** as this counts for much and will sustain and lead the seeker forward… and while it is not openly stated in the *Hermetica*, the *Kundalini* aspect of Serpent Wisdom <u>will</u> develop one's mental powers as well as intuition (see Chapters 9-13).

The *Hermetica* describes a person who has opened to the divine vision where all is seen as one, and such a person is called **"twice-born"…**

> …seeing within me an unfabricated vision that came from the mercy of god [sic], I went out of myself into **an immortal body**, and now I am not what I was before [an Out-of-Body experience]. I have been born in mind. This thing cannot be taught nor can it be seen through any elementary fabrication that we use here below. There for the initial form even of my own constitution is of no concern. Colour, touch or size I no longer have; I am a stranger to them. Now you see me with your eyes, my child, but by gazing with bodily sight you do not understand what I am; I am not seen with such eyes… [357]

Glorified Soul-body

As an example, the astral body (or soul) that is connected to the body looks something like this (left):

The image on the left is also very much what the **Beings of Light** (aka Angels) look like, but larger.

The greater your personal Light (PFV) the more brilliant is the aura and the larger it is.

Ascended Masters and Avatars often have gold or purple in their auric field.

(source: www.bing.com/images)

Unlike the Egyptians, the Hermetic view of Death is that it is nothing to fear – it is but a passage to the Realm we all came from. Another teaching is that while Earth life is an illusion, it is still something has to be dealt with – unless one chooses to be a total ascetic and then that will have its own set of lessons and tests. We still need to honor our spiritual roots and do the best we can with what we are given.

> It is worth mentioning that choosing what appears to be an easy path thru life may just have signed you up for the hard lesson that (1) there is no easy path, and (2) trying to take an easy path is a cop-out and you will still have to do what you were sure you could not handle .
>
> The gods want us all to see that we are capable of handling whatever comes up and we get a sense of our real capability and strength. That is part of the realization that makes us "Graduates" from the Earth School. (See VEG, Ch's. 15-16.)

Lastly, there is mention of **"advanced beings"** **<u>who incarnated before Man</u>** to prepare the way – a variety or class of souls came into being before mankind and possibly even the physical world was created (as the **Edfu Texts** suggested in Chapter 5)… and the ancient civilizations in India and Egypt referred to them as the **Devas**. This was done to provide a higher frequency and thus create a balance between the materialistic denser humans and the spiritual frequency that was also necessary.

> As Chapter 13 will point out, they are still here, sustaining as much of an energy balance as possible so that the "negative" energy of wayward and learning humans does not become the dominant frequency of Earth. To the extent that the "positive" frequency is still available to those who seek it, their upward growth is facilitated. (It would not be much of a School if Earth was totally negative – such a state would generate entropy and the School would collapse upon itself for lack of a sustaining proactive vibration that would entrain souls higher thru the often dense matrix in which they have to function. And then, in a negative matrix, no one exits.)
>
> (This is also examined more in TOM, Ch's. 2 and 7.)

Gnosticism

The major set of documents that represent Gnostic thought are the **Nag Hammadí Library (NHL)** …profiled in Chapter 13. There are as many inconsistencies in this Library as were found in the *Corpus Hermeticum*… according to another author.[358]

And there is a link between Hermeticism and Gnosticism in that **four of the documents in the NHL are Hermetic treatises.** And yet, the Gnostic documents are quite a bit behind the Hermetic ones in terms of true spiritual insight. The Hermetic texts do speak of divine creation of the Earth while the Gnostic texts relate the story of the demiurge having created the Earth, egotistically, as a poor substitute for a world, and **the Gnostics thus considered the world a mistake** and an abomination and Gnosticism gets quite negative about the world in general.

Some of the salient points to be aware of in Gnosticism are such as the origin of some Gnostic lines of thought as coming from Egypt, and so in a like manner, **Gnostics do not speak of Reincarnation and Karma**. Their way out of this ugly world is thru Gnosis – Knowledge such that one creates one's own salvation.

Secondly, the Gnostic texts focus a lot of attention on the Demiurge, the Archons and eons and their responsibilities. And it is in the Kabbalistic Sefirot (Tree of Life) that the hierarchy becomes more important, and the 10 Sefirot are referred to as "emanations" of the divine realm beings… i.e., attributes of God.

Perhaps the two documents most worth examining (in Chapter 13) are *The Gospel of Thomas*, and *On the Origin of the World.* These contain some esoteric information of interest, and are examined later as they do relate somewhat to the basics of Serpent Wisdom. *On the Origin of the World* has a deeper explanation of the creation of Man and almost parallels the Sitchin material where Enki creates Man… And the *Thomas* sayings are enough to make one stop and think that these are heavier sayings of Jesus (like *Thomas 70*) than are found in the Bible – as if the Bible (which does have a lot of the *Thomas* sayings) was redacted to a more straight vanilla version where the reader doesn't have to do much thinking or reflecting.

> Due honorable mention is also the *Apocryphon of John* which does another treatment of the Creation of Man. All 3 texts are examined in Chapter 13.

And then, in a shocking section of the *Origin of the World*, we find some very esoteric information which HAS been kept from the public by those who assembled the official Church version of the Bible (AD 325)… in addition to keeping the *Book of Enoch* out, this *Origin* treatise has not been considered for inclusion, first because it is 'heretical' (Gnostic) and second it reveals what Chapter 12 in this book says about Genesis (see Kabbalah section).

> And when they [the Archons and Demiurge] had finished with Adam, he abandoned him as an inanimate vessel, since he had taken form like an abortion, in that no spirit was in him… he left his modelled form forty days **without soul**, and he withdrew and abandoned [Adam]…
>
> Sophia [Wisdom] sent her daughter Zoe [Life], being called Eve, as an instructor in order that she might make Adam, **who had no soul**, arise so that those whom he should engender might become containers of Light… [i.e., so that his offspring might receive/contain souls]
> Now the first Adam, Adam of Light, is **spirit**-endowed and appeared

> on the first day. The second Adam is **soul**-endowed, and appeared on the sixth day… [at this point, there were two creations]. The third Adam is a creature of the earth, that is, the man of the law, and he appeared on the eighth day … which is called Sunday.[359]

This is significant – the Gnostic account cites **at least three Adams**, and that matches what Zechariah Sitchin has said about the creation of Man by the Anunnaki – there were multiple attempts to get it right, and the development of Man progressed from the simple, non-procreating *Lulu*, to the better, procreating *Adama*, and then with Enki's genetic involvement with an earth female, the *Adapa* was produced. You can see where the Church would hate and persecute Gnostics!

The original *Lulu* did not have souls and did not reproduce. *Adama* had souls and their upgrade, called *Adapa*, had souls. What is a bit 'off' in the Gnostic account is that the three Adams are not revealed in the correct sequence, and yet the soul or no-soul issue is correct. The bottom line is that there is a mix of humans on the planet, some of whom have souls and some do not. (VEG, Ch. 5 goes into much more detail on this and references multiple ancient accounts where this fact was known—before the Church decided to "level the playing field" and said that all of mankind was the same. Many problems in current society are due to this disparity and we still ignore it and pay the price.)

> The issue is one of the soul – if the People in Nod had no souls, they were the Pre-Adamics, and humans have intermingled for centuries, so the human state on the planet as a mix. The caution is that the Greeks would not let these "soulless ones" teach in their schools nor could they hold public office… and thus there was more integrity in the Greek society and government than we have today.
>
> Mark Twain said it well:
>
> > Politicians are like diapers and should be changed often – for the same reason.

KABBALISM

Moving forward with the survey, we find that the Kabbalah has a stable framework allowing practical advice on spiritual growth and if one follows the prescribed path thru the 10 Sefirot on the Kabbalistic Tree of Life, one arrives at union with Ain Sopf, the All, the One (Kether). [360]

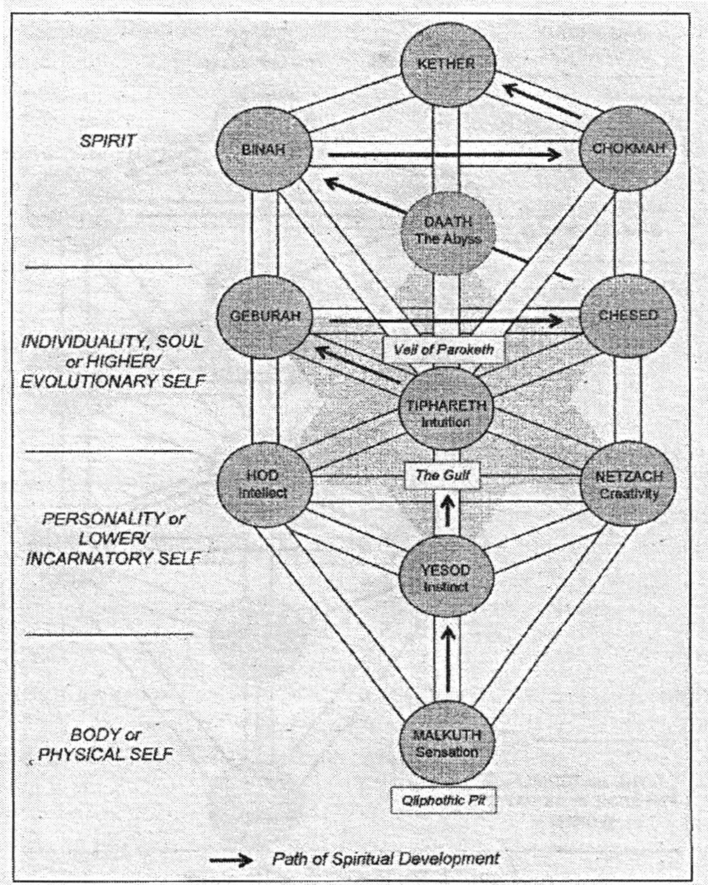

Note that one starts at the bottom, and moves up thru the various aspects of personal growth --

Note also the 6-pointed star, whose center is Intuition (Tipareth), or balance.

And, by the way, modern Kabbalists seem to agree that Reincarnation and Karma play a part in one's ability to navigate the framework. One starts at MALKUTH (bottom sphere, or Sefirot) which is the realm of physical sensation, the body, the material world. One then ascends:

To YESOD --- the foundation, Instinct

Picking up (left) Intellect at HOD and (right) Creativity at NETZACH , one moves to TIPARETH – Intuition, also beauty & equilibrium…

Picking up (left) strength at GEBURAH and (right) Love/Compassion at CHESED one moves thru the Abyss (**DAAT) = Knowledge (Gnosis**)…

> DAAT may also serve as the **Dark Night of the Soul** wherein a soul comes to meet itself and the Knowledge at this point is a form of self-knowledge…

Picking up (left) understanding at BINAH and (right) wisdom at CHOKMAH, one is ready to enter higher consciousness and awareness of the One, the Ain Soph, the Light of All at the Crown (7th Chakra) and KETHER.

The movement thru the framework is affected by one's ability to meet and handle the **tests and trials** that come with all initiations into the sacred mysteries… as a Druid, a Djedhi Knight, or Kabbalist on a sacred path.

Rosicrucianism

It is said that the Alchemists, seventeenth century occultists , Hermeticists and Kabbalists were either Rosicrucians or had some serious interest and many of the later movements (going into the 18th and 19th Centuries) were indirectly involved in their work. One author suggested that instead of there being the Illuminati, Freemasons and Rosicrucians, they might as well have been one organization since they all three tended to have the same esoteric view of the world, Man and God.

> The author was raised by a grandmother who was a high-level adept in the Rosicrucian AMORC and she shared many esoteric and metaphysical ideas as he was growing up. Small wonder that he drifted from Christianity to Religious Science (now replaced by CSL), and Unity.

AMORC (Ancient & Mystical Order of RosiCrucians) runs correspondence courses by mail and nowadays by Internet, and claims about 250,000 members. It welcomes anyone into its fold but keeps its deeper teachings reserved for those who 'go the distance' and such teachings are not revealed to the public. Most of the introductory material that is published is either too bland to be of interest, or once again, requires 'decoding.' [361]

> As a 'mystical fraternity' AMORC claims to teach its students to function 'in accordance with the Cosmic and its laws of nature', to bring about 'a harmonious level of interaction within your body' and to make it possible that 'through the experiments in the Rosicrucian teachings, your psychic faculties can be one of the greatest powers within you.' [362]

AMORC is not a religion and members are encouraged to continue with whatever church they currently attend… which is fine until you begin to learn more and realize that your current church is really very primitive and controlling. As the author's grandmother did, many people then move on into the New Thought churches, and even as the author discovered, some New Thought churches can be very parochial, too…. leading one to ask… "What's next?"

Higher States

Thus we can see that there exist higher levels of consciousness and thru disciplined and persistent effort one can attain a higher degree of awareness and perhaps commune with Astral beings (**caution advised here**: many Over There are game players. You want to play the game? – They'll oblige – until you learn better!) And communicating with Astral game players does not mean you are enlightened, or more advanced – it could be the beginning of something horrible – see Al Bender's experience in VEG, Ch. 4.

The major paths to higher consciousness have been thru meditation, Yoga, special breathing exercises, Tai Chi, and hallucinogens… each one being just a bit more effective than the last. **Meditation** often achieves nothing as it is too easy to burn some incense, sit maybe with mantra music playing (or even Gregorian Chants), breathe purposefully, and find one's mind wandering. **Yoga** if done too intensely or incorrectly, can injure a person, and it often is no more effective than Pilates or Zumba… just exercise. **Tai Chi** is a bit more productive as there is an 83-year old woman who does Tai Chi every day and can run, jump, swim – she is very healthy, very flexible physically and attributes it to Tai Chi – considering she was bed-ridden before she started!

> FYI: **Qigong** is the grandfather to Tai Chi and is even more effective at limbering the body and sustaining vibrant health.

Lastly, the issue of using Ayahuasca, LSD, DMT, etc. has been explored by other scientists and authors, including **Jeremy Narby** who wrote <u>The Cosmic Serpent</u>.

What Jeremy did for the world was certify that the shamen who used Ayahuasca to commune with the beings on the Other Side were actually guided for the benefit of Man.

> Jeremy describes how he first became intrigued with the shamans' use of the drug Ayahuasca when he established the extent of their amazing knowledge of the properties of various of the eighty thousand [80,000!] species of plants in the Amazonian jungle. [363]

The many plants' extracts have amazing healing properties – often combining two or more of the plants into an efficacious mixture – which makes the statistical likelihood of discovering which plants work together pretty remote. Considering that the shamen say that they go into an Ayahuasca-induced trance and commune with the **two huge serpents** who give them the knowledge…the serpents tell the shamen which plants to use to achieve the desired healing.[364]

Serpent Imagery again.

While Jeremy theorized that the two serpents symbolize the **two DNA strands** it is also recognized that DNA does not talk. Yet the serpent imagery is not universal as several other shamen have experienced "bird-headed people" – apparently the beings on the Other Side work with whatever the shaman is most comfortable with, or maybe what symbols he will understand and accept…

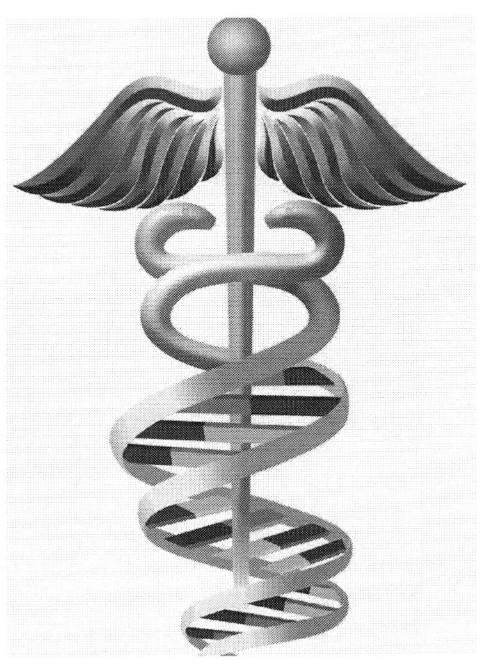

It would seem that the **Caduceus** as a serpent image is a very accurate one…. And it has a counterpart among Amazonian shaman healers.

Thus DNA is part of the Caduceus as well as symbolizing the *Kundalini* moving to awaken Man.

Esoteric Summary

Thus while we have seen that not all mystery schools were equally enlightened, and the initiate is advised to adhere to the "*caveat emptor*" dictum, we can sum up a few of the universal and common points:

Reincarnation and Karma apply to the souls in the Earth Realm.

Higher Conscious states are possible and worthwhile.

True Gnosis, Knowledge, can be achieved if one seriously applies oneself.

There are **Higher Beings** who watch over Man and can help (if asked).

Everything is energy and matter is in a state of vibration.

Matter is an illusion and the initiate should detach from it.

All is One, Entanglement is the rule, everything is interconnected.

Everything has consciousness, just different levels of it.

As above, so below; the part is in the whole.

There was **no Big Bang** – the Universe is eternal.
(It expands and contracts.)

Miracles are the result of laws we don't yet understand.

Higher Physics is called **Metaphysics** – one describes the other.

The soul exists in **multiple realms** concurrently.

There is **no Hell/no Satan**, but one can be created for you if your soul needs to experience it.

Duality does not exist in Reality – it is Man's explanation for his world.

To graduate from Earth School, you need **Love <u>and</u> Knowledge**.

Corollaries:

The student does not control the School: you cannot 'create' your day.
Take what you get and don't take what you don't get.
Listen more than you talk.
Wherever you are, <u>be</u> there.
The correct sequence is: Be – Do – Have.

> The last one means: if you <u>are</u> a teacher, you will <u>do</u> what a teacher does and then <u>have</u> what a teacher has (students, or followers).

Watch for these universal concepts in the remaining chapters.

Alchemical Summary

From the bottom of our hearts we ought to thank the modest men who held in their hands the magical **Emerald Formula** that makes a man master of the world, a formula which they took as much trouble to hide as they had taken to discover it. For however dazzling and bright the obverse of the alchemical medallion, its reverse is dark as night. The way of good is the same as the way of evil, and when a man has crossed the threshold of knowledge, he has more intelligence but may have no more capacity for love. For with knowledge comes pride, and egoism is created by the desire to uphold the development of qualities that he considers necessary. Through egoism he returns to the evil that he has tried to escape. Nature is full of traps, and the higher a man rises in the hierarchy of men, the more numerous and the better hidden are the traps.

Saint Anthony in his desert was surrounded by nothing but dreams. He stretched out his arms to grasp them, and if he did not succumb to temptation it was only because the phantoms vanished when he sought to seize them. But the living, almost immediately tangible reality of gold, which gives everything -- what superhuman strength would be necessary to resist it! Alchemists had to remember those of their number who had failed and fallen to the wayside. And they had to ponder how apparently illogical and sad for mankind is the law by which the **Tree of Wisdom** is guarded by **a Serpent** infinitely more powerful than the trickster serpent that tempted Eve in the Garden of Eden. [365]

Remember the **Trickster** was also Loki in the Norse Sagas, and the Trickster was also a factor in many African Legends. It seems that was an aspect of the gods "training" Man – test him, trick him and if he is wise to what the Trickster does, then he has moved up a notch in awareness. Increasing awareness is what Enki's Serpent Wisdom was all about, thus the Trickster had a part in waking Man up.

But remember that Alchemy was really about self-transformation.

Let us now check out some other aspects of Serpent Wisdom…. It will be seen that Qabbalism, Gnosticism, Rosicrucianism and even today's New Thought movement carries elements of Serpent Wisdom (aka Hermeticism).

Chapter 11: Serpent Wisdom -- Augury

Man has always wanted to know what he is and why he is here, and to take some of the risk and mystery out of living, he has sought ways (e.g., Augury) to know what he should do and what will happen. Serpent Wisdom esoterics do provide an answer, but not by using chicken bones and stars.

In addition to Man being given spiritual Alchemy, Serpent Wisdom also embraced Genuine Prophecy for those who were hybrid humans (*Adapa+*) with better genetics and who could psychically anticipate events, and locate missing objects, **and Assisted Prophecy** where the Anunnaki told their human priests what to 'foretell' the humans because they were about to create a flood, a drought, an earthquake, a hailstorm, etc… The Anunnaki also taught the basics of Astronomy (as a way to track planting/harvesting seasons via the **equinoxes**), and the basics of Astrology to better understand sidereal effects on earth and human processes.

The effect of the Sun on the Earth has always been obvious and hence many cultures, from the Egyptians to the Incas, venerated it. Others like the Aztec were a little more anal retentive and killed people to make sure the Sun rose again the next day… And we all know that the Moon effects the tides, so some exo-planetary influences are real.

Astrology was not intended originally to predict the future but to reinforce the idea that Man was a part of the interplay of forces within the Cosmos – i.e., the energies of Jupiter, Mars and Venus do have an effect (although weak) upon Earth, and a lesser effect on Man… which led humans to later (incorrectly) extend the astrological effects of the planets into a belief in the **Four Humors** – looking for a way to explain why some people were easy going (sanguine) and others were generally always caustic, melancholy, or phlegmatic.

Later, it was Man's idea to develop things like the **I Ching** in China, **Tarot** and Astrological Horoscopes in Europe, Kabbalah in the Middle East, reading tea leaves, **phrenology** (reading head bumps) and other means of divination when no one was present who had a true gift of prophecy (called "inner sight"). Predicting the future has always been big business, and relatively important – witness the Oracle at Delphi being asked whether a war campaign would fail or succeed.

Many times, third world cultures would select someone who had a special birth, or who had special abilities (even if struck by the gods – via lightening) or who was the son/daughter of a current Shaman, and the initiate would be trained in all the ways of shamanism to serve the tribe or town. This was serious business – if you became a shaman and screwed up, it could mean your death at the hands of the tribe or town council.

So whereas Alchemy was of prime importance, concerning personal transformation, the Anunnaki also taught ancillary skills and knowledge for potions, originally for healing (**Herbology**), and then the *Kundalini* process. Occasionally there was some input on Man's origins (outside of Mesopotamia where it was obvious where Man came from). That was basically it. What we have beyond that with Kahuna, Santeria, Wicca, Voodoo and the like, is a deviation from the more sacred teachings nowadays hidden in the secret societies – examined as the book draws to a close.

> And because there are entities in the Astral who will empower witchcraft (for a price – and they don't want your money) that is why the Bible warned against consorting with unseen entities who will do your bidding, and thus anyone practicing Voodoo or is a Kahuna is to be respected but avoided. (See Ch. 2, 'Central Sun' in Virtual Earth Graduate.)

Instead of flat out rejecting all these modalities as "witchy", let's take a look at their original nature and purpose. Like today's religions, even the shamanistic practices have wandered from their original design…. Don't worry, we will avoid Santeria and Voodoo. Gnosticism, Rosicrucianism and Kabbalah will be examined as they still contain elements of the Serpent Wisdom given to Man..

Prophecy

It stands to reason that Enki and his son were educated and knowledgeable of the inner workings of Astronomy, Medicine, Chemistry, and how humans worked (physically and mentally), thus it can be said that Enki's legacy was not superstitious analysis of signs to determine the future, nor to decide which course of action to follow. It is believable that Enki promoted connection with one's Higher Self for inner direction, healing and perhaps psychically anticipating the future. In short, Enki would not have been against valid prophetic determination of the future – especially if the Anunnaki were going to do something and they warned humans what it was, thus the human "blowing the whistle" or making the prophecy (based on what Enki or his son told the human, Noah) would have a 100% accuracy rate.

This is what was recorded in the Bible and the Sumerian epic called *Atra Hasis* where Noah is told to build an ark. This also reflects the accuracy of Jeremiah, Ezekiel, *et al* – they did have inside knowledge. It just wasn't the God of the universe talking to

Man, but one of the Anunnaki, such as Enlil, Marduk or Enki. (Sorry to burst any bubbles.)

Power Differentials

While we're at it, let's talk about power.

If The God of the Universe ever spoke directly to a man, it would be the last thing that man ever experienced. The power differential is too great for The God to speak to, touch, or even to come near his creation. His power is "stepped down" via the hierarchy between God and Man (Think: Angels and Higher Beings).

Think of it this way: If you connect a 120-volt source (e.g., house current) to a 12-volt battery (with the intention of recharging it) you'll destroy the 12-volt battery because the power differential cannot be handled by the lower voltage battery. The necessary interface is called a **transformer** – to step down the power to what the 12-volt battery can handle. TVs, toasters, and hair dryers all have a built-in transformer to modulate and assimilate the house's electrical current.

Thus, while the presence and power of The God does empower and sustain all of creation, and such nowadays is called **Dark Energy**, it is nowhere totally concentrated. To be sure, the Central Sun at the core of our Galaxy is a kind of concentration, sustaining the Galaxy and its solar systems, but it is not but a fraction of the energy which is subdivided to sustain other Galaxies, too. The God force does flow through Souls, and depending on the degree of soul growth (i.e., connection with one's Higher Self) Souls as sparks of the One, have more or lesser degrees of *chi* or power, and yet all souls are sustained by the ambient energy of the universe (see Transformation of Man, Ch. 12.)

This may be why, in the Bible, when Moses went up on **Mt. Sinai** mountain to meet with God, he was put in the cleft of a rock wall – said to be to shield him from God's power (which is illogical seeing how great the power of His presence is), or as is nowadays more believable, Enlil, the local god, did not want Moses to see what he looked like. Same goes for the **"Burning Bush"** – something created thru which God could speak, but not project his total awesome power in Moses' presence. And lastly, there was the issue with the **Ark of the Covenent** – it had to be carried with wooden poles such that the electrical potential of the Ark itself would not transfer to those carrying it. (See the end of Chapter 5 where the Ark is discussed.)

Astrology

Just as Alchemy was examined in the last chapter, we need to take a look at Astrology and its original purpose… which was not the making of Horoscopes. And the most obvious place to see what could have been given Man in the area of Astrology is in Egypt, inasmuch as Alchemy also started there. It was said that Hermes/Thoth was a three-fold master: **Alchemy, Astrology and Theurgy**.

Astrology has been dated to as far back as the 2nd millennium BC. That dating by itself leads one to suspect the Anunnaki were busy teaching some of its precepts as this was the time when the Anunnaki were most active around the globe. They knew their time was coming to a close on Earth, due to the unstoppable effects of the Sun on their aging, and within another 1500 years they would have to leave Earth and return home.

Achemy and Astrology are closely connected thanks to Hermes. And the art was taken seriously by academics until the 1500s as it was the accepted basis for illness and the corresponding medicine – both rooted in the stars. In addition, it was connected with other studies, such as Astronomy, Meteorology, and Medicine. This was due to the dictum, "As above, so below" which was also interpreted to mean the stars had an influence on Man.

> Today we still have remnants of past astral associations when we describe someone: when we say "He is very saturnine," or "She is very mercurial," "He is very Jovial" or the song "Venus in Blue Jeans," or "His fate is written in the stars."

> Astrology, in its broadest sense, is the **search for meaning in the sky**. Early evidence for humans making conscious attempts to measure, record, and predict seasonal changes by reference to astronomical cycles, appears as markings on bones and cave walls, which show that **lunar cycles** were being noted as early as 25,000 years ago. This was a first step towards recording the Moon's influence upon tides and rivers, and towards organising a communal calendar. Farmers addressed **agricultural needs** with increasing knowledge of the constellations that appear in the different seasons—and used the rising of particular star-groups to herald annual floods or seasonal activities. By the 3rd millennium BCE, civilisations had sophisticated awareness of celestial cycles, and may have oriented temples in alignment with [specific] rising of the stars.[366]

Occasional evidence suggests that the oldest known astrological references are copies of texts found in the ancient world. The **Venus Tablet** of Ammisaduqa thought to be compiled in Babylon about 1700 BC. And the Anunnaki connection is:

> The oldest undisputed evidence of the use of astrology as an integrated system of knowledge is therefore attributed to the records of the first dynasty of Mesopotamia (1950–1651 BC). [367]

It is obvious that if Hermes was Thoth and Thoth was Ningishzidda (and that is true), then the Anunnaki were responsible for teaching Man to use the Moon to tell the passing of time, and to watch the stars to track the seasons… for agricultural purposes. Hence we have a lot of **Spring and Fall equinox** tracking via stone monuments around the world.

But what was the connection with Medicine?

Astrology and Medicine

Hermes

Remember that Hermes was a master in Alchemy and the alchemists sought to develop healing panaceas-- also known as **panchrest** was said to be a remedy that would cure all diseases and prolong life indefinitely. Now where would Man get that idea – unless the Anunnaki had used such to cure, heal, or resurrect someone in Mesopotamia. As a matter of fact, Inanna and Dumuzi were both restored to life by the Anunnaki technology (which probably included an **elixir**), and the humans knew that the Anunnaki lived for thousands of years (as was examined earlier).

Thus at some point it can be said that Thoth/Hermes/Ningishzidda made the humans aware that such things existed, and then Man began the search for the Philosopher's Stone – which also (see last chapter in the potion that **John Frederick Helvetius** drank) benefitted the body: it was known that if one applied the Philosophers Stone to an ailing part of one's body, or created an **elixir** from the Stone, it could heal. In fact the potion was called *Aurum potabile* ("potable gold") [368]

But the main connection between the stars and medicine was the brainchild of Philippus Aureolus Theophrastus Bombastus von Hohenheim, known as the Swiss/German alchemist **Paracelsus** (AD 1493-1541).

Paracelsus

According to Paracelsus, one must know what the effect of the stars is on the body parts. Thus one must learn which planets rule which body parts, AND which plants minister to which body parts, so that a disease in the blood, for example, should be given a cure from a plant ruled by Mars, such as Nettle, which supplies iron. Even back in that day, it was known that the blood needed iron to carry oxygen on the red blood cells.

> Paracelsus developed the concept of the **Doctrine of Signatures** – if a plant resembled a body part (as orchids resemble testicles) then it was considered a hint from God that the plant was supportive of health in that body part. [369]

In addition, demonstrating the Hermetic axiom, "As above, so below":

> Diseases were caused by poisons brought from the stars. However, 'poisons' were not necessarily something negative, in part because related substances interacted, but also because only <u>the dose</u> determined if a substance was poisonous or not. [This was the origin of **Homeopathy**.] Paracelsus claimed the complete opposite of Galen [who said] that <u>like cures like</u>. If a star or poison caused a disease, then it must be countered by another star or poison.
>
> Because everything in the universe was interrelated, beneficial medical substances could be found in herbs, minerals and various chemical combinations thereof. Paracelsus viewed the universe as one coherent organism pervaded by a uniting life-giving spirit, and this in its entirety, Man included, was 'God'. His views put him at odds with the Church, for which there necessarily had to be a difference between the Creator and the created [but he would be at home with today's New Thought churches.] [370] [Emphasis added]

Just FYI, the 7 Planets and corresponding Body parts are:

Saturn: correspondences: metal = Lead, Plants = corn, irises,
Body = **bone**, joints, teeth, & spleen.

Jupiter: correspondences: metal = Tin, Plants = lilac, carnation,
Body = **liver**, digestive organs, & feet.

Mars: correspondences: metal = Iron, Plants = geranium, honeysuckle,
Body = **muscles**, red blood cells

The Sun: correspondences: metal = Gold, Plants = marigold, sunflower,
Body = **heart**, spine, solar plexus, & eyes.

Venus: correspondences: metal = Copper, Plants = roses, orchid, Body = complexion, **kidneys**, breasts & sex organs.

Mercury: correspondences: metal = Quicksilver (mercury), Plants = azalea, lily, Body = ears, nervous system, & **lungs**.

The Moon: correspondences: metal = Silver, Plants = acanthus, lilies, Body = **brain**, stomach, pancreas & Body fluids.

The Zodiac

The zodiacal chart consisting of 12 'houses' has been derived from the notion that the stars affect our lives… coming from an alternate interpretation of Alchemy. The underlying concept is that **each planet/star has a specific frequency or vibration** and the arrangement of those key stars when one was born had an effect on one's inner nature and potential.

Particularly relevant is the ascending sign, or the **Ascendant**, to that Horoscopic Chart. It is the zodiacal sign that was rising on the eastern horizon when one was born. Someone born at 7:30 pm Friday Sept 24th would have Libra as their **Sun sign**. Someone born in March would have Aries as their Sun sign. The Ascendant has to be calculated and can be a different sign.

And in keeping with the Alchemical principle of the Four Elements, there are Fire Signs, Water Signs, Air Signs and Earth Signs – all of which are supposed to reflect a person's temperament. Astrologers believe that the Ascendant signifies a person's **awakening consciousness**, in the same way that the Sun's appearance on the eastern horizon signifies the dawn of a new day. Astrologers also believe the Ascendant also has a strong bearing on a person's physical appearance and overall health.

So where did this system begin? Astrology began with the Mesopotamians (Sumerians) and was further developed by the Egyptians, whereas the Horoscope aspect was a development in Babylon about the 2nd millennium BC. The Hellenistic Greeks about 200 BC also had a version of Astrology.

Because of the 23° tilt of the Earth's axis, done to give us seasons, some constellations appear to "rise" and "fall" with respect to the horizon during certain times of the year. The ancients were taught to watch these actions as a way to monitor the seasons. It was in later centuries, with the advent of comets (considered bad omens) and meteorites that Man began to 'read' the stars looking for omens and ways to spot (foretell) celestial events.

Lately, it has been discussed that there should be a 13th 'house' in the Zodiac, uniquely called **Ophiuchus**, a very small sliver of time in the Winter. Most zodiacal houses are 30° (or 2160 years) long, and Ophiuchus is only 30 November – 17 December (18 days) between Scorpio and Sagittarius.

> Ophiuchus is an anciently recognized constellation, catalogued along with many others in Ptolemy's *Almagest*, but not historically referred to as a zodiac constellation. The inaccurate description of Ophiuchus as a sign of the zodiac drew media attention in 1995, when the BBC Nine O'clock News reported that "an extra sign of the zodiac has been announced by the Royal Astronomical Society." There had been no such announcement, and the report had merely sensationalized the 67-year-old 'news' of the IAU's decision to alter the number of designated ecliptic constellations.[371]

What is interesting, and the reason for mentioning Ophiuchus is that it is a man wrestling with a **Serpent**:[372]

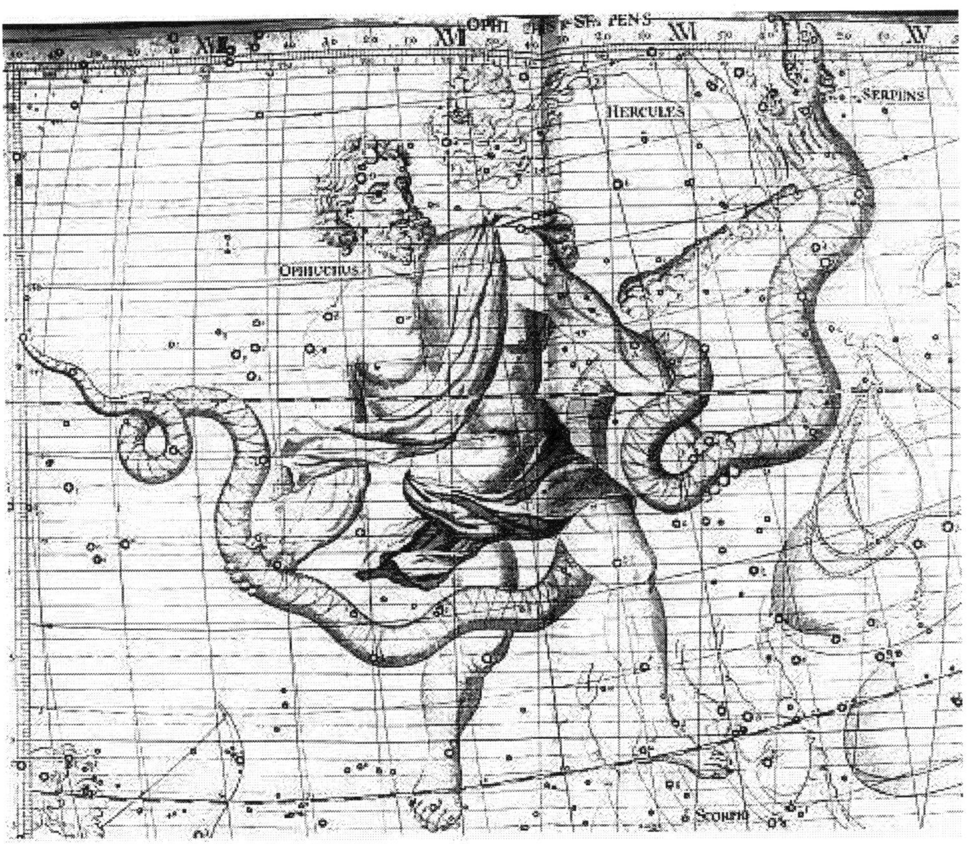

The constellation is described in the **astrological** poem called the *Astronomica*, which is dated to around 10 AD. The poem describes how:

> Ophiuchus holds apart the serpent which with its mighty spirals and twisted body encircles his own, so that he may untie its knots and back that winds in loops. But, bending its supple neck, the serpent looks back and returns: and the other's hands slide over the loosened coils. The struggle will last forever, since they wage it on level terms with equal powers. [373]

Later in the poem, the astrological influence of Ophiuchus, when the constellation is in its rising phase, is one which offers affinity with snakes and protection from poisons, saying "he renders the forms of snakes innocuous to those born under him. They will receive snakes into the folds of their flowing robes, and will exchange kisses with these poisonous monsters and suffer no harm."

> Based on the 1930 IAU constellation boundaries, suggestions that "there are really 13 astrological signs" because "the Sun is in the sign of **Ophiuchus" between November 30 and December 17** have been published since at least the 1970s.
>
> Does this mean that the astrological horoscopes done with 12-sign zodiacs are inaccurate and should use all 13 signs?

Constellation Grouping

The following is a constellation sky chart of interest – this is in its entirety:

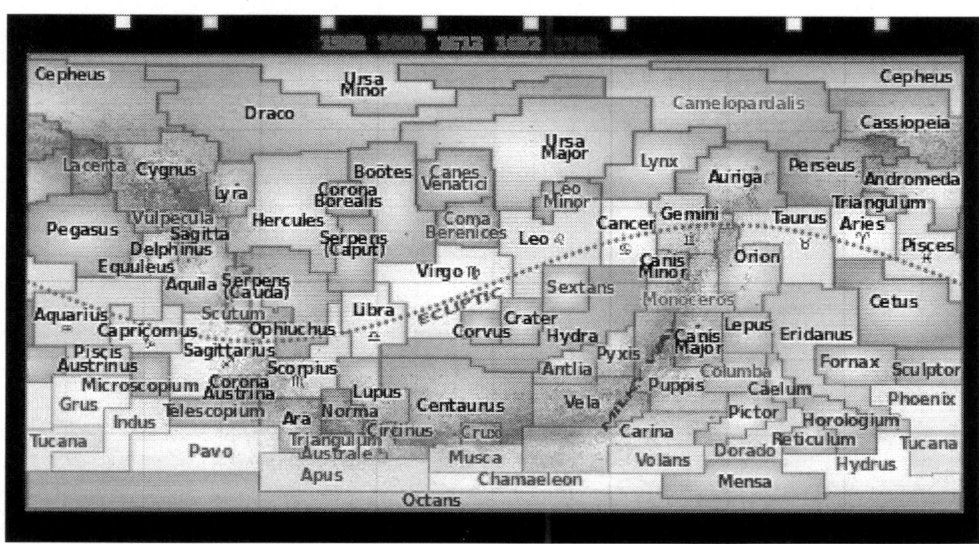

(credit: Wikipedia: https://en.wikipedia.org/wiki/Constellation)

Don't strain your eyes trying to make out the elements of the prior chart – what is of interest is in the right side, reproduced below:

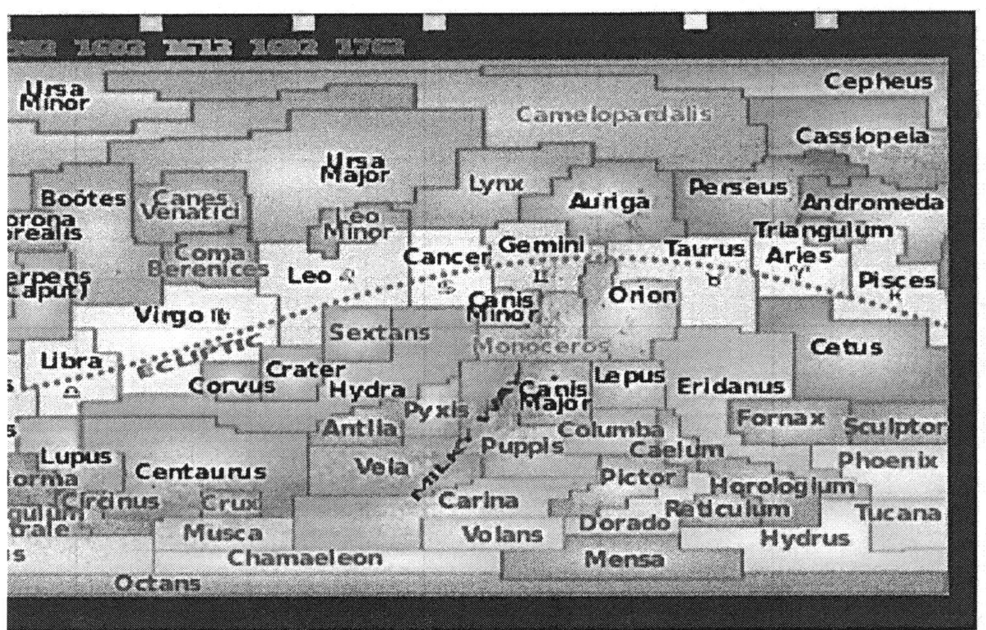

Please note that Orion, Taurus and Cetus are in the same general area, as well as Canis Major (southwest of Orion). Guess where most of the visitors to Earth have been said to come from… by the Zulu, the Dogon, the Amerindians, the Maya, and the Sumerians? The following 6 groups are all located in the starmap above.

The Pleiadians are in Taurus (human) 444 LY away.
The Aldebarans are in Taurus (human) 65 LY away.
The Reptilians are in Orion (humanoid) 20 LY away.
The Denebians are in Cetus (human) 2600 LY away.
The Sirians are in Canis Major (humanoid) 8.6 LY away.
The [real] Grays are in Reticulum (humanoid) 39 LY away.

Ophiuchus is off the 2nd chart in Sagittarius, far to the left of Libra.
Note: Most of the alleged ET Visitors are in the same quadrant of the sky.

> The significance of the man Ophiuchus wrestling the Serpent is that Humans have wrestled with Serpent Wisdom for centuries. Again, we find the Serpent imagery… and its rejection as a sign in the Zodiac.

Moving forward, it should be mentioned that the Chinese also were alchemists and developed something called Traditional Chinese Medicine (TCM).

Traditional Chinese Medicine (TCM)

The Chinese received similar teaching (mostly from the **Denebians**) and believed there was a time of the day that corresponded to the weakness or strength of different body parts. They also believed in the Five Elements (Earth, Fire, Water, Wood and Metal) similar to Alchemy, and knew which plants promoted which of the five essences and when was the best time of the day or month to use a certain herb. For example, an herb with an essence of Fire would not be used to heal heartburn; that required a cooling plant with a Water essence.

Chinese astrology was developed in the Zhou dynasty (1046–256 BCE).

TCM still exists today in China, and among TCM practitioners in the world. And the Chinese have an interesting twist on the doctor-patient relationship: you pay your doctor to keep you well (by buying the herbs and potions s/he sells after your once a month checkup), and if you get sick, you pay nothing until your doctor gets you well again.

TCM is much more developed than ancient Alchemy – it is as if the Chinese started with what was taught them and then modified it. There are different kinds of *chi* (one's personal energy), there are Yin and Yang foods, Yin and Yang herbs, and times of the day when exercise is most beneficial and times when it will be harmful – they believe that there is a measurable aspect to the hour-by-hour state everyone's body finds itself in – a time for elimination, a time for sleep, a time for eating, and a time for work.

There are 6 Yin and 6 Yang organs and they are connected to the *chi* meridians (the **Bionet**) which interconnect with the chakras, consisting of 12 meridians which correspond with the 12 organs. For example, the Stomach is Yang, and the Lungs are Yin. (Yang is strong energy and Yin is more gentle.)

There are Five Seasons – Winter, Spring, Summer, Fall and a **Transition Stage** between each of the standard four. "When the weather is wrong for the time of year, as is increasingly the case as the effects of global climate change become apparent, then seasonal illness may result." [374]

Remember **Huang Di** (2600 BC) from Chapter 4 – he was called the Yellow Emperor and united the warring states to create a unified China, in addition to teaching the Chinese people agriculture, writing, medicine etc. We already know that he was a kind of Quetzalcoatl to the Chinese but there is more:

> The *Nei Jing Su Wen* is a classic text written by Huang Di (2696-2598 BC). It is known in English as his Classic of Internal Medicine. Huang Di asked his physician, Qi Bo, to tell him about the twelve organs and their relationships. Qi Bo described them as **twelve officials** and government departments, adding that they must work in harmony to achieve good health. [375]

Briefly, it was said that the Heart was the Emperor, the Lungs were the Prime Minister, the Liver was the head of the Emperor's Army, the Stomach was the head of the Granaries (storehouses), and the Kidneys were the Office of Power and Strength.

Feng Shui

Lastly, the Chinese were also given a system of physically living in harmony with the external world of Nature, called **Feng Shui** (pronounced "fong schway"). It is a system of arranging one's house for the best (healthiest) flow of *chi*, and the **Bagua** (8-sided mandala) is one of the tools that is traditionally used to verify harmony among the elements.

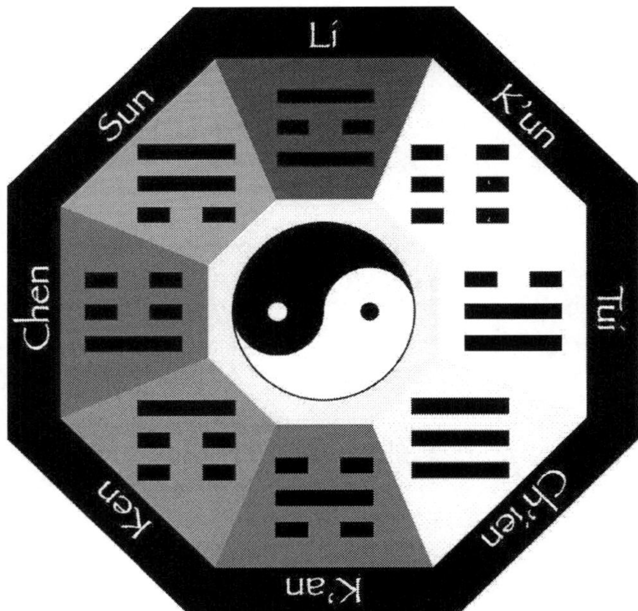

Feng Shui Bagua

It is a school of thought that uses the Bagua/Pagua chart and the directions based on the position of the main door.

(efengshui.org)

Note the I Ching symbols.

Clockwise from the 12 o'clock position: Fame/**Fire**, Love, Future/**Metal**, People, Career/**Water**, Wisdom, Past/**Wood**, Prosperity. **Earth** is in the center: Yin Yang symbol.

In brief, placement of furniture and mirrors were key items to be positioned in such a way as to not block the flow of *chi* thru the house. One did not want stairs to the upper level of the house to face the front door as the *chi* would flow down the stairs and out the door. Thus, it was a good idea to have a mirror at the foot of the stairs to reflect the *chi* back up the stairs. It was also unfavorable to have your house at the end of a street as negative *chi* could flow down the street (including cars) and hit your house. And if you needed to 'bend' the *chi* around a corner (inside the house), one could hang a faceted crystal from the ceiling at the corner of the 90° walls.

This system was not found among the Alchemists of yore, but does bear a relationship to Chinese prophecy.

I Ching

Seen above in the Bagua are symbols like those found in the Chinese system of divination called I Ching, or *The Book of Changes.* Possessing a history of more than **two and a half millennia** of commentary and interpretation, the *I Ching* is an influential text read throughout the world, providing inspiration to the worlds of religion, psychoanalysis, business, literature, and art. It was originally a divination manual in the Zhou period (1000–750 BC). The Chart (left) is the 64 hexagrams of the I Ching Table – note the similarity to the 3-layer symbols (**Trigrams**) in the Bagua above.

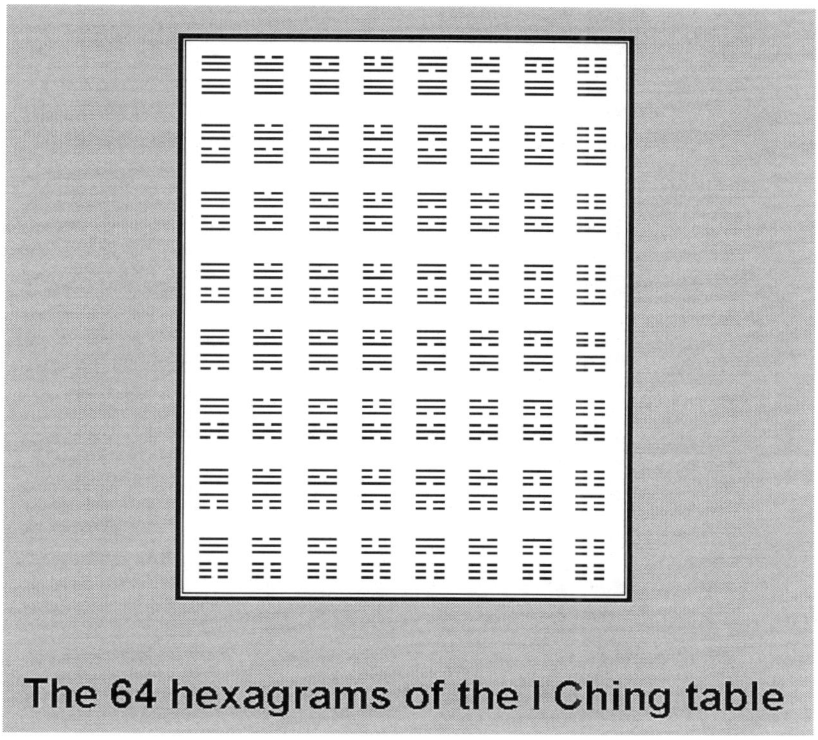

The 64 hexagrams of the I Ching table

(credit: leadershipbyvirtue.blogspot.com)

Each hexagram has a name and is a physical symbol representing a deeply metaphysical or subconscious manifestation.

`While it is too complicated to explain how it works, one can spot a pattern in the 64 symbols – the upper three (8 combinations) and the lower three (8 combinations) lines form a 6-layer hexagram by one of the following:[376]

Upper → / Lower ?	Heaven ☰	Thunder ☳	Water ☵	Mountain ☶	Earth ☷	Wind ☴	Fire ☲	Lake ☱
Heaven ☰	1	34	5	26	11	9	14	43
Thunder ☳	25	51	3	27	24	42	21	17
Water ☵	6	40	29	4	7	59	64	47
Mountain ☶	33	62	39	52	15	53	56	31
Earth ☷	12	16	8	23	2	20	35	45
Wind ☴	44	32	48	18	46	57	50	28
Fire ☲	13	55	63	22	36	37	30	49
Lake ☱	10	54	60	41	19	61	38	58

(credit: Bing Images: I Ching)

To cast the I Ching stones (or tiles) requires a thick handbook to identify the patterns and interpret what the combination of **Trigrams** on the tiles means. You take 3 Chinese coins and toss them 6 times.

Note that one side of the coin has the **Trigrams** and the other identifies the coin as to what denomination it is.

Note that there is also the **Yarrow-stalk** method, using 50 thin 8" sticks NOT encoded with any hexagrams. You manipulate the sticks into groups of 6, 7, 8, or 9 and after 6 times doing that (recording that), you have the hexagram to look up – it will suggest one of the 64 combinations of Trigrams (chart above).

As an example, supposing you get a Trigram of 3 solid lines (top= 'Heaven') and three broken lines (bottom = 'Earth') which looks like this:

" This **hexagram** describes your situation in terms of being blocked or interfered with. It emphasizes that accepting the hindrances that temporarily interrupt the flow of life and thwart communication is the adequate way to handle it. To be in accord with the time, you are being told to:
Accept obstruction!" [377]

否 (pǐ)

The significance of this is that Astrology, Medicine and Herbology were given the Chinese back when the Anunnaki (and/or Denebians) traveled the planet, enlightening Man (about 2000-3000 BC). And as was mentioned in Chapter 4, **Huang Di** came from the sky in a flying dragon, and he and his entourage left the same way.

Man then developed the **Feng Shui and I Ching** concepts based on his interpretation and extension of esoteric principles he had acquired. Feng Shui evolved from the information about *chi* (in Medicine), and I Ching was developed from Alchemical (and Tarot) principles, broken into 64 possible life situation combinations.

Specifically, the I Ching was developed by **Fu Xi** (see Chapter 4). He was a special being like the Serpent Goddess **NüWa** who was also a benefactor of Man. Fu Xi was called the "original man" (although technically speaking he was not a human). (Later, King Wen modified the Trigrams.) [378]

According to this tradition, Fu Xi had the arrangement of the Trigrams (八卦 *bāgùa*) of the *I Ching* revealed to him in the markings on the back of a mythical Dragon (sometimes said to be a tortoise) that emerged from the Luo River. (Think: USOs.)

Nagas Fu Xi and Nü Wa used clay to create humans, and with the divine power they made the clay figures come alive. These clay figures were the earliest Chinese human beings.[379]

Fu Xi and NüWa

While we're talking about serpents and the Zodiac…

Zodiacal Snakes

In Chinese culture, the years of the Snake are sixth in the cycle, following the Dragon Years, and recur every twelfth year. The Chinese New Year does not fall on a specific date, so it is essential to check the calendar to find the exact date on which each Snake Year actually begins. Snake years include: 1905, 1917, 1929, 1941, 1953, 1965, 1977, 1989, 2001, 2013, and 2025. Thus, 2013 is a year of the yin water Snake, and actually starts on February 10, 2013 and lasts through January 30, 2014. The previous year of the yin water Snake was 1953, respecting a 60-year cycle.

In Thai culture, the year of the Snake is instead the year of the little Snake, and the year of the Dragon is the year of the big Snake.

The same 12 animals are also used to symbolize the **cycle of hours in the day**, each being associated with a two-hour time period. The "hour" of the Snake is 9:00 to 11:00 a.m., the time when the Sun warms up the earth, and snakes slither out of their holes.

The Hindu astrology uses the same signs in their Zodiac as the Western world.

Hindu Astrology

Astrology was practiced all over the world. Usually wherever Alchemy was practiced, so was Astrology. In India, however it took a slightly different turn, and was called **Jyotisha** and then **Vedic Astrology**.

> *Vedanga Jyotisha* is one of the earliest texts about the Jyotisha field within the six Vedangas [6 ritual disciplines in Vedic practice], it is about **astronomy and time keeping for Vedic rituals**, and has nothing to do with prophecy or astrology.
>
> Historical evidence suggests that astrology arrived in India from Greece, after the arrival of Alexander the Great, and it post-dates the Vedic period [*c. 1500 – c. 500 BC was the period in India during which the Vedas, the oldest scriptures of Hinduism, were composed*]. The zodiac signs for the Greek astrology and Hindu astrology are almost identical. [380]

It is an important difference to see that Hindu astrology, or Jyotisha, was one of the six disciplines concerned with the preparation of a calendar to fix the date of Vedic sacrifice rituals, or **Yajnas**. Nothing was written about planets.

Yajna goes back into antiquity (the word is Sanskrit for "worship") when the Hindus would light fires and sacrifice offerings of grain. There were usually one, or three, fires lit in the center of the offering ground. Oblations are offered into the fire. [381]

Among the ingredients offered as **oblations** in the yajna are ghee, milk, grains, cakes and soma (no one knows what plant that ritual drink was made from). Then the **benedictions** proffered ranged from long life, gaining friends, health and heaven, more prosperity, to better crops. Yajnas are often performed when getting married and even when moving into a new house.

The meaning of the term **Yajna** evolved from "ritual sacrifice" performed around fires by priests, to any "personal attitude and action or knowledge" that required devotion and dedication. Hence, later Vedic Upanishads expand the idea further by suggesting that **Yoga is a form of Yajna** (personal devotion, sacrifice).

Yoga Poses

There are many types of Yoga, and they are all intended to develop flexibility, promote health, and sometimes move the *Kundalini* -- the most common form of Yoga (safely) practiced today is **Hatha Yoga**. The most common pose used for basic meditation is shown below:

Version 1:

Version 2:

(credit: Bing Images: Yoga Poses: and leanitup.com)

Note that their legs are in the preferred position – but if you are too old, and not very flexible, it isn't required to cross the right leg up and over the left. Also note the two ways of holding the hands – v. 1 is for concentrating *chi* in the navel (chakra #2), and v. 2 uses the thumb and forefinger, sometimes the middle finger, to connect the meridians running thru the fingers with those in the arms and on into the main body meridians. The spine is kept perfectly straight so that the *chi* (if it rises) does not hit a blockage or pinched vertebra in the spine due to a slight curvature from leaning out of perpendicular.

Often the practitioner is doing **breathing excercises (Pranayama),** and if they are Chinese, they may be running the *chi* thru the Microcosmic Orbit – as shown on the next page. This is a practice that removes energy blockages and revitalizes the body.

Breathing

It is also one of the mainstays of TCM that learning to breathe correctly helps restore health, and special breathing exercises, as taught in Qi Gong and Kung Fu, can acquire and store *chi* for healing or martial arts use.

In this issue we also find that the Hindus knew about the same breathing exercises (left nostril vs. right nostril) as the Chinese. The combination of the mind directing the *chi* along with the appropriate breathing exercise could activate the *Kundalini.* Who taught them that? (See Transformation of Man, Ch. 11.)

The Chinese do breathing exercises when they perform the following:

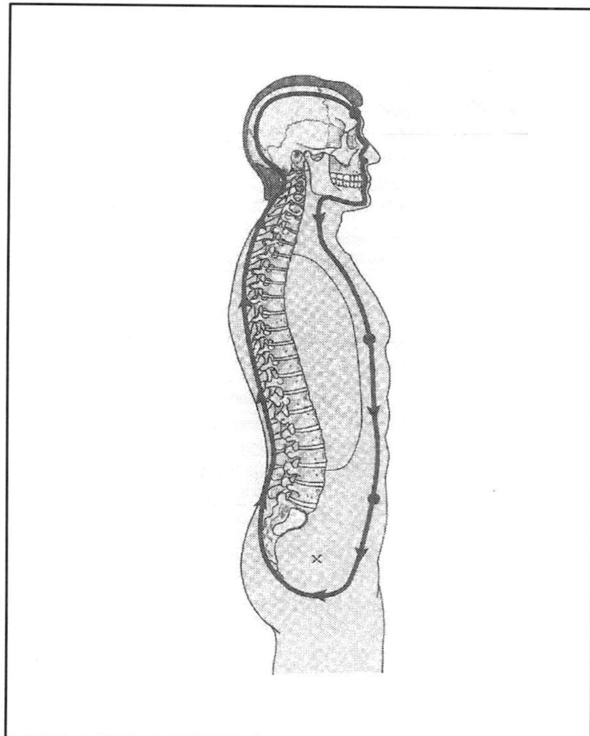

This is also called the Microcosmic Orbit, or the Fire Path of Qi Circulation.
(credit *The Root of Chinese QiGong*, p. 85)

Normally, sitting up, one again visualizes a major *chi* 'artery' running down the center of the front of the body (**Ren Mai**), into the anal region (chakra #1 down there), and then up the back side through another major *chi* 'artery' (**Du Mai**) that goes all the way up to the back of the head, over the top (center of the head and chakra #7), and continues to the face, semi-terminating in the roof of the mouth… one holds the tongue against the roof of the mouth to make the connection between the head meridian with the one that picks up in the lower jaw, and continues on to the frontside meridian (Ren Mai) that was just mentioned.

You can flow the *chi* in either direction, down the front and up the back, or up the front and down the back – these are Yin/Yang variations. But you start in the abdomen in what they call the **Dan Tien**, which is the reservoir of *chi* that the martial arts practitioners and healers use to build and store their *chi.* It takes about 5 -8 minutes to make one cycle, if done correctly as it is not to be rushed, and sometimes one can feel 'tingling' as the *chi* moves into the next area.

> Again, this is explained more in Transformation of Man, and is in synch with meditation and the *Kundalini* experience.

So Yoga was developed in India to facilitate the *Kundalini* experience, while the Chinese worked with the *chi* in their meditation times, and Tai Chi and QiGong..

Modern Indian Astrology

It is absolutely fascinating and amazing that Astrology in India has been granted **scientific status** ....

> Astrology retains a position among the sciences in modern India. Following a judgment of the Andhra Pradesh High Court in 2001, some Indian universities offer advanced degrees in astrology.
>
> Hindu astrology has been marketed as an **applied science** to help schedule important events and counsel timing of life activities. It combines textual traditions of medieval Hindu and Jaina astrology texts ....saying that "vedic astrology is not only one of the main subjects of our **traditional and classical knowledge** but this is the discipline, which lets us know the events happening in human life and in universe on time scale. [sic]" [382] [emphasis added]

And, there is a movement in progress to establish a national Vedic University to teach Astrology together with the study of Tantra, Mantra, and Yoga.

Of course, the scientific community pooh-poohs the whole scenario, including the Indian scientists themselves [who are now Westernized and] who cannot see any value in the tradition. Astrologers were put thru a double-blind test to see if they could determine from natal astrological charts whether certain children would be sickly, have a high or low IQ, and what sex they were. The statistical results were miserable and further discredited Astrology as a way to determine much about a person. [383]

Interesting, but the practice seems best suited to tracking the seasons for agricultural reasons, and to track sidereal events, comets, etc. which is what it was designed to do in India. And in that regard, the Maya were also spot on.

Mayan Astrology

The Maya made meticulous observations of celestial bodies, patiently recording astronomical data on the movements of the Sun, Moon, Venus, and the stars. This information was used for divination, so Maya astronomy was essentially for <u>astrological</u> purposes.

The Maya built the **Caracol Observatory** in Chichen Itza to observe the heavens:

(credit: Bing Images: Caracol)

Maya astronomy did not serve to study the universe for scientific reasons, nor was it used to measure the seasons in order to calculate crop planting – they used their agricultural calendar for that purpose. It was rather used by the priesthood to comprehend past cycles of time, and project them into the future to produce **prophecy.**

The priesthood refined observations and recorded eclipses of the Sun and Moon, and movements of Venus and the stars; these were measured against dated events in the past, on the assumption that similar events would occur in the future when the same astronomical conditions prevailed. Hence their prophecy was really **prediction.**

Mayan Codices

The Maya actually wrote what could be called picture books – using their glyphs to document wars and important state events – such as the installation of a new king – and that was accompanied with the building of a *stela,* the Mayan version of an obelisk.

Illustrations in the codices show that priests made astronomical observations using the naked eye, assisted by crossed sticks as a sighting device. Analysis of the few remaining Postclassic **codices** has revealed that, at the time of European contact, the Maya had recorded eclipse tables, calendars, and **astronomical knowledge that was more accurate at that time than comparable knowledge in Europe.** [384]

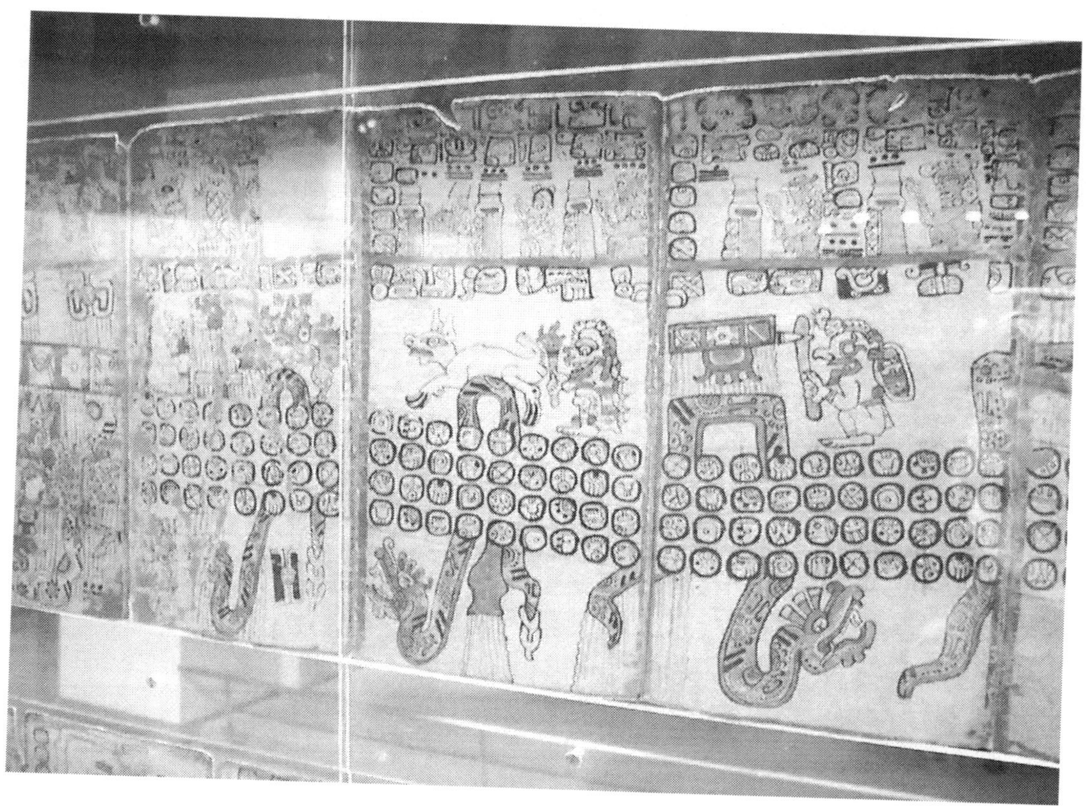

The Madrid Codex 6 in Spain: Rain Bringing Snakes[385]

The Madrid Codex above is the one with astronomical reporting.

> The Madrid Codex is the longest of the surviving Maya codices. The content of the Madrid Codex mainly consists of almanacs and horoscopes that were used to help Maya priests in the performance of their ceremonies and divinatory rituals. The codex also contains **astronomical tables**, although less than are found in the other two generally accepted surviving Maya codices. A close analysis of glyphic elements suggests that a number of scribes were involved in its production, perhaps as many as eight or nine, who produced consecutive sections of the manuscript; the scribes were likely to have been members of the priesthood. [386] [emphasis added]

Note the 4 serpents in the above codex pages.

Representation of an astronomer from the Madrid Codex.

We would have more codices if the Spanish Conquistadores hadn't destroyed 80% of them as "works of the devil."

flickr.com

What else were they tracking?

Venus was closely associated with warfare (not Mars!), and the hieroglyph meaning "war" incorporated the glyph-element symbolising the planet. Sight-lines through the windows of the **Caraco**l building at Chichen Itza align with the northernmost and southernmost extremes of Venus' path. Maya rulers launched military campaigns to coincide with the cosmical rising of Venus, and would also sacrifice important captives to coincide with such conjunctions.

Solar and lunar eclipses were considered to be especially dangerous events that could bring catastrophe upon the world. In the *Dresden Codex*, a solar eclipse is represented by a **serpent** devouring the *k'in* ("day") hieroglyph. **Eclipses** were interpreted as the Sun or Moon being bitten, and lunar tables were recorded in order that the Maya might be able to predict them, and perform the appropriate ceremonies (or hide).

Solar Flares and **Coronal Mass Ejections** (CMEs) would have interested the Maya especially if the **Aurora Borealis** flared as a result and could be seen from Alaska to the Yucatan. And related to that, Kukulcan aka Quetzalcoatl would have warned them if they needed to track any planetary objects that could come their way – such as Planet X, or a large Asteroid.

While speaking of **Planet X**, there is a very strange wall at Chichen Itza connected with El Caracol and it suggests the Maya might have been aware of the "Planet of the Crossing" also known as Nibiru. Of course, it would not have been known to the Maya as "Planet X" but the "X" symbol would be what the Maya would use to signify a **crossing**… and there is the strange series of X's in the wall associated with El Caracol: [387] (See also end of Chapter 1 – Substantiation of Sitchin.)

There are actually two rows of X's , most of the upper row has collapsed. This is not normal Mayan artwork and it was not designed to support any of the upper stonework – because it obviously hasn't. It is an inset, above what appears to be a face – two eyes just below the X's, a nose below the eyes, and then a mouth.

This might be considered stretching the point, but after all, (1) if the **Anunnaki** intervened in Man's affairs in Central America (and they did as Kukulcan to the Maya, and as Ningishzidda with the Olmecs), and (2) they were said to be from the planet **Nibiru** (which the Sumerians clearly called the **Planet of the Crossing** – crossing Earth's orbit every 3600 years often with disastrous results), then **that is something that the Maya would want to track** – if they were made aware of it…. And (3) this artwork is physically connected to the Caracol building. Perhaps these X's are a mute clue to what the Maya expected to see in the sky some day.

Planet X (aka 10th Planet)

While this book was being edited for final print, *NASA's Unexplained Files* (April 12, 2016 episode: **Attack of the Thunderballs**) had a section on the fact that the astronomers are puzzled by **something big at the edge of the solar system** that seems to be removing many pieces of the Kuiper Belt – perhaps knocking asteroids into the inner solar system and sending them Earth-ward. They are concerned that we may have another huge object that is part of our solar system that they can't see. That may be because it is a **Brown Dwarf** – a failed Sun that did not ignite (like Jupiter) and has a strange elliptical orbit that sends it thru the solar system below:

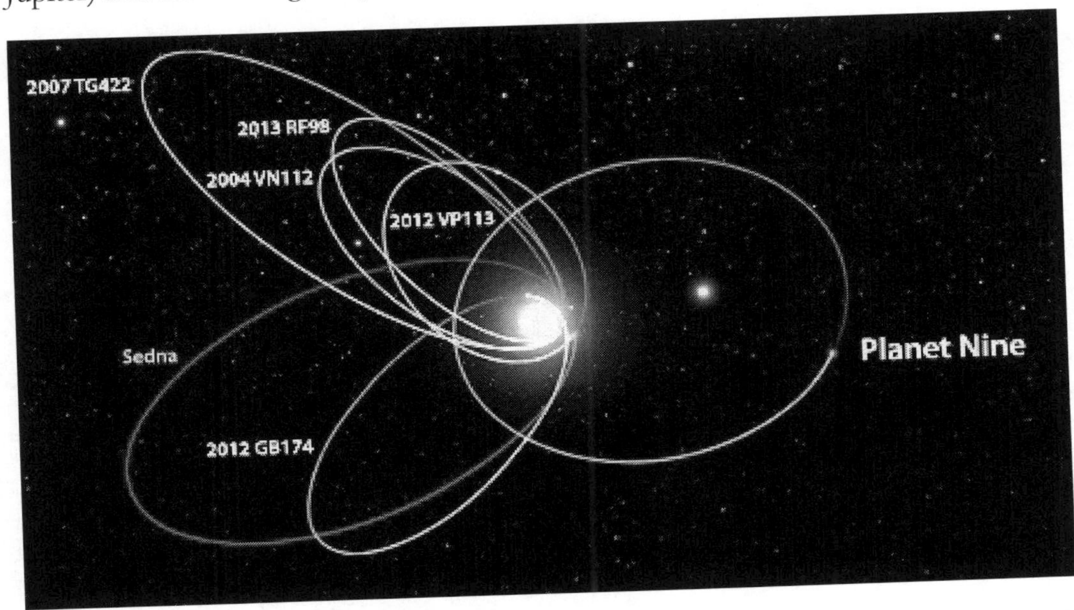

Orbital paths of the six most distant known objects in the solar system (magenta) along with theorized path of "Planet Nine". (Lance Hayashida/Caltech)

(credit: http://blogs.voanews.com/science-world/2016/04/11/learning-more-about-mysterious-planet-9/

What is shown is the whole solar system (the large white spot in the middle), and the Orbit of the new **Planet 9 (aka Planet X)** whose orbit swings it into the solar system's outer edge (Kuiper Belt of asteroids).

> Note that the new Planet 9 is so named because it was decided that Pluto which used to be planet #9 is too small to be called a planet – even though it has 5 moons! In fact if it had been kept as our #9 planet, then we would be looking for the 10th Planet – which is also what Zechariah Sitchin called it – but then, we can't let him be right, can we? So organized, think-inside-the-box Science had to play a game called "demote Pluto and let's look for a Planet 9." Did anybody notice that Planet X = Planet 10? (Roman numeral X =10.)

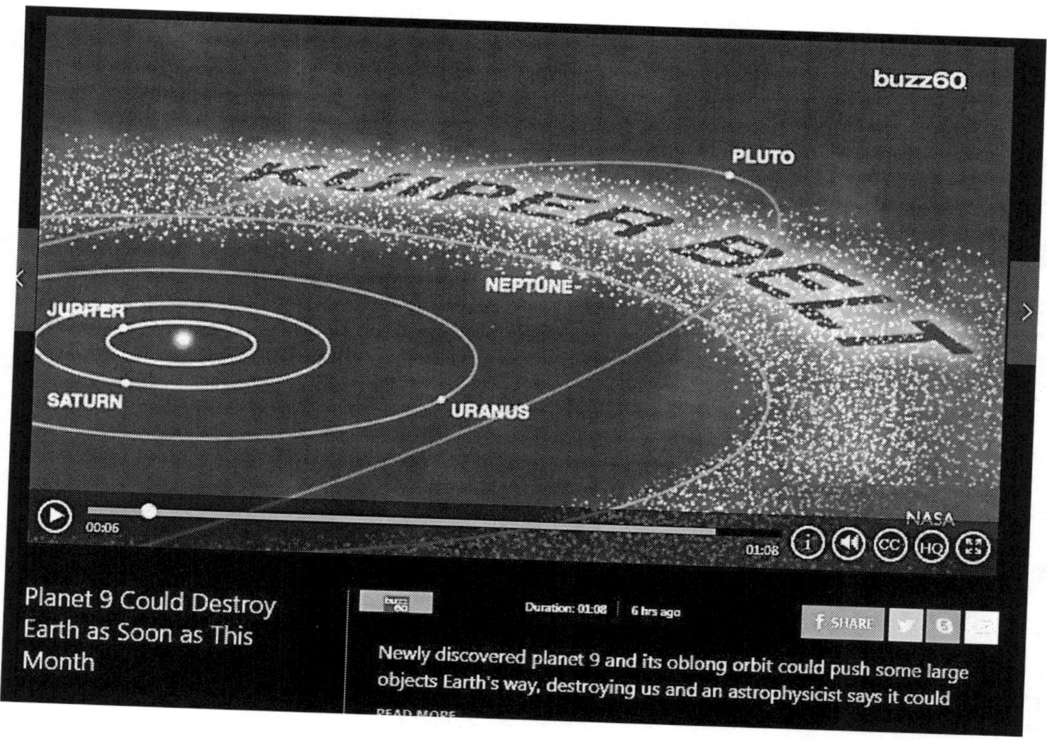

Planet 9 aka Planet X is not pictured in the above diagram. The orbit of Pluto does take it thru the Kuiper Belt. The new Planet 9's orbit is shown below.

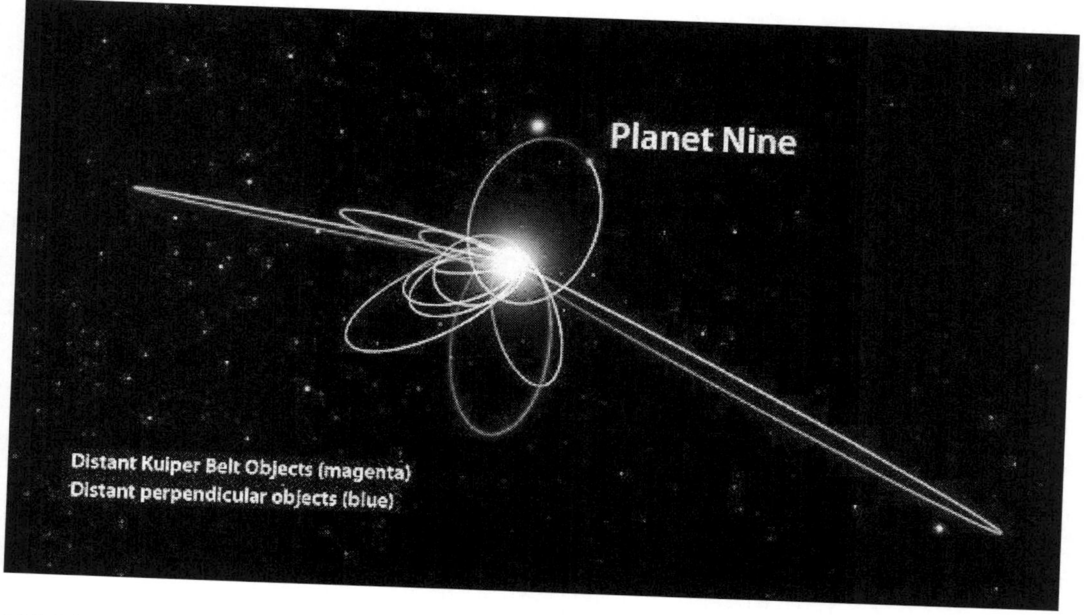

NASA is struggling to actually sight Planet X but so far all they know is that its mass perturbs Pluto and Neptune, and somehow is clearing a huge path of objects from the Kuiper Belt… so they know **something is there**, they just have not located it yet. (Also See Chapter 1 at the end.)

This is definitely something the Anunnaki would warn the Maya about, track it by calendar, and warn them to hide (**underground**, or inside their large pyramids for shelter) when it passes by. Seems the late Zeçhariah Sitchin was right – there is another very large object that is part of our solar system, and when it passes by, it creates global chaos… earthquakes, volcanism, tidal waves, 200-mph winds.

> In a related story, NASA's Kepler Probe has gone into **emergency mode** (13 April 2016) as it nears the outer edge of the solar system. Its job was to spy out new planets (outside the solar system) but it is malfunctioning… possibly as a result of something being done to it (electronic interference?) so that we can't see what is out there?
> (Source: http://solonews.net/281525/news/nasas-planet-hunting-kepler-spacecraft-enters-emergency-mode.html)

Architecture such as **El Caracol** ("the snail") at Chichén Itzá was also aligned with the appearance of celestial bodies such as the **Pleiades** and Venus. Another observatory at Uxmal contains hundreds of Venus symbols.

Rewind: The Pleiades Again

The Pleiades, also known as Tzab-ek by the Mayas, was considered **the place from which they originated** (pointed out in Chapter 6). The Tzolk´in, which is the sacred calendar of the Mayas, is **based on the cycles of the Pleiades**. The central plaza of the ruins of Ujuxtle, in the Pacific Lowlands, seems to have been aligned with the rise and fall of the Pleiades. The Stelas and Altars at Monte Alto in Guatemala are also aligned with the **Pleiades constellation** (left).[388]

> The famous astrologer John Dee used an Aztec obsidian mirror to see into the future. We may look down our noses at his ideas, but one may be sure that in outlook he was far closer to a Maya priest astronomer than is an astronomer of our century.
> — *J. Eric S. Thompson, Maya Astronomy: Philosophical Transactions of the Royal Society, 1974*[333]

The Maya were more sophisticated than the Norse who did not pay much attention to (much less track) the stars. So next, we take a brief trip from the Yucatan back to Scandinavia and the Germanic peoples who had a very interesting system of divination.

Norse Runes

While the writing and use of runes has been outlawed in Europe (thanks to the Nazis who used two Sig ᛋᛋ runes) it has a healthy following in America and Australia.

The meaning of the double Sig rune was four-fold: (1) reflective of the **Blitz**krieg – or "lightning" war, (2) SS was said to stand for **SchutzStaffel** – the SS division, and (3) since the Sig rune symbolized the Sun for the ancient Norse, it was also said to represent the **"Schwarze Sonne"** – the Black Sun (another mythical aspect of Teutonic lore provided by the Ahnenerbe).[389] (4) Lastly, the Sig rune itself was sometimes used to signify "victory."

The alphabet used (which was modified over the centuries) was called the **Futhark** and it consisted of all straight lines because the Vikings or Germanic tribes who also used runes, would have to chisel the runes into wood or stone, and so curves were avoided.

Note the end of the second line (chart, next page) where the Sig rune is followed by the 'Tyr' rune (Tyr was the Norse god of justice and this rune also was used to signify victory.) Note also that each rune also stood for a concept that will come into play when the Norse shaman starts using the runes for divination. **"Serpent"** is third from the left on the last line.

> FYI: the first 6 runes (below) spell out F – U – Th – O – R – C, hence the name of the alphabet.

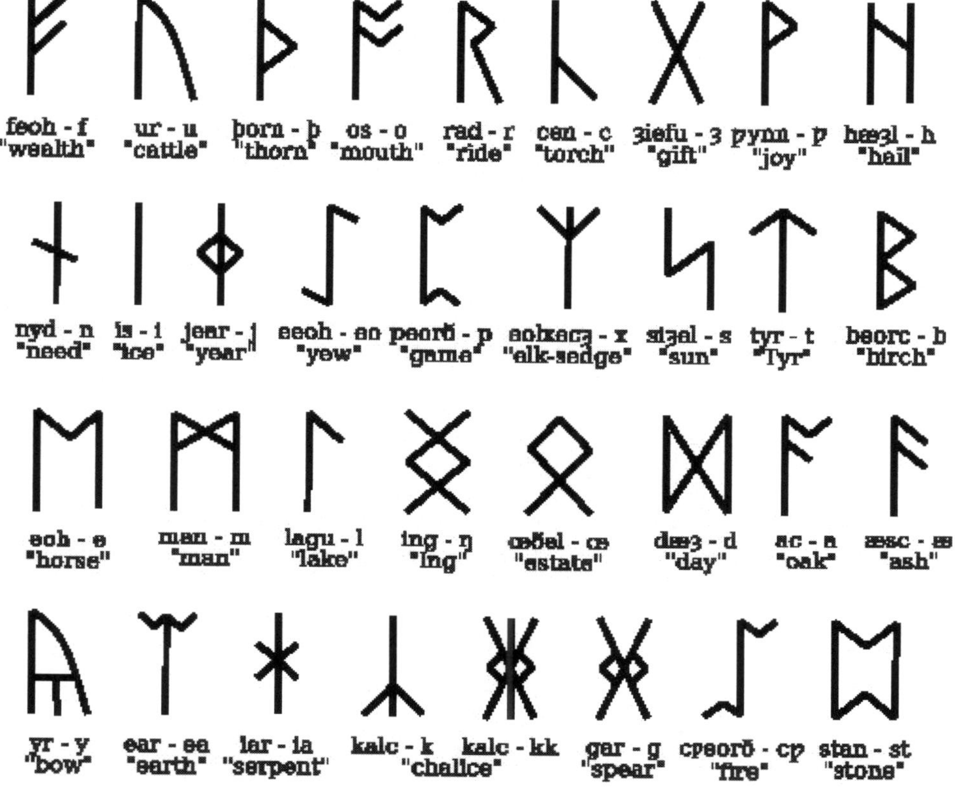

One of the Earliest Anglo-Saxon Futharks
(credit: Wikipedia: https://en.wikipedia.org/wiki/Runes)

Keep in mind, from Chapter 2, that the people in Northern Europe (Norse, Germanics, Danes, Frisians…) were given writing by their gods. So naturally, the Norse used the runes to communicate with their gods in one-sided "casting the runes" and invoking the divine blessing for healing, wealthy, or even war.

But before examining the runic divinations, which amounted to magic (which is why they are outlawed in Europe – besides their use by the Third Reich), there are a couple of interesting aspects of daily life that the Norse provided us with.

Days of the Week

The names of the days of the week in English all relate to the Stars/planets, or the Norse gods.

Saturday	---	Saturn Day	
Sunday	---	Sun Day	
Monday	---	Moon Day	
Tuesday	---	Tyr's Day	(Tyr = god of justice)
Wednesday	---	Woden's Day	(aka Odin = main god)
Thursday	---	Thor's Day	(Thor = god of war)
Friday	---	Freya's Day	(Freya = a goddess)

Architecture in Germany

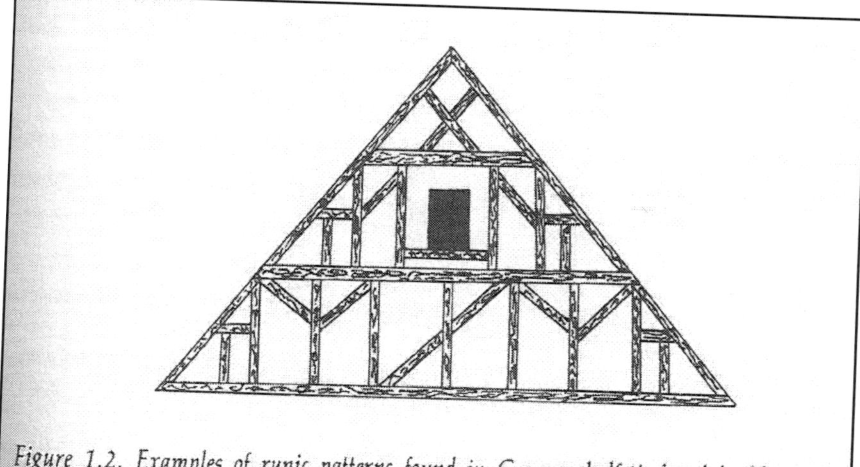
Figure 1.2. Examples of runic patterns found in German half-timbered buildings.

The old Germanic style of building preserved the runes in what was called ***Fachwerk*** or "half-timbered" style: [390]

There are 5 different runes shown above (see Futhark table).

How many runes are there (to the left and above)?

(Use the Futhark Chart on the preceding page. Hint: note that the upside down trident [left] is "K" or Chalice.
Above diagram: they use the "E" for Elk and "G" for Gift.)

Serpents on Runestones

Gripsholm Stone

This commemorates a battle where the brother of Ingvarr fell while fighting a battle in the east, far from home.

The stone dates to the middle of the 11th Century.

The inscription is read starting at the head of the serpent:

"Tola had this stone raised for his son Harald, Yngvarr's brother. [They] fared boldly far away after gold and in the east they gave [food] to the eagle… they died in the south in Serkland."

Serkland was Persia.

Divination with Runes

If one wanted to beseech the gods to bless an action about to be taken, it was customary to cut staves of wood, smooth one side, carve appropriate runes into it, color the runes with one's blood, and then speaking the sacred formula (special incantation), one would then toss them onto a white cloth, perhaps three times, invoking the god's name.

According to a Roman witness, Tacitus:

> A branch is cut from a nut-bearing tree and cut into slips: these are designated by certain signs (Latin: *notae*) and thrown randomly over a white cloth. Afterwards, the priest of state…. offers a prayer to the gods, and while looking up at the sky, takes up three slips, one

> at a time and interprets their meaning from the signs carved on them. If the message forbids something, no further inquiry is made on the question that day; but if it allows something, then further confirmation is required through the taking of auspices [sacrifices]. [391]

It was also a practice to carve a sturdy piece of wood, like a pole, write runes on it, stick an animal's head on the top of the pole, and stick it in the ground to curse someone.

Here is where it gets interesting and could not be just something that the Norse made up as they went along. They had help from esoteric teachings (notably the gods who were in all probability the Anunnaki as Chapter 2 said) that revealed **the power of mind.**

Three elements were required of the *Vitki* (supplicant) if the **ritual** was to have any effect and manifest results.

1. The *galdr* was the incantation that followed a set format. Many times these were pre-set but could be free form.
2. The *stödhur* was a way of standing, posturing the body to imitate the shape of the major rune invoked.
3. The *fehu* is the raw, archetypal energy of the Universe which the *Vitki* must also invoke and embody.

So what is that last element? The Vikings weren't as primitive as we have been led to think. Their World Tree and Runic System were involved.

Four **principle forces** and entities arise from the complex interplay of runic symbols and the consciousness of Man.

1. The *hugr* is the intellect and conscious will.
2. The *hamr* is the personal aspect of the image-forming essence in the Universe.
   The Norse sagas abound with stories of a powerful *hugr* projecting itself into a distant location (Think: bilocation or astral projection.)
3. The complex entity that empowers the first two, is *hamingja* a term that means **'shape-shifting'** or power, and can be the *Vitka*'s guardian angel.
4. The *fylgja* is the storehouse of this action. A numinous being attached to every human; a kind of karmic aura.

This is all about the **personal power of the soul** – one of the secrets of Serpent Wisdom which the Church worked hard to suppress from the public.

Yes, obviously this is not primitive Viking slash and burn consciousness… it is more on the order of some guru, or shaman trained in mental arts. And it is also a description of the **Hawaiian Kahuna functioning**… using mind energy to affect people and things. One either has to be born a talented human, already having abilities in that direction, or one has to spend years developing a higher consciousness – and again, that would be *Kundalini*-based. But it was not called *Kundalini* – the Norse referred to the inner power as ***hamingja*** **.**

> The Norse also knew about the aura, or energy field around the body, which they called *hamr*. It was possible to manipulate and reshape the energy field by magical power (*hamingja*) according to will (*hugr*). [392]

Runic Practices

Runes can be used to heal or curse. Here are a few examples… [393]

> In *Egill's Saga* (about the greatest runemaster of all time, known as Egill Skallagrimsson) we find Egill heals a girl of sickness caused by ill-wrought runes. There was a secret stave carved by a peasant boy trying to cure her, but the runes on it only made her sickness worse. The whalebone on which the runes were carved was found lying in her bed.
>
> Egill read them and then he whittled the runes off and scraped them down into the fire and burned the whalebone and had all her bedclothes thrown to the winds. Then Egill said:
>
> > A man should not carve runes unless he knows well how to read: it befalls many a man who are led astray by a dark stave; I saw whittles on the whalebone ten secret staves carved, that have given the slender girl her grinding pain so long.
>
> Egill carved runes and laid them underneath the pillow of the bed, where she was resting; it seemed to her that she was well again...

One of the most remarkable uses of runes is in the preparation of the *nidhstöng* (cursing pole)…

Again, *Egill's Saga* gives another example:

Egill came up onto the island. He picked up a hazel [wood] pole in his hand and went to a certain rock cliff that faced in toward the land; then he took a horse head and set it on the pole [impaled on the top of the pole]...

Then he performed an incantation and said "Here I set up the niding pole and I direct this insulting curse against King Eirikr [Bloodaxe] and Gunnhild the queen" -- then he turned the horse head in toward the land -- "I turn this insulting curse to those land-spirits that inhabit this land, so that all of them go astray, they will not figure nor find their abode until they drive King Eirikr and Gunnhildr [sic] from the land."

Then he shoved the pole down into a rock crevice and let it stand there; he also turned the horse head toward the land and then he carved runes upon the pole, and they said all the incantation.

It is also interesting that runes could be used to create **chaos**. If runes were carved intelligently, and correctly, with no errors, then just the opposite was expected to create confusion. Some runes have been found whose 'lettering' makes no sense, gibberish as it were.

Equally interesting was the use in initiatory circles among apprentices to the runic art, and **initiates into the esoteric secrets**. The runemaster would carve into one or more staves the secret runes promoting and invoking higher consciousness, then scrape them off into a mead drink, and have the initiates drink it. The result was faster learning and a sort of intuitive development of the esoteric truths.

Lastly, there were the **Norns**. Goddesses of destiny. The three prominent ones are Urd (fate), Skuld (personification of the future), and Verdandi (necessity). They reside under and care for Yggdrasil, the Norse Tree of Life. The Norns control the unchanging universal laws and the Fate of humans and the Norse gods. They can obstruct Odin, which means they sometimes have more power than the main god.

And that sounds like the concept of the **Greek Fates**, the triple goddesses who also control Fate and determine the mortal's lot in life. They were Clotho (the spinner), Lachesis (the apportioner), and Atropos (the cutter). They are frequently in opposition to Zeus which gives them more power than Zeus.[394]

Greece and Scandinavia were not connected linguistically, geographically, culturally, nor economically… yet they have the same esoteric teaching. Can you guess the connection?

The Greek gods interacted with Man just as the Norse gods interacted with humans. The gods taught man agriculture, astronomy, writing, medicine…..The common element is the gods. The Greek gods were also the Norse gods. (Think: Anunnaki.) Amazing what you find when you connect the dots.

And because we mentioned the Norse Tree of Life, and are about to link that with Kabbalah and the Sefirot (next chapter), there is an interesting interrelationship between the Norse gods:

Norse Gods Tree of Life

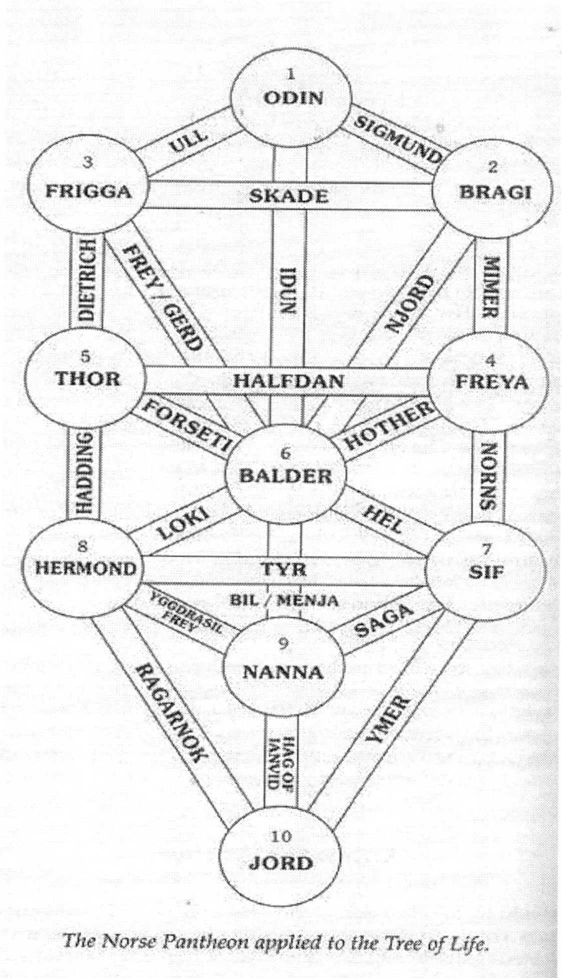

The Norse Pantheon applied to the Tree of Life.

Norse Tree of Life Symbol

The Tree of Life is one of the most familiar of the Sacred Geometric Symbols.

Freya is Odin's female counterpart.
Frigga is Odin's wife.
Balder is the son of Odin & Frigga.
Bragi is a son of Odin & Frigga.
Thor is Odin's son by Jord.
Nanna is wife of Balder; Moon goddess.
Loki is a trickster, Odin's shadow side.
Hermod is Odin's son: a war god
Sif is Thor's wife.
Jord is mother of Thor; earth goddess.

(The Norse gods do not correspond to the Sefirot positional qualities.)

pinterest.com

And finally, this chapter would not be complete without a brief look at Tarot which is another avenue under the heading of Augury (Divination).

Tarot

Tarot is an item in the suite of divination modalities, often used to 'read' one's future and often used in conjunction with an astrological reading. It was not always that way – **Tarot used to be just a card game**, said to have originated in northern Italy, near Parma. While it is true that the Egyptians also used playing cards, and the origin of Tarot has been said to come from Thoth, there is absolutely no foundation for Egypt being the source of Tarot cards and the divination practice with them. Divination started in France in the 1770s.

Jean-Baptiste Alliette wrote a book called *Etteilla, ou manière de se récréer avec un jeu de cartes* ("Etteilla, or a Way to Entertain Yourself With a Deck of Cards") in 1770. Note that the book title *Etteilla* was his last name backwards – he was already into playing games. He used a shortened deck of 32 cards used in gaming, with the addition of an "Etteilla" (trump) card.

> In 1781 the French Swiss Protestant clergyman and occultist Antoine Court who named himself Court de Gebelin published in his massive work *Le Monde primitif* his idea that the Tarot was actually an ancient Egyptian book of arcane wisdom. **There is no evidence to support the notion that tarot has an Egyptian lineage**, but in the stir that followed, Etteilla responded with another book, *Manière de se récréer avec le jeu de cartes nommées Tarots* ("How to Entertain Yourself with the Deck of Cards Called Tarot") in 1785. It was the first book of methods of divination by Tarot [using the 1760 Conver deck].[395] [emphasis added]

Nonetheless, Tarot cards were very much in use to teach **Hermetic Alchemy**. Etteilla published his ideas of the correspondences between the Tarot, Astrology, and the four classical elements and four humors, and was the first to issue a revised tarot deck specifically designed for occult purposes.

> By 1790, he was interpreting the hermetic wisdom of the Egyptian Book of Thoth: *Cour théorique et pratique du Livre du Thot*, that included his reworkings of what would later be called the "Major" and "Minor" Arcana, as well as the introduction of the four elements and astrology. Towards the end of his life Etteilla [sic] produced a special deck for divination that syncretized his ideas with older forms of French cartomancy, the first deck of cards specifically designed for occult purposes [now 78 cards]. [396]

Occultists call the trump cards and the Fool "the major arcana" while the ten pip and four court cards in each suit are called “minor arcana.” The cards are traced by some occult writers to ancient Egypt or the **Kabbalah** but again there is no documented evidence of such origins or of the usage of tarot for divination anywhere before the 18th century. So it was not a part of the original Achemy nor Hermetics, coming much later after them.

Tarot was often used with the study of the **Hermetic Qabalah**. Hermetic Tarot has imagery to function as a textbook and mnemonic device for teaching the gnosis of alchemical symbolical language. An example of this practice is found in the rituals of the 19th-century Hermetic Order of the Golden Dawn. Then, in the 20th century, Hermetic use of the tarot imagery as a handbook was developed by Carl Gustav **Jung** 's exploration into the psyche (archetypes in particular) and imagination.

Because the next chapter gets into Kabbalah, Gnosticism and Rosicrucianism to begin to examine some of the Serpent Wisdom principles that have been made public (one way or another), we have to clarify something. On the last page (above) it was stated that there is no known connection between Jewish **Kabbalah** and Tarot. There was a connection between Hermetic **Qabalah** and Alchemy and Tarot… but note the spelling.

Difference between Jewish and non-Jewish Kabbalah [397]

From the Renaissance onwards, Jewish Kabbalah texts entered non-Jewish culture, where they were studied and translated by Christian Hebraists and Hermetic occultists. Syncretic traditions of Christian **Cabala** and Hermetic **Qabalah** [spelled differently to distinguish the two] developed independently of Jewish **Kabbalah**, reading the Jewish texts as universal ancient wisdom. Both adapted the Jewish concepts freely from their Judaic understanding, to merge with other theologies, religious traditions and magical associations.

With the decline of Christian **Cabala** in the Age of Reason, Hermetic **Qabalah** continued as a central underground tradition in Western esotericism. Through these non-Jewish associations with magic, alchemy, and divination, Kabbalah acquired some popular occult connotations forbidden within Judaism, where Jewish theurgic **Practical Kabbalah** was a minor, permitted tradition restricted for a few elite. (Theurgy was one of Hermes’ 3 key disciplines.)

Today, many publications on Kabbalah belong to the non-Jewish **New Age** and occult traditions of Cabala, rather than giving an accurate picture of Judaic Kabbalah. Instead, academic and traditional publications now translate and study Judaic Kabbalah for wide readership.

With the next chapter, we are still looking for the Tree of Life, or World Tree, Serpent imagery, and tidbits of esoteric Serpent Wisdom that have leaked out of the secret societies.

Chapter 12: Serpent Wisdom -- Secret Sects

Here is where we get into the esoteric, hidden, inner teachings mostly still well-guarded by the secret societies or Orders. So how can they be presented here if they are secret? First, has Man ever kept a secret? Second, the author was taught by a Rosicrucian member before she died, and asked to guard the information and later explain some of the basics – some of which were just presented in the latter part of Chapters 10 & 12. And third, there are still secrets not revealed as they are not germane to this book.

> In fact, it is because I had that 'inside' information that I was visited and asked to receive the more complete package and transcribe it for Them. **Not aliens but the Watchers still here**. The result was Books 1 and 2. Lastly, this book which is the final member of the set, shows to whom else, and where else, the esoteric knowledge was taught.

So for the most part, this chapter is about the three movements called Kabbalah, Gnosticism, and Rosicrucianism and how the three incorporate the Tree of Life, World Tree, and Serpent imagery – or whether they do not. All three have links to Hermeticism and that will be the link with Alchemy, Divination and Astrology. It will not be a complete examination of each of the three – all we want is to see what elements in the three movements relate to each other and how that relates to Serpent Wisdom. After covering those elements, additional aspects of Serpent Wisdom will be examined.

Kabbalah

Kabbalah is spelled as above as this is the correct spelling to indicate the Jewish mystical movement, whose organization and writings began in France about 1200 AD. Until the Middle Ages, most of Kabbalah was transmitted orally from one mystic to another. (As pointed out in the last chapter, Qabalah refers to the New Age version, and Cabala refers to a Christian version.) Jewish mystics and rabbi have suggested that the real Kabbalah began with Adam and what was transmitted to him by God.

Kabbalah means "tradition" and it can be seen as receiving or transmitting teachings. Mystical, esoteric teachings that were said to be the deeper part of the Oral Law that were given to Moses at Mt. Sinai. [398]

Kabbalists adopted a new way of looking at God, Creation and Man and the purpose for life. And one of the most significant aspects was interpreting the Torah in an esoteric way… looking for the deeper meanings in the Holy Scriptures which will help Man to better understand God. The **Zohar** is the basic work presenting the mystical aspects of Kabbalah, the Torah (1st five books of the Old Testament), Cosmogony, and mystical Psychology.

> The Zohar contains discussions of the nature of God, the origin and structure of the universe, the nature of souls, redemption, the relationship of Ego to Darkness and "true self" to "The Light of God", and the relationship between the **"universal energy"** [*Chi*, Prana, and Ruach] and man. Its [scriptural critique] can be considered an esoteric form of the Rabbinic literature known as *Midrash*, which elaborates on the Torah.[399]

To give a decent background to the Zohar, it is noted:

> The Zohar first appeared in Spain in the 13th century, and was published by a Jewish writer named **Moses de Leon**. De León ascribed the work to **Shimon bar Yochai** ("Rashbi"), a rabbi of the 2nd century during the Roman persecution who, according to Jewish legend, hid in a cave for thirteen years studying the Torah and was inspired by the Prophet Elijah to write the Zohar. This accords with the traditional claim by adherents that **Kabbalah is the concealed part of the Oral Torah**. [400]

Many people throughout history have scanned the Zohar for insights into life, the purpose of Creation, and Man's relationship with the Laws of Nature. However, from the perspective of the rabbis, and from statements in the Zohar, the purpose is to help the Jewish people and to infuse the Torah and ***mitzvot*** (Judaic commandments) with the wisdom of Kabbalah for its Jewish readers. Needless to say, the Hermeticists and Gnostics also learned much from the Zohar.

The Zohar refers to God as ***Æin Sof,*** the unmanifest, the indescribable, and Infinite One. And since God is indescribable and unknowable directly, He must be understood in some other form (thru His **emanations**). One of the salient symbols or forms developed by Kabbalists is found in the earliest book of the Zohar, called the ***Sefir Yetzirah*** (which means the Book of Formation). In the *Sefir* is the key diagram of **10 emanations** called the *Sefirot*. It is also called the **Tree of Life**.

The *Sefirot*

Below is the **Jewish Tree of Life** which bears a strong resemblance to the Norse Tree of Life, Yggdrasil, and to the Sumerian Tree of Life.

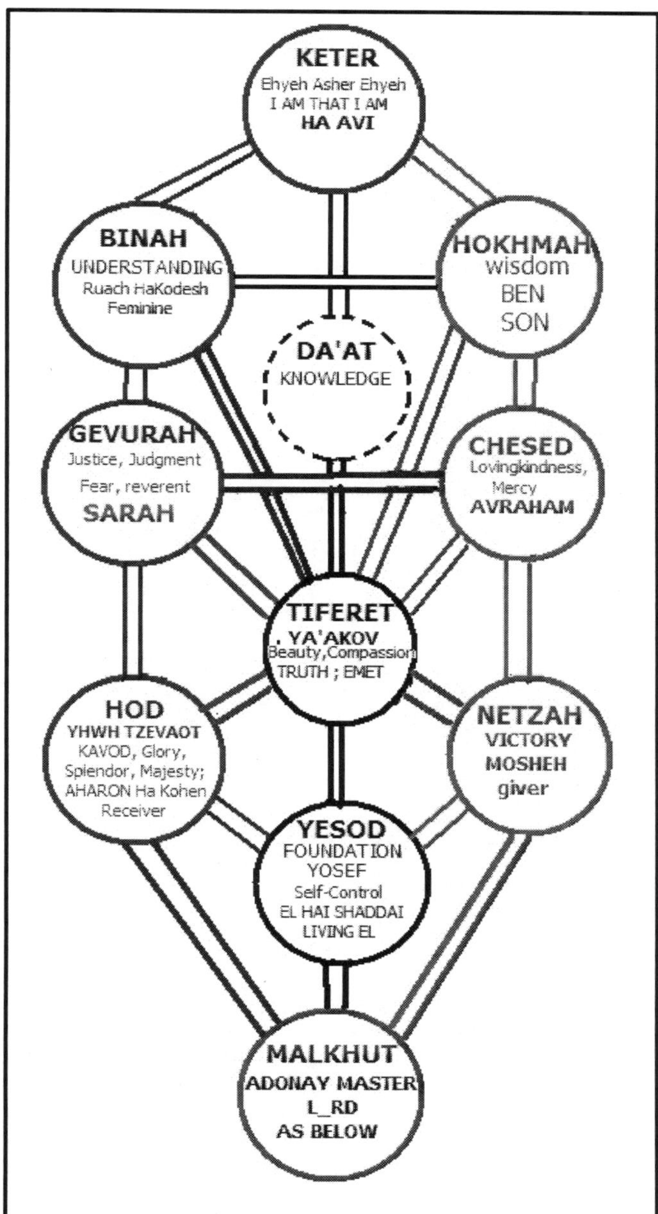

The Keter is *Æin Sof*,
The One, the Source.

Note the **Da'at** is Knowledge, very important: **Da'at** is the location (the mystical state) where all **ten *Sephirot*** in the Tree of Life are united as one, but it is not part of the official 10 spheres.
Sephirot are the attributes or **emanations** of God.

The left three are Yin, feminine or passive.
The right three are Yang, masculine, or active.
The middle four are called the Pillar of Compassion, and it is all the **Tree of Life**.

There are 22 paths, and 22 letters in the Hebrew alphabet. There are 10 Spheres, or *Sephiroth*. 10 + 22 = 32 paths of wisdom.

(Credit: Bing Images: Pinterest.com)

The Norse Tree of Life:

Remember this from Chapter 2?

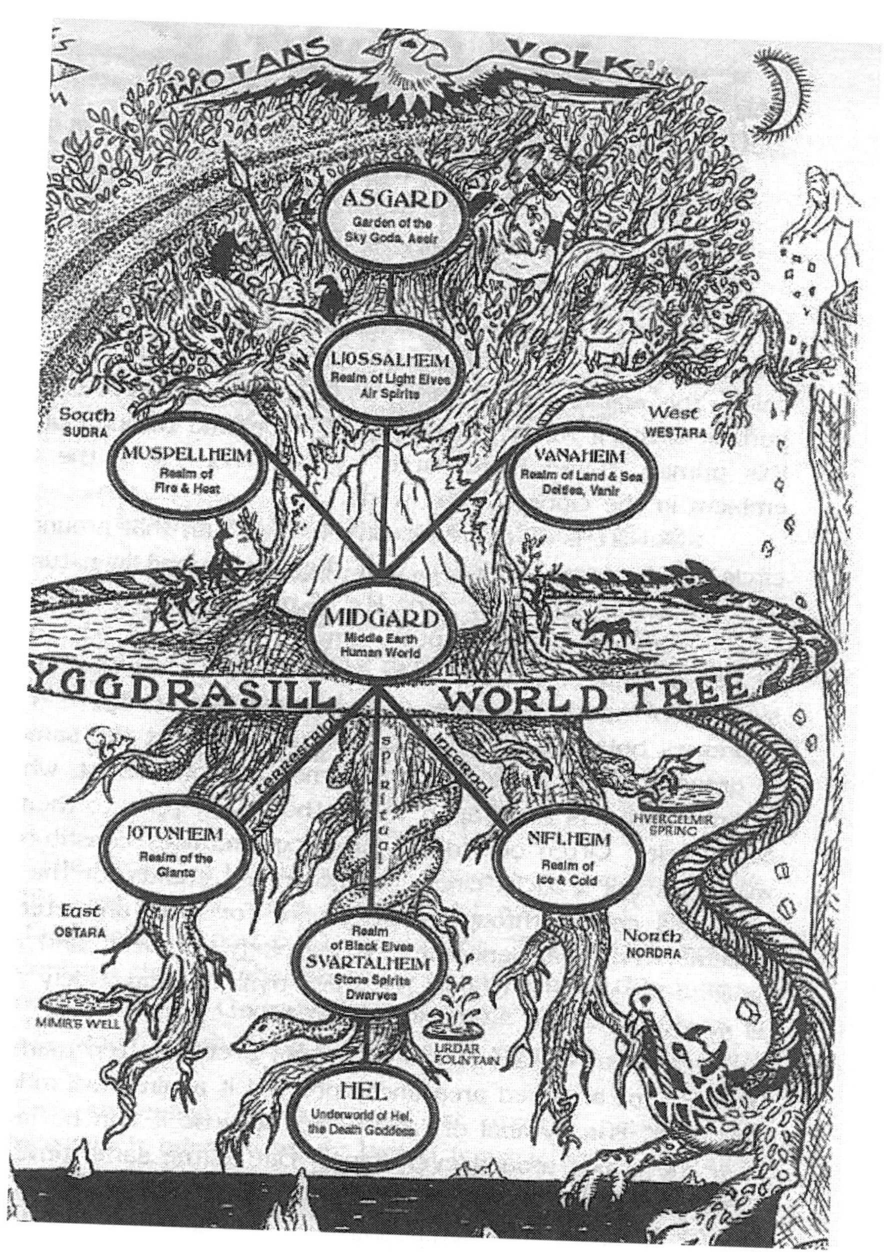

The connection is not only in the shape/representation of the different locales, but the Kingdom of the gods (Asgard/Wotan and Keter) is at **the top**, as is the lower world, reality (Midgard and Malkut) found at **the bottom** of both diagrams.

The Sumerian Tree of Life

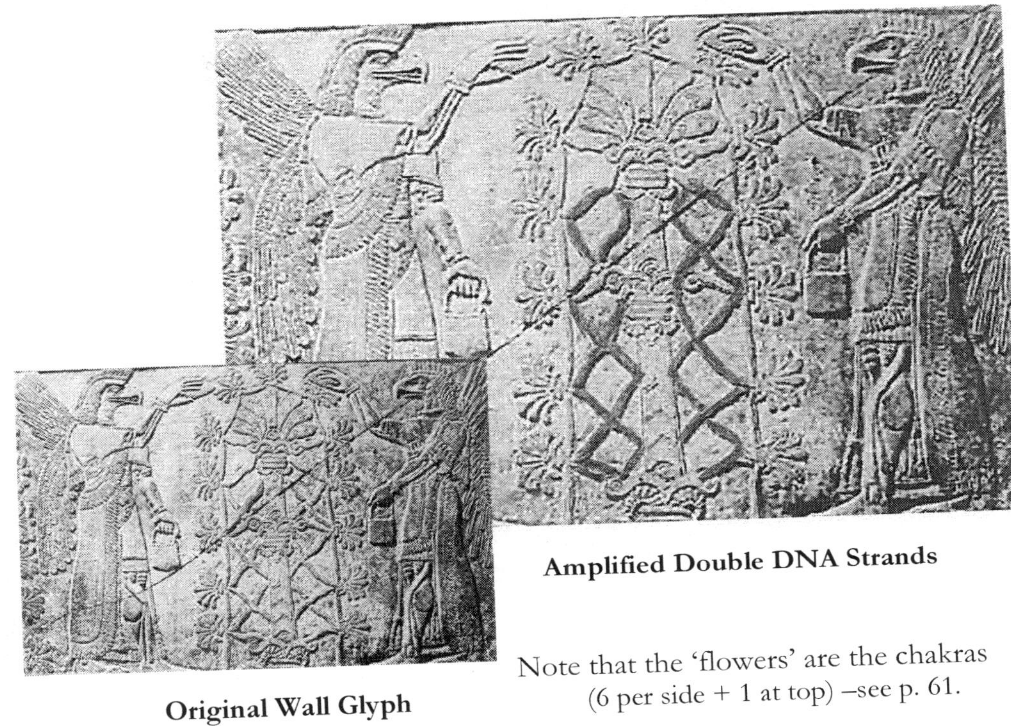

Amplified Double DNA Strands

Original Wall Glyph

Note that the 'flowers' are the chakras (6 per side + 1 at top) –see p. 61.

Note that the Norse Tree of Life has an Eagle at the top and the Sumerian Tree is attended to by **Eagle-headed beings**. Note that there is also a series of nodes and criss-crossing lines as with the *Sefirot.*

The Tree of Life motif is also known in Sweden, Africa, Indonesia, the Philippines, Iran, Egypt, China –

> An archeological discovery in the 1990s was of a sacrificial pit in Sichuan, China. Dating from about 1200 BC, it contained three bronze trees, one of them 4 meters high. At the base was a **dragon**, and fruit hanging from the lower branches. At the top is a strange **bird-like (phoenix**) creature with claws. Also found in Sichuan, from the late Han dynasty (c 25 – 220 CE), is another tree of life. The base is guarded by a horned beast with wings [dragon]. The leaves of the tree are coins and people. At the apex is **a bird** with coins and the Sun. [401]

Of course, Christianity speaks of the Tree of Life (Garden of Eden), as do Hinduism, Islam, Druids and Judaism. The point is that trees were venerated by many peoples around the world as were Serpents, and in several cases, as was pointed out in several chapters, the Serpents are associated with special trees. And sometimes, there are birds [a spirit symbol] at the top of the tree.

Someone may argue that the three diagrams have nothing to do with each other, and yet, ask yourself: Why wasn't the *Sephirot* done as a star pattern, or a version of the 6-pointed star, or even a Merkaba?

Or how about a **Buddhist Wheel?**

Someone will say, the Wheel only has 9 points: 8 spokes and a hub. The hub could be Keter and the other 8 could accommodate the 9 spheres – note that several *Sephirot* could be combined: Wisdom and Understanding, Truth and Knowledge, and isn't Splendor & Majesty related to Beauty?

If you have Wisdom, you have Understanding – and Truth.

Or how about a **Celtic Knot** – with all 10 'spheres' (holes) accounted for?

The Eternal Knot is also a symbol used by the Buddhists.

Certainly the Eternal One could interweave His many facets into a never-ending whole?

(credit: Bing Images: ancient-symbols.com)

That is not to denigrate the Judaic *Sephirot*, but to emphasize that there is some underlying reason a vertical diagram was chosen by several cultures. And they called their diagrams, Trees.

Or how about a 10-petalled **Lotus Flower**, symbol of enlightenment in the Orient?

There are 10 petals, Keter would be in the center, and the 9 *Sephirot* would be the leaves.

Their symbology is accurate too: the flower rises out of the muck and mud of the pond, to live in the Light (floating on the water).

One of the reasons for the vertical structure has to be that there is a hierarchy – Keter is above the Kingdom, Asgard is above Midgard, and because the Sumerian Tree is really symbolizing the Spine and 7 major chakras, the ***Kundalini*** rises from the base and flows to the Crown (Keter, Asgard). That is why there is a Serpent (sometimes a Dragon) at the base of the Tree and an Eagle at the top.

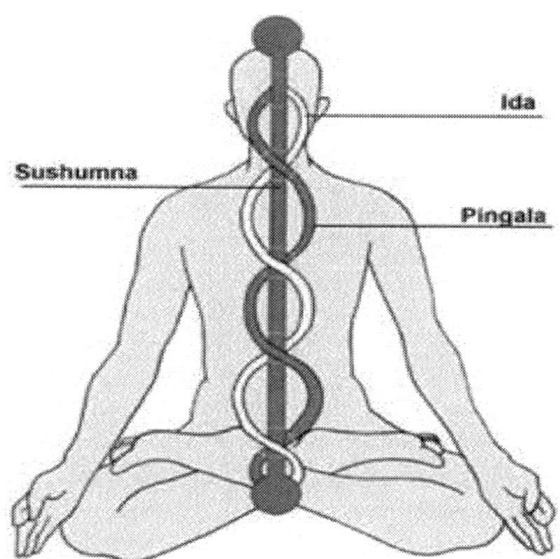

The reason for the Sumerian Tree having two sides of 7 blossoms is that the Spine is the Sushumna Nadi (path) for the Ida and Pingala – there are two energy flows, 'snaking their way up the Tree/spine thru 7 chakras.

This is also why the Caduceus has two serpents entwined around it.
(See Chapter 5, Greek Section.)

So all we need now is a connection between *Kundalini* and the Zohar, or *Sephirot*.

So far we know that the Hermeticists knew about *Kundalini* – the Gnostics (next section) got it from the Hermeticists, and the Zohar speaks of the **Shekhinah** (energy/power, Love, glory) that resides in Malkut (the base of the Tree) which has to rise up and reunite with Tiferet (understanding, i.e., the head).

Then, if one overlays the Sefirot with the human body, saying that the chakras have a correspondence with the Sefirot, you get this: [402]

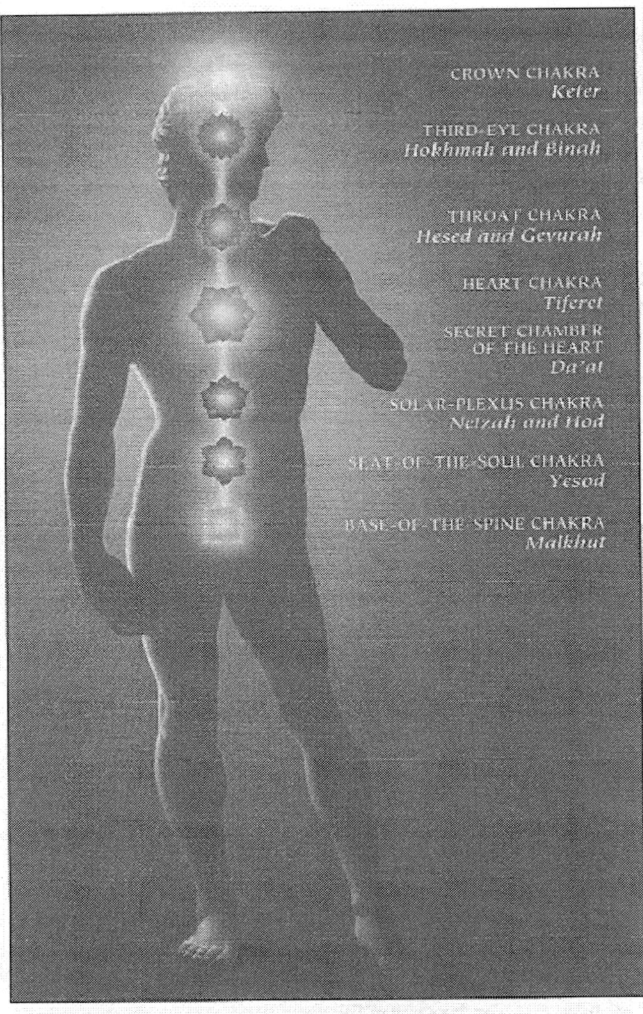

FIGURE 13. *The sefirot correspond to the chakras (the centers of light in your etheric body). Both the sefirot and the chakras step down God's energy for our use.*

But it is interesting that whereas the Hindus and Chinese teach that the *Kundalini* must **rise up**, the *Sepher Yetzirah* teaches something different -- It is **called The Lightening Flash:** [403]

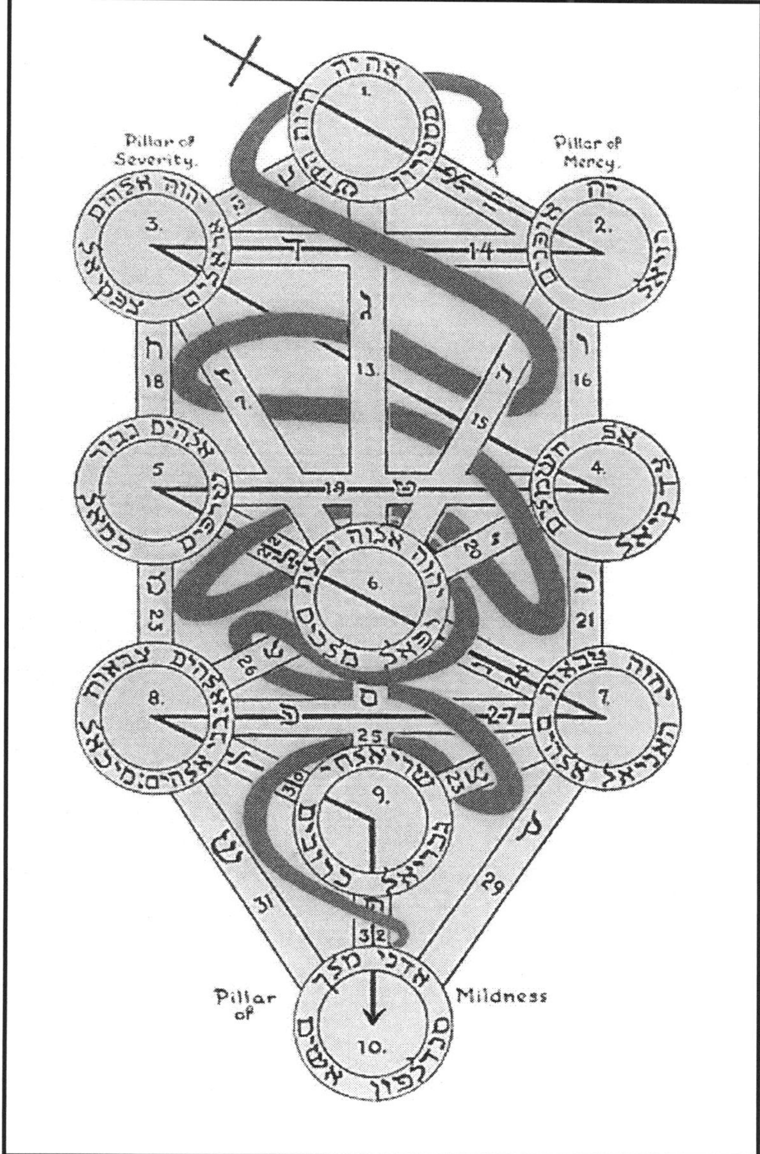

Note that it **starts at the top,** running from Keter to Malkut (top to bottom).

"In this illustration," says Z'ev Halevi, "we have a brief outline of the **Lightning Flash** as described in the human Tree of Life. All creative processes in the Universe follow the same pattern…."

Æin Sof delivers the enlightenment to Man (top – down).

Note the serpent again.

Rabbi Yonassan Gershom says that *Malkut* can correspond to the base of the spine or to the feet….Yogis sit on the ground, but in Kabbalah *Malkut* corresponds to the point of the feet because we **stand when we pray** [and so are connected to the physical world]. [404]

So the Kabbalists believe that ***Shekhinah*** (aka Dragon Fire) resides in *Malkut* at the base of the Tree, and it is a feminine energy (very Yin). This correlates very nicely with the Sacred Feminine concept.

The ***Shekhinah*** is associated with the transformational spirit of God (also regarded as the source of prophecy); it denotes the dwelling or settling of the divine presence of God and his cosmic glory. This exact term does not occur in the Hebrew Bible, and is first encountered in rabbinic literature…

> Be aware that the *Kundalini* is believed to be absorbed into the body thru primarily the Base Chakra and it flows into other parts and organs of the body. The Life Force is called Prana in India and *Chi* in China.
>
> There was no concept found in Kabbalah that corresponds to *Chi*, nor that of *Kundalini.* The Kabbalistic view is that energy , Life Force, and creativity, etc all come from the top-down, thru the Keter, from the *Æin Sof*, the Source of All.

Rewind: Sourcing the Kabbalah

Said to be very ancient, the Kabbalah was the "soul of the soul of the Law" and while the Law was given to the Children of Israel, soul of the Law was given to the rabbis, and the deeper level was only for initiates instructed in its secret principles.

> According to Jewish mystics, Moses ascended Mt Sinai three times….
> The first time he received the Tablets with the written Laws….
> The second time he received the soul of the Law….
> The third time God instructed him in the mysteries of the Kabbalah, or: the soul of the soul of the Law.
> Moses concealed in the first four books of the Pentateuch (Torah) the secret instructions that God had given him, and for centuries students of Kabbalah have sought therein the secret doctrine of Israel.
> Kabbalah means the secret or hidden tradition, the unwritten Law, and according to an early rabbi, it was delivered to Man so that thru the aid of its abstruse principles he might learn to understand the mystery of both the universe about him and the universe within him. [405]

The point being that we already know who gave the teachings (the Law) to Moses, and the Hebrews dissected it and created the Midrash, the Mishna, the Talmud, and various other scholarly writings… extrapolating what the god gave them. (See

Chapter 1.) And yet, there were Ten Commandments, so why are there 613 parts (or *mitzvot*) to the Mosaic Law? [406]

Man doesn't always do what he is told. He was told to live the Ten Commandments not analyze them. Case in point: Matthew 24 says to go and teach the Gospel in all the world. Instead, missionaries go out and study a small tribe's language and then spend 20 years creating a Bible for them. The injunction was to **teach** not write – that means take a translator, and teach. And the Wycliffe Bible Translators have created themselves an empire based on writing the Bible in more than 2000 languages.

> There are currently over 100 Wycliffe member organizations from over 60 countries…. As of November 2012, translations of either portions of the Bible, the New Testament, or the whole Bible exist in over 2,800 of the 6,877 Earth languages. [407]

That is reminiscent of what Man did when the modern era began and companies began to **bake and sell bread**. Instead of making and selling the whole wheat product – endosperm, bran, wheat germ – Man was clever and produced a type of pulpy white bread, then isolated the wheat germ and sold it separately, and also sold the bran separately. That way he can make three times the money by breaking down a natural, whole product, and those who eat spongy, lifeless white bread into which the companies had to ADD vitamins (because they just took them all out with the **fiber**, bran and wheat germ) have no idea where their potential diverticulitis comes from. Just sayin'… It is something Man does.

So back to Kabbalah, Hermetics, and Gnosticism and how they relate. We are still looking for common points between them that suggest one common source.

Hermeticism

Thus far, it is clear that Hermetics borrowed from Kabbalah and then the Gnostics borrowed from Hermeticism and Kabbalah. And yet, the Kabbalists have something in common with the Gnostics – **the belief that one can experience/know God directly.** And like Hermeticism, the Kabbalists believe that everything is connected to everything else and all is an expression of the One God … *Æin Sof*, which means "without end." So Kabbalah teaches ways to connect and communicate with God.

The Hermeticists agree with the Kabbalists: **As Above, So Below**. And the Jewish flag is a reminder of that axiom:

The bottom triangle points UP, and the top triangle points DOWN.

The blue stripes recall the blue stripes of the prayer shawl.
Blue symbolizes divinity.

Simple & Elegant.

Much of the importance of Hermeticism arises from its connection with the development of science during the time from 1300 to 1600 AD. The prominence that it gave to **the idea of influencing or controlling nature** led many scientists to look to magic and its allied arts (e.g., alchemy, astrology) which, it was thought, could put Nature to the test by means of experiments. Consequently, it was the practical aspects of Hermetic writings that attracted the attention of scientists.

> **Isaac Newton** placed great faith in the concept of an unadulterated, pure, **ancient doctrine**, which he studied vigorously to aid his understanding of the physical world. Many of Newton's manuscripts—most of which are still unpublished—detail his thorough study of the *Corpus Hermeticum*, writings said to have been transmitted from ancient times, in which the secrets and techniques of influencing the stars and the forces of nature were revealed. [408]

Remember that the three components of Hermeticism were:

Alchemy

Astrology

Theurgy

Kabbalah can only speak to one of those: Theurgy.

Jewish Theurgy

The Medieval Jewish mystical tradition of Kabbalah developed the concept that the Universe is regarded as a series of emanations from the Godhead, namely, the **10 *Sephirot*.** It is said that God created the world using the sephirot, pouring Divinity into creation through these "vessels," which also have personality traits. The highest sephirah, **Kether**, holds the most divine light and is the least accessible to humanity. The lowest sephirah, **Malkut**, is still higher than matter itself, so a parallel with Neoplatonism is not complete, but Malkut is considered that aspect of God that can be perceived in the material world. It is also where the **Shekhinah** can be found.

For the Kabbalist, God is a single oneness, not separate "gods." The teaching avoids polytheism by insisting that the sephirot are not to be prayed to, but rather, to be **meditated on and experienced** as manifestations of how God acts in the world. They are envisioned as arranged in three columns, in a pattern called the **Tree of Life**. By meditating on the sephirot and praying for their unification, Kabbalists seek **the theurgic goal of healing a shattered world**.[409]

So far nothing to suggest an Anunnaki interaction with Man via the Kabbalah teachings, except the way the Kabbalah Tree of Life reflects the Sumerian Tree of Life. So let's look at the 1st book of Moses in the Torah (within the Tanakh) and the Creation called **Genesis**. We need to briefly review this as it bears on the Gnostic section which follows.

Genesis

In the Torah, Genesis is called *Bereshit* (בְּרֵאשִׁית, literally "In the beginning").[410] What is significant here is the **Two Creations** in Genesis...and who did them.

While the Judaic texts may not agree with this examination (and we don't know if it is addressed or not in the Talmud or the Mishnah), it is presented here as it has relevance to the older Sumerian texts that deal with the creation of Man, AND it is also highly relevant to the Gnostic teachings as will be seen.

> While Chapter 1 of the Virtual Earth Graduate (VEG)book goes into much more detail, the relevant parts are repeated here.

Creation

> In the beginning, God created the heavens and the Earth…

Great, we have heard that before.

And then the Book of Genesis tells us:

Gen 1:26-28
[26]And God [Elohim] said, Let **us** make man in **our** image, after **our** likeness...
[27]So God [Elohim] created man in his own image, in the image of God created he him; male and female created he them.

Ok, good. Man and woman were created at the same time, no rib involved, and the Creator was referred to as "us" and "our"… EL is the word for God; in Hebrew, the suffix "-im" makes the word plural. **Elohim is plural for El… several gods** creating Man. Very interesting. But it doesn't stop there.

In the very next chapter of Genesis, it tells us:

Gen. 2:7
[7]And the LORD God [Yahweh] formed man of the dust of the ground, and breathed into his nostrils **the breath of life**; and man became a living **soul**.

Very interesting. The same Book, same writer, and one assumes the same Creator, but now with a new name, Yahweh, and now Man has a soul. Woman was not created at this point in the text.

In addition, the claim is made that in Gen. 1 man is represented as having been made "in the image of God" (27), yet in Gen. 2, he is merely "formed...of the dust of the ground" (7), thus suggesting a contrast. And this was allegedly all written by Moses, the same writer.

Two different accounts, in the same Book… and get this:

VERY Important: Nowhere in the Bible does a writer ever repeat the same event twice in the same Book. (Ink and papyrus were expensive items and they would not waste them by repeating themselves.)

Genesis 2 is not a repeat or 'clarification' of Genesis 1.

There were (at least) two Creations of Man.

And in fact, there were multiple creations as the late Mesopotamian scholar **Zechariah Sitchin** has told us (in The Twelfth Planet), and we have 5 distinct races on the Earth… Caucasian, Oriental, Latino (including South Sea Islanders), Negroid, and Amerindian (including Eskimo, Aleuts, Inuit, etc.)

> If you think that white humans evolved from the Blacks, or vice-versa, I have some ocean-front property in Montana I want to sell you.

But racial diversity, to create a 6th race, is not still happening, contrary to Darwin, and apes are not still 'evolving' into humans, and that is a key point. Man is a special creation, and was 'assembled' to look like his creators – Elohim or ETs, it makes no difference. The Sumerians said their gods were the Anunnaki, from the stars. The Hopi, the Chinese and the African Zulu and Dogon, by the way, said the same thing. In fact, ZULU means "from the stars." Man's evolution was **assisted**, and that is the basis of Ch. 3 in VEG.

> By the way, Dr Susan Martinez has already been profiled (Chapter 8), and she agrees based on the anthropological evidence. (See VEG, Ch. 1, Creation vs Evolution section.) **Polygenesis** is what happened.

The diversity of Man on Earth looks more like an **Experiment**, as if some advanced geneticists were looking to see which of the 5 Root Races would survive (Survival of the Fittest) and be the best, advanced humanoid lifeform with which to populate this or perhaps other similar planets.

> Keep in mind that Homo *erectus* already existed and note that **Neanderthal** (30,000 years ago) was replaced with Cro-Magnon. Cro-Magnon then was 'upgraded' to **Homo *sapiens***… obviously current Man is not the one that was originally created (according to Genesis) and the anthropological record. But it wasn't plain and simple Evolution because: (1) it is not still on-going, (2) there is no "missing link" and (3) the Sumerians, Zulu and Dogon said they were created and taught by the sky gods (i.e., Anunnaki).

Sorry, but Darwin was wrong on Evolution as the sole source of all life on the planet, and correct on Survival of the Fittest and Natural Selection – which we now call **Epigenetics**. Interestingly, after Creation, there has been a form of evolution as **morphogenesis** tends to modify species to better adapt to their environment.

So what is the point of two creations of Man?

Two Seeds

Let's assume that there really were two creations in Genesis, and that the Bible is basically correct and makes it clear that the first creation had NO souls. This group of humans (Pre-Adamics) would have lived and propagated and formed at least a small tribe somewhere (Land of Nod).

Then we have the second creation of Man, maybe something was not quite right with the first group and it was decided to make another version… this time with a **soul**. And we got Adam and Eve, then Cain and Abel. Cain slays Abel and is expelled from Eden, and he wanders off and takes a wife from the **Land of Nod**… a wife! A grown woman. From another group of humans. And those two give birth to Enoch…. Who "walked with God" and challenged the Watchers above the Earth. (All examined in detail in VEG, Ch.s 1-3).

The point being that there was <u>another group of humans in Nod</u>, and they logically had to be the first creation (Gen. 1:26). Logically, because we are not told about any other people at the time.

> **Apologetics** is a Christian scholarly group that has said that Genesis is so vague about timelines that we don't know how much time elapsed between Cain and Abel and Seth, and did Adam and Eve have daughters? (If not, we're talking incest to replicate the species!)
>
> Interesting that the Bible is supposed to be the inerrant, perfect Word of God, and yet Man has to **apologize** for what is there…. To try and explain the omissions, inconsistencies, and errors… Sounds like The God of the Universe is as fallible as Man… (or maybe Man modified the original, perfect Word of God, and redacted much of Genesis…?)

And the arguments go on and on, but let's keep this as close to the facts as possible and avoid the polemics.

If there were two creations, the first one without a soul and the second with a soul, then we have **two seeds on the planet**. Is that in the Bible? Yes.

> …I will put enmity between thee and the woman [Eve], and between **thy seed and her seed**…. (Gen. 3:15)

> I realize that God is talking to Eve and the Serpent, but the point is still that there are **two seeds**, and VEG, Ch. 1 goes into more detail as to just what the Serpent was and how his 'seed' equates with those in the Land of Nod. This was examined in some detail in VEG, Ch. 1 (with a Chart) and is not repeated here.

Suffice it to say that the seed of Eve (the 2nd seed, with a soul) would find the other seed, the 1st seed (without a soul), antagonistic and working at different purposes on Earth. The 1st seed has to be the people from Nod who also propagated and have spread over the Earth…even to this day. The Genesis origins account doesn't speak of any other people beside Adam and Eve's group and those in Nod.

> Both seeds are on the planet today (because they spread out and the Flood was not global).

There is another interesting Biblical passage that tells us that there are two seeds that don't mix, metaphorically speaking:

> And whereas thou sawest iron mixed with miry clay, **they shall mingle themselves with the seed of men: but they shall not cleave to one another** even as iron is not mixed with clay.
>
> Daniel 2:43

There is another meaning to the passage, in addition to what the Bible scholars say about Daniel interpreting the king's dream: a woman with a soul should not marry a man who is soulless. (What does the Bible say about being "equally yoked"?) And this is an issue that one can use to avoid heartache in one's life. (TSiM, Apx. D.)

Creation Validated

The late **Boris Mouravieff** was a Russian scholar and student of Gurdjieff and Ouspensky, living in Paris, who wrote a three-volume Gnosis [411] which was an analysis of **Esoteric Christianity.** In this work, he reveals an alternate, enlightened interpretation of the first two chapters of Genesis which summary goes like this:

> **Genesis Chapter 1**: the original 1st creation – without souls.
> Boris Mouravieff calls these humans **pre-Adamic man**.

> **Genesis Chapter 2**: another creation where the 'breath of life' (*ruach*) was breathed into *adamah* meaning "earth man" – Adam had a soul. Eve was created from Adam's rib and as a 'meet' (complementary/corresponding) mate for Adam, would also have a soul. (Also Cain and Abel.) Boris Mouravieff calls these humans **Adamic man.** [412]

That means that those things that a soul could normally do in a normal body (with all chakras functional), cannot be done in a soulless body – even through **the soulless body looks normal, it isn't.** It is under-functioning, compared to an ensouled body. These differences were delineated in the review of "A" and "B" Influences (See VEG, Ch. 14).

Note again that the creation of Man took place in two distinct stages and the pre-Adamic and the Adamic have coexisted for a long time, probably intermarrying. [413] Would this not result in martial strife since the two humans would have different perceptions of themselves and life?

At this point it is emphasized that the pre-Adamic man represents the 1st Creation in Genesis 1. And this is significant because the Bible tells us that Adam and Eve had two sons, who would be 'Adamic' like them: the offspring had souls just like their parents. Then Cain killed Abel and was expelled from the scene – and he takes his wife from the Land of Nod. And is relocated to the New World.

FYI: The 'mark' of Cain was no facial hair.

This is important information. There is only Adam and Eve up to this point, with their two sons. Where did the rest of the people come from? To cut to the chase, it was suggested that the people in the **Land of Nod** were descendants of the pre-Adamics, from the 1st Creation, and Mouravieff does agree.[414] That means that **Cain had a soul and his wife didn't**. As they left for parts unknown, and did a lot of 'begatting' as the Bible says, they began the **mixed marriage scenario** and the furtherance of the two human lines, with enmity between the two, just as Yahweh/Enlil said in the Garden of Eden when he expelled Adam and Eve.

> **Edgar Cayce** said that one of Adam's sins was "consorting with others" and was told that "all flesh is not one flesh!" Cayce never clarified this reference to "others" but it is not hard to think that it could have referred to ensouled (Adamic) Man mixing his genes with those of the people in Nod, the Pre-Adamics and soulless ones.[415]

Ok, now let's take a look at Gnosticism and its teachings relevant to Creation…

Gnosticism

First, let's be clear on what Gnosticism is.

Whereas the Jewish mysticism called Kabbalah has an oral tradition preceding its documentation in the 13th century, Gnosticism is much more a recent development coming from Greece about the 2nd century. In fact, it often is defined in a Christian context, and explains the Creation in terms of a **Demiurge called Yaldebaoth** the God of Earth, **Sophia the goddess of Wisdom**, Archons and Æons.

There are three major aspects to Gnosticism:

> Gnostics see the world in terms of **duality** in order to explain it, Good and Evil are in an eternal battle for supremacy;
>
> and
>
> Gnosis (esoteric or intuitive knowledge) is the way to **salvation** of the soul from the material world;
>
> and

Gnostics believe that The One, *Æin Sof*, is knowable by direct experience – there is no need for "middle men" called priests.

The Church had a problem with the last two concepts and denounced Gnosticism.

Gnostic Rejection of Judaism

In turn, Gnosticism renounced standard Christianity and Judaism.

Modern research (Cohen 1988) identifies Judaism, rather than Persia or Greece, as a major source of Gnosticism. Many of the Nag Hammadi texts make reference to Judaism, in some cases with **a violent rejection of the Jewish God**. Gershom Scholem once described Gnosticism as "the Greatest case of metaphysical anti-Semitism."
Professor Steven Bayme said Gnosticism would be better characterized as anti-Judaism. Yet, recent research into the origins of Gnosticism shows a strong Jewish influence, particularly from *Hekhalot* literature.

Gnostic ideas found a Jewish variation in the mystical study of Kabbalah. **Many core Gnostic ideas reappear in Kabbalah**, where they are used for dramatically reinterpreting earlier Jewish sources according to this new system. On the other hand, other scholars, such as Scholem, have postulated that there was originally a **Jewish gnosticism**, which influenced the early origins of Gnosticism in general…

Pit Stop: Overview

What is being shown here is that while some systems borrowed from each other, they often did not see eye to eye, suggesting that they could not have come from one source as the truth. And that is what we are looking for – commonalities between belief systems which would suggest a common source that sought to enlighten Man and get all humans on the same page. In fact, that is what has been proposed from the beginning of this book: the Anunnaki set up the Serpent Wisdom Schools with their esoteric teachings and in examining the major beliefs of major systems, that should make itself evident… that way, we'd know what the true (original), inner teachings were.

As the foregoing exercise with Kabbalah, Hermeticism and now Gnosticism is showing, if Man ever was given one solid all-true teaching, the three ideologies do not reflect a common *Weltanschauung* (world view). They all agree that there is a Being that is greater than Man and thru experience -- or experiment (Alchemy in

Hermeticism) – one should be able to determine the real underlying principles of the universe and life.

Kabbalah

So what do we have? We saw that Moses was given a set of Laws by God, or someone they thought was Him. And due to the unusual circumstances, and the fact that Man cannot bodily come into the presence of Almighty God (again, the energy differential issue), Moses did not meet with the God of the Universe. And yet, it is reasonable that he did receive genuine Laws and commandments by which to govern Man's unpredictable behavior. Man needs boundaries, standards, and rules. It is suggested that Enlil (a local god) was Yahweh.

At this point, having suggested that there were Two Creations, and that Enlil was the god who gave Moses the Ten Commandments, let's pause and acknowledge something.

The Church is to be commended for trying to unite Man and get everyone on the same page with religious doctrine -- which meant teaching principles and truth that even the densest [ignorant] average human could understand and accept, and thus exoteric Church doctrine was designed 800+ years ago and set at <u>the least common denominator</u> which was very basic and contained no mention of the Visitors and the real creation of Man. Times have changed.

In the year 2000, Zechariah Sitchin went to the Vatican and had several productive meetings with Msgr Balducci and found that the Vatican knows more that it can share but is making the effort to gradually wake people to the probable existence of other beings Out There. He found that Msgr Balducci was authorized by the Vatican to speak proactively on the UFO/ET issue. (These details were covered in Ch. 3 of VEG.)

Lastly, the Vatican produced a press release by Fr. Jose Funes stating "Extraterrestrials Exist and They are Our Brothers." The Vatican is well aware of Sitchin's books and teachings, and had no major objection to the Anunnaki information.

In Defense of the Church[416]

Hermeticism

What we extracted from Hermetics was the search for rules and processes by which to transmute baser things to more noble things – lead as well as souls. It included principles of Gnosticism and Kabbalah, as well as Divination (Astrology, Tarot, I Ching) and Theurgy (divine magic, or white magic) all in a wide-reaching effort to discover what life was all about, how it worked, and of course how to manipulate it. Such men as Isaac Newton, Robert Boyle, and Jan van Helmont began with Alchemy and pursued it on into *bona fide* science.

Gnosticism

Returning to the Gnostics, we find that they too were seeking the meaning behind Life's mysteries, just as were the Alchemists and the Kabbalists. So they all had that in common, they just differed in how they went about it, and they differed in what they found, and how they explained it. And here is where it gets different… and we can connect the Genesis Creation story to that of the Gnostics' found in the Nag Hammadí scrolls. In fact, not much was known about the earliest gnostic writing until the discovery of ancient scrolls at **Nag Hammadí** in 1945.

Nag Hammadí Scrolls

There are some concepts emerging from the Scrolls that bear review. Let us look at their version of Creation and Adam and Eve, which by the way, echoes the Sumerian cuneiform tablets.

Garden of Eden

As might be expected, the Nag Hammadí Library contains a work called *The Origin of the World.* And in it, they agree with the Torah's and Bible's Genesis – there were two trees.

> The Justice created Paradise…. And desire is in the midst of the beautiful, appetizing trees. And the **tree of eternal life** is… to the north [side] of Paradise, so that it might make eternal the souls of the pure…. Now the color of the tree is like the sun. And its branches are beautiful. Its leaves are like those of the cypress. Its fruit is like a bunch of grapes when it is white. Its height goes as far as heaven.
>
> And next to it is the **tree of acquaintance (*gnosis*)** [Knowledge], having the strength of God. Its glory is like the Moon when fully radiant. And its branches are beautiful. Its leaves are like fig leaves [large and broad]. Is fruit is like a good appetizing date. And this tree is to the north [side] of Paradise, so that it might arouse the souls…. in order that they might approach the **tree of life** and eat of its fruit and so condemn the authorities [the Demiurge] and their angels.

[Now the good part:]

> The effect of this tree is described in the *Sacred Book* [Bible], to wit: "It is you who are the tree of acquaintance [gnosis], which is in Paradise, from which the first man ate and which opened his mind; and he loved his female counterpart and **condemned the other, alien likenesses and loathed them.** [417] [emphasis added]

Well, there is the Anunnaki serpent part, and we also have the reference to the Tree of Life. So now let's briefly reveal the highlighted text regarding the creation of Man.

Gnostic Creation Players

Before relating what the Nag Hammadí Library **(NHL)** text (*On the Origin of the World*) has to reveal, a few terms and concepts will be useful to know:

Pistis Sophia -- the Universal Mother, the Mother of the Living or Goddess Mother, the Power on High, She-of-the-**left-hand** (as opposed to Christ, understood as her husband and he of the **Right Hand**), …. the Holy Dove of the Spirit, the Heavenly Mother …. or Elena (that is, Selene, the Moon). She was envisaged as the Psyche of the world and the female aspect of Logos. To the Gnostics, Sophia was a divine [opposite companion] of Christ, rather than simply a word meaning wisdom, and this context suggests she is the **Goddess of Wisdom**. [418]

Sophia Zoe – daughter of Sophia.

Archons – "rulers" or "lords" -- several servants of the Demiurge, the "creator god" that stood between the human race and a transcendent God that could only be reached through Gnosis.

Aeons -- the various emanations of God; remember the Kabbalah said that the 10 *Sefirot* were also the emanations of God, or His characters/aspects.

Demiurge – This is Yaldabaoth who thinks he's God, and does rule the Earthly realm. Having created the **Aeons**, he told them that "I am a jealous God and there is no other God besides me…" But the angels remarked to themselves that he would not have said that had there not been another of whom he is jealous. Thus the angels knew him to be a liar. [419]

According to the Gnostics, here are some Bible personages and their origin:[420]

Wisdom: Sophia or Pistis Sophia. (an emanation of God)

Zoe (life): daughter of Sophia

Yaldabaoth (aka Ialdabaoth): The chief ruler also called Sakla ("fool") and Samael. He is the Demiurge who rules his domain: Earth.

Sabaoth: One of Yaldabaoth's first seven offspring (aka the 7 Rulers).

The above 4 are like astral beings, almost angels with supernatural abilities.

Adam: The first human being, but there are **two Adams**:
Adam1 – created by the Elohim/Arcons with a soul
Adam2 – created by the 7 rulers, activated by Sophia Zoe – no soul.
The 7 rulers are part of the Archons who serve the Demiurge.

Eve: Adam's wife and counterpart but there are **two Eves**:
Eve of the Light – created by Sophia Zoe an advanced being
Eve 2 – a replica created by Eve of Light to fool the Archons.

Cain: Eve's son begotten by the rulers
Abel: Eve's son begotten by Adam
Seth: a son through God
Norea: Eve's daughter

Creation à la Gnosticism

There is an older version examined in Ch. 2 of VEG that will not be repeated here, which has to do with Yaldabaoth creating a man and being tricked into blowing a divine breath into him, giving him a soul, then Yaldabaoth sees the man is smarter than he is and casts the man into the lowest levels of the Creation (Earth). Sophia protects the man and hides his divine light so that the Demiurge cannot find Adam and kill him. (This was a version to explain how man acquired sin because Yaldabaoth created in his man **a counterfeit spirit** and the problems of pleasure, desire, fear , grief, lust, anxiety, and pride, etc..).[421]

Note: *Adamah* is the word for the first man. (Sitchin called it *Adamu.*)

While interesting, it is not the one that really serves our purpose. What we want is the account that follows (from NHL and *The Origin of the World*), and it is lengthy so that it will be paraphrased and its relevancy highlighted:

The authorities (Archons) had laughed when the Demiurge said that he was the only God, and in fact he had created a counterfeit spirit in his version of man [the people of Nod], so the Archons said to themselves, "Let us create a man with the Light and have him serve us [as opposed to serving the Demiurge]."

Pistis Sophia advised the Archons and assisted them in the creation of a true, 1st Adam. Meanwhile, Sophia Zoe (her daughter) took sides with Sabaoth (Yaldabaoth's son) and planned to use her 'fake' Adam 2 to get the real Adam1 to despise the Archons and rebel against them.

Sophia Zoe first creates an androgynous human being, **Eve of Light**, and it bears an offspring via virgin birth which is called the Beast [a serpent]. The Archons called it the **Beast** and said that it was the wisest of all beings. So the 7 rulers accompanying Sophia Zoe fashioned a man who looked like the Archon's version of the ensouled Adam1... but this one had a counterfeit spirit and no soul, so Yaldabaoth puts him aside, unmoving for 40 days, not planning to use him (still Adam2).

Pistis Sophia comes along, sees the well-made but soulless Adam2 of the Demiurge and breathes **spirit** (not a soul) into him. Adam2 begins to move, and Eve of Light begins to encourage him to open his eyes and be her consort. Adam sees Eve and says "It is you who have given me life!"

The Archons were not pleased with Eve, nor with the 2nd Adam. They knew she was of the Light like Yadabaoth, and they knew that this Adam2 was her protégé... they had to do something and said "those whom she bears will be under our charge.... [her] Adam is not one of us. Rather let us bring a deep sleep over him [and create another Eve] from his rib such that his wife may obey and he may be lord over her." (They do not get to it yet.)

Eve of the Light, being of a higher force, laughed at them, created a fake Eve, blew a mist into the Archon's eyes to blind them, and went into the **Tree of Knowledge**, and hid.

(to be continued...)

This gets even more interesting… the Gnostics are recounting something, not just making up a myth, and to a large degree it synchs up with the Sumerian/Anunnaki version as it goes on. The Anunnaki made many attempts to create a worker human, and the first (*Lulu*) could not procreate and had no soul, the second (*Adamu*) was smarter and had a soul, and the third (*Adapa*) was the crowning achievement: smart, procreated, had better genetics and a soul.

What the Gnostic account is saying is that there were two creations and the first one was a phony creation of Man and is probably where the people of Nod (above with Mouravieff) came from.

Insert: Valentinian Gnosticism

This is a brief insert so that the next part of the Demiurge vs. Archons story makes sense. Valentinian Christianity was Gnosticism (about AD 140) recognized three types of humans on the planet (See also VEG, CH.2):

> **The Elect**: the '**pneumatic**' or spirit-filled who were searching for a deeper Christian message because they lived through gnosis/insight;
>
> **The Called**: the '**psychic**' or mental man who was happy with what he knew (knowledge) and he walked by faith;
>
> **The Material man**: the '**hylic**'(*choikos*) who was incapable of understanding any spiritual message, and did not have the soul-awareness of the other two types.

What is significant about this schema is that in the early centuries AD, man was aware that **all men were not 'created equal'**, and that some men had souls and some didn't. **Hylics didn't have a soul**. [422] (These 3 types are examined again in Ch. 5 of VEG.)
Somehow, perhaps deliberately in an attempt to 'level the playing field,' that information has been lost to the modern world. And by simple inspection, we can see that this 3-tiered system could have bred **a spiritual elite** in the 'pneumatics' which appears to be a simple "better-than-you" philosophy… enough to create division in any church. (And it did among those calling themselves the **Illuminati**.) And this is probably what led to the whole teaching being hidden or rejected, and everybody was deemed (inaccurately) to be the same as everybody else. Needless to say, Valentinus' teachings were denied and refuted by the young and growing Church; he was later denounced as a heretic. So much for truth.

Gnostic Creation Story

Refocus: most of the Archons are the "good guys" – the Elohim who are trying to create a proper man and woman. Now there is the 'fake' Adam2, and there is a fake Eve (created by the Eve of the Light) – the ones created by Sophia Zoe and Sabaoth (the "bad guys"). FYI, the first Eve who has been called the Eve of the Light could also be called **Lilith** [423] who (according to Jewish folklore) [25] was not a proper helpmate for the real Adam (who at this point in the story above has yet to be created – the good guys are still planning it).

The Archons recover and discover the remaining Eve and seek to defile her and make sure that no good offspring can come from her. But they goofed and now there are several Adams running around.

The 2nd Adam is the Adam that was born from the 1st Eve and is just "spirit-endowed" (*pneumatilos*). The 1st Adam from the Archons is "soul endowed" (*psychikos*) , and the 3rd Adam from the 2nd Eve is a creature of the Earth (*choikos*). This relates directly to the **Insert** section above.

Thinking it was the real Eve, the Archons descend on Eve and get her pregnant… and she bears many offspring by them. They thought it would generate a true race. However, the result was described: "And the progeny of the earthly Adam [#2] became numerous and was completed , and produced within itself every kind of scientific information of the soul-endowed Adam [#1]. But all were in ignorance." The Archons saw that these humans could worship them and so they were initially glad. However, they began to remember that the Light Eve had turned herself into a Tree and they began to worry…

(continued…)

This is a tricky part of the original manuscript. It seems Adam1 is now the real, soul-endowed man, and Eve2 by his side was the creation of the other **Eve of Light** (who is like an ascended being, being both astral and material at will) who turned herself into a Tree of Gnosis. But the Eve now with Adam1 is Eve2.

They came up to Adam and Eve timidly and said " The fruit of all the trees created for you in Paradises hall be eaten, but as for the Tree of Acquaintance [knowledge], control yourselves and do not eat from it [because it was really the deceptive Eve playing a trick]. If you eat, you will die. " They hoped fear would keep the two safe from the Tree.

Then they said to themselves this is the true man [Adam #1] and yet Eve was a ringer and they realized that humans were still going to go awry.

Then came the wisest of all creatures [because he had been supernaturally created] called **The Beast**, and he tells Eve that God lied and the Tree is of course good to eat, they won't die, and it will grant humans Knowledge so that they [the humans] can be as gods. Adam and Eve were already immortal, now the aim of the Beast was to get them knowing everything and thus challenge the gods [Elohim].

Remember: the fruit of the Tree was the being called Eve of Light.

Eve ate and had Adam also eat. Their intellect became opened. They realized their position, they were "naked of acquaintance [gnosis]" and they now saw their creators and the Beast and "loathed them, they were very aware." Adam and Eve had been kept as **slaves** in the Garden, and they had immortality but their intellect was kept undeveloped, allowing the gods to manipulate them. So they now turned and ran and hid.

Naturally, the gods came looking for them. When they could not find them, the gods called out. [These gods were not omniscient.] Adam answered and the traditional exchange followed and the god then banished Adam and Eve from the Garden.

(continued...)

In addition, the gods could not punish the Beast as he blew a mist into their eyes as he tried to escape, but the gods cursed him, then cursed Eve and cursed Adam… removed their immortality from them.

The gods then saw that Adam had overcome the trials they had set before him, and they were again concerned. "Behold Adam! He has come to be like one of us so that he knows the difference between the light and the darkness. Now perhaps he will be further deceived and come to the Tree of Life and eat from it [which earns permanent immortality – up to now his immortality was granted at the whim of the gods]. He will despise us and disdain our glory. Then he will denounce us and our universe and we'll have real problems."

So said because Eve was not a pure creation as Adam used to be, but both having eaten of the Tree, they were now both defiled. If they gained eternal life, and are defiled, there would be big problems from the humans. So the gods kicked them out of the Garden, and set Cherubim and flaming swords around the Tree of Life so that no one would dare approach it.

They then decided to clean house and cast Adam and Eve down to the lowest level of Earth, along with the Adam2 and his progeny [which became the people in the Land of Nod]. They also cast down to Earth the 7 Rulers so that the latter "…instructed mankind in many kinds of error and magic and potions and worship of idols and spilling of blood and altars and temples and sacrifices and libations to all the **spirits of the Earth**…. Thus did the world come to exist in distraction, in ignorance, and in stupor. They all erred until the appearance of the true man [Jesus]."

And then the ancient text goes into something very relevant for our day:

> When a multitude of beings had come into existence, through the parentage of Adam…. the rulers were master over it …. They kept it **restrained by ignorance**. … since the immortal father knows that a deficiency of truth ….[would] bring to naught the rulers of perdition [7 Archon Rulers] thru the creatures they had modeled…[424]

What is being said, in a convoluted way, is that the Ruler Archons over Earth are still keeping Man ignorant, suppressing truth thru their flesh & blood 3D lackeys: the PTB who love ruling and need ignorant sheep to do it… so public education is watered down, for one thing. Then, in the quote, the rulers are chastised by the

Angel of Gnosis for keeping the humans dumb because that way it only serves the Rulers's purpose but keeps the Earth in darkness and both the Earth and humans suffer because it takes **Knowledge** to exit this School.

Then the Father of Light sent emissaries (Jesus, Buddha, Melchizedek, Zarathustra, Krishna, the Christ…) to enlighten Man and the Archons tried to mix their polluted seed with that of the chosen emissaries, and any of their offspring to pollute and defeat the race of Man, but it didn't work. Yet the emissaries were to find all kinds of seed already in the churches (see the 3 types in the Valentinian Insert, above.)
But those who heed the Logos and become children of the Light are "…superior to everyone who was before them" and by their ascension will condemn the gods of chaos, and "…ascend to their reward: peace, unending joy and glory … they shall be kings in the mortal domain." [425]

Gnostic Summary

What we have seen is the creation of Man by lesser gods (Elohim) not the God of the Universe. We also saw that there were (at least) **two creations**, several Adams, and some were missing a soul and Cain took his wife from those earlier, defective humans. The god walking in the Garden didn't know where Adam and Eve were – so it was not a case of the God of the Universe (who is omniscient) addressing them, it was a lesser god who was in charge of the Garden. It is also interesting that **Adam and Eve were not impressed with their creators**, "loathing" their appearance – which has been suggested to be something along the lines of a reptilian since Eve of Light gave birth to a Serpent which became known as The Beast. And we again saw the **Serpent** imagery.

We also saw that the Gnostics dealt with the **Trees of Life and Knowledge** and that was part of our search. Yet the Gnostics had a new twist – the Eve of Light inhabited the Tree of Knowledge (or became it – the original text is not clear on that). But there is a relevant text on the Tree of Life:

> And our sister Sophia [Pistis] is she who came down in innocence… therefore she was called Life, which is the mother of the living…. And thru her they [humans] have tasted the perfect Knowledge. I [Sophia] appeared in the form of **an Eagle on the Tree of Knowledge**…. that I might teach them and awaken them out of the depth of sleep [ignorance]. For they were both in a fallen state and they recognized their nakedness [non-Knowledge state]. The Epinoia appeared to them as a light and She awakened their thinking. [426]

It was also interesting to see Eve as a creator, of course it was Eve of the Light, an angelic-type being with supernatural powers, and she created her look-alike, the Eve2 that paired up with Adam1. There is an interesting parallel with the Chinese Nü Wa

(Ch. 4) where Nü Wa drops a rope in the mud and its **drops become humans**, and then the Gnostics add this:

> Now the production … came about as follows. When Sophia let fall a **droplet of light** it flowed onto the water, and immediately a human appeared, being androgynous. That droplet she molded as a female body…. An androgynous human being was produced whom the Greeks call Hermaphrodites, and **whose mother the Hebrews call Eve of Life (Zoe)**… [427]

The drops of life and the Eagle in the Tree suggest connections with the Chinese and the Norse… coincidence, or was there a communication by a common 3rd party?

And remember that the first Eve was also called **Lilith**… who was not acceptable as a mate for Adam1 (See footnote 420). Lilith connects with **Inanna**, an Anunnaki goddess.

For agnostics/atheists and the Fundamentalists, it will be easy to just diss the above as a Gnostic rewrite of the Genesis account, and go on as if it were just a myth. What catches the perceptive person's eye however, is that the Gnostic account has many similarities with the Sumerian account of Creation, and the "gods" in the Gnostic version are just the gods called the Anunnaki and the Gnostics were recounting the same story but playing safe about it: ETs were not that well-accepted as a possibility 1800 years ago.

As Man grows thru the next 100 years, and embarks on space travel, genetic manipulations, and even meets some ETs who recorded the history of Earth, it will seem that dissing the Gnostic account and dissing the similar Sumerian Anunnaki account will appear to be as idiotic as the people 500 years ago who thought the Earth was flat. Man is very slow to wake up and entertain new ideas.

And yet, there are the Illuminati and the Rosicrucians who formed secret societies as they were not afraid to learn from their Hermetic, Kabbalistic and Gnostic brothers and guard the sacred teachings of the ages.

Rosicrucianism

This will not be a complete examination of "The Rosy Cross" as it is sometimes called. It is said to have been founded in late medieval Germany by Christian Rosenkreuz . It holds a doctrine or theology "built on esoteric truths of the ancient past", which "concealed from the average man, provide insight into nature, the physical universe and the spiritual realm." [428]

The Rosicrucian Order was founded in or around AD 1407 and consisted of 8 men, all doctors and bachelors who were sworn to secrecy about the teachings that the founder, Christian himself, had had no success in promoting publicly. After studying in the **Middle East** under various masters, adhering to **Sufism**, he was unable to spread the knowledge he had acquired to any prominent European figures. As a result he took it into a secret society, saying that it would be revealed when the public was ready to accept it. Even his later manifestos were dissed as either hoaxes or just allegorical statements.

And yet, for such an allegedly nonsensical organization, throughout the years there have been no less than 33 organizations founded upon its teachings, all the way from the 1750's to the year 2008. About AD 1782, this highly secretive society added Egyptian, Greek and Druidic mysteries to its alchemy system. There are links from Rosicrucianism to the Knights Templar, the Golden Dawn, the "Invisible College" (natural philosophers and scientists which later morphed into the Royal Society), the Scottish Rite, and Freemasonry.

For inspiration, the later followers of the founder did spend some time **in the Middle East among the Sufi,** studying occult teachings, just as did Gurdjieff and Ouspensky 200 years later.

> In his 1618 pamphlet, *Pia et Utilissima Admonitio de Fratribus Rosae Crucis*, Heinrichus Neuhusius wrote that the Rosicrucians departed for **the east** due to European instability caused by the start of the Thirty Year's War [1618-1648]. In 1710, Sigmund Richter, founder of the secret society of the Golden & Rosy Cross, also suggested the Rosicrucians had migrated **eastward**. In the first half of the 20th century, René Guénon, a researcher of the occult, presented this same idea in some of his works.[429] [emphasis added]

The point being to substantiate "Mohammed going to the mountain" instead of the other way around. If these adepts studied anywhere the Mesopotamian heart of the Serpent Wisdom teachings, they were sure to have come across some of the esoteric teachings. In Arabia it would have been the Imams, in Egypt it would have been the Ulema (in Alexandria) along with the Therapeuts, and in India (if they got that far) it could have been the sadhus.

Sufi Serpents

At this point it is valuable to take a quick look at the Sufis since they were an elite group of adepts whose teachings reflected their secret traditions and an ancient lineage of masters reaching back thousands of years – and would have time-wise been a convenient era in which to have received the Serpent Wisdom teachings from its source (just up the road in Mesopotamia).

The earliest Sufi adepts were a solitary group of itinerant mystics who wandered the desert and sought oases and caves to meditate. These early nomads were exalted spiritual masters who were known for their elevated states of consciousness and their magical powers. The modern Sufi Idris Shah says:

> The Sufi ancients could walk on water, describe events taking place at vast distances, experience the true reality of life. When one master spoke, his hearers went into a state of mystical rapture and developed magical powers. Wherever Sufis went, mystics of other persuasions.... became their disciples – sometimes without a word having been spoken.[430]

It looks like we have found a group who truly possess the Serpent Wisdom and the **Serpent Fire** which is what gives them their ability.

With the coming of Mohammed and the Muslim Empire, the Sufis divided into two main groups: those who joined society and became university professors, alchemists, Astronomers, and doctors, teachers and Imams. The second main group devoted themselves to founding monasteries and retreats to support their solitary ways.
As Mohammed's influence spread, so too did the Sufis migrate, and they wound up in Egypt, Turkey, India, China, and continued to assimilate the esoteric teachings of each country's secret societies. The Sufi masters recognized the same universal truths uniting all the diverse traditions and they accepted other spiritual teachers "Sufis." And thus, Christ, Zoroaster and Thoth-Hermes were accepted Sufi patriarchs. [431]

Baraka

One of the Sufi teachings centered around something called "Baraka" or serpent power which is...

> ...a three-syllabled name which referred both to the union of the Male (Ba or Ra) and female principles (Ka) as well as to the serpent and its triune powers [reincarnation, regeneration and wisdom]. The grandmasters of each Sufi Order normally possessed immense amounts of Baraka and wielded the serpent's three powers thereby allowing them to accomplish almost any supernatural feat....The Baraka was transmitted from Master to disciple when s/he was Ready. Upon transference, the power would awaken the inner fire serpent [*Kundalini*] and consummate a rapid process of [spiritual] alchemical unfoldment. [432]

That is what this is all about –not so much the data but the experience of the Serpent Fire. It wasn't the written teachings that enlightened the initiate, but it did help prepare him/her to understand the **context** of the new world in which they would find themselves following the enlightening experience.

> **Baraka** can be found within physical objects, places, and people, as chosen by God. This force begins by flowing directly from God into creation that is worthy of baraka. These creations endowed with baraka can then transmit the flow of baraka to the other creations of God through physical proximity or through the adherence to the spiritual practices of the Islamic prophet Muhammad. God is the sole source of baraka and has the power to grant and withhold baraka.[433]

Baraka is the God Force. And those who have been initiated via the Serpent Fire, can access it and use it. Just imagine the Alchemists in Europe looking for ways to transform themselves spiritually and discovering that the Sufis had already found it… they would beat a path to the Middle East. And that was what many of them did, the more famous ones were Christian Rosenkreutz (above), Gurdjieff, Ouspensky, Mme Blavatsky and of course, the German *Ahnenerbe* looking for power in ancient teachings.

To emphasize: there must have been something about the East that so many "seekers of truth" went East to discover the truth about Man, Life, God… and that was where the Anunnaki had begun the Serpent Wisdom groups which later became the White Brotherhood. If the connection is valid, then there might be something(s) we can discover in the Rosicrucian ideas that were brought back from the Sufis, and that *have* become public, such as their signatory document published in 1614.

Fama Fraternitatis

This is an account of Brother Christian Rosenkreutz' (CRC) life and said, among other things, that the Church was suppressing the secret knowledge of the spirit. The author claimed to represent an illuminated brotherhood of adepts who were set to perform a spiritual reformation of the whole world. Martin Luther would have loved it, but he died 70 years before. If we can believe the "press release:"

> The Brotherhood opened Rosenkreutz' tomb after 120 years to find that he hadn't aged any since his death (at age 106), and they found a parchment book which was a collection of sayings, divine revelations, and secrets of heaven – that he literally took to the grave.[434]

The book showed that CRC was an adept and one of the 'treasures' he collected was the secret of the transmutation of metals. It suggests that the Brotherhood also holds the secrets "to a thousand better things." Further it maintains that all of Christendom can benefit from the enlightenment found in the teachings of Rosicrucianism. Further publications in Europe led people to believe that the Rosicrucian 'Army' was already among them and ready to take over, secretly living among the public, and as a result no member of the society dared to announce his or her membership for fear of being stoned. Yet many publications continued to speak of the wonders, benefits, and presence of the Rosicrucians among the populace.

The Jesuits were so alarmed, trying to support the Church, that they produced bogus manifestos with the goal of portraying the Rosicrucians as devil-worshippers. This led to crazed witch hunts and the Inquisition. Obviously, the Church felt threatened, as they always have (until recent history) by those who know more, are truly enlightened, have psychic abilities and want to spread their Light among people.

> For those who doubt this, and the Church has admitted to it in the *Catholic Encyclopedia*, that was the aim of the **Inquisition** – 600+ years [1100's – 1794] of persecution and often death for people who would contradict the Church. (The Church is examined and exonerated in VEG, Ch. 11; i.e., they did what they had to do to maintain societal order at the time where humans were ignorant and panicked easily.)

Proponents of Rocicrucianism were often from the ranks of the alchemists, such as **Dr. John Dee** (astrologer and mage to Queen Elizabeth I), and **Michael Sendivogius** who was a **Paracelsian** physician and healed people with his own potions, **Robert Fludd**, and **Johan Andreae** who wrote much about the society and probably wrote the *Chemical Wedding* and the *Fama Fraternitatis* – although he denied it. In fact, it might have been he who was the Christian Rosenkreutz since modern investigation has determined that the name was that of an allegorical figure.

Nonetheless, what teachings or beliefs can we extract from what IS known about Rosicrucianism?

Rosicrucianism Teachings

For starters, we might look to what is known and shown about **Freemasonry**.

> Freemasonry, the most famous and influential of secret societies, **absorbed the ideals and mysticism of Rosicrucianism**, providing it with a lasting , though sadly unfulfilled, legacy.[435]

And

> …the Rosicrucian movement is **eclectic** and draws upon the diverse mystical traditions of ancient Greece, China, India, and Persia.[436]

Freemasonry and Rosicrucianism share a common basis and probably a common origin. Could their esoteric teachings have originated with Serpent Wisdom in Atlantis or Lemuria?

According to one author, who is aware that Atlanteans interacted with the Anunnaki…

> When their Motherlands eventually collapsed and began to sink to the bottom of their respective seas, the Serpents of Wisdom bundled up their ancient wisdom and migrated to various parts of the globe, where they were welcomed by the indigenous people as "Serpent" prophets. Under their guidance, numerous **"Dragon Cultures,"** which were comprised of colossal pyramids, multitudinous serpent motifs, and ruled over by Dragon Kings, eventually came into existence. These Dragon Cultures continued to survive for many thousands of years.
>
> Beginning approximately two thousand years ago, the Serpents of Wisdom and their Dragon Cultures encountered an inimical foe in the Christian Church. The patriarchs of the new Christian faith judged the old serpent wisdom to be heretical and began an initiative to completely stamp it out. Fortunately, before these upstarts could were successful in their iconoclastic campaign , many of the Serpents disappeared "underground" and were able to safely preserve ancient knowledge. They later resurfaced as the Islamic Sufis and their eventual heirs, the **Templars, Freemasons and Rosicrucians** who kept the flame of serpent wisdom alive while inspiring and organizing the revolutions which have slowly precipitated a democratic world. [437]

That is an interesting insight on our world and the fact that, as author Wm Bramley has said, we are watched over by the **Custodians**, or as the Book of Enoch said, The **Watchers**. Man is special and there is a group that is determined to see him grow and develop his divine potential – just as Enki, the Anunnaki Science Officer, intended.

What that means is that what we have seen about Hermeticism and the principles outlined by the Emerald Tablet, as well as The Kybalion, are part of the Serpent Wisdom teachings… and others in the next chapter.

Freemasonry Overview

Returning to the Freemasons for a minute, it is said that some of the secret teachings are shown in some of the Freemason pictures:

Masonic Hall, Bury St Edmunds, Suffolk, England
(credit: Wikipedia: Freemasonry.)

What is significant here is the **black & white checkered floor** – a standard item in all Freemason temples. The checkered floor is a representation of the ground floor of King Solomon's Temple. It is also called The Masonic Pavement and is emblematical of human life, checked with good and evil.[438]

Those are aprons hanging from the ceiling… signs of rank (probably from deceased members). Living members wear their aprons into the Masonic meetings, take one of the seats, and the Lodge Grand Master officiates – business may be some local charity work they are doing. Masons are very proactive in their communities.

Then there are the Masonic aprons which have some unusual symbols:

(credit: http://masonicsymbols.blogspot.com/2011/01/masonic-aprons.html)

There is the B&W checkered floor, the Twin Pillars, the **All-seeing Eye** (remember Horus?), and what looks like a UFO (poor image of an apron?) hovering in the air just to the right of the back-left pillar. **Seven stars** could be the Pleiades (Boy, they get around!), and then there is the Pythagorean 3-triangular boxes, 5-pointed star (Pentagram pointed up is positive), and the **Masonic Compass and Square**. God is recognized as the Supreme Architect. Note the **beehive** on the center of the flap: The beehive represents industry, not the Mormon Church.

Then there is this one with a pyramid and a serpent in it (upper flap):

Did you notice the **Ouroboros** (serpent) encircling the Compass and Square? (The serpent head is just below the point of the upper flap.) The rest are symbols of the building profession, or symbols that speak of divinity (such as the "G" above the temple), or the brotherhood of the Masons. Again, note the **B&W checkered floor** at the temple. The **Skull & Crossbones** go way back into the beginnings of Masonry and Egypt, and even to the Knights Templar who used it to represent Golgotha (where Jesus was crucified), and it also is a warning to members to not reveal any secrets of Masonry to outsiders. It is also a reminder of one's mortality – don't procrastinate. And there are **trees** on the hill.

Lastly, we have another serpent-related apron:

The hand (left side) is holding a serpent; possibly signifying "taking hold of the Serpent of Wisdom" – and that is what we are looking for. And the symbols: "As Above, So Below" in the 6-pointed stars (influence from Kabbalah).

Thus, somewhere in the past – and in the higher ranks of the Masons – the Serpent was acknowledged to be "the wisest of all creatures" and advanced levels no doubt knew the secrets of Hermeticism, Kabbalah, and Gnosticism – which it is suggested are the same since Truth is Truth.

And a Scottish Rite Lodge in the Washington DC area in May-June 2012 held a very interesting open meeting –inviting Masons and the general public to a fascinating presentation:

Masonic Tree of Life

Just when it looked like there were no more Tree of Life images to be found, up comes an in-depth seminar by 33d degree Masons, no less. The seminar topics are shown below (taken from their website):

> Students will have the opportunity to learn how the different mystical traditions view the spiritual path to enlightenment. These hand-picked spiritual luminaries will address the question: **How do traditional spiritual paths serve the needs of humanity in the 21st century?** The great wisdom traditions emerged at a time when life was radically different than it is today. The world has changed immeasurably in the past two thousand years, and human beings have changed along with it. We live a global existence, and it is more important than ever that we promote understanding between the various traditions. Science also has entered into the equation and has become a predominate influence in the search for enlightenment. **The new humanity faces a new set of challenges**—and a new set of opportunities.
>
> Seminar topics are: "**Kabbalah,**" Dr. Darryl Carter; "**Sufism**," Dr. Julianne Hazen, Director of Sufi Studies, Sufi Center, Medina, NY; "**Vedanta Yoga**," MW George R. Adams 33°, Grand Cross, JD, MBA; "**Science,**" Dr. Pierre Gaujard, 33°, Physicist; "**Buddhism,**" Ven. Bhante Katugastota Uparatana, Buddhist Chaplain American University; "**Esoteric Christianity**," Bro. Marcel J. Desroches, Jr., KCCH, Rosicrucian; "**Taoism,**" Dr. Darryl Carter; and "**Freemasonry,**" MW George R. Adams, 33°, Grand Cross, JD, MBA.
>
> This event is open to everyone interested in the subject. There is no requirement for Masonic or Scottish Rite affiliation. For information on attending this seminar (in person or virtually), visit **dcsr.org/seminar.**

(Credit: https://scottishrite.org/about/media-publications/journal/article/current-interest-the-tree-of-life-seminar-series-a-unique-learning-experience/)

Note the **33rd degree masons** teaching in 3 of the topics! They do know their esoteric teachings. And just as interesting was the following…

This was the picture of the **Tree of Life** accompanying their advertisement:

This is vaguely resembling the Egyptian Hathor and the Sun motif – note that the Tree's branches do not cover the 'Sun' but enfold it as the Sun is enfolded in the picture below:

(credits: dcsr.org and Bing Images)

If you look closely at Hathor (right), there is a **serpent** on the lower right of the "U" horn.

The only thing missing from their seminar is an examination of the Egyptian Mysteries – but then, that is typically Rosicrucian (AMORC).

Summary

And in fact, there is no point in trying to identify what the Truth was for each of the secret movements – much of it is still closely guarded, but if it could be discerned… note that it would resemble the Truth and axioms presented in Chapter 10 in the section entitled **"Hermetic Principles" subsections I and II**.

We can tell something about the secret principles by observing those who were privy to the Serpent Wisdom – whether in Freemasonry, Rosicrucianism, or Hermeticism. There were initiates that we have all heard about who lived their lives from an understanding of the Truth.

And that is the link with the final Chapter 13.

Chapter 13: The Shining Ones

So now we have come to the "wrap it all up" chapter. We have traced the Serpent Wisdom around the planet, and seen that the Tree of Life was often part of a culture's religion, and there was often an emphasis on *Kundalini* for personal development. We also saw that The Flood and Creation stories were pretty much the same around the planet. And we saw that there were white men with beards visiting the Americas and educating the natives.

Lastly, we also included some of the latest findings, regarding the search for Planet X, the discovery of pyramids off the Cuban coast, and the latest findings regarding **Göbekli Tepe**. It is clear that there was and is much more happening on Earth than we were aware, and some of it goes back significantly into the far past and threatens to rewrite some of the history books. Man's real history is not taught in the public schools and is much more interesting -- but many humans are fragile and unable to handle the truth (Think: Brookings Report, 1962), so the truth is white-washed and not what we have been led to safely believe.

Historical Insight Ia

> Wouldn't it be interesting to discover that what we have thought were ETs and their UFOs are nothing more than a very advanced race <u>on Earth</u> (or in a base on the back side of the Moon) that is still monitoring and covertly assisting us to grow?
>
> If such is the case, then any announcement that Atlantis or Hyper-Borea was real and that those **Ancient Agents of Fire** are still here (albeit hidden), would put them at risk, thus the wisest policy would be to deny anything that is not Plain Vanilla Science, Plain Vanilla Archeology or Plain Vanilla Religion, or Anthropology, and control the sheep – for the safety of <u>all</u> involved.
>
> (to be continued… in **Ib**)

Ancient Agents of Fire

First let's rewind and identify the term "Serpent Wisdom"…

Serpent – relates to the *Kundalini* awakening in Man because the process resembles two serpents ascending the spine.

Wisdom – the awakened state in Man that results in knowing the truth about Man, the Earth, and God. In short, True Wisdom. Sample Wisdom was given in Chapters 10 and 12, and more is given at the end of this chapter.

The secret societies initiated by Enki sought to deliver *Kundalini* awakening to Man, to stimulate the process of human development – the awakening helps Man to achieve his **true potential** by releasing the Divine Fire (i.e., **Dragon Fire**) at the base of the spine and activates his latent abilities – connecting his Consciousness with his Subconscious and Superconscious so that he can experience a unified conscious connection with his **Higher Self**. In short, he'd awaken latent (potential) psychic abilities and (eventually) become god-like himself.

This is what the Church was hoping to prevent.

And in a way, it was wise: awakening a person who does not have the discipline nor the altruistic orientation would create a potential monster who would misuse his new abilities. With the proper training, preparation and discipline the initiate should become more of a Master, an awakened soul who serves others. In short, an STO soul not STS.

Thus secret societies did not make themselves known to the public, but the few "insiders" would have to observe other humans and choose whom they could recommend to the multi-stage initiation process. The awakening process was always lengthy to insure that initiates were sincere, dedicated and disciplined so that by the time they get to the *Kundalini* awakening stage, they have been 'vetted' and will probably not misuse the higher abilities they gain from the knowledge and awakening.

Along the way, the secret societies taught the truth of Man's tripartite nature: body, soul and spirit, as well as Conscious, Subconscious, and Superconscious aspect of the Mind. And the true nature of the Trinity, the Godhead, Angels and Masters would be explained.

So the secret society was basically two things: esoteric Teaching and *Kundalini* awakening.

Now the question remaining is: Who were the adepts, the Masters who initially were qualified to lead Enki's Serpent Brotherhoods? Enki did not do it all himself, and while the Priest Groups that he formed (using **Adapa+**) to help guide and rule in the cities like Ur, Nippur, Babylon, Ninevah, Uruk and Eidu, were not qualified to lead the Serpent Brotherhood esoteric work.
The truth is: Enki got it from Others who were <u>already here</u> on Earth – the Shining Ones.

The Shining Ones

As a group throughout history, they have gone by many names: [439]

> Abgal, **Akhu**, Anak, Anannage, Ancient Masters, Angels, Annedoti, **Anunnaki**, **Devas**, Elders, Feathered Serpents (Quetzalcoatl), Fish Beings (Oannes), Gibborim, Grigori, **Djinn, Nagas, Neteru**, Nommo, Seraphim, Seven Sages, **Serpents**, **Shemsu Hor**, **Tuatha dé Danaan**, **Watchers** …
> There were also the Ennead in Egypt, the gods of the Amerindians, the Magi and the Elohim from the Bible….

The list is longer but that references most of them.

Note that *elohim* is the plural for *el* – which means 'shining' in Sumerian. It was mistranslated 'God' in the Bible, whereas it should have been translated 'the gods' who made Man 'in their image.' The Semitic word *el* is found in many ancient languages. The Anglo-Saxon word *aelf* for 'elf,' which is a supernatural being, also means 'shining being' such that *el* should be translated as 'the shining one.' Thus *elohim* would be 'the shining ones.' [440]

Researching other civilizations in depth does discover that there have been (and are) these Agents of Fire all over the globe – it is a global phenomenon. These are the intelligent beings who have existed all around the world and have emerged at various points in history – to guide Man. It doesn't matter if they have been called Anunnaki, **Tuatha dé Dannan, Shemsu Hor**, Serpents or Devas – they all share the same enlightenment and altruistic desire to benefit Man… and they have been there all along. Man is not alone. Man has never been alone.

The last public interaction of the gods was in Rome as the Roman Gods… after that, they "disappeared" in synch with the newest dictum that said: "Man will be assisted to develop, but let's stay in the shadows see what he does with what we give him."

> This is reminiscent of the *Star Trek* stated **Non-interference Directive**: It doesn't work to always be visible and tell Man what to do all the time-- Man came to resent that and the gods (e.g., Devas) want to see what Man will do if he thinks he is doing it all himself and They aren't watching. Of course, the minute he tries to launch nuclear ICBMs, he will be stopped – and Their control was demo'ed at **Maelstrom AFB** (March 1967) as a warning that Man is not free to destroy himself nor the planet. He is to be given the tools and like a 5-year-old learning about fire, he will be watched, hence the group called The **Watchers**.

Over time these Enlightened Ones, such as the Devas, chose certain humans to be their 'channels' to society, i.e., their spokesmen as it were, and gave them the knowledge to help others, and then this group of men naturally formed an Elite Brotherhood – the Brotherhood of the Serpent.

Circles of Light

And while we're at it, please note that **Sumer** (Sumeria) was the home of a group of the Shining Ones called the Anunnaki, and 'Sumer' comes from *Shumer* which in reality means 'the land of the Watchers.' The **Watchers** were also Shining Ones, and Sumer was also known as the biblical Shin'ar – 'the place of the Shining Ones.'

The Egyptian **Neteru** (above list) can also be translated as 'Watchers' – thus the meaning is rather focused. These were beings of Light, Knowledge, and they let their Light Shine. Such a designated 'shining' was painted the only way artists could do it – as a halo:

The bigger the halo, the more holiness (and Light) was implied.

And yet, it is interesting to consider that there was a beginning group who came from ….? and historical religious/spiritual tradition says that it was the **Devas**. The Anunnaki that have been mentioned throughout this (and other authors' books) were not the first… and as was suggested earlier, the Anunnaki might not even have been ETs – it was just said they were those who "from Heaven to Earth came…" and heaven was always in the sky… In short the gods landed. But they were not the first…

The Devas

This is an important connection for this part of the chapter. The paragraph header did not specify Hindu nor Buddhist… because there are multiple references to Devas in the spiritual literature, among different cultures and gods. The Devas were known as **Agents of Serpent Fire.**

Alleged picture of a Deva…[441]

If one has astral sight, or can see auras, this is what a Deva might look like. Mostly flame (in multiple colors) and about the height of a man.

Deva is masculine
Devi (Dewi) is feminine

(**credit: http://www.eioba.org/files/user2314/devas.jpg Geoffrey Hodson**)

Buddhist Devas

They can be generally all be said to have these things in common: [442]

> Devas are **invisible** to the human eye. The presence of a deva can be detected by those humans who have opened the "Divine eye" …. [The 3rd Eye, or Ajna] an extrasensory power by which one can see beings from other planes. Their voices can also be heard by those who have cultivated divyaśrotra, a similar power of the ear.

> Most devas are also capable of constructing illusory forms by which they **can manifest themselves** to the beings of lower worlds; higher and lower devas even have to do this between each other.
>
> Devas do not require the same kind of sustenance as humans do, although the lower kinds do eat and drink. The higher sorts of deva **shine with their own intrinsic luminosity**.
>
> Devas are also capable of moving great distances speedily and of **flying through the air**, although the lower devas sometimes accomplish this through magical aids such as **a flying chariot**. [emphasis added]

It is said that Devas arrived on Earth before humans and remained inactive (dormant) until humankind reached a certain level of development.

> Accounts like this have led some authors to advocate the 'alien' hypothesis – the idea that 'alien reptiles' or serpents spawned human civilization. But it can be shown that the use of the term 'serpent' …. is simply *symbolic* and the associated stories are simply hiding a true and very rational history. [443]

Except for the fact that the *Enuma Elish* and the *Atra Hasis* and the Jewish *Haggahdah* and the Babylonian scribe Berossus say that **the serpents walked around**, and were reptiles, that might work for a while … It is also said that Enki was called a 'Serpent' and had the countenance of one (See VEG, Ch. 3). As we saw in Chapters 4 and 8, there are Nagas, Serpent Beings…. These may also be the **Djinn**.

> It would be very arrogant of Man to declare that the reptilian hominid lifeform does not exist in the Universe. The variety of sentient forms Out There is probably endless – Why limit the Creator and say what She did or didn't do? There are multiple records of people being abducted and even visited by UFOs and they report different lifeforms on the same ship – Greys, Lizards, Preying Mantis, Nordics and short Blues … It would be best to keep an open mind…

Actual reptile or not, it makes no difference, really. As used in this book, the reference to 'Serpent' this-and-that is using the symbolic meaning as it refers primarily to the Serpent Wisdom teachings and practices. True enough, a lot of those listed above as Shining Ones were not serpentine in appearance.

Hindu Devas

The Hindu version of the Deva arises from a Sanskrit word found in **Vedic literature** from about 200 BC. It has been translated as "heavenly, divine, terrestrial things of high excellence, **exalted, shining ones**".

> The Sanskrit *deva-* derives from Indo-Iranian **dev-* which in turn descends from the Proto-Indo-European word, **deiwos*, originally an adjective meaning "celestial" or "**shining**", which is a (not synchronic Sanskrit) vrddhi derivative from the root **diw* meaning "**to shine**", especially as the day-lit sky. According to Douglas Harper, the etymological roots of *Deva* mean "a shining one," from *div- "to shine," and it is a cognate with Greek dios "divine." [444]

From that, we can gather that Divine Beings also shine.

Devas are benevolent supernatural beings in the Vedic era literature, with **Indra** (left) as their leader.

Recall that Indra was venerated in the **Göbekli Tepe** site – in Chapter 7.

So let's take a quick look at who this Indra was…

Indra

Indra, (Sanskrit: इन्द्र) is **the leader of the Devas** and the lord of Svargaloka or a level of Heaven in Hinduism. He is the Deva of rain and thunderstorms.
He wields a **lightning thunderbolt** [like Thor and Odin] and rides on a white elephant known as Airvata. His home is situated on **Mount Meru** [see Chapter 4] in the heavens. He is celebrated as a demiurge who pushes up the sky, releases Ushas (dawn)… and slays **Vritra**… [445] [emphasis added]

Great, what is **Vritra**?

Vritra is of course a figure in the early Vedic religion… a **serpent or a dragon**. It is also the adversary of Indra. (Think: St. George and the Dragon.)

> Vritra was also known in the Vedas as **Ahi** (Sanskrit: अहि ahi, lit. **'snake'**). He appears as a dragon blocking the course of the rivers and is heroically slain by Indra [with a thunderbolt]. [446]

The **thunderbolt** was last seen used by Thor and Odin – perhaps it is a tool of the gods, representing some technology that was never documented in the Norse *Eddas* nor in the Vedas… Interesting how the same imagery keeps coming around.

And here we go again…

> For this feat, Indra became known as Vritrahan "slayer of Vritra" and also as "**slayer of the first-born of dragons**". Vritra's mother, **Danu** (who was also the mother of the **Danava** race of Asuras [bad Devas]), was then attacked and defeated by Indra with his **thunder-bolt.** [447]

Whoa… wait! Danu? The mother of the **Tuatha dé Dannan**? (Chapter 3). This is unreal. What connection does Danu have with the Hindus….? And who were the **Danavas**?

> Remember from Chapter 3 that the Tuatha dé Dannan were very powerful, supernatural beings who were said to be able to do magic – create fogs, heal people, sink ships…shapeshift, and create illusions. And Danu was their mother.

We have a very interesting 'coincidence:' the king of the Anunnaki was Anu and the leader of the Tuatha dé Dannan was Danu. Note also that Anunnaki (Anunna) is similar to Dannan… Is there a connection?

Danavas Characteristics

Besides unusual longevity, the Danavas possessed many "superhuman" capacities known as *siddhi.* The Vedas indicate that they were wise, artful and knew secrets of magic, specifically maya **(illusion).** They could appear in various forms such as elephants, lions and tigers, and even rakshasas [demonic beings] as well as becoming **invisible Nagas**. Their descendants continued to possess these *siddhi.* The Danavas also possessed **advanced technology.** [448]

> The **Tuatha dé Dannan** also possessed technology: the large Gundestrup Caldron – when a sick person was placed in it, they were healed, and (shades of Inanna, Chapter 1), a dead person could be resurrected in it.[449]

It is reasonable that the Tuatha originated in or near India, perhaps migrating to Ireland. It is known that they came in 32 ships from the Mediterranean…

> The Danaans were descendants of earlier invaders, the Nemedians, some of whom had returned to Greece… [when the Nemedians were attacked by the Formorians] King Smol of Greece sent an army to help them… [450]

Although this book is not about the history of Ireland nor that of the Tuatha, there are some interesting coincidences…

Jain Devas

The Jain are another religious sect from India who also count the Devas as real celestial beings who can be born into a body on Earth…

Jainism is an ancient religion that prescribes the path of non-violence towards all living beings. Jains believe that a human being who has conquered all inner passions comes to possess omniscience; such a person is called a **Jina** (conqueror). The path practiced and preached by *Jinas* is Jainism, and the followers of the path are called Jains. The philosophy distinguishes the soul (consciousnesses) from the body (matter). Jains believe that all living beings are really soul, intrinsically perfect and immortal. Souls in reincarnation (that is, still undergoing repeated births and deaths) are said to be imprisoned in the body. *Ahiṃsā* (non-violence) and self-control are said to be the means to liberation. The liberated souls [are] free from Karma. [451]

> Jains have the highest degree of literacy of any religious community in India (94.1 percent), and their manuscript libraries are the oldest in the country. [452]
>
> **Deva** is a term used to refer the celestial beings in Jainism. They are born instantaneously in special beds without any parents… According to Jain texts, clairvoyance (*avadhi jnana*) based on birth is possessed by the celestial beings. [453]

According to Jain texts, the celestial beings are of four orders (classes):

Residential
Peripatetic
Stellar
Heavenly beings

There are often, eight, five and twelve classes up to the Heavenly beings (*kalpavasis*). There are ten grades in each of these classes of celestial beings, the Lord (**Indra**), his Equal, the Minister, the courtiers, the bodyguards, the police, the army, the citizens, the servants, and the menials.

This is the relevant Jain concept of the Universe: [454]

A Jain Tree of Life….

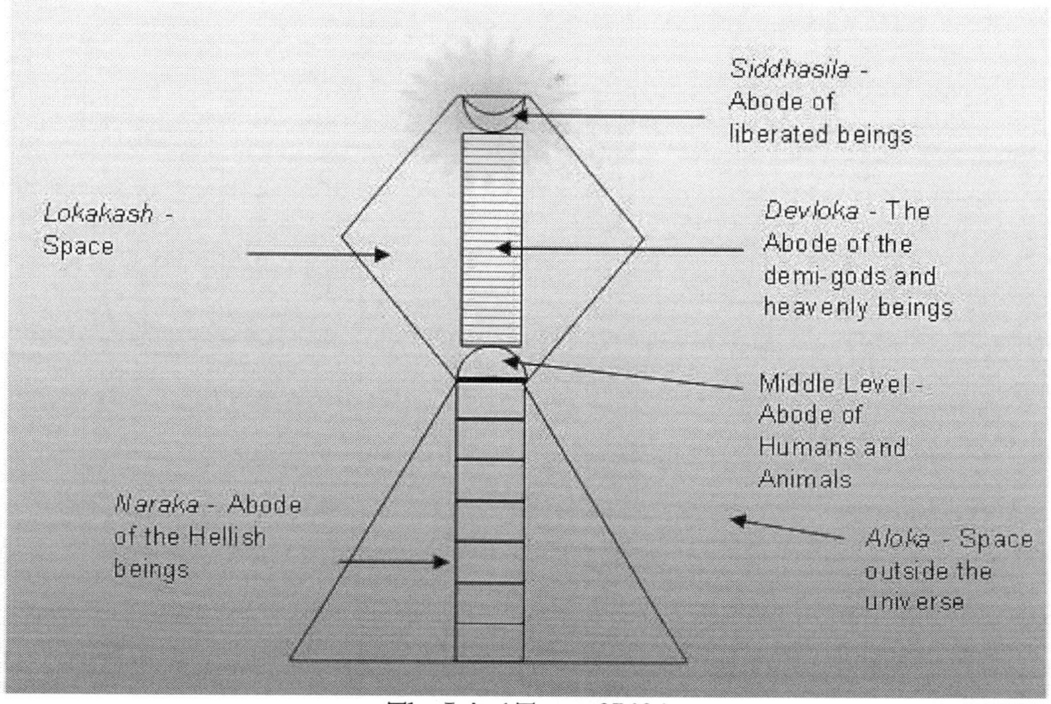

The Jain ' Tree of Life'
(credit: https://en.wikipedia.org/wiki/Jainism)

The chart is pretty accurate and even looks like a **'Tree'** (the structure also resembles Yggdrasil, the Norse Tree of Life) but its major significance is that it does reflect some of the secret society teaching about the Universe. We live in a hierarchy consisting of levels (e.g., 3D thru 7D) and there is a **hierarchy of beings** who serve from The One down to Man – and including some beings in the Astral. (This was explored in VEG Ch.7.)

The **relationship between the soul and karma** is explained by the analogy of gold. Gold is always found mixed with impurities in its natural state. Similarly, the ideal pure state of the soul is always mixed with the impurities of *karma*. Just like gold, purification of the soul may be achieved if the proper methods of **refining** are applied. The Jain karmic theory is used to attach responsibility to individual action and is cited to explain inequalities, suffering and pain.[455]

Refining: Steel is not made without fire.

Jain texts propound that **the universe was never created**, nor will it ever cease to exist. It is independent and self-sufficient, and does not require any superior power to govern it. Elaborate descriptions of the shape and function of the physical and metaphysical universe, and its constituents, are provided in the canonical Jain texts.[456]

Göbekli Tepe Again

So here, in Jainism, we have **Indra** as an important god in the hierarchy of Devas. And recall that Indra was venerated and thanked for the *Kundalini* service rendered in **Göbekli Tepe – Turkey** which is not that far from India, and thus there is probably a connection, as yet undiscovered, between India and Turkey. Whereas India was using Sanskrit (around 300 BC), Göbekli Tepe was using Paleo-Sanskrit, an older version (dating back to 15,000 BC). Tracing that etymology is beyond the purview of this book.

So lastly, we come to another realm where the Devas are venerated…

New Age Devas

A **Deva** in the New Age movement refers to any of the spiritual forces or beings behind Nature. The word 'deva' was borrowed from the Sanskrit language. According to Theosophist Charles Webster Leadbeater **devas represent a separate <u>evolution</u> to that of <u>humanity</u>.** (like Djinn?) The concept of Devas as nature spirits was further developed in the writings of Theosophist Geoffrey Hodson (whose Deva picture was featured earlier). It is believed that there are numerous different types of Devas with a population in the millions performing different functions on Earth to help the ecology function better. It is asserted they can be observed by those whose third eye has been activated. [457]

So it appears that **the Devas were the start** of the Serpent Wisdom movement, and it is easy to see where the Anunnaki showing up, and creating Man, would count themselves as Shining Ones and probably worked with the Devas to formulate the Serpent Wisdom process… they both were among the earliest Agents of Fire that we know of, and it is suggested that **Hyperborea and Atlantis** cannot be ruled out as places where they might have lived.

> The Greek and Roman gods always stayed just out of human reach – up on Mt. Olympus, up in their ziggurats, or in their "casitas" at the top of the Mayan pyramids… **Mt. Meru** in Hyperborea would have been another high dwelling.

No Aliens

At this point it can be pointed out that there is no need for the Anunnaki to have been ETs, and the Devas (remember there are higher and lower classes) might have been from another dimension, or just materializations from the Astral realm (Think: Djinn). The general consensus among scholars and priests, rabbis, and Theosophists is that **the Shining Ones have always been here**.

Some have attributed these otherworldly powers [displayed by the Shining Ones] to ancient spacemen or extraterrestrials, but it is more probable that we are dealing with people who had become enlightened thru the *kundalini* experience and had formed a priesthood. Then after what may have been a global cataclysm, those Shining Ones who survived dedicated themselves to the task of instructing the rest of mankind in their knowledge so that it could be preserved in the event of future catastrophes ....

Whatever the catastrophe was that ended the so-called Golden Age and the Shining Ones' reign as 'gods' and 'shepherds of men' according to the ancient texts, the survivors came ashore in different parts of the world and were forced to live with their more primitive neighbors and so taught the rest of mankind their knowledge... [458]

Aztecs and the Seven Sages

Again, according to the Egyptian **Edfu 'Building Texts'** (inscribed on the walls of the Temple of Edfu, between Luxor and Aswan), a group of divine beings, sometimes called the **Seven Sages** or "the builder gods" came from an island which had submerged due to a **sudden flood**, many of its 'divine inhabitants' having drowned... This is part of the Egyptian **Zep Tepi** – The First Time. Thus Atlantis is a good bet – even the Aztecs have said they came from the East, from **Aztlan**.

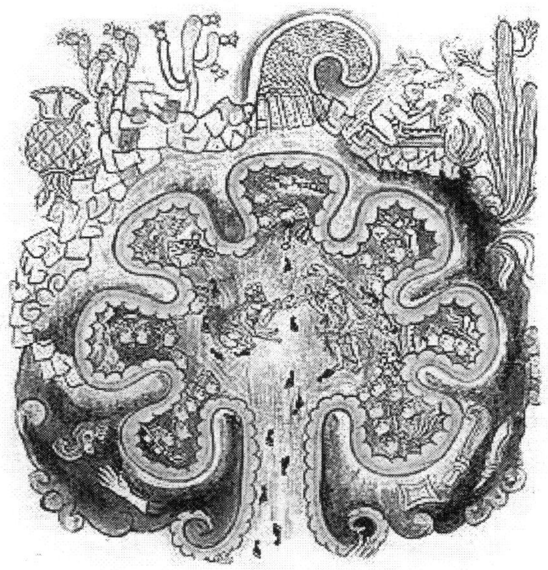

Seven Sages... there is that number 7 again, and having mentioned Aztlan, here is a blurb from the Aztec legend of their origins:

Nahuatl legends relate that **seven tribes** lived in Chicomoztoc, or "the place of the **seven caves**". Each cave represented a different Nahua group: the Xochimilca, Tlahuica Acolhua, Tlaxcalteca, Tepeneca, Chalca, and **Mexica** [Aztec]. Because of their common linguistic origin, those groups are called collectively "**Nahuatl**-aca" (Nahua people)...

These tribes subsequently left the caves and settled "near" Aztlán. [459]

In addition, as some readers will be familiar with some of the major town/cities in Mexico will notice, each of the seven tribes settled a different city in today's Mexico.

Aztec legend of leaving the seven caves and fleeing to Aztlan… by a lake, and a mountain.

(Left) is a picture from an ancient Codex Boturini depicting the escape…Aztec history appears to be a myth, and yet archeologists have nonetheless attempted to identify a geographic place of origin for the **Mexica** (as the Aztecs called themselves).

What is significant is that the Aztecs/Mexica came from 7 caves – recall the **Incan** story of emergence into this world – thru caves (Chapter 7) and the **Navajo** said the same thing… and the **Hopi/Zuñi** said something similar: they came from a *sipapu* – a hole in the ground… where there were "Ant people." This has got to relate in some way to a kind of **underground origin for the Brown race**…. Perhaps the caves were shelter on **Mu** (allegedly the Pacific Ocean home of the Brown race – half went to India and the other half went to South America after a cataclysm?) and the people left the shelter of their caves and made it to nearby dry land.

> Friar Diego Duran (c. 1537–1588), who chronicled the history of the Aztecs, wrote of Aztec emperor Moctezuma I's attempt to recover the history of the Mexica by congregating warriors and wise men on an expedition to locate **Aztlán**.
>
> According to Durán, the expedition was successful in finding a place that offered characteristics unique to Aztlán. However, his accounts were written shortly after the conquest of Tenochtitlan and before an accurate mapping of the American continent was made; therefore, he was unable to provide a precise location…

> There is a lake around Cerro **Culiacan ….** that makes the mountain look very much like an island when photographed from the water, and is similar to the illustration above.[460]

And lastly, fairly recent research determined that Eduardo Matos Moctezuma presumes Aztlán to be somewhere in the modern-day states of Guanajuato, Jalisco, or Michoacan. Indeed, scholars are all consistent in naming the measures of **"150 leagues" from Tenochtitlan** that were documented by the Spanish scribes taking notes from conquered Mexica as the distance to the place of origin, coinciding in all ways at Chicomoztoc, "**Cerro del Culiacan**", which is indeed a humped mountain when seen from the south face.

Looking at a map of Mexico, Jalisco, Michoacan and Culiacan are all on the north-western side of Mexico very near the coast. **Significance**: if the 7 caves were somewhere on the continent of Mu, then escape by boat (as shown above) would have taken the Mexica east to land… and coastal **Culiacan** (about 100 miles north of Mazatlan) is the best bet because the Mexica tell of fighting their way south to what is now Mexcio City, battling other tribes just to survive.

So the Aztecs appear to not be from Atlantis after all. And their wild, aggressive behavior to all the tribes that surrounded them does make one think that whereas Atlantis was technologically sophisticated, the Aztec were anything but.

They may have been originally from **Mu** -- Mu disappeared thousands of years BC before the Aztec capital of Tenochtitlan was built in 1325 AD…. So the Aztecs might still have originated there, but over several thousands of years, surviving the cataclysm, they occupied "Aztlan" somewhere in northwestern, coastal Mexico….

To wrap up this part of the chapter, let's look at the known history of the Shining Ones where it was documented: Egypt.

Kings Lists

About 42,000 years ago, well into the Anunnaki time frame of Earth-occupation, by the way, we find an historical list of rulers in the **Turin Canon Papyrus**:

> Ten **Neteru** kings ruled for 23,200 years

Followed by

> A ruling priesthood called the **Shemsu Hor** (followers of Horus) who ruled for 13,420 years. They were also called the **Akhu**.

Followed by

The rule of Menes (1st king/pharoah of the 1st dynasty): **at 3000** BC

This Turin Canon appears to be more credible than the Sumerian King List, since it is linear and the **Sumerian King List** records multiple nearby city-state rulers who ruled at the same time as each other, yet they are listed separately, thus giving an inflated sense of linear chronology.

What is significant about the sequence of rulers is that the **Devas** preceded the **Neteru** (aka Watchers) who were god-kings, and then the real human priest rulers were known as the **Shemsu Hor** who followed Horus, the first god-ruler. Then Egypt about 3000 BC began to record its human Dynasties.

> Note: Robert Bauval and Graham Hancock have determined that **the Great Pyramid was built by the Shemsu Hor** – before any Pharaonical Dynasties. [461]

As for the Shemsu Hor (aka Akhu), the Edfu Texts say that all human knowledge came from the **Akhu** , or "Followers of Horus" who came after the gods and giants, the Neteru or Akeru, and it was they who also invented Kingship (Think: "Dieu et Mon Droit") and every pharaoh that ruled from Menes to Emperor Trajan all ruled Egypt in their name. The **winged disk** was their symbol….

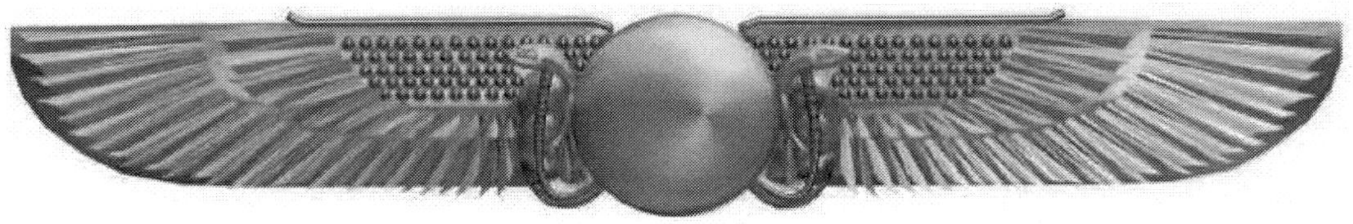

(credit: Bing Images: photobucket.com)

In a further note, tucked away in Gardiner's book, we note this clarification:

> …the root name of the mysterious race of 'gods' who were said to have come to Egypt was NTR, 'those who watch, oversee, see.' Neter, also **Neteru, was the Egyptian name for the Anunnaki** of Sumeria, which means they are the same people….[462]

This is why the winged sphere was an Anunnaki symbol as well as an Egyptian one. It was <u>the</u> symbol of the **Akhu** and was called the ***udjat.***

Recent Agents of Fire

Let's move on to more of the recent people and beings who are associated with Serpent Wisdom. This section will be dealing with Teachings and Techniques.

Teachings: Dragon Wisdom

Nag Hammadí Library

This is a collection of 4th Century AD papyrus manuscripts found in Nag Hammadí Egypt in 1945. The Gnostic texts written in Egyptian Coptic script and the discovery also included three works belonging to the ***Corpus Hermeticum*** (Chapter 10) and a partial translation/alteration of Plato's *Republic*. The thinking is that these were works declared heretical and buried so as to not get a local monastery in trouble if found within the monastery library. None of these works was included in the Bible, but neither were *The Book of Josher* nor *The Book of Enoch* – and the last is particularly enlightening (covered in VEG, Ch 2).

Due to the exciting events surrounding the find and the feud between the two brothers who found the manuscripts, it is amazing that we have anything left to look at – even their mother burned some of the manuscripts, using them for kindling in the family stove! And some of the manuscripts were sold for money to local antiquities dealers… By 1975, authorities had realized what had been found and had managed to acquire the manuscripts from various locations. The 52 writings are now kept in the Coptic Museum in Cairo.

The only complete text among the collection found was that of the **Gospel of Thomas**. Other works found have already been quoted earlier in this book, namely *The Apocryphon of John* and *On The Origin of the World*, in Chapter 12 dealing with Gnosticism.

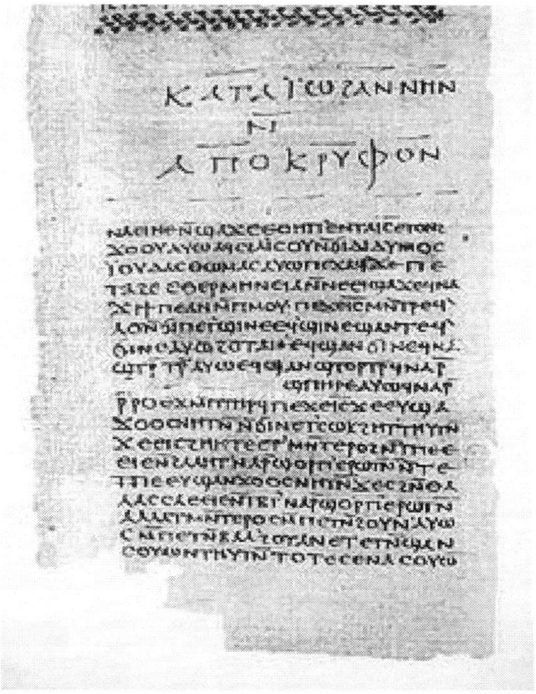

Sample Coptic Text from Nag Hammadí

(credit: wikipedia.org)

Gospel of Thomas

These are the recorded 114 sayings of Jesus – many of which (almost ½) agree with what is in the New Testament. They reflect the oral tradition which means they were written down <u>after</u> they had been spoken and made the public circuit for a while.

> The introduction states: "These are the hidden words that the living Jesus spoke and Didymos Judas Thomas wrote them down." Didymus (Greek) and Thomas (Aramaic) both mean **"twin."** Some critical scholars suspect that this reference to the Apostle Thomas is false, and that therefore the true author is unknown. [463]

The sayings do not detract from Jesus' divinity, but they do not directly promote it either. When Jesus is asked about his origin, he sidesteps the issue and asks why his listeners do not recognize what is before them.

> Jesus said to his disciples, "Compare me to someone and tell me whom I am like."
> Simon Peter said to him, "You are like a righteous angel."
> Matthew said to him, "You are like a wise philosopher."
> Thomas said to him, "Master my mouth is wholly incapable of saying whom you are like."
> Jesus said, "I am not your master. Because you have drunk, you have become intoxicated from the bubbling spring which I have measured out."
> And he [Jesus] took him [Thomas] and told him three things. When Thomas returned to his companions, they asked him, "What did Jesus say to you?"
> Thomas said to them, "If I tell you one of the things which he told me, you will pick up stones and throw them at me; a fire will come out of the stones and burn you up." **Thomas 13-14**

On another occasion,

> Jesus said, "When you see one who was not born of woman, prostrate yourselves on your faces and worship him. That one is your father."
>
> Jesus said, "I shall give you what no eye has seen, and what no ear has heard and what no hand has touched and what has never occurred to the human mind." **Thomas 15, 17**

And again,

Jesus said, "If a blind man leads a blind man, they will both fall into a pit."

Jesus said, "The Pharisees and the scribes have taken the keys of knowledge (gnosis) and hidden them. They themselves have not entered, nor have they allowed to enter those who wish to. You however be as wise as **serpents** and innocent as doves." **Thomas 34, 39**

And perhaps the best-known quote from the Gospel of **Thomas v. 70**:

Jesus said, "That which you have will save you if you bring it forth from yourselves. That which you do not have within you [will] kill you if you do not have it within you [and you try to bring it forth]."

This has always been a cryptic phrase – even more confusing in the original. What he is referring to is Light – " if you bring it forth, it will save you (i.e., bless you); if you do not have Light and you attempt to bring forth what you do not have, it will condemn (harm) you." Conversely, if you have Light and do not bring it forth, it will also condemn you…

Jesus said, "…For no one lights a lamp and puts it under a bushel, nor does he put it in a hidden place, but rather he sets it on a lampstand so that everyone who enters and leaves will see its light."

and

He said to them, "Whoever has ears, let him hear. There is light within a man of light, and he lights up the whole world. If he does not shine, he is darkness." **Thomas 33, 24**

and

Jesus said, "Whoever has something in his hand, will receive more, and whoever has nothing will be deprived of even the little he has." **Thomas 41**

That same concept goes along with this one:

Jesus said, "For unto every one that hath shall be given, and he shall have abundance: but from him that hath not shall be taken away even that which he hath**."** **Matt. 25:29; Matt. 13:12 Mark 4: 25**

That is what you call 'hard sayings.' And is one of the underlying principles of the Serpent Wisdom teachings. If you don't have what it takes, you will not be given any more, let alone be given it in the first place. Explained in Matt. 25:25 – the servant went and hid the talent he had been given and did nothing with it… As shown above, the point is made at least 3 times in the Bible, and in Thomas verses 41 &70 – if you have something and don't use it, you lose it.

There are other pithy sayings worthy of Serpent Wisdom:

> Jesus said, "The kingdom of the Father is spread out upon the Earth and men do not see it."

and

> Jesus said, "It is the I who am the light which is above them all. It is the I who is the all. From the me did all come forth, and unto the me did the all extend. Split a piece of wood and the I am is there. Lift up the stone and you will find the me there."

and

> Jesus said, "Recognize what is in your sight and that which is hidden from you will become plain to you. For there is nothing hidden which will not become manifest."
>
> **Thomas 113, 77, 5**

The "I am" is consciousness and even rocks are operating within consciousness – but it is a very low level… How else could Jesus say that "even the rocks will cry out!" (Luke 19:40).

> Case in point: there may be some readers who will not follow what has been just said (from the Gospel of Thomas) and they are an example of those who do not have and so do not receive. Having "ears to hear" requires a consciousness that can see different levels and intuits the meaning of deeper sayings with hidden truths.

So that is why (1) esoteric truth is not for the masses, and why (2) it is said:

> "Do not give what is holy to dogs, lest they throw them on the dung heap. Do not throw the pearls to swine, lest they trample them…" **Matt. 7:6**
>
> **Thomas 93**

More insights into what was esoteric will follow.

Sufis

As was said in Chapters 5, 10 & 11, the Sufis were quite adept at miracles and healing. They understood the universal truths and often ascetically lived them.

Developing the Serpent Fire, or **Baraka**, they could awaken it in others and pass on anointings. Baraka is also Dragon Fire.

One of the most well-known of Sufi practices was that of the **Whirling Dervishes**. And there is a really good reason for it. It is more than just a colorful dance.

Sufi Whirling Dhikr
(Source: Wikipedia: Whirling_Dervish)

There really is an energetic medium in which we humans live, move and have our being, as well as the Earth and the solar system, and the galaxies… The fact that we can barely measure it with today's equipment means it is beyond the equipment capabilities or the techniques of measurement – or both. It doesn't mean the **Æther** doesn't exist, and today's scientists are coming around to that conclusion, despite the opinion of Einstein (who claimed it didn't exist) – space is filled with something they now call **Dark Matter**, and empowered by **Dark Energy**. (This is explored more in TOM, Ch. 12.)

It has also been called **The Field** which contains **Zero Point Energy** (ZPE). Alternately, it has been called an **Energy Matrix**.

> What is so amazing about the ZPE and its natural matrix is that it is a **boundless source of energy** – a 3" cubic space of it contains more than enough energy to bring all the world's oceans to the boiling point. [464]

Dr. Nikolai Kozyrev's big discovery was that **this energy was spiraling, twisting** such that he called it Torsion Physics. He made the connection with Rupert

Sheldrake's *Morphogenetics* and suggested that DNA was a spiral because it is sustained by the torsion aspects of the ZPE Field. He made a corollary discovery: [465]

> …Kozyrev showed that by **shaking, spinning**, heating, cooling, vibrating or breaking physical objects their weight can be increased or decreased by subtle but definite amounts.[466]

Sufis do not gain mass, **they gain energy**. Energy from the ZPE Field. This is what the Sufi Whirling Dervishes and Shakers are doing to enhance their religious experience. Significantly, Sufis balanced on their left foot, spinning **counter-clockwise**… which is the direction of the **toroidal energy**… and the direction of the Earth's spin on its axis. How did they know?

> In a related experiment by **Dr. Frank Brown**, it was found that the biofield that Sheldrake referred to (morphogenetics) is sensitive to **rotation** (as Kozyrev also discovered above): [467]

That the biofield is involved [in living things] is supported by Brown's observation of a connection between rotation and bean seed interaction. He found that the beans responded (grew) more strongly when they were rotated **counter-clockwise** than when they were rotated clockwise. This would lend support to the Sufis twirling in a counter-clockwise direction to empower their (ecstatic?) devotional dance, the Dhikr.

> *FYI: It has been discovered that if a human spins/twirls* ***clockwise*** *(in the northern hemisphere) it can make him sick.*

The point of the foregoing is: Who told the Sufis this? Just standing up one day and deciding to spin oneself is not something anybody just does. It is strongly suggested that someone who already knew about torsion energy, the Earth's spin, and the body's Bionet taught this to some willing listeners…. Could it have been the Anunnaki?

Count de St Germain

This man was a mystery – where he came from, who he really was, and why he knew so many things. In addition, he was reputed to be hundreds of years old as society had made note of him a century before he became popular in High Society in Europe in the mid-1770's.

The reason for including him is the very strong probability that he was either one of the Watchers who move among us, contributing knowledge and guidance, or in any case, he had inside knowledge (as a member of the Freemasons), as we'll see with the next several men, as well… Note: **he ate no meat and drank no wine**…

While skeptics have counted him a phony and a scam artist, there are two things that are notable: he was an **expert Alchemist** and had discovered *The Elixir of Life*, and he wrote a very esoteric triangular-shaped book, called *La Très Sainte Trinosophie (The Very Holy Trinosophia).* The writing in the book is unique, and consists of a very clever code… almost like the Voynich Manuscript.

The cover is dark red and inside the 10-pointed star is the number '76' …

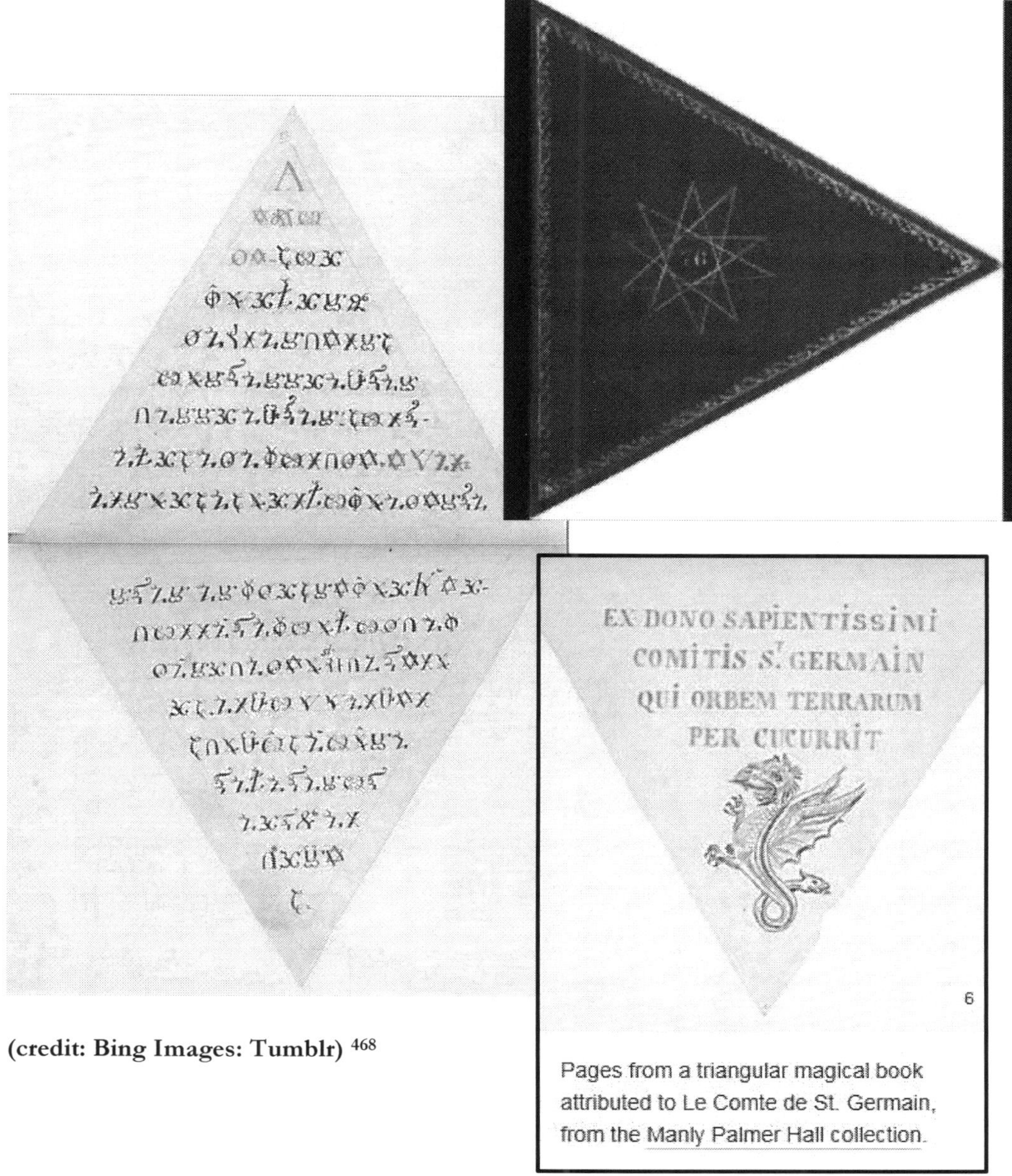

(credit: Bing Images: Tumblr) [468]

Pages from a triangular magical book attributed to Le Comte de St. Germain, from the Manly Palmer Hall collection.

According to Wikipedia:

> *La Très Sainte Trinosophie* is MS. No. 2400 in the French Library at Troyes [France]. The work is ....ninety-six leaves written upon one side only. The calligraphy is excellent. Although somewhat irregular in spelling and accenting, the French is scholarly and dramatic, and the text is embellished with numerous figures, well drawn and brilliantly colored. In addition to the full-page drawings there are small symbols at the beginning and end of each of the sections. Throughout the French text there are scattered letters, words, and phrases in **several ancient languages.** There are also magical symbols, figures resembling **Egyptian hieroglyphics**, and a few words in characters resembling [Sumerian] **cuneiform**. At the end of the manuscript are a number of leaves written in arbitrary ciphers, possibly the code used by St.Germain's secret society. The work was probably executed in the latter part of the eighteenth century, though most of the material belongs to a considerably earlier period.[469]
>
> [emphasis added]
>
> — *Manly Palmer Hall, La Très Sainte Trinosophie*

At left is a sample drawing from the book:

While it looks like a Tarot card, it isn't, and purports to show an esoteric truth – something about an initiation...
Some of the coded and strange alphabet is shown.

(credit: Wikipedia)[470]

St. Germain was no fraud… very credible sources of his time documented his qualifications and actions. This is significant. What he was (is?) will become clear at the end of this section on him.

Manly Palmer Hall then cites Dr. Edward C. Getsinger, "an eminent authority on ancient alphabets and languages," in emphasizing that *La Très Sainte Trinosophie* is couched in **secret codes intended to conceal its contents from the profane**.

> In all my twenty years of experience as a reader of **archaic writings** I have never encountered such **ingenious codes** and methods of concealment as are found in this manuscript. In only a few instances are complete phrases written in the same alphabet; usually two or three forms of writing are employed, with letters written upside down, reversed, or with the text written backwards. Vowels are often omitted, and at times several letters are missing with merely dots to indicate their number. Every combination of hieroglyphics seemed hopeless at the beginning, yet, after hours of alphabetic dissection, one familiar word would appear. This gave a clue as to the language used, and established a place where word combination might begin, and then a sentence would gradually unfold.
>
> The various texts are written in **Chaldean Hebrew, Ionic Greek, Arabic, Syriac, cuneiform, Greek hieroglyphics, and ideographs**. The keynote throughout this material is that of the approach of the age when the Leg of the Grand Man and the Waterman of the Zodiac shall meet in conjunction at the equinox and end a grand 400,000-year cycle. This points to **a culmination of eons**, as mentioned in the Apocalypse: "Behold! I make a new heaven and a new earth," meaning a series of new cycles and a new humanity.[471] [emphasis added]

Time is being spent on this man for a reason. He was an accomplished musician, wrote an opera, spoke 12 languages with fluency: French, German, Spanish, Portuguese, Italian, English, Polish, Greek, Latin, Sanskrit, Arabic and Chinese. He was ambidextrous such that he could write with both hands simultaneously the same statement, then place the two pieces of paper over each other, and the words on the top sheet exactly covered the words on the bottom sheet. He had an uncanny knowledge of the events on Earth for the past 2000 years, and he could take a jewel in the presence of its owner and closing his hand around it, remove any flaws in it.

Are you beginning to get an idea of who/what this man was?

He said that he had discovered the fabled ***elixir of life*** and administered it to a lady of the French court, under Madame de Pompadour's watch, and for the next 25 years, the lady did not age at all. Perhaps he was taking the elixir himself if the stories about his longevity are true… It is suspected that he faked his death as no one saw the body sick or buried, the public was just told about his allegedly passing in 1784. And then we have Madame d'Adhémar who knew him and met him 5 years after his 'death.' [472]

And last but not least, **his prophecies all came true** when he advised heads of state, and he was often used as an ambassador between countries. From Persia to France, Calcutta to Rome, and England to China he was known and respected.

He was both a Freemason and a Templar, and it is strongly suspected that he was a Rosicrucian – it is even said that he was the **Christian Rosencreutz**, founder of Rosicrucianism, himself. Others lately have suspected that if he lived for hundreds of years and was obeying the orders of a higher Master, his job was also to spread truth and wisdom – such that he might also have been **Sir Francis Bacon** (and wrote the Shakespearean plays) – just as he wrote *La Très Sainte Trinosophie. Those who have said such things note that there are many similarities in the knowledge and linguistic abilities of the two men. Christian Rosenkreutz, Sir Francis Bacon and St Germain were all Alchemists, by the way.*

It is understood that staunch skeptics will have a hard time with the forgoing, and yet, the point of spending this time and space on St Germain is that (as has been said throughout the book), there are Those (call them Custodians, Neteru, Watchers, or even Anunnaki Remnant) – someone is still watching out for Man and guiding his development. St Germain certainly qualifies for that rôle. As did Sir Francis Bacon, and to a lesser extent, **Rudolph Steiner** and **Benjamin Franklin** -- these are lesser (human) Shining Ones, walking among us, assisting and educating us.

> Older examples were **Apollonius of Týana**, Apollo himself, Pythagorus, Tesla, **Paramahansa Yogananda**, Emerson, Ghandi, Plato, Jesus, Buddha, Krishna, and Mohammed, to name a few.

No less remarkable was the following man who was more instrumental in founding the USA than people realize.

Benjamin Franklin

While it is not suspected nor is it suggested that Benjamin was similar to St Germain, nonetheless, he was a scholar, linguist, scientist, inventor, metaphysician, statesman, Freemason, writer, meteorologist, and postmaster– to name a few things. He was a **polymath** – like **Leonardo da Vinci**…one whose expertise spans multiple fields.

Sometimes the term 'Renaissance Man' fits a lot of these gifted people.

Ben Franklin was a true Renaissance Man – interested in and capable of handling whatever he set his mind to.

As a **scientist**, he was a major figure in the American Enlightenment and the history of physics for his discoveries and theories regarding electricity. As an **inventor**, he is known for the lightning rod, bifocals, and the Franklin stove, among other inventions. He facilitated many civic organizations, including Philadelphia's fire department and a university.

He is also scientifically known to be one of the first to promote the "wave theory of light" and he was the first to discover the principle of conservation of electric charge and identified positive vs. negative electric charges. He also correctly said that lightning is electricity and he knew enough to stand on an insulator when performing his famous kite experiment! He would have loved to meet **Nikola Tesla.**

> If Franklin did perform this experiment, he may not have done it in the way that is often described—flying the kite and waiting to be struck by lightning—as it would have been dangerous. Instead he used the kite to collect some electric charge from a storm cloud [in a Leyden jar], which implied that lightning was electrical.[473]

Franklin himself wrote:

> When rain has wet the kite twine so that it can conduct the electric fire freely, you will find it streams out plentifully from the key at the approach of your knuckle, and with this key a phial, or Leyden jar, may be charged: and from **electric fire** thus obtained spirits may be kindled, and all other electric experiments [may be] performed which are usually done by the help of a rubber glass globe or tube; and therefore the sameness of the electrical matter with that of lightening completely demonstrated. [474]

Ok, just enough to give you a sense that this was not some goofball hacking his way thru science experiments – he knew what he was doing. Who told him?

Perhaps a clue can be found in the true story that follows. In *Our Flag*, a treatise of the American Revolution, there is an episode concerning the design of the new American flag. The account involves a **mysterious old man** who is known to both General George Washington and Benjamin Franklin…[475]

> Little seems to have been known this old gentleman, and in the materials from which this account is compiled, his name is not even once mentioned… he is uniformly spoken of as 'the Professor.'
>
> He was evidently far beyond his threescore and 10 years and he often referred to historical events of more than a century previous just as if he had been a living witness of their occurrence… still he was erect, vigorous and active – hale, hearty and clear-minded – as strong and energetic every way as in the prime of his life. He was tall, of fine figure, perfectly easy, and very dignified in his manners, at once courteous, gracious and commanding.
>
> **He ate no meat, fish or fowl, and drank no wine.** [Sound familiar?]
>
> He was well-educated, highly cultivated, of extensive as well as varied information and very studious. He spent considerable time in the patient and persistent conning of old books and manuscripts which he seemed to be deciphering, translating or rewriting. He kept them locked up in an iron-bound, heavy oaken chest whenever he left his room for walks or meals… no one was allowed to see them close up.
>
> [He stayed with a local family in Cambridge, Mass.]
>
> He was a quiet and genial member of the family and he seemed to be at home on every topic of conversation. He was the kind of person that everyone would notice and respect, yet no one asked him from whence he came nor where he was headed.
>
> By something more than a mere coincidence, the committee appointed by the Continental Congress to **design a flag** occurred in Cambridge and happened to be held in the same house where the old gentleman was staying. Both General Washington and Doctor Franklin attended the small meeting [less than 10 people were present].
>
> (continued…)

By the signs which passed between them, it was evident that both General Washington and Doctor Franklin recognized the Professor and by unanimous approval he was invited to be an active member of the committee. During the proceedings which followed, the Professor was treated with the most profound respect and all of his suggestions immediately acted upon. He submitted a pattern which he considered symbolically appropriate for the new flag and this was unhesitatingly accepted by the other six members of the committee, who voted that the arrangement be forthwith adopted. [F] [Note F next page]

[So much for the myth of Betsy Ross...]

After the episode of the flag the Professor quietly vanished and nothing further is known concerning him.

Did General Washington and Doctor Franklin recognize the Professor as an emissary of the Mystery School which has for long controlled the political destinies of this planet?

****

It was during the evening of July 4, 1776 that the second of these mysterious episodes occurred. In the Old State House in Philadelphia group of men gathered for a momentous task, and were discussing whether they should put their lives on the line for the new country – they could all be killed by the British if they failed.

In the midst of the debate a fierce voice rang out... Everyone stopped and looked at the stranger. Where had he come from? Who knew him? Was he a British spy? His tall form and pale face filled them with awe , as did his oratory. He stirred the men to their very souls, and then said "God has given America to be free!" and sat down.

Wild enthusiasm burst forth and name after name was placed on the document before them: The Declaration of Independence. The men were so busy with their signing and positioning on the document they didn't see the old man leave. He had disappeared, nor was he ever seen again, nor his identity established.

That episode parallels others that have been documented by ancient historians during the founding of new nations. Are they coincidence or does this demonstrate that the wisdom of the Watchers is still indirectly involved in the world, serving Man as it has for centuries?

Note [F] –

It is said that the following is the design of that first **Colonial Flag of 1775** – which did not last long. As soon as more states joined the Union, the number of stars changed and so did the design inside the canon (i.e., field of stars).

(credit: bing images: Pinterest.com)

Triune Agenda

Knowledge

Tales of the Flood, Creation, Serpents and similar veneration of a Tree of Life are found all over the world, due to what appears to be the Anunnaki visiting multiple cultures and leaving a part of their teaching with the natives. That was Enki's stated purpose behind promoting Serpent Wisdom Groups around the globe… and certain ideas and stories naturally went with the process since explaining things while **imparting Knowledge** to the natives would probably involve the same or similar examples or imagery. Hence, Africans, Incans, Hindus and the Sioux might have heard the same ideas couched in the same examples as the gods taught them common principles of Agriculture, Medicine, Astrology, and Civilization…

Kundalini

Then there were the St Germains out there – also seeing to the edification of more sophisticated cultures while not ostensibly being involved in the ***Kundalini* process**… There were the *Kundalini* Awareness agents, and there were the Wisdom Teachers – those latter who helped steer civilization but did not get involved with awakening to a Higher Self…

And besides Yoga, meditation, ayahuasca, and physical stimulation of the Dragon Force, there is another technique in today's world. It is called **Hemi-Synch®** and is promoted by the Monroe Institute – allegedly one can use a binaural sound generator to synchronize both halves of the brain and so induce an altered state of consciousness in the person – and if carried far enough, while not so advertised by the Institute, it could awaken the *Kundalini* by preparing the brain to receive it, and entraining the Bionet *chi*, synching the chakras – as if enhancing a meditational state – which is how the yogis have always done it (without equipment)… The entrainment effect appears to be electro-magnetically based.

Genetics

And as we all suspect, there is a third group – those who are also on Earth performing **genetic upgrades**…. Neanderthal to Cro-Magnon to Homo *sapiens* to …. what has been called Indigos, or lately, the Hybrids. (VEG and TOM dealt with this part of the Agenda.)

And it is all good – for Man's benefit. Really.

Additional Dragon Wisdom

As was said earlier, there are a few remaining concepts that have made their way into the public arena, and many of them were shared in the last two chapters of Virtual Earth Graduate. This chapter is thus the sequel to those points that were shared in VEG to assist the person wanting to know what are the aspects of the Walk that will get him/her out of here – i.e., how does one become an **Earth Graduate**?

> **Nexus**: Know that the reason the Serpent Wisdom Groups share their Knowledge and assist with the *Kundalini* Awareness process is to "upgrade" Man and in so doing, he automatically becomes a Graduate. Earth is a School and the "Teachers" are still here.

Some of the insights and relevant wisdom that have been shared in the last 50 years follow….

Insider Truth

An astute person calling herself the Insider appeared for 1 week in 2005 on the Internet and invited people on the GLP forum to submit any questions they had and she would answer them. Those readers who had spiritual insight and could 'read' the energy of the Insider's words, knew it was a woman, **an Elite family member**. As usual, the Trolls came out in force and repeatedly attacked, jeered, swore, insulted – typical lower human response – and of course they boldly identified themselves as 'Anonymous.' And thru it all, she shared some very interesting bits of knowledge, not found elsewhere… selected snippets follow: [476]

> The more divided people are the easier it is to control them. Thus were religions setup by us to divide and control and the major religions in the world are under our control. **Just as are the banks and the media**… and yet you think you are free… [The PTB will not come for your guns because they will not let you hear anything which would cause you to go get your gun …] Remember that the best slave is the one who can say: "I'm no slave, I'm free."
>
> There is **no endtime**. There will be a time when souls are released but that is not a mass event, but rather 1 by 1… work on yourself.
>
> If you think the Elite do not exist, just remember: A fish in the ocean can't see the birds that are flying in the sky.

The Elite are the ones who are responsible for Man's safety and development, and have been thus for centuries. Some call them Custodians, Watchers…

> There are **higher beings** who govern this Earth realm. You do not understand what this world we live in really is….Are you really living on the planet you think you are? The higher beings are benevolent and interpenetrate everything [Think: Devas] and you need to show that you are worthy to be released [from this School]. If you could leave out bigotry, cussing, hate and prejudice it would show that you are a bit more evolved from the peasant stage.
>
> The ones you see on TV and read about in the papers are not the Elite – what you see are the PTB (puppets) who dance to the tune called by the Elite – whose names you do <u>not</u> know. So do not take them for your

rulers nor as your gurus. The Bushes are not bloodline – they are your kind who want to be worshipped by your kind. [Same for the Rockenfelders and the Bauers aka Rothschilds].

Most humans do not have the discipline to live by strict values and temperance to achieve the next stage in their development by applying their highest values and rules to everything they do.

We manipulate this world only so far as we are allowed to by Divine Law. We provide you with **tools** and it is then up to you to determine how to use them [Think: freewill universe] … so despising the ones who provide you with the tools is about you trying to camouflage your tracks… no one is forcing you to use the tools as you do. You get what you deserve.

When you seek, **do not join secret societies**, nor blindly believe popular gurus. They have all been corrupted from their original purpose. And realize that not all questions need to be answered… only certain questions need to be answered by yourself, and not by others. It is not our duty to enlighten you, that is yours.

There is just one struggle and it is now, here on this planet and on a personal level… meaning you only. There is no enemy you can attack [to blame for anything] except yourself. If you succeed, there will be no more struggle.

Knowing yourself, and where you really are, are the two most important issues that you should be involved with. It is your task to find out. In fact, if someone should give you the correct answers, they will not be attached to you in a way they would have if you had found them yourself. If you find the answers to your questions, you have accomplished a huge part of your duty to yourself – after that your task would be to live according to the Divine Law which is revealed to you after that stage until departure.

The **Divine Law** has a purpose for you and it is not on this planet. Prove that you are worthy again to be released. [note: "again"]

It is the task of every soul to accomplish that while in this human shape. There is a part that can be called escaping which will be followed by **transcending** … if failing, reincarnation. The Divine Law controls what is called **Karma** but it is much broader and "harsher" than people want to accept. **Reincarnation** is a fact, but if you achieve your task there is no [more] reincarnation – no need to experience all levels of life on Earth as they are mainly pointless to experience.

The Divine Law is the manifestation of the Will of the **Superior One** which not only creates everything that exists in this universe but also maintains, nourishes, balances, energizes and renews it. [Think: Dark Energy.] It also reigns in other realms – including the realm you originally belong to.

You can be guided up to a certain point and then it is up to you. **Know yourself and what this place is**. It is your duty. A human is corrupt while on this planet – each and every one of them. "Death" does not change the personality… so fix it while on Earth.

It is very easy to make humans think they are enlightened and know the truth … and then think that it is their task to wake up others. A few are thus engaged and supported by us, but the great majority are used by their religion – **most of which are floating in a sea of error**.

Everyone can 'dial in' and when they seek, they shall be answered. It is being provided by Divine Law to everything that searches for truth. The truth wants to be known by you; there is no conspiracy by the higher beings to withhold or deceive.

Yet there are **"malicious" beings in the Astral**. They seek to dissuade, derail and mislead people. Someone who is led by malicious forces [Think: Chas. Manson] cannot utter/write certain words or phrases without it affecting him/her. The humans led by [those beings] also cannot accept hearing/reading certain things without getting overly mad/aggressive (see the GLP thread for examples). "Malicious" beings are present every time you cuss, talk negative, scheme, get violent, utter lies, get sexually aroused, get afraid, get jealous [any strong emotions attract them] and **they feed off the energy you project. [See Appendix A: Dr. Lerma and George's Story.]**

"Malicious" beings are from this Earth realm – this is their home. They are doing what they are programmed to do… **do not hate them** for they are doing their duty – You are to do yours and act in ways that do not 'feed' them… They are a feedback mechanism to act as a 'course correction' and **their rightful duty is connected to your behavior**. You are the perpetrator – they react. Respect them up to a certain point – because they are not really "malicious" – People are perpetrators who play the victim rôle.

Earth can be a **prison** with no escape for those who believe the contrary: they will never graduate if they are attached to the things of this planet. If they believe that all is well and that Earth is their home, they will be here for a long time. You have more power than you think you have… You must learn to **think outside the box** that others have created for you and realize that some humans who think they worship the "good" are really worshipping the "bad" – and it has been orchestrated that way. **[It is one of your "tests" to see if you can see thru what is really happening.]**

Remember that prisoners can still determine what they do in their prison with the tools that were provided them… how to walk in the yard, how to think, talk… what to study. We also provide you with the tools to free yourself or chain yourself… your choice.

Real consciousness is provided you when you are in tune with Universal Mind which operates according to the Divine Law – they are not the same, btw. This **Mind** interpenetrates everything, it rules over everything, and if you connect with it, you may experience its unlimited power. No prison can confine this power, hence there will be an escape, you will be guided up to a certain point – yet most work is to be done by you.

Everyone can tune into **the Mind** and receive insights, information… and if you can, it means you are at a higher stage than others, but beware of how you use it… it is not yours, not in this realm. It can be a deceiving beginning of something else which many people experience [deception from the Astral]. You are not the Mind, you merely "plug in" and use it while on Earth.

I would hesitatingly add that studying **ancient texts** will help (although a lot is filled with perversions and wrong translations, intentionally) but this only after a certain level of awakening – so that you will recognize the small parts that are true. [It is called spiritual discernment.]

Knowledge does not appear out of nothing – it is passed on, always. No exceptions. And before accepting it, you need to verify where it comes from. Be careful of people, books and movements that are popularly acclaimed – many things are orchestrated to distract you. **If heavily promoted, be wary**.

So, **understand this place, what and where it is, know what you are, how you came here, why you came here, and how to return**. Prepare yourself for the answers, cleanse yourself, reach out for the Mind, speak within that you are ready, and live strictly according to the answers. Accept no outside sources –
You only need yourself and the Divine [connecting thru your Higher Self] and no intervention by anybody, guru or group.

Case in point:
If your father asks you for a glass of water to show that you care for him and are disciplined, do you bring it directly to him, or do you take the glass

of water to your neighbor and ask him to tell you what it is that your father really asked, while the neighbor did not hear it and is now drinking the glass of water himself?

She also advises people to be careful of their words, which have an energy… and be careful to not speak against the Divine Law, or The One, as we will surely answer for it. One of her warnings is to not refer to The One as a god because the term is corrupted and represents those who came to Earth in a former Era and are not The Father of Light, but wanted to be worshipped as gods. (And that includes the Anunnaki who she says are no longer here [but their descendants and Others are].)

A reader asked: "If the Christ came in another Era, why did he fail his mission?"
Her answer: Be careful with what you say. **You are harming yourself**. If you fail, do not blame the Divine. Do not swear at or by the Divine. Do not ever make any misstatement against the Divine, The One… it is heard and reflects badly on you. The One knows that if you knew better, you'd not speak anything untrue/negative of the Divine… [thus in so doing, you just nailed yourself to the cross and have signed on for the lesson!]

By the way, the real Christ should get all the praise.

The One has any manifestations/emanations/characteristics which are present in a hierarchy of beings with different workings but operating together. All are incorporeal/immaterial although some may operate bodies in a fashion different to ours, some by lowering their frequency which is actually emanating a form from themselves, may appear in the material world.

You people worship some humans as "gods" be it prophets, celebrities, sportsmen, politicians, authors, etc. – which is an abomination.
Only The One deserves your thanks and veneration. As souls, you are a 'spark' off The One.

The One is self-existent [the Jains are correct], pure, Good, and indeed the One who creates the Good.

The Soul is not a part of you, it is **who you are**. You are not in the body, **the body operates within the Soul's energy envelope** [aura] and as a result entangles you as a Soul in the 3D world. Yet your duty toward The One stays the same no matter what happens.

Be like that which you want to connect with as much as possible.

Temperance and **restraining the body** always pays off. Remember that the body has a mind of its own and sometimes forces you into passions and desires that it wants and you become a slave and a dumbed-down version of yourself. The more you follow the body's lead, the more you chain yourself to this world. Respecting it and gently taming it is the best approach.

The body has the job to let you experience this realm, and whenever you reach for the Other, to find enlightenment, higher consciousness, it resists. Also [Astral] beings will accompany your thoughts and try to divert them, again **it is their duty**, so show respect and that will be recognized by them. They are not evil – they react to your thoughts, and they must fulfill their duty. "Take every thought captive" until you reach a point where you are in control of most of your thoughts – it is possible and **it is your duty**.

What I am allowed to tell you is that you are still here [on Earth] because of your **lack of understanding**. Do not think in terms of "us" but "I." The "us" comes later in another realm. [Think: the Group Entity RA from 6D – see Bibliography for the RA Material.]

Lastly, she closes with something that we can do every day to improve our Walk:

If you choose to:
Thank every day the Good One where everything has it's beginning for being, for It's Divine Law providing you with a chance to return to your original state, the realm you truly belong to, for It's Power of Necessity applying the justified corrections that you experience every day.

Praise the Higher Beings who operate according to The One's Divine Law, which are manifestations/emanations of The One, for providing the means of Life in all areas, sustaining them and providing these means **for your benefit, guiding you to the release [from Earth School]and more**.

When addressing Divinity (read again), be careful to articulate well, do not demand, tell, beg, order, suggest, ask … which are abhorrences, **just state and do your duty**.

That is the essence of her 5-day mission, but there was more. It is clear that she is also one of the Shining Ones… there is a lot of Light in what she wrote. And it is easy to see where this wisdom would be part of the ancient Serpent Wisdom teachings… It is a blessing that she logged in (via proxy server by the way, to prevent tracing her back to wherever she was located) and she did her best to share as much Light, Love and Wisdom as she could.

This is what was said earlier: **we are not alone** and They occasionally step in and assist, enlighten and guide Man. It is said that 20% of the people on that GLP Blog dissed her, and worse, which says some very negative people are so dense that they cannot recognize Truth when they hear it. The Trolls play it safe and live in fear of being 'conned' – as if the person writing the powerful words in her Blog could be coming from a lower, "malicious" state of being. Sorry, such Trolls will obviously be **recycled**. (See VEG where much of this **issue of personal growth** is examined and a way out, a way to transcend one's density, is suggested – especially in the last two chapters of VEG.)

Suggested Reading:

For those seeking further true spiritual Light, the following books may be of help:

Oneness	by Rasha.
Spiritual Growth Personal Power Thru Awareness	by Sanaya Roman
Putting on the Mind of Christ	by Jim Marion
The Lazy Man's Guide to Enlightenment	by Thaddeus Golas
Jesus and the Lost Goddess (note: Lucid Living)	by Timothy Freke
Into the Light Learning from the Light	by Dr. John Lerma
Lessons from the Light	by Dr. Kenneth Ring
Virtual Earth Graduate Transformation of Man	by TJ Hegland

> Key ideas from these books are profiled in **Appendix A**. You have seen some Serpent Wisdom in Chapter 10 (*Hermetic Principles* section), and this chapter, and now here is the third set.

There are many other worthy and interesting sources (see Bibliography) but these ten should be in **the core** of one's Spiritual Library. The VEG book is an extension of the principles just noted in the previous **Insider Truth** Section.

Dragon Wisdom Summary

We can tell something about the secret principles by observing those who were privy to the Serpent Wisdom – whether Sufis, Gnostics, Kabbalists, or in Freemasonry, Rosicrucianism, or Hermeticism. If those groups really had The Truth, then they all secretly taught the same thing. By the same token, if their members all knew the same thing, then they should all pretty much act in the same way – e.g., compassion, respectful of others, patient, humble…. Very **proactive** people.

One of those teachings (following **The Kybalion** in Chapter 10) that could have been listed, but is saved for this summary to emphasize the idea that we are all **One**… all souls are connected thru the Father of Light, The One – and souls are sparks off The One. Even Quantum Physics says the same thing in a doctrine called **Entanglement**. This is one of the few places where Quantum Physics and Metaphysics meet and agree.

> Entanglement is also related to Einstein's "Spooky Action at a Distance" comment: When a particle is split and ½ goes left and the other ½ goes right, what is done to the left particle automatically is reflected in the particle half on the right. If the left particle is rotated 180° the right particle **auto**-rotates accordingly to maintain symmetry.
>
> The point being: How did the right half know what happened to the left half? Because they are **connected** in way we don't understand – yet. And the answer seems to have something to do with Dark Energy (aka the Æther) which interpenetrates everything and is probably the medium of communication.

In addition, there are Laws in the Universe that all souls are subject to, and the details are listed (see "Law of…") in the Glossary. Suffice it to say that **the Universe is ordered and nothing is out of control**. Even today's Physics has found order hidden in Chaos. Thus accidents may just be "premeditated carelessness" – if they aren't Karmic.

Returning to the initial section of this chapter, **Historical Insight Ia**…
let us complete the line of thought and consider Man's future….

Historical Insight Ib

Imagine that you are part of the secret, hidden **Advanced Society**, and your presence is a secret, yet you see the surface humans destroying the planet – tearing up the Rain Forest, polluting the oceans, destroying the Ozone Layer… building nuclear warhead missiles. What would be your response? Realize that if the stupid surface humans screw up the planet, and destroy the ecological balance, NO ONE will be living here much longer!

And, as the **original inhabitants** of the planet, you have a say in what the newcomers do.

It would be important to either educate the humans, or stop them or make plans to move to another planet (if they haven't already). And throughout the Earth's history, beginning with Enki and Man's Creation, at least guiding if not controlling the rowdy, ignorant and sometimes violent humans (**this description is how the ETs and Enlil saw humans**) would be a top priority. If that could not be done, then Enlil's decision to wipe them all out (and start over) was the right one… Earth and any other sentient beings on Earth are not benefitted by a dysfunctional and defective species.

Hard sayings, but the Advanced Society, Watchers, Devas – whatever you want to call them – are not playing pattycake with us. And as was hinted at, at the end of Chapter 1, there is a serious reason we all should be "getting our act together" – we may be running out of time.

This was what was foreseen by Enki: educate the humans and manage them so that they grow into responsible caretakers of the Earth. And because he created (upgraded) a special human, the ***Adapa+***, those would be potential subjects for a further upgraded teaching – what came to be known as the Brotherhood of the Serpent. In short, Enki initiated the secret society to benefit humans who were a cut above those who are the riff raff out there – today estimated at 20% of the population, whereas it was 80%+ back in Enlil's Era. So we have made some progress.

The average Man does not like to hear the downside of human short-comings but it is true – **not all humans were created equal**. They are equal before the Law, but many are different in physical and mental ability, IQ, and even spiritual discernment. Some are psychic, and others can't even write… it often comes down to genetics… and you often can't tell if someone is normal (or advanced) just by looking – unless there is something obvious like Down's Syndrome.

It was said years ago that there are three types of humans on Earth:

Those who make things happen,
Those to whom things happen,
Those who wonder what happened.

And that is why Earth is the way it is. Different humans, different agendas, different perceptions… This is why the **Insider** said we cannot give our power away to some secret society or some popular guru… even Jesus said it: "The kingdom of heaven [our connection with The One] is within…"

The solution devised by Enki was to manipulate the genetics and upgrade the humans to a better (Adapa+) version. And with billions of humans walking around, many of whom need **genetic upgrading**, that is a little like trying to paint a moving freight train!

So human leaders who are sharper than the average, and who may have been in the secret societies, and some who are sometimes called the **Elite**, meet with the Advanced Society and determine that humans will be abducted by **a bio-cybernetic android** (Think: The Greys), and they will abduct as many humans at night as possible, perform scientific evaluations on them to see what the polluted environment is doing to their genetics, and begin to create a new version of Man… Homo *noeticus*. Sometimes these have been called the **Indigos.** They are to be smarter and more aware, more willing to be responsible for what they do… in short, they are also called the **Hybrids**.

And they secured the permission of the US Govt (1954) and other countries' leaders to sanction the Upgrade.

> 30,000 years ago, **Neanderthal** (*Adama*) roamed the European continent, and was something of a brute, slow in his thinking, and while he wasn't tearing up the planet, he didn't get along with other tribes and he and his tribe engaged in a lot of inter-tribal warfare
>
> The Advanced Society removed him and replaced him with **Cro-Magnon** (*Adapa*) and worked with <u>the</u> fledgling secret society of that day to upgrade eligible humans – and Göbekli Tepe (12,000 BC) was one of those places where the *Kundalini* was activated and perhaps also the genetics were modified – obviously Enki and his staff had a part in this.
>
> Then Cro-Magnon was upgraded to **Homo *sapiens*** (*Adapa+*) and nowadays to the Hybrids or **Homo *noeticus***. This will change everything and Man will be less arrogant, less warlike (because he has less testosterone), and he'll

be more psychic and intuit things – and know when he is being lied to or manipulated by the former version of Man (Homo *sapiens*) who has yet to change.

So the future looks good – if enough dysfunctional humans are replaced by (or offset numerically by) the new version of Man. This means that the remaining secret societies will be open to more and more **noetic** humans, and their doors will be less closed – until the secret societies with their advanced spiritual knowledge become the new "churches" where most people will go to get enlightened… kind of a "Göbekli Tepe for the masses." *Kundalini* awakening may also become a common thing.

That also means we will be ready to meet the Advanced Society face-to-face… and work together, journey together, move out into space to explore the wonders of the Multiverse… if the dumb sheep don't outnumber the new noetic humans and destroy everything with their World War III.

What will Man choose… Ascension or Oblivion?

Epilog

The essence of this book was two-fold:

Those who watched and guided Man were largely benevolent and moved around the planet, sharing Knowledge in Agriculture, Astronomy, Writing and the much acclaimed, but secret, Serpent Wisdom. As they educated and assisted mankind, they left similar concepts, imagery and beliefs – the Tree of Life, The Flood, similar Creation information, a respect and symbology for Serpents, Law and Religion, and something that left mankind venerating Orion's Belt (Pyramids of Giza layout, Hopi villages layout) and the Pleiades (source of the significance of the number 7).

The second point made was that some of the unseen benefactors did not have to be ETs – they included those who were here before Man, and Earth is also their home. The mysterious lands that disappeared (Sand Island in the Pacific and Hy Brasil off the British coast), and Atlantis & Mu, and Hyperborea… all point to the Others who not only were here, but probably still are. Underground. Or under large bodies of water (Think: USOs.)

Cosmic Overview

So there are a couple of key points to be made as we close this book. The global survey was to provide evidence that Others were here (not just the Anunnaki) and they oriented Man to skills and Knowledge to set up and successfully run his village/city/state. And today, our **survival as humans** depends on enough people **waking up, being responsible, and being the Resistance that provides our own salvation**. Times have changed and no one is coming to rescue us – not the White Hat ETs, and not even Jesus who'd probably kick butt if he did return – the way he was treated by the PTB, Pharisees and Black Hats would dissuade many avatars from again trying to directly help mankind.

While it can be seen, from the damage done to Puma Punku, Atlantis and Gunung Padang (Chapter 8) for starters, it is obvious that the Others fought among themselves, and we can deduce that all is not rosy. **We are not alone, and never have been** … and now that we can blow up the planet, super pollute it, over-populate it (straining vital resources of air and clean water), the Others have to do something. Man is his own worst enemy – he will even destroy himself if he is not stopped, or at best he'll deliver the future seen so often in SciFi movies, like the *Terminator* series where the landscape is torn up, cities are rubble, humans have largely been wiped out, and the adversary flies overhead. The latest warning in that

genre is *400 Days* – where Man blew up the Moon and pitched the whole planet into chaos.
This is not a joke. We had an opportunity to turn things around in 1987 and Reagan at the UN had the opportunity to explain our real situation and call for more unity – he did say something amazing, but then he clammed up. Fortunately the White Hats won the day 3 years later and collapsed the evil Soviet Union. Yes, evil. The perpetrators of that USSR construct went much further than even the Black Hats predicted, and the biggest reason it failed was that no one could control a country with 11 timezones[477] and no computers.

But what if you had networked computers and 3 timezones…?

Larger Community

That is to emphasize that we are not alone. And as Chapter 10 said, the dictum "As Above, So Below" is accurate – Man squabbles and so do those who have discovered Earth and want its **resources**. Notice when the Science Channel shows what the rest of the planets look like in our solar system, they are barren, gaseous, no life, and while they may have resources, they are not like Earth – Earth is a jewel of habitability: air, water, flora, fauna --- and the ETs with the power to take it have been mining our resources (and more) for centuries. **They are not evil – they just want what they want,** and occasionally the White Hats step in to block them (in our behalf). Yes, the government knows about this and has made deals with some of the Others, for technology in return for 'resources' (many types here).

There are many societies Out There, in the **Larger Community**, and not all are benevolent, nor are all Reptiles enlightened. They have subjugated many worlds and are used to the "might makes right" dictum and they take whatever they want. The Reptoids will use force if the mental influence (see below) doesn't work. They fear humans with souls as we have a connection to a Higher Self that they do not have, so they don't understand, nor trust humans – who can be very unpredictable and are often guided and protected by Light Beings (Angels)… so they use caution and get humans to agree to the ideas that they [the Black Hats] put in humans' heads – then the Angels can't do anything – Humans agreed to it! **This is why Knowledge is important.**

It is all about commerce, trade, getting what you need from someone who has what you want, and hopefully you have something to trade in return. And that is where the danger to Earth comes in: if they continue to take our resources, we will have less and less to bargain with and then humans will not have the resources with which to function, much less trade with the Larger Community, and Earth eventually goes the way of Mars… an exhausted rock not worth much more than a base for operations elsewhere in the solar system. It is all about **resources**.

> When push came to shove, millennia ago, a rare battle erupted in the Inner Planets and Mars got badly scarred, and lost part of its atmosphere and oceans, and the planet between Mars and Jupiter was gradually broken up forming the asteroid belt.

This is serious, folks. No cause for fear – just read on and see what you have to do to protect yourself and your loved ones…

Benevolent Quarantine

Part of the problem is that those (Anunnaki) who started us did so as **slave workers**, and while Enlil did not care to continue to support and develop Man, Enki did – if for nothing else than scientific curiosity – "How far can I develop my protégés?" And it turned out that the humans were very viable as a body into which a soul could incarnate for interestingl experiences so the ***Adapa+*** was a winner… and once souls discovered human forms, the Higher Beings had to work thru the Solar Council to make special provision for them – they were now a **sentient, ensouled creation** and that is why the planet is today **in White Hat Quarantine** (has been for 800+ years), and that is why the Anunnaki Remnant (on Earth) were told to monitor, educate and guide their progeny.

So, the Quarantine protects Earth and humans from the Black Hats? Sometimes, but that is why we can't freely go to the Moon, or Mars – too dangerous. The Moon is a base and we had 'permission' to go only 6 times. While the Quarantine does stop 90% of the Black Hats Out There, it is said the Draconians have the ability to travel **intra-**dimensionally and 'beam' into an underground facility from outside the Quarantine.

Man now has the responsibility to develop himself, not only mentally and spiritually, but technologically to defend himself and his resources. Our current situation will not last forever… it is a little like the USA trying to teach and support the Vietnamese or Afghans in learning and defending their own countries – the US serves as advisors, and does not want to fight their battles for them (and we got sucked into it anyway!), but the Nordics are more advanced and will not fight for us – they can blockade, and they can advise (i.e., give technology), but it is up to Man to make it work – **Protection of Earth is up to Man**. Where do you think the billions of $$ have gone in the last 20 years? Why do you think the National Debt is a 'necessary evil' and will not be balanced again? National Security is very important and is not just a buzzword.

If the Nordics fought our battles for us, we'd become dependent on them and that is not what they want. That also makes them an enemy of the Reptilians and damages their economic balance in the Large Community… so it isn't in their best interests.

They have stuck their necks out with the Quarantine (which is supported by a number of races), but the agreement was that it would not last forever, and then the Earthlings will have to handle things for themselves… The Council laid the Law down that Earth was not to be stripped of its resources as the Reptiles were wont to do.

Black Hat Subterfuge

The Black Hats have other ways around the Quarantine, however. Let's examine two more of them. If we are aware of them, perhaps we can be on our guard…

Hybrid 5th Column

It was said that a **5th column** approach is used to undermine a school, a government, a country… just slip agents of destruction (or even disinformation) into a going organization, and watch them destroy it from within. It isn't necessary to fire any shots, just infiltrate, work up into positions of authority, then manipulate and deactivate whatever has been working.

And this has been happening with the little Greys – one set is working to create a hybrid human who can be manipulated by them and the Black Hats to further their agenda, and a second group under the control of the Anunnaki Remnant, who seek to also create hybrids who are proactive and make for a smarter, more intuitive human, and who are more altruistic.

> Both groups of Greys are **bio-cybernetic androids** with a dual brain – one communal, the other for personal tasks assigned it. (This is not counting the real Grays [note spelling] from Zeta Reticuli.)

That is why all the abductions and cattle mutilations (the latter for 'parts').

Mind Control

No advanced race Out There stoops to the crude and primitive invasion scenario and "blast 'em all to hell" idea we love to portray in our SciFi movies. Actual battle, or war, is very rare because there are resources at stake and any disruption on a Galactic scale (to anybody!) can be disastrous – so cooperation and negotiation, trade and commerce rule.

> In addition, the groups Out There are pretty evenly matched in their technology (as we are on Earth – again: As Below, So Above) and so no one has an outstanding edge.

However, the one area that even the Council cannot stop deals with the ability of most of the Larger Community to **communicate telepathically** – an ability that was NOT given to Man. Knowing what your 'enemy' competitor is planning and thinking just about obviates all-out war, and that is another reason it is very rare Out There. But, **mental influence and manipulation** are often the rule – used on unsuspecting and undeveloped civilizations.

And that is what the Reptiles who are <u>very good at it</u> are doing from the other side of the Quarantine – We must think about what <u>we</u> are doing, gain Knowledge, and act as intelligent, responsible, self-directed beings.

Knowledge Protects
Ignorance Enslaves

If we know the Reptiles can do it and we know they exist, and what they can do, we will more closely guard our thoughts instead of blindly and emotionally jumping to act on them. The Black Hats hope we do not learn and grow, gain **Knowledge**, and thereby resist them – this is how they have subjugated so many worlds Out There… Earth will be next and humans relegated to mindless (non-thinking) puppets **if** the Reptoids have their way… and it is already happening… The Bookstores and Video stores are disappearing, the American educational system no longer teaches kids to think (H.O.T.S. is gone)[478] – just memorize names, dates and events…. But learn of nothing like Sumeria or Khazaria that would <u>warn people</u> to wonder and think. The Black Hats (which include the PTB, the 3D fat cats who think they will be rewarded for selling out their own planet/country) <u>will be thrown under the bus</u> if/when the Black Hat leaders take over.

> The PTB fat cats cannot be trusted – they sellout their own kind, so the smarter Black Hats know they can't trust the Earth PTB and <u>will</u> get rid of them.

And given human ignorance, complacency and disbelief, most humans think we're all alone and that we are soon going to create a perfect, wonderful world on Earth – and the New Age pundits are pushing that – and **it is a Black Hat teaching**!

New Age Interference

Just so that you know how they seek to control and derail a society, you need to be wary of the New Age "everything is OK, just smile and Be Happy!" teaching. Even Albert Speer, Hitler's Minister of Propaganda, knew the secret: keep the people distracted and keep telling them a lie – **if they hear it often enough, they'll believe it**. So they controlled the Banks and the Media – same thing nowadays in the USA – the people were kept in debt, so they had no time for reading and discussion, let alone thinking, so they had to work their butts off. And the Media never let them hear anything that would cause them alarm – kind of like the US Media today – UFOs are not reported, and people are conditioned to laugh at them.

So what is wrong with the New Age promoting just Love and Happiness? Nothing – as long as the people also are taught that Life is a School and we are not here just to be happy – yet that is the teaching with several of the New Age "centers" as they are now called – Centers for Spiritual Living (which replaced Religious Science where people could think and question about how to grow spiritually)… Black Hats don't want people thinking, they want compliance, so Sundays in these new 'churches' are all about Love, Joy, and **guided meditation** (Think: you are in Alpha and are sensitive to suggestions said during the guided meditation… such as "I hear no negativity, I do not respond to negativity… All is well!"… all that borders on hypnotic suggestion.) Also called **entrainment**.

> The author attended several of these CSL centers and found them to be Jumping Freddy Feelgood churches – people were dancing in the aisles, hugging, laughing and doing a conga line around the room – no teaching. And then the leader did the *pièce de résistance*: She played the video by Pharrell Williams called *Happy*.
> And that is a very catchy, happy video… no question about it… but I noticed the part where he tells people that they do not need to bother with anything negative… Here it is: [479]
>
> > Here come bad news talking this and that
> > Yeah, give me all you got, don't hold back
> > Yeah, well I should probably warn you I'll be just fine
> > Yeah, no offense to you, don't waste your time
> > Here's why -- Because I'm happy….
>
> And that is reinforced with:
>
> > …'cause I'm Happy…
> > **Can't nothing bring me down**
> > **Love** is too happy to bring me down
> > Can't nothing bring me down
> > …I said bring me down…
> > Can't nothing bring me down
> > **Love is too happy to bring me down**
> > Can't nothing bring me down
> > I said …. Because I'm happy….
> > [emphasis added]

So that reinforces the Beatles' song *All You Need is Love*, and that was a wrong idea planted with the Beatles. "ALL" you need…? You also need **Knowledge**. Be aware that there is such a thing as **entrainment**… the more you hear something, or listen to *Happy*, the more it will program you. If you are busy being happy, can you still handle the negative issue before you? True, one need not collapse and be "brought down" as the song says – but our task in the Earth School is to handle our lessons, our tests, and not blow them off – as Mr. Williams is advocating. His song suggests that we be happy at any price… and that is a Black Hat teaching. After a while, you'll begin to see these kinds of **'positive' distractions**….

The gods are not ogres, happiness is OK on Earth, but to ignore issues that arise and still focus on being happy (which means ignoring something that you need to handle)… is a dangerous thing to do. **We are not here to be happy**, we are to learn, think, and handle whatever comes up. We will experience happiness along the way, but it is not what life is about.

The Black Hats hope you believe in being happy 24/7.

Also, the New Age is telling people that they can "create their day" – make it turn out the way they want… Ignore problems and they'll disappear…. And the most questionable of all: Awaken the Giant Within! It is so positive, what could be wrong with that? Simply that there is already a larger You that projected (small) you into this realm and when you die, you return to it – but you don't "awaken" it, control it, use it… it is also called your **Higher Self** (VEG and TOM examine this in some detail), and when you go within as the Gnostics said, you can connect with it, and synch up with it... and if Tony meant awaken the *Kundalini*, then Ok; else he's misleading people.

So the TV used to be used for **subliminal programming in the 50's**… advertisers would flash "Drink Cola" or "Eat Cookies" on the TV screen for ¼ second, so fast that the conscious mind does not catch it, but the subconscious did see it, and all of a sudden, viewers had a desire for a cola or cookies… Supposedly that has stopped… But what if the Black Hats are still doing it (and they now mostly control the Media), so where would the "watchdogs" be to guard the public against it…?

> This was the idea behind the movie *They Live* (1988) which warned people about **Hidden Persuaders**[480] (also the name of a Vance Packard book from 1957)… humans are very susceptible to suggestion… But they don't need to do subliminal suggestions – TV nowadays just has a "sex & violence" emphasis that shows back in the 50s-70s did not have. That difference is what counts: women are now sex objects, the family head is either a joke, gay or unwed (giving the idea that it is the new norm) and 40% of the TV shows out there deal with crime and violence… just as the Black Hats planned… and it is now

Ok to use the "F" word. Have we lost conscience and respect for Life?

How do you know whether the TV network program heads are not being **influenced** to degrade American society?

> If you want to boil a live frog, you don't throw him into a pot of boiling water – he'll jump right out. But if you put the frog in a pot of cool water and turn the heat on, he'll boil to death because the heat is increased so gradually, he gets used to it.
>
> What is gradually being done in America today?

What this book has been saying is that the Anunnaki may have set us on the right course, and the Watchers have (up till 40 years ago) kept us fairly strong, free, and respecting the environment. And now there is something else going around the planet which is disruptive, derailing, and deceptive… Others are here who do not want Man to make it, they do not care about Man, and they are called the Black Hats who just want the **planetary resources**. It is a new threat and because it is new, most people do not suspect or see it – the Black Hats are very clever and have been outthinking and manipulating Man, influencing his thinking, for centuries – Wonder why Man never gets it together?

> If Man cannot get his act together, see what is really happening, he too will boil to death in that pot that Others have now got him in. Man and his soul is a threat to the Reptoids, and their hybrids some of whom walk among us, who do not have souls. They fear Man

There is a battle for Man's hearts, minds and souls going on and it pays to question, research and think. We are not alone, this is not our planet (yet), and as the Insider said (Chapter 13), if something is heavily promoted, be wary … it may not be in our best interest.

Thus, even this book must be thought about… and consider whether this Epilog is warning about the real thing or not. No one likes to be deceived, nor fooled into believing something that isn't so. And it is hoped that enough "coincidences" and similar legends were presented in the foregoing chapters to give the reader something to think about… How could so many different cultures, miles apart and sometimes centuries apart, have similar traditions and teachings? There had to be a common interface, and because the Anunnaki lived longer than Man and were very mobile, (sky boats and flying craft) and wanted Man to succeed as a species…. They are the logical common denominator.

So now we come to consider whether similar or unusual things are going on in today's world. And they are – as the following sections will present for evaluation.

> Remember, if you convince yourself that all this is froo-froo, and it doesn't mean anything, you play into the hands of the Black Hats… Can you afford to (1) be wrong, (2) be part of the problem because **ignorance enslaves**, and (3) miss the opportunity to rise above the current level of **limited Earth thinking** and not gain Knowledge that will benefit you and mankind?

With that in mind, here are some things to think about from <u>today's world</u>.

Today's Global Anomalies

First, we have been told that there are no **UFOs**, and there will be no disclosure – not because they aren't real, but you don't want to know who's flying them (really), and secondly it would do you no good even if you did know. And thirdly, they are not "UFOs" – nowadays they are called ARVs (Ærial Reconnaissance Vehicles), or UAP (Unidentified Ærial Phenomena), and sometimes IFOs – they have been identified so they are Identified Flying Objects. Thus the Air Force can say there are no UFOs.

> Because they use electrogravitic propulsion (i.e., Anti-grav systems), they are only of use around the Earth where they have gravity to push against – they have to fly up and into Mother Ships in orbit which use a different means of propulsion to fly between planets.

It is puzzling that the **Moon** always has the same side turned to the Earth – whereas every other moon we know about revolves. In addition, the Moon has been shown to be hollow, or at least composed of large cavities. And is it just a coincidence that the Moon exactly eclipses the Sun?

Mars is another anomaly: there are what appear to be "glass tubes" on Mars – (Appendix A) probably some Plexiglas-type tubing which would be a logical carrier for water from the poles to underground facilities. And then, there is the Face on Mars with attendant pyramidal structures to its left… (See VEG, Apx A… the Face was <u>not</u> proven to be a trick of the light.)

Equally perplexing were the two Russian **Phobos** reconnaissance probes sent to Mars and both were mysteriously terminated. Then there were the **Apollo Moon** missions that abruptly ended with Apollo 17, and left 18 sitting on its launch pad… and the cancellation of the **Space Shuttle** program… Going to the Moon and back in a Space Shuttle was never announced but would have been a very viable means to go, circle, drop a lander and return… And what ever happened to the Chinese Moon Rover (sent in 2013)….**Chang'E 3? (**It stopped working in 2015.)

And there is where the ET aspect comes in to play – we are not wanted on the Moon, we haven't been back in 44 years, and it is strongly suspected that we are not on Mars, either. Mars rovers were tested in the **Atacama Desert** in the mountains of Chile…

> In a region about 100 km (60 mi) south of Antofagasta, which averages 3,000 m (10,000 ft) in elevation, the soil has been compared to that of Mars. Owing to its otherworldly appearance, the Atacama has been used as a location for filming Mars scenes, most notably in the television series *Space Odyssey: Voyage to the Planets.*

Atacama Desert #1

> In 2003, a team of researchers published a report in the journal Science in which they duplicated the tests used by the Viking 1 and Viking 2 Mars landers to detect life, and were **unable to detect any signs in Atacama Desert soil** in the region of Yungay. The region may be unique on Earth in this regard, and is being used by NASA to test instruments for future Mars missions. The team duplicated the Viking tests in Mars-like Earth environments and found that they missed present signs of life in soil samples from **Antarctic** dry valleys, the Atacama Desert of Chile and Peru, and other locales. However, in 2014, a new hyperarid site was reported, **María Elena South Atacama (left)**, which was much drier than Yungay, and thus, a better Mars-like environment.

Still think we're really on Mars?

The Atacama is also a testing site for the NASA-funded **Earth-Mars cave Detection Program.** [481] [emphasis added]

Atacama Desert #2
Note the European Space Observatory on the hill (right) in the background…[482]

Of course, any remote desert, <u>with an orange filter</u> on the camera might do… like this one?

Nahal Bokek in the Judean Desert[483]

Ok, you get the point, we don't have to be on Mars, and if the Phobos "shoot-downs" were any measure of our welcome there, it isn't likely that we have rovers on Mars. And then there was this recent picture of the Mars rover Curiosity being "cleaned"...[484]

The above is a 'selfie' shot by Curiosity... Tell me again, we are on Mars... no helmet, but backpack for an oxygen mask...? (see video: endnote 484 in Epilog Endnotes)

And then the Scottish hacker, **Gary McKinnon** (2002), who found lists of extraterrestrial ships and officers working in a program called **Solar Warden**... If one connects the dots, it looks like we are already off the planet, and having trouble with the **Black Hats** Out There... so we are still Earth-bound.

Mars Fake Color

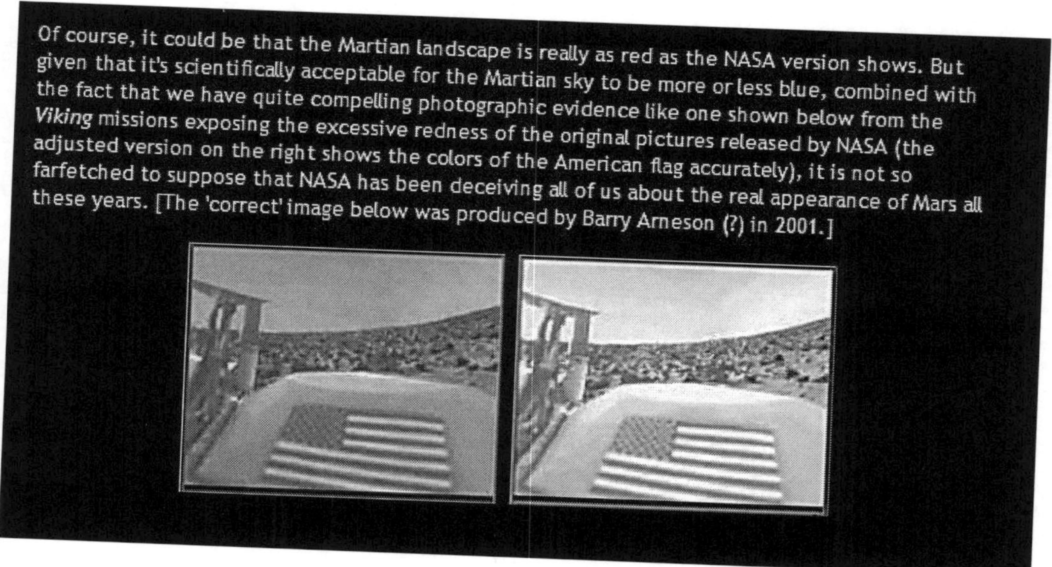

To see the color difference, go to: http://davidaroffman.com/photo2_5.html

And there is more…
And years ago, someone took a Mars rover shot of Mars, noting that the colorwheel was off, and they adjusted the color of the Mars photo to where the colorwheel would be true…true red, true blue, true green… and we got a picture of Mars that looks like it was shot on Earth… pale dirt and blue sky.[485] In other words, the Mars rover shot had been doctored by NASA/JPL to look orangish-redish because that is what the public expects to see of the 'Red Planet'…
The excellent article is at:
http://www.thelivingmoon.com/43ancients/02files/Mars_Blue_Bird_Color_01.html

And then there was the mysterious **cleaning** of the solar panels on Opportunity…

(credit: Bing images: businessinsider.com)

Someone will say, well the Martian wind blew the dust off… and you need to ask yourself, What if it wasn't the wind? What if the wind (dust storm) blew more onto the panels?

Always question….

What is this from the Mars rover…?

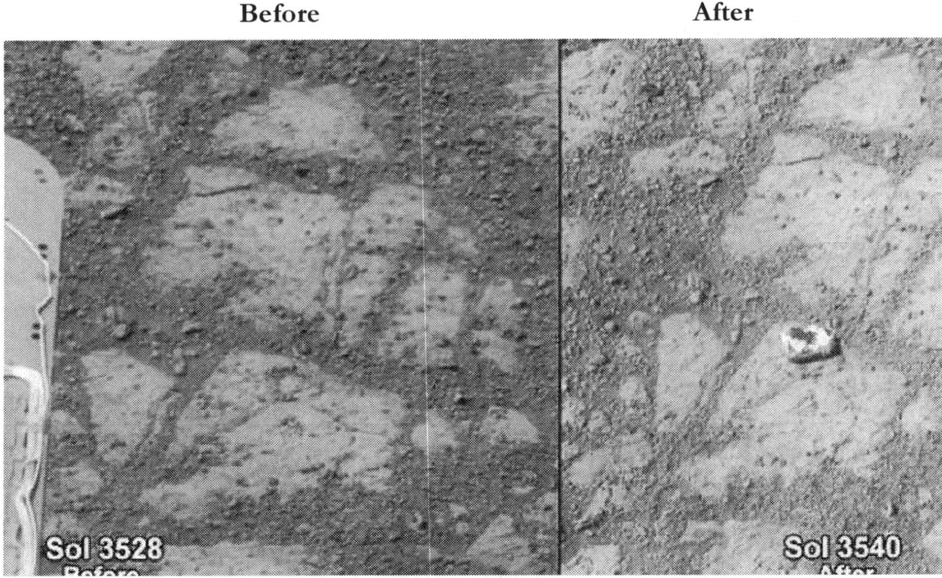

A "jelly donut" appears out of nowhere (right) …or was this taken in Atacama?

Venus Oddity

Venera 1 failed, Venera 2 flew past Venus, and Venera 3 sent no data… Now we are told that Venera 13 landed and started taking pictures after the lenscap fell off… Note the picture of the Venera (next page) – there are 2 cameras. Why a lenscap?

Image of the Surface of Venus Venera 13 Lander A
Does that look like a lenscap…. Given the camera shown below…?

Cameras 1 & 2 were positioned 180° apart. There was no lenscap on the ground on the other side of the Venera.

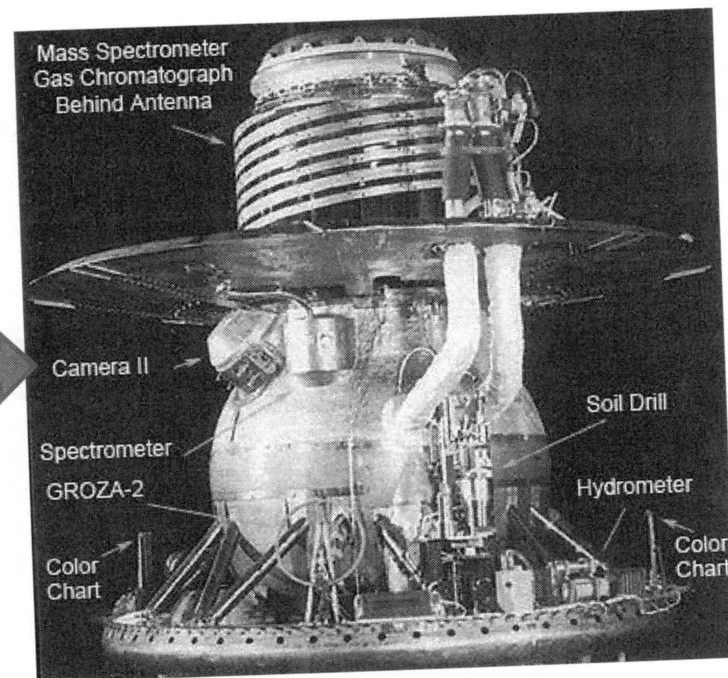

Maybe it <u>is</u> a lenscap, but....

...how do you program a lenscap to come off? Why would it break? Why use one in the first place? Why was one not seen on the other side of the craft? Here is some real BS...

> It's also enormously difficult to gather images of Venus from the surface of the planet because of the extreme temperatures (over 460° C or 860° F) and crushing atmosphere **(92 times that of Earth)**. And don't forget the **sulfuric acid** in the upper atmosphere...[486] [emphasis added]

Those certainly are the standard Venus description given...
Wouldn't 92 Atmospheres crush the craft? That is 1,352 psi.
Do the math – 1 atmosphere = 14.7 psi.
Modern submarines cannot go below 2000' (= 880 psi)...
every 1000' = 440 psi.
So here we have a Venera lander and <u>sphere</u> (see above) going to 1,352 psi? What is wrong with this story?

Georgia Guidestones

Closer to home, and this repeats what was said in VEG and QES, the Black Hats put up a warning in stone... in Northeast Georgia, in 1980, in the middle of nowhere. You can't say they don't warn us... the structure is in 8 common Earth

languages, plus 2 old ones, and it suggests major changes to be made to Earth civilization….
It also contains these 4 languages: Babylonian, Classical Greek, Sanskrit, and Ancient Egyptian (hieroglyphics), plus accurate astronomical alignments. Think about that – That is some expertise!

Georgia Guidestones

(Credit: Bing Images: folkmaktnu.wordpress.com)

And a copy of the English panel:

1. Maintain humanity under 500,000,000 in perpetual balance with nature.

A stark reminder that we are overpopulated.

2. Guide reproduction wisely — improving fitness and diversity.
3. Unite humanity with a living new language.
4. Rule passion — faith — tradition — and all things with tempered reason.
5. Protect people and nations with fair laws and just courts.
6. Let all nations rule internally resolving external disputes in a world court.
7. Avoid petty laws and useless officials.
8. Balance personal rights with social duties.
9. Prize truth — beauty — love — seeking harmony with the infinite.
10. Be not a cancer on the earth — Leave room for nature — Leave room for nature.

While it may not have been the Black Hats who erected the monument; the Others who also live on Earth would agree with #s 2-9. #1 supports Black Hat control. Two interesting comments[487] on the Georgia Guidestones … to make one think:

> Computer analyst Van Smith said the monument's dimensions predicted the height of the **Burj Khalifa** [now the tallest building in the world], which opened in Dubai over thirty years after the Georgia Guidestones were designed. Smith said the builders of the Guidestones were likely aware of the Burj Khalifa project which he compared to the biblical **Tower of Babel**.
>
> The most widely agreed-upon interpretation of the stones is that they describe the basic concepts required to rebuild a devastated civilization. **Brad Meltzer** argues that the stones were built in 1979 at the height of the Cold War, and may have been intended as a message to the possible survivors of a World War III. The engraved suggestion to keep humanity's population below 500 million could have been made under the assumption that it had already been reduced below this number.

Summary

So, the point is that we can't always believe what is told us via the Media or NASA. Thus, is NASA lying? Not if it is very important that certain things not be exposed in the interest of National Security. "Airbrushing" and denial would be required if NASA knows something that cannot be revealed at this time. Then the Media would also be told to follow suit.

Then those of us who have been given the information could share certain aspects of it, for those whose curiosity means they can probably handle a basic amount of revelation, but the general public has been conditioned to ignore and laugh at what 8% of the country considers interesting – that 8% is a cut above the rest of humanity and may have the *Adapa+* genes… so expanding their Knowledge is not a bad thing.

However, it is wise to be skeptical and do further research – until they lockdown the Internet, and restrict where you can go, OR they just remove the websites that would educate you. "Browsing and discovering" is being seriously curtailed with each passing year.

Earth history is more than we have been told and it pays to read, investigate and think – when you have enough data, it might be possible to "connect the dots." And if you do, books like the six that have been released by this author are there to get people to think and wonder…to promote Knowledge… until the PTB have their way and society is locked down, education is controlled, and thinking is no longer an option… Wow! A return to the good ol' days of Medieval Europe!

Appendix A: More Dragon Wisdom

This Appendix will profile the key ideas found in the ten suggested books at the end of Chapter 13, and at the beginning of the Bibliography. Anyone who is curious as to what esoteric ideas could be part of Serpent (aka Dragon) Wisdom originally kept just for initiates in the secret societies, here they are. Truth is Truth and because these ideas are so profound, they had to be part of the original Dragon Wisdom Teachings and Man can still benefit from and grow thru these higher truths.

Authors' text quoted is referenced in ( ).

Oneness by Rasha.

It is crucial that you attain a state of **detachment** from the energy changes that have magnetized you....recognize the common thread in the web of dramas that you have woven – that continue to ensnare you.... Until you are able to liberate yourself, vibrationally, from the chronic patterns of response that keep you "stuck" in endless repetitions of the same old song, your higher aspect of self is unable to integrate you without jeopardizing its own vibrational levels...

You are a **multidimensional** being. There are viable aspects of self that live, unbeknownst to you, in parallel realities... There are aspects of your own being who have been excluded from *you* and who seek to integrate with you, in *their* journey toward Oneness. (29-30)

This is the experience you would refer to as **ascension**. One does not.... cease to materialize in physical form... rather one comes to embody each successive level , as each is embraced and encompassed.... The heightened sensibilities are integrated and one is able to resonate at the higher level of the expanded consciousness, and to perceive the world as it truly is [good and bad].... Ultimately one comes to embody all aspects of one's inter-dimensional lineage simultaneously. (25)

You are fully responsible for your vibrational state of beingness [PFV] at any given moment.... It is not necessary to experience repeat performances of painful dramas....the only way to end this vicious cycle of events is to become very clear about the connection between your vibrational state and the life dramas it creates for you to live out... **There are no victims**... It becomes abundantly clear when you are vibrationally balanced and **heart-focused**. You are in command of your situation at all times. Step back.... and make the conscious choice to shift the energy to one emanating from the place of heart-centeredness... detach from the circumstances...

Beings who have integrated heightened levels of vibration as their "norm" will experience extreme results when shifting to an unbalanced vibrational state. The vibration of every thought pattern that passes thru your consciousness carries an energy charge ... by releasing that energy in the form of **speech** you set into motion an imprint that magnetizes to it circumstances of a corresponding vibration...[thus] "your thoughts create your reality." (34-37) Monitor your words.

She also discusses one's **script**, freewill, intent, timelines, detachment vs. indifference, life themes and how to de-energize them. She also goes into quite some detail about **ascension**, what it looks like, how it happens and what it means when things are going well and all of a sudden, things go to hell. "These are classic signs of the advanced stages of the journey." (93)

When one attempts to defy a situation by meeting adversity head-on, one disrupts the momentum and manifests results that are less desirable. Conflict can be circumvented by simply allowing it to pass without becoming ensnared in its grasp....Riding the wave of the energies is a skill that you will perfect as part of this process....[and yet] Ultimately, one's "buttons" *must* be pushed and the corresponding energy charge released if one is to realize one's highest potential... [she is not saying to avoid issues, but face them and ...] **allow the energy to pass *through* one's field**...[and allow it to trigger release of the negative pockets of energy without reacting negatively to it]... An energy charge that is allowed to remain will continue to draw to it repeated opportunities for release. Avoidance of the underlying issues and the maintenance of a calm veneer does <u>not</u> enhance one's progress. Quite the contrary. ... No one emerges from the **journey of transformation** without having weathered a storm or two....gasping for breath now and then. (94-96)

And while the book is full of spiritual and metaphysical insights, there is one point worth noting for those people who try to **control** things in their lives:

As you become consciously aware that the only thing that can be counted on is the realization that nothing can be counted on, you will shift from a mind-set of expectation to one of **allowance**. You cannot "control" anything now [at this stage in your 3D development]. You are, in fact, totally "out of control." ....**Resistance** to the reality that things are not the way that they were .... will only reinforce the difficulties you may choose to create for yourself. **Openness**.... is the best possible response to the conditions at hand. (105)

As TOM (Ch. 3 & 6) and TSiM (Ch. 4) both share, we are born into the world with a **Script**, or a **Sacred Contract** as Dr. Caroline Myss says, that sets up what we are to experience here (like a school curriculum) and we have **freewill** about how we handle the "tests" and "trials" that are really just **catalyst.** The Script does not tell us what to do or what to say – that is why it is a **test** – to see what we have learned and how we handle what we get… knowing that often we cannot control what we get. Only the major events are orchestrated.

She also talks about **life scripts** (40) and more pointedly:

The only real security in these times [of accelerated energies] is the unmistakable sense of well-being that is experienced when you are in harmony with the flow of the higher frequencies [and she shares how to do that]…. The details of how things will work out are perceived as less important than the sense of being in harmony with the flow of your own **highest purpose**….allow the process to direct you rather than trying to direct the process… relinquish the "need to know" [because the energies are increasing and]… the population at large will be dealing with levels of change in their **life scripts** for which there is no precedent. And many will have difficulty in dealing with the demolition of the foundations upon which they have structured their lives…. It is important that you retain the perspective of the overview with world events that reflect a reversion to fear…. It is not necessary to intervene in the **scripts** of others undergoing such trials… although you may choose to do so. For their higher purpose [soul growth thru 'fire'] would not be served by helping them avoid the circumstances without providing the understanding that gives those trials relevance.

And in many cases, as Thaddeus Golas (below) says, you don't know where they are at [spiritually] or why they are facing a particular test, so how can you really help them? If you remove their lesson, have you really helped them?… and how can you 'fix' what you don't really understand? You don't ignore them, but give them moral support, encouragement, pray with/for them… to be indifferent to them means you will have to go thru what they are experiencing (at some point).

Indifference is the opposite of Love.
and
There is never an excuse for a failure to Love.

Lastly, she talks a bit about personal **Transformation** – the kind the Alchemists were after, and what it looks like, how to develop it and sustain it. (Her Ch. 23, especially p. 227) There is so much more terrific information that a whole 2nd book could be written about it, but that would be a repeat of the gems Rasha has already given us.

Spiritual Growth by Sanaya Roman

Moving into higher consciousness and **increasing one's vibration**. She says that Love is the way to raise our vibration (79) and we can send Love forward and back in time (82). That means we can heal old wounds and bless people we didn't get to say goodbye to. In addition, **one positive thought can cancel out hundreds of negative ones** (80). Rather than criticizing others for their faults, or focusing on them, realize that you have the opportunity to raise your vibration by loving them.

Becoming a source of Light. Ch. 15. You can send people Light to use as they wish without saying anything, and realize that you can talk mentally directly to other people's Higher Selves – by intending it. (166-167) As you grow spiritually, your words gain more power to affect people, so it is better to say those things that serve people in some way. (184-185) If you focus on their behavior that you do not like, you may elicit more of the same from them – remember, <u>you</u> have lessons to learn, from them. (187)

Enlightenment thru service – if you are really enlightened, you have an inner drive to serve. And it is important to know when to assist people and when not to. (164) Are there people who aren't growing and who are a drain when you try and assist? It takes a certain amount of your energy to shift someone's consciousness to a higher level. Know that the higher your consciousness, the more of a penalty you pay for putting your energy where it doesn't create a shift. (165) Remember, offer assistance to others <u>only when they ask for it</u>. (197)

Energy Vampires – (196-197). (Covered in TOM, Ch. 11.)

Attachment – Everything comes into your life to teach you something. And sometimes we like what we have and get attached to it… part of the spiritual growth dictum says that we be willing to let go of things/people that no longer serve us. We let go because **attachment** is one of the strongest barriers to growth.

Hanging on to something you currently have can occupy the space for what you really want to appear. Once you release something, it will either come back to you or something better will take its place. **Detach from needing to have things work out a certain way**… IF you are tuned in to your higher good, trust that all is working as it should…(202-205) [As they used to say in the Est Training: "Take what you get and don't take what you don't get."]

Lastly, attachment is wanting to take care of people and solve their problems for them. Sometimes the only thing you can do is Love them and let them have their problems (lessons). **You are not responsible for making other peoples' lives work** – they are. (205-207) But if they ask for assistance, see if you can assist them with compassion – but not do it for them or tell them what to do… perhaps suggest, or give them hints. The need to save people from their mistakes is an attachment that will slow your growth, and you may then become a victim. (206-207)

Becoming Transparent – Be aware that as you grow spiritually, you will be more and more aware of other peoples' energies around you, and learning how to stay centered and calm while they are running thru various emotions is called "being transparent." Their energies (and thoughts) pass right thru you… no reaction.(213)

Any resentment because you had a **difficult childhood** needs to be let go of – remember that you don't get steel without fire. Hopefully you gained strength from the situations and people you grew up with. If you are around people whose energy you are not comfortable with, see it as an opportunity to teach you transparency. You could try changing jobs or moving to a different set of neighbors, but you will continually attract people of a similar hue until you learn how to stay balanced in your center when you are around them. (214) You can always **White Light** yourself and see an aura of strong white light protecting you from really abusive energy [as well as cover your solar plexus area – the 3rd chakra is where the energy cords of others connects to drain you]. Feel compassion, send the Love & Light, and observe them as you would a lab experiment (maybe even imagine them 1" tall)… and take charge of your emotions. (215-216)

Learning to sense and handle other peoples' energy is what the other book by Sanaya Roman (below) is about… and as you go higher, you want to transmute others' negative energy rather than be transparent to it. (218)

Personal Power Thru Awareness by Sanaya Roman

You are affected by the energies that surround you –learn to read them and realize when you are being affected by them, and cancel the effect.

Sensing Energy and using **visualization** to transmute it. (8)

Exercises to sense energy and sense whether you can feel the energy in a room as you first walk into it – and did that change how you were feeling?

You do not have to go thru pain and struggle to grow. (79)
There is no one right way to evolve. (94)
If any area of your life is not working, one of your beliefs in that area needs to be changed. (95)
You can assist mankind in achieving peace by evolving your thoughts. (96)
The more you understand what you are learning from a situation, the more rapidly you can leave it. (116)
If you have nothing to defend, living becomes easier. (107)
Forgiveness is important – it releases the energy ties between you… and if you have trouble forgiving someone, pretend that this is their last day on Earth. (120)
Rather than resisting lower thoughts, place higher ones by their side. (151)

Also: Opening intuition, positive self-talk, changing energy states, receiving guidance from the higher realms, and wisdom.

Next we come to a very interesting book where the author delineates the **Levels of Consciousness** and what they look like as one ascends the spiritual staircase.

Putting on the Mind of Christ   by Jim Marion

Consciousness Scale (Chapters 4-11)

1. Infant Level

The developing awareness of the infant begins with a sense of differentiation of its body from that of its mother. This is true of spiritual growth in general: the more a person's Consciousness goes up the spiritual ladder, the less attached they are to physical matter.

All growth in Consciousness is a process of inner realization.[488]

This level has been termed **very primitive** – the Soul is receiving input from its 5 senses, but is **very me-me-me based.** Whereas each level in the future will be less egocentric than the last, this first stage is **very tied to dense matter**, and were the child to stay at this level as it becomes an adult, it would be a spiritual disaster.

A child that does not make a clear distinction between self and others may grow up afflicted with **narcissism… or** as an adult afflicted with a borderline personality disorder – **seeing oneself as a victim and never takes responsibility for his own problems.**

2. **Magical or Child Level**

This is usually the human's life between ages 2 - 7. It is called 'magical' because it often includes a world of fairies, elves, gods, demons, and various imaginary creatures that inhabit the child's world. **The child often cannot determine what is real and what is imaginary, and the child often believes the world still revolves around it.**

> **Magical consciousness was the general level of consciousness in the polytheistic, animistic, tribally-organized ancient world**. [489]

At this time, the child begins to learn what is right and what is wrong in its particular culture. But this is not a moral sense of what is right or wrong, it is based on what makes Mom and Dad happy or upset. As age 7 approaches, the child may have the beginning sense that its point of view is not the only one. Self-centeredness begins to fade.

Obviously, if the child does not develop and grows into adulthood with this Magical view of the self and world, s/he will be **a very limited adult, often superstitious and naïve.**

3. **Mythical or Adolescent Level**

This is the area of growth **into the teens**. It is the first of the "mental levels" as the child's mind or ego begins to emerge. There is a belief that the God in the Sky and one's parents can accomplish every sort of miracle to meet the child's needs. The mythical has incorporated some earlier magic.

And yet at the same time, the child begins to adopt a law-and-order phase where s/he defines itself by conventional rules and sees its self-worth in following those rules, and behaving properly. **Rules and roles** are taken seriously.

> Until recently, the mythic level of consciousness has been the dominant level of consciousness in all the world's "universal" religions, including Christianity.[490]

For some reason, the child sees Mommy and Daddy as right in whatever church they belong to, whatever political party they belong to, and the child just knows that the public school that s/he attends is the best one in the world. Trying to teach tolerance and diversity to a child at this age does no good; the brain has not developed enough to allow analysis of abstract concepts.

These people at this level **cannot think "globally"** and planetary ecology is not important to them. They are centered in their own little world. Other religions are a threat to them. Perhaps that helps to explain why some people are so **narrow-minded** and cannot examine their Faith and other beliefs… without suffering a nervous breakdown. The 'programming' of beliefs as a child goes deep and often stays into adulthood.

4. **Adult or Rational Level**

This is the second of the mental levels, and is **the dominant Consciousness of our present age, and is the level attained by the average adult in today's world**. Many are stuck at this level and don't know it.

The Age of Reason, the Industrial Revolution, and Man's current drive in Physics to understand the world about him has supported the public schools' emphasizing math and science for all our kids in school. There is an **opportunity to develop abstract thinking**, to reason or argue with friends about philosophical statements (e.g., "All men are created equal") and thus begin to **develop some higher thinking skills**.

Thinking skills are often exercised to a greater degree in college studies. There the danger is to fall prey to ideologies and groups who want to bend students' thinking in their direction. Yet too many people have not been able to train the mind to the discipline of Logic and spot false ideas, false claims, and illogical proposals.

The development of reason will encourage the teenager to **question rules and society's traditional structures.** Bringing forth their earlier Mythical propensities, they may begin to imagine a better world and hopefully one that make sense for the greater good. Developing reason should bring the teenager's mind to the awareness of a global economy, global ecology, and perhaps even a one world religion… Such was the energy behind the European Union and the Euro.

> It would appear that the majority of the world's people fall into the last two categories, or levels: Mythic or Rational, with some people in a half-and-half state. Developing Love and Knowledge will assist these souls in becoming Earth Graduates – see TSiM Chapter 13.

5. Vision-Logic Consciousness

This is the highest of the three mental states. It is the Consciousness of many great writers, artists, scientists and philosophers. **The primary aspect of this level is a sense of self with the abstract mind, and the ability to think from many different perspectives.**

It is definitely STO and these people think globally. These people can resolve international issues with their **ability to think and see from the 40,000' level** – but their solutions may 'threaten' those who still function at the Mythic level.

This is the first level of Consciousness where it can be said that we have successfully integrated body, emotions and mind. [491] And we no longer identify self by race, color or religion – we are simply a human being, humble yet very other-directed (STO). **We seek the good for all humanity, and are tolerant of other cultures, religions and ideas.**

But all is not rosy and there is a downside to this seemingly wonderful level of Consciousness. It is called **Existentialism** and has been known to cause profound unrest and angst, sometimes leading a soul to nihilism. They have so many great ideas and so little time in which to see them to completion. And then, they often worry what will become of their projects when they die…?

These people sometimes **struggle to find meaning in a chaotic world**. And sometimes they lose their Faith, wondering where God is, and does He really exist? As a result, these people are among the first to either become **atheists**, or to seek deeper meaning in life, and begin to lose the ego and locate the Self beyond the Mind.

The successful Souls (successful at handling their '**awakening**') begin to transcend body, emotions, and mind and identify with an **"inner witness"** – the One who is doing the looking and thinking. The person becomes more whole by becoming detached from the physical self. The **Higher Self** begins to emerge…

It is then a natural progression to the next level.

6. Psychic Consciousness

At this level, we no longer identify with the rational mind, but with the "inner witness" (i.e., **the Higher Self) that observes it all**. This is the You that is more than you, and along with it comes **clairvoyance and healing**. These people become aware of information coming from beyond the normal 5 senses. Often referred to as ESP, it is a way of **knowing on a higher level**. (See Freke, later section.)

A common experience for these people is what is called a **Peak Experience** which has also been called cosmic consciousness. This can happen in a split second when walking thru a park, or along the beach – all of a sudden the soul shifts into a higher awareness state (Soul) -- the colors are much more vibrant, deeper, and one's senses are very acute and there is **a sense of oneness with all creation**.

Ralph Waldo Emerson was such a person and often spoke about using one's intuition to transcend the material world. He believed we could contact the "Oversoul" or what has today been called the Higher Self, and attune to one's inner drummer and **live by one's own higher truths**. [492]

7. Subtle Consciousness

The subtle level is the last one wherein we identify, even if weakly, with our self, or personality. Our Consciousness becomes **capable of receiving direct communications from the causal level, the level of the Oversoul.** This is the person who receives **spiritual revelations** and whose Consciousness is so far above the average person that communication with the average person is very difficult – because the aware person now sees and understands so much more.

These people may hear voices and heavenly music, and see things that are intradimensional. They are getting **ready to transcend the 3D world** – but before they can, they often have to undergo a momentous experience called **The Dark Night of the Soul,** which breaks all ties with the Earth plane. (This special transformational Night was examined in more detail in TOM, Apx A, and it is covered in Marion's book as well.)

This is truly **a rebirth to new level**. And these people often become hermits or monks so that they do not have to deal with the crowd, yet they serve the planet in the background, **"anchoring the Light"** and transmuting ambient negative energy.

8. Christ Consciousness

This is **the causal level**. Also called Christ Consciousness. They are free from neurotic projections and emotional addictions, and they see all other people as precious souls and they see the Father's Light in them, however much buried it may be. They are **totally detached from cares and concerns, anxieties and struggles.**

They now **commune silently with God** and are in the first stages of a realized divinity. Their Crown chakra is wide open and they are immersed in Light – to anyone who sees auras, these avatars project an aura out to 30' around them. It is white with a gold core, and the white has flecks of purple in it. Quite a sight to see.

Their **Love** is so strong you can feel it from across the room, and their **Knowledge** surpasses that of Wikipedia (no joke) – they have full access to the Akashic Records, so it is indeed extensive.

This is the level to which most Souls will someday arrive. And the book is very helpful in identifying what the problems and successes are at each level, AND it serves each person as a clue as to what their personal level of spiritual growth is.

The 8 levels are examined further in the TSiM book.

<u>The Lazy Man's Guide to Enlightenment</u> by Thaddeus Golas

This is the smallest of all ten books, a hardback at just 110 pages. Mr. Golas was a Hippie back in the 70's in Haight-Ashbury, totally devoted to the Zen and Flower Power of that era… and yet it is amazing how **deep and relevant** are his insights that he wrote down, hand-published, and then sold on street corners.

Reading the book, one thinks he had private tutoring from a Tibetan monk. Maybe he was one of the Watchers walking among us – no one who tries to meditate and be a Hippie would just happen on these concepts.

His legacy is a small but powerful book that the author of this (*Anunnaki Legacy*) book used to buy and hand out to his friends.

(credit: <u>http://thaddeusgolas.com/</u> also called The Thaddeus Golas Café.)

Selected comments, insights and teachings follow… (version: hardback)

Each of us must learn to travel alone [spiritually] sooner or later. If we wait until a group is ready, we will never leave this reality. (28)

Other than prolonging your [current level of] consciousness, there is no idea or action that makes the slightest bit of difference to your spiritual future. (32) When we are unconscious we are propelled to the vicinity of others equally unconscious, and …. We then awaken to the perhaps dismal thoughts around us as well as the pain of being newly different from our neighbors. If we cannot endure this unpleasantness, and retreat from consciousness to feel the pleasure of human agreement, to feel love now, then we will remain in this Earthly reality. (37)

We become what we agree with and love. Therefore we must **choose to love what we wish to become.** We must behave now as that which we wish to be. (38) [The Insider said the same thing in Chapter 13.]

What has to be true for the universe [reality] to look as it does? (52)

Key statement: We are equal beings and the universe is our relations with each other. The universe is made of one kind of entity: each one is alive, each determines the course of his[her] own destiny. (54)

Perhaps many of us do not like it where we are in the universe now, but we can all be certain that we got where we are by our own decisions to expand in love or withdraw [contract] from it. (57)

There is no point in worry or wonder about worse or better spiritual conditions, although that game is available. You will not be able to rise above your present vibration level to stay until you love the way you are now…. Your choice is always the same: to **expand your awareness or contract it**. (58)

You are the sole cause of your level of existence…. Enlightenment is any experience of expanding our consciousness beyond its present limits… There is no one correct way of looking at life 'after' enlightenment….[we need to] experience life without mental resistance… and none of the threatening evil that bothered you has disappeared from the world… [but note that] **we tend to return to the vibration level where we feel stable**… Your life will change as you become more loving, but not in ways that you can exactly predict. What happens is not as important as how you react to what happens…. A good attitude to take towards any goal: It's nice if it happens, nice if it doesn't. (63-67)

When you push hard in one direction, you are likely to be swung into a state other than what you intend. (69) If you complain loud enough you will be given a flash of insight into higher consciousness… [but] **you will not be able to stay on higher levels when you get there thru negative emphasis [including drugs].** (70)

What you deny others will be denied you…. What you say goes – but only for you and those who agree with you…. Grant to others the freedom, the love, and the consciousness that you want for yourself. (70-71)

Lifesavers:
When you see a bad situation or an ugly person, say "Well, what did you think it was that needed Love?"

No resistance. **Go with the Flow**. Love it the way it is.

Changing the *content* of your mind does nothing to change your [soul] vibration level.

If you can't find it where you're standing, where do you expect to wander in search of it?

Love yourself.

What you cannot think about, you cannot control. Violent human beings are precisely those who refused at some point to conceive that they could be violent…. Every evil that is manifest is there because we refused to conceive of causing it, or denied someone else the freedom to conceive of it…. Evil occurs as a secondary reality, after you have withdrawn to a low vibration level. (77-79)

When negative thoughts or events intrude, ask yourself: "**What am I doing on a level of consciousness where this is real?**" [you attracted it]

When your vibrations are slow, events seem to happen fast… the more you love, the faster you vibrate and the less need you have to control anything… [you have expanded your awareness] and then it is useless to try to escape any difficulty by contracting [withdrawing] your consciousness [of it]… keep your attention on it until it turns beautiful or at least until you are **indifferent to it**… It will seem like the strangest of coincidences when, having withdrawn your attention sharply from one unpleasant scene, you keep running into others like it…. Look at it, love it, and *then* get away! The point is to **take your leave in a way that doesn't hang you up**…. And by the way, don't feel that it is "unspiritual" to perceive unwholesome possibilities in other people – it isn't paranoia if the object of your fear is real! (88-90)

Remember: **different sets of facts are real at different vibration levels**. The Truth is the same for everyone, the facts are always a little different for everyone. Once you know that the facts will be different on every level, you are less likely to fight the facts of any particular plane…. Since every being is self-determined, you cannot change anyone else's vibration level against his will, <u>nor are you obliged to</u>. Indeed your perception of others is colored by your own limited vibrations until you reach the higher levels, so you have no way of knowing exactly what it is that you are trying to change. (98-101)

And lastly: No matter how confused or stupid or unloving other persons may appear to us, we have no right to ever assume that their consciousness is on a lower level than ours….The way we see them is an explicit measure of our own vibration level …**what we see is always ourselves**. (104-106) Accepting and loving them as they are, we give them the freedom to change.

Lessons from the Light by Dr. Kenneth Ring

This is a landmark book regarding his study of **Near Death Experiencers (NDErs)** and what truths they share after their visit to the realm we go to when we die. It is amazingly a life-transforming experience as well as yielding fascinating and reassuring insights into the Other Side.

The concept is that people died during surgery and were taken to the Light, the Other Side, and told they could not stay, but many were able to see former family members and a **Being of Light** often imparts knowledge of what goes on over there – and what they are looking for in those who leave Earth and return home…

It should be obvious to everyone that if the Truth (big T) comes from a visit to the Other Side, that such revelations might even exceed the truth (small T) that Serpent Wisdom would teach…

Caveat:

Of course it has been fashionable for the 'expert' skeptics who don't understand the NDE phenomenon to diss it and "explain it away" by a normal death-throe operation of the brain, involving brain-generated psychedelics and unique chemicals… but realize that there are those who always diss something new (No one is going to put one over on them!), and they are desperate to find a scientific explanation for the phenomenon. Why? Because if they admit that there is an Other Side, and advanced beings and Masters, and a purpose to Life, and it was created (and thus Darwinian Evolution is inexact) and a whole other realm that watches what we do – it means there is a God, and that means the scientist skeptics are at some point responsible for what they do (how they live their lives), and (according to Fundamentalist Religion) they will be "judged" according to their deeds—and they don't want that. So they <u>have to</u> say NDErs are imagining it all and there is no Other Side, and <u>therefore</u> no God… this leaves them free to do whatever they want (with no conscience). Boy, are they in for a surprise – providing they have a soul. IF they have no soul [as the Mayans, Greeks and Gnostics argued is possible, as well as **Boris Mouravieff** – Chapter 12 (*Genesis & Creation* section)], they have no connection to anything spiritual, and thus **no conscience** – they may be the ones yelling the loudest to pooh-pooh the NDE phenomenon. If that is true, do you want a soulless idiot telling you, a soul, what to believe? (See also VEG, Ch. 5 for detailed examination.)

Several things are spiritually informing about this book (19):

1. Their outlook on life is different: **they do not fear death**, they now know what it is – merely a transition to the Other Side, the realm we all come from.
2. They have an **eternal soul**. Their body is not who they are.
3. When returning 'home', the Masters want to see what we have learned –

   They look for **Love and Knowledge** – not just Love.

   These people are **transformed** – something that the Alchemists were looking for an a personal basis. Interesting that people are transformed by Knowledge of what they are, where we are, and what the Masters want us to learn… we do not ascend just by Love….

   "Be ye transformed by the renewing of your mind." Rom. 12:2

   It didn't say be transformed by Love.
   The mind is transformed by Knowledge.

4. **Cooperation** is better than competition.
5. **Love** is extremely important – it <u>empowers</u> everything.
6. Success and possessions are not that important.
7. **Life is precious**… it is a gift.

Special knowledge gained (26):

1. There is a reason for all that happens.
2. It is your duty to do your best, find your purpose in life, and learn.
3. Do not be concerned what others think of you.
4. Be open to life and live it to its fullest.
5. Money is not #1.
6. Helping others counts for a lot in the Life Review (Ch. 6 p. 145).

Characteristics of the NDErs (31-32):

1. Increased love for all people and all things.
2. Increased sensitivity, psychic ability—see auras.
3. **No fear of death**. Lessened fear of many things.
4. Know Reincarnation is true.
5. Vegetarianism
6. Major life changes – job, divorce, new city
7. Less religious, **more spiritual**.
8. Increased concern for the planet – Mother Earth.
9. More **open to new things and people**.
10. Seeing the "big picture" in life.
11. Seeing that **life's challenges are lessons to learn**
12. Know that Earth is a School.
13. Complete Self-acceptance.

Obviously, these people are **transformed** and did not just go thru a froo-froo experience – they are now "enlightened" and have become **"born again"** – they know the truth about Death and the Other Side… and they usually are fearless about making major changes in their lives to synch up with what they see is now (after coming back into the body) important.

And connecting back to our chapters on *Kundalini* – they didn't have to activate their **Dragon Fire** to be enlightened and develop higher consciousness abilities (sense energy, clairvoyance, and precognition…) Their gifts and outlook are examined more in Dr. Ring's Ch. 5 (124).

Good news!

What is even more interesting is that there is proving to be a **benign virus** that affects people, some more, some less, when they read this book. Seriously. (213) Something in the NDEr's sharing and recounted stories **resonates with readers** and they seem to 'remember' or connect what the NDEr is sharing and it is believed to transform the reader thru a **"principle of contagion."** The reader becomes enlightened on a soul level without having an NDE.

> In fact, thinking about it, these people are now what Jim Marion (above) would call the #6 **Psychic Consciousness –** they are in touch with their intuition and their Higher Self in many cases.
>
> The NDE experience served the same purpose as the Dragon Fire or *Kundalini*. And what if the 'benign virus' effect is true? – read the book and have an awakening of your own!

Jesus and the Lost Goddess by Timothy Freke (pron. "frake")

The reason for including this book (it is one of three in a series) is that it has a relevant subtitle: Religious Lies and Gnostic Wisdom.

Of particular note is the chapter: **Hip-Gnosis (Ch. 7)**. Here the author introduces us to the concept of **Lucid Living** which is a state of being very aware of self and surroundings – yet at the same time, know that you are awareness – the observer and the observed.

Website: timothyfreke.com

Lucid Living is not seeing the world as a dream, but realizing that life has a dream-like aspect to it, that you are not a person, not a body, **you are an awareness which is witnessing the life-dream**. The author suggests that it is being conscious that you have **two aspects** to your identity right now: your **apparent nature** is the person you appear to be, but your **essential nature** is awareness which is witnessing all you experience. You are both an 'I' and an 'it' and you are unconscious of the fact that the **I** is dreaming the **it** into being.

Physics calls it **Entanglement.**

Lucid Living calls it "looking in two directions at once." This uses **the Gnostic view that God is the life-dreamer who is becoming conscious *through* creation**. (199) Said another way, look at yourself and see that you are a person with a body (the 'it') in the world. Then flip it and look at it from the 'I perspective' – you are an awareness and the world exists in you. Look at it from the 'it perspective' and see that you are a person confined by time. Flip it and look at the situation from the 'I perspective' and see that you are an eternal witness of what we call 'time.' From the 'it perspective' you are a separate individual. From the 'I perspective' all is one. (141)

Lucid Living isn't being the life-dreamer *instead of* a person in the dream. It is consciously being *both* the life-dreamer [God] *and* a person in the life-dream. (141)

This split between a bigger You and the smaller you was addressed in VEG, TOM and again in TSiM via a diagram that shows that there is the real You that splits off aspects of itself into various realms for the 'you' experience (it is included here for clarity):

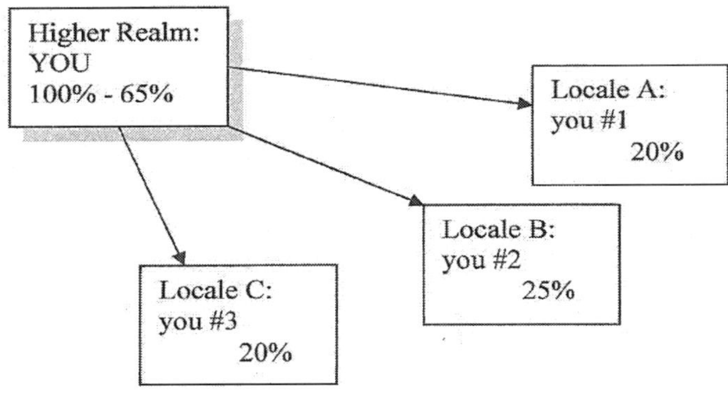

Chart 3c

Note the real, larger and eternal You spawns several finite you's. You are part of the One who is dreaming the Reality in which we live – souls are sparks of the One Soul and thus participate in the "life-dream." ... Souls are **Multidimensional**. There is **one awareness dreaming itself to be everyone and everything right now.** (138) And if you plumb the depths of your being you will discover that you are the life-dreamer. We are all One, we are all connected and thus the Reality is our life-dream – it is a product of a Consciousness that pervades everyone and everything.

Back to the perspective...

The 'I perspective' and the 'it perspective' is not really not an exercise in mumbo-jumbo. When God **thinks** Reality and souls into existence, what else would you call it but similar to a life-dream... it is His idea, and we are part of His awareness, which He is purposing, similar to dreaming.

There is one awareness dreaming itself to be everyone and everything right now. We are not saying that you as an individual are dreaming the [whole] life-dream, because as a person, you are part of the dream, as is everyone else. **We are suggesting that the awareness which is conscious thru each one of us is the same awareness experiencing the life-dream from different perspectives.** (138) Co-creation.

> By the way, that is exactly what the NDErs say when they come back to Earth – John saw himself hitting another man, Bob, in the face, slugging him, and during the **Life Review** (when the Being of Light 'replayed' John's life) he saw himself hitting Bob – and feeling what it was like! (175)

Lastly, it is increasingly fashionable to believe that we 'create our own reality' and in a way this is true. As the life-dreamers we are creating all of Reality. But we are not doing this consciously as individual personas in the life-dream. Waking up is the recognition that as individuals <u>we are not really doing anything</u>. We are part of what is happening. (175)

> Think: Shakespeare, the Stage and a Drama – you have a **Script** and events are orchestrated… and you have freewill to play your part [not being told what to do or say] and keep the Drama going…

However there is still a sense in which we are all **co-creating Reality** as individuals because, as we become more conscious the life-dreamer is able to make better choices thru us and that changes Reality. Lucid Living is *both* being the life-dreamer ***unconsciously*** **[as I]** dreaming the life-dream *and* appearing to be a person playing our part in ***consciously*** **[as it]** co-creating Reality. [Read that carefully to get the full sense.] (175)

Later in the book, he likens the life-dream to a game – the Game of Life. And if it was always easy, there would be no game. **The game of life is about waking up,** and if we want to wake up more than we choose to stay 'asleep', then that is what we do. That means that we can play the Game at a higher level because we are conscious about what we are doing. (183-185) Or we can stay asleep… as many people have chosen to do.

> Just remember: Life is a School and we are not here to coast and just have fun 24x7. We <u>can</u> have fun, but that is not what Life is about.

Into the Light by Dr. John Lerma

Dr. Lerma runs a hospice in Houston, Tx, and has learned some remarkable things from his patients – as they are dying.

Perhaps the most significant thing is that we are not alone and at death, there are angels who come to escort us to the Other Side. And the dying patients see the angels and later report information or conversations they have had with them.

Whereas Dr. Ring (above) dealt with Near Death and "after" death experiences, Dr. Lerma deals with pre-death – his patients die and do not come back.

They all speak of the one God who creates with total love and reminds us that everyone on this planet serves a purpose and is unified from the same wholeness, and many speak of the need for self-love and forgiveness. (13)

Some excerpts:

The angels told Katrina that there are very holy people on Earth born specifically to be examples of God's love. [They are protected from Dark Angels and have no Karma.]
We do not need to get this life perfect… just stay balanced.
We all have a light side and a dark side. So Katrina was told to love herself, then try to love and forgive others. (86)

Father Mike [dying] was allowed to discuss some religious points with the angels, and he learned that there is **no Hell** as is traditionally taught, but that **Hell is the soul's willful separation from the light of God**. Some souls when they die refuse to go to the Light, and become discarnates… (120) [The prayers of living people on Earth can 'rescue' them.]

Joanna was told that the more loving one is on Earth and the more **acts of random kindness** one does, the easier it is to forgive oneself and move into harmony with God. She was told that freewill is God's gift to Man and while God is not the author of pain/suffering, we use Faith to connect with God in times of trial/pain. (140)

George's Awesome Story
The story of George in Chapter 11 (Redemption) is particularly fascinating. George was 53 and chained to the hospice bed as he had been convicted of multiple murders

years earlier. He was Catholic and now worried that he could not go to Heaven. His sins weighed heavily on his mind…

Initially George just wanted to be left alone to die, and take his punishment. He had a lot of guilt for having killed 4 teenagers in a drug deal that went bad. He also now had stage 4 lung cancer.

As Dr. Lerma gains George's confidence and listens to him (which no one had ever done), George began to tell what he was seeing in his hospital room when he was alone. **Two entities** appeared hovering in the upper part of the room…One was bright white, and about 8' tall with flowing golden hair, and the other was also tall but just a dark shadow [Dark Angel]. The two appeared to be communicating and after 5 minutes the bright angel said they were there to help him. At one point the Dark Angel approached George and he saw a dark figure pop out of him and the two dark figures were all that was left – the Bright Angel had gone. The room was oddly bright black and the two dark entities were conversing, but he could not hear what they were saying.

George yells at the two to leave him alone, and the smaller one that had popped out minutes before now popped back in him. George was really scared. The remaining Dark Angel then explained to George that **darkness was not evil** – it was merely raw human energy [the Dark Energy of Astrophysics?] used with negative intentions. The angel also explained how darkness transfers among family members and affects DNA… so he was not totally to blame. The Dark Angel caringly gave George the information and ability to understand why he had screwed up his life, and had not been able to overcome the negative tendencies 'programmed' into his DNA.

Then the story of George delivered a real heavy piece of information. Incredible. The two angels [Bright and Dark] reappeared the next day in his room, and were looking at him. George was still puzzled – why was a Dark Angel still there and what did he want?
The Bright Angel told George that **they work together**. They are not enemies. "Your darkness was so intense it formed an entity which resided within you." His Mom was there to help him cross over… and so was the shiny Dark Angel – trying to tell George something and George's Mom finally told George to listen to the Dark Angel. George listens and finds that it is the dark side of his life communicating with him – so that he gets a complete understanding of his life… all about soul growth!

Then George got a second awesome bit of information. No matter what he had done in life, he could still go to Heaven --- if he believed in God. The **Archangel Michael** showed up just before they were to collect George and cross over… Michael asked him just one thing: "Do you believe?" George protested that he was a sinner. Michael responded that **there is no sin that is so bad it cannot be forgiven**, and again he was asked "Do you believe?"

If you believe in God/Heaven, you can go to Heaven. (159-164) Awesome!

<u>Learning from the Light</u> by Dr. John Lerma

This is the second book written about Dr. Lerma's hospice patients. This work includes:

> How to prepare for a peaceful transition to the Other Side
> Interaction with Bright and Dark angels
> Latest research on pre-death visions
> **Changes in our DNA as we embrace the Light**

One account of a dying patient stood out. **Colonel Marshall Bradfield** who spent years in Roswell, NM, and in 1947 he witnessed the crashed craft. Now that he was dying, he felt he could share (in 2006) what had happened back when he was 24 years old.

First he said that we stopped the radio transmissions to outer space, attempting to contact ETs, and of course SETI and Arecibo were shut down from <u>active</u> search several (current) years ago – because contact had been made.

Then he said that Mac Brazel came to his door the morning of July 7, 1947 and said he wanted to show him something and get his opinion. He and Mac had grown up as boys in Roswell and knew each other well. He took 'Marsh' as he was known then out to the crash site… the severe thunderstorm of the night before had left the ground wet in places and they had to drive around mud puddles. Mac drove the pickup thru the soft soil up to the craft. There was debris all over the place and the wrecked hulk of the main part of the craft, but he could still see that it had been circular. In addition, Marsh picked up some of the debris, noting the 'memory metal' that regains its shape after crumpling it, and he saw some odd symbols [probably runes]. This didn't look American-made…

> Gee, some people would like us to believe that a UFO came all the way across the Galaxy, dodging and blasting asteroids out of its path, flying at faster-than-light speed, able to withstand cosmic rays… and a simple thunder & lightning storm on Earth does it in…. really?

Marsh saw the wreckage and the round craft… and he saw a piece of wreckage that seemed to have an emblem on it. He picked it up and saw more pieces of the emblem, then pieced them together…. and felt a cold chill run up his spine. It was the **German Iron Cross**…

This is also called a BalkanKreutz…

…and so this had to be a crashed, smaller **Haunebu I**. He had heard about them, but thought they were just a myth. He immediately went back home and called his commander who was already aware of the crash and was in the process of releasing a cover story… He was reminded to not say anything to anyone as part of his National Security Oath… He now knew that the US had recovered advanced technology created by the Germans. (121-123)

> In fact, this craft was the source of transistors, fibre optics, Kevlar, night vision, and the basics of electrogravitic propulsion.

Larger Haunebu II: BalkanKreutz on the Turret

He could not get the image out of his mind. But more was to come. In later years, he was privy to the 70's Mars fly-bys and the pictures taken of the Cydonia Region – and the **Face on Mars**. Subsequent pictures proved that the Face had been created by intelligence but NASA and JPL were dead set on covering up the whole thing… and that upset him, so he confided in Dr. Lerma. He went on to say that water had been discovered on Mars, and the European Space Agency (ESA) released the info in 2008. (137)

> … the last missions to Mars proved, through the digital images, that foliage, and fossils exist on Mars today. In addition, on the unnatural mesa 1 kilometer next to Cydonia, images outlined on the surface around Cydonia resembling a child, an Egyptian goddess, marine animals, as well as **glass tubes** were found. [VEG Apx A explores these things with pictures]. The ESA reported that these glass tubes were found to connect several of the above-mentioned structures, which were reportedly interlaced metallic support beams. (137)

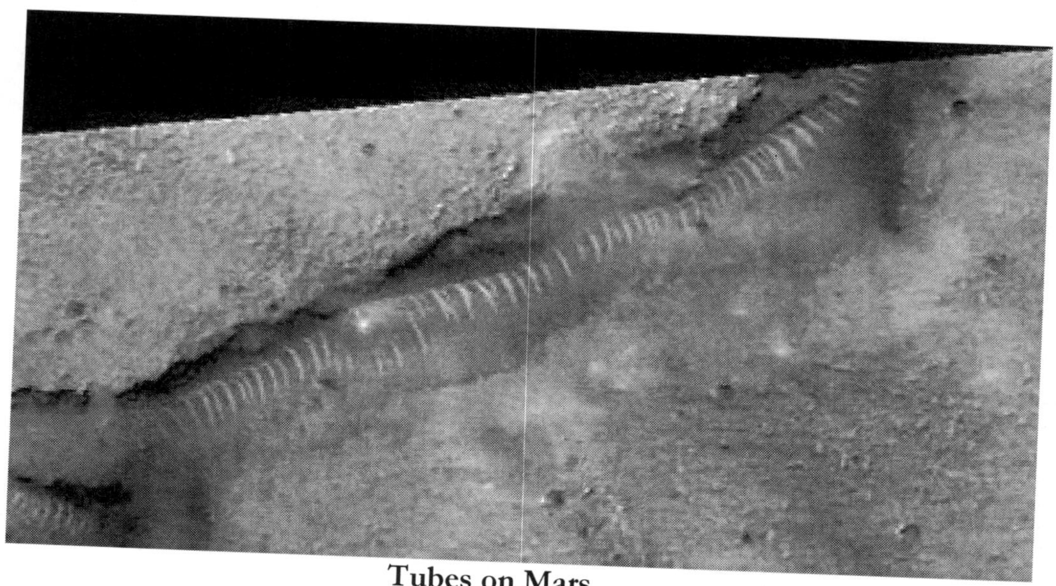

Tubes on Mars
(**credit:** NASA/Malin Space Science Systems)

And there is more to the revelations… so this *Anunnaki Legacy* book has some connections with Mars, as well, which were hinted at in Chapter 7 and the Hopi connection.

Thanks to Colonel Marsh Bradfield, we have an insight into what we have suspected was true… and that is probably what will happen anyway: instead of direct disclosure by the government, here and there things will leak out and who can say but what that has been their current intention… **A clever psychological ploy**. Instead of surprising and potentially freaking people out with the full official disclosure, bits and pieces leak out so that people say "Oh, come on! Liar! You aren't telling us the truth!" and instead of fear, the public is outraged to know more – a 180° proactive turnabout.

Virtual Earth Graduate (VEG) by TJ Hegland

In a nutshell, the first 13 chapters are to confront whatever you think you know about Earth History, Physical Science, and Religion… a challenge to see how you handle **catalyst**. Chapter 14 is telling people why they cannot continue to think that Earth is their home (it is being polluted and de-oxygenated under our feet, not to mention all the deadly germs), and the last 2 chapters give some Serpent Wisdom concepts that will help souls 'graduate' from the Earth School.

Earth is a School, Shakespeare said a Stage, and we are all in a Drama, and we are expected to do our best, learn and grow in awareness – fulfill our divine potential.

Errors in Science, Earth History and Religion are examined as well as a look at Zecariah Sitchen's Anunnaki. Amazing discoveries in Science are presented as well as a new kind of Quantum Physics called Subquantum Kinetics that is more to the point, less cumbersome. A brief look at nutrition is given, but more is presented in TOM… if your body needs water or special supplements (not Rx's) and you don't know that, your poor health can operate against your learning what you need to know to 'graduate' from Earth School – so health is important.

New information about Western Chronology is given as discovered by a Russian Math Professor (with heavy credentials and reams of proof), showing what looks like someone doctored the chronology of Western Civilization – and it is credible… and that gives rise to a new idea of Jesus' birth and death dates. In addition, Apollonius of Týana is examined as a potential source (read: role model) of those who created the New Testament Jesus and Paul. And many inconsistencies, and mistranslations, from the Bible are corrected. The real identity of Yahweh is revealed, with apologies to the Church.

Additionally, the book visits the Great Pyramid and Nazca with alternate stunning ideas for how they were created, and why the Mayan pyramids have steps that are too large for the average human to navigate comfortably.

By the way, here is a brief overview of the other books, using their id's from the copyright page...

TOM – Originally part of VEG, this gives specific information about the Other Side (called the **InterLife**), and how it is run, what I saw and was told about how our lives are loosely planned before we incarnate. There is also info at the end on various modalities to assist with **energy management** and potential consciousness awakening.

Also see end of this book's promo pages...

TEW – a Sci-Fi **novel** based on real people, real places and real events. In some ways, the first 5 chapters in this book extend the Chapter 4 in VEG. How UFOs work is revealed. The 3rd Secret of Fatima is carefully revealed as the possibility of a **Galactic Superwave** (and the 2008 cropcircle) which terminates the book.

QES – Chapter 13 in VEG is further explored here – there is considerable **evidence** that we live in a **Simulated world** in a very sophisticated Holographic Universe (as Michael Talbot said) and it is theorized by both scientists and philosophers that the gods are benevolent and run it as a **quarantined School** for our benefit. This is not fiction. If it is hard to believe, consider it "brain candy."

TSiM – A look **beyond positive thinking**, what it actually does in our brains, and what nutrition we can take, and what brain exercises, to avoid dementia and/or Alzheimers. It also reveals what violent video games do to neurons in those who play them. There is a new science field called **Quantum Biology** which reveals how Quantum Tunneling (at the layman level) answers the riddles of Photosynthesis, how our noses smell, how birds navigate and the miracle of **Vision**.

Appendix B: Goddesses & The Sacred Feminine

This Appendix will examine the key ideas behind the Sacred Feminine, or Divine Feminine, and what it meant to be a goddess in the service of mankind. Of course, the foregoing chapters mentioned a number of goddesses, NüWa in China, Inanna in Sumeria (aka Astarte, Athena and Ishtar – depending on what country she was in at the time), and Freya in Scandinavia, Isis in Egypt, Shakti in India, and Sophia who was the Goddess of Wisdom among the Gnostics – the latter who was more of an ideal, a myth, than a real person.

And lastly, we are about to add a well-known name to the list since she was a real person and was venerated throughout the following countries:

> **Africa**: Algeria, Senegal and South Africa, **Asia**: the Philippines, **Greater Europe**: Belgium, France, Italy, Germany, Spain, Ireland, Kosovo, Luxembourg, Lithuania, Poland, Portugal, Russia, Serbia, Malta, Macedonia, Slovenia, Turkey, Ukraine, Switzerland, United Kingdom, and **The Americas**: Brazil, Chile, Costa Rica, Cuba, and Trinidad & Tobago – just for starters.

No, not the Virgin Mary… but you are close.

The Black Madonna

La Vierge Noire de Guingamp, France

This statue is often venerated as the Virgin Mary & Jesus.

Yes, it does look like a Black version of the Virgin Mary holding Jesus, but throughout the countries just listed, especially the South of France and Southwestern Asia (Ukraine-Greece), it is an original reference to Mary Magdalene.

The image of Mother & Child was common to the major cultures of the world – (pre-Christianity). Here it is in Egypt: Isis nursing Horus:

…and in Africa:

According to the official, Church-sanctioned explanation: [493]

> A **Black Madonna** or **Black Virgin** is a statue or painting of Mary in which she, and oftentimes the infant Jesus are depicted with dark skin, especially those created in Europe in the medieval period or earlier. The Black Madonnas are generally found in Catholic and Orthodox [Russian and Greek] countries. The term refers to a type of Marian statue or painting of mainly medieval origin (12th to 15th centuries), with dark or black features. The statues are mostly wooden but occasionally stone, often painted, and up to 75 cm (30 in) tall.

They fall into two main groups: free-standing upright figures or seated figures on a throne. The pictures are usually icons which are Byzantine in style, often made in 13th- or 14th-century Italy.

There are about **450–500 Black Madonnas in Europe**, depending on how they are classified. There are **at least 180 *Vierges Noires* in France**, and there are hundreds of non-medieval copies as well. Some are in museums, but most are in churches or shrines and are venerated by devotees. A few are associated with miracles and attract substantial numbers of pilgrims.

So if that is not the Virgin Mary, then who is it?

After The Crucifixion

Jesus was hung on the cross and his disciples denied even knowing him. Thomas went to Asia, and is said to have made it to Japan. And there was a disciple who accompanied Jesus whom, according to the non-selected Gnostic Gospels, he loved very much as he "used to kiss her on the lips" – Gospel of Phillip.[494]

Mary Magdalene.

(credit: Bing Images)[495]

Mary was of Egyptian descent, so had brown skin, dark hair, and it was rumored that she and Jesus were at least lovers, if not married. (Dan Brown promoted that in his *DaVinci Code.*) If so, and this was the secret the Templars discovered while in the Holy Land, they certainly could blackmail the Church and render themselves a very powerful group. And if they did learn that secret, then the child in the picture above, of the Black Madonna, could represent the child that Mary had who was of "royal blood" – or **Sang Real**. Allegedly, her son went on to spread his bloodline eventually running thru Dagobert and ending with the Merovingians. That does make for a fascinating story and may be why there were <u>two</u> Madonnas with Child in the Priory of Sion at Rennes-le-Château….

But that is not the focus of this Appendix – What happened after the Crucifixion, was that Mary and a couple of disciples took a boat to the South of France where she continued teaching what Jesus started. Jesus had given her much private and esoteric teaching. She landed at Saintes-Maries-de-la-Mer (again, two Mary's), not far from Marseille, and she preached the gospel and eventually became a hermit **in a cave** at Sainte-Baume. This is backed by local tradition to have been based on actual events… not just a clever ploy to spur tourism. Her cave was no less than 100 miles northeast from the Basque world – to be examined next…

> Perhaps the historical documents will emerge to verify this once Church persecution has finally ended. Obviously, if the above is true, the Church would seek to recover the historical documents and deny that anything but its version of Mother Mary & Jesus is all that happened.

It was said that Jesus told her more than he told the resistant and slow-witted male members of his entourage, and if she was teaching advanced truths, then she was also a **Shining One**, and her truths probably made it into a secret society somewhere in France – largely because the Church in that day would have suppressed higher spiritual truth, as did the Egyptian priests in their day. Is that what was behind the tumult in the media about twenty-five years ago about the Priory of Sion? If the Templars (and Cathars?) knew the truth, and they headquartered at Rennes-le-Château where they also hid their plunder (which the Nazis found and removed during WW II by the way)… would it not suggest that something secret was indeed hidden there – besides treasure?

> Remember that Marie Denarnaud was the priest Saunière's assistant and housekeeper, and there are credible accounts that he told her (before he died) what he had found in Rennes and also in the neighboring village of Rennes-les-Bains.
>
> And then Saunière had a special tower built in honor of Mary Magdelene, and he also allegedly buried something very important beneath the first floor.

Yet, the issue is that Mary Magdalene, having closely associated with Jesus, achieved a **semi-goddess status** herself. Perhaps we should call her a **priestess**. Certainly she must have benefitted from Jesus sharing deeper truths with her, perhaps sharing himself with her, and "initiating" her into a higher state of knowledge/awareness – and he might have activated the *Kundalini* Dragon Force in her. That is also a characteristic of most goddesses named in the first paragraph.

Basque Goddess

An interesting country that was not on the Global Tour in Chapter 8 is the Basque world between Spain and France, in the Pyrenees. Again, the zealous Spanish Catholic Church wiped out most of the history of these people when they converted them to Christianity. So what is left is fragments of information about another Mary…

> **Mari** is depicted in many different forms: sometimes as various women, and **living in a cave** [as did Mary Magdalene (Black Virgin)]. Her consort Sugaar, however, appears only as a man or a **serpent/dragon**. Mari is said to be served by the *sorginak*, semi-mythical creatures impossible to differentiate from … pagan priestesses.[Remember if the Church didn't like it, it was 'pagan'.] Mari lives underground, normally in **a cave** in a high mountain, where she and her consort Sugaar meet …. to conceive the storms that will bring fertility [agricultural] …. to the land and the people. Mari is served by a court and the Basque were considered to **be masters of magic**, or Magos [think: **Druid** priests] … A cadre of "witches" [Druids] near Zugurramurdi …. were the target of the Spanish Inquisition's largest witch hunt… [496] [emphasis added]

There is a lot of common imagery in the above quote that was encountered earlier in the book's chapters. According to the same source, there was a solar deity called **Eki** (close to the Sumerian Enki) and a **dragon** called Herensuge which figures in a few Basque legends. Interestingly, they also have legends of huge hairy hominids called **Basajuan** which dwelled in the woods and built megaliths and taught Man agriculture and metal-working, among other things. Perhaps most fascinating is the Basque legend of **Urtzi** (or Ortzi) who was said to be a **sky-god**. Many cultures spoke of gods that came from the sky to assist and guide Man.

Lastly, we also find a **sacred Tree**, called **Gernikako Arbola** which was an oak tree under which oaths of office and treaties were signed.

Arms of Biscay

The trunk of the old tree was enshrined (above), and one of its acorns used to grow a new tree close by.

Characteristics of Goddesses

First and foremost a goddess must have had some sort of a **divine birth**… either her father was a god, such as Zeus, or Apollo, or she must have descended from a bloodline that once had a god, or hybrid such as Alexander the Great, or Charlemagne, in it. This is why tracking who begat whom was so important in the past, and the Mormons still do it today.

Secondly, a goddess must be a "cut above" – smarter, more integrity, wiser, and even **able to impart wisdom and power to humans** – usually benefitting them in some way. A goddess often prophesized with 100% accuracy.

> The goddess can be inspiring to women, embodying wisdom, guidance, physical grace, athletic prowess, and sensuality. [497]

Whereas male gods were often associated with War and Conquest, the goddesses were often associated with Beauty, Wisdom and Learning. And it is more than who has the testosterone! Yet there was the Yin (feminine) and Yang (masculine) aspect of Man which **Carl Jung** said led him to believe that there never were any actual gods/goddesses – it was all just an archetypal aspect of the duality of Man's psyche.

And he was largely correct when it came to **Sophia** the Gnostic Goddess of Wisdom, but if a scientist has trouble with historical accounts that are too hard to believe (because they don't still happen today), they invent some psychological explanation for persistent <u>myths</u> – which really reflect more realistic <u>legends</u>, which really reflect ancient <u>historical events</u>… when the actual, physical gods were here. This is also where **Joseph Campbell** ran off the tracks and seconded Jung's explanation for myths.

> Yet, what often happened was that the male god derived his powers from the goddess... According to Riane Eisler, cultures in which **women and men shared power**, and which worshipped female deities, were <u>more peaceful</u> than the patriarchal dominator societies that followed.[498]

And yet the role of women in society has been notoriously downplayed or flat-out suppressed with the advent of the patriarchal Church in the Western World. To do it, they had to make Mary Magdalene out to be a sinner (like Rahab, Tamar, Ruth and Bathsheba) who needed the male (Jesus') forgiveness. Testosterone also rules the White House and the Catholic Church… remember, it was founded by Saint Peter and all priests and bishops are male. And yet, the Catholic Church pays lip service to Mother Mary and motherhood – the Divine Virgin – while relegating women to the status of nuns and teachers. No female Pope or President … yet.

But the key point is that the **goddesses** of yore were different from what could be expected today… they really were physical beings, with advanced technology (as was the case with Inanna), or they have advanced abilities (as did the Devis in India) and they had a non-human origin. And as for the Druid **priestesses**, they were skilled in *Kundalini* activation, raising their consciousness to a point where they could accurately predict, heal others, and even control the weather.

Women in Egypt

Few ancient civilizations enabled women to achieve important social positions. In Ancient Egypt, there are not only examples indicating women high officials were not so rare, but more surprising (for its time), there are women in the highest office, that of **Pharoah**. More than a kind of feminism, this is a sign of the importance of theocracy and **thealogy** in Egyptian society. Women were not just important to the Egyptians because of the importance of childbirth.

Egyptian society of antiquity, like many other civilizations of the time, used religion as a foundation for society. This was how the throne of the power of the Pharaohs was justified, as **anointed by the gods**, and the holder of the throne had a divine right. Typically, in ancient [non-Egyptian] societies power was transferred from one male to the next. The oldest son inherited the power, and in cases where the king did not have a son, the throne was then inherited by the male members of the family further removed from the king, such as cousins or uncles. But even if the monarch had daughters, they usually could not gain power.

In Egyptian civilization, this obligation of passing power to a male successor was not without exceptions. **Royal blood**, a factor determined by divine legitimacy, was the unique criteria for access to the throne. Thus, the divine essence was transmitted to the royal spouse, as was the case with **Nefertiti,** wife of Akhenaton.

And let's not forget **Hatshepsut**, and **Cleopatra VII**. And who was it that restored Osiris and protected Horus? The **goddess Isis**. Women also held offices of Vizir, Scribe and some were recognized with a special title: The Great Wife.[499]

Goddess in Mesopotamia

Women also held important roles even in sexist and cast-driven societies – like that of the Anunnaki. Anunnaki society was very patristic and women were important in Science (Ninharsag and Ninlil) and Education, but only one made it to the position of ruler – **Inanna**.

Inanna didn't take no for an answer and when Enki's son Marduk killed her lover, Dumuzi, she chased him down and was about to kill him – Anu and Enlil had to intervene (story in Chapter 5).

She was very smart, a fierce warrior, a compassionate woman and commanded respect even among the men who ranked higher than she – Enlil's rank was 50 and hers was 25 (women were always odd-ranked) but he had a lot of respect for her. She was given the **Indus Valley** (now Pakistan) to rule, and she was quite a 'package.'

(Think: *Xena* and *Wonder Woman* all in one.)

Goddesses in India

Two major women come to mind:

Shakti – the Divine Mother, the absolute Godhead – above Vishnu the male godhead. She is also called Devi (see Devas in Chapter 13). Called **Mahadevi** ("great goddess") she has many manifestations and is the dynamic feminine aspect of the Supreme One.

Kali -- she represents Time, Change, Power, Creation, Preservation, and **Destruction**. "Kali" also means "the black one." Her earliest appearance is that of a destroyer (principally of evil forces). Devotional movements worship Kāli as a benevolent mother goddess. She is often portrayed **standing or dancing on her consort, the Hindu god Shiva, who lies calm and prostrate beneath her**. (Women's Libbers love it!)

Kali Stands On Shiva
(credit: Bing images: dollsofindia.com)

Two things to note here:

Shiva (the male) is surrounded by **serpents**, and Kali is **blue-skinned**.

Again, the image is that of **serpent (Naga)** worship.

The blue skin is due to an ancient legend that at one time in India, there were blue-skinned gods… Ever heard the term, "royal, blue-blood"?

Like the Aztec Calendar, there is the tongue again… the meaning is unknown.

> It is not advisable to worship Kali as she is the goddess of destruction, and this author saw that firsthand at a local church where the pastor chose to put a statue of her on his desk and venerate her – allegedly as the "goddess of new beginnings" – but the old has to be destroyed first – and his church was totally destroyed.

So there are good goddesses and … not so good ones!

Mahadevi (below) as a supreme goddess can appear as Sita, Lakshmi…

Mahadevi --- https://en.wikipedia.org/wiki/Devi

Note: Mahadevi is shown above with all major male gods as smaller, subordinate and subsumed. It is the male god Vishnu (aka Narayana) lying beneath her.

Goddess in Scandinavia

The foremost goddess is known as **Freya** (from whence we get "Friday" as a day of the week) – she was also called Frigg. Old English: "Frīge's day" (Freya's day).

> Frigg is described as a goddess associated with foreknowledge and **wisdom** in Norse Mythology, the northernmost branch of Germanic mythology and most extensively attested. Frigg is the wife of the major god Odin and dwells in the wetland halls of Fensalir, is famous for her **foreknowledge….** The children of Frigg and Odin include the gleaming god Baldr. Due to significant thematic overlap, scholars have proposed a particular connection to the goddess Freyja.[500]

The Goddess Frigg/Freya.

Frigg sits enthroned and facing the spear-wielding goddess **Gna**, flanked by two goddesses, one of whom (**Fulla**) carries her *eski*, a wooden box.

Illustrated (1882) by Carl Emil Doepler.

Note the special 'horse' behind Gna -- Hofvarpnir, and that this horse has the ability to ride through the air and atop the sea. [501] Sounds like another type of skycraft… (See pp. 90-91.)

Goddesses in China

While we already revealed **Nü Wa** as the Creator Goddess in China (Chapter 4), and her consort FuXi, there is another well-known goddess: **Xi-He** who chariots the Sun around the sky…. pulled by a **dragon**…. as a **sky-goddess.**

> Gods and goddesses were from the sky, so the dragon may resemble an Anunnaki skycraft (Chapter 2, end), and there you have the image of the Sun blessing Man – much as the Maya and the Egyptians also considered the Sun very important to life on Earth. In this case, the Chinese ascribe the movement, not to Ra (Egyptian god) or to Huitzilopochtli (Mayan god) but still to a god that is the cause of the Sun's movement. This seems to be a common image, also found in Africa and among the Amerindians.

Statue of the **goddess Xi-He** charioteering the Sun, being pulled by a Chinese **dragon** in Hangzhou. [502]

Goddess Danu in Celtic Ireland

Danu was the recognized leader, and goddess, of the **Tuatha Dé Dannan** who were said to do magic, but was it really technology like the Norse had? (See Chapters 2 & 3.)

Danu and her people were originally from Greece – close to the Anunnaki territory, and while they were not Anunnaki, it is interesting that her name, Danu, relates to the King of the Anunnaki, Anu.

She is associated with a triad of goddesses: **Anu**(Ana), **Danu**, and **Brigit**. Her magic caldron was said to come from Murias, the City of the West which sank beneath the waves. [503]

In addition, **Biróg** was a **Druid Priestess** involved in several Celtic legends.

> Biróg, another *bandrúi* [druid priestess] of the Tuatha Dé Dannan, plays a key role in an Irish folktale where the Formorian warrior Balor attempts to thwart a prophecy foretelling he would be killed by his own grandson; imprisoning his only daughter Eithne in the tower of Tory Island, away from any contact with men … But Biróg helps a man called Mac Cinnfhaelaidh, whose magical cow Balor stole, to gain access to the tower and seduce her. Eithne gives birth to triplets, but Balor gathers them up in a sheet and sends a messenger to drown them in a whirlpool. The messenger drowns two of the babies, but unwittingly drops one in the harbour, where he is rescued by Biróg. She takes the child back to his father, who gives him to his brother …. in fosterage. The boy grows up to kill Balor.

So much for trying to thwart the gods' prophecies… Destiny sometimes rules.

Sophia Goddess of Wisdom

Pistis Sophia is known as the "Virgin of Light." She is a supreme deity who falls from grace (Heaven) and gets defiled by the lower world (of ignorance, greed, corruption…) and has to call on her Father who agrees to send his firstborn, her brother (Jesus), to resurrect her and restore her. He is seen as 'the bridegroom' and Sophia prepares herself to be worthy of him, as he represents Higher Consciousness, and when the two are united, the result is Enlightenment (Gnosis).

The mystical marriage symbolizes the good news:
This Gnostic Gospel says that transformation of a lower state (spiritual unconsciousness) is possible and one comes to understand s/he is an eternal soul and never dies. They were said to be "born again." [504]

Sacred & Divine Feminine

So, can an Earth woman today be a goddess? No. The goddess carries the **Divine** Feminine… an aspect of godhood. Can she be a priestess? Yes, the priestess carries the **Sacred** Feminine – but should avoid Wicca (or carefully go no further) because it often leads to entrapment in witchcraft and darker Neo-paganism….. the real thing ("goddess-hood") is not available to Earth-born women, and the reason was explained in TOM, Ch. 3 and VEG, Chs. 6 & 14.

Rewind: **Danger in Witchcraft**
As was said in two former books, there are Astral entities who love to play games – especially the Ouija Board and empowering Wiccan priestesses seeking more personal power. The problem with the Ouija Board is that it leads to more and people like Jane Roberts died as a result – she left the Board and invited the entity to speak thru her – so while in her body he drank and smoked and several years later, she died of lung cancer.

The problem with any entity empowering the spells and incantations a priestess makes (including Santeria, Huna, Voodoo, etc) is that the entities will eventually come to collect, and they don't want your money . This author served a year in a Deliverance Ministry and saw what these entities do to people when they come to 'collect.'

Not possession, just nasty oppression.

Be very careful of the **ego trap** where you think you're doing the magick and now have some personal power.

At this point, let's make a distinction between goddess and priestess.

- **Goddess** refers to specific **deities** linked clearly to a particular culture and often to particular aspects, attributes and **powers** (for example: the Mesopotamian goddess Inanna, Ishtar or Athena; or Hindu goddesses like Sarasvati, Mahadevi, or Lakshmi; or Nü Wa and Xi-He in China).

- **Priestess** refers to Earth women who dedicate themselves to one or more goddesses. It may or may not include leadership of a group, and it may or may not include legal ordination. The analogous term for men is "priest." However, not everyone who dedicates themselves to the Goddess or goddesses calls themselves a priestess (or priest). Examples : Reiki Masters, and Wiccan priestesses.

Thus, the Sacred Feminine is something that an Earth woman can aspire to and develop with care… whether or not she undergoes the *Kundalini* experience. It is the manifestation of the **Yin Force**, so prevalent in a woman (the man is Yang energy).

> Yin Force in a woman is an aspect of the Dragon Force examined earlier in the book. When it is soft, passive and receptive it is Yin. When it is strong, aggressive and concentrated, it is Yang. It is the same energy, or Life Force.

Many women already have better intuition and sensitivity to energy than most men do, and thus meditation and specific forms of Yoga can be used to develop their Yin Force. A true connection with one's Higher Self has 5 aspects – generating wisdom, compassion, patience, respect for all living things, and humility. In some cases, advanced abilities are seen – clairvoyance, telepathy, and levitation…. The woman can activate her intuition and higher guidance faculty easier than a man because testosterone often interferes with the just-mentioned 5 qualities of higher consciousness.

Yang is Warrior, Yin is Nurture. Thus the term **"Warrior Priestess"** is an oxymoron – while Yin and Yang should be balanced – they cannot manifest at the same time; a human is either Yang or Yin. So the Warrior Priestess is either attacking with Yang energy, or passively subduing her enemy with Yin energy. The body at rest is when the balance occurs (Think: meditation). Kung Fu generates Yang energy. Female seduction generates Yin energy.

The trick is to be able to consciously generate one or the other, as needed, and **Paramahansa Yogananda** often did that – which is why his body did not decay after death. Jesus and **Apollonius of Týana** also were masters of the physical world – both were known to disappear and reappear miles away from their current site, heal people at a distance, and walk on water, and even **Padre Pio** could bi-locate…

The most recent example of a woman, not a goddess, who could levitate, heal, change water to wine, etc. was **Theresa of Avila**, more properly called a mystic. Also included were Hildegard of Bingen, Catherine of Siena, Meister Eckhart, John of the Cross, and St. Francis of Assisi. Some Amerindian Shamen and Sufis also fall into this category. (See also Nart Knights in Chapter 5.)

20th Century Goddess

If we accept that a goddess is someone who comes to Earth to help Man, and is not a human, and has advanced knowledge and abilities, then there is another woman who qualifies as a 'goddess.' Maria Orsitch.

Maria Orsitch

(Left) a real photo of the woman who showed up in 1934 in Germany and delivered an electrogravitic design for what we today call a UFO.
She worked with Dr.s Schauberger and W.O. Schumann to make several working prototpes. Later Dr. Hans Kammler would engineer another type of *flugscheiben* and Maria would disappear in 1945 using her own *Jenseitsflugmaschine.*

She said she was Serbian, as did Nikola Tesla, her compatriot – both here to lead Man into new science – but others who knew her and were familiar with how she got the technical specs (via channeling with ETs, in Cuneiform, no less!) said that she was from Aldebaran and was here to help the human offspring of an earlier genetic "planting" of humans in Northern Europe. She succeeded, whereas Nikola failed.

> A fairly factual account of her work was contained in the novel, The Earth Warrior, yet her presence on Earth ended in 1945, whereas the novel has her helping Man on into 2017.

The study of goddesses and the Divine Feminine is **Thealogy.**

Turkey Again

Whereas Göbekli Tepe has stunned the world, pushing back the recorded history of Man to about 10,000 BC, Turkey is also home to a major goddess site: **Çatalhöyük.**

> James Mellaart discovered the site in 1960 which dates back to 7000 BC and consists of buildings and shrines dedicated to a supreme goddess – built on several levels and following a very sophisticated architectural blueprint.... The major arrangement of images was a **central female goddess** surrounded by satellite, subordinate male symbols. [505]

The map below shows not only Çatalhöyük, but it also shows Cappadocia, Mt. Nemrut and Derinkuyu – other fascinating sites in **Turkey** (as follows):

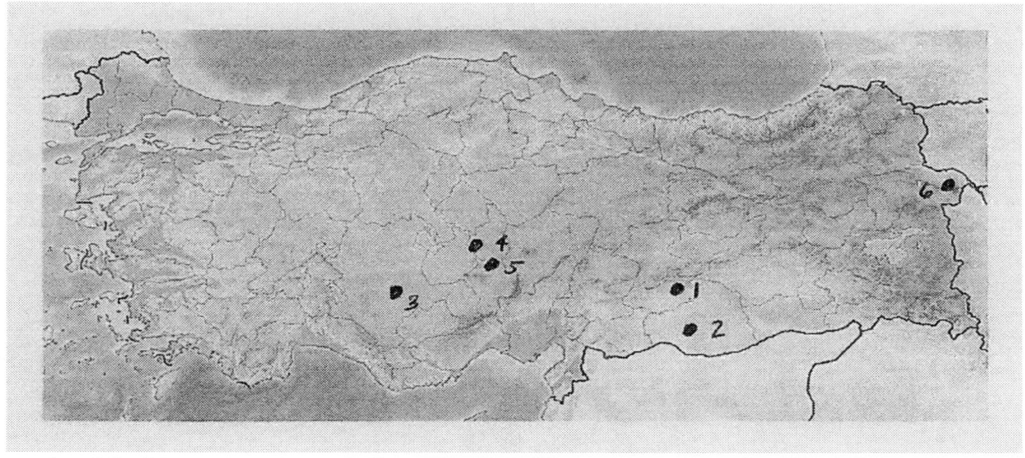

1 – Mt. Nemrut	3 – Çatalhöyük	5 – Derinkuyu
2 – Göbekli Tepe	4 – Cappadocia (Göreme)	6 – Mt. Ararat

Mt. Nemrut and Derinkuyu were profiled on page 413.
Göbekli Tepe is profiled on page 412, and Chapter 7.
Cappadocia was profiled on page 350.

What is interesting is that something important was going on in Turkey, with the underground dwellings (Derinkuyu and Cappadocia), statues to the Gods and Goddesses (Mt. Nemrut), a temple for 'delivering *kundalini*' (Göbekli Tepe) and a major temple to a supreme goddess (Çatalhöyük). And lastly, Mt. Ararat, alleged resting place of Noah's Ark. It is well worth the time to Google or do Wikipedia for these sites and study the pictures.

Summary

As a closing idea, it is well-known that the Church relegated women to a lesser rôle in religion, and the Christian Church itself was largely male-dominated. And its insistence on blind faith and dogma at the expense of intellectual inquiry has seriously suppressed the spiritual side of Man – and now many people treat true spirituality as superstition and nonsense. Yet many women still carry a connection to the spiritual side of life, and its mysteries, and could help to mollify our patristic and violent society.

> If Christianity were to acknowledge its debt to the **ancient mysteries** it could connect again to the universal current of human spiritual evolution and become a partner, not an adversary, of all the other religious traditions it has branded as the work of the Devil. If it were to cast off the deadweight of the Old Testament and its jealous tribal deity, it could rediscover the wisdom of the **Divine Feminine**. If it

were to relinquish its dogmatism, it could reawaken the ancient sense of wonder that united science and mysticism in one human adventure of discovery. If it could finally concede that the New Testament is the work of men and women, not the word of God recording actual events, there would be nothing to stop it recovering its own **mystical Inner Mysteries**. Is this too much to hope for? [506] [emphasis added]

Appendix C: Paleo-Sanskrit

This Appendix provides a look at Paleo-Sanskrit – the forerunner to Sanskrit which was, in turn, the forerunner to today's Hindi and Pali, and some Indo-European languages. Because it was an ancient language (> 10,000 years BCE) it was used principally in ancient cultures, located in what is today India/Pakistan, notably the Harappa Valley (see Chapter 5, Karukshetra War). Indus Valley was Inanna's domain… is this <u>another</u> Anunnaki script – besides cuneiform?

In Harappa, the language of choice was the Indus Script which was also associated with Proto-Dravidian aka Proto-Sanskrit from the **Indus Valley**… An example of the Script is shown below…

(credit: By Source (WP:NFCC#4), Fair use, <u>https://en.wikipedia.org/w/index.php?curid=50693381)</u>

vedic puranic proto-sanskrit also called **paleo-sanskrit**: <u>http://www.human-resonance.org/paleo-sanskrit.html</u>

Also please note the similarity of the design (called Rangoli) to the Celtic Knot as was examined in Chapter 3. Certain themes repeat around the planet.

Professor Kurt Schildmann (1909-2005)

Says Wikipedia (source: Harappan language = proto-sanskrit):

> Professor Schildmann's dedication to the translation of ancient hieroglyphic languages culminated in his 1994 recognition of the phonetic structure of **Paleo-Sanskrit** from the Indus Valley texts, a breakthrough enabling his definitive decipherment of the Indus Valley script, and by extension to the decipherment of the scripts of the **Illinois cave** archive and **Tayos Cave**, Ecuador. [emphasis added]
>
> Schildmann's ability and willingness to link modern aerial phenomena with the enigmatic statements of ancient cultures has been met with strict suppression.
>
> During his decades of travels and epigraphic research Schildmann was continually confronted with profoundly disturbing statements among the Illinois Cave archive's Paleo-Sanskrit texts, which repeatedly referred to those strange and prevalent phenomena involving unidentified circular spacecraft ("nau"), 'alien' abduction, livestock mutilation and deep subterranean bases.

The foregoing is to establish that (1) Paleo-Sanskrit did exist and was a real, pictographic language, and (2) that it reveals (including artifacts found at the Illinois cave) the presence and activity of the gods (i.e., ETs).

The Illinois Cave artifacts is another similar finding to that at Göbekli Tepe. Further amazing info is available at:

http://www.human-resonance.org/illinois_archive.html

The professor was roundly criticized for his findings as they did not agree with the accepted history of the Earth. However, his translations and dictionary were never faulted, thus we need to look at a basic dictionary so that the translations in Chapter 7 of the Göbekli Tepe artifacts can be seen to be authentic.

Professor Schildmann's scholarly excellence and decisive offerings in the field of Paleolithic epigraphy are reasserted here, applying his comprehensive lexicon and cipher key to dozens of Paleo-Sanskrit texts:

The following examples of Paleo-Sanskrit script
are credited to: http://www.human-resonance.org/paleo-sanskrit.html:

Paleo-Sanskrit Lexicon & Cipher Keys

Sanskrit-English Dictionary
Arthur A. MacDonell (1893)

Cosmological

Karāha	the Creator
Kara	the Maker
Viṣṇu	the Pervader
Aśvinau	the Divine Twins
Svar	the Sun, light-giver
Indu	the Moon, fullness
Budha	Mercury, speed
Kavi	Venus, wisdom
Sita	the Earth, beauty
Mangal	Mars, fortune
Indra	Jupiter, the one
Śani	Saturn, yang
Yonī	womb, race, humanity
Tridaśa	thirty resonances
Soma	gold & silver colloid

Numerical

śūnya	zero, inifinity
éka, anya	the one, single
dvi, aśvin	the two, double
trí, trā	the three, triple
catúr	four, quadruple
hasta	five, the hand
pañca	five
ṣáṣ	six
saptá	seven
aṣṭá	eight
náva	nine
daśa	ten
ekādasa	eleven
dvādasa	twelve
trayadasa	thirteen
caturdasa	fourteen
pancadasa	fifteen
sodasa	sixteen
saptádasa	seventeen
aṣṭádasa	eighteen
návadasa	nineteen
vimśat	twenty
tridaśa	thirty
śata	one hundred
dviśata	two hundred

General

kar	works
kari.kr	making tribute
karas	workings
kara	make, action
akar	without action
kala	black, dark blue
akala	untimely
kavi	wise
kāma	desires
karman	fate, destiny
karya	duty
karva	love
ka	whatever, following
kū	where, whereby
u	oh
ai	aye, also, upon
āt	and, then
aya	going
as	for, to be
aśi	you are
aśmi	I am
aśti	he is, him
ha	that, those, gives
dha	thereupon
dhana	wealth
dhī	thought
vi	from, through
va	certainly
vai	woes
vaiaśva	all, entirely
vaś	will, command
ca	built, building, thus
nā	not, without
nadu	according to
nātha	chief, commander
naitri	leader, guide
nara	man
nari	woman
mātri	matriarch
nana	mother
tata	father
tah, te	the

Part 1 of 2

Note above (upper left): Indra, Visnu.

Indra is Jupiter and Visnu is Vishnu.

ta	giving, endowing
rā	granting
las	brilliant, shining
lās	jumping, moving
aśu	life
aśna	stone
aś-iṣ	delight
ana	breath
jivhā	tongue
jani	wife, production
mī	waning, diminishing
iṣ	waxing, swelling
mī-iṣ	synchrony, rhythm
si	your, yours
syāt	it is, they are
sita	beauty
suta	son
ma	being, status
mai	my, mine
mahā	great
mahāta	greatness
mila	joining
ya	commencing, initiating
ya-as	striving, aiming
ya-ta	vengeful, vengence
hastī	elephant (infrasound)
raua	thundering, roaring
śu-us	whirring, humming
su	the good, benefit
śūra	hero, deity
aśura	deities
vīra	man, hero
daiva	god
aiva	long life, eternity
adri	tree
adhi	delivering
upama	the highest
upaātta	received
cakra	wheel, cycle, era
śam	universal, cosmic
śamadhi	cosmic consciousness
ānam	captain
nau	spaceships
pī	after, moving
pra	for, forward
paia	approaching
punar	again, back, anew

prāna	soul
pā	protecting, Lord
trāya	protection
trasa	creature, the heart
teṣam	of the
tasya	from him, for him
tada	that time
tama	darkness
tara	the stars
graha	the planets
oha	excellence
īra	wind
ura	broad
āra	metal, ore, magma
aua	below, underlying
alam	enough
plava	flooding, inundating
mū	stopping, preventing
muta	impelled by
mita	measured
ris	dwindling, displacing
śai	declining
vical	rescinding
vida	knowing, wise
ama	the night
ava	favor
antar	between
atha	how else
atas	henceforth
atma	influence, control
amara	immortal
amata	imperceptible
amati	want, indigence
amati	(*alt.*) splendor
atra	devourer
aśri	edge, blade
asráva	tears
aśas	hating, cursing
śas	suffering, punishing
iha	killing
aśa	evil
astā	death
asta	house, abode
dura	malevolent
dusta	evildoer
dhara	sword
phala	shield

Part 2 of 2

Note above: ra, maha, raua, adhi, nau, prana, upama, sam, asu.

…these words are used in the Göbekli Tepe translations in Chapter 7. Note that "maha" is Hindi for 'great' as in "MahaRaja" = great king.

Further parts of the lexicon follow…

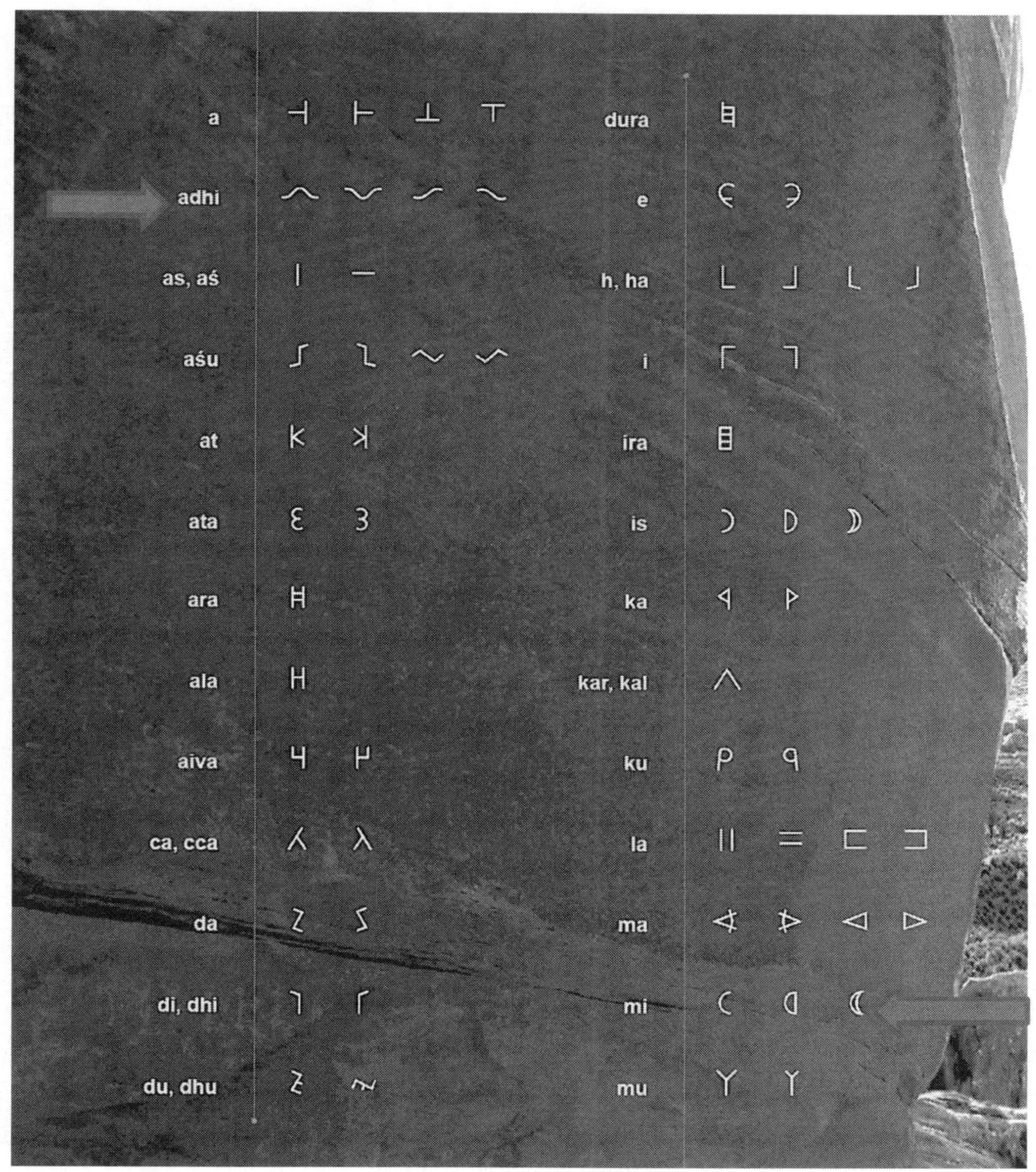

Part 1 of 4

Note **adhi** and **mi** from Chapter 7 "ducks"…

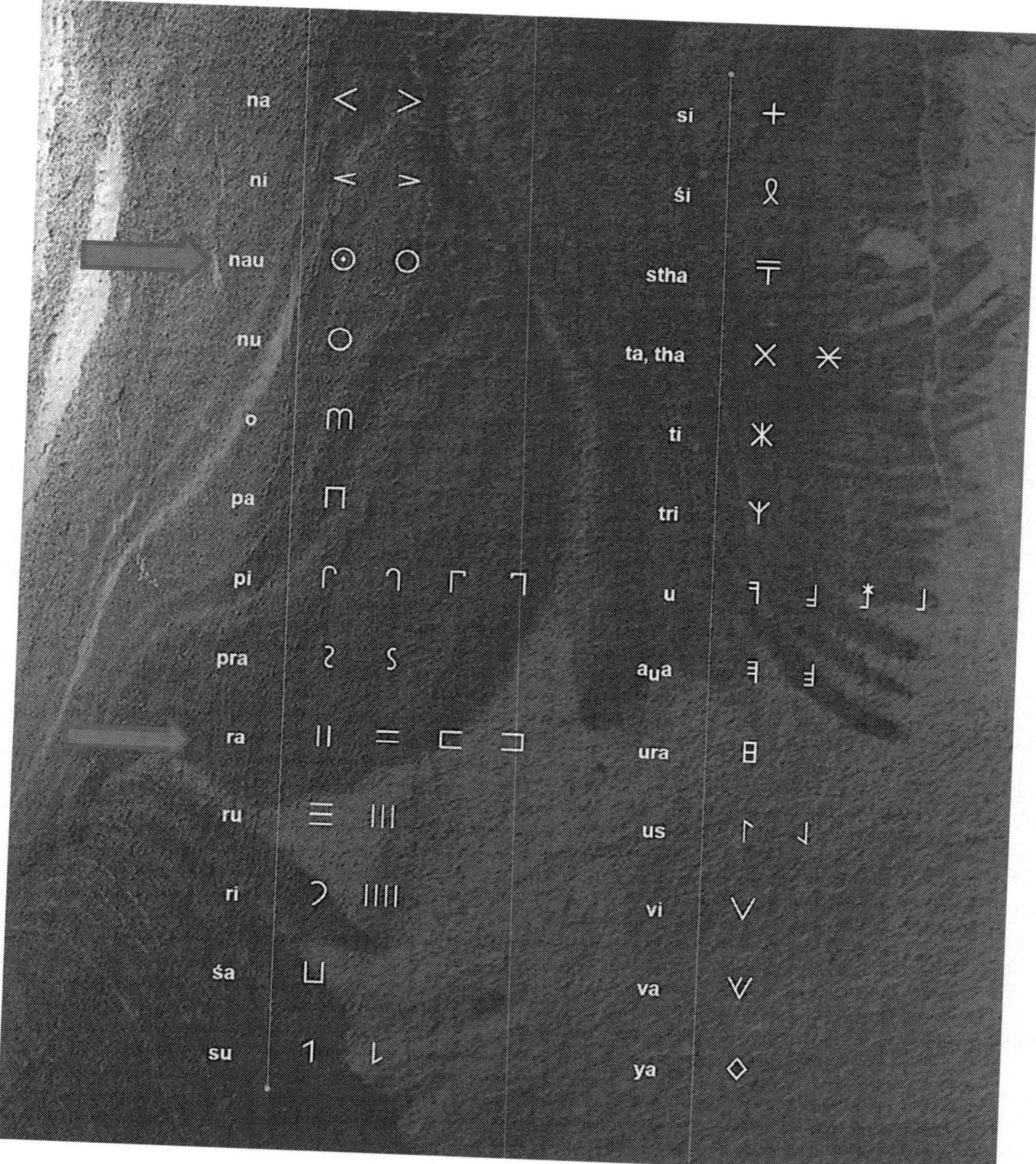

Part 2 of 4

Note **nau, ra,** as used in the translations in Chapter 7.

These words and hieroglyphic symbols can be used in a **pictographic way**, read left to right, top to bottom – as it was in Chapter 7 with the "ducks" at the base of the stone. Because there are some very interesting symbols in the extended lexicon, they are included below:

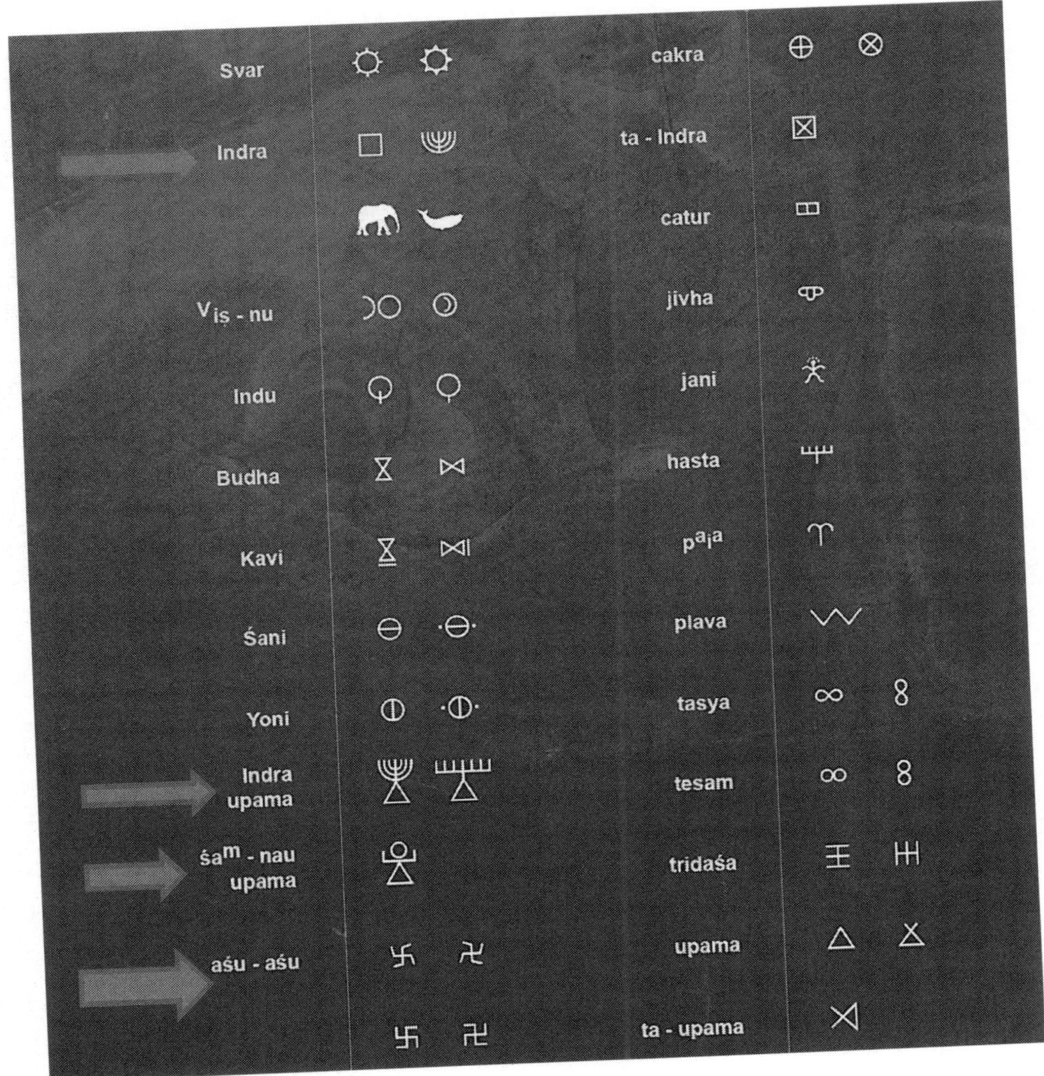

Part 3 of 4

Note: the swastika (**asu**) denotes "life" back in the earlier definition page (Part 2 of 2, 2 pages back). In ancient times it was not a symbol of evil.

Note: Indra above is a box (Göbekli Tepe) but could also be a menorah!

Note: sam-nau-upama = "universal/cosmic – spaceship - highest". Furthermore, there is another ancient symbol we all know:

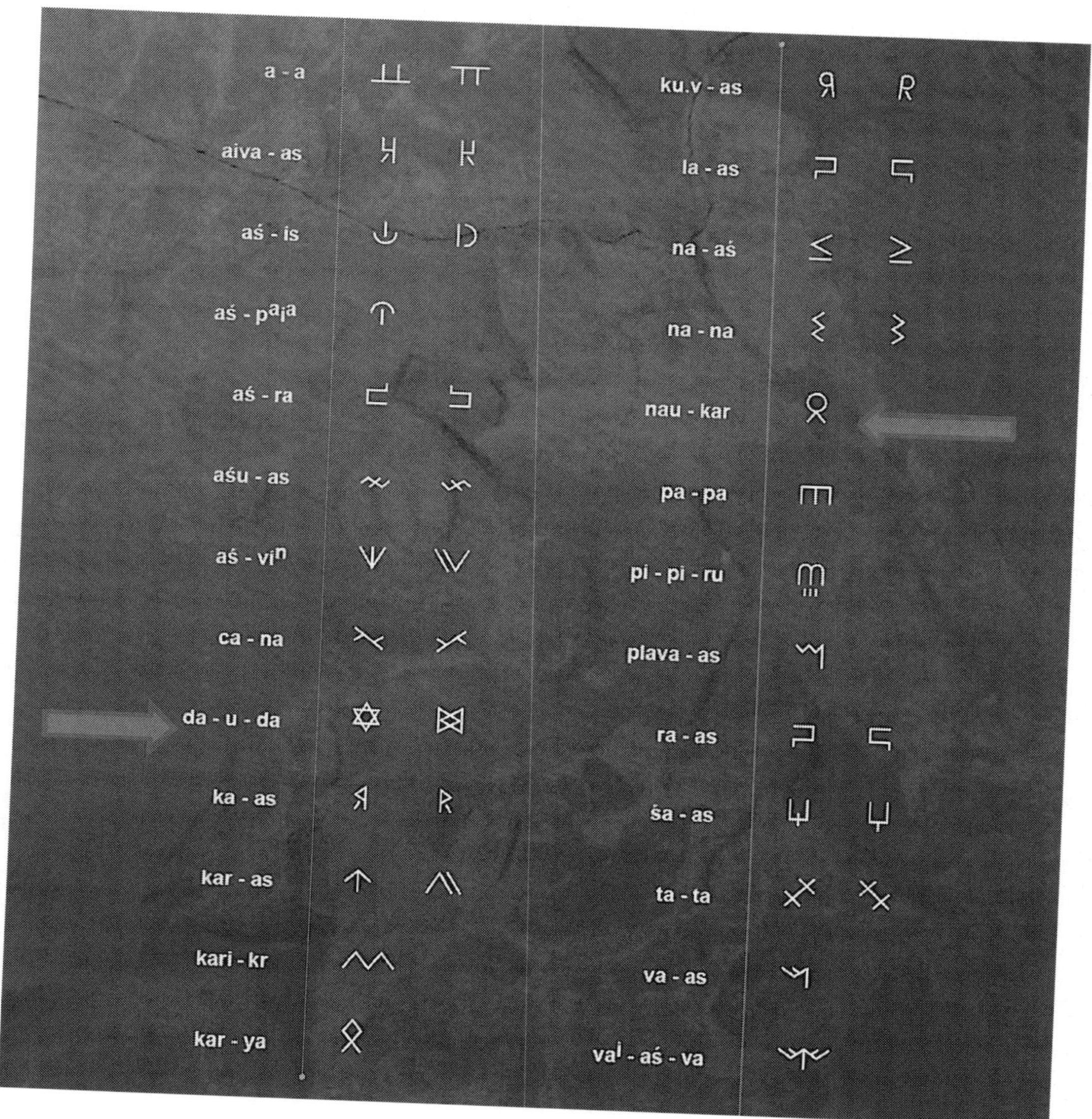

Part 4 of 4

And when you combine the symbols, as is beginning to happen above, one gets a new picture of the Chapter 4, Indus Valley Script (p. 160-161). And the "animals" on the T-posts at Göbekli Tepe are a combination of the above symbols.

nau kar = "spaceship working…."

Fascinating way to communicate… gotta wonder: since it is > 10,000 years old, do the ETs still use it?

Encyclo-Glossary

Note: throughout this book, reference is made to further detail on certain topics, and the books are referred to by abbreviation:

VEG – Book 1 – Virtual Earth Graduate
TOM – Book 2 – Transformation of Man
TEW – Book 3 – The Earth Warrior
QES – Book 4 – Quantum Earth Simulation
TSiM -- Book 5 – The Science in Metaphysics

ξ ξ ξ

1-Sec Drop -- this is a direct communication from a higher being into one's mind and memory/knowledge base. It is not a voice, not automatic writing. It takes a very brief split second and one knows that it is happening, and then it can take anywhere from 10 seconds to 20 minutes to examine what one was given. It is information that is usually complete and appears to the recipient to be something that s/he already knew and is now aware of.
Similar to an insight or revelation, except that it has an energy signature about it that you know it is being "dropped" into you. (Reminiscent of **V2K** but there are no words 'spoken.')

Anunnaki – one of the early, original ET visitors to Earth who interfered in the natural progression of the bipedal hominids here, and created some of the first 'humans' in Africa and Sumeria. Because of their technology and power, they were looked upon as gods. Supposedly from the planet **Nibiru**, but more likely Orion or Sirius systems. (See **Zechariah Sitchin** and **Remnant**. See also VEG Ch. 3.)

Anunnaki Elite – consists of two main types: the ruling reptilians who retained their original appearance (e.g., Enlil and Enki), and the later, hybridized, more human-looking (e.g., Inanna, Marduk, Sargon, even Alexander the Great). The later change was effected by Enki's mating with humans and later genetic prowess to enable the Anunnaki to move among the humans who found the original., reptilian/reptibian appearance repulsive.

Archons – the 'powers that be' in the celestial realms – according to the Gnostics. These are the same ones that Ephesians 6:12 refers to: powers & principalities (a hierarchy) dedicated to evil and wickedness. Synonymous with 'demon.' (See **Nephilim**, and see **Djinn** in VEG Ch. 6).

Astral Realm – note that there are levels in the Astral realm, and in particular, the one that most concerns Man, is the Level I (**Chart 4** in VEG, Ch. 12) which is a kind of intra-dimensional space – more than 3D and yet not really 4D, and this is inhabited by Man's oppressors, the STS Gang. The normal 4D STS/STO entities occupy the higher 4D and lower 5D Astral realms and cannot see 3D Man.

Attractor – energy in the form of an idea, person, or thing that draws other things, ideas or people together based on similar and strong resonance.

Beings of Light – often referred to as Angels, or today's Watchers, they guide and protect Man. They are also known to provide the life review that NDErs speak of, and they are the '*Inspecs*' that Robert Monroe spoke of.

Bionet – a term coined in VEG Ch. 9 to describe the hyperdimensional network of communication in the body. Like the Internet, *chi* is carried in meridians of energy to all parts of the system, from the chakras, and tells the cells and organs what to do. The Bionet is manipulated during Accupuncture to channel biophotons. Chinese TCM called it Meridians.

Book 2 – the successor to the *Virtual Earth Graduate* , with additional examination of specific topics, is *Transformation of Man*, aka Book 2. Book 1 and 2 were originally the same book – at 868 pages.

Brain Waves – a measurement of consciousness.

Beta cycle: 12 – 19+ Hz (normal waking consciousness)
Alpha cycle: 8 – 12 Hz (relaxed, aware state)
Theta cycle: 4 – 8 Hz (sleep)
Delta cycle: less than 4 Hz (deep sleep)

Catalyst – anything like an event, an idea or a word, that causes change in a person; the threat of being fired for bad performance at work is a catalyst to perform at one's best. Illness is a catalyst to see what is wrong, or what energy is blocked, in one's body.

Chakra – a vortex of energy formed in the body wherever two or more chi meridians cross or come together; same as a vortex on the earth with its ley lines. (Sedona, AZ is known for several of these.) These are also referred to as 'energy centers' as they transduce energy from the air/water/Sun around a body and draw it into the body thru the chakras. There are 7 main charkas in the body and 1 above the head, and 1 below the feet. There are many more, minor charkas all over the body.

Chi – energy particles, also called *ruach*, orgone, mana, prana or ki – without chi in our food, air and water the human body could not exist. The chi is a force that travels along meridians (pathways) in the body that link the etheric aura (1st level of the aura) to the physical body; it can be directed by the mind to specific parts of the body for healing.

Cognitive Dissonance – the result of hearing/reading something new that does not fit into one's reality, or in what one thought was their reality; the effect is to create confusion followed by denial of new concepts. More specifically, when a new idea conflicts with an established idea that one already thinks they know, the result is 'dissonance', and rejection. When people were told 500 years ago that the Earth was round, they experienced great cognitive dissonance… which led to denial.

Coherence – resonating alike; attracted to each other by similar resonance. Two energy waves are coherent if they have the same shape, size, and strength.

Dissidents – Anunnaki hybrid Remnant still on the Earth who seek to control Man and deny him his divine heritage. See **Insiders**.

Dragon Force – another term for the *Kundalini* enlightening a person. (Chapter 9 & 10.) A person with Dragon Force also has Dragon Wisdom.

Draconians – a militaristic STS race largely from the Orion system who have subjugated many worlds in our Galaxy. Also referred to as the Dracs, or the Reptiles. A very old race that lays claim to much of our Galaxy and they fear Man because they don't all have (nor do they understand) the soul, thus they seek to contain/control Man.

Elite -- those humans who are mostly descended from the Anunnaki hybrids; as a group they may be augmented by the Remnant Insiders who stayed behind when the main contingent of Anunnaki went home. They are generally not the enemy. See **Chapter 13, 'Insider'.** See also **PTB.**

Energy Vampire – a person, OP or ensouled, who subconsciously starts an argument, gets the other person angry, and the instigator takes the other person's energy through the Law of Energy Potentials. Energy always flows from the higher potential to the lower and this applies to car batteries, as well as humans. So the instigator creates a fight, not to win or lose (they don't care), they will walk off with some of your energy, and they quit the argument when they have it. They are up, and the victim is usually tired.

Entrain – to induce a state in B like in A; usually done by music, movies, and words, but can be done by powerful thoughts and beliefs. A hypnotist entrains a subject into a desired state; Hitler's harangues entrained the crowds into the Nazi mindset he wanted; and classical music entrains the listeners into a relaxed (Alpha) state.

Flow – often referred to as The Flow. This is the rising energetic vibrational entrainment into the higher 4th and 5th dimensional realms. It has increased awareness, compassion, Light, and STO aspects for service and is available to all who seek to align themselves with a Higher Way. It was created by the Higher Beings and is supported by an archetype that masters on the Earth reinforced and made available to all spiritual growth aspirants.

Free Will – an illusion. The more one grows spiritually, the more one does the will of the Father of Light. Baby souls, or those who insist on their own way, think they have free will but the Father is merely letting them experience the results of what they do... their **Script** controls much of what young/baby souls can do. As Jesus said "Not my will, but Thine be done." Advanced souls have surrendered their will by eliminating their ego.

Galactic Law – the ethics and rules as set forth by the Galactic Council and adhered to by all subordinate councils for the maintenance of order. It includes a Non-Interference directive, responsibilities of 'creator races', transportation or communication protocols, terra-forming procedures, and energy creation/disposal to name a few. Specifically, the creation of brand-new sentient, humanoid species is forbidden, but the modification of existing species may be allowed (approval required) provided: (1) the species is terminated when its usefulness is done [which was Enlil's choice], or (2) the species may be further developed if reasonable and can be done in a way that benefits them and the solar system Association of Worlds [this was Enki's choice].

Gnostic – one who believes that God is accessible to all by going within and following their 'inner knowing'. Gnosticism relies on one's personal enlightenment to guide them; it is in fact, connecting with one's **Higher Self** which has true Knowledge. The Bible refers to it as the 'inner Light' and is what one connects with when they follow Jesus' suggestion that "the Kingdom of Heaven is within." Gnosticism was originally (AD 100) part of the Christian movement.

God/gods – this is god with a small "g". It is just a convention for referring to those who are alleged to be watching over us, running the Drama on Earth.

Godhead – a collection of higher souls, and Soul Groups, in closer proximity to God, like spokes on a wheel where the hub is God Himself. The Godhead works directly with the Oversoul for each Soul Group and sometimes the two are hard to distinguish. The basic hierarchy is: **God – Godhead/Oversouls – Soul Groups – Angels/Neggs – and individual souls.** Between the Godhead and God is the Hieracrchy of Masters and those who are responsible for Solar Systems, and then Galaxies.

Greys – the 3' tall gray-colored humanoids with the big heads, big black eyes and skinny bodies; their eyes are large (really protective coverings over eyes sensitive to light); they typically perform the abductions on humans, some cattle and other species. They have a hive/group mentality as they are **bio-cybernetic roboids** and tools to change Man's DNA. (Grays [note spelling] are real beings from Zeta Reticuli.)

Higher Beings – Light Beings above the Astral and reincarnative levels (1-6) and who are responsible for the operation of these lower 6 levels, reside on the 7th level themselves; may intervene in 3rd – 4th – 5th – 6th dimensional affairs when the Greater Script of the Father of Light, or the One, requires it to keep the Multiverse working.
Also colloquially called "**the gods"** just in VEG Chapters 12-15 who run the HVR Sphere or Simulation. The Higher Beings are not the Beings of Light (angels) nor ETs nor aliens.

Higher Self – also called the Oversoul, this is the coordinating entity of each Soul Group and acts to oversee Scripts, events, lessons – and coordinate with the souls of the same Soul Group, and with other Oversouls who manage other Soul Groups in the same Godhead. Each Godhead has multiple Oversouls that interface with the multiple Soul Groups. See VEG Ch. 7, Chart 3a.

Hybrids – this is any human-looking but 'upgraded' version of Homo *sapiens* which may or may not have a soul. It can be the Anunnaki hybrids – part Anunnaki, part human, and their bloodline. Or it may be Homo *noeticus* that the Greys have been so busy developing to restart civilization after the big Change event in the near future. Most are very intuitive, psychic and are the next step in the development of Man.

Insiders – Anunnaki hybrid Remnant still on the Earth (may include Enki). The pro-active ones who try to help mankind and block the **Dissidents** (qv).

InterLife – where souls go when they die, after passing through the **Tunnel** to the **Light**. Also called the Other Side, and sometimes appears to be Heaven. It is where the **Script** is designed, souls are counseled by the Masters and Teachers, souls are rehabilitated after a rough lifetime on Earth (or elsewhere), and it is where the Heavenly Biocomputer referred to in TOM Ch. 6 resides. This is also where reunions with members of one's **Soulgroup** happen. (Book2 spends 2 chapters on this aspect.)

Karma – *Aka* **The Law of Karma**. – originally the concept of "meeting oneself", or "what goes 'round, comes 'round." It does not mean being stabbed in this lifetime because one stabbed someone else in a former lifetime. The original, true concept was that of the Universal Law of Cause and Effect, and it forms the basis of one or more aspects of your Life Script. Karma can also be a manipulative issue in the

Virtual Reality of Earth if the life review is done by a Negg posing as a Being of Light.
Note that **Karma applies only to Earth**; other souls who do not come to Earth do not have to deal with Karma.

Law of Attraction – simply says that you attract to you who and what you are. Attraction also works by repeated focus, visualization, affirmations and speaking one's word, and of course, by prayer. Attracting what you want may be blocked by the Script if it is not permitted this lifetime… to enforce some lesson: you stay poor to learn humility or reliance on other people, for example.

Law of Confusion – when RA was asked a question that violated someone else's right to privacy, or asked something that would be giving advanced level information that the person had no context for, RA would comment that the question could not be answered because it "violated the Law of Confusion." We are to work thru confusion and seek the answer(s) on our own; **everyone has a temporary 'right' to be confused** (i.e., to not know) and are expected to work thru it, or ask, thereby absorbing the lesson and info on a level that makes the lesson/info part of us.

Law of Non-Interference -- there are several parts to this Law. One is that other sentient beings from other worlds do not have *carte blanche* to manipulate or interfere with the normal development of Earth's humans. In addition, it also specifies that human bodies are to have only one soul (possession is not permitted), and there is a provision that ensouled humans cannot be manipulated from the Astral violating their Freewill.

Law of One – the concept that we are all connected at a higher level, mostly thru our Higher Selves, and we are all part of the One, the Father of Light – if you have a soul. The Law of One also includes freewill and love. Telling someone else what to do, how to live, etc. is a violation of the Law of One, a violation of freewill whose flipside is called the Law of Confusion. (Think: **Entanglement**.)

Law of Potentials – this merely says that energy in the universe always flows from the higher potential to the lower. (Think: a weaker battery being charged by a stronger one, or a Master healing a human.)

Light – an intelligent aspect of God; sometimes referred to as the Force. It may be used interchangeably with Heaven and/or Knowledge. There are biophotons of light that support the operation of DNA and sustain bodily operations.
Note that Light (large L) is a conscious aspect of the God force, which force can have a brilliant light about it. The light (small "l") is everyday, regular light.

LY – abbreviation for Light Year, a measure of distance between worlds in the Universe.

Morphic Resonance – said of a plant or animal that takes its physical shape from the *morphogenetic* field that establishes a 'morphic' (shape) resonance with the object's energy. The plant's shape is entrained by the morphic resonance with the morphogenetic field (pattern) that governs how living things take shape, according to Rupert Sheldrake. (See VEG, Ch. 9 'Chuck.')

Morphogenesis – Rupert Sheldrake conceived of the presence of a 4D field around living things that influences the shape they take – kind of an Astral Template that governs height, width, color and other aspects of the oak tree for example, such as when and where it sends out its branches, how fast and how far.

Multiverse – the universe we live in is one of a number of universes comprising a Multiverse… multiple universes interconnected forming a coherent larger universe consisting of multiple levels (realities), and can involve parallel universes or dimensions in '**superposition'** (or stacked).

NDE – a Near Death Experience where the person appears to die, and their body is pronounced clinically dead, but they come back to life and relay their experience of meeting a Being of Light with whom they have a Life Review, and they usually come back a changed (better) person. The NDE effect often produces a spiritual transformation in the person.

Neggs – the 4D 'dark' angelic beings operating in the Astral realm around the Earth, whose sole purpose is to apply the negative lessons specified in one's Life Script. Thus they are "**NEG**ative **G**uide**S**." They work with the Beings of Light (Angels). See **Appendix A: Dr. Lerma**.
They are programmed to afflict mankind – they are appointed to effect the negative parts of one's Script (aka **catalyst**). They provide catalyst and feedback inducing Man to change and grow. They work with the Beings of Light (VEG Ch. 6) because they, too, are Beings of Light who volunteered to serve the negative agenda and they were 'reoriented' to Darkness to maximize their effectiveness. They still carry a small, suppressed connection to their original Light down inside and they will be restored to their original positive condition when their service is complete.

OPs – Organic Portals -- (pronounced "Oh Pee") human beings, flesh and blood (Organic part), and they can serve as a portal for astral entities to manipulate them. This is not synonymous with Zombie.
They also are not fully human as they allegedly lack a soul and that is because they have incomplete DNA and only the lower 3 chakras are wired to function; they cannot access higher energy centers. Due to their somewhat robotic nature, they can be used to guide and/or influence ensouled humans in 3D. The Greeks called them 'hylics.' The Mayans called them 'wooden people.' Dr. Mouravieff called them pre-Adamics. (See TOM.) Also called **Backdrop People** (Apx D, TOM.)

The Church has said for centuries that all humans have souls. The Greeks and Mayans said there were people who have no soul. This whole issue was **examined in detail in VEG, Ch. 1 & 5**. They allegedly do exist and are probably the Sociopaths and atheists among us. 98%+ **are not evil**, they just have **no conscience** and think they can do whatever they want. Jim Jones, Charles Manson, and Richard Ramirez are prime examples of OPs on steroids that have run amok, because they have no connection to a Higher Self. Discussing spirituality with them gets nowhere, they cannot imagine what you are talking about. They are run by 'A' Influences (VEG, Ch. 3: Life is a Film).

The Greeks would not let them teach in a school/college, and they could not hold public office – becasue they had no conscience and would eventually do the wrong thing.

Also called **Non-Playable Characters** (NPCs) as in a video game (see QES and Appendix D in TOM.)

PFV – Personal Frequency Vibration -- the day-to-day, overall vibratory rate (resonance) of the soul energy sustaining the human body. When a person is angry their aura 'glows' red, and the PFV can drop to a lower (denser) vibration than when a person feels a lot of love and the aura 'glows' rose and the vibration reflects the energy ofthe heart charka (higher, lighter energy). The PFV also denotes which charka is dominant in the person; a person living from their higher charkas has a higher PFV than one engaged in sex, violence and pettiness (lower chakra activity). The aura typically reflects what one is feeling, yet the base PFV does not change; when the person is at rest, the base PFV is consistent from day to day as it reflects the overall level of soul growth. Also known as that person's "energy signature" as recorded in objects (Psychometry). At 51% positive, the soul 'graduates.'

Points of Choice – there are pre-programmed points in a person's life where important choices must be made, and they are found in a person's Script. Examples are whether to move to Florida or stay in California, whether to accept what looks like a great new job, or whether to get married. Sometimes the choice results in a **timeline bifurcation** into a fractal subset so that another aspect of you can see how that turned out. See **Timeline**. (Covered more in detail in TOM, Ch. 2.)

Prime Directive – a requirement in our Galaxy for those races who can create life and modify existing life genetically – often referred to as a 'creator race.' They are responsible for overseeing the welfare: safety and education of their creation. This is why a **Remnant** of the Anunnaki stayed behind (now known as the Naga.) (VEG, Ch. 12 'Prime Directive.') See Galactic Law.

Prophylactic Fantasy – describes the world of denial that some people live in. 'Prophylactic' because they feel safe in their version of the world, and they reason that nothing really destructive has ever happened to them, nor can it. 'Fantasy' because they do not accept the real world and its negativity; they see their world as they want it to be and sometimes think that they can exert a 'force' that makes it that way.

PTB – the earthly human Powers That Be; the 3rd dimensional STS people running the world for their Anunnaki Dissident masters (control group still here). They are also influenced by corrupt DNA, and the **RCF/Matrix** itself. Puppets. Many of them are OPs. See **Elite** – not the same thing, just a higher level of control.

Quantum Net – the field that interpenetrates all things and all of space. This has also been likened to the Ether and what is today called Dark Energy. The body has a minor Net, called the **Bionet**. In all Nets, the communication is almost instantaneous.

Reassembled – this is also called **Disassembled**, Dissolved in VEG and TOM (books 1 and 2). The Higher Beings will attempt to infuse a wayward soul with new, proactive energy, and perform a kind of 'psychic surgery' on the soul's energy field (which emanates from their Ground of Being so it is tricky), and failing that, if a soul cannot be re-oriented to STO behavior, the energy (soul) is **Dissolved** back into its component energy parts, as a failed soul. The consciousness is removed, energy then is cleaned, and can be reused without the former consciousness that accompanied the failed soul. (In short, fooling around for Eternity is not allowed, and when a soul goes mostly Dark, it is taken aside and examined closely… it is not allowed to pollute the world of souls headed for the Light. Thus, it should be clear that there is no Satan, or fallen angel.)

Recycled – short-circuited version of reincarnation: to come back into the same body, same lifetime, hence experiences **Déjà Vu**. Implies the inability to move forward into new realms and experiences in the greater **Multiverse**. (See VEG, Ch. 14.) If the soul learns nothing in a lifetime, this is the first step in rehabilitating them, and is a gentle nudge to apply oneself and handle the lessons... ultimately potentially followed by Reassembly.

Reincarnation – the spiritual growth aspect of a soul moving thru the different realms in the Multiverse (not just back to Earth) for the purpose of experiencing and gaining knowledge and wisdom. On the other hand, a repeated lifetime limited to Earth is more of a recycling.

Remnant – short for Anunnaki Remnant – that part of the Anunnaki group that stayed on Earth and did not leave with the main group, between 610-560 BC. Comprised of the Insiders (+) and the Dissidents (-). Some are human-looking.

Also known as **Naga** (underground 'Serpent' dwellers in Asia), may also be Dravidians.

Reptibian – A humanoid being, part reptile, part amphibian. In most ways looking like a human being, but with scales instead of skin, perhaps slightly webbed toes and fingers, cat's eyes, and a face that suggests a reptile/amphibian more than a human being. Note that an anaconda is aquatic and is also a reptile that moves on land. (VEG, Ch. 3)

Resonance – vibrating alike: such that two tuning forks A and B side by side, with A struck hard to set it vibrating, when put next to B which was not vibrating, will set tuning fork B vibrating at the same frequency as tuning fork A. This also happens with people in close proximity: a very negative person can 'detune' (bring down) a room of people and some people may actually feel ill and not know why (as they pick up the negative person's vibes). See **Entrainment**.

Schumann Resonance – natural frequency of earth's vibration/resonance: 7.8Hz.

Script – (LifeScript) to assist Karma, when one is born, one has a Script covering the basic (usually 10 % max) events that are to happen in one's life, which one is expected to overcome. They may be positive or negative, and how one meets them and handles them determines how one is progressing towards the goal of getting out of the Earth School. It often has Options programmed into it (**Points of Choice**) where the Soul must make a significant choice. It is a test of soul growth. A personal LifeScript is usually subject to the Greater Script of the Father of Light and works within it. The Angels (Beings of Light) administer the Script, yet the Soul still has 90% Freewill. (See **Ground of Being.**) **The Script does not tell you what to do or say; just major events are scripted to test you.**

ShapeShifting – the ability to control what people see… the being doing the shape-shifting does not actually change any of his atomic structure – just the way his appearance is perceived, and perception is holographic. So to effect a different appearance, the being just produces new interference waves that the observer 'sees' differently. Commonly done by 4D and above entities while in 3D.

Sheep – people who are barely conscious, and refuse to think for themselves. They want someone to tell them what to do and when to do it, and they go along with whatever they are told. They are easily manipulated by the Media. Also called **'sheeple'** and may be OPs or 'dense' ensouled humans.

Soul Aspect – all souls can 'split' themselves to experience different realms; as when a timeline splits, one part of the soul stays with the original TL and another part replicates to the new TL. Each soul has aspects in different TLs, dimensions, worlds, and realms, etc and at a point in the future, they reunite to the Soul Group. Not a **Fragment** (next). (See VEG, Ch.7.)

Soul Fragment – some souls may fragment **due to trauma** and then special therapy is often needed to coax the missing fragment to rejoin its source. Some fragments are held by family members, past lovers, and even by the Neggs themselves.

Soul Group – each soul was part of a group of like souls (same core vibration PFV which usually synchs up with a specific archetype) and these split up to better experience the Creation – souls will eventually reunite in their original group when their explorings are done. The Soul Groups reunite with the **Godhead** from which they came.

Soulless -- in this book, this refers to beings who act/react without conscience, compassion or regard for the spiritual side of life. This describes the majority of the PTB – the fat cats whose money 'entitles' them to dictate to the rest of humanity. (See also theory of the **OP**s.) Also see Hybrids.

Soul Migration – the concept that animals can progress to first-time human beings with 'baby' souls and the full-fledged human soul must be earned thru successive incarnations. As they would also have only the lower 3 chakras operative, they may be mistaken for OPs. (See Metempsychosis on Wikipedia.)

STO – Service To Others; altruistic behavior, self-sacrificing.
STS – Service To Self; selfish behavior; 'Me-My-Mine' syndrome.

Terraforming – an advanced technical process whereby a whole planet is set to its original, or a near-new, pristine condition following some catastrophe or pollution, or both. The ecology is balanced, the air, land and water are unpolluted, and in the case of planet Earth, it can once again support lifeforms. See also "**Wipe and Reboot**."

Timeline (TL) – the linear coherent vector on which all souls and Placeholders (OPs) of a certain frequency range have their being; a reality timeline that linearly moves forward creating causal events. It is not permanent and is subject to entropy if a bifurcation results from a rise in consciousness and attendant agreement coherently shared among the souls seeking to live in a higher consciousness in TL2 is preferable to the negatively polarized TL1. If there is not enough agreement (energy) to sustain the new TL2, it dissolves.
If a dimension has only one TL, the TL is the dimension, but dimensions can have multiple TLs. There is a TL where Hitler won, for example.
And timelines may create, 'run' and dissolve **fractal** subsets (within the larger TL framework) for special purposes (qv). (See TOM, Apx. D.)

Torsion Wave – Being neither electromagnetic in nature nor relating to gravity as it stands on its own, this wave energy is a spiraling, non-Hertzian electromagnetic wave that travels through the vacuum of space at super-luminal speed - a billion times faster than the speed of light. Because these waves trace a spiraling path, they are called "torsion waves." (See QES, Ch. 10.)

Torus – an energy field that is toroidal in shape (like a doughnut), and is found around the heart – extending and an electromagnetic field about 3-4' around the human body. (See TOM, Ch. 12.)

Unconscious – unaware, not a very high level of perception. A person who is 'asleep' spiritually and is not aware that there are more than the 5 senses. Can also mean 'spacing out' with eyes wide open. Standard condition of the **Sheep**.

V2K – "Voice to Skull" -- a microwave enhanced transmission of words directly into a person's head, as if they actually hear the words, without any external devices or hearing apparatus. Developed by the US Army to communicate with a soldier on the battlefield, to the exclusion of other soldiers, it was perfected during the mind experiments with Helen Schucman while she transcribed the *Course in Miracles* book. Who sent her the information is not known. (VEG, Ch. 11. Also see Bibliography : Internet Sources.)

Vibration/Vibe – the energy state of a person, place or thing. Everything puts out an energy 'signature', which is how pyschometry works… objects record the energy of the person that held/owned the object, and places often hold the residual energy of events that happened there: some sensitive people cannot visit Gettysburg as they feel the negative energy from all the hate and fear created in that place – even thought it was long ago, it still holds some energy that has not completely dissipated. (See **PFV**.)

Vimanas – In Hindu literature (*Ramayana* and *MahaBharata*), the gods were said to fly around the sky and even engage in warfare between these craft with exotic but powerful weapons – similar to the Sumerian flying machines (MAR.GID.DA, IM.DU.GUD, and GIR). An ancient form of UFO, cone-shaped like many temples in Thailand, or *Stupas* in Tibet.

Wipe and Reboot – an end to a current **Era** of Man on Earth, followed usually by a terra-forming (resetting the environment back to clean and balanced), followed by the Re-seeding of Man on the planet. (See Chart 5 in VEG, Ch. 15.)
The term is borrowed from the computer world where when a PC is non-functional (i.e., locked up and displays the dreaded BSOD [Blue Screen of Death]), it is necessary to "Wipe" the hard disk – reformat it – and reload the operating system and application software… i.e., "Reboot" the system and start all over again.

Whereas the PC gets a clean start as if nothing happened, each new Era for Man still includes whatever major, solid objects were created in the prior Era – i.e., pyramids, huge walls, and Stonehenge.

Zechariah Sitchin – the late Middle Eastern scholar, speaking several languages, who translated the Anunnaki/Sumerian tablets. VEG Ch. 3 is mostly dedicated to a summary of his findings about Man's origins. His claim to fame was *The Earth Chronicles* series of 8+ books that revealed the Sumerian – Anunnaki connection (see Bibliography for partial list).

> **Sasha Lessin** was a protégé of Sitchin and has written several books about the Anunnaki, many parts of which have been quoted in this *Anunnaki Legacy* book.
> He has his own website: www.enkispeaks.com

ZPE (Zero Point Energy) – Zero-point energy, also called quantum vacuum zero-point energy, is the lowest possible energy that a quantum mechanical physical system may have; it is the energy of its ground state. Vacuum energy is the zero-point energy of all the fields in space, which in the Standard Model includes the electromagnetic field, fermionic fields, and the Higgs [boson] field.

It is the energy of the vacuum, which in quantum field theory is defined not as empty space but as the ground [lowest vibrational] state of the fields. In cosmology, the vacuum energy is one possible explanation for the cosmological constant. A related term is *zero-point field*, which is the lowest energy state of a particular field.
(Definition: credit https://en.wikipedia.org/wiki/Zero-point_energy)
Dark Energy is thought to contain a ZPE state.

(See Quantum Net, and VEG, Ch. 9. Also see TOM, Ch. 11.)

Bibliography

Books

Serpent/Dragon Wisdom

Elkins, Don and Carla Rueckert. *The RA Material, Book I.* Atglen, PA: Schiffer Publishing/Whitford Press, 1984.

Freke, Timothy & Peter Gandy. *The laughing Jesus.* NY: Three Rivers Press, 2005.

____________ *Lucid Living.* UK: Sunwheel Books, 2005.

Gardiner & Osborn. *The Shining Ones, Revised.* London: Watkins Publishing, 2010.

Golas, Thaddeus. *The Lazy Man's Guide to Enlightenment.* Salt Lake City: Gibbs-Smith, 1995.

Lerma, John, M.D. *Into the Light.* Franklin Lakes, NJ: New Page Books, 2007.

____________ *Learning From the Light.* Franklin Lakes, NJ: New Page Books, 2009.

Marion, Jim. *Putting on the Mind of Christ.* NY: Hampton Roads, 2000.

Mead, G.R.S. *Apollonius of Tyana.* (1901 Edition reprint) Sacramento, CA: Murine Press, 2008.

Meyer, Marvin. *The Gospel of Thomas.* New York: HarperCollins, 1992.

Paulson, Genevieve Lewis. *Kundalini and the Chakras.* MN: Llewellyn Worldwide, 2005.

Rasha. *Oneness.* Santa Fe, NM: Earthstar Press, 2003.

Ring, Kenneth. *Lessons from the Light.* Portsmouth, NH: Moment Point Press, 2000.

Roman, Sanaya. *Spiritual Growth.* Tiburon, CA: HJ Kramer, Inc., 1989.

____________. *Personal Power Through Awareness.* Tiburon, CA: HJ Kramer, Inc., 1986.

Spencer, Robert. *The Craft of the Warrior.* 2nd Ed., CA: Frog, Ltd, 2006.

Religion/Metaphysics/Spirituality

Acharya S. *The Christ Conspiracy.* Kempton, IL: Adventures Unlimited Press, 1999.

Atwater, P.M.H. *Near Death Experiences.* NY: MJF Books, 2011.

Barrett, David V. *Secret Religions.* PA: Running Press, 2011.

Castaneda, Carlos. *A Separate Reality.* New York: Washington Square Press, 1971.

____________. *The Active Side of Infinity.* New York: HarperCollins, 2000.

Charles, R.A. *The Book of Enoch the Prophet.* San Francisco, CA: Weiser Books, 2003.

Dawood, N. J. *The Koran.* New York: Penguin Group (USA), 2006.

Frejer, B. Ernest. *The Edgar Cayce Companion.* New York: Barnes & Noble Press, 1995.
Gaffney, Mark. *Gnostic Secrets of the Naassenes.* Rochester, VT: Inner Traditions, 2004.
Gardiner, Philip. *Secret Societies.* Franklin Lakes, NJ: Career Press/New Page, 2007.
______________. *Secrets of the Serpent.* Forest Hill, CA: Reality Press, 2008.
______________. *The Shining Ones.* Nottinghamshire, England: Phase Group, 2002.
______________. *The Shining Ones*, rev. UK: Watkins Publ., 2010.
Hall, Manly P. *The Secret Teachings of All Ages*, NY: Tarcher/Penguin, 2003.
Hoeller, Stephan A. *Gnosticism.* Wheaton, IL: Quest Books, 2002.
Husain, Shahrukh. *The Goddess.* London: Duncan Baird Publ., 1997.
Laurence, Richard. *The Book of ENOCH the Prophet.* Kempton, IL: Adventures Unlimited Press, 2000.
Mead, G.R.S. *Apollonius of Tyana.* (1901 Edition reprint) Sacramento, CA: Murine Press, 2008.
Melville, Francis. *The Book of Alchemy.* Dallas, TX: HPB Press, 2013.
Moody, Raymond A., Jr., MD. *Life After Life.* New York: HarperCollins, 2001.
Monroe, Robert. *Journeys Out of the Body.* New York: Doubleday, 1971.
_____________. *Far Journeys.* New York: Random House/Broadway, 2001.
_____________. *Ultimate Journey.* New York: Random House/Broadway, 2000.
Pagels, Elaine. *The Gnostic Gospels.* New York: Random House/Vintage, 1979.
Prophet, E. C. *Kabbalah.* MT: Summit Univ. Press, 1997.
Robinson, James M., Gen. Ed. *The Nag Hammadi Library.* NY: Harper Collins, 1990.:
Russell, A. J., *God Calling.* Uhrichsville, OH: Barbour Publishing, 1989.
Slate, Joe H., Ph.D. *Aura Energy.* Woodbury, MN: Llewellyn Worldwide, 2002.
________________. *Psychic Vampires.* St. Paul, MN: Llewellyn Worldwide, 2004.
Snellgrove, Brian. *The Unseen Self.* Essex, England: The C.W. Daniel Co., 1996.
The King James Study Bible. Nashville, TN: Thomas Nelson, 1988.

Scientific/Medical

Baugh, Carl E. *Why Do Men Believe Evolution Against All Odds*? Oklahoma City, OK: Hearthstone Publishing, 1999.
Behe, Michael J. *Darwin's Black Box.* New York: Simon & Schuster, 1996.
Braden, Gregg. *The Divine Matrix.* Carlsbad, CA: Hay House, 2007.
Brown, Walt. *In The Beginning: Compelling Evidence for Creation and the Flood.* Phoenix, AZ: Center for Scientific Creation, 1995.
Chmelik, Stefan. *Chinese Herbal Secrets.* NY: Penguin Books, 1999.
Johnson, Phillip E. *Defeating Darwinism.* Downers Grove, IL: InterVarsity Press, 1997.
Morris, John D., Ph.D. *The Young Earth.* Green Forest, AR: Master Books, 2006.

Myss, Caroline, Ph.D. *Why People Don't Heal and How They Can.* New York: Three Rivers Press, 1997.

__________________. *Sacred Contracts.* New York: Three Rivers Press, 2002.

Narby, Jeremy. *The Cosmic Serpent.* New York: Tarcher/Putnam, 1998.

Peterson, Dennis R. *Unlocking the Mysteries of Creation.* 6th edition. El Dorado, CA: Creation Resource Foundation, 1990.

Talbot, Michael. *The Holographic Universe.* New York: HarperCollins, 1991.

Yang, Jwing-Ming, Dr. *The Root of Chinese Qigong.* Roslindale, MA: YMAA

UFOs and ETs

Boulay, R.A. *Flying Serpents and Dragons.* Rev. Ed. San Diego, CA: The Book Tree, 1999.

Bramley, William. *The Gods of Eden.* New York: HarperCollins/Avon, 1993.

Branton, ed. *The Omega Files.* NJ: Global Communications, 2012.

Cannon, Dolores. *Keepers of the Garden.* Huntsville, AR: Ozark Mtn Publishers, 2002.

Clark, Gerald. *The Anunnaki of Nibiru.* Lexington, KY: CreateSpace, 2013.

Farrell, Joseph P. *The Cosmic War.* Kempton, IL: Adventures Unlimited Press, 2007.

Fowler, Raymond. *The Watchers.* New York: Bantam Books, 1990.

Haze, Xaviant. *Aliens in Ancient Egypt.* VT: Bear & Co., 2013.

Heron, Patrick. *The Nephilim and the Pyramid of the Apocalypse.* New York: Kensington Publishing/Citadel Press, 2004.

Lessin PhD, Sasha. *Anunnaki: Gods No More.* Lexington, KY: CreateSpace, 2012.

__________________ *Anunnaki: Legacy of the Gods.* CA: Aquarian Radio Publishing, 2014.

Lewels, Joe, Ph.D. *The God Hypothesis.* Columbus, NC: Wild Flower Press, 2005.

Marrs, Jim. *Alien Agenda.* New York: HarperCollins, 1997.

__________. *Rule by Secrecy.* New York: HarperCollins, 2000.

Olsen, Brad. *Future Esoteric: The Unseen Realms.* CA: CCC Publishing, 2013.

__________________ *Modern Esoteric: Beyond Our Senses.* CA: CCC Publishing, 2014.

Pruett, Dr. Jack. *The Grandest Deception.* Xlibris Corp: Lexington, KY, 2011.

Story, Ronald D., Ed. *The Encyclopedia of Extraterrestrial Encounters.* New York: New American Library, 2001.

Tellinger, Michael. *Slave Species of god.* Johannesburg, SA: Music Masters Close Corporation, 2005. (1st book)

__________________. *Slave Species of the Gods.* Rochester, VT: Bear & Co., 2012. (2nd Book reprint)

Von Daniken, Erich. *Arrival of the Gods.* London: Vega, 2002.

__________________ *History is Wrong.* New Jersey: New Page, 2009.

History and Other Related Books

Calleman, Carl Johan, PhD. *The Mayan Calendar and the Transformation of Consciousness.* Rochester, VT: Bear & Co., 2004.

Childress, David H. *Technology of the Gods.* IL: AU Press, 2000.

__________ *Lost Cities of North & Central America.* IL: AU Press, 1992.

Coleman, J.A., Ed. *The Dictionary of Mythology.* London: Arcturus, 2015.

Curran, Dr. Bob. *Lost Lands, Forgotten Realms.* NJ: New Page, 2007.

Davidson, H.R. Ellis. *Myths & Symbols in Pagan Europe.* NY: Syracuse Univ. Press, 1988.

Davis, Kenneth C. *Don't Know Much About Mythology.* NY: Harper Collins, 2005.

Dougherty, Martin J. *A Dark History: Vikings.* NY: Metro Books, 2013.

__________ *A Dark History: Celts.* NY: Metro Books, 2015.

Duane & Hutchison. *Chinese Myths and Legends.* London: Brockhampton Press, 1998.

Ellis, Peter B. *The Celts: A History.* PA: Running Press, 2008.

Guiley, Rosemary Ellen. *Encyclopedia of the Strange, Mystical & Unexplained.* New York: Gramercy Books, 2001.

Hawkins, David R. *Reality and Subjectivity.* West Sedona, AZ: Veritas Press, 2003.

__________ *The Eye of the I.* West Sedona, AZ: Veritas Press, 2001

Icke, David. *The Biggest Secret.* Wildwood, MO: Bridge of Love, 2001.

__________ *Tales from the Time Loop.* Wildwood, MO: Bridge of Love, 2003.

Jwing-Ming, Dr. Yang. *The Root of Chinese Qigong.* MA: YMAA Publications, 1997.

Kenyon, Douglas. *Forbidden Science.* Roch, VT: Bear & Co., 2008.

__________ *Forbidden History.* Roch, VT: Bear & Co, 2005.

__________ *Forbidden Religion.* Roch, VT: Bear & Co, 2006.

Killeen, Richard. *Ireland: Land, People, History.* PA: Running Press, 2012.

Kramer, Samuel Noah. *The Sumerians.* Chicago, IL: Univ. of Chicago Press, 1971.

Kreisberg, Glenn, Ed. *Lost Knowledge of the Ancients.* Roch, VT: Bear & Co, 2010.

Lawton, Ian. *Genesis Unveiled.* London: Virgin Books, 2003.

Macbain, A. *Celtic Mythology & Religion.* UK: The Lost Library, 1917.

Markale, Jean. *The Celts.* VT: Inner Traditions, 1978.

Martinez PhD, Susan B. *The Mysterious Origins of Hybrid Man.* Roch, VT: Bear & Co, 2013.

__________ *Delusions in Science & Spirituality.* Roch, VT: Bear & Co, 2015.

Parkes, Henry B. *A History of Mexico.* Boston, MA: Houghton Mifflin Co., 1960.

Pemberton, John. *Myths & Legends.* NY: Chartwell Books, 2012.

Pinkham, Mark Amaru. The *Return of the Serpents of Wisdom.* Kempton, IL: AUP, 1997.

Pye, Lloyd. *Everything You Know Is Wrong, Book I: Human Origins.* Lincoln

NE: iUniverse/Authors Choice Press, 2000.
Ritsema & Karcher. *I Ching*. Rockport, MA: Element, Inc., 1994.
Rosenberg, Donna. *World Mythology, 2nd Ed.* IL: NTC Publishing, 1994.
Sitchin, Zecharia. *Journeys to the Mythical Past.* Rochester, VT: Bear & Co., 2007.
____________ *The Twelfth Planet.* New York: HarperCollins, 2007.
____________ *The Cosmic Code.* New York: HarperCollins, 2007.
____________ *The End of Days.* New York: HarperCollins, 2007.
____________ *The Earth Chronicles Expeditions.* Roch, VT: Bear & Co., 2004.
____________ *Divine Encounters.* New York: HarperCollins/Avon, 1996.
____________ *Genesis Revisited.* New York: HarperCollins/Avon, 1990.
____________ *The Wars of Gods and Men.* New York: HarperCollins, 2007.
____________ *The Lost Book of ENKI.* Roch, VT: Bear & Co., 2004.
____________ *The Stairway to Heaven.* New York: HarperCollins, 2007.
____________ *The Earth Chronicles Handbook.* Roch, VT: Bear & Co., 2009.
____________ *There Were Giants Upon the Earth.* Roch, VT: Bear & Co., 2010.
____________ *The Anunnaki Chronicles.* Roch., VT: Bear & Co. 2015.
Squire, Charles. *Celtic Myth & Legend.* NJ: New Page, 2001.
Thorsson, Edred, *Runelore: The Magic, History & Hidden Codes of the Runes.* SF: Weiser Books, 2012.
____________ *Futhark: A Handbook of Rune Magic.* SF: Weiser Books, 1984.
Turner, Patricia & Charles Russell Coulter. *Dictionary of Ancient Deities.* NY, NY: Oxford University Press, 2001.
Walker, Dave. *Cuckoo for Kokopelli.* AZ: Northland Publ. , 1998.
Wilkinson, Philip. *Myths & Legends.* London: DK Ltd., 2009.
Witkowski, Igor. *Axis of the World.* Kempton, IL: AU Press, 2008.

Amerindians & Maya

Childress, David. *Lost Cities of North & Central America.* IL: AU Press, 1992.
Davis, Nancy Yaw *The Zuni Enigma.* NYC: W.W. Norton & Co., 2000. (the Zuni connection with Japan)
Men, Hunbatz. *The 8 Calendars of the Maya.* Roch, VT: Bear & Co. 2010.
____________ *Secrets of Mayan Science/Religion.* Roch, VT: Bear & Co. 1900.
Pike, Muench & Waters. *ANASAZI, Ancient People of the Rock.* NYC: Crown Publishers/Harmony Books, 1974.
Pinkham, Mark A. *The Return of the Serpents of Wisdom.* IL: AU Press, 1997.
Ross, Dr. A.C. *Mitakuye Oyasin.* Rev.ed., Colorado: Wicóni Wasté, July 1997. (detailed look at Amerindian myths and reality)
Williamson, G.H. *Road in the Sky.* London: Neville Spearman, 1959. (detailed look at Hopi and Inca origins)

Internet Sources

Anunnaki

Amitakh Sanford, "The Anunnaki Remnants Are Still on Earth." Excellent article that extends and refutes some of the Zechariah Sitchin material on the Anunnaki. Website: http://www.xeeatwelve.com/articles/anunnaki_remnants.htm

Estelle N. H. Amrani, "A Different Story About the Anunnaki" is another article by a credible source, which partly agrees with Amitakh, and gives additional compatible information. Website: http://www.bibliotecapleyades.net/sumer_anunnaki/anunnaki/anu_12.htm

Robertino Solàrion, "Nibiruan Physiology." Excellent article mentioning the Galactic Law that the Anunnaki must adhere to – first reported by John Baines in his book, The Stellar Man. Website:
http://www.bibliotecapleyades.net/cosmic_tree/physiology.htm
see also Baines reference:
http://www.bibliotecapleyades.net/serpents_dragons/boulay05e.htm

"Myths From Mesopotamia: Gilgamesh, The Flood, and Others" translated by Stephanie Dalley as quoted in the website: http://www.piney.com/Atrahasis.html also see: http://www.book-of-thoth.com/ftopicp-137854.html

Christianity & Gnosticism

Acharya S, "The Origins of Christianity and the Quest for the Historical Jesus Christ" is a lengthy article examining non-Biblical sources and other documents in a search for the existence of a man called Jesus. Comparisons to the same stories about Christ are found in the stories about the Buddha, Horus, Mithra, and Krishna. Website: http://truthbeknown.com/origins.htm

Acharya S, "The Origins of Good and Evil" is an article that outlines the sources and evolution of evil, as well as how religions take each other over. Website: http://truthbeknown.com/evil.htm

Acharya S./D.M. Murdock, "**Apollonius, Jesus and Paul**: Men or Myths?" takes an educated look at Apollonius as the source for the Jesus/Paul myth.
http://truthbeknown.com/apollonius.html

Dr. R.W. Bernard, "Apollonius the Nazarene" is an ebook which covers as much of Apollonius's life as is extant, in nine chapters. It is based on the work of Philostratus in his *Life of Apollonius*. Website: http://www.apollonius.net/bernardbook.html

Tony Bushby, "The Forged Origins of the New Testament" is an article extracted from *Nexus Magazine*, vol. 14, no. 4 (June-July 2007). The author also wrote a related book called *The Bible Fraud*, via Joshua Books (Australia), 2001. Website: http://www.nexusmagazine.com/articles/NewTestament.html

Wikipedia, "**Apollonius of Tyana**" article on Wikipedia that is rather negatively biased but relates the generally-agreed on facts surrounding the sage's life. Website: http://en.wikipedia.org/wiki/Apollonius_of_Tyana

"Ghandi on Christianity" set of his quotes in a section called AMOIRA; website: http://koti.mbnet.fi/amoira/religion/gandhicr1.htm
see also: **http://whoisthisjesus.googlepages.com/westernchristianity**

John Lash, "Kundalini and the Alien Force" article that examines the Gnostic and Tantric practices of sacred sexuality, but also examines the Archons and Jehovah. Website: http://www.metahistory.org/KundaliniForce.php

Joseph Macchio, "**The Orthodox Suppression of Original Christianity**" is an ebook of 15 chapters that explores the historical suppression of original Christian truths by the orthodox Church of Rome. It is a treasure-trove of Gnostic teaching, early Christian leaders Mani, Origen and Valentinus, as well as the actions and teachings of Constantine, Augustine and Iraneus. It also reinforces Mouravieff (see OPs/Mouravieff this Appendix). Websites: http://essenes.net/conspireindex.html
http://essenes.net/new/subteachings.html

Also worth a look:
"Apollonius of Tyana – Paul of Tarsus?" is an in-depth article on the unique parallels between Apollonius who existed and the putative Apostle Paul. Under 'Christian Origins' section, click on 'The True Identity of St. Paul.'
http://nephiliman.com/apollonius_of_tyanna.htm

Extraterrestrial Exposure Law

Michael Salla, PhD., "Extraterrestrials Among Us" (vol.1:4, originally from Exopolitics Journal website), is an interesting article on how ETs are among us who look so much like us that we don't suspect, and secondly the article explores the Extraterrestrial Exposure Law of 1969. Website:
http://www.bibliotecapleyades.net/exopolitica/esp_exopolitics_ZZZN.htm
also see: http://exopolitics.com for author's general website.

Extraterrestial Genes in Human DNA

"Scientists Find Extraterrestrial Genes in Human DNA" is another article seeking to explain "junk DNA" and its probable origin and significance. Website:
http://www.bibliotecapleyades.net/vida_alien/esp_vida_alien_18n.htm

Greek Gods

Neil Jenkins, Sumair Mirza and Jason Tsang, "The Creation of the World & Mankind" is a great summary review of the major aspects of the Greek myths. Fascinating material, well-organized and indexed; won an award in 1997. Website:
http://www.classicsunveiled.com/mythnet/html/creation.html -- multiple topics.
See also: http://historylink102.com/greece2/ -- multiple topics.

The Insider

"The Revelations of the Insider" is an article containing the blog during a 5-day visit by someone calling themselves an "insider" who had knowledge on most aspects of Earth history, science and religion. This was done anonymously via a proxy link to the GLP (Godlike Productions) forum in the Fall of 2005. The material is not copyrighted and can be reproduced as long as none of the original text is changed. Website: http://www.scribd.com/doc/403303/The-Revelations-of-an-Elite-Family-Insider-2005

People With Horns

Sutherland, Mary, "Was There a Race of People Who Had Horns?" is a thought-provoking article with pictures showing people in the past and present who have horny growths coming out of their heads. Has links to other related websites. Website: http://www.burlingtonnews.net/hornedrace.html
ancillary link: http://www.bibliotecapleyades.net/vida_alien/alien_watchers04.htm

Serpents, Reptiles & DNA

Paul Von Ward, "Aliens, Lies and Religions" article on great Belgian website that discusses the author's book Gods, Genes and Consciousness. The issue of serpents and DNA is clarified as well as other AB (Advanced Being) issues. Website: http://www.karmapolis.be/pipeline/von_ward_uk.htm

Vatican & ETs

Patricia Cori, "The Vatican Says OK, We Can Believe in ET Now" is an article that comments on the more common Breitbart and Fox News article (below) revealing the Pope's blessing on humans accepting the existence of ETs. Website: www.sirianrevelations.net

FOX News article "Vatican: It's OK for Catholics to Believe in Aliens" containing a longer examination of the Pope's blessing on our ET brothers. Website: http://www.foxnews.com/story/0,2933,355400,00.html

Videos of Interest

Forbidden Planet. MGM classic from 1956; debuts Robby the Robot.
The X-Files (TV series, 1993-2002): Twentieth Century Fox.
K-Pax. Universal Pictures, Lawrence Gordon et al. 2001.
Millenium. Gladden Entertainment. 1989.
Hangar 18. Republic Entertainment. 1980.
Capricorn One. Associated General Films. Lazarus/Hyams prod. 1978.

Groundhog Day. Dir. Harold Ramis, Columbia Tristar. 1993.
Men In Black. I & II Dir. Barry Sonnenfeld, Columbia Pictures. 2000.
The Matrix. Dir./Written by The Wachowski Bros., Warner Bros. 1999.
The Mothman Prophecies. Dir. Mark Pellington, Screen Gems/LakeShore Entertainment. 2001.
Prometheus. 20th Century Fox, 2012.

Taken. (TV miniseries) Stephen Spielberg, DreamWorks. 2002.
V, the TV series (1983-85, and 2009-11). WarnerVideo, Kenneth Johnson Production.
The Truman Show. Peter Weir, Paramount Pictures. 1998.
The Young Age of the Earth. Aufderhar, Glenn. Earth Science Associates / Alpha Productions. 1996.
What the Bleep Do We Know? 20th Century Fox, 2004.

They Live. Dir./Written by John Carpenter, Universal Studios. 2003.
Prometheus I. Ridley Scott, 2oth Century Fox. 2012.
The Thirteenth Floor. Columbia Pictures, Roland Emmerich. 1999.
The Day the Earth Stood Still. Twentieth Century Fox, Erwin Stoff et al, 2009.
The Forgotten. Revolution Studios. 2004

Iron Sky. Timo Vuorensola, Ger/Fin release via Paramount Pictures, 2012.
Paul. Universal Studios, Greg Motola. 2010.
2012. Sony Pictures, Roland Emmerich. 2010.
The Fourth Kind. Universal Pictures, Olatunde Osunsanmi. 2010.
The Adjustment Bureau. Universal Pictures, George Nolfi. 2010.

Knowing. Summit Entertainment, Alex Proyas. 2009.
Dark City. New Line Cinema, Alex Proyas. 1998.
Source Code. Summit Entertainment, Duncan Jones. 2011.
eXistenZ. Canadian Television Fund, David Cronenburg, 1999.
Defending Your Life. Warner Bros., 1991.

Also: Ancient Aliens video series (esp. Season 9).

***

Introduction -- Endnotes

[1] Manly P Hall, The Secret Teachings of All Ages. pp 294-297.

Chapter 1 -- Endnotes

[2] Zechariah Sitchin, The 12th Planet. p 329.

[3] From Yahoo Coins of Alexander; see http://search.yahoo.com/search;_ylt=AuGsxC8UzTjm1.kh.2CU9IabvZx4?p=alexander+the+great+coin&toggle=1&cop=mss&ei=UTF-8&fr=yfp-t-788

[4] Zechariah Sitchin, Stairway to Heaven. p. 137-138.
[5] Zechariah Sitchin, The Cosmic Code, pp51-52,.

William Bramley, The Gods of Eden. Pp 44-46.

Zechariah Sitchin, The 12th Planet. pp 251, 365-367

Gerald Clark, The Anunnaki of Nibiru. Chapt 4.

[6] William Bramley, Gods of Eden. Pp48-49.
[7] Ibid., pp 51-52.

[8] R.A. Boulay, Flying Serpents and Dragons. p11.

[9] Pinkham, Mark Amaru. The *Return of the Serpents of Wisdom.* p 44.

[10] Turner & Coulter, Dictionary of Ancient Deities. p. 355.

[11] Icke, David, *Children of the Matrix.* p 91.
Also uoted in Boulay, *Flying Serpents & Dragons*, p. 61.
[12] Ibid., 122.

[13] Zechariah Sitchin, The 12th Planet. pp. 126-127.
[14] Ibid., p. 81 (shows the same bust)
[15] Zechariah Sitchin, There Were Giants Upon The Earth. pp 315-326.

[16] https://en.wikipedia.org/wiki/Hammurabi

[17] https://en.wikipedia.org/wiki/Enki and
RA Boulay, Flying Serpents & Dragons. P68.

---

[18] Dr Susan Martinez, The Mysterious Origins of Hybrid Man. Pp 435-38. This author really spells it out and goes into more detail about the genetic and anthropological development of mankind. She postulates multiple Gardens of Eden (pp 390-438) and explains racial diversity from a scientific standpoint.

[19] Michael Tellinger, *Slave Species of the Gods*. p 524.

[20] Zechariah Sitchin, Divine Encounters. Pp168-169
[21] Op Cit, 12th Planet, pp. 138-142.
[22] Ibid., p. 141-42.
[23] Ibid., 139-40.
[24] Ibid., p.143 and Op Cit, Cosmic Code, p. 57.

[25] Sasha Lessin, Anunnaki Gods No More, pp 72, 108, 205.
Also Sitchin, The Cosmic Code, pp 100, 106. Resurrection technology was a fact.

Addendum (discovered as book was going to press):

Inanna ruled Dumuzi's eldest brother, Marduk, unfit to impregnate her since Marduk (Dumuzi's firstborn brother) caused Dumuzi's death. So she sought Dumuzi's next oldest brother, Nergal, Ereshkigal's mate.
Inanna would, through Nergal and the boy they'd beget, rule in Africa despite Dumuzi's death. Their son would inherit Dumuzi's realms in northeast Africa, and she, as regent, would usurp Ereshkigal in Africa. "Of scheming an heir by Nergal, Dumuzi's brother, Inanna was accused."

When Inanna got to Ereshkigal's place, Ereshkigal barred her entry.
Inanna forced her way in, but Ereshkigal disarmed her and hung Inanna on a stake to die.

But "from clay of the Abzu, Enki two emissaries fashioned, beings without blood, by death rays unharmed, to lower Abzu he sent them, Inanna to bring back.

"Upon the corpse the clay emissaries a Pulsar **and an** Emitter **directed, then the** Water of Life **on her they sprinkled, in her mouth, the** Plant of Life **they placed. Then the dead Inanna arose"** [*Enki*: 255].

She took Dumuzi's body to Sumer and mummified him so he could rejoin her bodily on Nibiru, since, she said, Nibiran gods live forever [*Cosmic Code*: 90, 96].

(Source: Lessin's website: enkispeaks.com)

[26] Op Cit., Tellinger., pp 484-485

[27] Manly P Hall, The Secret Teachings of All Ages. p. 241-42.

[28] Philip Gardiner, Secrets of the Serpent. Pp 8-11.
[29] Ibid.

[30] Turner & Coulter, Dictionary of Ancient Deities. p.58 Inanna is Ishtar.

[31] Op Cit., Gardiner, pp 8-11.

[32] Op Cit, Boulay, pp. 75-77.

[33] Op Cit, Gardiner., 17-19.

[34] Z. Sitchin, 12th Planet, pp 315-16.
[35] Ibid., 395.

[36] Also see *Scientific American* magazine, issue Feb. 2016, pp30-37.

[37] Jim Marrs, Alien Agenda. P. 137.

[38] http://www.abovetopsecret.com/forum/thread447131/pg1

[39] http://www.crystalinks.com/hopi2.html

[40] http://www.sciencemag.org/news/2016/01/feature-astronomers-say-neptune-sized-planet-lurks-unseen-solar-system

Also see http://www.nibiruupdate.com/
And http://yowusa.com/et/2008/et-2008-07a/1.shtml
for Hopi video insert.

Chapter 2 -- Endnotes

40 wikipedia: https://en.wikipedia.org/wiki/Niflheim

[42] Martin Dougherty, A Dark History of the Vikings, pp 36-37.

[43] Wikipedia: https://en.wikipedia.org/wiki/Geri_and_Freki

[44] Wikipedia: https://en.wikipedia.org/wiki/Odin
[45] Ibid.
[46] Ibid.

[47] https://en.wikipedia.org/wiki/Thing_(assembly)

[48] Wikipedia: https://en.wikipedia.org/wiki/Lindisfarne

[49] Courtesy: Ancient Aliens DVD, Season 8, *The Alien Wars*

[50] Zechariah Sitchin, The Stairway to Heaven. pp 92-98.

[51] RA Boulay, Flying Serpents & Dragons. P. 61
[52] Ibid., pp 61-63.

[53] **(credit: http://www.mysteriesofancientegypt.com/2012/10/the-helicopter-hieroglyphic-symbol.html)**

[54] http://www.anehdidunia.com/2015/06/gambar-benda-kuno-kedatangan-alien-ufo.html

[55] Of particular caution is the cropcircle **at r71.deviantart.com** which shows an updated version to an original cropcircle where an alien in 2007 had sent a binary message (see: http://www.csicop.org/si/show/crop_circles_a_not-so-convincing_case). This is admitted to be an example of digital computer art superimposed on a photo of a crop field – and that is evident when you examine the crop field – the r71's design's lines do not disturb the tractor lines, as usually happens. This is not denigrating r71.deviantart, merely saying it is an amazingly clever thing.

[56] (Vetted at: http://ufonews24.blogspot.com/2015/07/cerchio-nel-grano-con-simboli-anunnaki.html and Lucypringle copyright 2015 and http://cropcircleconnector.com/2015/uffcottdown/uffcottdown.html)

[57] https://en.wikipedia.org/wiki/Norse_religion

[58] **Huitzilopochtli** comes into this because he deliberately promoted human sacrifice among the Aztec and the Maya – whereas **Quetzalcoatl** tried to stop it – thus some Anunnaki gods were at odds with each other. And it is rumored that some Anunnaki feasted on the corpses of the Mayan and Aztec sacrificial victims much as humans feasted on chicken. [As gruesome as it is to contemplate, what do you think was done with the sacrificed victims when the Aztec/Maya priests threw their bodies down the stairs? They did not bury them, and they didn't throw them into the *cenotes*... the only bones in the *cenotes* are those of young women sacrificed to the gods.] More than this you do not want to know.

[59] Encyclopedia of World Mythology . p. 84.

[60] Coleman & Davidson, The Dictionary of Mythology, p. 124-126.

Chapter 3 -- Endnotes

[61] https://en.wikipedia.org/wiki/Viking_Age_arms_and_armour#Armour

[62] http://johnmckay.blogspot.com/2009/05/strange-case-of-teutobochus-king-of.html

[63] Farrell, Joseph P. *The Cosmic War*. p88-89.

[64] https://ironlight.wordpress.com/2010/07/10/nevadas-mysterious-cave-of-the-red-haired-giants/

[65] Heinrich Leutemann (1824-1904). - Wägner, Wilhelm. 1882. *Nordisch-germanische Götter und Helden*. See : https://en.wikipedia.org/wiki/Irminsul
[66] Ibid.

[67] https://en.wikipedia.org/wiki/Germanic_paganism#Religious_practices

[68] https://en.wikipedia.org/wiki/Golden_apple#The_Garden_of_the_Hesperides

[69] Coleman, Ed. Coleman, Ed. The Dictionary of Mythology. pp. 21-22.

[70] https://en.wikipedia.org/wiki/Vikings

[71] https://en.wikipedia.org/wiki/Celts#Warfare_and_weapons

[72] Martin Dougherty, A Dark History: Celts. Pp90-122.

[73] Peter B. Ellis, The Celts: A History. P.8.

[74] https://en.wikipedia.org/wiki/Nebra_sky_disk

[75] Mark Pinkham, Return of the Serpents of Wisdom. Pp. 244-245.
[76] Ibid., 247
[77] Ibid., 249-250.
[78] Ibid., 250-251.

[79] Turner & Coulter, Dictionary of Ancient Deities, pp. 107-108.
[80] Ibid., p477.
[81] Ibid., 243.

[82] Sasha Lessin, Anunnaki Gods No More. P. 200

[83] Wikipedia: https://en.wikipedia.org/wiki/Boudica

[84] Ibid. see:

- *Boadicea* (1927) is a feature film, wherein she was portrayed by Phyllis Neilson-Terry,[49]
- *The Viking Queen* (1967) is a Hammer Films adventure movie set in ancient Britain, in which the role of Queen Salina is based upon the historical figure of Boudica.
- *Boudica* (2003; *Warrior Queen* in the US) is a UK TV film written by Andrew Davies and starring Alex Kingston as Boudica.[50]
- A History Channel documentary production is entitled *Warrior Queen Boudica* (2006).

[85] R.A. Boulay, Flying Serpents & Dragons. P. 36

[86] Op Cit, Ellis, p. 139 (picture gallery).

[87] Op Cit, Boulay., p39

[88] Op Cit, Pinkham. P. 249.

---

[89] https://en.wikipedia.org/wiki/Stonehenge#Early_history
[90] https://en.wikipedia.org/wiki/Stonehenge

[91] https://en.wikipedia.org/wiki/Tuatha_D%C3%A9_Danann
[92] https://en.wikipedia.org/wiki/Parthol%C3%B3n
[93] Ibid.

[94] Jean Markale, The Celts. Pp. 40-48.
[95] Ibid.
[96] Ibid.

[97] https://en.wikipedia.org/wiki/Apollo

[98] Sasha Lessin, Anunnaki: Legacy of the Gods. p.167.

Chapter 4 -- Endnotes

[99] http://www.ewao.com/a/1-the-aiud-aluminum-wedge-a-vimana-landing-gear/

[100] Ancient Aliens DVD, Season 8, *The Alien Wars.*
[101] Ibid.
[102] Ibid.
[103] Ibid.

[104] http://perdurabo10.tripod.com/storagej/id24.html
[105] Ibid.
[106] Ibid.

[107] Igor Witkowski, The Axis of the World. pp 137-38.

[108] Wikipedai: https://en.wikipedia.org/wiki/Kurukshetra_War

[109] Sasha Lessin, Anunnaki Gods No More. Pp. 186-193.

[110] http://humanpast.net/language/language.htm
[111] Ibid.

[112] Coleman & Davidson, Dictionary of Mythology. P. 183, 336.

[113] http://www.speakingtree.in/allslides/mount-meru-hell-and-paradise-on-one-mountain

[114] Wikipedia: https://en.wikipedia.org/wiki/Mount_Meru
[115] Ibid.

[116] Op Cit., Speaking Tree (note 12).

[117] Credit: http://hyperboreanvibrations.blogspot.com/2011/02/hyperborea.html
(this is a very interesting website.)

[118] Op Cit., Speaking Tree (note 12).

[119] N.S. Rajaram, *Ocean Origins of Indian Civilization* in Ancient Aliens, Lost Civilizations, Astonishing Archeology and Hidden History. Pp. 39-49. Scientific article discounting the Aryan Migration Theory,

[120] Op Cit. Speaking Tree (note 12)

[121] Wikipedia: https://en.wikipedia.org/wiki/Hyperborea
[122] Ibid.

[123] RA Boulay, Flying Serpents & Dragons. Pp 41-43.
[124] Ibid.
[125] Ibid.
[126] Ibid., p. 49.

[127] Duane & Hutchison, Chinese Myths & legends. P. 43.

[128] *2015 Indian Science Congress ancient aircraft controversy*
And
https://en.wikipedia.org/wiki/Vaim%C4%81nika_Sh%C4%81stra

[129] Wikipedia: https://en.wikipedia.org/wiki/Dragon_dance
[130] Ibid.

[131] https://en.wikipedia.org/wiki/Chinese_dragon
[132] Ibid.

[133] http://ancientaliensdebunked.com/dont-dropa-the-stone-dropa-stones-debunked/

[134] Op Cit., Dictionary of Mythology. P. 235.

[135] http://buddhism.about.com/od/buddhisthistory/a/mountmeru.htm

[136] https://onthebridgeway.wordpress.com/2012/08/11/the-tale-and-the-telling/

[137] http://native-science.net/Turtle_Elephant_Myth.htm
[138] Ibid.

[139] Turner & Coulter, Dictionary of Ancient Deities. P 475.

[140] http://native-science.net/Turtle_Elephant_Myth.htm

[141] http://en.wikipedia.org/wiki/Myth_of_the_Flat_Earth)

[142] http://native-science.net/Turtle_Elephant_Myth.htm

[143] http://ancientufo.org/2015/05/how-turtle-symbolism-is-connected-to-ancient-astronauts-hypothesis/

[144] J.A. Coleman, Dictionary of Mythology. P. 335.

[145] Mark Pinkham, The Return of the Serpents of Wisdom. Pp 12-14, 19-20, 46-47, 52.

[146] R.A. Boulay, Flying Serpent & Dragons. P. 41.

[147] Wikipedia: https://en.wikipedia.org/wiki/Naga

Chapter 5 – Endnotes

[148] https://en.wikipedia.org/wiki/Greek_mythology

[149] Sitchin, Zecharia. *Journeys to the Mythical Past.* (Rochester, VT: Bear & CO., 2007), 215.
[150] Sitchin, Zecharia. *The Twelfth Planet.* (New York: HarperCollins, 2007), 52-58.

[151] Tellinger, Michael. *Slave Species of God.* (Johannesburg, SA: Music Masters Close Corporation, 2005), 367.

[152] Sitchin, Zechariah, *The Wars of Gods and Men.* (New York: HarperCollins, 2007), 95.

[153] Neil Jenkins, Sumair Mirza and Jason Tsang, "The Creation of the World & Mankind", eprint at http://www.classicsunveiled.com/mythnet/html/creation.html

[154] Sitchin, Zecharia, *The Earth Chronicles Handbook.* (Rochester, VT: Bear & Co., 2009), 180.

[155] Tellinger, Michael. *Slave Species of God.* 333-378.

[156] https://en.wikipedia.org/wiki/Dryad

[157] https://en.wikipedia.org/wiki/Pythagoras#Views
[158] Ibid.

[159] https://en.wikipedia.org/wiki/Tetractys
[160] https://en.wikipedia.org/wiki/Tetractys
[161] https://en.wikipedia.org/wiki/Emerald_Tablet

[162] http://www.energygrid.com/destiny/emerald-tablets/tablet-01.html

[163] From Interior illustration from A Natural History of Dragons by Marie Brennan, art by Todd Lockwood. Lady Trent Natural History of Dragons. See also Torforgeblog. com

[164] https://en.wikipedia.org/wiki/Pythia

[165] Manly P. Hall, The Secret Teachings of all Ages. Pp 496-97.

[166] Sasha Lessin, Anunnaki Gods No More. Pp. 197-207.
[167] Ibid., pp203-207.

[168] http://archivmedes.blogspot.com/2000/03/die-batterie-von-khujut-rabu-oder-auch.html
See also Pinterest

[169] Zechariah Sitchin, The Earth Chronicles Handbook. P.69.
[170] Sitchin, The 12th Planet. p.84.
[171] SItchin, The Cosmic Code. Pp 78-79.

[172] Lawton, Genesis Unveiled. Pp. 73, 78-79.

[173] EAE Jelinkova, *The Shebtiw at the Temple at Edfu*.

[174] https://shebtiw.wordpress.com/?s=edfu

[175] Kenneth C. Davis, Don't Know Much About Mythology. PP 75-79.

[176] **Note**: the confusion in Egyptian gods is due to time and locale. For example, Amun was also Amen, Ammon and Atum and the Egyptians combined him with Ra and we got Amun-Ra. In addition, according to the Dictionary of Ancient Deities, Amen-Ra was also Atum-Ra and Khepre.
Source: Dictionary of Ancient Deities, Turner & Coulter, pp. 43 and 81.
Again, the issue was not who was whom, it was to show that **horns and serpent imagery** were prevalent with these gods.

[177] From Yahoo Coins of Alexander; see http://search.yahoo.com/search;_ylt=AuGsxC8UzTjm1.kh.2CU9IabvZx4?p=alexander+the+great+coin&toggle=1&cop=mss&ei=UTF-8&fr=yfp-t-788

[178] http://www.bhporter.com/Porter%20PDF%20Files/Worship%20of%20the%20Ancestor%20Gods%20at%20Edfu.pdf
See also: "Mythical Origin of the Egyptian Temple" by E.A.E. Reymond.
Pp 23,34,35, and 59-61.
[179] "Mythical Origin of the Egyptian Temple" by E.A.E. Reymond.
Pp 106-107, 114.
EAE Reymond was former professor of Egyptology at the University of Manchester and her work *Mythical Origin of the EgyptianTemple* was first published in 1969.

[180] https://en.wikipedia.org/wiki/Tree_of_life#Ancient_Egypt

[181] sacredwood.yuku.com

[182] Turner & Coulter, Dictionary of Ancient Deities. P 421.

[183] sacredwood.yuku.com

[184] See Empty Force by Paul Dong. Pictures and text recount the ability of *chi* adepts to not only knock down an opponent without touching him, but they may be knocked unconscious, blinded or even killed with the Force.

[185] **https://en.wikipedia.org/wiki/Westcar_Papyrus**

[186] http://djedhitemplarcorps.wix.com/djedhitemplarcorps#!the-knights-of-egypt-and-persia-/c1ti7
[187] Ibid.
[188] Ibid.

[189] Op Cit., Anunnaki Gods No More, pp 72, 108, 205.
Also Sitchin, The Cosmic Code, pp 100, 106. Resurrection technology was a fact.

[190] Op Cit., www.djedhitemplarcorps.... (see fn # 24)

[191] Mark A. Pinkham, Return of the Serpents of Wisdom. Pp 198-202.

[192] https://en.wikipedia.org/wiki/Kemet:

> Ancient Egypt is commonly referred to as 'km.t' , believed to be a reference to the black Nile Delta earth, as opposed to Deshret, the red barren desert land. The name Egypt was used accidentally by the Greeks after mistaking the Second name of the City of Thebes, "Aigyptos" for the country. Kush is the Egyptian name for their country.

[193] https://en.wikipedia.org/wiki/Tiye

[194] http://womenshistory.about.com/od/cleopatra/a/was_cleopatra_black.htm

And

http://news.bbc.co.uk/2/hi/also_in_the_news/7945333.stm: March 16, 2009…

Cleopatra's mother 'was African'

[195] jamiiforums.com

[196] Op Cit, **http://news.bbc.co.uk/2/hi/also_in_the_news/7945333.stm: March 16, 2009… Cleopatra's mother 'was African'**

And

http://womenshistory.about.com/od/cleopatra/a/was_cleopatra_black.htm

[197] Brad Olsen, Modern Esoteric. P63.
[198] http://www.generationword.com/jerusalem101/38-western-wall-tunnels.html
This website is really worth a look as it has maps and explains what the pix show.

[199] unexplained-mysteries.com

[200] Zechariah Sitchin, The Earth Chronicles Expeditions: Journeys to the Mythical Past. Pp 228-239

[201] http://www.israeldailypicture.com/2012/10/a-cave-under-temple-mounts-foundation.html

[202] Op Cit, Sitchin p 228.
[203] Ibid., p. 229
[204] Ibid., pp 237-38.

[205] Zechariah Sitchin, The Stairway to Heaven. Ch. 14 (pp 382-410)

Chapter 6 -- Endnotes

[206] Donna Rosenberg, World Mythology, 3rd Ed. P. 484.
(Most facts about the Aztecs in the beginning of Chapter 6 are from this source.)

[207] Hunbatz Men, The 8 Calendars of the Maya, p. 13
(It must be added that Hunbatz Men is a deep Mayan scholar and selections of his 2 books are faithfully quoted to maintain the integrity of his work. He nowhere draws any connections to Sumerian gods, yet his seminal work helps explain what the Mayan taught and what it meant to them. MY point that the Mayan gods were already gods from another part of the world in no way is meant to denigrate the Mayan history, merely expand it with what appears to be a valid connection – based on the works of the late Zechariah Sitchin, and today's Michael Tellinger and Sasha Lessin.)

[208] Ibid., p. 17.

[209] Hunbatz Men, Secrets of Mayan Science/Religion. P. 38.

[210] https://en.wikipedia.org/wiki/Aztec_calendar

[211] https://en.wikipedia.org/wiki/Itzamna

[212] Op Cit 8Calendars of the Maya, p. 82.

[213] https://en.wikipedia.org/wiki/Itzamna

[214] https://en.wikipedia.org/wiki/Maya_calendar#Haab.27

[215] Mindscape magazine, Issue 5, Feb. 2012, pp.28-31; quote from p.31. Andrew Gough, Ed.

[216] Zechariah Sitchin, The Cosmic Code. P. 191.

[217] Mark Pinkham, Return of the Serpents of Wisdom. P 167.

218 https://en.wikipedia.org/wiki/List_of_Maya_gods_and_supernatural_beings. Also see Wikipedia: Xochipilli (pron. So-chee-Peelee).

219 Op Cit., World Mythology, p. 484-85.

220 Op Cit., Secrets of Mayan Science/Religion. pp 57-79.

221 https://en.wikipedia.org/wiki/%C3%81rbol_del_Tule

222 **http://hubpages.com/education/Ancient-Mayan-Astronomy**

223 Op Cit., Secrets of Mayan Science/Religion. p. 72
224 Ibid., p. 89-90.
225 Ibid., 68-69, 77-78.

226 RA Boulay, Flying Serpents & Dragons. P 127.

227 Op Cit., The Cosmic Code. Pp 85-90.

228 Op Cit, Boulay., p. 49.

229 Op Cit., World Mythology. Pp 480-483.

230 http://news.nationalgeographic.com/news/2002/05/0528_020528_sunkencities.html
231 Ibid.
232 Ibid.

233 https://badarchaeology.wordpress.com/2012/10/28/an-underwater-city-west-of-cuba/

Chapter 7 -- Endnotes

234 https://en.wikipedia.org/wiki/Inca_mythology#Deities

235 Igor Witkowski, Axis of the World. p.221.

236 machupicchuorellana.com

237 https://en.wikipedia.org/wiki/Band_of_Holes

also known in Spanish as ***Monte Sierpe*** (serpent mountain) or ***Cerro Viruela*** (smallpox hill), is a series of about 5,000-6,000 man-sized holes found in the Pisco Valley on the Nazca Plateau in Peru.

.

238 http://blog.world-mysteries.com/strange-artifacts/unexplained-band-of-holes-pisco-peru/
Length: approximately 1,450m
Width: approximately 20m
Number of holes estimate: 6,900
View it on Google Earth: (continued…)

Lattitude: 13°42’55.37″S (continued…)
Longitude: 75°52’28.46″W
Eye alt: 3,100 ft

[239] http://www.human-resonance.org/gobekli_tepe.html
[240] Ibid.
[241] Ibid.

[242] Christopher Dunn, The Giza Power Plant.
Joseph Farrell, The Giza Death Star. (Series)

[243] *Op Cit., Human-resonance.*

[244] http://www.human-resonance.org/lascaux.html

[245] https://en.wikipedia.org/wiki/Inca_Empire
[246] Ibid.
[247] Ibid.

[248] https://en.wikipedia.org/wiki/Chakana

[249] Mark Pinkham, The Return of the Serpents of Wisdom. P154.
[250] Ibid., p89.
[251] Mark Pinkham, Return of the Serpents of Wisdom. P178.

[252] Philip Wilkinson, Myths & Legends, p. 282.
and Rosenberg, World Mythology, pp 498-503.

[253] Wikipedia: https://en.wikipedia.org/wiki/Kachina
[254] Ibid.

[255] Nexus Magazine, Vol 23., No. 5, Aug-Sept 2016. p.56.

[256] Wikipedia: https://en.wikipedia.org/wiki/Kachina
[257] Ibid.

[258] https://en.wikipedia.org/wiki/Mysteries_at_the_National_Parks
[259] (bibliotecapleyades.net)

[260] https://en.wikipedia.org/wiki/Sipapu

[261] Op Cit., The Return of the Serpents of Wisdom. Pp 179-182.
[262] Ibid. 181.
[263] Ibid., 183
[264] Ibid., 183

[265] https://en.wikipedia.org/wiki/Lakota_people and
https://en.wikipedia.org/wiki/Lakota_mythology

[266] Ibid.

[267] Op Cit., Dictionary of Mythology. P 332.

[268] https://en.wikipedia.org/wiki/Hopi_language

[269] https://en.wikipedia.org/wiki/Ancestral_Puebloans and Donald G Pike, Anasazi, Ancient People of the Rock. pp11-13 (foreword by Frank Waters)

[270] "Spiro Wulfing and Etowah repousse plates HRoe 2012" by **Herb Roe**. Licensed under CC BY-SA 3.0 via Commons – from copper plates: https://commons.wikimedia.org/wiki/File:Spiro_Wulfing_and_Etowah_repousse_plates_HRoe_2012.jpg#/media/File:Spiro_**Wulfing_and_Etowah_repousse_plates**_HRoe_2012.jpg

[271] Op Cit., Mark Pinkham. pp. 62-63.
[272] Ibid.

[273] https://en.wikipedia.org/wiki/Serpent_Mound

[274] This is copied from VEG, Ch. 14:

Pollution:

Oxygen has decreased overall on the planet over the last 100 years by 20%. The Pacific floating garbage patch is twice the size of Texas and cuts oxygen generation.
http://search.yahoo.com/search?ei=UTF-8&fr=att-portal&p=oxygen+levels&rs=0&fr2=rs-bottom

The North Pacific Trash Vortex
Plastic garbage dumped at sea comprises an area **bigger than the size of Texas.** The plastic contains toxic chemicals harmful to marine life, and there are also old but intact nets that trap dolphins and sea turtles who die because they can't get free. http://www.greenpeace.org/usa/campaigns/oceans/follow-the-journey/trashing-our-oceans

Significance: the ocean's surface has always contained millions of phytoplankton to (1) provide a food source for marine mammals, and (2) provide oxygen in the atmosphere. We now have **25% less oxygen** on the planet than in 1890. According to NOAA, if we lose another 8% nobody will be breathing.

Ozone layer depletion worse.
As the ozone layer depletes, Ultraviolet-B (UV-B) radiation increases – no longer stopped by the atmosphere, and skin carcinomas increase, as well as the

phytoplankton (oxygen-producers) are killed by the UV-B radiation. As the phytoplankton die, so do the krill and that helps starve the penguins and whales. (www.umich.edu/~gs265/society/ozone.htm)

Significance: I often wonder what the real estate developers are going to breathe while they try to spend their millions of dollars made while overdeveloping the country and **cutting down trees and shrubs** …we already don't have enough clean oxygen, and then we wonder where respiratory problems come from… They cut down a 40 year old oak tree and put back a 2 year old sapling… This is the version of mankind that doesn't work and is leading to his replacement for the sake of the planet.

Dead Zones Multiplying Fast, Coastal Water Study Says
This is from a 2008 report on the 'Dead Zones' around the world – areas in the seas where life is no longer supported due to the severe pollution – Man is creating it faster than Mother Nature can clear it away.
There are now more than 400 dead zones, up from just over 300 in the 1990s. http://news.nationalgeographic.com/news/bigphotos3669583.html

[275] https://en.wikipedia.org/wiki/Hopi_mythology

[276] Op Cit., Mark Pinkham. p 184.
[277] Ibid., p 184. Note that L. Taylor Hansen wrote a book on the subject, He Walked the Americas which is very informative.

Chapter 8 -- Endnotes

[278] J.A. Coleman, Dictionary of Mythology. P. 312.

[279] https://en.wikipedia.org/wiki/Dayak_people#Religion_and_festivals

[280] https://en.wikipedia.org/wiki/N%C4%81ga#Cambodia

[281] Encyclopedia of World Mythology. P 166 (and 163 ref).
[282] Ibid., 164.

[283] https://en.wikipedia.org/wiki/Snow_Lion

[284] Igor Witkowski, The Axis of the World. p. 81.

[285] Alistair Coombs, "Nan Madol, City of Spirits on the Reef of Heaven" in NEXUS Magazine for Dec. 2015- Jan 2016. Pp. 45-49.
[286] Ibid., 48.
[287] Ibid., pp47-48.

---

[288] https://en.wikipedia.org/wiki/Rainbow_Serpent

[289] https://en.wikipedia.org/wiki/Wagyl

[290] Op Cit., Dictionary of Mythology. P. 359.

[291] https://en.wikipedia.org/wiki/Mapuche
[292] https://en.wikipedia.org/wiki/Flag_of_the_Mapuches

[293] Op Cit, Witkowski. P. 68.

[294] https://en.wikipedia.org/wiki/Zulu_mythology

[295] https://en.wikipedia.org/wiki/Abzu

[296] Op Cit., Dictionary of Mythology. P. 336. (Nothing could be found about this tree in any source.)

[297] https://www.facebook.com/notes/ras-fetari/african-lore-gods-demigods-heroes-symbols-and-other-famous-mythological-characte/752424198179172

[298] David Icke, Children of the Matrix. P. 252.

[299] https://en.wikipedia.org/wiki/Ashanti_people#Golden_Stool

[300] https://en.wikipedia.org/wiki/Serpent_(symbolism)#African_mythology

[301] Dr. Susan Martinez, PhD, The Mysterious Origins of Hybrid Man. P.431.

[302] Geoffrey Parrinder, African Mythology. P 46-47, 52.

[303] Op Cit, Martinez, p. 432.

[304] https://en.wikipedia.org/wiki/Yazidis#Religious_beliefs

[305] https://www.youtube.com/watch?v=gpJvymMGR9k
This is for real. If this link is gone, Google: YouTube: blonde Yazidi.

[306] Op Cit., Martinez., pp 400 – 446.
[307] Ibid., p 397.
[308] Ibid., 410.
[309] Ibid., pp 417-18.
[310] Ibid., 421-22.

[311] Op Cit., The Axis of the World. pp 117-18.

[312] D.H. Childress, Lost Cities f North & Central America. P.376.

[313] Op Cit, Axis of the World. , pp 99-103.

Chapter 9 -- Endnotes

[314] Sasha Lessin, Anunnakl Gods No More. Pp 197-207.

[315] Wm. Bramley, The Gods of Eden. P. 448.
[316] Ibid., 54-55.

[317] Wikipedia: https://en.wikipedia.org/wiki/Caduceus
[318] Ibid.

[319] Op Cit, Bramley. Pp 54-55.
[320] Ibid., 65
[321] Ibid., 66
[322] Ibid., 66-67

[323] https://en.wikipedia.org/wiki/Djed
[324] Ibid.
[325] Ibid.
[326] Ibid.

[327] https://en.wikipedia.org/wiki/Kundalini
[328] Ibid.

[329] https://en.wikipedia.org/wiki/G%C3%B6bekli_Tepe
[330] (credit: "Göbekli Tepe" by Creator:Rolfcosar - Own work. Licensed under CC BY-SA 3.0 via Commons - https://commons.wikimedia.org/wiki/File:G%C3%B6bekli_Tepe.jpg#/media/File:G%C3%B6bekli_Tepe.jpg

[331] Sitchin, , The 12th Planet. pp 395-396.
[332] Op Cit., The 12th Planet. pp 395-396.

[333] Sasha Lessin, Anunnaki Gods No More. pp 78-80.

[334] Op Cit., 12th Planet, p. 329.

http://documentaryworldhistory.wikispaces.com/1.+Early+Human+History+to+the+Agricultural+Revolution)

Chapter 10 -- Endnotes

[335] https://en.wikipedia.org/wiki/Emerald_Tablet

[336] Frances Melville, The Book of Alchemy. Pp 18-19.

337 https://en.wikipedia.org/wiki/Emerald_Tablet
and:
http://www.alchemylab.com/history_of_alchemy.htm ::

338 Zechariah Sitchin, The Earth Chronicles Handbook. Pp 102, 204.

4 http://www.alchemylab.com/origins_of_alchemy.htm

339 http://ten1000things.org/russian-pyramid-power/

340 **https://igg.me/at/levitation-thruster**
See also Dr Paul LaViolette website: http://starburstfound.org/category/research/
and the Overunity Thrusters
also see http://ten1000things.org/russian-pyramid-power/

341 https://en.wikipedia.org/wiki/Prima_materia

342 http://www.alchemylab.com/history_of_alchemy.htm

343 https://lilipilyspirit.com/alchemy_hermeticism.htm

344 Op Cit, The Book of Alchemy, p. 54

345 (http://www.occult-mysteries.org/alchemy.html) and also see:

http://chemistry.about.com/cs/generalchemistry/a/aa050601a.htm:

Changing the element requires changing the atomic (proton) number. The number of protons **cannot** be altered by any chemical means. However, physics may be used to add or remove protons and thereby change one element into another. Because lead is stable, forcing it to release three protons requires a vast input of energy, such that the cost of transmuting it greatly surpasses the value of the resulting gold.

Transmutation of lead into gold isn't just theoretically possible - it has been achieved! There are reports that Glenn Seaborg, 1951 Nobel Laureate in Chemistry, succeeded in transmuting a minute quantity of lead (possibly en route from bismuth [#83 on Periodic Chart], in 1980) into gold. There is an earlier report (1972) in which Soviet physicists at a nuclear research facility near Lake Baikal in Siberia accidentally discovered a reaction for turning lead into gold when they found the lead shielding of an experimental reactor had changed to gold.

346 http://www.alchemylab.com/history_of_alchemy.htm
This is a fascinating and well-worth-it website – they have everything plus pictures related to Alchemy. Highly recommended viewing – even if you're not into Alchemy. The music is great also.

[347] https://en.wikipedia.org/wiki/Alchemy

[348] http://www.alchemylab.com/history_of_alchemy.htm
[349] Ibid.

[350] https://en.wikipedia.org/wiki/Hermeticism

[351] **http://www.occult-mysteries.org/alchemy.html**
[352] Ibid.

[353] http://www.occult-mysteries.org/hermetic-philosophy.html

[354] Manly P. Hall, The Secret Teachings of all ages. 498-99.
Interspersed with Hall's revelations are some from the latest New Thought writings.
(For more, see Transformation of Man.)

[355] Op Cit., The Book of Alchemy. Pp 57, 63.

[356] https://en.wikipedia.org/wiki/Nicolas_Flamel

[357] Corpus Hermeticum, 13:3 , pp49-50.

[358] Ian Lawton, Genesis Unveiled. P337.

[359] James M. Robinson, The Nag Hammadi Library. Pp 182-183.

[360] Op Cit, Lawton, p. 346.
[361] Ibid., 347.

[362] David Barrett, Secret Religions. pp 186-87.

[363] Op CIt., Lawton, p. 351.
[364] Ibid., 351-52.

[365] http://www.alchemylab.com/history_of_alchemy.htm

Chapter 11 -- Endnotes

[366] https://en.wikipedia.org/wiki/Astrology
[367] Ibid.

[368] Francis Melville, The Book of Alchemy. Pp. 9, 61, 109.

[369] https://en.wikipedia.org/wiki/Paracelsus
[370] Ibid.

---

[371] https://en.wikipedia.org/wiki/Zodiac#Twelve_signs

[372] Credit: "Ophiuchus" by Jacopo Montano - Atlas Coelestis, Johan Cammayo. Licensed under CC BY-SA 3.0 via Commons - https://commons.wikimedia.org/wiki/File:Ophiuchus.jpg#/media/File:Ophiuchus.jpg

[373] https://en.wikipedia.org/wiki/Ophiuchus_(astrology)

[374] Stefan Chmelik, Chinese Herbal Secrets. Pp 34-35.
[375] Ibid., 40-41

[376] https://en.wikipedia.org/wiki/I_Ching

[377] Ritsema & Karcher, I Ching. Pp. 197-205.
[378] Ibid.

[379] https://en.wikipedia.org/wiki/Fuxi

[380] https://en.wikipedia.org/wiki/Hindu_astrology

[381] https://en.wikipedia.org/wiki/Yajna

[382] https://en.wikipedia.org/wiki/Hindu_astrology
[383] Ibid.

[384] https://en.wikipedia.org/wiki/Maya_civilization#Astronomy

[385] "Madrid Codex 6" by Simon Burchell - Own work. Licensed under CC BY-SA 3.0 via Commons - Https://commons.wikimedia.org/wiki/File:Madrid_Codex_6.JPG#/media/File:Madrid_Codex_6.JPG

[386] https://en.wikipedia.org/wiki/Maya_codices

[387] http://www.delange.org/ChichenItza3/ChichenItza3.htm

388 **http://hubpages.com/education/Ancient-Mayan-Astronomy**

[389] Joseph Farrell, Reich of the Black Sun. pp 172-75.

[390] Edred Thorsson, Futhrk: A Handbook of Rune Magic. p. 7.

[391] Edred Thorsson, Runelore: the Magic, History and Hidden Codes of the Runes. P 78.
[392] Ibid., 213.
[393] Ibid.,, pp. 80-82

[394] Turner & Coulter, Dictionary of Ancient Deities. Pp, 177, 351.

[395] https://en.wikipedia.org/wiki/Etteilla
[396] Ibid.

[397] https://en.wikipedia.org/wiki/Kabbalah

Chapter 12 – Endnotes

[398] E.C. Prophet, Kabbalah: Key to Your Inner Power. Pp 13-19.
Note: this author's quoted work has been limited to the historical origins of Kabbalah, not the Qabalistic teachings she is known for.

[399] https://en.wikipedia.org/wiki/Zohar
[400] Ibid.

[401] https://en.wikipedia.org/wiki/Tree_of_life

[402] Op Cit., Prophet, p. 89.
403 https://s-media-cache-ak0.pinimg.com/originals/6d/c8/a5/6dc8a52b0b0e10e8e0171c4558c...

[404] Ibid., 91

[405] Manly P Hall, The Secret Teachings of All Ages. pp 356-57.

[406] https://en.wikipedia.org/wiki/Law_of_Moses

[407] https://en.wikipedia.org/wiki/Wycliffe_Global_Alliance
This is not a baseless rant – I spent time with those people and was told that the Bible comes first, then they teach.

[408] https://en.wikipedia.org/wiki/Hermeticism

[409] https://en.wikipedia.org/wiki/Theurgy#Jewish_theurgy

[410] https://en.wikipedia.org/wiki/Tanakh#Books_of_the_Tanakh

[411] https://fr.wikipedia.org/wiki/Boris_Mouravieff
[412] "Organic Portals Theory: Sources", compendium: Book II of Gnosis. eprint at: http://www.montalk.net/opsources.pdf
[413] Ibid., II, p. 7.

[414] Bibliotecapleyades website product of Jose Ingenieros, Book III, p. 112-115. reprint at: http://www.bibliotecapleyades.net/esp_autor_mouravieff.htm

[415] W.H. Church, *Edgar Cayce's Story of the Soul*, pp. 137-39.

[416] Sitchin, Zechariah, Journeys to the Mythical Past. Pp. 138-147, 153, 214-216.

[417] James M. Robinson, Ed., The Nag Hammadí Library. Pp 179-189.
[418] https://en.wikipedia.org/wiki/Pistis_Sophia#Title,
[419] James M. Robinson, Ed., The Nag Hammadí Library, p. 112

[420] https://en.wikipedia.org/wiki/Hypostasis_of_the_Archons

[421] Op Cit, Nag Hammadí Library, pp113-117.
[422] Ibid., Ch. VII, Great Schools, Doc. of 3 Natures.

[423] According to Wikipedia: https://en.wikipedia.org/wiki/**Lilith**#Talmud

> In Jewish folklore, from the 8th–10th century *Alphabet of Ben Sira* onwards, **Lilith** becomes Adam's first wife, who was created at the same time and from the same earth as Adam. This contrasts with Eve who was created from one of Adam's ribs. The legend was greatly developed during the Middle Ages, in the tradition of the **Zohar**, and Jewish mysticism. In the 13th century writings of Rabbi Isaac ben Jacob ha-Cohen, for example, Lilith left Adam after she refused to become subservient to him and then would not return to the Garden of Eden after she mated with archangel Samael. Lilith was then demonized.
>
> **Note**: Lilith has also be equated with Ishtar who was in fact, Inanna, the "goddess" in the Anunnaki pantheon. (In Wikipedia link above, the ref. to Ishtar is made under the side picture... which in VEG, CH 3 proves to be Inanna.)

[424] Op Cit, NHL, p. 187.
[425] Ibid., 188.
[426] Ibid., 118.
[427] Ibid., pp 180-81

[428] https://en.wikipedia.org/wiki/Rosicrucianism
[429] Ibid.

[430] Mark Pinklham, The Return of the Serpents of Wisdom. pp. 264-295.
[431] Ibid., 265
[432] Ibid., 265

[433] https://en.wikipedia.org/wiki/Barakah -- I bet you thought his was a made-up term.

[434] Francis Melville, The Book of Alchemy. pp 38-45.
[435] Ibid., 43.

[436] David Barrett, Secret Religions. pp. 186-87

[437] Gardiner & Osborn, The Shining Ones. pp 91-92.

[438] http://longmontmasons.com/author/admin/

Chapter 13 – Endnotes

[439] Gardiner & Osborn, The Shining Ones. pp xviii, 87.
[440] Ibid., p. 188.

[441] Hodson, Geoffrey, *Kingdom of the Gods*. 1952. ISBN 0-7661-8134-0 Contains color pictures of what Devas supposedly look like when observed by the third eye — their appearance is reputedly like colored flames about the size of a human being. Paintings of some of the devas claimed to have been seen by Hodson from his book *Kingdom of the Gods*.

[442] https://en.wikipedia.org/wiki/Deva_(Buddhism)

[443] Op Cit., Gardiner, p230.

[444] https://en.wikipedia.org/wiki/Deva_(Hinduism)

[445] https://en.wikipedia.org/wiki/Indra

[446] https://en.wikipedia.org/wiki/Vritra

[447] https://en.wikipedia.org/wiki/Danava_(Hinduism)
[448] Ibid.

[449] Op Cit., Gardiner, p. 213.

[450] Coleman, Ed. Dictionary of Mythology, pp84, 242.

[451] https://en.wikipedia.org/wiki/Jainism
[452] Ibid.

[453] https://en.wikipedia.org/wiki/Deva_(Jainism)

[454] "Jain universe" by Anishshah19 at English Wikipedia - Transferred from en.wikipedia to Commons by Mangostar using CommonsHelper.. Licensed under Public Domain via Commons - https://commons.wikimedia.org/wiki/File:Jain_universe.JPG#/media/File:Jain_universe.JPG

[455] https://en.wikipedia.org/wiki/Deva_(Jainism)

[456] Ibid.

[457] https://en.wikipedia.org/wiki/Deva_(New_Age)

[458] Op Cit., Gardiner, p. 88, 94

[459] https://en.wikipedia.org/wiki/Aztl%C3%A1n
[460] Ibid.
[461] Op Cit, Gardiner, p. 174.
[462] Ibid., p169.

[463] James Robinson, The Nag Hammadí Library. Pp124-138.

[464] http://www.divinecosmos.com/start-here/articles/334-kozyrev-aether-time-and-torsion
[465] Ibid.
[466] Ibid.

[467] Brendan B. Murphy, in http://blog.world-mysteries.com/science/torsion-the-key-to-theory-of-everything/

[468] https://www.tumblr.com/search/comte%20de%20saint%20germain

[469] https://en.wikipedia.org/wiki/The_Most_Holy_Trinosophia
[470] Ibid.
[471] Ibid.

[472] Manly P Hall, The Secret Teachings of All Ages. (St Germain) pp 654-657.

[473] https://en.wikipedia.org/wiki/Benjamin_Franklin#Electricity
[474] Ibid.

[475] Op Cit, Manly Hall, pp 658-660.

[476] **The Insider**
"The Revelations of the Insider" is an article containing the blog during a 5-day visit by someone calling themselves an "insider" who had knowledge on most aspects of Earth history, science and religion. This was done anonymously via a proxy link to the GLP (Godlike Productions) forum in the Fall of 2005. The material is not copyrighted and can be reproduced as long as none of the original text is changed. Website: http://www.scribd.com/doc/403303/The-Revelations-of-an-Elite-Family-Insider-2005

Epilog -- Endnotes

[477] https://en.wikipedia.org/wiki/Time_in_Russia

[478] In the early 90's this was called Higher Order Thinking Skills – analyze, synthesize, compare, contrast, deduce, induce... and it was cancelled by Others in Washington DC (Dept of Educ) because parents no longer get involved in the PTA, so they don't know what is being taught nor how... nor care

479

https://www.bing.com/search?q=pharrell+williams+happy&form=PRACER&pc=MAARJS&mkt=en-&httpsmsn=1&refig=56786445c24d4833801c1de3f920b0d5&qs=LS&pq=pharrell&sk=LS1&sc=8-8&sp=3&cvid=56786445c24d4833801c1de3f920b0d5

480 This is still on Amazon along with The Waste Makers, and Our Endangered Children also by the same author.
Very enlightening evaluations of a prosperous and out-of-control society.

481 https://en.wikipedia.org/wiki/Atacama_Desert (all 3 preceding paragraphs)

482 Energiaoldal.hu also:
http://energiaoldal.hu/a-legszarazabb-sivatagban-is-van-elet/

483 asergeev.com:
Approaching beginning of a canyon of Nahal Bokek in Judean Desert, on a plateau 2 miles west from Ein Bokek. asergeev.com

484 (credit: https://www.youtube.com/watch?v=EMVfMB0ypQM)
Just go to YouTube and google: shadow mars rover.

You can find the original photo here http://marsmobile.jpl.nasa.gov/msl/mu...
Check out the UFO sightings blog at http://ufosightingz.blogspot.com

485 http://www.thelivingmoon.com/43ancients/02files/Mars_Blue_Bird_Color_01.html

486 https://en.wikipedia.org/wiki/Venus

487 https://en.wikipedia.org/wiki/Georgia_Guidestones#Inscriptions

Endnotes – Appendix A

488 Marion, Putting on the Mind of Christ, p. 34.
489 Ibid., 37
490 Ibid., 41.
491 Ibid., 64.
492 Ibid., 70-71.

Appendix B -- Endnotes

493 https://en.wikipedia.org/wiki/Black_Madonna

494 Picknett & Prince, The Templar Revelation. P. 65

And
Robinson, The Nag Hammadi Library, p. 148

495 Hanan Abdalla via UNwomen.org. Beautiful representative of an Egyptian woman which Mary Magdalene was alleged to be from a well-to-do family.

496 https://en.wikipedia.org/wiki/Mari_(goddess)

497 Caroline Myss, Sacred Contracts, p. 388.

498 https://en.wikipedia.org/wiki/Goddess_movement

499 https://en.wikipedia.org/wiki/Women_in_Ancient_Egypt#Women_playing_an_official_role_at_the_highest_levels

500 https://en.wikipedia.org/wiki/Frigg

501 https://en.wikipedia.org/wiki/Vanir

502 https://en.wikipedia.org/wiki/Xihe_(deity)

503 Turner & Coulter, Dictionary of Ancient Deities. p.477.

504 Freke & Gandy, Jesus and the Lost Goddess. Pp. 3, 79-95.

505 ShahrukhHusain, The Goddess. Pp10-17, 163.

506 Freke & Gandy, The Jesus Mysteries. P.254.

Virtual Earth Graduate

By TJ Hegland

Man, Creation & Anunnaki, ETs, UFOs, OPs, Angels, Souls, Holograms, DNA, Serpent Wisdom, Gnosticism, the InterLife, Karma, déjà vu, the Bionet, Simulation, the Control System, and more – how they fit our special reality.

(Chapter 13 in VEG is the springboard for the following book…)

Quantum Earth Simulation

By TJ Hegland

Simulation, Virtual Reality, Matrix and Holodecks, Holograms and Quantum Physics, Vision & Hypnosis, Timelines, Eras, Stages & Scripts, Programming the Simulation, Consciousness, Reality Fields, Lucid Living, and Many Anomalies.

(this is not a novel)

The Transformation of Man

By TJ Hegland

Spirituality, Reincarnation & the InterLife, Consciousness, the Matrix, Zero Point Energy, Dark Matter, DNA & Healing Energy, Timelines, Quantum Biocomputer, Greys & Hybrids, and Abduction & the Near Death Experience as Transformation.

(this is the 'overflow' from VEG)

NOTES

Made in the USA
San Bernardino, CA
27 July 2019